Crime and Criminal Justice in Modern Germany

Studies in German History
Published in Association with the German Historical Institute, Washington, D.C.

General Editors:

Hartmut Berghoff, Director of the German Historical Institute, Washington, D.C.
Uwe Spiekermann, Deputy Director of the German Historical Institute, Washington, D.C.

CRIME AND CRIMINAL JUSTICE IN MODERN GERMANY

Edited by

Richard F. Wetzell

berghahn
NEW YORK · OXFORD
www.berghahnbooks.com

First published in 2014 by

Berghahn Books

www.berghahnbooks.com

©2014 Richard F. Wetzell

Library of Congress Cataloging-in-Publication Data

Crime and criminal justice in modern Germany / Edited by Richard F. Wetzell.
p. cm. — (Studies in German History ; 16)
Includes bibliographical references and index.
    ISBN 978-1-78238-246-1 (hardback : alk. paper) — ISBN 978-1-78238-247-8
(ebook)
    1. Criminal justice, Administration of—Germany—History.   2. Crime—
Germany—History.   I. Wetzell, Richard F., editor of compilation.
KK7962.C75 2013
364.943—dc23

                                                                2013017866

British Library Cataloguing in Publication Data

A catalogue record for this book is available from the British Library

Printed on acid-free paper.

ISBN: 978-1-78238-246-1 hardback
ISBN: 978-1-78238-247-8 ebook

Cover image: "Der Kleine Frauenmörder" [The little murderer of women] by George Grosz, 1918, oil on canvas, 66.8 cm

x 66.8 cm. Private collection, courtesy Ralph Jentsch, Rome. ©Estate of George Grosz/Licensed by VAGA, New York, NY.

CONTENTS

PART IV. CRIMINAL JUSTICE IN NAZI AND POSTWAR GERMANY

INTRODUCTION
Crime and Criminal Justice in Modern Germany

Richard F. Wetzell

Historians of nineteenth- and twentieth-century Germany have been relative latecomers to the history of crime and criminal justice. In both modern British and French historiography, crime and criminal justice have been major topics of research since the 1970s: in France, research in this area was pioneered by Michel Foucault, in Britain, by E. P. Thompson and other social historians.[1] In the field of German history, the significance of this subject was first recognized by historians of the early modern era, who developed a rich literature on this topic over the last twenty-five years.[2] Historical research on crime and criminal justice in nineteenth- and twentieth-century Germany, by contrast, has only begun to flourish in the last ten years. It is the aim of this volume to make some of the results of this recent boom in research accessible to a general audience.

There is a notable asymmetry between the early modern and modern German historiographies of crime and criminal justice. Whereas most early modern studies have focused on the criminals themselves, their socioeconomic situations, and the meanings of crime in a particular urban or rural milieu, late modern studies have tended to focus on penal institutions and the discourses of prison reformers, criminal law reformers, criminologists, and psychiatrists. Simplifying somewhat, one might say that early modernists have studied crime and criminal justice primarily with the tools of social history and historical anthropology, while late modernists have most often used the tools of cultural history, intellectual history, and discourse analysis.[3] To some extent, this difference in approaches reflects the effect that the "scientization of the social" began to have on criminal justice in the last third of the nineteenth century.[4] Compared with what we know about the

---

Notes from this chapter begin on page 21.

early modern era, our knowledge of the history of crime and criminal justice in the various German states in the first two-thirds of the nineteenth century is very limited. Although we are beginning to learn more about the important transformations of criminal justice that took place in this period,[5] most late modern research on crime and criminal justice picks up after the German unification of 1871, a fact that is reflected in this collection.

The essays collected here do not just provide pioneering contributions toward a history of crime and criminal justice in Germany from about 1871 to the 1950s, but connect the history of criminal justice to the larger questions of German political history from the Kaiserreich to the two postwar Germanies, examine the increasingly close but difficult relationship of criminal justice to psychiatry and social welfare, analyze the representations of crime and criminal justice in the media and literature, and also use criminal justice history to illuminate German social history, gender history, and the history of sexuality.

Criminal Justice in Imperial Germany

A central part of the founding of Imperial Germany in 1871 was the ambition to establish a uniform legal system throughout the German Reich. This ambition manifested itself in the quick passage of a Reich Penal Code (Reichsstrafgesetzbuch, 1871), which superseded the penal codes of the individual German states and was modeled on the Prussian Penal Code of 1851,[6] a Reich Law on the Organization of the Courts (Gerichtsverfassungsgesetz, 1877), and a Reich Code of Criminal Procedure (Strafprozessordnung, 1877).[7] Despite wide-ranging support for the establishment of a unified prison system, the goal of a Reichsstrafvollzugsgesetz (Reich Prison Law) remained elusive, and prisons continued to be administered by the individual states.

From the 1960s until quite recently, Imperial Germany's criminal justice system was often portrayed as an instrument of authoritarian rule and class justice. Studies that advanced this interpretation tended to focus on the use of criminal justice to persecute Social Democrats during the era of the Anti-Socialist laws (1878–1890) and drew heavily on contemporary Social-Democratic critiques of "class justice."[8] Many were primarily interested in criminal justice in the Weimar Republic or Nazi Germany and were therefore looking for continuities that would explain the left/right disparities in Weimar political trials or the complicity of the judiciary in the crimes of the Nazi regime.[9] This interpretation is currently undergoing vigorous revision. Kenneth Ledford has argued that the Prussian Supreme Administrative Law Court brought "meaningful rule of law" to Germany. In a series of cases, the Prussian court protected individual rights by ruling against the state in challenges to police actions such as prohibitions of assembly directed against Social Democrats and the Polish minority in Eastern

Prussia. To be sure, as the embodiment of a procedural and formalist conception of the rule of law, the court also frequently upheld police powers in these kinds of cases. Nevertheless, within the limits of legal formalism, Ledford concludes, the court "provided a lively and capacious stage for Prussian citizens to vindicate their individual rights."[10] Likewise, in his work on literary censorship in Imperial Germany, Gary Stark has shown that public prosecutors who prosecuted publishers or authors for libel or obscenity were frequently disappointed by the verdicts: agile defense attorneys, impartial judges, and press coverage of the proceedings ensured that in over two-thirds of press trials the sentences imposed were lighter than prosecutors had requested, and in 20–30 percent of all cases the defendants were acquitted. In Prussia, Saxony, and Baden administrative law courts set important limits on police censorship of theaters by frequently allowing the performance of dramas that the local police had tried to ban.[11] Ann Goldberg's study of *Beleidigungsprozesse* in Imperial Germany has demonstrated that defamation lawsuits served not only to protect state power and social hierarchies, but were also used by social outsiders such as Jews and people interned in lunatic asylums to protect their honor. Imperial Germany, she has argued, had a "hybrid legal culture" that combined authoritarian elements with the liberal legal principles of the rule of law so that "the traditional idiom of honor" could be harnessed to "a democratic politics of rights."[12] In sum, while Imperial Germany's authorities did use the judicial system, even after the expiration of the anti-Socialist law, for political purposes (through prosecutions for libel or lèse majesté, for instance), recent work has shown that such efforts were frequently stymied by independent judges, increasingly assertive defense attorneys, the due process guarantees of German criminal procedure, and the influence of public opinion. The Kaiserreich's judicial system was characterized by the rule of law and therefore imposed significant limitations on the power of the authorities.

Benjamin Hett's opening chapter provides two important arguments for the revisionist position that the Kaiserreich's criminal justice system came much closer to the ideal of the *Rechtsstaat* (rule of law) than that of authoritarian justice. First, Hett shows that a significant number of the Kaiserreich's critics of criminal justice—most of them criminal defense lawyers, who could hardly be suspected of authoritarian leanings—did not think that the problem with German justice was authoritarianism or class justice; instead, they criticized the randomness of verdicts and the influence of public opinion, an assessment confirmed by Hett's analysis of two major turn-of-the-century criminal trials. Second, the critics' increasing concern with the influence of public opinion derived from the fact that the 1877 Code of Criminal Procedure had instituted most of the items on the liberal reform agenda, such as public trials and the use of juries.[13]

In other words, far from criticizing an authoritarian justice system, a substantial number of liberal jurists were beginning to grow uncomfortable with some of the achievements of liberal penal reform. In particular, some liberal defense lawyers were becoming quite critical of juries, doubted the reliability of witnesses, and thought that the oral proceedings overtaxed most judges.[14] Whereas some thought that solutions to these problems would be found in better use of psychology and forensic science (such as fingerprinting, blood tests, or photographic evidence) in the courtroom, others stressed the need for procedural reforms, such as abolishing juries or replacing them with mixed panels of lay and professional judges, as well as curtailing oral proceedings by using more documentary evidence. Far from functioning as an instrument of the authoritarian state, Hett argues, the Kaiserreich's criminal justice system was "moving out of control of the state" both because the liberal features of German criminal procedure increased the influence of public opinion and because German prosecutors, judges, and defense lawyers were eager to harness public opinion for their own purposes.[15]

The insight that the Kaiserreich's liberal jurists were not concerned about its legal system's being too authoritarian, but about the unintended consequences of the liberal penal reforms that had been achieved, applies not only to Imperial Germany's debates on criminal procedure but also to contemporary debates on the reform of substantive criminal law. The penal reform movement that was led by criminal law professor Franz von Liszt starting in the 1880s was not concerned that punishments were too arbitrary (the classic liberal charge against authoritarian justice) but that they were too uniform. When the reformers demanded that criminal sentences ought to be calibrated to the personality of the offender rather than the severity of the offense, they were taking aim at a key feature of liberal criminal justice that nineteenth-century liberal reformers had regarded as a guarantee against judicial arbitrariness: namely, the imposition of uniform prison sentences for any given offense, as prescribed in the penal code, regardless of the person of the perpetrator.[16]

Both the "literature of judicial error" examined in Hett's chapter, which focuses on reforming criminal procedure, and Liszt's "modern school of criminal law," which called for the revision of substantive criminal law (the penal code), were movements of middle-class legal professionals. The literature of judicial error was mostly penned by practicing criminal defense lawyers, whereas the penal reform movement was led by criminal law professors. Although these middle-class critics failed to detect a class bias in the Kaiserreich's judicial system, the charge of "class justice" was frequently raised by the socialist labor movement.[17] As Andreas Fleiter's chapter shows, however, the Social Democratic Party's (SPD) attitudes toward criminal justice were more complex than the rhetoric of class justice suggests. To be sure, the Anti-Socialist Laws passed in 1878 blatantly instrumentalized criminal justice for the purpose of political persecution and resulted in the imprisonment of thousands of Social Democrats.[18] It was above all this political persecution that was branded as "class justice" by the SPD. While prominent party leaders were usually sentenced to *Festungshaft* (minimum-security detention with numerous privileges designed for offenders of conscience), rank-and-file party activists were often sentenced to regular prison. The experience of detention in regular prisons did not, however, lead socialists to declare their solidarity with common criminals as fellow victims of class justice. On the contrary, although socialists demanded the abolition of private property, they condemned individual lawbreaking and drew a sharp distinction between socialist "political prisoners" and "common criminals," whom they disparaged as members of the *Lumpenproletariat.*

During the period of the Anti-Socialist Laws (1878–1890) and into the 1890s, the SPD party leadership's interest in criminal justice was mainly limited to two issues: the treatment of political prisoners and the regulation of prison labor. By the turn of the century, however, the criminal law reform movement had firmly placed penal reform on the national political agenda, so that the SPD had to take a position on criminal justice and penal reform in general. The party's new interest in penal reform also resulted from the rise of a revisionist wing within the SPD. Whereas orthodox socialists such as August Bebel expected that a crime-free socialist future was close at hand, the revisionists did not regard the revolution as imminent and therefore argued that the party must take a position on penal reform in the present political system and were generally inclined to support key elements of the "modern school's" penal reform agenda.

Germany's late-nineteenth-century penal reform movement, which was very much part of an international movement, called for a fundamental transformation of the criminal justice system.[19] Instead of retributive justice, criminal justice was to serve the purpose of defending society against crime. The penal reformers around Franz von Liszt meant this quite literally: the criminal justice system was to take whatever measures were necessary to ensure that each individual offender would not break the law again in the future. Therefore the reformers' key demand was the individualization of punishment. During the sentencing phase of criminal trials (that is, after the accused had been found guilty of having committed a criminal offense), the offender's sentence should no longer be determined by that criminal offense but by the person of the offender, more precisely, by the offender's future dangerousness. If a first-time offender and a multiple recidivist committed the same crime, they should therefore receive different sentences. Whereas for a first-time offender a suspended sentence (probation) might be sufficient, a recidivist ought to receive an indeterminate sentence whose duration would depend on the progress of his rehabilitation.[20]

The reformers' shift in focus from offense to offender inescapably led them to become interested in criminological research on the causes of crime.[21] Only if one understood what caused someone to commit a crime, could one hope to prevent that person from committing future infractions. Although some reformers were quite interested in the social causes of crime, the reform movement's goal of protecting society through individualized penal sanctions meant that individual causes of crime loomed larger than did social ones. Hence criminology increasingly came to study "the criminal" rather than the causes of crime more generally.

But where could the criminal be studied? Most easily, of course, in prison. Starting with Cesare Lombroso, the Italian founder of criminal anthropology, almost all criminological studies of criminals were conducted on prison populations by prison doctors or by psychiatrists who worked in the psychiatric wards of prisons.[22] As a result of the "criminological turn," prisons became much more than institutions of detention; they became places of scientific observation: criminological laboratories.[23] This transformation of prisons into sites of scientific discovery lent new authority not only to prison doctors and psychiatrists but also to regular prison officials, who argued that their experience with prisoners gave them unique expertise in a range of issues including how to categorize criminals, how to rehabilitate different types of criminals, and how to combat crime. To be sure, prison officials had claimed special expertise since the beginnings of modern prison reform in the early nineteenth century.[24] What changed at the century's end, however, was that prison reform became more closely connected to the general reform of criminal justice.

The reason for this change was simple. In classic nineteenth-century criminal justice, judges pronounced sentences according to the penal code's provisions for the offense committed and did not have to think about the administration of the punishment in prison or the personality of the offender. By the turn of the century, however, penal reformers were demanding that judges impose the penal sanction that offered the best chance of preventing the individual offender from committing future offenses, so that judges had to start thinking about the offender's personality and the administration and probable effect of the punishment. Even though the penal reformers' agenda met considerable resistance, the demand for the individualization of punishment began to inflect sentencing practices in German courtrooms. As a result, what happened in the courtroom and what happened in prison (or, as we shall see, in homes for delinquent youth or psychiatric wards for abnormal offenders) was becoming much more closely connected. And by the same token, prison reform, criminal law reform, and criminology were becoming more integrated as part of what Franz von Liszt called "die gesamte Strafrechtswissenschaft" (the penal sciences).

By the late nineteenth century, therefore, prison officials regarded themselves as experts not just on matters of prison administration and prison reform, but on the larger subjects of penal reform and criminology. Having fully absorbed the penal reformer's shift in focus from offense to offender as well as the demand for the individualization of punishment, they began to divide offenders into different categories. Not surprisingly, one of the most important criteria for categorizing offenders was gender, the central focus of Sandra Leukel's chapter. As Leukel shows, prison officials' newfound interest in female criminals and the treatment of women in prison was closely related to the changing social position of women in German society, which gave rise to fears of an increase in female crime. There were calls for separate prisons for women and the hiring of female staff to supervise female prisoners, but both of these were long-standing if largely unrealized demands. What was new in the turn-of-the-century debates was the demand that women's treatment in prison be adapted to women's special nature. Whereas earlier calls for separate facilities had primarily reflected disciplinary strategies, now these demands became the starting point for developing a gender-specific penal regime adapted to the "peculiarities" of women that would include different dietary, work, and rehabilitation regulations for female prisoners. As Leukel demonstrates, the Kaiserreich's debate over the proper treatment of women in prison was shaped by the confluence of the penal reformers' call for the individualization of punishment and the larger phenomenon of women's emancipation in German society. Perceiving the latter as a threat, some prison reformers sought to stabilize the gender hierarchy by transforming the penal system's treatment of women.

Penal Reform

The penal reform movement's demand for the individualization of punishment based on each offender's dangerousness was a call to break the prison's near monopoly as the standard penal sanction (the death penalty was very rarely imposed)[25] by introducing a spectrum of other sanctions from the realms of education, medicine, and welfare. Whereas in classic criminal law, prison sentences represented *Freiheitsstrafen*—deprivations of liberty for the purpose of retribution and general deterrence—the reformers insisted that an offender's penal sanction ought to transform the individual offender in such a way that he or she would not commit further crimes. As a first step, this meant dividing offenders into categories and assigning each category the most appropriate sanction from an array of penal, educational, medical, and welfare measures. The reform movement divided offenders into five main categories: (1) first-time "occasional" offenders were to have their prison sentences suspended on probation or replaced by fines, on the expectation that such measures were sufficient to deter them from future crimes; (2) "habitual" offenders (recidivists) who appeared "corrigible" were to serve a prison term during which they would undergo rehabilitation; (3) habitual offenders who appeared "incorrigible" were to be detained indefinitely (with periodic review) to "incapacitate" them for the protection of society; (4) mentally abnormal offenders were to receive therapeutic treatment in psychiatric facilities instead of prison sentences; (5) juvenile offenders were to be sentenced to correctional education (*Fürsorgeerziehung*) in special homes for wayward youth instead of prison.[26]

The penal reform movement was thus pursuing a radical agenda: seeking to replace standard fixed prison sentences with a range of individualized preventive measures drawn from a variety of non-penal forms of state intervention, includ-ing education (for juvenile delinquents), medical treatment (for abnormal offenders), and the workhouse (for incorrigible habitual criminals). Depending on the category of criminal, this transformation of the penal sanction could result in less punitive sanctions (such as suspended sentences or fines instead of prison for first-time offenders) or harsher, more repressive punishments (such as indefi-nite detention for habitual criminals). In short, the modern school's penal reform agenda was, from the outset, Janus-faced. For certain categories of criminals, it could, in fact, be hard to determine whether or not they were better off under the modern school's proposals: for whereas juveniles or mentally abnormal offenders were now to be spared imprisonment, their correctional education or psychiatric treatment might be more interventionist than a prison term. Because of this ambivalence, the penal reform movement's agenda could be and was attacked from both left and right: whereas left-liberal critics accused the reformers of rein-troducing the police state, conservative critics charged them with undermining retributive justice and individual responsibility.[27]

The revision of the penal code therefore turned out to be a drawn-out proj-ect that began with a first reform commission in 1906 and continued through several reform commissions and draft codes during the Weimar Republic and the Nazi regime, without a comprehensive revision of the penal code coming to pass before 1945. In West Germany, the reform process ultimately resulted in the *Grosse Strafrechtsreform* (Comprehensive Penal Reform) of 1969–1970. In the meantime, however, beginning in late Imperial Germany and intensify-ing during the Weimar Republic, significant parts of the penal reform agenda were implemented through piecemeal reforms. The modern school's demand that first-time occasional criminals should not go to prison was realized through the introduction of suspended sentencing and the increased use of fines. Suspended sentencing was first introduced administratively in most German states between 1895 and 1903; and in 1920, Germany's largest state, Prussia, authorized judges to suspend sentences at their discretion. In 1923, the *Geldstrafengesetz* (law on fines) drastically increased the use of monetary fines for minor offenses. The reformers' demand that juvenile offenders should be subject to education rather than punishment resulted in the creation of special Juvenile Courts (Jugendger-ichte) in Berlin and other cities starting in 1908, which led to the passage of a comprehensive Juvenile Justice Act (Jugendgerichtsgesetz) in 1923. Finally, even though the modern school's demand for the indefinite detention of incorrigible criminals was only realized after the Nazi seizure of power, its call for the differ-ential treatment of corrigible and incorrigible habitual criminals was reflected in the 1923 passage of new prison guidelines, which introduced the so-called progressive system in all German prisons.[28]

These transformations of criminal justice during the Weimar years are exam-ined in the chapters by Wachsmann (on prisons), Finder (on juvenile justice),

and Rosenblum (on the role of *Gerichtshilfe* in suspended sentencing). As Wachsmann shows, the development of the Weimar prison was significantly influenced
by social and political forces. In the early Weimar years, for instance, the hyperinflation triggered a crime wave, which provided a strong impetus for prison
reform. During the 1920s, German prison reformers made significant progress in
transforming the prison into an educational institution committed to prisoners'
rehabilitation and reintegration. But their reforms also met with considerable
resistance from prison personnel and fully succeeded only in the few institutions that were run by reform-minded wardens. The new prison guidelines of
1923 introduced the "progressive system" (*Stufensystem*), in which prisoners
could advance through three stages, with increasing privileges in each stage. But
although the progressive system was originally conceived as a tool for rehabilitating prisoners, it turned out that it could also be used to institutionalize the
distinction between supposedly corrigible and incorrigible prisoners. Whereas
most prison reformers insisted that prisoners must not be labeled incorrigible
unless rehabilitation efforts had failed, other prison officials began to assess
corrigibility at the outset and excluded supposedly incorrigible prisoners from
advancing beyond the first stage of the progressive system. The assessment of
corrigibility at the intake point increasingly took the form of criminal-biological
examinations. These examinations gathered extensive data about the prisoner's
body, mental health, life history, family, and milieu, but their concluding "social
prognoses" (assessments of corrigibility) were usually little more than moral judgments dressed up in medical terminology.[29] The bifurcation of the prison system,
in which supposedly incorrigible prisoners were excluded from rehabilitative
programs, accelerated after the world economic crisis of 1929, when conservative prison officials found it convenient to argue that scarce resources must be
reserved for reformable prisoners.[30]

The penal reformers' call for the individualization of punishment was also
reflected in the development of juvenile justice, which is the subject of Gabriel
Finder's chapter.[31] As Finder shows, the juvenile courts' abridgment of normal
judicial procedures as well as their focus on the *person* of the offender (rather
than the *offense*) made these courts unusually hospitable for forensic psychiatric
experts, who regarded juvenile delinquency as a medical rather than a moral
condition. Already in the Wilhelmine period the rate of forensic examinations
increased, and forensic psychiatry gradually became entrenched in the juvenile
courts. In a dozen large cities every juvenile defendant underwent a psychiatric examination. Nevertheless, psychiatrists' lobbying efforts to make psychiatric examinations mandatory for all juvenile defendants failed. Instead, the
Juvenile Justice Act of 1923 gave juvenile court judges discretionary authority
to order psychiatric examinations "in appropriate cases" and to impose "educative remedies" (*Erziehungsmassregeln*) instead of punishment where they
saw fit. Whether this discretionary authority should be interpreted broadly or

restrictively remained the subject of dispute. Thus, even though the Juvenile Justice Act gave forensic psychiatry and educative measures a firm foothold in juvenile justice, it also circumscribed both. Weimar juvenile judges limited the role of psychiatry and education in juvenile justice not only because they wished to defend the principle of retributive justice or to uphold their authority against the encroachments of psychiatrists but also, as Finder argues, because they were committed to the rule of law, that is, to the principles of individual responsibility and due process.[32]

The penal reform movement reconfigured not only the relationship between criminal justice and psychiatry but also that between criminal justice and welfare.[33] As part of this reconfiguration, the boundary between criminal justice and welfare was eroded in two ways: First, some types of delinquents could now be sentenced to welfare measures instead of prison terms. This was the case for juvenile delinquents, who could be placed in homes for wayward youth (*Fürsorgeerziehung*), and for first-time offenders, who could be sentenced to probation under the supervision of local welfare offices; in the reformers' agenda, it would also eventually apply to incorrigible habitual criminals, whose indefinite detention was to resemble internment in a workhouse rather than prison. Second, because the shift from offense to offender in the sentencing phase of criminal trials necessitated the collection of information about the offender's background and personality, criminal courts began to turn to welfare agencies to help them collect this information. These efforts resulted in the development of *soziale Gerichtshilfe* (social court assistance), which is examined in Warren Rosenblum's chapter. Pioneered in Bielefeld during World War I and more widely introduced after the war, Gerichtshilfe sought to bring the expertise of private and public welfare agencies to bear on criminal justice. In 1920, the Prussian Ministry of Justice gave judges the power to suspend the prison sentences of offenders who seemed capable of rehabilitation under the supervision of a welfare agency. To help the judge decide whether a defendant should be eligible for the suspension of his or her sentence, the Gerichtshilfe's "court assistants" were to provide the court with a "social diagnosis" of the offender by gathering information about his or her personality and milieu from family, school, church, and other sources. Ideally, the Gerichtshilfe agents would also provide the offender's welfare supervision during the probationary period.

As Rosenblum shows, the introduction and development of Gerichtshilfe was closely connected to broader critiques of the criminal justice system from the left and the right. When leftist critics argued that the judiciary's "remoteness from life" (*Lebensfremdheit*) and legal formalism had created a "crisis of trust in justice" (*Vertrauenskrise der Justiz*), Gerichtshilfe seemed to offer the ideal remedy because it sought to bring the facts of defendant's actual lives to bear on their legal treatment.[34] But when conservative critics charged that excessive lenience had emasculated (*verweichlicht*) Weimar criminal justice, Gerichtshilfe became a major culprit because these critics blamed the increase in suspended sentences on the "social diagnoses" delivered by Gerichtshilfe agents and criticized the welfare supervision of defendants as no more than a slap on the wrist. Because Gerichtshilfe was implicated in these opposing critiques, the struggle over who would control the new institution became highly contentious. This struggle eventually turned on the alternative whether Gerichtshilfe should be controlled by municipal welfare offices or the prosecutor's office. In Rosenblum's analysis, this battle developed into a conflict that pitted judges and prosecutors who defended retributive justice and judicial supremacy against welfare officials who advocated a welfarist approach that focused on social diagnosis and rehabilitation. Unlike Finder, then, who explains the judiciary's resistance to forensic psychiatry primarily as a defense of the rule of law, Rosenblum interprets the judiciary's resistance to the intrusion of welfare offices as a defense of judicial supremacy and retributive justice. This difference in interpretation may be attributable to the difference in the samples of judges: whereas Finder focuses on juvenile court judges, Rosenblum looks at regular judges and prosecutors. But it also nicely illustrates the fact that the penal reform movement's push for the integration of criminal justice into the broader arenas of medicine, education, and welfare was criticized and resisted from two rather different perspectives: on the one hand, by jurists who were concerned that the reforms were undermining important rule-of-law principles, especially the due process guarantees designed to protect the individual against the power of the state, and on the other hand, by jurists who regarded the reforms as a threat to the principle of retributive justice, the supremacy of the law, and the control of jurists (rather than psychiatrists or welfare workers) over criminal justice.

Constructions of Crime in the Courts, Media, and Literature

Crime and criminal justice attracted considerable public attention during the Weimar years, especially in the Berlin press. Berlin reporters such as Paul Schlesinger, Moritz Goldstein, and Gabriele Tergit transformed court reporting into a prominent journalistic genre and made it a major feature of the capital's daily press. Their reporting was strongly influenced by the "criminological turn," that is, by the endeavor to understand the causes of crime. But whereas Weimar-era criminology was characterized by a strong tension between searching for genetic explanations of crime and recognizing the role of environmental factors, Weimar Berlin's court reporters tended to attribute the deeds of the accused primarily to social factors. As Daniel Siemens has demonstrated, although the reporters were generally deferential toward psychiatric expert opinions presented in court, they did not usually adopt their conclusions and, instead, presented sympathetic portraits of the defendants as normal people who fell victim to circumstances.[35]

Two sorts of trials attracted particular attention at the time (and have likewise attracted special attention from historians): political trials and murder trials, especially those involving sexual crimes. The political violence of the early Weimar years, which ranged from communist insurrections on the left to Hitler's Beer Hall Putsch on the right, resulted in a great number of trials for political crimes. These trials quickly gave rise to contemporary criticism from leftist authors who criticized the judiciary for "being blind on the right eye," that is, for imposing much harsher sentences on left-wing than on right-wing political criminals.[36] Starting in the 1960s, this line of argument was taken up by historians who seized on the Weimar judiciary's right-wing bias as an explanation for the subsequent complicity of the judicial system in the crimes of the Nazi regime.[37] This long-standing focus on the reactionary political views of Weimar judges has recently been challenged by studies that approach the history of Weimar political justice from a broader perspective. In his study of the left-wing lawyer Hans Litten, Benjamin Hett has pointed out that Weimar judges were part of a larger judicial system that included the parliament, the justice ministries, a critical press, and highly skilled private lawyers, all of whom significantly affected judicial culture. Especially in political cases, aggressive defense lawyers made use of the extensive right to call witnesses and mobilized the press and lobby groups.[38] In his work on Weimar political trials, Henning Grunwald has called for studying the entirety of the proceedings rather than just the verdict and shifting the focus from the judges to the ideologically committed defense lawyers on the left and the right, who often radically redefined their roles. Instead of serving the interests of the client (working toward an acquittal or a minimal sentence), these lawyers stage-managed the trials to generate maximum propagandistic impact for the benefit of their political party. From this perspective, purposely provoking the court into rendering a harsh verdict could be counted as a *victory* for the defense.[39]

Despite the prominence of political trials, the most famous trials of the Weimar era were those involving *Lustmord* (sexual murder). The most sensational among these were the trials of several serial sexual murderers, including Carl Grossmann, the "Blue Beard" of Berlin (1921–1922), Fritz Haarmann, the "butcher of Hannover" (1924–1925), and Peter Kürten, the "vampire of Düsseldorf" (1930–1931), on whom Fritz Lang's famous film *M* was based.[40] The chapters by Sace Elder, Eva Bischoff and Daniel Siemens, and Todd Herzog all examine famous murder trials from the Weimar era by analyzing the narratives about perpetrators and victims that were constructed in court, in medical expert testimony, in the press, and in literary works.

Arrested in August 1921 and tried a year later, Carl Grossmann was accused of having murdered as many as twenty women in his apartment; it was widely concluded that the murders had been sexually motivated. By focusing on the gap between press narratives and witness narratives, Sace Elder's chapter illuminates the social history and the cultural construction of crime, gender, and class in postwar Berlin. Whereas the press marginalized Grossmann's victims as prostitutes or hapless country girls, the narratives of female witnesses reveal that Grossmann's victims represented a cross-section of women from his neighborhood, including married women and mothers. The fact that these women accompanied Grossmann to his apartment in the hope of employment, a handout, or trading sex for money thus reveals working-class women's dire circumstances rather than a criminal subculture of pimps and prostitutes. As Elder shows, the neighbors' failure to intervene when they heard screams coming from Grossmann's apartment also reveals a broad cultural acceptance of violence against women among the urban working class.

Whereas Elder's study of the Grossmann case focuses on the narrative constructions of the victims, Eva Bischoff and Daniel Siemens's analysis of the 1928 murder trial of Karl Hussmann centers on the narrative constructions of the perpetrator. The Hussmann trial presents an interesting case because unlike Grossmann, Haarmann, and Kürten, Hussmann was acquitted.[41] To explain why, despite considerable circumstantial evidence, Hussmann was not regarded as a sexual murderer (*Lustmörder*), Bischoff and Siemens examine the trial's press coverage and the psychiatric expert opinions. The press coverage was very different from that of the Grossmann and Haarmann trials. To prevent sensationalist coverage, the court had agreed to cooperate with the press in return for the press's refraining from reporting on the case's sexual aspects. This clearly worked to Hussmann's advantage. According to Bischoff and Siemens, the main reason why the medical experts did not construct Hussmann as a psychopathic homosexual *Lustmörder* was that they could not envision a member of their own social class as a sexual psychopath. (Grossmann, Haarmann, and Kürten were all working class.) As this chapter demonstrates, the medical explanations of crime that were making inroads into Weimar's courtrooms remained amazingly malleable because psychiatric definitions of abnormality were often little more than bourgeois moral judgments couched in medical language.[42]

The portrayal of crime in literature and film was no less influenced by the criminological turn than the court reporting in the popular press.[43] In his 1924 novella *Die beiden Freundinnen und ihr Giftmord*, the distinguished Weimar novelist Alfred Döblin went further than Weimar's newspaper reporters in exploring the tensions involved in identifying the causes of crime. Döblin's "case history" was based on the 1923 trial of Ella Klein and Margarete Nebbe for the murder of Klein's husband and the attempted murder of Nebbe's husband.[44] Döblin spent much of his book recounting the arguments presented at trial, at which experts who attributed the women's crimes to certain physiological or psychological abnormalities, such as childhood traumas and homosexuality, clashed with those who found the causes in social conditions, such as spousal abuse, poverty, and society's stigmatization of homosexuality. But as Todd Herzog shows in his chapter, Döblin then went on to argue that it was in fact impossible to construct a coherent narrative or causal explanation of the case. Connecting the Weimar Republic's crisis of faith in justice to a larger modernist crisis of narrative, Döblin was suggesting that the traditional case history failed to explain the cause of criminality because, in Herzog's words, its emphasis on the individual "fails to look beyond the borders of individuality, fails to look precisely at this border that goes into crisis in modernity." In short, Döblin was trying to come to grips in literary terms with the same tension that characterized criminological research in the Weimar years, namely the great complexity of the interaction of biological and social factors, whose unraveling was becoming more, not less, elusive the more criminologists studied the subject.[45]

Criminal Justice under the Nazi Regime

The history of criminal justice under the Nazi regime poses the problem of continuity and change with particular starkness. Until quite recently, the historiography of law under National Socialism was characterized by two strands of interpretation.[46] Presenting the Nazi seizure of power as a radical break in German legal history, the first interpretation argued that the Nazi regime "perverted" the judicial system and transformed Germany from a *Rechtsstaat* (state governed by the rule of law) into an *Unrechtsstaat* (state governed by injustice). Early apologetic versions of this interpretation portrayed the legal profession in the Nazi era as a passive "tool" (*Werkzeug*) that was "defenseless against the penetration of state-sponsored injustice into the judicial realm";[47] later, critical versions presented German jurists as having played an *active* role in the process of perverting justice.[48] While the apologetic version was clearly counterfactual, even the critical version of the "perversion of justice" thesis greatly underestimated the continuities across 1933. Stressing these continuities was the hallmark of the second strand of interpretation, which we might call the "continuity thesis." In an early version of this thesis, Social-Democratic legal scholar Gustav Radbruch (who had served as justice minister in the early Weimar Republic) argued that the German judiciary's willingness to enforce unjust Nazi laws was best explained by German legal positivism, in the sense that legal positivist jurists accepted the laws passed by the legislator without any reference to natural law or other norms.[49] This thesis, however, proved hard to maintain in the face of considerable evidence that, far from merely implementing Nazi law in a legal-positivist manner, German judges had frequently used their judicial discretion to push Nazi policies beyond what was dictated by strict adherence to the law. This critical view of the judiciary formed the basis of a new version of the continuity thesis, which attributed German judges' participation in Nazi injustice not to their supposed legal positivism but to their ideological affinity for Nazism, which this version of the thesis traced back to right-wing, anti-Republican attitudes among the German judiciary in the

Weimar period.[50] The problem with this interpretation, which virtually became orthodoxy in the 1980s and 1990s, is that it concentrates almost exclusively on the continuities in right-wing ideology among the judiciary without examining the broader but more complex continuities in German legal history across the 1933 divide.

Moving beyond these two master narratives, the most recent work on the history of criminal justice under the Nazis paints a complex picture of ruptures and continuities.[51] There can be no doubt that the Nazi seizure of power brought about a number of significant changes in criminal justice. First, the Nazis used the justice system for the persecution of their political opponents, whose activities were criminalized, and the racial persecution of the Jews, through laws such as the Nuremberg Laws (1935), which, among other things, criminalized sexual relations between Jews and Gentiles as *Rassenschande* (race defilement).[52] Second, the Nazis attacked the Weimar penal reform movement for having emasculated criminal justice and called for the strengthening of retribution instead of rehabilitation.[53] Over time, especially after the outbreak of the war, this emphasis on retribution led to ever more draconian punishments, including the escalating use of the death penalty even for minor offenses.[54] Third, the Nazis made a clear break with legal tradition by eroding several of the due-process guarantees that were at the core of the rule of law. In particular, they permitted the use of analogy in criminal law, thus making it possible to prosecute acts that were not mentioned in the penal code but could be construed as "analogous" to acts that were illegal under the code.[55] Finally, the Nazi regime created an extra-legal detention system under the control of the SS and the police: the concentration camps. The concentration camp system allowed the regime to circumvent the remaining due-process guarantees of regular criminal justice by detaining people indefinitely without charges or trial.[56] The categories of people interned in concentration camps expanded over the course of the Nazi regime and included the regime's political enemies (socialists and communists), racial minorities (Jews, Sinti and Roma), homosexuals, Jehovah's Witnesses, people labeled as "asocials" (vagrants, beggars, and the so-called work-shy) as well as certain categories of criminals ("habitual criminals").[57] Even defendants who were acquitted in a regular criminal trial were sometimes rearrested by the Gestapo for detention in a concentration camp immediately after their acquittal. In all these ways, the Nazi seizure of power brought about drastic changes in criminal justice and completely destroyed the rule of law.

Despite these ruptures, however, there were also important elements of continuity across 1933. Chief among them was the continuity in personnel. With the exception of those dismissed for racial or political reasons, most German judges, prosecutors, and lawyers continued to serve under the Nazi regime and enforced Nazi laws, often with enthusiasm. Their support of the Nazi regime is best explained not by their adherence to legal positivism, but by the same combination of factors that explain why most members of the German elites supported the Nazis, including conservative nationalism, anti-Communism, and anti-Semitism as well as conformity and careerism.

Just as important, however, is another line of continuity that is often overlooked, namely that connecting Nazi penal reforms to the pre-1933 penal reform movement. For even though the Nazis attacked Weimar penal reformers as weakkneed humanitarians who had undermined criminal justice, they actually implemented parts of their penal reform agenda. Perhaps the clearest example of this was the Law against Habitual Criminals of November 1933, which introduced the indefinite detention of "dangerous habitual criminals," a measure the penal reformers had been calling for since the turn of the century. The same law also introduced medical treatment for mentally abnormal offenders, another one of the reformers' long-standing demands.[58] More generally, the Nazis pushed the logic of the modern school's demand that punishments should depend on the personality of the offender (rather than the offense) further than anyone previously had: Nazi legislation started to define certain "criminal types" (*Tätertypen*) that were to receive particular punishments. This strategy became especially prominent in the rapid succession of decrees and laws passed after the outbreak of the war. The "criminal types" that were created in these decrees included the *Volksschädling* (national parasite) of the Volksschädlingsverordnung of 5 September 1939, the *jugendlicher Schwerverbrecher* (juvenile serious criminal) of the Verordnung zum Schutz gegen jugendliche Schwerverbrecher of 4 October 1939, and the *Gewaltverbrecher* (violent criminal) of the Gewaltverbrecherverordnung of 5 December 1939;[59] the trend found its culmination in the catchall criminal type of the *Gemeinschaftsfremder* (community alien) in the 1944 draft for a Gemeinschaftsfremdengesetz, which, however, never became law.[60] To be sure, all these criminal types were in part defined by certain acts, but their definitions included attempts to describe personality types whose antisocial tendencies supposedly warranted especially draconian punishment. That the definitions of these personalities sometimes drew on criminal-biological categories fit in well with Nazi eugenics and biopolitics.

The observation that Nazi criminal law was gradually shifting from a *Tatstrafrecht* (offense-based criminal law) toward a *Täterstrafrecht* (offender-based criminal law) is not meant to suggest that Nazi criminal law was the logical outcome of the modern school's penal reform agenda. At least two crucial differences between the penal reform movement and Nazi criminal justice must therefore be pointed out. First, Franz von Liszt and his fellow reformers were fully committed to the due-process guarantees that nineteenth-century liberals had fought for (Liszt famously called the criminal code the "Magna Carta of the criminal"); the Nazis, as we have seen, were not. Second, the Nazis realized only the repressive side of the penal reform agenda, whereas the pre-1933 reform movement had always combined its call for the indefinite detention of incorrigible habitual criminals with a commitment to rehabilitating everyone who could be reformed and to replacing punishment with educational and therapeutic measures for juveniles and abnormal offenders. That said, the experience of Nazi criminal justice certainly revealed the enormous danger posed by the increase in judicial discretion that the modern school's agenda required.

Robert Waite's chapter on juvenile justice in Nazi Germany presents a revealing case study that illustrates many of the key features of Nazi criminal justice.[61] Focusing on the Verordnung zum Schutz gegen jugendliche Schwerverbrecher (Decree for the Protection against Juvenile Serious Offenders) of October 1939 and its implementation during the war, Waite's analysis demonstrates the ambivalent relationship of Nazi legal reform to the pre-1933 penal reform movement. On the one hand, the 1939 Decree was a blatant attempt to roll back the special treatment for juvenile offenders that the penal reform movement had fought for and achieved in the Juvenile Justice Act of 1923; for the 1939 Decree made it possible to try certain juvenile offenders as adults to impose adult punishments on them. On the other hand, the very strategy by which this rollback was accomplished, namely, the invention of the criminal type of the *jugendlicher Schwerverbrecher*, employed the penal reform movement's strategy of individualizing punishment by matching penal sanctions to the offender rather than the offense. The chapter's account of juvenile justice between 1939 in 1945 also illustrates the process of cumulative radicalization by which criminal justice became ever more draconian and ultimately escalated into state terror.

Postwar Criminal Justice

In some respects, Germany's defeat and the fall of the Nazi regime utterly discredited the country's criminal justice system. Everyone knew that most German jurists—whether prosecutors, judges, or professors of law—had eagerly cooperated with the Nazi regime in almost every conceivable way. And yet Germany's criminal justice system survived the war relatively intact and quickly began functioning again, mostly with the same prosecutors, judges, and law professors. Whereas the major war criminals were tried by the Allies at the Nuremberg War Crimes Trial of 1945–1946 and a number of successor trials, the task of prosecuting lower-level Nazi crimes fell to German courts.[62] Their reluctance to prosecute the crimes of the Nazi regime was, of course, closely related to their disinclination to face up to their complicity in the Nazi regime.[63] As mentioned earlier, the question of how to explain that complicity found its first answer in Gustav Radbruch's thesis that German jurists' legal positivism had rendered them defenseless against the Nazis' arbitrary and criminal laws. This thesis was eagerly endorsed by the legal profession because it provided an impersonal explanation that conveniently avoided the sensitive questions of jurists' ideological affinities to Nazism and their personal responsibility. The fact that Radbruch was a Social Democrat who had been dismissed from his professorship by the Nazis only strengthened the exculpatory power of the "legal positivism thesis."[64] This thesis also played an important part in the renaissance of natural law that took place in postwar West Germany. For if the Nazis' crimes had been made possible by legal positivism, so the argument went, then the remedy must lie in an appeal to the eternal values of natural law, which were often given a Christian inflection. This renaissance of natural law had a tangible effect on judicial practice. When German courts judged Nazi crimes after the war, they often did so on the basis of natural law arguments.[65]

Even though most German jurists gave themselves an easy pass for their participation in the Nazi regime, the Allies were initially quite intent on denazifying both Germany's jurists and its criminal laws. Whereas denazification authorities in the Soviet zone of occupation conducted a serious purge of jurists, most jurists in the Western zones of occupation and later West Germany survived the denazification proceedings virtually unscathed. Only one German professor of criminal law permanently lost his professorship as a result of denazification; for all others, denazification brought at most short interruptions of their careers.[66] The task of purging criminal law of Nazi elements proved to be a difficult one because it was not always easy to decide whether Nazi-era changes in criminal law were specifically National Socialist or in line with pre-1933 legal traditions. One of the questions, for instance, was whether the 1935 changes made to the penal code's article 175, which aggravated the criminalization of male homosexuality, should be considered National-Socialist in content and therefore voided or not. In 1957 West Germany's highest court decided that the 1935 version was fine and should be kept on the books.[67]

As Petra Gödecke shows in her chapter on the beginnings of penal reform in West Germany, the legacy of the Nazi period and the denazification process had a depoliticizing effect on professors of criminal law. Most retreated from politics and penal policy and turned toward "pure scholarship" in the form of jurisprudence and legal philosophy. As a result, only a minority participated in the resumption of penal reform efforts in the postwar years. Law professors who had been closely associated with the Nazi regime generally stayed out of these debates altogether. This did not mean that those who participated were untainted; many had also been complicit with the Nazi regime. The postwar penal reform debates reproduced the conflict between the supporters of retributive justice and the advocates of the individualization of punishment that had characterized German penal reform since the Kaiserreich. As Gödicke demonstrates, the triumph of retributivism in postwar penal reform discourse was due to a confluence of factors: First, the general renaissance of natural law made it easier to base criminal justice on the metaphysical foundation of retributive justice. Second, postwar jurists wrapped their return to retributive justice in the flag of democracy by arguing that the West German constitution's (*Grundgesetz*) protection of human dignity was an endorsement of free will, individual responsibility, and retributive justice. Finally, the retributivists sought to discredit the modern school's penal reform agenda by associating it with Nazism. That this smear was disseminated by criminal law professors who had themselves been deeply implicated in the Nazi regime is one of the great ironies of German postwar legal history. To be sure, as we have seen, Nazi criminal justice did indeed draw on parts of the modern school's agenda; but it was also strongly shaped by retributivism. Presenting Nazism as the logical outcome of the penal reform movement was therefore a gross distortion. Gödecke's story ends in the late 1950s. When West Germany passed a set of comprehensive reforms of the penal code ten years later, in 1969–1970, that set of reforms did indeed implement significant elements of the modern school's agenda: individualizing punishment, strengthening rehabilitation, and increasingly replacing prison sentences with alternative sanctions. Nevertheless, these reforms remained constrained by a criminal justice system based on the general principle of retributive justice.

Whereas Petra Gödecke's chapter examines the discourse of legal academics in the Western zones of occupation and West Germany, Jennifer Evans's chapter focuses on the practitioners of juvenile justice in Berlin-Brandenburg and the Soviet zone of occupation, later the GDR.[68] The social dislocations of the early postwar years made juvenile waywardness and petty crime a widespread and pressing social problem, especially in large cities like Berlin.[69] The response of the East German authorities abandoned the punitiveness of Nazi juvenile justice in favor of a renewed focus on rehabilitation and reintegration. In doing so, however, they drew on the established institutions and approaches of juvenile justice as they had coalesced during the Weimar years. The turn toward rehabilitation did not signal a retreat of state power but brought with it an intensification of the state's intervention in the lives of individual youths. Even though the two German states sometimes sought to use penal policy as a tool in the Cold War, juvenile justice in both states was quite similar. Despite the East German state's revolutionary rhetoric it was just as wedded to bourgeois sexual norms and gender stereotypes as the West German state. The gendering of juvenile justice was perhaps most evident in the role of sexuality in the definitions of male versus female waywardness and delinquency. For girls, sexual promiscuity by itself was considered evidence of juvenile delinquency or at least waywardness. For boys, juvenile delinquency was usually defined in terms of petty theft and shirking work; only if boys were suspected of homosexuality or homosexual prostitution did sexuality become an issue. Similarly, although GDR juvenile justice policy touted its lofty goal of creating socialist citizens, in practice it was just as focused on inculcating a strict work ethic as juvenile justice in the capitalist West.

Conclusions

The history of criminal justice in modern Germany has become a vibrant field of historical research. The chapters in this volume not only lay the groundwork for writing a history of crime and criminal justice from the Kaiserreich to the early postwar period, but demonstrate that research in criminal justice history can make important contributions to other areas of historical inquiry. Thus the conclusion that Imperial Germany's criminal justice system came much closer to the liberal ideal of the rule of law than historians have long assumed sheds new light on long-standing debates about the Kaiserreich's political culture. Criminal justice forms an essential element of political rule. Yet penal codes, institutions, and practices also represent great forces of inertia that tend to survive political regime changes with only minor modifications. This paradoxical combination of political relevance and inertia makes criminal justice an excellent lens for examining the complex mixture of continuity and change across different political regimes. As we saw, the study of criminal justice and penal reform under different political regimes demonstrates that it can be difficult to distinguish a legal system's "progressive" or "liberal" features from its supposedly "repressive" ones. Many features of criminal justice, and indeed of the modern state, are politically ambivalent, harboring both emancipatory and repressive potentials, whose activation depends on the political circumstances.

The study of the influence of criminology, psychiatry, and other human and social sciences on criminal justice elucidates the larger process of the "scientization of the social," that is, the increasing use of scientific expertise in almost all areas of social life.[70] As several chapters show, the history of modern criminal justice is inextricably interwoven with the history of psychiatry, in particular with the ambition of psychiatrists to provide medical remedies for social problems. Private and public welfare agencies, too, sought to harness scientific expertise to find better solutions to social problems. Since penal reformers integrated welfare services into the work of the courts as well as the spectrum of penal sanctions, criminal justice became so closely intertwined with welfare that it seems fair to say that the history of the modern welfare state cannot be written without studying the history of criminal justice. Yet the "scientization of the social" must not be understood as a one-way street of science penetrating criminal justice. The history of modern penal reform is not one of criminal jurists simply ceding authority to medical doctors, for instance, but one of disciplinary boundary disputes. Most of the time, jurists kept the upper hand as they learned to integrate scientific, especially medical, knowledge into penal reform proposals, legislation, judicial practice, and the administration of punishment. Although over the first half of the twentieth century medical doctors and welfare workers came to play a larger role in criminal justice than ever before, criminal jurists were remarkably successful in assimilating new types of knowledge in order to buttress their dominant position in the criminal justice system.

Criminal trials reflect the society in which they take place and therefore provide an important source for the social and cultural history of their times. Several chapters demonstrate how the study of criminal trials illuminates the social and cultural history of the Weimar Republic, for instance. Others show that the history of criminal justice can profitably be combined with media history and the history of literature because the representations of crime and criminal justice in the press, literature, and other media provide a rich topic of research that sheds new light not only on criminal justice but on social and cultural history more generally.

Much remains to be done, not only in fleshing out the history of criminal justice in modern Germany but in unlocking the power of criminal trials as historical sources. The records of vast numbers of criminal trials remain unexplored, ready to be discovered—to teach us not only about courtroom practices and legal culture but about a great variety of historical topics ranging from the history of sexuality to economic history. Finally, more comparative work in the history of crime and criminal justice should help us better discern which aspects of the story were specifically German.

Notes

1. Michel Foucault, *Surveiller et punir: Naissance de la prison* (Paris: Gallimard, 1975); translated as: *Discipline and Punish: The Birth of the Prison* (New York: Pantheon, 1978); for a lucid analysis and critique of Foucault's book, see David Garland, *Punishment and Modern Society: A Study in Social Theory* (Chicago: University of Chicago Press, 1990), 131–175. The first British studies dealt with the eighteenth century: E. P. Thompson, *Whigs and Hunters: The Origin of the Black Act* (New York: Pantheon, 1975) and Douglas Hay, Peter Linebaugh, John Rule, E. P Thompson, and Cal Winslow, eds., *Albion's Fatal Tree: Crime and Society in Eighteenth-Century England* (New York, Pantheon, 1975); but British research on crime and criminal justice quickly expanded to include the nineteenth and twentieth centuries: see Michael Ignatieff, *A Just Measure of Pain: The Penitentiary in the Industrial Revolution 1750–1850* (New York: Pantheon, 1978), David Garland, *Punishment and Welfare: A History of Penal Strategies* (Aldershot: Gower, 1985), Clive Emsley, *Crime and Society in England 1750–1900* (Harlow: Longman, 1987; 2nd ed., 1996); W. J. Forsythe, *Penal Discipline, Reformatory Projects and the English Prison Commission 1895–1939* (Exeter: University of Exeter Press, 1990). For a recent comparative survey, see Clive Emsley, *Crime, Police, and Penal Policy: European Experiences 1750–1940* (Oxford: Oxford University Press, 2007).

2. See Gerd Schwerhoff, *Historische Kriminalitätsforschung* (Frankfurt am Main: Campus, 2011); Andreas Blauert and Gerd Schwerhoff, eds., *Kriminalitätsgeschichte: Beiträge zur Sozial- und Kulturgeschichte der Vormoderne* (Konstanz: UVK Universitätsverlag Konstanz, 2000).

3. See Rebekka Habermas and Gerd Schwerhoff, "Vorbemerkung," in *Verbrechen im Blick: Perspektiven der neuzeitlichen Kriminalitätsgeschichte*, ed. Habermas and Schwerhoff, (Frankfurt am Main: Campus, 2009), 10–12.

4. See Lutz Raphael, "Die Verwissenschaftlichung des Sozialen als methodische und konzeptionelle Herausforderung für eine Sozialgeschichte des 20. Jahrhundert," *Geschichte und Gesellschaft* 22 (1996): 165–193; Kerstin Brückweh, Dirk Schumann, Richard F. Wetzell, and Benjamin Ziemann, eds., *Engineering Society: The Role of the Human and Social Sciences in Modern Societies, 1880–1980* (Houndmills: Palgrave Macmillan, 2012).

5. Recent studies on the nineteenth century include Rebekka Habermas, *Diebe vor Gericht: Die Entstehung der modernen Rechtsordnung im 19. Jahrhundert* (Frankfurt am Main: Campus, 2008); Desiree Schauz, *Strafen als moralische Besserung: Eine Geschichte der Straffälligenfürsorge 1777–1933* (Munich: Oldenbourg, 2008); Sylvia Kesper-Biermann, *Einheit und Recht: Strafgesetzgebung und Kriminalrechtsexperten in Deutschland vom Beginn des 19. Jahrhunderts bis zum Reichsstrafgesetzbuch 1871* (Frankfurt am Main: Vittorio Klostermann, 2009). See also Rebekka Habermas, "Rechts- und Kriminalitätsgeschichte revisited—Ein Plädoyer," in *Verbrechen im Blick: Perspektiven der neuzeitlichen Kriminalitätsgeschichte*, ed. Habermas and Schwerhoff, (Frankfurt am Main: Campus, 2009), 19–41.

6. Excellent introductions to Imperial Germany's criminal justice system are provided in Benjamin Hett, *Death in the Tiergarten: Murder and Criminal Justice in the Kaiser's Berlin* (Cambridge: Harvard University Press, 2004), 11–54, and in Eric Johnson, *Urbanization and Crime: Germany 1871–1914* (New York: Cambridge University Press, 1995), 15–51. On the 1871 German penal code (*Reichsstrafgesetzbuch*) and its origins, see Sylvia Kesper-Biermann, *Einheit und Recht*, 270–371, and Werner Schubert and Thomas Vormbaum, eds., *Entstehung des Strafgesetzbuchs*, 2 vols. (Baden-Baden, 2002; Berlin, 2004). An analysis focusing on public criticism of the judicial system (*Justizkritik*) is provided by Uwe Wilhelm, *Das Deutsche Kaiserreich und seine Justiz: Justizkritik—politische Strafrechtssprechung—Justizpolitik* (Berlin: Duncker & Humblot, 2010). For a survey of German criminal justice in the nineteenth and twentieth centuries, see Thomas Vormbaum, *Einführung in die moderne Strafrechtsgeschichte* (Berlin, 2009). The classic work on the history of German criminal justice, first published in 1947 but still worth consulting, is Eberhard Schmidt, *Einführung in die Geschichte der deutschen Strafrechtspflege*, 3rd ed. (Göttingen: Vandenhoeck, 1964). A good collection of sources, with commentary, is Wolfgang Sellert and Hinrich Rüping, *Studien- und Quellenbuch zur Geschichte der deutschen Strafrechtspflege, vol. 2: Von der Aufklärung bis zur doppelten Staatsgründung* (Aalen, 1994).

7. See Kenneth Ledford, "Lawyers, Liberalism, and Procedure: The German Imperial Justice Laws of 1877–79," *Central European History* 26 (1993), 165–193.

8. For the contemporary charges of class justice, see Detlef Joseph, ed., *Rechtsstaat und Klassenjustiz: Texte aus der sozialdemokratischen "Neuen Zeit" 1883–1914* (Freiburg: Rudolf Haufe, 1996); Karl Liebknecht, "Rechtsstaat und Klassenjustiz" [1907], in Liebknecht, *Gesammelte Reden und Schriften* (Berlin: Dietz, 1958–1971), 2, 17–42; Erich Kuttner, *Klassenjustiz* (Berlin, 1913).

9. See Heinrich Hannover and Elisabeth Hannover-Drück, *Politische Justiz 1918–1933* (Frankfurt: Fischer, 1966), 22–26; Bernt Engelmann, *Die unsichtbare Tradition: Richter zwischen Recht und Macht 1779–1918* (Cologne: Pahl-Rugenstein, 1988), 1, 187–318, esp. 233; Johnson, *Urbanization and Crime*, 26, 29, 39–40.

10. Kenneth F. Ledford, "Formalizing the Rule of Law in Prussia: The Supreme Administrative Law Court, 1876–1914," *Central European History* 37 (2004): 203–224, quote 224; see also Ledford, "Lawyers, Liberalism, and Procedure."

11. Gary D. Stark, *Banned in Berlin: Literary Censorship in Imperial Germany, 1871–1918* (New York: Berghahn Books, 2009), 1–20.

12. Ann Goldberg, *Honor, Politics, and the Law in Imperial Germany, 1871–1914* (Cambridge: Cambridge University Press, 2010), 11.

13. See also Hett, *Death in the Tiergarten*, 1–5, 220–228.

14. On German lawyers see Kenneth Ledford, *From General Estate to Special Interest: German Lawyers 1878–1933* (Cambridge: Cambridge University Press, 1996).

15. For a broader analysis of the culture of the criminal courtroom in Imperial Germany, see Hett, *Death in the Tiergarten*; on the press coverage and public resonance of the era's criminal trials see Philipp Müller, *Auf der Suche nach dem Täter: Die öffentliche Dramatisierung von Verbrechen im Berlin des Kaiserreichs* (Frankfurt am Main: Campus, 2005); an illuminating study of a ritual murder case is provided by Helmut Walser Smith, *The Butchers Tale: Murder and Anti-Semitism in a German Town* (New York: Norton, 2002).
16. On the penal reform movement, see Wetzell, "From Retributive Justice to Social Defense: Penal Reform in Fin-de-Siècle Germany," in *Germany at the Fin de Siècle: Culture, Politics, and Ideas*, ed. Suzanne Marchand and David Lindenfeld (Baton Rouge: Louisiana State University Press, 2004), 59–77; Christian Müller, *Verbrechensbekämpfung im Anstaltsstaat: Psychiatrie, Kriminologie und Strafrechtsreform in Deutschland 1871–1933* (Göttingen: Vandenhoeck, 2004), 125–169; Wetzell, *Inventing the Criminal: A History of German Criminology, 1880–1945* (Chapel Hill: University of North Carolina Press, 2000), 31–38; Silviana Galassi, *Kriminologie im Deutschen Kaiserreich: Geschichte einer gebrochenen Verwissenschaftlichung* (Stuttgart: Steiner, 2004), 339–414; Monika Frommel, "Internationale Reformbewegung zwischen 1880 und 1920," *Erzählte Kriminalität: Zur Typologie und Funktion von narrativen Darstellungen in Strafrechtspflege, Publizistik und Literatur zwischen 1770 und 1920*, ed. Jörg Schönert (Tübingen: Niemeyer, 1991), 467–495; Schmidt, *Einführung*, 355–399. On the broader context of social and moral reform see Andrew Lees, *Cities, Sin, and Social Reform in Imperial Germany* (Ann Arbor: University of Michigan Press, 2002).
17. Joseph, ed., *Rechtsstaat und Klassenjustiz*; Liebknecht, "Rechtsstaat und Klassenjustiz."
18. On libel prosecutions of the Social-Democratic press see Goldberg, *Honor, Politics, and the Law*, 81–114; on the history of political criminal justice, see Dirk Blasius, *Geschichte der politischen Kriminalität in Deutschland, 1800–1980* (Frankfurt: Suhrkamp, 1983). The standard account of the SPD during the era of the antisocialist laws remains Vernon Lidtke, *The Outlawed Party: Social Democracy in Germany, 1878–1890* (Princeton: Princeton University Press, 1966).
19. On the international aspect, see Sylvia Kesper-Biermann and Petra Overrath, eds., *Die Internationalisierung von Strafrechtswissenschaft und Kriminalpolitik (1970–1930): Deutschland im Vergleich* (Berlin: Berliner Wissenschaftsverlag, 2007), and Peter Becker and Richard F. Wetzell, eds., *Criminals and Their Scientists: The History of Criminology in International Perspective* (Cambridge/New York: Cambridge University Press, 2006).
20. Wetzell, "From Retributive Justice"; Müller, *Verbrechensbekämpfung*, 125–141; Wetzell, *Inventing the Criminal*, 31–38; Schmidt, *Einführung*, 370–381. The penal reform movement's seminal programmatic text is Franz von Liszt, "Der Zweckgedanke im Strafrecht," *Zeitschrift für die gesamte Strafrechtswissenschaft* 3 (1883), 1–47.
21. On the history of German criminology see Wetzell, *Inventing the Criminal*; Peter Becker, *Verderbnis und Entartung: Eine Geschichte der Kriminologie des 19. Jahrhunderts als Diskurs und Praxis* (Göttingen: Vandenhoeck, 2002); Galassi, *Kriminologie im Deutschen Kaiserreich*; Mariacarla Gadebusch Bondio, *Die Rezeption der kriminalanthropologischen Theorien von Cesare Lombroso in Deutschland von 1880–1914* (Husum: Matthiesen, 1995); Ylva Greve, *Verbrechen und Krankheit: Die Entdeckung der "Criminalpsychologie" im 19. Jahrhundert* (Cologne: Böhlau, 2004); Karsten Uhl, *Das "verbrecherische" Weib: Geschlecht, Verbrechen und Strafen im kriminologischen Diskurs 1800–1945* (Münster: Lit, 2003). Especially on post-1945 criminology, see Imanuel Baumann, *Dem Verbrechen auf der Spur: Eine Geschichte der Kriminologie und Kriminalpolitik in Deutschland 1880 bis 1980* (Göttingen: Wallstein, 2006). On the international context, see Becker and Wetzell, eds., *Criminals and Their Scientists*.
22. On Lombroso see Mary Gibson, *Born to Crime: Cesare Lombroso and the Origins of Biological Criminology* (Westport, Conn.: Praeger, 2002).
23. The history of German prisons in the period 1870–1918 is not well researched; one of few works that includes coverage of this period is Sandra Leukel, *Strafanstalt und Geschlecht:*

Geschichte des Frauenstrafvollzug im 19. Jahrhundert (Baden und Preussen) (Leipzig: Leipziger Universitätsverlag, 2010). On the general history of German prisons, see Silke Klewin, Herbert Reinke, and Gerhard Sälter, eds., *Hinter Gittern: Zur Geschichte der Inhaftierung zwischen Bestrafung, Besserung und politischem Ausschluss vom 18. Jahrhundert bis zur Gegenwart* (Leipzig: Leipziger Universitätsverlag, 2010); Norbert Finzsch and Robert Jütte, eds., *Institutions of Confinement: Hospitals, Asylums and Prisons in Western Europe and North America, 1500–1950* (New York: Cambridge University Press, 1996); Thomas Krause, *Geschichte des Strafvollzuges* (Darmstadt: Wissenschaftliche Buchgesellschaft, 1999).

24. See Thomas Nutz, *Strafanstalt als Besserungsmaschine: Reformdiskurs und Gefängniswissenschaft 1775–1848* (Munich: Oldenbourg, 2001); Martina Henze, *Strafvollzugsreformen im 19. Jahrhundert: Gefängniskundlicher Diskurs und staatliche Praxis in Bayern und Hessen-Darmstadt* (Darmstadt und Marburg: Hessische Historische Kommission Darmstadt, 2003); Falk Bretschneider, *Gefangene Gesellschaft: Eine Geschichte der Einsperrung in Sachsen im 18. und 19. Jahrhundert* (Konstanz: UVK, 2008).

25. On the history of the death penalty, see Richard Evans, *Rituals of Retribution: Capital Punishment in Germany 1600 to 1987* (Oxford: Oxford University Press, 1996), and Jürgen Martschukat, *Inszeniertes Töten: Eine Geschichte der Todesstrafe vom 17. bis zum 19. Jahrhundert* (Cologne: Böhlau, 2000).

26. Wetzell, "From Retributive Justice"; Müller, *Verbrechensbekämpfung*, 125–169; Wetzell, *Inventing the Criminal*, 31–38; Wetzell, "The Medicalization of Criminal Law Reform in Imperial Germany," in *Institutions of Confinement*, ed. Finzsch and Jütte, 275–284; Schmidt, *Einführung*, 370–381; Liszt, "Der Zweckgedanke."

27. Wetzell, "From Retributive Justice," 71–74, 76.

28. On penal reform during the Weimar Republic see Müller, *Verbrechensbekämpfung*, 180–227; Vormbaum, *Einführung*, 153–183; Schmidt, *Einführung*, 405–424.

29. On the criminal-biological examinations, see Thomas Kailer, *Vermessung des Verbrechers: Die Kriminalbiologische Untersuchung in Bayern, 1923–1945* (Bielefeld: Transcript, 2011); Oliver Liang, "The Biology of Morality: Criminal Biology in Bavaria, 1924–1933," in *Criminals and their Scientists*, ed. Becker and Wetzell, 425–446; Wolfgang Burgmair, Nikolaus Wachsmann and Matthias Weber. "'Die soziale Prognose wird damit sehr trübe . . . ' Theodor Viernstein und die kriminalbiologische Sammelstelle in Bayern," in *Polizeireport München*, ed. Michael Farin (Munich: Belleville, 1999); Liang, *Criminal-Biological Theory, Discourse and Practice in Germany 1918–1945* (Ph.D. diss., Johns Hopkins University, 1999).

30. On the history of German prisons in the Weimar era (and beyond), see also Kai Naumann, *Gefängnis und Gesellschaft: Freiheitsentzug in Deutschland in Wissenschaft und Praxis 1920–1960* (Münster: Lit, 2006). On the history of German prisons during the Nazi era, see Nikolaus Wachsmann, *Hitler's Prisons: Legal Terror in Nazi Germany* (New Haven and London: Yale University Press, 2004).

31. On the history of German juvenile justice and youth welfare, see Edward Ross Dickinson, *The Politics of German Child Welfare from the Empire to the Federal Republic* (Cambridge, Mass.: Harvard University Press, 1996); Christine Dörner, *Erziehung durch Strafe: Die Geschichte der Jugendstrafe 1871–1945* (Weinheim and Munich: Juventa, 1991); Elizabeth Harvey, *Youth and the Welfare State in Weimar Germany* (Oxford: Clarendon Press, 1993); Marcus Gräser, *Der blockierte Wohlfahrtsstaat: Unterschichtjugend und Jugendfürsorge in der Weimarer Republik* (Göttingen: Vandenhoeck, 1995); Detlev Peukert, *Grenzen der Sozialdisziplinierung: Aufstieg und Krise der deutschen Jugendfürsorge von 1878 bis 1932* (Cologne, 1986).

32. On the relationship of psychiatry to criminal justice, see also Richard F. Wetzell, "Psychiatry and Criminal Justice in Modern Germany, 1880–1933," *Journal of European Studies* 39 (2009): 270–289. On the role of experts in criminal justice, see Desiree Schauz and Sabine Freitag, eds., *Verbrecher im Visier der Experten: Kriminalpolitik zwischen Wissenschaft und Praxis*

im 19. und frühen 20. Jahrhundert (Stuttgart: Steiner, 2007); Alexander Kästner and Sylvia Kesper-Biermann, eds., *Experten und Expertenwissen in der Strafjustiz von der Frühen Neuzeit bis zur Moderne* (Leipzig: Meine-Verlag, 2008).

33. See Warren Rosenblum, *Beyond the Prison Gates: Punishment and Welfare in Germany, 1850 to 1933* (Chapel Hill: University of North Carolina Press, 2008); Young Sun-Hong, *Welfare, Modernity, and the Weimar State, 1919 to 1933* (Princeton: Princeton University Press, 1998).

34. On the *Vertrauenskrise*, see Daniel Siemens, "Die 'Vertrauenskrise der Justiz' in der Weimarer Republik," in *Die Krise der Weimarer Republik. Zur Kritik eines Deutungmusters*, ed. Moritz Föllmer and Rüdiger Graf (Frankfurt am Main: Campus, 2005), 139–164; Siemens, *Metropole und Verbrechen: Die Gerichtsreportage in Berlin, Paris und Chicago, 1919–1933* (Stuttgart: Steiner, 2007), 114–144; Henning Grunwald, "Die 'Vertrauenskrise der Justiz' in der Weimarer Republik: Justiz als Krisendiagnostik," in *Krisis! Krisenszenarien, Diagnosen und Diskursstrategien*, ed. Henning Grunwald and Manfred Pfister (Stuttgart: Fink, 2007), 177–199; Robert Kuhn, *Die Vertrauenskrise der Justiz, 1926–1928: Der Kampf um die "Republikanisierung" der Rechtspflege in der Weimarer Republik* (Cologne: Bundesanzeiger, 1983); Claudia Schöningh: *"Kontrolliert die Justiz". Die Vertrauenskrise der Weimarer Justiz im Spiegel der Gerichtsreportagen von Weltbühne, Tagebuch und Vossischer Zeitung* (Munich: Fink, 2000).

35. Daniel Siemens, *Metropole und Verbrechen: Die Gerichtsreportage in Berlin, Paris und Chicago, 1919–1933* (Stuttgart: Steiner, 2007), esp. 213–214, 221–223; Siemens, "Explaining Crime: Berlin Newspapers and the Construction of the Criminal in Weimar Germany," *Journal of European Studies* 39 (2009): 336–352; Sling [Paul Schlesinger], *Richter und Gerichtete* (Berlin: Ullstein, 1929); Moritz Goldstein, *George Grosz freigesprochen: Gerichtsreportagen aus der Weimarer Republik* (Hamburg: Philo, 2005); Gabriele Tergit, *Wer schießt aus Liebe? Gerichtsreportagen* (Berlin: Das neue Berlin, 1999); Kathrin Kompisch, "Gewaltdarstellungen in der Massenpresse der Weimarer Republik am Beispiel des Falles Fritz Haarmann (1924)," in *Repräsentation von Kriminalität und öffentlicher Sicherheit: Bilder, Vorstellungen und Diskurse vom 16. bis zum 20. Jahrhundert*, ed. Karl Härter, Gerhard Sälter, and Eva Wiebel (Frankfurt am Main: Klostermann, 2010), 487–508. On press representations of crime in the Imperial period see Johnson, *Urbanization and Crime*, 53–107.

36. Emil Julius Gumbel, *Vier Jahre politischer Mord* (Berlin: Verlag der neuen Gesellschaft, 1922).

37. Hannover and Hannover-Drück, *Politische Justiz 1918–1933*.

38. Benjamin Carter Hett, *Crossing Hitler: The Man Who Put the Nazis on the Witness Stand* (Oxford/New York: Oxford University Press, 2008), esp. 121–127; Hett, "Hans Litten and the Politics of Criminal Law in the Weimar Republic," *Modern Histories of Crime and Punishment*, ed. Darkus Dirk Dubber and Lindsay Farmer (Stanford: Stanford University Press, 2007), 175–197. For another important study of an anti-Nazi lawyer, see Douglas G. Morris, *Justice Imperiled: The Anti-Nazi Lawyer Max Hirschberg in Weimar Germany* (Ann Arbor: University of Michigan Press, 2005).

39. Henning Grunwald, *Courtroom to Revolutionary Stage: Performance and Ideology in Weimar Political Trials* (Oxford: Oxford University Press, 2012); Grunwald, "From Courtroom to 'Revolutionary Stage': Performing Ideology in Weimar Political Trials," in *Das Gericht als Tribunal oder: Wie der NS-Vergangenheit der Prozess gemacht wurde* (Göttingen: Wallstein, 2009), 41–52; Grunwald, "Der Gerichtssaal als 'revolutionäre Tribüne': Ideologische Selbst-Inszenierung im Medium politischer Prozesse der Weimarer Republik," *Paragrana* 15 (2006): 211–225.

40. See Sace Elder, *Murder Scenes: Normality, Deviance, and Criminal Violence in Weimar Berlin* (Ann Arbor: University of Michigan Press, 2010); Hania Siebenpfeiffer, *"Böse Lust": Gewaltverbrechen in Diskursen der Weimarer Republik* (Cologne: Böhlau, 2005); Kerstin Brückweh, *Mordlust: Serienmorde, Gewalt und Emotionen im 20. Jahrhundert* (Frankfurt/Main: Campus, 2006); Maria Tatar, *Lustmord: Sexual Murder in Weimar Germany* (Princeton: Princeton

University Press, 1995); Kathrin Kompisch, "Wüstling—Werwolf—Teufel: Medienbilder von Serienmördern in der deutschen Massenpresse 1918–1945" (Ph.D. diss., University of Hamburg, 2008); Amber Marie Aragon-Yoshida, *"Lustmord* and Loving the Other: A History of Sexual Murder in Modern Germany and Austria (1873–1932)" (Ph.D. diss., Washington University in St. Louis, 2011). On Fritz Lang's film *M,* see: Anton Kaes, *M* (London: BFI, 2000) as well as Christoph Bareither and Urs Büttner, eds., *Lang: "M-Eine Stadt sucht einen Mörder": Texte und Kontexte* (Würzburg: Königshausen & Neumann, 2010). See also the forthcoming dissertation by Kathrin Kompisch (Hamburg).

41. Haarmann and Kürten were convicted and executed; Grossmann committed suicide before his trial concluded. All of them confessed to at least some of the murders.

42. See Wetzell, *Inventing,* 136–137, 168–178, 297–300.

43. On literary representations of crime, see Todd Herzog, *Crime Stories: Criminalistic Fantasy and the Culture of Crisis in Weimar Germany* (New York, 2009); Isabella Classen, *Darstellung von Kriminalität in der deutschen Literatur, Presse und Wissenschaft: 1900 bis 1930* (Frankfurt am Main: Lang, 1988); Birgit Kreutzahler, *Das Bild des Verbrechers in Romanen der Weimarer Republik: Eine Untersuchung vor dem Hintergrund anderer gesellschaftlicher Verbrecherbilder und gesellschaftlicher Grundzüge der Weimarer Republik* (Frankfurt am Main: Lang, 1987); Klaus Petersen, *Literatur und Justiz in der Weimarer Republik* (Stuttgart: Metzler, 1988); Joachim Linder und Claus-Michael Ort, eds., *Verbrechen—Justiz—Medien: Konstellationen in Deutschland von 1900 bis zur Gegenwart* (Tübingen: Niemeyer, 1999); Jörg Schönert, ed., *Erzählte Kriminalität: Zur Typologie und Funktion von narrativen Darstellungen in Strafrechtspflege, Publizistik und Literatur zwischen 1770 und 1920* (Tübingen: Niemeyer, 1991); Stefan Andriopoulos, "Die Zirkulation von Figuren und Begriffen in kriminologischen, juristischen und literarischen Darstellungen von ›Unfall‹ und ›Verbrechen‹," *Internationales Archiv für Sozialgeschichte der deutschen Literatur* 21 (1996), 113–142; Karsten Uhl, "Die Gewaltverbrecherin im kriminologischen und literarischen Diskurs des frühen 20. Jahrhunderts," in *Frauen und Gewalt: interdisziplinäre Untersuchungen zu geschlechtsgebundener Gewalt in Theorie und Praxis,* ed. Antje Hilbig, Claudia Kajatin, and Ingrid Miethe (Würzburg: Königshausen und Neumann, 2003).

44. On the trial and the larger subject of *Giftmord* (murder by poison) in the Weimar era, see Siebenpfeiffer, *Böse Lust,* 95–150.

45. See Richard F. Wetzell, "Criminology in Weimar and Nazi Germany," in *Criminals and Their Scientists,* ed. Becker and Wetzell, 401–423.

46. For surveys of the historiography, see Thomas Roth, *Verbrechensbekämpfung und soziale Ausgrenzung im nationalsozialistischen Köln: Kriminalpolizei, Strafjustiz und abweichendes Verhalten zwischen Machtübernahme und Kriegsende* (Cologne: Emons, 2010), 19–34; Jürgen Zarusky, "Walter Wagners Volksgerichtshof-Studie von 1974 im Kontext der Forschungsentwicklung," in Walter Wagner, *Der Volksgerichtshof im nationalsozialistischen Staat,* 2nd, expanded edition (Munich: Oldenbourg, 2011), 993–1023; Joachim Rückert, "Justiz und Nationalsozialismus: Bilanz einer Bilanz," in *Fünfzig Jahre Institut für Zeitgeschichte: Eine Bilanz,* ed. Horst Möller and Udo Wengst (Munich, 1999), 181–213; Michael Stolleis, "Recht im Unrecht," in Stolleis, *Recht im Unrecht: Studien zur Rechtsgeschichte des Nationalsozialismus* (Frankfurt am Main, 1994), 7–35, translated into English as "General Introduction," Stolleis, *The Law under the Swastika: Studies on Legal History in Nazi Germany* (Chicago: University of Chicago Press, 1998), 5–24; Gerhard Werle, *Justiz-Strafrecht und polizeiliche Verbrechensbekämpfung im Dritten Reich* (Berlin: de Gruyter, 1989), 5–56; Michael Stolleis and Dieter Simon, "Vorurteile und Werturteile der rechtshistorischen Forschung zum Nationalsozialismus," in *NS-Recht in historischer Perspektive* (Munich: Oldenbourg, 1981), 13–51, translated into English as "Biases and Value Judgments in the Study of National Socialist Legal History," in Stolleis, *Law under the Swastika,* 25–39.

47. Hermann Weinkauff, *Die Deutsche Justiz und der Nationalsozialismus* (Stuttgart: Deutsche Verlags-Anstalt, 1968), 19, 30–31, also esp. 37–38. In the same vein: Hubert Schorn, *Der Richter im Dritten Reich* (Frankfurt am Main: Klostermann, 1959). On Weinkauff see Daniel Herbe, *Hermann Weinkauff (1894–1981): Der erste Präsident des Bundesgerichtshofs* (Tübingen: Mohr Siebeck, 2008).

48. See Martin Broszat, "Zur Perversion der Strafjustiz im Dritten Reich," *Vierteljahreshefte für Zeitgeschichte* (1958), 390–441; Ilse Staff, ed., *Justiz im Dritten Reich: Eine Dokumentation* (Frankfurt: Fischer, 1964); Redaktion Kritische Justiz, ed., *Der Unrechtsstaat: Recht und Justiz im Nationalsozialismus*, vol. 1 (Frankfurt: Europäische Verlagsanstalt, 1979); vol. 2 (Frankfurt, 1984). Closely related to the perversion thesis is the topos of "degenerated law"; see Bernd Rüthers, *Entartetes Recht: Rechtslehren und Kronjuristen im Dritten Reich* (Munich: Beck, 1988); Rüther also speaks of the "perversion of the law" (13). For critical appraisals of the perversion thesis, see Werle, *Justiz-Strafrecht*, 5–7, and Wolfgang Naucke, "NS-Strafrecht: Perversion oder Anwendungsfall moderner Kriminalpolitik?" *Rechtshistorisches Journal* 11 (1992): 279–292, reprinted in Naucke, *Über die Zerbrechlichkeit des rechtsstaatlichen Strafrechts* (Baden-Baden: Nomos, 2000), 361–376.

49. Gustav Radbruch, "Gesetzliches Unrecht und übergesetzliches Recht," *Süddeutsche Juristenzeitung* 1 (1946): 105–108; reprinted in *Gustav Radbruch Gesamtausgabe*, vol. 3, *Rechtsphilosphie III* (C.F. Müller, 1990), 83f.

50. See Ingo Müller, *Furchtbare Juristen* (München, 1987), translated as Ingo Müller, *Hitler's Justice: The Courts of the Third Reich* (Cambridge, Mass: Harvard University Press, 1991); Ralph Angermund, *Deutsche Richterschaft 1919–1945* (Frankfurt: Fischer, 1990); Udo Reifner and Bernd-Rüdeger Sonnen, eds., *Strafjustiz und Polizei im Dritten Reich* (Frankfurt am Main: Campus, 1984).

51. A recent overview is provided in Thomas Roth, "Kriminalpolitik im NS-Regime: Ein Überblick," in Roth, *Verbrechensbekämpfung*, 44–69; see also Vormbaum, *Einführung*, 183–218. Two foundational works are Lothar Gruchmann, *Justiz im Dritten Reich 1933–1940: Anpassung und Unterwerfung in der Ära Gürtner* (Munich: Oldenbourg, 1988) [2d ed. (1990)] and Werle, *Justiz-Strafrecht*. See also Joachim Vogel, *Einflüsse des Nationalsozialismus auf das Strafrecht* (Berlin: Berliner Wissenschafts-Verlag, 2004). On the later period, see Sarah Schädler, *'Justizkrise' und 'Justizreform' im Nationalsozialismus: Das Reichsjustizministerium unter Reichsjustizminister Thierack, 1942–1945* (Tübingen: Mohr Siebeck, 2009). On the Volksgerichtshof (People's Court) see the 2011 edition of Walter Wagner, *Der Volksgerichtshof im nationalsozialistischen Staat*, which includes a report on recent research by Jürgen Zarusky.

52. See Cornelia Essner, *Die "Nürnberger Gesetze" oder die Verwaltung des Rassenwahns 1933–1945* (Paderborn: Schöningh, 2002), and Alexandra Przyrembel, *"Rassenschande": Reinheitsmythos und Vernichtungslegitimation im Nationalsozialismus* (Göttingen: Vandenhoeck, 2003).

53. Wetzell, *Inventing*, 179–180.

54. On the death penalty under the Nazi regime see Evans, *Rituals of Retribution*, 613–737.

55. Wolfgang Naucke, "Die Aufhebung des strafrechtlichen Analogieverbots 1935," in *NS-Recht in historischer Perspektive* [1981], 71–108, reprinted in Wolfgang Naucke, *Über die Zerbrechlichkeit des rechtsstaatlichen Strafrechts* (Baden-Baden: Nomos, 2000), 301-335.

56. See the section on "polizeiliche Verbrechensbekämpfung" in Werle, *Justiz-Strafrecht*, 481–618. On the police, see Patrick Wagner, *Volksgemeinschaft ohne Verbrecher: Konzeptionen und Praxis der Kriminalpolizei in der Zeit der Weimarer Republik und des Nationalsozialismus* (Hamburg: Christians, 1996); Patrick Wagner, *Hitlers Kriminalisten* (Munich: Beck, 1992); Deutsche Hochschule der Polizei et al., eds., *Ordnung und Vernichtung: Die Polizei im NS-Staat* (Dresden: Sandstein, 2011).

57. On the concentration camps, see Jane Caplan and Nikolaus Wachsmann, eds., *Concentration Camps in Nazi Germany: The New Histories* (London: Routledge, 2010). On the targeted groups,

see Robert Gellately and Nathan Stoltzfus, eds., *Social Outsiders in Nazi Germany* (Princeton: Princeton University Press, 2001) as well as Michael Burleigh and Wolfgang Wippermann, *The Racial State: Germany 1933–1945* (Cambridge: Cambridge University Press, 1991).

58. Christian Müller, *Das Gewohnheitsverbrechergesetz vom 24. November 1933* (Berlin: Berliner Wissenschafts-Verlag, 1997), Nikolaus Wachsmann, "From Indefinite Confinement to Extermination: 'Habitual Criminals' in the Third Reich," in *Social Outsiders in Nazi Germany*, ed. Gellately and Stoltzfus, 165–191; Wachsmann, *Hitler's Prisons*, 128–144; Werle, *Justiz-Strafrecht*, 86–108.

59. On these Verordnungen see Werle, *Justiz-Strafrecht*, 233–280, 284–302. On the Verordnung zum Schutz gegen jugendliche Schwerverbrecher, see Robert Waite's chapter in this volume. On the role of *Tätertypen* in Nazi criminal justice, see, for instance, Vormbaum, *Einführung*, 185–88, 204.

60. On the Gemeinschaftsfremdengesetz see Werle, *Justiz-Strafrecht*, 619–680; Schädler, '*Justizkrise' und 'Justizreform'*, 280–316; Walter Fuchs, *Franz Exner (1881–1947) und das Gemeinschaftsfremdengesetz* (Berlin: Lit, 2008); Matthias Willing, *Das Bewahrungsgesetz (1918–1967)* (Göttingen: Mohr Siebeck, 2003), 187–208; Wolfgang Ayass, '*Asoziale' im Nationalsozialismus* (Stuttgart: Klett-Cotta, 1995), 202–209.

61. On juvenile justice under the Nazi regime, see Frank Kebbedies, *Ausser Kontrolle: Jugendkriminalpolitik in der NS-Zeit und der frühen Nachkriegszeit* (Essen: Klartext, 2000); Jörg Wolff, *Jugendliche vor Gericht: Nationalsozialistische Jugendstrafrechtspolitik und Justizalltag* (Munich: Beck, 1992); Ulrike Jureit, *Erziehen, Strafen, Vernichten: Jugendkriminalität und Jugendstrafrecht im Nationalsozialismus* (Münster: Waxmann, 1995).

62. A good introduction to the Nuremberg Trial is provided in Michael Marrus, *The Nuremberg War Crimes Trial 1945–46: A Documentary History* (Boston: Bedford Books, 1997).

63. See Marc von Miquel, *Ahnden oder amnestieren? Westdeutsche Justiz und Vergangenheitspolitik in den sechziger Jahren* (Göttingen: Wallstein, 2004), and Miquel, "Juristen: Richter in eigener Sache," in *Karrieren im Zwielicht: Hitlers Eliten nach 1945*, ed. Norbert Frei (Frankfurt am Main: Campus, 2001), 181–237; Annette Weinke, *Die Verfolgung von NS-Tätern im geteilten Deutschland* (Paderborn: Schöningh, 2002).

64. On Radbruch's biography, see Arthur Kaufmann, *Gustav Radbruch* (Munich: Piper, 1987).

65. See Jörg Requate, *Der Kampf um die Demokratisierung der Justiz: Richter, Politik und Öffentlichkeit in der Bundesrepublik* (Frankfurt am Main: Campus, 2008), 43–56.

66. See Petra Gödecke's chapter in this volume.

67. See *Die Geschichte des § 175: Strafrecht gegen Homosexuelle*, ed. Freunde eines Schwulen Museums (Berlin: Verlag Rosa Winkel, 1990).

68. See also Verena Zimmermann, *Den neuen Menschen schaffen: Die Umerziehung von schwererziehbaren und straffälligen Jugendlichen in der DDR (1945–1990)* (Cologne: Böhlau, 2004); Wolfgang Hofmann, Kristina Hübener, and Paul Meusinger, eds., *Fürsorge in Brandenburg* (Berlin: be.bra Wissenschaft Verlag, 2007). On juvenile justice in postwar West Germany, see Kebbedies, *Ausser Kontrolle*.

69. See Jennifer V. Evans, *Life among the Ruins: Cityscape and Sexuality in Cold War Berlin* (London and New York: Palgrave Macmillan, 2011).

70. See Raphael, "Verwissenschaftlichung"; Benjamin Ziemann, Richard F. Wetzell, Dirk Schumann, and Kerstin Brückweh, "The Scientization of the Social in Comparative Perspective," in *Engineering Society*, ed. Brückweh, Schumann, Wetzell, and Ziemann, 1–40; Raphael, "Embedding the Human and Social Sciences in Western Societies, 1880–1980: Reflections on Trends and Methods of Current Research," ibid., 41–56.

Part I

CRIMINAL JUSTICE IN IMPERIAL GERMANY

Chapter 1

JUSTICE IS BLIND
Crowds, Irrationality, and Criminal Law in the Late Kaiserreich

Benjamin Carter Hett

A Prussian prosecutor knows no fear . . . Justitia still rules in Prussia; Justitia still has the blindfold over her eyes.[1]

The blindfold of Justitia symbolizes the most dreadful problem of legal life; Justitia strikes blindly about her, and often, for the sake of false problems and theories, destroys all human happiness, in the manner of a terrible force of nature.[2]

Early in 1901, a Berlin lawyer named Ludwig Flatau published a surprising pamphlet. The surprise did not lie in the title—"More Protection for the Administration of Justice!"[3]—as commentators of all political stripes had been questioning the practical independence of Germany's courts for years. Nor was there anything surprising or novel about some of Flatau's social prejudices, directed toward eastern Europeans and eastern Germans (among whom "the level of cultivation closely approaches the Slavic regions of Austria");[4] against women; and indeed, against the "the broad masses" anywhere, whose chances of ever acquiring "enlightenment" were "the slimmest imaginable."[5] No, the surprise in Flatau's pamphlet came in the dangers to the integrity of judicial decision-making that he identified. For Flatau, the institutions of German justice now resembled nothing so much as "a fortress whose defensive bulwarks are all set out in one direction," while standing utterly defenseless against new threats that he considered inherent in a "modern, democratic society": "Below the masses, above the strong financial powers."[6] The *demos*, in proletarian or plutocratic form, Flatau argued, was now just as able to exert a corrupting influence on the courts as Frederick the Great had been. The core of his argument rested on the examples of two recent, highly publicized German trials. The trial of a Jewish man for perjury in the West-Prussian town of Konitz had demonstrated the baleful influence of "popular currents led astray by agitators," whereas the trial of the millionaire August Sternberg in Berlin exemplified the American-style danger of "a giant fortune concentrated in one hand."[7]

Flatau's pamphlet was part of a new and quintessentially modern discourse in Wilhelmine Germany. "The masses have come of age," wrote a radical nationalist politician, "through elementary schooling, mass conscription, universal suffrage and the cheap oil lamp."[8] In the years after 1890, a complex of mutually reinforcing technological, social, and political factors combined to create an entirely new kind of mass involvement in public life generally, and in politics in particular. Newspapers became less expensive to print; by virtue of the railways, easier to distribute; and with "elementary schooling and the cheap oil lamp," more widely read. Popular participation in politics, measured not only by voting but by membership in a plethora of political organizations and lobby groups on right and left, increased dramatically. This democratic surge represented both a crisis and an opportunity for the cozy elite of German politics.[9]

Related to the democratic surge was the notorious mood of revolt, or *Aufbruchstimmung* in German-speaking Europe. This mood took many forms: the Nietzsche cult;[10] the various movements of secession in the visual, literary and performing arts; and social movements such as the feminist and gay rights movement (the latter especially conspicuous in Germany).[11] There were secessionists in the legal world as well. Flatau wrote of secessionist trial lawyers who did not respect the older traditions of the bar;[12] Berlin lawyers could be seen calling for their champagne glasses to be refilled in the course of a jury trial.[13] Part and parcel of this secession was a rejection of sober rationality in thought and behavior. At a more serious level, the rationality of outcomes in criminal trials appeared to be threatened in two ways. The first involved the rationality of factual determination: German lawyers were becoming increasingly afraid that the procedural structures of their system were defenseless against the seeming tide of superstition and ignorance from "below." The second was in some respects more insidious: it involved the rationality of legal conclusion. Even in cases where the facts were not disputed, German lawyers were increasingly coming to believe that the law, even when exhaustively codified, could not offer final and indisputable resolution. Such a notion was heresy in the context of late-nineteenth-century legal positivism, which held law to be a closed formal system of logical concepts, cleanly separable from morals, politics, or history. Some critics of positivism were beginning to argue that rather than clinging to the mantle of Olympian formalism, law should seek closer ties with the natural feelings of "the people"; judges should decide individual cases freely on such an intuitive basis.[14] Thus a three-cornered struggle emerged, which would become characteristic of the predicament of German criminal law until 1933. The state was forced to defend its stake in the rational administration of justice against anti-rationalist currents from the political left as well as right. Lawyers of a rationalist bent contributed by formulating a new literature on the sources of judicial error. This literature was assembled from the observation of many cases in which the court system, through its openness to public opinion and the broad scope it gave for the gathering of evidence and the extensions of appeals, seemed to have been blown badly off course.

The continuities in German life from the Wilhelmine to the National Socialist era have long been a staple of historiography.[15] The history of German law has been no different; most historical work has been concerned with demonstrating that the principal continuity between Kaiserreich and Nazism has been that of *Klassenjustiz* and *Weltfremdheit*, of class justice and "being out of touch." Such accounts see the justice system as an instrument of a quasi-authoritarian state in the Imperial period, unwilling or unable to adjust to a democratic republic in the 1920s and thus welcoming the advent of the Nazi regime in 1933.[16] A related, but more theoretically inclined literature, has dealt with the role of legal positivism as either an excuse or explanation for the conduct of German judges in the early twentieth century.[17] This essay seeks to recast these questions. On the one hand, the historiography's charges of authoritarianism and class justice miss what was clear to so many contemporaries of Imperial and Weimar justice: trial outcomes were not dictated by rulers or by judges' social and political biases, but were frighteningly random. The debate in legal theory, on the other hand, tends to obscure the complexity of the interactions of political and jurisprudential philosophy. What was at issue, from the beginning of the twentieth century until the 1930s, was a contest about the ends and the rationality of law. There was no simple formula by which one could infer political positions from jurisprudential ones; the irrationalist challenge to the legal framework of Wilhelmine Germany came from right as well as left, from mass agitation as well as sophisticated legal theorists. The defense of rationality could coincide with a defense of state power (and before 1918 it virtually always did), but it could also go hand in hand with a defense of the liberal heritage of the nineteenth century. Perhaps the chief continuity from the Imperial period through the Weimar period was that the administration of criminal justice moved steadily beyond the control of the state. In this essay I wish to explore the roots of this process in the last Wilhelmine years and demonstrate the (often surprising) links between the intellectual and practical history of law in this period. While the *legal-theoretical* narrative of creeping irrationality is familiar (some have suggested too familiar) to legal historians,[18] the story of irrationality *in practice* is much less familiar. I seek to show how it developed and suggest the somewhat subterranean connections to the legal theories of such well-known scholars as Hermann Kantorowicz and even Max Weber.

The essay begins by surveying several of the court cases that gave birth to the literature of judicial error; I will then demonstrate how these cases merged in the liberal mind to form a new and disturbing account of how the courts worked.

I will conclude with a look at the connection between the literature of judicial error and the more theoretical concern with the rationality of law-finding that animated German jurists after 1900.

Ritual Murder

In the late nineteenth century, the medieval legend of Jewish "ritual murder"—the Christian folk belief that Jews required the blood of a Christian child, usually a boy, for the making of matzo for Passover—underwent a revival in central and eastern Europe. Various explanations have been offered for why this should be so. The revival might have come from the dissemination of early modern folk tales by *Germanisten* like the brothers Grimm; it was certainly given wings by the growth in political and racial anti-Semitism after the 1870s. And if one considers the geography and timing of episodes of ritual murder accusations, it is clear that they always arose in small and isolated rural communities that were hard hit by the great depression of the 1870s to the 1890s.[19]

In Germany, two ritual murder cases became the objects of significant public, political, and judicial attention. The first was the 1891 murder of a small boy named Johann Hegmann in the village of Xanten on the lower Rhine; the second was the murder, nine years later, of a *Gymnasium* student named Ernst Winter in the West Prussian town of Konitz. The Xanten case set a pattern that the Konitz affair would largely follow. Soon after Johann Hegmann's body was found, local opinion, fanned by anti-Semitic activists and journalists who flocked to Xanten, began to attribute the murder to a Jewish butcher named Adolf Buschoff. Prussian authorities, administrative and judicial, were torn between catering to anti-Semitic opinion and preserving the authority of the state. Thus the local prosecutors brought Buschoff to trial, while promising the jurors from the beginning that the evidence would exonerate him (as it in fact did). An anti-Semitic publisher named Heinrich Oberwinder brought out a pamphlet on the case in which he alleged that authorities as highly placed as Prussian Justice Minister Ludwig Hermann von Schelling had given way to a Jewish conspiracy in their handling of the case. This was too much for the Prussian Justice Ministry, and Oberwinder was brought to trial for libel in Berlin. One of the judges, however, displayed sympathy with Oberwinder's position, the evidence exposed the official ambivalence about the Hegmann murder, and though he was convicted, Oberwinder soon received royal clemency.[20] In the prosecution of Oberwinder, as in the case against Buschoff, the Prussian justice system thus displayed a willingness to cater to anti-Semitic opinion as a means of containing it. These cases therefore demonstrated that the integrity of judicial decision-making was vulnerable to any current of public opinion that was vocal enough to worry the men at the ministerial green tables. The Xanten case and its aftermath became the starting point for a new narrative of the baleful influence of mob opinion. But the full flowering of this narrative came only with the Konitz case.[21]

Konitz (today in Poland and known by the Polish name of Chojnice) was a town of approximately eleven thousand inhabitants, a few hundred of them Jewish, the rest evenly divided between Catholics and Protestants.[22] Until 1900, Konitz's principal claim to fame was its *Gymnasium*. One of the pupils was an eighteen-year-old named Ernst Winter, who enjoyed a precocious reputation as a ladies' man. On Sunday, 11 March 1900, Winter disappeared after he had left his *Pension* hinting at a rendezvous. Two days later his body was found in Konitz's Mönchsee, *sans* head and limbs.[23] At first, suspicion for the killing centered on the non-Jewish butcher Gustav Hoffmann. Hoffmann had a plausible motive for the crime. His fourteen-year-old daughter had been receiving Winter's attentions; it was conceivable that Hoffmann had caught Winter with his daughter *in flagrante* and killed him in a rage.[24] That the dismemberment of Winter's body appeared to have been carried out by a skilled hand also added to the suspicions of Hoffmann, as indeed did "certain spots" on Winter's clothing that made it appear likely that shortly before his death he had had "intercourse with a female person."[25] But, inspired in part by previous ritual murder cases, and in part by the claims of a notoriously weak-minded Jewish rag dealer named Alexander Prinz (known in Konitz as "dumb Alex"), stories began to circulate that "the Jews" were responsible, that here was another ritual murder. The evidence: Winter's body had been found near the synagogue and the home of the Jewish butcher Adolf Levy; the body seemed not to contain any blood; and the murder occurred at a time suspiciously close to Passover. These rumors led to a wave of anti-Semitic disturbances in Konitz and across West and East Prussia, Posen, and Pomerania. Jews were jeered on the streets; the windows of Jewish shops and homes were broken. The climax came on 10 June, when the synagogue in Konitz was robbed and then burned down.[26]

Once again, Prussian officialdom displayed a desire to cater to and contain all shades of opinion. Troops were dispatched to maintain order in Konitz, closely followed by two well-known Berlin police detectives, Inspector Alexander Braun and Commissar Wehn. These officials were less than impressed with what they found in Konitz. Inspector Braun said later, "The investigations were dreadfully difficult because the people were so uncommonly agitated. Either one heard, 'I will testify only against the Jews,' or else 'leave me in peace, I don't want to know anything about the case.'"[27] In his reports, he complained of "the accusations of ritual murder against the Jews, which mock all Christian feeling," and he said that these accusations must "be kept out of the discussion."[28] The Chief Prosecutor for the Marienwerder Court of Appeal district, which included Konitz, agreed. He wrote to Justice Minister Karl von Schönstedt on 24 April 1900 to say that he had "taken the opportunity to ensure that officially everything (not absolutely necessary for the investigation) might be avoided that could give more nourishment to the starkly apparent arousal of the population against the Jews." On the other hand, he showed the characteristic desire of Prussian prosecutors to have it all ways when he added, "I do not exclude the possibility that the murder was committed by Jews, and in particular by butchers, for revenge or out of jealousy."[29] A few days later he wrote that "the Jews" had "occasionally contributed to the suspicions by their statements and their behavior."[30]

The "arousal of the population" did, however, most certainly find its way into the legal processing of the case. Part of the reason, as in Xanten, lay in the vulnerability of the judicial institutions to surges in popular opinion, especially when a case had to be built largely on witness testimony. In the days and weeks after the discovery of Winter's body, the burghers of Konitz came forward with all manner of fantastically contrived stories that implicated Jewish families in the killing, especially the butcher Adolf Levy and his son Moritz. Communal resentments or hatreds played a role in the witnesses' attitudes; but so did money. Anti-Semitic activists offered a reward for information on the killing, which the Prussian government gradually topped up until it reached the staggering sum of 32,000 Marks. Many in Konitz were willing to risk a perjury conviction for this kind of sum. The second part of the explanation for the legal reaction in Konitz lay with the prosecutors. Konitz's First Prosecutor Settegast and his successor Schweigger did not share the Berlin detectives' aversion to the anti-Semites; in fact, they seemed at times to be working hand in glove with the agitators and journalists who descended on Konitz after the murder. In a report to Justice Minister Schönstedt, which fiercely criticized Settegast's handling of the case, Settegast's superior Chief Prosecutor Wulff complained that "[Settegast] has not kept himself sufficiently independent of the influence of the press."[31]

As in the Xanten case, no one was ever convicted of Winter's murder; but the authorities busied themselves with a remarkable number of incidental prosecutions of Jewish and non-Jewish citizens of Konitz for perjury or for being an accessory to the killing.[32] And like the Xanten case, the Konitz murder also found its way into Berlin's courtrooms. Reporters from the *Staatsbürger Zeitung*, the pre-eminent anti-Semitic newspaper of Wilhelmine Germany, based in Berlin, had been prominent among the agitators in Konitz in the spring of 1900. On 28 July, First Prosecutor Hugo Isenbiel at Berlin's Superior Court I reported to the Prussian Justice Minister that he had raised an indictment against the responsible editor of the *Staatsbürger Zeitung*, Paul Bötticher, and its publisher, Wilhelm Bruhn. The indictment charged the two men with the libel not only of a number of officials, but also of several Jewish private citizens—including Adolf and Moritz Levy.[33] To be sure, Isenbiel did not display any excess of sympathy for the Jews of Konitz; he showed himself to be as ready to make gestures toward anti-Semitic opinion as had earlier prosecutors. "It might not appear desirable," he wrote to the minister, "to bring a prosecution solely because of the libel of a few Jewish citizens," and so the police and judicial authorities in Konitz,

Marienwerder, and Berlin should also be involved as private prosecutors (*Neben-kläger*). At the same time, Isenbiel was just as anxious to make gestures in other directions: referring to a libel prosecution of the Catholic Center Party's flagship newspaper *Germania,* which Chief Prosecutor Wulff had just launched, Isenbiel said it was not proper that *Germania* alone be prosecuted while the *Staatsbürger Zeitung* was overlooked.[34]

Whether it was wise for the state to fight the battle of Konitz in a Berlin court-room was another question. It was clear from the outset that the defense would seek only to make propagandistic points. Shortly before the appointed trial date of 16 October 1900, the defense raised a series of evidentiary motions to establish that the investigations in Konitz had been carried out incompetently, that public confidence in the administration of justice had thereby been severely shaken, and that the Levys, the businessmen Gustav Caspari in Konitz and Großmann in Lütow were "more or less suspected of having participated in the murder of Ernst Winter."[35] Isenbiel believed that, while the third ground was relevant to the case, because of the libel of the persons involved, the first two grounds were inad-missible, as they could only be matters of the judgment of poorly informed and partisan individuals. And yet the logic of the case drew him inexorably into fight-ing on these "inadmissible" grounds. Thus he wrote to Justice Minister Schön-stedt that he wanted to call the Konitz officials and the Berlin police officers as witnesses before the court to establish that these officials "acted in a thoroughly dutiful and legal manner . . . and in no way committed a bending of the law, and that none of them issued any kind of instruction to work in a definite pattern of sheltering the Jews." Isenbiel wanted the court to be able to assess the demeanor and credibility of these witnesses from personal observation. Instead, to Isenbiel's vexation, the chamber decided to have depositions taken before trial and then introduce into evidence those which seemed valuable. No trial date could be set until all the depositions had been taken.[36]

After these depositions and several other procedural delays (a result of official complaints by Ernst Winter's father, which once again showed the openness of the justice system to delay due to procedural generosity), the trial of Bötticher and Bruhn opened before the second criminal chamber of Berlin Superior Court I on 30 September 1902, almost two years after the original trial date. Bötticher was charged with twenty-six and Bruhn with two counts of libel under the terms of §§ 185 and 186 of the Reich Criminal Code.[37] The authorities clearly conceived the trial as an exercise in public relations. Isenbiel's correspondence with the min-ister showed that this had been his concern all along; presiding judge Superior Court Director Opitz announced early in the trial that all official witnesses had been released from their duty of confidentiality "in order to document that from the state or any official side there is nothing to hide."[38] But because the defense was also playing to the gallery and stubbornly insisted that the Levys had been involved in the killing and that authorities had sought to protect "the Jews," the logic of the case forced the prosecution to counter these allegations. The defense maintained, for instance, that higher officials had instructed the police and the prosecutors in Konitz not to pursue leads against Jewish suspects. Defense attorney Hahn claimed that reports by First Prosecutor Settegast in Konitz and Chief Prosecutor Wulff in Marienwerder from March to June 1900 showed that these officials recommended against prosecuting Moritz Levy for fear of further agitating the crowds in Konitz. Settegast denied that he had said any such thing, but Wulff's evidence came close to substantiating the claim. He had "advised First Prosecutor Settegast that the investigation must be extended in all directions" and that "if it took only a one-sided direction against the Jews a great excitement could, and would be bound to, arise (*könne und müsse . . . entstehen*)."[39]

Settegast admitted that "the chief prosecutor asked me to leave these investigations to the police, since so sharp a procedure on my part could perhaps create bad blood, as I was already suspected of anti-Semitic inclinations." He denied that he had been told simply to drop investigations of Jews. But he admitted that people in Konitz could have gotten a different impression from him in casual conversations at the time, and that his daughter had said similar things among acquaintances.[40] Indeed, Settegast's anti-Semitic tendencies emerged clearly from the record. Later in his testimony he admitted that on the very first day of the investigation he had requested the official documents from the Xanten case, along with those of another "ritual murder case" from the town of Skurz. Not a single day had gone by, he said, in which he did not interrogate a Jewish person: "He had even investigated anonymous denunciations, had not even scorned to question people who claimed to be able to find the culprit by spiritualist means, in short, he had not neglected a single clue against the Jews."[41]

After eight days, the Bötticher and Bruhn trial reached the closing arguments. The defense maintained until the end that Winter's death had been a ritual murder and that the authorities were sheltering "the Jews."[42] The court was not persuaded. After deliberating for several hours, it convicted both defendants and denied them the protection of § 193 of the Criminal Code, the justification of acting in defense of a public interest. Bötticher was sentenced to a year, Bruhn to six months in prison.[43] Their applications for royal clemency were stubbornly resisted by Isenbiel and eventually rejected. In a demonstration of how alienated the anti-Semitic movement had become from the symbols of the Wilhelmine state, the *Staatsbürger Zeitung* vowed that it would carry on the struggle against "everything un-German, and the fatherland-less rabble, without concern for whether higher places approve or not."[44] But like the Xanten case, if the long trail of prosecutions arising out of the Winter murder demonstrated anything, it was the rudderlessness of German criminal justice. The system was driven from pillar to post by conflicting official desires to harness and contain public opinion and an increasingly forlorn desire to preserve the authority of the state.

The Flower Medium

We began this essay with Ludwig Flatau, who seized on the Xanten and Konitz cases as evidence of a new kind of threat to the justice system, a threat from below. This kind of rhetorical operation became increasingly common in the years after 1900, even as the props of the rhetoric became more diverse. The threat from below was not limited to appearing in the form of recirculated medieval anti-Semitic legends; other forms of popular "stupidity" and "superstition" could also confound the courts of the modern age. One example was the spiritualist Anna Rothe, the "flower medium," so named for her supposed ability to pull flowers out of thin air. Rothe was brought to trial in 1903 for defrauding the credulous patrons of her séances. As in the cases of Xanten and Konitz, a defense strategy that made full use of the scope that the laws of criminal procedure allowed defendants forced the prosecution to fight on ground that was less than congenial. In a manner analogous to those earlier cases, the defense argued that Rothe had not committed fraud because the representations she had made were *true*. As a result, in addition to eighty-nine prosecution witnesses, the court summoned forty witnesses requested by the defense: Rothe's satisfied customers, convinced that they had received communications from their dead aunts on the best way to cope with back pain or heard their late spouses reveal the identity of a son's secret lover.[45] The court was not persuaded. In its judgment it went to rather absurd lengths to debunk Rothe's performances. The judges held that hers was a clear case of fraud. Their reasoning was simple. The scientific experts all said that there was no room in the scientific worldview for the existence of spirits; therefore, Rothe had promised something to her patrons that she could not deliver. She had taken money from them to do so. These actions fulfilled the legal definition of fraud. The court sentenced her to eighteen months' imprisonment.[46]

The judgment provoked criticism from a wide spectrum of editorial opinion. This criticism came in three distinct forms. One was that the law should not seek to protect the credulous; another was that it was undignified to use a courtroom as a forum to debate the merits of spiritualism. A third came from lawyers who argued that, for various reasons, the court had erred in law in reaching the decision it did. What was striking about virtually all of the reactions to the case from the liberal press, lawyers, and the legally well-informed, was the manner in which the Rothe case was incorporated into a larger narrative together with the cases of Xanten and Konitz: a narrative of the baleful influence of the masses on the courts, a narrative of liberal despair. Journalist Hugo Friedlaender lamented that despite all of the tremendous progress of modern science, "when one looks more closely at the life of the people, one comes to the recognition that we are still stuck in the middle ages."[47] Maximilian Harden, editor of the idiosyncratic weekly *Die Zukunft*, complained that the "modern worldview" had not yet penetrated from the heights to the "dark quarters of the masses."[48] The celebrated trial lawyer Erich Sello linked the Rothe case not only to the murder of Ernst Winter, but also to another case that had grown out of anti-Semitic riots: the burning of the synagogue in Neustettin in the 1880s, a case in which, as a young lawyer, he had made a name for himself by securing acquittals for several Jewish defendants. "How desperately thin," Sello wrote, "even in our much-praised days, is the veneer of culture that covers the age-old swamp of moral and intellectual barbarity":

> The evil spirits of hatred, of horror, of superstition still lurk under this surface, as they did a thousand years ago, ready to break their weak chains at any moment . . . Anyone who thinks back on the frenzy of persecution, which the fire at the Neustettin Synagogue, and fifteen years later the murder of the *Gymnasiast* Winter, unleashed, even in classes of the population which counted themselves with pride among the cultivated, will no longer regard the horrors of the witch persecutions as . . . a sinister legend from the past whose return in our golden age of enlightenment and tolerance is no longer to be feared.[49]

Sello was also the author of the most penetrating legal analysis of the Rothe case, an analysis that bore a message similar to Flatau's. Sello argued that the Rothe case had demonstrated the vulnerability of legal institutions to ill-founded popular opinion. There were two branches to this claim. The first was that the judges had given time to arguments and to evidence that insulted a courtroom by their very presence in it. "Did it have to be?" he asked. "I know that I am not the only one who regarded the serious discussion of this tomfoolery [*Possen*] as a demeaning of the administration of justice, and who felt a little ashamed as a jurist."[50] But the court had also let the barbarians through the gate by means of an error of legal interpretation. Sello quoted the critical sentence of the decision: "The court holds that those who went to the defendant to see appearances from the spirit world, and instead received conjurers' tricks, have been materially injured; they did not receive that which they could claim contractually." Sello disagreed. The state would only protect *legitimate* contractual interests with the laws of fraud. Contracts that were either immoral or impossible to perform fell outside of the protection of the fraud paragraph. The Imperial Supreme Court, for instance, had held in 1889 that a prostitute who did not receive payment for her services could not claim to have been defrauded. And Franz von Liszt, in his textbook on criminal law, wrote simply, "If the 'claim' in which the disappointed party is injured is not recognized by the law, the possibility of fraud is excluded." Therefore, Sello concluded, so long as no one wished to claim that the summoning of spirits lay within the realm of legally protected interests, Rothe had been unjustly condemned.[51] The court's decision amounted to a statement that it sought to enforce the expectation of *genuine* appearances from the spirit world. And so, as with the Xanten and Konitz cases, the court seemed to have been hijacked, forced to give a platform to views better left in obscurity, forced even, as in some of the Konitz prosecutions, to legitimate those views.

A Narrative of Judicial Error

In the last decade before World War I, cases in which an irrational public opinion seemed to strongly influence court proceedings began to be pulled together as supporting evidence to form a general narrative of judicial error. This was a new narrative, which appeared in a new kind of literature. German legal academics had long been hostile to studying individual trials. Franz von Liszt, professor of criminal law at Berlin University, wrote in a pamphlet on law reform in 1906 that "appeals to the many 'individual cases' prove nothing at all."[52] Practitioners increasingly complained of this scholarly shortsightedness. "We lack a science of the application of law," wrote Bremen lawyer Richard Finger in 1912, "as a sub-genre of legal science; and we especially lack a literature of the application of law."[53] Some worked to fill the gap. A number of lawyers began producing a body of work that proceeded from an observation of the defects in individual trials to broad diagnoses of defects in the system to various recommendations for reform. Their writings offered a remarkably unanimous characterization of the justice system. The problem with the courts was not that they were too harsh or indeed too lenient. It was not that their practice betrayed a consistent bias, at least in political or social terms. The problem was that outcomes were random; as Richard Finger put it, Justitia was truly blind, wielding her sword carelessly and—in every sense—without judgment.

This new literature of judicial error began with the wellspring of all criminal cases: human perceptions and opinions. Its strongly negative assessment of the capacities of ordinary people as informants, witnesses, and consumers of newspapers reflected its roots in the characteristic *fin de siècle* discourse of the degeneracy of the masses.[54] But in one respect the new lawyers' literature was different from the books of Gabriel Tarde, Gustave Le Bon, Max Nordau, or Cesare Lombroso. Sociological, criminological, and legal discourses saw the "dangerous classes" as the raw material or subject matter of scientific inquiry and (more importantly) of legal processing, that is to say, entirely distinct from the institutions of justice. The new literature of judicial error, by contrast, raised the alarm level a notch precisely because it saw that these distinctions were vanishing.

Sello, for instance, devoted a 1910 pamphlet to what he called "The Psychology of the *Cause Célèbre*,"[55] which was chiefly an indictment of the effects of public opinion on the courts. The phenomenon of mass suggestion characteristic of the *cause célèbre* was, he said, "a sickness of the entire population, just one of the many symptoms of a general illness of our social organism, a symptom of that general neurasthenic disposition of our time that grabs for ever newer and greater sensations."[56] Sello believed that this sickness found its way into the courts chiefly through the press. When crimes were especially bloody or when they caused serious damage to the economic, political, or religious interests of a community, public opinion could be whipped up all the more easily by irresponsible journalists. Then "it [is] all the worse for the objective determination of the truth," Sello wrote. "[T]he sources from which the judge is supposed to shape his verdict will run all the cloudier."[57] If it sounded as though Sello were writing about Xanten or Konitz, he was. In a rhetorical illustration entirely typical of the genre, he told his readers that they did not need to travel back in time to the witch persecutions to see such hysteria at work: "Have we not ourselves experienced them with a shudder: . . . the trial concerning the Xanten child-murder, the Konitz and Polna ritual-murder trials, haunted by the horror story of Jewish ritual murder, as in ages past?"[58] The cultural stereotypes typical of liberal gentlemen played a role in Sello's assessment of public opinion:

> Just like the less educated, in comparison to the more highly educated, children and women, too, are . . . as a result of their general mental disposition, in which the power of imagination is uppermost, more commonly victims of mass suggestion than grown-ups and men. . . . So must one be shaken to the core by the inexhaustible quantities of sources of error which flow together to make the task of finding the truth more difficult to the point of impossibility.[59]

Once such ill-formed public opinion had served to set the investigative machinery in gear—through denunciations or the evidence of witnesses in police or judicial investigations—that machinery could all too easily run off in its own directions. This problem was illustrated by Hamburg-area lawyer Julian Witting in an article inspired by the 1900 child-molestation trial of millionaire banker August Sternberg (which had also served as one of Flatau's examples) and the much-quoted claim by First Prosecutor Isenbiel that the state prosecutor's office was the "most objective authority."[60] The legality principle, Witting reminded his readers, which was one of the cornerstones of liberalized criminal law, required the prosecutor to investigate any case that was brought to his attention. Often enough, the prosecutor wished to "kill the case" at this stage, but was reluctant to face the victim's or complainant's official protest to the chief prosecutor (as in the Winter case) and the long reports the complaint would require of him. So instead the prosecutor raised the indictment and told himself "the motions chamber can always turn it down." But the motions chamber did not always do so. Rather, the judges—like the prosecutor—would tell themselves that the case was legally or factually uncertain, so they should bring it before the proper judge. Witting pointed to the dangerous desire to court public opinion that could drive such cases: "Cases even occur in which an indictment is raised and a trial opened, even though not one of the officials involved seeks a conviction." His examples were Xanten and Konitz.[61] The authorities might bring such a prosecution out of the laudable motive of seeking public education. But such a practice raised another danger. To bring about the necessary "clarification," the limits on admissible evidence had to be set as widely as possible. This led in turn to the distended, years-long proceedings characteristic of the Konitz cases; and "this latitude is easily transferred to other 'sensational' trials."[62]

These problems were not confined to the pretrial stages. Lawyers in Wilhelmine Germany increasingly began to find that once a case came to trial, there were all manner of procedural rules and courtroom habits that could cause or fail to prevent errors of justice. Strikingly, the new criticisms were generally directed at rules or institutions that had represented benevolent progress to earlier generations of liberal lawyers. Trial by jury had long been a classic liberal *desideratum* in the criminal courtroom, but in the literature of judicial error this institution began to come under scrutiny. If ordinary people were unsuitable for supplying evidence in criminal trials, surely they were all the more unsuitable for judging them. In view of the acquittal statistics for Wilhelmine jurors, which were much higher than for professional judges sitting without lay colleagues,[63] it was not surprising that a judge like Otto Schwarz should be sufficiently skeptical of juries that he inserted an editorial favoring their abolition into his outline of the laws of criminal procedure.[64] Nor was it very surprising that a police officer like Hans von Tresckow should look at juries with disdain, quoting in his memoirs "the words of a high justice official" who told him "juries are good for a guilty person, they mostly get acquitted. But if a really innocent person ever comes before the jury, they will convict him sure as death."[65] What *was* surprising was the ambivalence, ranging to hostility, with which defense counsel regarded juries.

Sello was prominent among these critics, calling himself "a fundamental opponent of the jury court, at least in the form obtaining in Germany." He hoped indeed that his position would counter the "vulgar prejudice" that a lawyer supported amendments to the criminal law only in so far as they would help his clients get acquitted, as the probability of acquittal was "by long experience greatest in the jury courts."[66] In *Cause Célèbre*, he contrasted the credulous vulnerability of the juror to press and community opinion with the professional judge, who had "daily experience of dutiful practice in seeking and pronouncing the law."[67] Sello wished to see a lay element incorporated in all courts of first instance, including the criminal chambers, but with the lay elements joined with the professional judges in one unit instead of sitting separately as a jury.[68] The famous defense lawyer Fritz Friedmann did not advocate the abolition of the jury court, but he thought it needed reform, as he believed that juries were more likely to convict wrongly than to acquit wrongly. Above all, he thought that juries should be sequestered during the entire length of the trial to insulate them from public and press opinion.[69] Max Alsberg, arguably the greatest trial lawyer in German history,[70] supported the general notion of a jury court—"[T]here are some professions that do not lend themselves to being carried out professionally"[71]—but he could not avoid reservations. In 1911, he wrote a pamphlet about a pornog-raphy trial he had conducted in Bavaria. With the sarcastic condescension of the big city lawyer stuck in the provinces, Alsberg poked fun at the jurors' complete lack of interest in the proceedings, their desire to be finished as soon as possible so that they could get back to their fields, and their efforts to bribe him so that he would reject them from the jury pool.[72] His assessment of the weaknesses of jurors, especially in such a case as a prosecution for "spreading immoral writings," said much about the attitudes of judicial insiders: "The juror who comes from enlightened circles would likely want nothing to do with stamping out the distribution of pictures with fire and sword," he wrote. But jurors were unequal in their understanding of literature and art, an inequality that was "certainly not to be found among professional judges. The academic education which the professional judge has enjoyed always creates a certain common foundation. The lay judges completely lack a comparable equal foundation." Alsberg thought that the remedy was to ensure that along with regular judges or regular jurors, lay judges were appointed for each case, based on no other criteria than that they were social and professional equals (*Standesgenossen*) of the defendant.[73] In other words, the cultivated had to be insulated from the opinions of the great unwashed.

At first, the literature of judicial error was scattered and piecemeal, a composite of newspaper editorials and articles in legal journals and general periodicals like *Die Zukunft*. But in the last Wilhelmine years, several Berlin lawyers began the task of assembling the strands of the new narrative into broadly synthetic accounts. The most prominent among them were the trio Johannes Werthauer, Erich Sello, and Max Alsberg. Their works, though widely different in style, were strikingly similar in their fundamental message: that the danger facing the courts was not consistent political bias but rather randomness of outcomes, which were a product of human and procedural weaknesses, in other words, of irrationality.

Werthauer was first into the field with a pamphlet entitled *Moabitrium: Scenes from the Administration of Justice in the Big City*.[74] It took the form of an account of a day's business in a busy Berlin criminal chamber. That this account was ostensibly fictional was telegraphed, at least to initiates, by the fact that the chamber was designated as the twenty-first. In actuality, Superior Court I, the largest Berlin trial court, had no more than twelve criminal chambers in the Wilhelmine years. But Werthauer's stories were written to serve a serious purpose. As a young lawyer he had been shaken by how frequently innocent people were convicted, and even when he succeeded in securing acquittals for clients he believed to be innocent, he "recognized that this was actually a matter of chance, that the system was so flawed that even correct judgments actually rested on erroneous functioning."[75] Thus in *Moabitrium*, Werthauer's theme was the frightening arbitrariness of justice. The first chapter, "Proceeding I against Müller et al. for theft," tells the story of husband and wife greengrocers, August and Mieze Müller. The Müllers become the innocent victims of a fraud artist who sells them stolen shirts for resale. Things go badly for them from the start. Their lawyer tells them their reputation as honest business people, carefully cultivated over ten years and well known in their street, counts for nothing; big city judges do not know the defendants, and character evidence is irrelevant. The lawyer warns them they should make arrangements for someone to take over their shop in the event that they are convicted, "because one can really never know how it will come out, justice is not only blind in the sense that it should judge with no respect for persons, but also in that it cannot know the right thing to do on its own, as it wasn't there and thus can only rely on third persons."[76] The Müllers are convicted and sentenced to one-and-one-half-year's hard labor—a half-year over the minimum for receiving stolen goods—largely because their failure to confess angers the presiding judge. The young con man who sold them the goods confesses and receives a milder sentence.

If the Müllers are innocents who do not know how to work the system, the second chapter presents their foil. It concerns the trial of a man named Adam Schoppach, who is a *schwerer Junge*, a professional breaking-and-entering artist. Schoppach is arrested the day after he has committed a robbery from a shop on Potsdamer Straße—but the arrest is not for the robbery. Schoppach is arrested for assaulting a schoolteacher on Rosenthaler Straße. A search through the "criminal album" reveals him as a possible suspect, and the police know that one of his girlfriends lives near the scene of the assault. As he is waiting to be interrogated at the police station, Schoppach overhears that he is also being sought for the robbery on Potsdamer Straße. Thinking quickly, he realizes that if he confesses to the assault, he will have an alibi for the robbery, which would carry a much more serious penalty in view of his record. He maintains this "confession" at trial. After some pressure from the presiding judge, he "admits" that he carried out the assault with a knife and not a brass knuckle as he had previously claimed. The judge is pleased with Schoppach's willingness to confess and gives him a light sentence of four months in jail.[77]

The pattern is repeated in case after case. Hardened criminals know how to work the system, are cunning enough to lie, even to their apparent disadvantage, when they recognize that they will be better off in the long run. Innocent and inexperienced people fall victim to their naiveté, the prejudices of the court, the dishonesty of more calculating witnesses, and the inadequacies of the evidence. The lessons of the chapters are summarized in the table of contents. The point of the Müllers' case was "limited possibility for individual judgment of the inhabitants of the big city." The lesson of Adam Schoppach was thus: "Big city alibi. Dependence of the criminal law on the statements of people involved. Limitation of proof of recognition. Exaggeration of the importance of confession." Other dangers included an inadequate recognition of the importance of psychology and the inability of judges to understand the daily life of social classes remote from them.[78] Having established a theme, Werthauer returned to it repeatedly in later years. The titles of his later books alone convey the message. In 1912 he published *Wie leicht man sich strafbar machen kann* (How Easy it is to Become Indicted), which warned non-jurists of the many traps the criminal law can set for the unwary. Werthauer followed this book in 1919 with *Strafunrecht* (The Injustice of Criminal Law), which set out both a critique and an ambitious program of criminal law reform.[79]

Erich Sello was the next lawyer to publish a synthetic treatment of judicial errors. His book, *Die Irrtümer der Strafjustiz und ihre Ursachen* (The Errors of Justice and Their Causes), was conceived as a magnum opus. Published in 1911, though Sello had been at work on it since 1897, it was supposed to be just the first in a multivolume study. It rested squarely on the belief that the positivistic, scientific spirit of the time could be turned to account in the reform of the courts. "My book," he wrote, "should, if it is just to its task, present a collection of practical examples of the lessons of judicial errors taken from experience, and in this sense supplement the material derived from modern experimental research."[80] It consisted of a collection of brief narratives of criminal cases drawn not only from Germany, but from across Europe and North America. Each one, Sello believed, was a case of a judicial error. It was his conviction that the courts were prone to errors to a degree that could only arouse "disquiet and horror."[81] Many of the themes of Sello's collection had been raised by Werthauer: above all, the dangers of false confessions, and the overemphasis that the system placed on them. It made little difference, said Sello, that confessions—"the pride of every inquisitor"—could no longer be extracted from prisoners under torture. "Months of investigatory custody, the reference to a milder judgment in return for a confession, the spiritual torture of the eternal interrogations, are able even today to tempt confessions especially from weaker defendants."[82] Another theme in Sello's collection was errors of medical evidence, above all, the failure of experts and courts alike to recognize that a defendant was mentally ill. But most striking was that, like Werthauer, Sello did not believe the errors of justice worked only one way, to convict the innocent. Though he had only presented such cases in his book, he went as far as to say, "I obviously do not fail to recognize that their number would be considerably outweighed by faulty verdicts in favor of the defendant." Fixing the sources of the one problem would fix those of the other. "The effort that we apply to this task, if it helps us to a deeper insight into the nature of the sources of error in this field . . . will teach us to avoid frivolous acquittals no less than frivolous convictions."[83] The best remedy was science. In his conclusion, Sello wrote, "I am not of the despairing opinion that the administration of justice is damned for all time to remain the prey of error to the dreadful extent that it has up to now." Salvation lay with "the microscope and the photographic apparatus," with blood tests and fingerprints, and with psychology, which would "more and more become the common property of the criminalist."[84] Indeed, for Sello, psychology was the queen of the criminalistic sciences. Earlier, he had written that anyone who thought he could make a career in criminal law without studying psychology would be better off "simply hanging up the trade. . . . He might, as paradoxical as it sounds, sooner dispense with the study of law than with that of psychology."[85]

Max Alsberg was Sello's heir in the combination of skill and combativeness that he brought to the courtroom; and at an early stage in his career he showed himself to be Sello's heir as a scholar of the bar as well. In May 1913, a few months after Sello's death, Alsberg published a collection of cases with a title and method strikingly similar to Sello's *Errors of Justice*. Alsberg did not seek to imitate Sello's "grandly conceived and grandly carried out, though sadly uncompleted, work." Indeed, Alsberg thought that one lesson of Sello's collection was that there was insufficient data for a comprehensive, scientific explanation of judicial errors. However, justice could still be "approached scientifically," and Alsberg's goal was to throw the spotlight on the inadequacy of *remedies* for error. Thus, his book—*Justizirrtum und Wiederaufnahme* (Judicial Error and Retrial) focused on the remedy of *Wiederaufnahme*, the application to open a new trial on the basis of new evidence. The book had two parts. The first was an extended essay by Alsberg, which addressed in turn "the dangers of the criminal trial," "the inadequacy of the remedy of revision" for jury and criminal chamber decisions, and "the limited value of the application for a retrial for the elimination of judicial errors." The second part of the book comprised a collection of cases designed to illustrate the systemic weaknesses. Some of them were trials Alsberg himself had conducted; some of them were submitted by eminent lawyers from all over Germany, among them Alsberg's Berlin colleagues Karl Liebknecht, Siegfried Löwenstein, and Johannes Werthauer.[86] Thus the book reflected the new literature's enthusiasm for learning from experience. As Alsberg wrote, "the life of the law thus gets its say in the second part of this book."[87]

If Sello had concentrated largely on psychology, Alsberg emphasized legal-procedural shortcomings. His view of the principle of orality (*Mündlichkeit*, one of the cornerstones of the Code of Criminal Procedure and a key demand of nineteenth-century legal reformers) was typical. For Alsberg, requiring the oral presentation of all evidence placed excessive demands on the power of the judge to quickly grasp the essential point of a proceeding. It was too easy for the judge to overlook a critical factor in the heat of the moment. More extensive use of documentary evidence, as in civil trials, was the remedy.[88] Ironically, this reform would mean a return to the documentary trials of the *ancien regime*, against which an earlier generation of liberals had struggled. Similarly, Alsberg saw a great weakness in the lack of a procedural mechanism to ensure that the presiding judge brought out exculpatory evidence in his interrogation of the defendant.[89] But this "defect" could be seen as the flipside of the defendant's right to decline to testify in paragraphs 136 and 242 of the StPO.[90] Like many, Alsberg believed that the laws of procedure placed too much emphasis on the principle of "free evaluation of the evidence." Criminal procedure went further in this point than did the civil laws. The Code of Civil Procedure (Zivilprozeßordnung) required the court to state the evidentiary basis for its decision, and the Imperial Supreme Court regularly overturned civil judgments that lacked such a foundation. The Code of Criminal Procedure, by contrast, stipulated only that the grounds for the court's decision "should" be given when the decision rested on circumstantial evidence; the lack of such grounds did not, however, render a decision invalid. Alsberg argued that too many judges took the principle of free evaluation to mean the freedom to write vague or unsupported judgments.[91] Finally, like many Wilhelmine legal commentators, Alsberg was alarmed at the courts' vulnerability to biased or perjurious witnesses and to the inability of honest witnesses to render an accurate account of what they knew: "Through the scientific study of witness testimony, it is ever more strikingly revealed how easily a precise functioning of perception and memory can be disturbed."[92]

Conclusion

For all their differences in points of detail, the writings of Werthauer, Sello, and Alsberg taught one basic lesson: the procedures of the justice system were inadequate to protect the courts from a wide array of human failings. The result was that the courts' decisions were frighteningly arbitrary. Far too often the guilty went free, whereas the innocent were sent to hard labor or the scaffold. The stories these lawyers told were informed by a hard-earned pessimism, garnered in the arena, from too much experience with fumbling jurors and witnesses, arbitrary judges, and cases that dragged interminably in the manner of *Jarndyce v. Jarndyce*.

The dynamic of action and reaction was at work on a more intellectual plane as well—in the realm of legal theory, which in the first decade of the twentieth century was beginning to respond to Germany's recent experience of legal codification. The tempo of codification, modernization, and reform of the law had been accelerating in German-speaking Europe throughout the nineteenth century.[93] After German unification in 1871 there came a final flurry: the Reich Criminal Code in 1871 and the complex of laws of 1877 (the Code of Criminal Procedure, Code of Civil Procedure, Judicial Code, and the Lawyers' Ordinance, all in force in 1879). After two decades of academic debate and legislative wrangling, the capstone was set on this process by the passage of the monumental Civil Code in 1896 (in force in 1900).[94] The new German codes represented the jurisprudential state of the art: they were modern, thorough, comprehensive, the fruits of a centuries-long central European tradition of serious thought about the law by some of the world's foremost thinkers. Must they not, then, provide answers to all conceivable legal questions, so that a judge need only be a "high state bureaucrat with an academic education . . . armed only with a thinking machine, admittedly of the finest sort," his only furniture a green table, able to produce on demand "with the aid of purely logical operations" and with "absolute precision" the "result pre-determined by the legislator"?[95] Not surprisingly, German legal scholars soon concluded that the new codes offered no such panacea. In part, this view reflected practical experience, the realization that, as Oskar Bülow wrote, the utmost of human experience, caution, and imagination could not hope to keep pace with "the freely striving human will, the inventive desire for gain, the cunning of egoism and of crime," which would always throw up unanticipated legal problems.[96] More cynically, but not implausibly, Max Weber speculated that the calls for a "free law" at the beginning of the twentieth century reflected the resentments of jurists who feared being relegated to the status of "subsumtion machine."[97]

The calls for a "free law" came from a new generation of liberal and left-leaning lawyers and law professors, above all from the Czernowitz professor Eugen Ehrlich, the Cassel trial lawyer Ernst Fuchs, and the Freiburg *Privatdozent* (eventually law professor at Kiel) Hermann Kantorowicz.[98] The Free Law movement sought, to varying degrees, a law that was less driven by the formalism and syllogistic logic of nineteenth-century positivism, a law in which the judge played a more critical and creative role, a law that was in closer touch with popular opinion and desires. This movement had everything to do with the perceived threats to the rationality of factual determination we have surveyed thus far, and not just because Hermann Kantorowicz cut his teeth in legal practice with a spell as an associate in Erich Sello's office.[99]

Both sides of the debate over free law acknowledged that at issue were attitudes toward the rationality of law and the place of popular opinion in it. Kantorowicz wrote that "the anti-rationalist outlook" went "hand in hand" with the Free Law movement;[100] and he sought a jurisprudence that would "express the free law that lives in the people."[101] Max Weber, for his part, had nothing but contempt for popular opinion and, logically, for juries, which he dismissed as an example of irrational "Khadi justice." For Weber, the popular and the intellectual tide of irrationality were two sides of the same coin; this assessment led him to some pessimistic conclusions. First of all, Weber worried that "judges or administrators" could not meet the demands of the propertyless classes for social and economic equalization without "assuming the substantively ethical and hence non-formalistic character of the Khadi," that is, giving up everything that was inherent in "lawyers' law." More generally, he was concerned that "the rational course of justice and administration is interfered with not only by every form of 'popular justice' . . . but also by every type of intensive influencing of the course of administration by 'public opinion', that is, in a mass democracy, that communal activity which is born of irrational 'feelings' and which is normally instigated or guided by party leaders or the press."[102] Finally, he was troubled by the "anti-formal tendencies [that] are being promoted by the ideologically rooted power aspirations of the legal profession itself."[103] For Weber, these several "interferences" were "as disturbing as, or under certain circumstances, even more disturbing than, those of the star chamber practices of an 'absolute' monarch."[104]

Max Weber also noted that the trend toward utilitarianism in criminal punishments meant that "increasingly nonformal elements" were being introduced into legal practice.[105] Although one can only speculate about the judicial thought processes in individual cases, there is no doubt that precisely in the years during which Franz von Liszt and the "sociological school" of criminal jurisprudence were advocating a relativistic turn in sentencing practices, the general severity of the sentences handed out by German courts was in steep decline.[106] As there were no essential changes to the sentencing provisions of the Reich Criminal Code in the Imperial period, the evolution in sentencing results had to indicate that judges were thinking differently and more independently of the statute, in precisely the manner the "free lawyers" wished them to. Historians have pointed to many other examples of judicial decisions, before and after World War I, which seemed to flow from an antiformalist orientation.[107] The significance of this trend was that the administration of justice, both before and after 1918, was moving simultaneously out of the control of the state and beyond the reach of formal logic as nineteenth-century jurists had conceived it. The dangers of this trend only became clear with the advent of a state that was both more determined to impose its will than either the Imperial or the Weimar states had been, and at the same time embodied the unreason, superstition, and hate that had shown themselves at Xanten and Konitz.

Notes

This chapter, written especially for this volume, draws on material from the author's *Death in the Tiergarten: Murder and Criminal Justice in the Kaiser's Berlin* (Cambridge, Mass.: Harvard University Press, 2004).

1. First Prosecutor Schweigger at the perjury trial of Moritz Levy, Konitz, West Prussia, 1901. Hugo Friedlaender, "Die Ermordung des Gymnasiasten Ernst Winter in Konitz," in Hugo Friedlaender, *Interessante Kriminalprozesse von Kulturhistorischer Bedeutung*, vol. 3 (Berlin, 1911), 128.
2. Richard Finger, *Die Kunst des Rechtsanwalts. Eine systematische Darstellung ihrer Grundfragen unter besonderer Berücksichtigung der Ehrengerichtlichen Rechtsprechung*, 2nd ed. (Berlin, 1912), 96.
3. Ludwig Flatau, *Mehr Schutz für die Rechtspflege! Legislative Betrachtungen über einige Prozesse aus der letzten Zeit* (Berlin, 1901).
4. Ibid., 17, 69.
5. Ibid., 82.
6. Ibid., 11, 21.
7. Ibid., 21.

8. Geoff Eley, *Reshaping the German Right: Radical Nationalism and Political Change after Bismarck* (Ann Arbor, 1991), 104.

9. This is a theme that many historians have taken on. See *inter alia* ibid.; David Blackbourn, *Populists and Patricians: Essays in Modern German History* (London and Boston, 1987), 217–245; David Blackbourn, *The Long Nineteenth Century: Germany 1780–1918* (London, 1997), 411–416; Margaret Lavinia Anderson, *Practicing Democracy: Elections and Political Culture in Imperial Germany* (Princeton, 2000).

10. Steven E. Aschheim, *The Nietzsche Legacy in Germany, 1890–1990* (Berkeley, 1992).

11. Blackbourn, *Long Nineteenth Century*, 351–399.

12. Flatau, *Mehr Schutz*, 74.

13. Benjamin Carter Hett, "Death in the Tiergarten, and Other Stories: Murder and Criminal Justice in Berlin, 1891–1933" (Ph.D. diss., Harvard University, 2001), 145–241.

14. The classic texts of the so-called Free Law Movement are Oskar Bülow, *Gesetz und Richteramt* (Leipzig, 1885); Eugen Ehrlich, *Freie Rechtsfindung und Freie Rechtswissenschaft* (Leipzig, 1903); Hermann Kantorowicz, *Der Kampf um die Rechtswissenschaft* (Heidelberg, 1906). See also Karl Larenz, *Methodenlehre der Rechtswissenschaft*, 6th ed. (Berlin, 1991); Franz Wieacker, *Privatrechtsgeschichte der Neuzeit. Unter besonderer Berücksichtigung der deutschen Entwicklung*, 2d ed. (Göttingen, 1996).

15. The classic book on the subject remains David Blackbourn and Geoff Eley, *The Peculiarities of German History: Bourgeois Society and Politics in Nineteenth Century Germany* (Oxford, 1984).

16. One of the classic works in this vein is Heinrich Hannover and Elisabeth Hannover-Drück, *Politische Justiz 1918–1933*, 2nd ed. (Bornheim-Merten Lamuv, 1987). The Hannovers' work built on a literature mainly of Weimar legal intellectuals; for a good explanation of the contours of the field, see Robert Kuhn, *Die Vertrauenskrise der Justiz (1926–1928). Der Kampf um die Republikanisierung der Rechtspflege in der Weimarer Republik* (Cologne, 1983). A more recent work that, in its first chapter, makes a similar argument is Eric A. Johnson, *Urbanization and Crime: Germany 1871–1914* (Cambridge, UK, 1995).

17. This question is to legal theory what that of continuities is to German historiography. See Gustav Radbruch, "Gesetzliches Unrecht und übergesetzliches Recht," in Gustav Radbruch, *Rechtsphilosophie*, 8th ed. (Stuttgart, 1975); Hermann Weinkauff, *Die Deutsche Justiz und der Nationalsozialismus. Ein Überblick* (Stuttgart, 1968); R. M. Dworkin, ed., *The Philosophy of Law*, *Oxford Readings in Philosophy* (Oxford, 1977); Lon L. Fuller, *The Morality of Law* (New Haven and London, 1969). For more recent (and in the latter two cases more nuanced) treatments, see Ingo Müller, *Hitler's Justice: The Courts of the Third Reich*, trans. Deborah Lucas Schneider (Cambridge, Mass, 1991); Markus Dirk Dubber, "Book Review: Judicial Positivism and Hitler's Injustice: *Hitler's Justice: The Courts of the Third Reich*, by Ingo Müller," *Columbia Law Review* 93 (1993), 1807–1831; Vivian Grosswald Curran, "Fear of Formalism: Indications from the Fascist Period in France and Germany of Judicial Methodology's Impact," *Cornell International Law Journal* 35 (2001), 101–187.

18. Curran, "Fear of Formalism," 159–161.

19. Georg R. Schroubek, "Zur Tradierung und Diffusion einer europäischen Aberglaubensvorstellung"; Albert Lichtblau, "Die Debatten über die Ritualmordbeschuldigungen im österreichischen Abgeordnetenhaus am Ende des 19. Jahrhunderts," in Rainer Erb, ed., *Die Legende vom Ritualmord. Zur Geschichte der Blutbeschuldigung gegen Juden* (Berlin, 1993), 21, 267–292; Christoph Nonn, "Zwischenfall in Konitz. Anti-Semitismus und Nationalismus im preußischen Osten um 1900," *Historische Zeitschrift* 266 (1998), 387–418; Julius H. Schoeps, "Ritualmordbeschuldigung und Blutaberglaube. Die Affäre Buschoff im niederrheinischen Xanten," in Jutta Bohnke-Kollwitz et al., eds., *Köln und das rheinische Judentum* (Cologne, 1984), 286–299; Arthur Nussbaum, *Der Polnaer Ritualmordprozess. Eine kriminalpsychologische Untersuchung aus aktenmässiger Grundlage* (Berlin, 1906).

20. See Schoeps, "Ritualmordbeschuldigung," 286–290; GStA Rep. 84a/16771, *Strafsache gegen Heinrich Oberwinder wegen Beleidigung*; Hugo Friedlaender, "Der Xantener Knabenmord," in Hugo Friedlaender, *Interessante Kriminalprozesse von kulturhistorischer Bedeutung*, vol. 1 (Berlin, 1910), 69–70.

21. The murder in Konitz has recently become the subject of a very fine social-historical study: Helmut Walser Smith, *The Butcher's Tale: Murder and Anti-Semitism in a German Town* (New York, 2002).

22. *Berliner Tageblatt*, 1 October 1902 A.

23. Paul Block, "Das Räthsel von Konitz III," *Berliner Tageblatt*, 10 November 1900 A; Friedlaender, "Die Ermordung des Gymnasiasten Ernst Winter in Konitz," in Friedlaender, *Kriminalprozesse*, 76.

24. Nonn, "Zwischenfall," 391.

25. *Berliner Tageblatt*, 30 September 1902 M.

26. Friedlaender, "Die Ermordung des Gymnasiasten," 78.

27. Friedlaender, "Die Ermordung des Gymnasiasten," 105.

28. Friedlaender, "Die Ermordung des Gymnasiasten," 105.

29. OSA Marienwerder to JM, 24 April 1900; GStA Rep. 84a/57471, *Ermordung des Gymnasiasten Ernst Winter in Konitz*, Bd. 1, 29, 30.

30. OSA Marienwerder to JM, 2 May 1900; GStA Rep. 84a/57471, *Ermordung des Gymnasiasten Ernst Winter*, 51.

31. OSA Marienwerder to JM, 2 May 1900; GStA Rep. 84a/57471, *Ermordung des Gymnasiasten Ernst Winter*, 52.

32. Paul Block, "Konitzer Auslese," *Berliner Tageblatt*, 12 November 1900 A; Friedlaender, "Die Ermordung des Gymnasiasten," 118, 36.

33. Isenbiel to JM, 28 July 1900; GStA Rep. 84a/16784, *Strafsache contra Boetticher und Genossen*, 1–2.

34. Isenbiel to JM, 22 June 1900; GStA Rep. 84a/57471, *Ermordung des Gymnasiasten Ernst Winter*, 273–274.

35. Isenbiel to JM, 2 November 1900; GStA Rep. 84a/16784, *Strafsache contra Boetticher und Genossen*, 7–11.

36. Ibid.

37. Justus Olshausen, *Kommentar zum Strafgesetzbuch für das deutsche Reich*, 9th ed., vol. 1 (Berlin, 1912), 743, 52, 59.

38. *Berliner Tageblatt*, 2 October 1902 A.

39. *Berliner Tageblatt*, 6 October 1902 A.

40. *Berliner Tageblatt*, 2 October 1902 A.

41. *Berliner Tageblatt*, 3 October 1902 M.

42. *Berliner Tageblatt*, 10 October 1902 M.

43. *Berliner Tageblatt*, 12 October 1902 S.

44. Isenbiel to JM, 6 July 1903; *Staatsbürger Zeitung*, 14 October 1903, 15 November 1903; GStA Rep. 84a/16784, *Strafsache contra Boetticher und Genossen*, 77–78; 90; 92.

45. *Berliner Tageblatt*, 21 March 1903 M.

46. Hugo Friedlaender, "Das spiritistische Medium Anna Rothe," in Friedlaender, *Kriminalprozesse*, 241–242.

47. Friedlaender, "Das spiritistische Medium," in ibid., 208.

48. Maximilian Harden, "Anna Rothe & Co.," *Die Zukunft*, 4 April 1903, 43.

49. Erich Sello, "Der Prozess Rothe," *Die Zukunft*, 18 April 1903, 93–94.

50. Sello, "Der Prozess Rothe," 95–96.

51. Sello, "Der Prozess Rothe," 98.

52. Franz von Liszt, *Die Reform des Strafverfahrens* (Berlin, 1906), 14. The context of this remark is Liszt's rebuttal of an argument favoring abolition of the jury court on the basis that many individual cases showed that "experiences [with juries] had been very bad." Liszt maintained the more traditional liberal view of the virtues of the jury court. As we shall see, defense lawyers who otherwise shared Liszt's liberal orientation but who had personal experience of arguing in front of juries were generally much less enthusiastic about the old institution, an interesting illustration of the difference between theory and practice. Liszt imparted his disdain for learning from the courts to his students. One of the last of them, the distinguished historian of criminal law Eberhard Schmidt, not only never referred to cases in his magisterial *Einführung in die Geschichte der deutschen Strafrechtspflege*, but criticized the Wilhelmine courts for judging individual cases in isolation: "The individual criminal case was treated in isolation rather than from a point of view that took into account the whole of criminality and the whole of criminal justice"—a curious criticism indeed of the work of trial courts. Eberhard Schmidt, *Einführung in die Geschichte der deutschen Strafrechtspflege*, 3rd ed. (Göttingen, 1995), 403.

53. Finger, *Kunst des Rechtsanwalts*, 10.

54. The literature on this subject is, of course, vast. See, for instance, George L. Mosse's introduction to Max Nordau, *Degeneration* (Lincoln and London, 1993); Susanna Barrows, *Distorting Mirrors: Visions of the Crowd in Late Nineteenth Century France* (New Haven and London, 1981); Daniel Pick, *Faces of Degeneration: A European Disorder, c. 1848–c. 1918* (Cambridge, 1989). Richard Wetzell has demonstrated the role of this discourse in the shaping of German criminology: Richard Wetzell, *Inventing the Criminal: A History of German Criminology 1880–1945* (Chapel Hill, 2000), chaps. 1 and 2.

55. Erich Sello, *Zur Psychologie der cause célèbre. Ein Vortrag* (Berlin, 1910).

56. Ibid., 43. For a thorough exploration of the theme of nervousness in Wilhelmine Germany, see the recent book by Joachim Radkau, *Das Zeitalter der Nervosität. Deutschland zwischen Bismarck und Hitler* (Munich, 2000). Radkau takes these witnesses as something more than stereotyped cultural pessimists. Radkau, *Zeitalter*, 203–204.

57. Sello, *Psychologie*, 19.

58. Ibid., 20–21. Polna was a town in Bohemia near the Moravian border. In two trials in 1899 and 1900 a Jewish man named Leopold Hilsner was prosecuted for the murder there of a non-Jewish woman named Agnes Hruza. Hruza's body had been found with a stab wound in the throat on the day before Easter 1899; the same kinds of allegations grew up against Hilsner as against Buschoff in Xanten and Levy in Konitz. Unlike his German equivalents, however, Hilsner was convicted of Hruza's murder, and of a second one as well, although the prosecution eventually dropped the claim of ritual murder and presented the cases as sexual murders. Hilsner was sentenced to death, reduced to lifelong imprisonment. See Arthur Nussbaum, *Der Polnauer Ritualmordprozess. Eine kriminalpsychologische Untersuchung auf aktenmässiger Grundlage* (Berlin, 1906).

59. Sello, *Psychologie*, 30–31.

60. Julian Witting, "Justizchronik," *Die Zukunft*, 12 January 1901, 83–86.

61. Ibid., 84.

62. Ibid., 85.

63. Benjamin Carter Hett, "The 'Captain of Köpenick' and the Transformation of German Criminal Justice, 1891–1914," *Central European History* 36 (2003), 1–43.

64. O. G. Schwarz, *Strafrecht, Strafprozess. Ein Hilfsbuch für junge Juristen* (Berlin, 1907), 249.

65. Hans von Tresckow, *Von Fürsten und anderen Sterblichen. Erinnerungen eines Kriminalkommissars* (Berlin, 1922), 201.

66. Erich Sello, "Strafprozessreform," *Die Zukunft*, 17 December 1904, 380.

67. Sello, *Psychologie*, 40.

68. Sello, "Strafprozessreform," 380–381.

69. Fritz Friedmann, *Hau ist kein verstockter Mörder! Kritische Studie* (Berlin, 1907), 27–28. Friedmann had made similar arguments earlier, in a pamphlet titled "Über die Schwurgerichte," which he discusses briefly in his memoirs: Friedmann, *Was ich erlebte*, 1, 210.

70. The best source of information on Alsberg is Jürgen Taschke, ed., *Max Alsberg: Ausgewählte Schriften* (Baden-Baden, 1992).

71. Max Alsberg, *Der Fall des Marquis de Bayros und Dr. Semerau. Ein Beitrag zur Lehre von der unzüchtigen Schrift und unzüchtigen Darstellung* (Berlin, 1911), 36.

72. Ibid., 8.

73. Ibid., 39–40.

74. Johannes Werthauer, *Moabitrium. Szenen aus der Grosstadt-Strafrechtspflege*, ed. Hans Ostwald, vol. 31, *Großstadt-Dokumente* (Berlin and Leipzig, 1908).

75. Johannes Werthauer, *Strafunrecht. Beitrag aus der Praxis zur Ermittlung und Beseitigung der strafrechtlichen Uebelstände, insbesondere zur Ersetzung des Strafgedankens durch den Erziehungsgedanken* (Berlin, 1919), 4.

76. Werthauer, *Moabitrium*, 16–17.

77. Ibid., 25–29.

78. Ibid., 6–7.

79. Johannes Werthauer, *Wie leicht man sich strafbar machen kann* (Berlin, 1912); Werthauer, *Strafunrecht*.

80. Erich Sello, *Die Irrtümer der Strafjustiz und ihre Ursachen,* vol. 1, *Todesstrafe und lebenslängliches Zuchthaus in richterlichen Fehlsprüchen neuerer Zeit* (Berlin, 1911), 1.

81. Ibid., 2.

82. Ibid., 466.

83. Ibid., 468.

84. Ibid., 467.

85. Erich Sello, *Die Hau-Prozesse und ihre Lehren. Auch ein Beitrag zur Strafprozeßreform* (Berlin, 1908), 130–134.

86. Max Alsberg, *Justizirrtum und Wiederaufnahme* (Berlin, 1913), iii, xiii–xiv.

87. Ibid., xv.

88. Ibid., 3–4.

89. Ibid., 7–11.

90. E. Löwe, *Die Strafprozessordnung für das Deutsche Reich*, 12th ed. (Berlin, 1907), 420, 590.

91. Alsberg, *Justizirrtum*, 26–29.

92. Ibid., 30.

93. See *inter alia* Uwe Wesel, *Geschichte des Rechts. Von den Frühformen bis zum Vertrag von Maastricht* (Munich, 1997); Wieacker, *Privatrechtsgeschichte;* Schmidt, *Einführung.*

94. On the Civil Code, see Michael John, *Politics and the Law in Late Nineteenth-Century Germany: The Origins of the Civil Code* (Oxford, 1989); Wieacker, *Privatrechtsgeschichte.*

95. Hermann Kantorowicz, *Der Kampf um die Rechtswissenschaft*, ed. Thomas Vormbaum, *Juristische Zeitgeschichte* (Baden-Baden, 2002), 5.

96. Bülow, *Gesetz und Richteramt*, 30–31.

97. Max Weber, "The Formal Qualities of Modern Law," in Max Weber, *Max Weber on Law in Economy and Society*, trans. Edward Shils and Max Rheinstein (Cambridge, Mass., 1954), 309.

98. On the Free Law movement, see, apart from the classical text cited in note 14, Karlheinz Muscheler, *Relativismus und Freirecht. Ein Versuch über Hermann Kantorowicz* (Heidelberg, 1984); Larenz, *Methodenlehre.*

99. Karlheinz Muscheler, *Hermann Ulrich Kantorowicz. Eine Biographie* (Berlin, 1984), 32.

100. Kantorowicz, *Kampf,* 23–24.

101. Ibid., 45.

102. Max Weber, "The Rational and Irrational Administration of Justice," in Weber, *Law*, 355–356.

103. Max Weber, "The Formal Qualities of Modern Law," in ibid., 321.

104. Max Weber, "The Rational and Irrational Administration of Justice," in ibid., 355–356.

105. Max Weber, "The Formal Qualities of Modern Law," in ibid., 306–307.

106. Franz Exner, *Studien über die Strafzumessungspraxis der deutschen Gerichte* (Leipzig, 1931), 19.

107. A common example is the *Aufwertungsjurisprudenz* of the Imperial Supreme Court in the 1920s. See Ludwig Bendix, "Die Rechtsbeugung im künftigen deutschen Strafrecht," *Die Justiz* 2, no. 1 (1926), 42–75; Wieacker, *Privatrechtsgeschichte*, 520.

Chapter 2

PUNISHMENT ON THE PATH TO SOCIALISM

Socialist Perspectives on Crime and
Criminal Justice before World War I

Andreas Fleiter

August Bebel, co-founder and recognized leader of the Social Democratic Party (SPD) in Imperial Germany, had a clear idea about the fate of crime under socialism. In his best-selling book *Die Frau und der Sozialismus* (Woman and Socialism), published in 1879, he wrote:

> Neither political nor common crimes will be known in the future. Thieves will have disappeared, because private property will have disappeared, and in the new society everyone will be able to satisfy his wants easily and conveniently by work. Nor will there be tramps and vagabonds, for they are the product of a society founded on private property, and, with the abolition of this institution, they will cease to exist. Murder? Why? No one can enrich himself at the expense of others, and even the murder for hatred or revenge is directly or indirectly connected with the social system. Perjury, false testimony, fraud, theft of inheritance, fraudulent failures? There will be no private property against which these crimes could be committed. Arson? Who should find pleasure or satisfaction in committing arson when society has removed all cause for hatred? Counterfeiting? Money will be but a chimera, it would be "love's labor lost." Blasphemy? "Nonsense! . . . Thus all the fundamental principles of the present "order" become a myth.[1]

Bebel also knew, however, that "unfortunately, we do not yet live in those joyous times in which humanity can breathe *freely*."[2] But until then, what should humanity do about crime? This chapter seeks to illuminate socialist attitudes toward the crime problem by addressing a series of questions, including the following: What role did German socialists assign the fight against crime? What

---

Notes from this chapter begin on page 76.

position did they take regarding the state and its penal policies as well as toward prisoners? What was the impact of the criminalization of the Social Democratic Party (SPD) through the Anti-Socialist Law and the resulting imprisonment of many Social Democrats? How did socialists react to the development of modern criminology, which sometimes included a eugenic agenda? All these questions are, of course, directly connected to socialists' views regarding state and society, as well as their political strategies and experiences in this society.

Socialist calls for legal reform have been discussed by a few older studies, which have examined their content but not their historical context.[3] By contrast, the more recent historiography on criminology and criminal justice before World War I rarely goes beyond a middle-class perspective. According to these studies, the bourgeoisie regarded criminality as a negative mirror image of its own identity, which it increasingly pathologized to exculpate society from its responsibility for the existence of crime. The perspectives of the workers' movement, whether Social Democratic or anarchist, are rarely mentioned.[4] Michel Foucault, on the other hand, argued that the early workers' movement included acts of resistance against the bourgeois "colonization" of delinquency to "reverse this monotonous discourse on crime, which sought both to isolate it as a monstrosity and to depict it as the work of the poorest class."[5] Foucault's thesis of a clear-cut dichotomy between bourgeois and working-class conceptions of crime is, however, questionable. Michael Schwartz, for instance, has shown that "socialist eugenics," too, spoke of a "criminal" underclass and shared many of the penal reform demands made by bourgeois criminology.[6]

We therefore need to examine socialist conceptions of crime and punishment more closely to discern why socialists accepted so much of the explanatory system of "bourgeois" criminology, even though they possessed the theoretical tools to criticize it and fundamentally opposed bourgeois society. A reconstruction of the criminological discourse alone cannot adequately answer this question. To do so would risk reifying the discourse into a historical subject. Instead, this chapter will analyze socialist conceptions of crime and punishment as the products of complex power relations and of a process of interaction in a concrete historical context.[7] The discussion among German socialists was far more extensive, more contested, and more nuanced than the widespread but simplistic thesis that without private property there would be no crime would initially lead one to believe.

Wilhelm Weitling, Karl Marx, and Friedrich Engels

In the first decades of the nineteenth century, Germany experienced unprecedented levels of social distress, which provoked radical protest movements. In the early 1840s, the tailor's apprentice and early socialist Wilhelm Weitling, for example, believed that pauperism could only be abolished by a social revolution.

Therefore, one should not hesitate to incite the immiserated urban masses to launch a long-term guerrilla war. For Weitling, crime was thus a political tool for liberating society, but only until the revolution occurred. As soon as the new social order had been established, further crimes would be considered crimes against the whole people and would no longer be tolerated.[8] Reacting to Weitling, Karl Marx and Friedrich Engels initially also regarded crime as something positive. Engels, however, in his 1845 book *The Situation of the Laboring Class in England* (*Die Lage der arbeitenden Klasse in England*), conjured up a new "proletariat," who was qualitatively different from the "mob," the ordinary poor. This proletariat, especially factory and mine workers, had already overcome "the first stage of opposition to social circumstances, the immediate rebellion of the individual by means of crime," by organizing itself in solidarity and carrying out its actions in a targeted, planned, and disciplined manner.[9]

To describe the rest of the lower classes, Marx and Engels coined the term *Lumpenproletariat* (literally, ragged proletariat). In the wake of various failed revolutions, they wrote in the *Manifesto of the Communist Party* (1847–1848), the "*Lumpenproletariat*, the passive degeneration of the old society's lower classes, will be partially injected into the movement through a proletarian revolution; by its nature, it will be more willing to sell itself for use by reactionaries."[10] The *Lumpenproletariat* simultaneously served as an aggregate category reflecting various social prejudices and as an analytical category that explained the failure of revolutionary movements within the lower classes.[11] To be sure, Marx and Engels saw the immediate causes of crime in alcohol, demoralization, hedonism, and moral decay, which they described in much the same terms as bourgeois reformers and conservatives.[12] Their search for underlying causes, however, led them to regard deprivation and misery as "the necessary consequences of modern industry."[13] Marx's and Engels's solution to this problem was the transformation of society according to socialist principles. Those social strata that did not share this view were doomed. In this sense, their proletariat was not only set off from those above it in the social order, but also from those below it. On the path to revolution, the proletariat could no longer be confused with the mob and thus could no longer be discredited.[14]

Middle-class social reformers and authorities looked for other answers to the problem of crime. For them, crime was above all a product of corrupting social influences against which the delinquent individual had not built up sufficient resistance. Around the middle of the 1830s, the view became dominant that strict solitary confinement would lead prisoners to engage in self-contemplation and improve their conduct. In the new cellular prisons operating on the "penitentiary system" that had been pioneered in the United States and England, religion and work were the most important techniques of moral rehabilitation.[15] This penitentiary system found a critic in Wilhelm Weitling, who asserted that solitary confinement would lead to insanity and condemned it as worse than the

Inquisition.[16] For Weitling, the only proper penal policy was the establishment of communism. Then, only a "natural vestige of human sickness and weakness" would remain, and these misdirected desires would be treated as illnesses. For these cases, Weitling developed a system of "philosophical healing," which physicians would follow in treating the sick until their complete recovery. As a last resort, those who still did not improve would be excluded from society by exiling them to distant islands, so that they could not infect future generations with their sickness through mixing (*Vermischung*) and contact.[17] Weitling followed his utopian model of society to its logical conclusion. Although he regarded human desires as a constant, he could not imagine any resistance to the rules of the ideal society that could result from a rational decision or external circumstances. Every violation must therefore have its origin in the individual and yet be outside that individual's rational control, hence pathological.

Marx and Engels never produced as detailed a theory of punishment as Weitling. Like him, they criticized the cellular prison in *The Holy Family* (1845) as a system that "sooner or later would result in the insanity of the criminal." In addition, they argued, solitary confinement combined judicial punishment with a kind of theological torture, which in its desire to convert the prisoner was worse than a quick execution and still resulted in the destruction of the person. In fact, Marx and Engels held that an effective fight against crime by means of punishment was impossible. In a critique aimed at Hegel, they wrote that "a theory of *punishment* that recognizes the *human being* in the criminal can do this only *abstractly*, in the imagination, because *punishment* and *constraint* go against *human* behavior."[18] In the materialist ideology of Marx and Engels, existence determined consciousness. Thus human weaknesses and desires would be overcome under socialism, and crime itself would disappear along with all its social causes. There would no longer be a *Lumpenproletariat*, whether it degenerated, was swept up in the revolution, or perished with the counterrevolution.

Early Social Democracy:
Darwinism, Penal Reform, and Prison Labor

German socialists' desire to develop a comprehensive scientific theory of the development of society led them to take great interest in Charles Darwin's theory of evolution. Darwinism seemed to offer the opportunity to base the materialist view of history on natural science, thereby overcoming ideological obstacles such as religion.[19] Darwinism did not influence the development of Marx's own theory, in part because Marx had largely developed his theory of society before Darwin published his theory. The same was true of Engels, whose popular writings disseminated the theory of evolution within the workers' movement: It was Engels's theory of society that determined his interpretation of Darwinism, not the other way around. Marx and Engels drew a sharp distinction between the laws of social science and those of natural science, especially when they addressed the fatalistic element of Darwinism, the "struggle for survival."[20]

In the works of August Bebel, however, the realms of society and nature were no longer separated; instead, socialist and Darwinist theories were blended. Bebel saw society as fundamentally shaped by the "struggle for existence" and in a constant state of development. For Bebel, crime was not simply the result of an unjust social order but an indicator of society's stage of development. The increase of crime proved this: "The struggle for existence takes on its most brutal and violent form and thrusts men back into their most primitive state, where they regard one another as mortal enemies."[21] Bebel regarded the accumulation of capital as a barrier to humankind's natural development because it deprived many individuals of the freedom that was necessary for them to develop their full capacities. Still, Bebel countered Darwinist notions of the inevitability of the struggle for survival with a greater emphasis on environmental factors and drew on the Lamarckian idea of the heritability of acquired characteristics to argue against the omnipotence of natural selection.[22]

This synthesis of natural science and social theory was no longer a purely materialist one, as natural science concepts began to shape socialist thinking. Thus, as early as 1875, the socialist newspaper *Leipziger Volksstaat* remarked:

> There can be no doubt that all crime results either from poverty (need) and educational neglect or from an abnormal . . . physical and mental constitution, that is, either from social or physiological causes. In other words: the "criminal" becomes criminal either due to his nature or due to social conditions. . . . Crime is a *disease*—a disease of *society* or a disease of the *individual*.[23]

With this statement, the anonymous author not only contradicted the dominant jurisprudential view that free will was a precondition for legal responsibility, guilt, and punishment, but also deviated from the socialists' focus on the social causes of crime. At the same time, the expectation that socialism would soon be established rendered socialists insensitive to the possible consequences of the application of scientific progress to social problems.[24]

Socialist conceptions of such developments varied significantly, however. Bebel did not pursue the issue of crime and punishment any further. The present, he believed, would soon be overcome, and the socialist future, with its freedom for the development of the individual, would be free of crime.[25] An 1878 essay in Karl Höchberg's journal *Die Zukunft*, which offered the most extensive socialist discussion of the prison system for some time, objected to this view. To be sure, while society was on the path to the ideal state, criminal justice was to be restricted to "unavoidable self-defense." Nevertheless, the article argued, at a time of overcrowded prisons and lively penal reform debates, socialists "as practitioners in the sense that they have experienced punishment" must take part in discussions of crime and criminal justice rather than leaving them up to jurists and prison officials.[26] Instead of a revolutionary perspective, the text outlined an evolutionary path lasting many years. For precisely this reason, the text did not limit itself to theoretical criticisms, but made concrete, practical suggestions for penal reform. The article called for individualized punishment on the model of the so-called progressive system, the introduction of release on probation, and made detailed suggestions regarding the ventilation and heating of the cells, prison food, education, and calisthenics, thus sharply criticizing the current penitentiary system. The article's reform proposals clearly endorsed the notion of a therapeutic criminal justice system that was increasingly being advocated in German penal and prison reform circles.[27] But only two of the demands in this essay had an impact on the socialist party's official policy regarding the prison system in the first decades after the founding of the Reich: those concerning the regulation of prison labor and the treatment of political prisoners.[28]

German workers' organizations had long raised the demand that prison labor be regulated. When the Lassallean and Marxist wings of the German labor movement merged in 1875 to form the Sozialistische Arbeiterpartei Deutschlands (Socialist Workers' Party of Germany), re-named Sozialdemokratische Partei Deutschlands (SPD) in 1890, this demand was included in the new party's Gotha Program. In 1869, Friedrich Wilhelm Fritzsche, a member of the leadership of Ferdinand Lassalle's Allgemeiner Deutscher Arbeiterverein, had called for the prohibition of certain prison industries in a speech in the Reichstag of the North German Confederation. Fritzsche argued that if convicts were to practice the trades that they had learned in prison after their release, they would endanger the morals of young workers and children: "The negative example that released convicts typically provide has such a corrupting effect on these younger colleagues that it is no wonder that such factories literally become schools for criminals." Fritzsche also railed against other consequences of prison industry, including competition for work in the free market, pressure on wages, and a general fall in product prices. His criticism stemmed from craftsmen's traditional concerns about prison work, which they viewed as dishonorable.[29] Social Democracy represented the interests of several specific industries and their workers; here, Fritzsche was defending the interests of workers in his own trade, cigar-making. A general prohibition of productive prison labor was never envisaged. The Social Democratic suggestions, which resembled those made by other parties, aimed primarily at getting prison labor to produce for the state's own consumption, for example, by producing military uniforms or agricultural goods. The minimal demands were that prison labor be paid and that it be offered at usual market prices. The Social Democratic Party made such a proposal in the Reichstag in 1885 and regularly reintroduced the proposal until 1902, but it was never adopted.[30]

The Impact of the Anti-Socialist Law:
Political Prisoners versus "Common Criminals"

The criminal justice issue that the Social Democratic Party was most concerned about was the treatment of political prisoners. This interest was, of course, closely related to the political persecution endured by the party during the twelve long years of the so-called Anti-Socialist Law, passed in 1878 and kept in effect until 1890, which made socialist and social-democratic organizations illegal and led to the imprisonment of countless party activists. The Social Democrat Ignaz Auer calculated the collective toll of the prison sentences served by party members during these years thus: "A thousand years prison for the rapture of reaction. . . . A thousand years of devastated domestic happiness, ruined health, terrible poverty for woman and child, and all too often, the destruction of one's livelihood in their wake!" Even without the passage of special laws, the Social Democrats and their press were repeatedly prosecuted and sentenced to prison for *lèse majesté*, blasphemy, and libel.[31] As a result, up to the turn of the century, Social Democratic discussions of the penal system consisted mainly of demanding various privileges for their incarcerated comrades and insisting on their equal treatment in the various federal states. Concretely, such criticism included demands for the self-provisioning, self-clothing, and self-employment of political prisoners, all of which was at the discretion of the heads of the penal institutions. Social Democrats hoped that such matters could be regulated in a future prison law that would regulate prisons across the Reich, which they and other parties had repeatedly proposed in order to address an omission made at the founding of the Reich.[32] The 1871 Reich Penal Code (Reichsstrafgesetzbuch) had imposed a unified penal code on all of Germany and had also standardized the categories of detention by establishing detention in a *Zuchthaus* for serious crimes, detention in a *Gefängnis* (prison) for lesser crimes, and *ehrenhafte Festungshaft* (honorable detention in a fortress) for "honorable" offenders. But the unification of substantive criminal law was not accompanied by a unification of the prison system. The individual federal states retained a free hand in administering their penal institutions, as the unification of the penitentiary system was postponed indefinitely.[33]

In addition to being recognized as honorable, *Festungshaft* involved many comforts and privileges that had to be fought for in the ordinary penal system, which did not recognize political prisoners as a separate category. Whereas prominent socialists tended to be sentenced to *Festungshaft*, rank-and-file party activists were often sentenced to regular prison. Thus August Bebel experienced his 1872–1873 *Festungshaft* in the Hubertusberg fortress, where he served time together with Wilhelm Liebknecht and other socialists, as a period of rest, during which he recovered from tuberculosis, read, and wrote a great deal.[34] Socialists who were less prominent suffered more under the penal system. Johann Most, for example, tells of comrades who at Plötzensee prison were put into prison uniforms and thrown into communal confinement, while he enjoyed the privilege of being kept in solitary confinement.[35] Indeed, socialists were mainly concerned that they should not be considered the same as, let alone inferior to, "common" criminals. Bebel argued that a common criminal broke the law out of self-interest, while a political criminal acted out of idealism.[36] Johann Most called his fellow prisoners "rogues and ruffians."[37] If socialists asked for better treatment than common criminals, this was not only to ease the conditions of their imprisonment; for them, the distinction between "political" and "common" criminals was a matter of principle. In this sense, their own prison experience did, of course, affect their image of common criminals.

Political and common criminal prisoners were usually separated by a gap in social status, education, and interests. Many Social Democrats found direct interaction with criminals correspondingly difficult, even shocking. In addition, there were preconceptions on both sides. Social Democrats, having read the *Communist Manifesto*, thought that most criminals were part of the *Lumpenproletariat* and were thus agents of reaction. Among the criminal convicts, on the other hand, the criminalization of the Social Democrats by the authorities had consequences as well. Thus the imprisoned socialist Johann Most found himself called a "terrorist" by fellow inmates, who jeered at and stole from him.[38] The two groups of prisoners distanced themselves from each other in mutual mistrust.

As political assassinations and anarchist actions shook Europe in the 1880s, the authorities intensified the criminalization of the Social Democrats.[39] Social Democrats reacted to their stigmatization in two ways. On the one hand, they charged the state and individual representatives of authority with being criminals.[40] On the other hand, they worked to distance themselves from common criminals but also from anarchist practitioners of the "propaganda of the deed," to whom a revolution of the masses seemed possible and necessary. Thus the *Sozialdemokrat* clarified in 1883: "To do away with private property in general is *revolutionary*. To do away with a specific article of private property is, as a rule, the *act of a scoundrel.*"[41] In their conflict with bourgeois authority, the Social Democrats viewed themselves as the morally superior force and thought that time was on its side. Therefore, despite their revolutionary perspective, they restricted themselves to a strictly law-abiding strategy. In fact, Social Democrats suspected that political actions and disturbances that did not follow this strategy were the result of targeted provocations on the part of reactionary forces.

This position was reflected in the definition of *Lumpenproletariat* as formulated by Wilhelm Liebknecht at the 1892 Party Congress. Several fellow socialists were angry that the Party newspaper *Vorwärts* had described rioters as *Lumpenproletariat* in reports on disturbances in Berlin. Liebknecht, however, insisted that *Vorwärts* had to distance itself from those who caused the unrest in order not to give the SPD's enemies any opportunity to use the disturbances as a pretext to pass a new emergency law. As much as he demanded the abolition of private property in general, his moral condemnation of individual law-breaking was strong: "In any event, our fellow party members did not break windows or engage in looting in the February riots. Whoever did that deserves the name *Lumpenproletarier*, and in a much more negative sense than that used by Marx. (Lasting, lively acclamation and applause.)"[42] In the words of labor historian Gerhard A. Ritter, Social Democracy was an "emancipatory movement with strong concepts of bourgeois morality and propriety broadened by the specific concept of the honor of solidarity in the labor struggle and in the political battle."[43]

Socialist analyses of crime often referred to want and misery and to the unjust nature of existing social conditions as causes of crime and called for society to be reshaped accordingly.[44] Nevertheless, socialist discussions of the penal system were mainly shaped by the SPD's struggle against the oppression exerted by the Anti-Socialist Law. The Party leadership's focus on the treatment of political criminals, however, hardly reflected the interests and needs of the social strata for which the leadership claimed to speak. The culture of the workers' movement was not the culture of the workers. Though workers did embrace some of the Party's official views on crime and punishment, especially regarding the social causes of property crime and the issue of class justice, many misdemeanors were tolerated more by SPD voters than by the moralizing party rhetoric.[45] Nevertheless, the Marxist theorist Rosa Luxemburg noted that among ordinary workers, too, a process of self-segregation from a kind of underclass was taking place:

> The workers themselves, especially the better-off ones, those who are organized, like to believe that, all in all, the existence and the struggle of the proletariat are part of the realms of honorability and prosperity. . . . Everyone knows that there are homeless shelters, that there are beggars, prostitutes, secret police, criminals, and "shady characters." But all that is typically viewed as something distant and foreign, as something that lies outside society itself. Between the virtuous workers and these outcasts there stands a wall, and one seldom thinks of the miserable ones on the other side of the wall crawling around in excrement.[46]

The socialist movement could not and did not wish to include the entire proletariat. Although socialist leaders claimed that their movement had an educational and disciplinary mission, they often did not make good on this claim during their time in prison and, instead, kept distance between themselves and ordinary criminals.

The SPD's commitment to Marxist social theory at its 1891 Erfurt Congress had only indirect effects on its analysis of crime. To be sure, Marx and Engels had not contributed much to a theoretical investigation of the problem. For Engels, the respective morality of a society and thus its crime was tied to its stage of economic development. "In a society where the motives for stealing have been removed," he wrote, "how we would laugh at the preacher of morality for solemnly proclaiming the eternal truth: 'Thou shalt not steal!'"[47] By contrast, in the first volume of *Das Kapital* (1867), Marx analyzed the laws on beggary and the first prisons in the fifteenth and sixteenth centuries as "blood legislation against the expropriated" and "laws for the depression of workers' wages." In his 1875 critique of the Socialist Party's Gotha Program, Marx criticized the demand for the regulation of prison work: "One should at least clearly articulate that one does not wish to see the common criminal treated like livestock out of fear of competition, and that one does not wish to cut off their only means of improvement: productive work. That is the least that one could expect of socialists."[48] Following Marx's critique, this demand was dropped when the SPD formulated its Marxist Erfurt Program in 1891, which hardly touched on criminal justice at all.[49] Socialist positions began to become more nuanced in the course of reacting to the discipline of criminology, then in the process of forming.

Socialists and Criminology

The beginnings of a systematic empirical approach to criminality go back to the first half of the nineteenth century. Already in 1835, the Belgian moral statistician Adolphe Quetelet, whom the socialists frequently cited, claimed in his work on "social physics" that criminality was socially determined.[50] In the late 1870s, the Italian psychiatrist Cesare Lombroso caused a huge sensation when he claimed to have deciphered the morphology of the so-called born criminal through anthropometric and craniological screenings. German psychiatrists and jurists criticized Lombroso's criminal anthropology on the grounds that the approach gave too little consideration to social causes of crime.[51] Social Democrats intensified this criticism. To be sure, in a review of 1893, the leading Marxist theoretician Karl Kautsky conceded that "[t]he notion that some kind of criminal type actually exists cannot simply be dismissed. But this type is not the cause of the crime, but rather an effect of the same causes that make the déclassé into a criminal."[52] In this sense, criminal anthropology could perhaps be useful in the future. Otherwise, however, Kautsky had only criticism and derision for Lombroso. Kautsky viewed crime as exclusively conditioned by society and reminded readers that the bourgeoisie, too, especially the factory owners, committed murder when they exploited members of the proletariat, working them to death in their factories.[53]

The teachings of early criminal anthropology faced methodological problems, and their monocausal interpretations left them vulnerable to attack. Criminal anthropology underwent further modifications by the Italian jurist and criminologist Enrico Ferri, who placed social influences like education, family, and economic factors alongside biological and physical factors at the center of his criminal sociology. In the process, he removed the major objections of the socialists. Ferri, who came from a middle-class family, gained considerable credibility in the eyes of socialists when he risked his academic career by declaring his support for the Socialist Workers' Party of Italy in 1893.[54] In socialism, Ferri saw "a further development of Darwinian teachings," according to which the survival of the *best*—not the best *adapted*, as under capitalism—would be ensured. Given Ferri's hereditarian belief in the natural inequality of human beings, the existence of individuals biologically destined to be criminals appeared to him a fact of nature as well as a scientific fact.[55] While, as Kautsky noted in a review, equating nature with society was not genuinely Marxist, this was nevertheless a widespread tendency.[56]

The blueprint for a Marxist-materialist analysis of criminality was provided by an extensive study of crime in France published in the leading socialist weekly *Neue Zeit*, which Kautsky edited. The study was carried out by the French socialist Paul Lafargue, a son-in-law of Karl Marx. Lafargue invoked Marx and Quetelet to demonstrate correlations between the organization of society, economy, and crime, supporting his hypotheses by comparing crime statistics with serial economic data. In a biting criticism of criminal anthropology, he concluded that criminality was exclusively the product of social conditions.[57] His strategy of analyzing criminality through the use of large statistical studies became widely accepted, with German socialists frequently making use of the crime statistics of the German Empire that became available after 1882.[58] Nevertheless, many socialists remained committed to a Darwinist view of society. Thus the Dutch criminologist and socialist Willem A. Bonger (1876–1940), whose 1905 work *Criminalité et conditions économiques* was perhaps the most extensive and most sophisticated criminal study of this type and widely read in Germany, could not divorce himself from the idea that the organization of society hindered the natural evolution of humanity.[59]

The socialists' contradictory attempt to bring together Marxism and Darwinism developed from discussions regarding two primarily bourgeois conceptions. On the one hand, socialists argued against a moralistic, often theological interpretation of criminality, which viewed crime as a moral decision based on free will and as part of a process of moral decay that was blamed on social developments, urbanization, secularization, industrialization, and also on the rise of Social Democracy, with its materialist ideology of revolution.[60] Socialists expended considerable effort using statistics to refute this charge, stressing their own efforts at instilling discipline and preventing crime,[61] and argued that natural science had revealed the idea of free will to be a fiction.[62] On the other hand, the socialists also criticized Social Darwinist theories, such as Ernst Haeckel's, which viewed social developments as the result of the process of selection, regarded social differences as a product of nature, and opposed social-political interventions as counterproductive because they interfered with the process of natural selection.[63] Socialists, by contrast, insisted on drawing a distinction between society and nature because only such a distinction made it possible to conceive of capitalism as a changing and changeable social construct. The inherent ambivalence of the socialist worldview thus combined with a belief in science that only became stronger as the socialist movement developed.

Prostitution, Alcohol, and the *Lumpenproletariat*

The socialist views of criminality and of the *Lumpenproletariat* were also closely bound up with the issues of prostitution and alcohol. According to Marx and Engels, prostitution was a "necessary social institution of the bourgeois world" in which bourgeois men exploited proletarian women to be able to sustain the bourgeois institution of marriage.[64] But within these rational explanations lurked resentments about the degenerative effects of prostitution. Thus the Social Democratic writer and activist Paul Kampffmeyer (1864–1945) noted in 1905: "Manners become coarser, an ambivalent tone enters into social interactions, a dirty joke sneaks into popular tunes and into children's conversations. A moral contagion is transmitted from class to class in the large city." He further warned that prostitution "seizes the body of the social organism and smites it with disease and death."[65] Admittedly, society could be held responsible for driving a proletarian woman to prostitution, but in the end, this meant the way "down into the *Lumpenproletariat*, from which there is no escape."[66] And it was here that prostitution produced the embodiment of the *Lumpenproletariat* criminal: the pimps, whom socialists saw as "parasitic elements," "sworn enemies of society," "dehumanized men" akin to beasts, and the "*pestilence* of capitalist society."[67] In short, for many socialists, the *Lumpenproletariat* was now no longer merely a political-moral problem, but also an objective, biological danger to the health of society.

Many socialists also believed that alcohol played a role in harming health, undermining morality, and causing crime. Thus, in 1890, Karl Kautsky stated: "It is obvious that the same social conditions that create crime also lead to drink. It is therefore easy to understand why a large number of criminals have given themselves over to drink." Once again drawing a line between the proletariat and the *Lumpenproletariat*, however, he also insisted: "Not the militant industrial proletariat, but rather the *Lumpenproletariat*, the decaying petty bourgeoisie and farmers, and those members of the wage-earning classes that have still not achieved class consciousness . . . are the ones who in large part fall victim to alcohol."[68] Kautsky thus articulated a party line that allowed the party to defend itself against the accusations of the temperance movement but also took into consideration the role of drinking in proletarian and socialist subculture; during the time of the Anti-Socialist Law, only taverns were available as meeting places. For this reason, the party leadership actually had a rather indifferent stance toward alcohol.[69]

Advocates of abstinence within the party, however, soon viewed alcohol not only as a substance that numbed pain and pacified the masses in a time of class struggle. They also worried about hereditary factors and thus about the future of coming generations. For the League of Abstinent German Workers (Deutscher Arbeiter-Abstinentenbund), founded in 1903, it was clear that the "restoration of all social relationships, on the one hand, and the elimination of everything that damages protoplasm (the fabric of life) and the unfolding of the innate positive qualities of the individual, on the other, are the only sure ways to prevent the development of crime by eliminating the conditions that give crime life."[70] Here it becomes evident that for all of their attention to the social causes of crime, some socialists already wished to emphasize supposedly physiological factors. From there, it was no longer much of a stretch to endorsing biological explanations of crime and of the *Lumpenproletariat*. When, in 1909, the SPD Reichstag deputy Edmund Fischer (1864–1925) called for the party finally to distance itself from the view of the *Lumpenproletariat* as formulated by Marx and instead embrace modern biological viewpoints, he clearly reflected a development that had been simmering below the surface for some time.[71]

A biological approach to social problems was characteristic of a group of socialist intellectuals who were a minority within the Social Democratic Party but who significantly influenced discussions regarding crime and criminal justice.[72] What is more, even intellectuals, such as Kautsky and Bonger, who consistently employed materialist arguments, did not hesitate to assert that the reproduction of the hard, biological core of degenerates would have to be regulated under socialism.[73] Voices such as that of Michael Sursky, who criticized criminal sociology and its biologization of crime, calling it "the fighter for the interests of the ruling classes," remained isolated. This was also the case because Sursky's arguments were hardly academic in nature, but exclusively ideological.[74] Within the movement, scientism and the adoption of Darwinist evolutionary views had already erased the border between the biological and the social, even for declared Marxists. This trend was facilitated by the socialists' feeling of moral superiority toward those underclasses not organized within the workers' movement. Their elitist moral views made lower-class needs and ways of life appear foreign to them.

Penal Reform and Prison Reform

In the years before World War I, socialists viewed criminal justice and the penal system as institutions that served to protect the ruling classes. These institutions would perish along with the social order and with criminality. "Where to put remaining evil-doers is a question that we need not worry too much about at present," wrote H. Dietz in 1887.[75] This assessment proved to be too simplistic. The question of how to deal with chronically criminal elements did become more important for socialists as more of them came to believe that such chronically criminal individuals actually existed and that they posed a general and immediate danger to society. Although Social Democrats had committed themselves in the Erfurt Program to waiting patiently for the collapse of capitalism, they could not avoid becoming embroiled in the political discussions regarding criminal justice reform and prison reform in the German Reich.

In addition, two specific issues continued to shape the demands of the socialists regarding the penal system: the treatment of political prisoners and prison labor. Because Social Democrats were subject to continued judicial prosecutions and the promised law unifying the prison system across the Reich was never passed, the SPD continued to voice its reform demands regarding the treatment of political prisoners.[76] Regarding the issue of prison labor, the party took its cue from Marx's pronouncement, in his critique of the Gotha program, that this problem was considered irresolvable under capitalism. SPD leaders criticized craftsmen's demands for the abolition of productive prison labor, which were attributed to their backward, petty bourgeois consciousness. Karl Liebknecht, speaking before the Prussian parliament in 1912, argued:

> We can demand only one thing: that the unfair competition of convict labor be abolished. (Hear hear! from the Social Democrats). But the competition of prison labor [as such] must not and cannot be removed. Indeed, more work should be performed in the prisons—work that should be in every way the same as the work done by free workers, so that the prisoners, once released, can make use of the skills acquired in prison.

Liebknecht's suggested solution was accordingly pragmatic: He wanted to mechanize prison labor and organize it along the lines of large factories because big industry could handle the competition and released prisoners would do better as factory workers than as craftsmen.[77]

Social Democrats also took positions on several other issues related to the penal system. They condemned corporal punishment, still used in the prisons and workhouses of several states as a means of enforcing discipline, as the epitome of cruel and barbaric punishment. Prison food, hygiene, and housing also met with socialist criticism, sometimes based on firsthand experiences.[78] Finally, socialists spoke out against deportation, which had been suggested as an alternative to normal punishment, not least because they feared that they themselves might then be deported to the colonies as political criminals.[79] A comprehensive Social Democratic position regarding criminal justice and the prison system, however, was developed only when a general public discussion of penal reform began to take place in the German Reich and the Social Democrats found themselves increasingly unable to bridge the contradictions between fundamentalist Marxist rhetoric and practical opportunities, between utopian views of the future and ordinary political discussions.

In 1882, Franz von Liszt, then a young Marburg professor of criminal law, published a programmatic article entitled "The Idea of Purposiveness in Penal

Law" (*Der Zweckgedanke im Strafrecht*), which called for legal punishments to serve the purpose of protecting society rather than providing retribution for a crime. In Liszt's reform program, the array of penal sanctions included indefinite, potentially lifelong detention for incorrigible habitual criminals, rehabilitative prison sentences for corrigible habitual criminals, as well as fines and probation for occasional criminals.[80] In many respects, Liszt's proposals were close to the political positions of the Social Democrats. "Every crime," Liszt wrote in 1898, "is the product of the character of the criminal and the social conditions surrounding the criminal at the moment of the crime," adding that "the social factors play a much larger role than the individual factor." Therefore, an effective penal policy required above all "the reshaping of the decisive social conditions." In the present social situation, this entailed "a social policy that aims to slowly but surely improve the entire position of the working class."[81] Liszt's application of Darwinist evolutionary theory to society was also not foreign to socialists. Moreover, some of his students joined the SPD. These included Hugo Heinemann (1863–1919), for example, who later taught criminal law and penology in the SPD's party school and espoused positions explicitly identified with Liszt.[82] For radical materialists, however, the Liszt school of criminal law did not go far enough. Thus, in 1904, Michael Sursky noted: "Criminologists needed to make but a single further step in order to recognize the genuine causes of crime," but "they could not and would not do this, because this step leads to socialism."[83] From another perspective, Wolfgang Heine (1861–1944), a lawyer and socialist member of the Reichstag, noted the internal contradictions of the sociological approach to penal law. He remarked that, despite its claims to be humane, it would inevitably lead to more severe penalties because it emphasized the protection of society at the cost of the individual.[84]

What began to be at issue was the position that the Social Democrats should take regarding the concrete legal reforms then taking shape. Despite some criticism of Liszt's positions, German legal scholars at the turn of the century had reached a consensus that the German penal code needed to be reformed to incorporate his "new school" of criminal law. Thus as early as March 1901, the Reich Office of Justice (Reichsjustizamt) announced plans to revise the Reich penal code, and in April 1906 a reform commission was charged with producing a new draft code.[85] Heinrich Wetzker, writing in the reform-oriented *Sozialistische Monatshefte* in 1902, therefore criticized the Erfurt Program as inadequate regarding matters of criminal justice. Although socialism would eliminate large-scale crime, he noted that "the current methods of fighting crime . . . are of such importance that we cannot afford to neglect them." Precisely because the current system of incarceration encouraged crime, he argued, the Social Democrats had to take a stance.[86] Wolfgang Heine added pragmatically: "Meanwhile it is not worth bothering with . . . matters of the future since it is clear that in the *present*, when we can have a political impact, crime has not yet been eliminated."[87]

Whereas twenty-five years earlier Dietz had still been convinced that socialism was near, Heine now openly expressed Social Democracy's new orientation: practical, pragmatic reform policies focused on the problems of the present.

The SPD's position on penal and prison reform was shaped by yet another factor, however. When, in late February 1904, Social Democratic newspapers revealed the improper treatment of prisoners in the Plötzensee prison, the authorities charged them with libel. The Social Democratic lawyers Karl Liebknecht and Hugo Heinemann used the trial that followed, the so-called Plötzensee trial, to assemble a comprehensive body of evidence on the penal system that was meant to convince the public of the necessity of reforms.[88] The government's libel charge was withdrawn in the course of the trial, and Heinemann summed up the case with satisfaction: "Thus concrete examples have demonstrated that our penal system's practices, through no fault of those in charge, can render mentally deficient inmates permanently unfit for the struggle for survival."[89]

The Social Democrats had now been so active on this issue that it became necessary to take a public position regarding the penal system. Accordingly, the issue was placed on the agenda of the 1906 Party conference in Mannheim. The lawyer Hugo Haase (1863–1919) delivered his first significant party congress speech on the subject and introduced a resolution. Haase used most of his speech to criticize the judicial persecution of Social Democracy and the unions. Not until the end did he turn to the question of crime in general. Here Haase, too, criticized Liszt's modern school by arguing that crime would be eliminated only through socialism. Nevertheless, he argued, the causes of crime in the existing social order could be reduced through a resolute social policy: for example, by implementing the eight-hour day, securing the freedom to form political coalitions, and adopting policies on housing, tariffs, and education that promoted social welfare. For the prison system specifically, Haase called for the unification of policy across the Reich, special institutions for youths and for the mentally deficient, early release, and the creation of work for those released.[90] On the one hand, Haase's resolution represented a compromise because it combined fundamental criticism with concrete proposals for reform while leaving out sensitive points such as indefinite sentencing and lifelong imprisonment, which would have required agreement regarding the state's punitive powers. In this respect, the speech's positive reception at the Party conference is understandable. On the other hand, congress chair Paul Singer overestimated the agreement regarding these proposals, which he used to justify the rapid passage of the resolution—the mass-strike debate had set the proceedings behind schedule—to be able to present an official SPD position in the discussions regarding the new Reich penal code.[91]

Indeed, not everyone was satisfied with the results of the Mannheim Congress. Edmund Fischer, for example, was convinced that Social Democracy must work toward practical goals rather than just hope for a socialist future. In his view, the current penal system should be reshaped according to the spirit of socialism and humanity, but also according to modern science. As a consequence, Fischer supported many of the modern school's penal reform proposals, such as psychiatric diagnosis, indefinite detention, and special legislation for psychopaths.[92] Because he defined the *Lumpenproletariat* biologically, he also supported eugenic measures such as sterilization, thus placing himself on the radical wing of general German criminology.[93] The medicalized view of alcoholism provided the basis for even more radical positions, even within the socialist movement. For if alcoholics and criminals were ill, logic commanded that they be treated until their recovery. Thus the socialist physician Otto Juliusburger (1867–1952) of the League of Abstinent German Workers demanded: "All people who demonstrate antisocial behavior under the influence of alcohol, from those who disturb the peace through excessive noise all the way to violent criminals and lechers, must be placed indefinitely in special educational institutions under social-ethical supervision."[94]

These positions represent the extremes. The overwhelming majority of socialists were not inclined to concede any further power to the current state because they were in constant conflict with its authorities and were fundamentally opposed to its political form. They gave voice to their perceptions of the state's class character and their own traumatic experiences by leveling the charge of "class justice." Just as law could not exist independently of the existing social order, socialists reasoned, judges could not issue verdicts independently of their class background. The result of the application of this class law, which discriminated against the working class and resulted in its political persecution, therefore constituted class justice. Social Democrats' experiences with the Kaiserreich's judiciary supported their theoretical analysis.[95] The drafts of the new Reich Penal Code seemed to confirm all of their fears, especially the passages regarding the right of combination, and appeared to represent "a dangerous attack on Social Democracy and the labor movement." The passages increasing the sentencing discretion of judges also proved alarming. Socialists feared that this would become a means of intimidation through which political opponents and striking workers could be locked up as incorrigible habitual criminals.[96] But even Siegfried Weinberg (1880–1932), who embraced a radically materialist position, admitted:

> We know that, in addition to those cases in which punishment is abused in order to harass political or social opponents of the ruling classes, there are also cases in which society is forced to adopt measures to defend itself against those who wish to do it harm. We also must recognize that these are often nothing more than *either sick people* who belong in institutions *or victims of the capitalist system* and the misery it causes. Based on this recognition, we must say that the best penal policy is a comprehensive social policy, one very different from that of the current state.[97]

According to the internal logic of this argument, bourgeois reformers' proposals for altering the penal code had to be rejected for the moment, but under socialism, they could well prove useful.

This did not mean, however, that concrete reform measures and proposals could not be assessed without ideological reservation and, if appropriate, advocated in the present.[98] Granted, the prison system seemed to socialists to be a remarkably ineffective way to prepare an individual for the struggle for survival. But Karl Liebknecht acknowledged in 1912:

> The penal system is the way it is, and we have to make do with it. Still, the particular difficulty our prison reformers face is how to shape punishment within the legal framework in such a way that the deprivation of freedom does not have damaging effects. Instead, the punishment should employ the force of the authorities to produce effects that reduce and weaken the undesirable tendencies of the convict while strengthening those tendencies beneficial to society.[99]

Using this approach, Social Democrats before World War I arrived at several suggestions for reform, some of them quite concrete. They made proposals regarding prison hygiene, education of prison officials and physicians, accident compensation, and measures to integrate released prisoners. They also promoted a graduated penal system along American lines and called for separate juvenile prisons as well as therapeutic treatment of mentally ill prisoners.[100] Social Democrats also called for the extension of conditional pardoning (*bedingte Begnadigung*), which had been introduced by decree in Prussia in 1895 and provided young first offenders the possibility of a suspended sentence, to a significantly broader range of offenders.[101] Reform proposals suspected of involving an extension of state power faced criticism, however. Thus Wolfgang Heine's support for removing the legal requirement that the public prosecutor's office must always file charges (*staatsanwaltschaftlicher Anklagezwang*) was harshly censured by Siegfried Weinberg. Despite practical justifications for the reform, Weinberg argued that this would be too large a concession to the class state and to its public prosecutor, the embodiment of class justice, and amounted to neglecting "the democratic virtue of mistrust."[102]

The socialists' main problem lay in weighing the interests of the individual against those of society, both in the present and in the future. Most socialists did not worry about this, however, since this problem would no longer exist under socialism. Some of the proposals could, on occasion, be quite radical. Because the socialist understanding of criminality rested squarely on Darwinism, it seemed quite conceivable, even scientifically proven, that some degenerate individuals were not physically up to the "struggle for existence," and therefore must become criminals. Paul Hirsch (1868–1940), writing in a popular scientific brochure first issued in 1897 and reprinted in 1907, considered how these few degenerate individuals could be rendered harmless in the society of the future and how the hereditary transmission of their criminal dispositions could be prevented:

> The most certain and easiest way to achieve the weakening and gradual removal of this disposition is to cross such individuals with other, healthy elements. Based on the

current state of the science of genetics, however, we may assume that we will not reach our goal in this manner. . . . Just as in the case of consumption, syphilis, and other hereditary diseases, the disposition toward crime would finally stop being transmitted if all those afflicted were forced to live and die childless. To be sure, this is a harsh measure that affects the individual very severely, but the individual must subordinate himself to the needs of society. The individual's rights end where they collide with the duties to society.[103]

Socialists' pre–World War I argumentation regarding penal and prison reform was fraught with paradox. On the one hand, regarding the present, they espoused what might be described as orthodox liberal positions, upholding individual rights and seeking to minimize incarceration. On the other hand, they laid claim to the modern school's agenda of preventive and individualized punishment for use in the socialist future—even as they claimed that these would no longer be needed in a society without crime.

Conclusion

Marx and Engels shared the terminology of middle-class social reformers to describe crime and the deprivation that they believed caused it. Although their conclusions were entirely different—predicting the fall of the existing social order—in their attempt to condemn existing society, Marx and Engels demonized the subproletarian social strata. Their conception of the *proletariat* as a positive political force led them to distinguish it from the *Lumpenproletariat*, which they blamed for failed revolutions. The socialist workers' movement later used the concept of the *Lumpenproletariat* to distance itself from other movements such as anarchism and to cast itself as a culture-bearing movement in the fight against state oppression. For this, the socialist movement paid the price of becoming rather distant from the lower strata of society.

Because they were convinced that socialism would soon establish a perfect society free of crime, socialists initially avoided a fundamental discussion of crime and criminal justice and limited themselves to criticizing the existing penal system. As a rule, up until the 1890s, Social Democratic calls for prison reforms dealt almost exclusively with the treatment of political prisoners. By the 1890s, however, the burgeoning field of criminology was producing large-scale statistical studies of crime, which socialists greeted as scientific proof of their conviction that society was responsible for crime. At the same time, socialist analyses of society were also undergirded by Darwinist ideas, and socialists had great difficulty maintaining the boundary between what is biological and what is social. The idea that society was characterized by a Darwinist "struggle for existence" was present in every socialist analysis of crime, including those of declared Marxists. Because socialist discussions about crime gradually became dominated by academically trained intellectuals who had joined the socialist movement, they were increasingly colored by the kinds of biological arguments developed in the academic field of criminology. The *Lumpenproletariat* was now seen as a concrete biological danger for society, and socialists morally condemned it in accordance with bourgeois values.

Around the turn of the century, the socialists began to give serious thought to which penal and prison reforms they might support, in the present, in a state that they fundamentally rejected, and to the proper treatment of those who would still commit crimes under socialism in the future. While the Mannheim Party Congress Resolution of 1906 represented a compromise between perspectives for the future and concrete calls for reform, some socialists were prepared to support more far-reaching reforms in the present. The overwhelming majority of social-ists, however, looked to the future. Those who conceded that this future would not be completely without crime were willing to support radical measures against a perhaps biologically determined core of degenerate enemies of society that they would not accept in the existing class society.

In these debates it is noticeable that it was exclusively revisionist Social Dem-ocrats, often writing in the *Sozialistische Monatshefte*, who embraced a pragmatic and sometimes biological, but no longer revolutionary Marxist approach to crime and criminal justice and were prepared, in the present, to take more radical steps in the fight against crime than their fellow party members who were ortho-dox Marxists. This set of issues was ideologically explosive because it touched on the sensitive area of the state's use of violence and raised a series of fundamental questions: To what degree could the masses be organized? What revolutionary or illegal actions were legitimate? What political strategy would lead to success?[104] But it is important not to confuse cause and effect. Revisionism did not give rise to new positions regarding crime and criminal justice. Both resulted from dissatisfaction with the theoretical potential of orthodox Marxism and from the attempt to bridge the gap between radical theory and social reformist practice.

Although the socialists had no intention of defending the existing social order, they had nevertheless adopted the rules of modern industrial society, including its order and discipline, and acted, politically, according to new standards and techniques. But it was not Imperial Germany's workers, the workers' movement, the SPD's electoral supporters, or even all SPD members who regarded the *Lum-penproletariat* as the opposite of their own identity, but the Party's leaders and functionaries, academics and intellectuals. Two psychological aspects should be noted here. First, socialist activists who agitated for their goals among subprole-tarian strata often reaped only contempt; as a rule, they did not find the potential revolutionaries who would work for socialism with them in these strata. Second, as the sociologist Erving Goffman has pointed out, stigmatized individuals often adopt the majority society's attitude toward individuals who are more strongly stigmatized then they are. According to Goffman, "the more [the stigmatized individual] separates himself structurally from the normals, the more like them he may become culturally."[105] Thus the fact that socialists drew such a strong distinction between themselves and the *Lumpenproletariat*, even though they themselves were persecuted and despised, also had external social psychological causes.

Does this mean that, ultimately, even the socialists signed on to the creation of the "carceral continuum," which, according to Michel Foucault, produced the "disciplined individual" that was so well-suited to working in factories?[106] Did the socialists fail when confronted with the colonizing claims of bourgeois criminological discourse? Posing the question in this way makes the mistake of proceeding retrospectively from the results of developments, instead of assessing them in their historical context. The essentially trivial conclusion that even libertarian or abolitionist theories of crime develop disciplinary practices when they become incorporated into a political movement should not be taken as evidence of the constant reproduction of a single criminological discourse. Otherwise, one underestimates not only the political volatility and uniqueness of individual statements, but also the historical dynamic in the production of the criminological discourse. If Social Democracy rejected a political justification of crime as impractical, it did so for good reason. Instead, Social Democracy viewed crime essentially as an indicator of the existing society's disintegration and a harbinger of the approaching revolution. Until such a time, its approach to criminal justice and penal policy focused on concrete, progressive reforms and appeared quite radical in the general discussion in the Kaiserreich. Through its interventions in the reform debates and through its general political success, the SPD did have an impact on bourgeois criminology and penal reform. Above all, Social Democracy raised the issue of social inequality as a problem that had to be addressed.

Notes

Translated by Keith D. Alexander and Richard F. Wetzell. This chapter is a significantly revised version of an essay that originally appeared in German in the *Mitteilungsblatt des Instituts für soziale Bewegungen* 26 (2001), whose editor kindly gave his permission for this new publication.

1. August Bebel, *Woman and Socialism*, authorized translation by Meta L. Stern (New York, 1910), 436–437.
2. August Bebel, *Die Frau und der Sozialismus*, 59th ed. (East Berlin, 1946), 532–533, 534 (emphasis in the original). A similar passage is found in the first edition: August Bebel, *Die Frau und der Sozialismus* (Zurich-Hottingen, 1879), 128–129.
3. Alfred Oborniker, "Strafrecht und Strafvollzug im Lichte der deutschen Sozialdemokratie," parts 1 and 2, *Archiv für Kriminalanthropologie* 30 (1908), 201–235; 31 (1908), 1–31; Theodor Gartner, "Sozialdemokratische Partei und Strafrecht" (Ph.D. diss., Albert-Ludwigs-Universität Freiburg/Br., 1927); Alfred Behrle, *Die Stellung der deutschen Sozialisten zum Strafvollzug von*

1870 bis zur Gegenwart (Berlin, 1931); Manfred Worm, *SPD und Strafrechtsreform: Die Stellung der Sozialdemokratischen Partei Deutschlands zur Strafrechtsreform unter Berücksichtigung ihrer Wandlung von einer Klassenkampfpartei zur Volkspartei* (Munich, 1968). I omit the issue of capital punishment in this chapter. On socialist attitudes toward the death penalty, see Richard J. Evans, *Rituals of Retribution: Capital Punishment in Germany, 1600–1987* (Oxford, 1996), 455–461.

4. See Peter Becker, "Kriminelle Identitäten im 19. Jahrhundert: Neue Entwicklungen in der historischen Kriminalitätsforschung," *Historische Anthropologie* 2 (1994), esp. 142–157 esp. 156–157; Monika Frommel, "Internationale Reformbewegung zwischen 1880 und 1920," in *Erzählte Kriminalität: Zur Typologie und Funktion von narrativen Darstellungen in Strafrechtspflege, Publizistik und Literatur*, ed. Jörg Schönert (Tübingen, 1991), 485–486; Richard F. Wetzell, "The Medicalization of Criminal Law Reform in Imperial Germany," in *Institutions of Confinement: Hospitals, Asylums and Prisons in Western Europe and North America, 1500–1950*, ed. Norbert Finzsch and Robert Jütte (Cambridge, 1996), 282–283. In the more recent studies of the history of German criminology, socialists hardly play a role. On this, see the works cited in the section on criminology below. Studies focusing on the socialists touch upon the issue but without systematic analysis: Richard J. Evans, "The 'Dangerous Classes' in Germany from the Middle Ages to the Twentieth Century," in Richard J. Evans, *Proletarians and Politics: Socialism, Protest and the Working Class in Germany before the First World War* (New York, 1990), 10–12, 18–19; Eric A. Johnson, *Urbanization and Crime: Germany 1871–1914* (Cambridge, 1995), 61–78.

5. Michel Foucault, *Discipline and Punish: The Birth of the Prison*, trans. Alan Sheridan (New York, 1978), 285–292, quote 288–289.

6. Schwartz concentrates on the Weimar Republic: "Kriminalbiologie und Strafrechtsreform: Die 'erbkranken Gewohnheitsverbrecher' im Visier der Weimarer Sozialdemokratie," *Juristische Zeitgeschichte* 6 (1997), 13–68.

7. Foucault further developed his own discourse analysis on this point. See Achim Landwehr, *Geschichte des Sagbaren: Einführung in die historische Diskursanalyse* (Tübingen, 2001), 75–89.

8. Wilhelm Weitling, *Garantien der Harmonie und Freiheit*, ed. Bernhard Kaufhold (orig. 1842; East Berlin, 1955), 21–26, 205–208, 259–60; see Weitling's 1849 leaflet about the tasks and goals of the *Befreiungsbund*, esp. Point 5: Hermann Schlüter, *Die Anfänge der deutschen Arbeiterbewegung in Amerika* (Stuttgart, 1907), 52–56.

9. Karl Marx, Friedrich Engels, *Werke*, 43 vols., ed. Institut für Marxismus-Leninismus beim ZK der SED (East Berlin, 1956–1967), 2, 504–506, quote 478; 356–359, 430–432, 453–455 (henceforth, *MEW*). See also crime as "der Kampf des isolierten Einzelnen gegen die herrschenden Verhältnisse," in *MEW*, 3, 311–312.

10. *MEW*, 4, 472.

11. *MEW*, 7, 26; 8, 160–161. See Robert L. Bussard, "The 'Dangerous Class' of Marx and Engels: The Rise of the Idea of the 'Lumpenproletariat,'" *History of European Ideas* 8 (1987), 675–692; Hal Draper, *Karl Marx's Theory of Revolution*, vol. 2, *The Politics of Social Classes* (New York, 1978), 453–478, 628–634; Arno Herzig, *Unterschichtenprotest in Deutschland, 1790–1870* (Göttingen, 1988), 112–114; Gertrude Himmelfarb, *The Idea of Poverty: England in the Industrial Age* (London, 1984), 387–392; Michael Schwartz, "'Proletarier' und 'Lumpen': Sozialistische Ursprünge eugenischen Denkens," *Vierteljahreshefte für Zeitgeschichte* 42 (1994), 537–570.

12. See for example Engels on the Irish: *MEW*, 2, 260, 293–296, 320–323, 353–359, 412–413. Other authors are referred to by Himmelfarb, 312–317; Martin J. Wiener, *Reconstructing the Criminal: Culture, Law and Policy in England, 1830–1914* (Cambridge, 1990) 23–37; also: Dirk Blasius, *Bürgerliche Gesellschaft und Kriminalität: Zur Sozialgeschichte Preußens im Vormärz* (Göttingen, 1976), 52–65.

13. *MEW*, 1, 398; 2, 356–359, 430–431; 3, 310–312, quote 312. See also *MEW*, 1, 120, 143.

14. On the development of these expressions, see Werner Conze, "Proletariat, Pöbel, Pauperismus," in *Geschichtliche Grundbegriffe*, 33–36, 41–44, 52–53.

15. For an overview, see Norval Morris and David J. Rothman, eds., *The Oxford History of the Prison: The Practice of Punishment in Western Society* (New York, 1995). On the German penal system, see Thomas Berger, *Die konstante Repression: Zur Geschichte des Strafvollzugs in Preußen nach 1850* (Frankfurt/Main, 1974); Blasius, *Gesellschaft*, 66–78; Wolfgang Dreßen, *Die pädagogische Maschine: Zur Geschichte des industrialisierten Bewußtseins in Preußen/Deutschland* (Frankfurt/Main, 1982), 271–340; Sebastian Scheerer, "Beyond Confinement? Notes on the History and Possible Future of Solitary Confinement in Germany," in *Institutions of Confinement*, ed. Finzsch and Jütte, 349–359; Thomas Nutz, *Strafanstalt als Besserungsmaschine: Reformdiskurs und Gefängniswissenschaft, 1775–1848* (Munich, 2001); N. Hermann Kriegsmann, *Einführung in die Gefängniskunde* (Heidelberg, 1912), 24–78.

16. Weitling, 209.

17. Ibid., 204–205, 214–219, quote 216.

18. *MEW*, 2, 187–202, quotes 198, 190.

19. Kurt Bayertz, "Naturwissenschaft und Sozialismus: Tendenzen der Naturwissenschafts-Rezeption in der deutschen Arbeiterbewegung des 19. Jahrhunderts," *Social Studies of Science* 13 (1983), 362–367.

20. Hans-Josef Steinberg, *Sozialismus und deutsche Sozialdemokratie: Zur Ideologie der Partei vor dem 1. Weltkrieg*, 5th edition (Berlin, 1979), 43–46; Richard Weikart, *Socialist Darwinism: Evolution in German Socialist Thought from Marx to Bernstein* (San Francisco, 1999), 15–79; Ted Benton, "Social Darwinism and Socialist Darwinism in Germany: 1860 to 1900," *Rivista di Filosofia* 73 (1982), 110–120.

21. Bebel, *Frau*, 1st ed., 93–96, quote 94.

22. Bebel at this point explicitly disputes Haeckel's negative selectionism. Weikart, 131–152; Benton, 98–102.

23. "Über Verbrecherthum und seine Ursachen," *Der Volksstaat*, 13 October 1875 (henceforth, *VS*) (emphasis in the original). An abridged version of this essay was reprinted as "Das Verbrechen und seine Ursachen," *Freiheit*, 19 July 1879.

24. Bayertz, 375–381; on the visions of the future of early social democracy, see Lucian Hölscher, *Weltgericht oder Revolution: Protestantische und sozialistische Zukunftsvorstellungen im deutschen Kaiserreich* (Stuttgart, 1989), 203–220.

25. Bebel, *Frau*, 1st ed., 128–129; "Über Verbrecherthum"; on Bebel's "Zukunftsstaat," see Hölscher, 307–318.

26. "Strafhaft, Strafverfahren und Strafvollzug im Lichte des Socialismus: Unter besonderer Berücksichtigung eines für das Deutsche Reich zu schaffenden Strafvollzugs-Gesetzes," *Die Zukunft* 1 (1878), 642–643, quote 634. It was not possible to identify the author of this essay. Because the essay is, in part, written in the first person plural, group authorship seems plausible. See Behrle, 15–18.

27. "Strafhaft," passim, esp. 674–675, 747–752, 754–756. The essay refers especially to the penal system in Saxony as administered by Eugene d'Alinge in the Zwickau prison (ibid., 679). D'Alinge saw himself as an opponent of any dogmatic penal system and pursued a flexible policy of individualization; this did not prevent him from being heavily criticized by Social Democrats: "Ein deutsches Gefängnis," *VS*, 1 March 1873. Johann Most and Bebel, too, served time in Zwickau in 1874–1875 but had no cause to complain. August Bebel, *Aus meinem Leben* (orig. 1911, 1914; Bonn, 1997), 375–377, 383–384. See in general Kriegsmann, 64–65, 70–78.

28. "Strafhaft," 672, 737–741, 755.

29. *Stenographische Berichte über die Verhandlungen des Reichstages des Norddeutschen Bundes*, 1. Legislaturperiode, 1869, 29 May 1869, quote 1144. For similar remarks, see *Stenographische*

Berichte über die Verhandlungen des Deutschen Reichstages (henceforth, *RT*), 3. Legislaturperiode, II. Session, 4. Sitzung, 14 February 1878, 38–39, 43. An example of the early rejection of prison work: *Die Verbrüderung*, 32 (19 January 1849), 128. As a demand within present society, it is in the Gotha Program: *Programmatische Dokumente der deutschen Sozialdemokratie*, ed. Dieter Dowe and Kurt Klotzbach (Berlin, 1973), 173.

30. *RT*, 4/II/74, 7 July 1879, 2105–2106; *VS*, 15 September 1876; "Moderner Sklavenhandel," *Der Socialdemokrat*, 25 November 1882 (henceforth, *SD*); Behrle, 10–12.

31. *Nach zehn Jahren: Material und Glossen zur Geschichte des Sozialistengesetzes*, vol. 2, *Die Opfer des Sozialistengesetzes* (London, 1890), 136. For the years 1890 to 1910, *Vorwärts* counted an additional 1,118 years *Gefängnis* and 11 years *Zuchthaus*. Alex Hall, *Scandal, Sensation and Social Democracy: The SPD Press and Wilhelmine Germany, 1890–1914* (Cambridge, 1977), 64–72.

32. Bebel, *Leben*, 473; Johann Most, *Die Bastille am Plötzensee: Blätter aus meinem Gefängnistagebuch*, 2nd ed. (Braunschweig, 1876), 76–77; "Die trockene Guillotine," *VS*, 14 April 1875; *SD*, 20 October 1881; "Zur Festungshaft in Hubertusburg," *VS*, 6 July 1873; *VS*, 2 May 1875; "Behandlung der politischen Gefangenen in Preußen," *VS*, 5 May, 7 May, 12 May 1875; *VS*, 13 June 1875; *SD*, 2 January 1881. See also Auer, who at the end of the 1890s declared that the treatment had gotten even worse in comparison to that of the 1870s. *RT*, 9/IV/155, 18 January 1897, 4122–4123; *RT*, 9/V/29, 21 January 1898, 756–760; see also Stadthagen: *RT*, 9/V/74, 31 March 1898, 1941–1943; *RT*, 10/I/39, 22 February 1899, 1057–1061. Berger, 212–235.

33. Kriegsmann, 123–128.

34. Bebel, *Leben*, 367–382, esp. 371–372.

35. Most, *Bastille*, 41–42; see also Liebknecht's examples in his speech before the Reichstag: *RT*, 2/II/56, 29 January 1875, 1414–1418; "Zur Behandlung politischer 'Verbrecher,'" *VS*, 22 September 1875; see the report by Wolfgang Wunderlich: "Aus dem Tagebuch eines politischen Zuchthäuslers," *SD*, 12 July–13 September 1890.

36. Bebel, *Leben*, 471.

37. *Bastille*, 7–9, 16, 19, 42. Critically interpreted by Sigrid Weigel, *"Und selbst im Kerker frei . . . !" Schreiben im Gefängnis: Zur Theorie und Gattungsgeschichte der Gefängnisliteratur, 1750–1933* (Marburg, 1982), 49–53.

38. Cited according to *Freiheit*, 7 May 1887. See also *SD*, 10 June 1887. The report by the Social Democrat Leuschke in *VS* hints at rejection by fellow prisoners. "Behandlung," *VS*, 22 September 1875. Also compare the report of prisoner K. M. in *Hinter Kerkermauern: Autobiographien und Selbstbekenntnisse, Aufsätze und Gedichte von Verbrechern. Ein Beitrag zur Kriminalpsychologie*, ed. Johannes Jaeger (Berlin, 1906), 348–354.

39. Werner Conze and Dieter Groh, *Die Arbeiterbewegung in der nationalen Bewegung: Die deutsche Sozialdemokratie vor, während und nach der Reichsgründung* (Stuttgart, 1966), 116–118; Evans, *Rituale*, 456-9; Joachim Wagner, *Politischer Terrorismus und Strafrecht im Deutschen Kaiserreich von 1871* (Heidelberg, 1981), 56–88; Dirk Blasius, *Geschichte der politischen Kriminalität in Deutschland, 1800–1980: Eine Studie zu Justiz und Staatsverbrechen* (Frankfurt/Main, 1983), 55–69.

40. "Die Gesellschaft des organisierten Massenmordes," *SD*, 9 May 1880; "Aus der Verbrecherwelt," *SD*, 31 October 1880. After December 1881, portraits of members of the "guild of brigands of law and order" (*Ordnungsbanditenzunft*) were published at irregular intervals in the category "criminal album." These included, for example, the judges in the 1881 Leipzig trial against Bebel and Liebknecht: *SD*, 22 December 1881. See Vernon L. Lidtke, *The Outlawed Party: Social Democracy in Germany, 1878–1890* (Princeton, 1966), 110–138, 261; Wagner, 88–115, 133–135.

41. B. Combattant, "Diebstahl und Revolution," *SD*, 22 March 1883 (emphasis in the original); "Gesindel und Revolution," *SD*, 26 February 1886; "Verrohung der Gesellschaft," *SD*, 6 March 1884. See also *MEW*, 7, 536; Johnson, 76–77.

42. *Protokoll über die Verhandlungen des Parteitages der Sozialdemokratischen Partei Deutschlands, abgehalten zu Berlin vom 14. bis 21. November 1892* (Berlin, 1892), 107–108, 272–275, quote 275; see *Vorwärts*, 13 March 1892. An interpretation of this discussion is also given in Schwartz, "Proletarier," 547–549; see Richard J. Evans, "'Red Wednesday' in Hamburg: Social Democrats, Police and Lumpenproletariat in the Suffrage Disturbances of 17 January 1906," *SH* 4 (1979), 14–15, 23–26.

43. Gerhard A. Ritter, *Die Arbeiterbewegung im Wilhelminischen Reich: Die sozialdemokratische Partei und die freien Gewerkschaften, 1890–1900*, 2nd ed. (Berlin-Dahlem, 1963), 221. See also Brigitte Emig, *Die Veredelung des Arbeiters: Sozialdemokratie als Kulturbewegung* (Frankfurt/Main 1980), 210–213, 232–240; Adelheid von Saldern, *Auf dem Wege zum Arbeiter-Reformismus: Parteialltag in sozialdemokratischer Provinz Göttingen 1870–1920* (Frankfurt/Main, 1984), 148–163.

44. See the report of the *SD* about a speech by Liebknecht before the Saxon parliament in 1880: *SD*, 21 January 1880; "Die Neider des Zuchthauses," *VS*, 10 April 1874; *VS*, 8 March 1876; "Wiederherstellung von Zucht und Sittlichkeit," *SD*, 3 October 1880; "Sozialreform," *SD*, 27 September 1883; "Zur Kriminalstatistik des Deutschen Reiches," *Die Neue Zeit* 5 (1887), 85–91 (henceforth, *NZ*); Karl Lübeck, "Verbrecher und Verbrechen," *NZ* 4 (1886), 368–374. Manfred Worm's thesis regarding the latent principle of retribution in Social-Democratic thought seems to be untenable and lacking sources to support it: Worm, 34.

45. Ralph Jessen, "Gewaltkriminalität im Ruhrgebiet zwischen bürgerlicher Panik und proletarischer Subkultur, 1879–1914," in *Kirmes—Kneipe—Kino: Arbeiterkultur im Ruhrgebiet zwischen Kommerz und Kontrolle, 1850–1914*, ed. Dagmar Kift (Paderborn, 1992), 235–244, 251; Michael Grüttner, "Working-Class Crime and the Labour Movement: Pilfering in the Hamburg Docks, 1888–1923," in *The German Working Class, 1888–1933: The Politics of Everyday Life*, ed. Richard J. Evans (London, 1982), 54–75; Michael Grüttner, "Die Kultur der Armut. Mobile Arbeiter während der Industrialisierung," *Jahrbuch Soziale Bewegungen 3* (1987), 24–29; Richard J. Evans, "Proletarian Mentalities: Pub Conversations in Hamburg," in Evans, *Proletarians*, 152–155, 166; idem, *Kneipengespräche im Kaiserreich: Stimmungsberichte der Hamburger Politischen Polizei, 1892–1914* (Reinbek, 1989), 182–224. See also the report by Paul Göhres on "the many Social Democrats who share the broad masses' not very high level of morality": *Drei Monate Fabrikarbeiter und Handwerksbursche: Eine praktische Studie* (Leipzig, 1891), 196–197. Franz Mehring, "Zur 'Gerichtschronik' der Parteipresse," *NZ* 23 (1904–1905), 793; U. Flüchtig, "Zur Gerichtschronik der Parteipresse," *NZ* 24 (1905–1906), 819–822.

46. Rosa Luxemburg, "Im Asyl," (orig. 1912), in Rosa Luxemburg, *Gesammelte Werke*, vol. 3, *Juli 1911 bis Juli 1914* (East Berlin, 1978), 84–90, quote 86.

47. *MEW*, 20, 87.

48. *MEW*, 23, 761; 19, 32.

49. See Point 8 of the demands: *Programmatische Dokumente*, 179.

50. Adolphe Quetelet, *Sur l'homme et le développement de ses facultés, ou essai de physique sociale*, vol. 1 (Paris, 1835), 10. On early statistics on crime and morality, see Monika Böhme, *Die Moralstatistik: Ein Beitrag zur Geschichte der Quantifizierung in der Soziologie, dargestellt an den Werken Adolphe Quetelets und Alexander von Oettingens* (Cologne, 1971).

51. There are a number of newer studies available regarding the development of criminal anthropology and Lombroso's biography. For the Italian context specifically, see John A. Davis, *Conflict and Control: Law and Order in Nineteenth-Century Italy* (Houndmills, 1988), esp. 314–334; Daniel Pick, *Faces of Degeneration: A European Disorder, 1848–1918* (Cambridge, 1989); Peter Becker, *Verderbnis und Entartung: Eine Geschichte der Kriminologie des 19. Jahrhunderts als Diskurs und Praxis* (Göttingen, 2002), 291–322. On the reception in Germany, see Mariacarla Gadebusch-Bondio, *Die Rezeption der kriminalanthropologischen Theorien von Cesare Lombroso in Deutschland von 1880 bis 1914* (Husum, 1995); Richard F. Wetzell, *Inventing the Criminal:*

A History of German Criminology (Chapel Hill, 2000), esp. 39–71; Silviana Galassi, *Kriminologie im Deutschen Kaiserreich: Geschichte einer gebrochenen Verwissenschaftlichung* (Stuttgart, 2004), 140–225; Christian Müller, *Verbrechensbekämpfung im Anstaltsstaat: Psychiatrie, Kriminologie und Strafrechtsreform in Deutschland 1871–1933* (Göttingen, 2004), 72–80.

52. Kautsky, "Eine Naturgeschichte des politischen Verbrechers," *NZ* 11 (1892–1893), 70.

53. See ibid., 69–70; cited according to "Der Alkoholismus und seine Bekämpfung," *NZ* 19 (1890–1891), 51. Kautsky's position was criticized by Friedrich Große, "Zur Naturgeschichte des politischen Verbrechers," *NZ* 12 (1893–1894), 205–213; see the further contributions to the discussion: Karl Kautsky, "Lombroso und sein Verteidiger," *NZ* 12 (1893–1894), 241–250; Otto Lang, "Noch einmal der Fall Lombroso," *NZ* 12 (1893–1894), 373–376.

54. See Enrico Ferri, "Kriminelle Anthropologie und Sozialismus," *NZ* 14 (1895–1896), 452–459; idem, *Das Verbrechen als sociale Erscheinung: Grundzüge der Kriminalsociologie*, trans. Hans Kurella (3rd ed., 1892; Leipzig, 1896), esp. 62–67, 84–100. Ferri, who worked as a socialist agitator until returning to a professorship in 1906, changed his political views repeatedly. He later openly sympathized with fascism. On Ferri, see Pick, 145–147; Thorsten Sellin, "Enrico Ferri (1856–1929)," in *Pioneers in Criminology*, ed. Hermann Mannheim (1958; London, 1960), 277–300; see also James Edward Miller, *From Elite to Mass Politics: Italian Socialism in the Giolittian Era, 1900–1914* (Kent, OH, 1990), 58–76, 89–93, 106–110. On the discussion of criminal anthropology and sociology among Italian socialists: Davis, 334–342; Delia Frigessi, "Scienza socialista e scienza borghese tra 'Archivio di psichiatria' e 'Critica sociale'," in *Le radici del socialismo italiano* (Milan, 1997), 223–234.

55. Ferri, *Socialismus und moderne Wissenschaft*, trans. Hans Kurella (1894; Leipzig, 1895), 39–48, 68–80, 8–24, 31–35.

56. "Darwinismus und Marxismus," *NZ* 13 (1894–1895), 709–716. Kautsky's own relationship with Darwinism was contradictory and is strongly debated in academic research. Although he castigated Ferri for mixing nature and society, Kautsky's own work also contains similar tendencies. Weikart, 162–188.

57. Lafargue, "Die Kriminalität in Frankreich von 1840–1886: Untersuchungen über ihre Entwicklung und ihre Ursachen," *NZ* 8 (1890), 11–23, 56–66, 106–116.

58. See, for example, Kautsky, "Lombroso," 244; Lang, "Fall," 374–376. The recourse to statistics is what distinguishes this work from earlier essays: J. S., "Der Einfluß der Jahreszeit auf die Kriminalität," *NZ* 12 (1893–1894), 719–722; H. L., "Ziffern des Verbrechens, insbesondere die starke Abnahme der Vermögensdelikte," *NZ* 21 (1901–1902), 267–271, 312–317; S. Weinberg, "Der werdende Verbrecher: Eine kriminalistische Studie," *NZ* 21 (1902–1903), 16–21; Heinrich Wetzker, "Die Zunahme der Verbrechen," *Sozialistische Monatshefte* 6 (1902), 518–527 (henceforth, *SM*); Siegfrieda, "Ortsüblicher Tagelohn und Kriminalität in Preußen," *NZ* 24 (1905–1906), 636–638.

59. W. A. Bonger, *Criminalité et conditions économiques* (Amsterdam, 1905), 340–345, 349–350, 721–726. See the socialist discussions: M. Sursky, "Aus der neuesten Literatur über die wirtschaftlichen Ursachen der Kriminalität," *NZ* 23 (1904–1905), 628–634; Robert Michels, "Review of: *Criminalité et conditions économiques* by W. A. Bonger," *Kritische Blätter für die gesamten Sozialwissenschaften* 2 (1906), 290–291. Bonger came from an educated middle-class family and joined the Socialist Party in 1897. On Bonger's biography, see H. Bonger, "Korte Levensschets van Prof. Mr. W. A. Bonger," in *Verspreide Geschriften* von W. A. Bonger, Deel 1, *Criminologie en Criminele Statistiek* (Amsterdam, 1950), ix–xxv; J. Valkhoff, "Bongers Werken," in Bonger, *Geschriften*, Deel 1, xxxvi–xcii.

60. Two examples should suffice here: G. von Rohden, "Von den sozialen Motiven des Verbrechens," *Zeitschrift für Sozialwissenschaft* 7 (1904), 509–531; F. A. Karl Krauß, *Der Kampf gegen die Verbrechensursachen: Übersichtlich dargestellt für alle Volks- und Vaterlandsfreunde* (Paderborn, 1905), esp. 9–14, 17–68, 147–149.

61. "Kriminalstatistik," 88–90; "Notiz: Statistik der Verbrechen und Vergehen im Deutschen Reich von 1882 bis 1887," *NZ* 7 (1889), 141–142; Georg S., "Die weibliche Lohnarbeit und ihr Einfluß auf die Sittlichkeit und Kriminalität: Ein nachträglicher Beitrag zur lex Heinze," *NZ* 18 (1899–1900), 754–756; Karl Kautsky, "Die Aktion der Masse," *NZ* 30 (1911–1912), 115–116.

62. See W. A. Bonger, "Cesare Lombroso," *NZ* 28 (1909–1910), 356–357.

63. The secondary literature on the subject is now very comprehensive. For a good synthesis see: Mike Hawkins, *Social Darwinism in European and American Thought, 1860–1945: Nature as Model and Nature as Threat* (Cambridge, 1997), 132–145.

64. Sybille Krafft, *Zucht und Unzucht: Prostitution und Sittenpolizei im München der Jahrhundertwende* (Munich, 1996), 131–133. Quote Bebel, *Frau*, 59th ed., 233. General female criminality was not part of social democracy's main interests. An exception: Siegfried Weinberg, *Über den Einfluß der Geschlechtsfunktionen auf die weibliche Kriminalität* (Halle, 1907).

65. Paul Kampffmeyer, *Die Prostitution als soziale Klassenerscheinung und ihre sozialpolitische Bekämpfung* (Berlin, 1905), 35, 37. See also similar passages in Karl Kautsky, *Der Einfluss der Volksvermehrung auf den Fortschritt der Gesellschaft* (Vienna, 1880), 77–84; Heinrich Lux, *Die Prostitution, ihre Ursachen, ihre Folgen und ihre Bekämpfung* (Berlin, 1892), 21–23; Paul Hirsch, *Verbrechen und Prostitution als soziale Krankheitserscheinungen* (Berlin, 1897), 54; Georg S., 749–756; Edmund Fischer, "Die sexuellen Probleme," *SM* 13 (1909), 961–962. Middle-class criminologists shared the same views: Peter Becker, "'Gefallene Engel' und 'verwahrloste Menschen': Über 'Erzählmuster,' Prostituierte und die Kriminalistik des vorigen Jahrhunderts," in *Konstruktion der Wirklichkeit durch Kriminalität und Strafe*, ed. Detlev Frehsee, Gabi Löschper and Gerlinda Smaus (Baden-Baden, 1997), 340–346.

66. Lux, *Prostitution*, 12; See Hirsch, 24–29; Kampffmeyer, 35; Edmund Fischer, "Die Überwindung der Prostitution," *SM* 10 (1906), 240–241.

67. Kampffmeyer, 33, ibid.; Lux, *Prostitution*, 26, Liebknecht, *Protokoll Parteitag 1892*, 274; Mehring, ibid., 794.

68. Kautsky, "Alkoholismus," 52, 115.

69. See the following overview: Hasso Spode, *Die Macht der Trunkenheit: Kultur- und Sozialgeschichte des Alkohols in Deutschland* (Opladen, 1993), 235–241.

70. Quoted in Otto Juliusburger, *Gegen den Strafvollzug* (Berlin, [1905]), 13. See Otto Lang, *Die Arbeiterschaft und die Alkoholfrage* (Vienna, 1902); idem, *Alkoholgenuß und Verbrechen: Ein Vortrag* (Bremerhaven, 1892).

71. "Das Lumpenproletariat," *SM* 13 (1909), 1133–1139. Fischer came from a poor background and worked himself up as an autodidact to become a woodcarver, journalist, and writer.

72. On socialist eugenics, but with an emphasis on the period after 1918: Michael Schwartz, *Sozialistische Eugenik: Eugenische Sozialtechnologien in Debatten und Politik der deutschen Sozialdemokratie, 1890–1933* (Bonn, 1995); Doris Byer, *Rassenhygiene und Wohlfahrtspflege: Zur Entstehung eines sozialdemokratischen Machtdispositivs in Österreich bis 1934* (Frankfurt/ Main 1988). On the socialist roots of racial hygiene: Peter Weingart, Jürgen Kroll, and Kurt Bayertz, *Rasse, Blut und Gene: Geschichte der Eugenik und Rassenhygiene in Deutschland* (1988; Frankfurt/Main, 1992), 105–129; Weindling, 117–126, 94–96.

73. Karl Kautsky, *Vermehrung und Entwicklung in Natur und Gesellschaft* (Stuttgart, 1910), 261–267; Bonger, *Criminalité*, 726. Compare esp. to Kautsky: Schwartz, *Eugenik*, 36–51.

74. M. Sursky, "Die kriminal-soziologische Schule als Kämpferin für die Interessen der herrschenden Klassen," *NZ* 22 (1903–1904), 641–648, 682–686.

75. H. D., "Gefängniswesen und Vollzug der Freiheitsstrafen in Deutschland," *NZ* 5 (1887), 295.

76. Arthur Stadthagen in *RT*, 11/I/117, 12 January 1905, 3694–3708; *RT*, 12/II/132, 22 February 1911, 4825–4837; Wilhelm Schröder, "Politische Gefangene in deutschen Gefängnissen," *SM* 12 (1908), 218–227.

77. *Stenographische Berichte über die Verhandlungen des Landtages, Haus der Abgeordneten*, 21. Legisl., V. Session, 19. Sitzung, 21. Februar 1912, 1363–1366, zit. 1365 (henceforth, *HdA*); also reprinted in Karl Liebknecht, *Gesammelte Reden und Schriften*, 10 vols., ed. Institut für Marxismus-Leninismus beim ZK der SED (Berlin/East, 1958–1968), 5, 22–25, quote on p. 24. See m.s. [= Max Schippel], "Innungen und Gefängnisarbeit," *NZ* 9 (1890–1891), 443–447; Siegfrieda [= Siegfried Weinberg], "Die Gefängnisarbeit," *NZ* 25 (1906–1907), 864–872.

78. August Bebel, *RT*, 10/I/175, 23 March 1900, 4935–4938, 4941; See also *VS*, 4 Mai 1870; "Zur Naturgeschichte der besten der Welten," *SD*, 20 September 1883; "Zur Frage der Prügelstrafe," *Socialpolitisches Centralblatt* 3 (1893), 465–467 (henceforth, *SC*); H. Lux, "Untersuchung der Kost in den preußischen Gefängnissen," *NZ* 7 (1888), 359–358.

79. Review of Strosser-Stursberg, *Die Anlage von Strafkolonien und die Prinzipien des gegenwärtigen Strafvollzugs* (Düsseldorf, 1880), *Jahrbuch für Sozialwissenschaft und Sozialpolitik* 2 (1881), 153–156; Ignaz Auer, *RT*, 9/V/29, 31 January 1898, 756–760; Michael Sursky, "Rezension von *Der Bankrott des modernen Strafvollzugs und seine Reform*, von Max Treu," *NZ* 23 (1904–1905), 325; Wolfgang Heine, "Stafrecht, Strafprozess und Strafvollzug," *SM* 10 (1906), 750.

80. Franz von Liszt, "Der Zweckgedanke im Strafrecht," in *Strafrechtliche Aufsätze und Vorträge*, 2 vols. (Berlin, 1905), 2, 173, 169–173, 178. On Liszt and his school, see: Richard F. Wetzell, "From Retributive Justice to Social Defense: Penal Reform in Fin-de-Siècle Germany," in *Germany at the Fin de Siècle: Culture, Politics, and Ideas*, ed. Suzanne Marchand and David Lindenfeld (Baton Rouge, 2004), 59–77; Monika Frommel, *Präventionsmodelle in der deutschen Strafzweck-Diskussion: Beziehungen zwischen Rechtsphilosophie, Dogmatik, Rechtspolitik und Erfahrungswissenschaften* (Berlin, 1987), 42–114. Another interpretation, which identifies lines of conflict between psychiatry and legal studies, can be found in Müller, 125–141.

81. Franz von Liszt, "Das Verbrechen als sozialpathologische Erscheinung," in *Strafrechtliche Aufsätze*, 2, 234, 235, 236, 246.

82. Other students of Liszt's included Siegfried Weinberg and Gustav Radbruch. The latter admittedly did not join the SPD until 1918. See Heinemann's essays: "Entwurf zu einem schweizerischen Strafgesetzbuch," *SC* 3 (1893), 61–63; "Das Strafensystem in dem Entwurfe eines Schweizerischen Strafgesetzbuches," *SC* 3 (1893), 73–76; "Sozialpolitisches in dem Entwurf eines schweizerischen Strafgesetzbuchs," *SC* 3 (1893), 88–90; "Die verwahrloste und verbrecherische Jugend," *SC* 3 (1893), 157–159; "Strafrecht und Sozialpolitik," *SC* 3 (1893), 463–465; "Der österreichische Strafgesetzentwurf und die arbeitende Klasse," *AfsGS* 7 (1894), 359–409. In 1892, Heinrich Lux cited without comment multiple pages from an essay by von Liszt regarding the social origins of crime and their remedy. Lux, ed., *Handbuch*, 159-60; compare Franz von Liszt, "Die gesellschaftlichen Ursachen des Verbrechens," *SC* 1 (1892), 59–60.

83. Sursky, "Schule," 685; I. Ingwer, "Zur Reform unseres Strafgesetzes," *Der Kampf* 2 (1908–1909), 67.

84. "Zur Reform des Strafrechts," *SM* 7 (1903), 22–35; Oborniker, 216. Here, too, Worm's interpretation that Heine, like many other Social Democratic jurists, did not wish to forgo guilt and retribution seems hardly tenable. Worm, *SPD und Strafrechtsreform*, 55–59.

85. Wetzell, "From Retributive Justice"; Richard F. Wetzell, "Criminal Law Reform in Imperial Germany," (Ph.D. diss., Stanford University, 1991), 95–154, 213–223, 280–287.

86. Wetzker, "Der Punct 8 unseres Programms," *SM* 6 (1902), 610.

87. Heine, "Reform," 24 (emphasis in the original). Both refer to Wetzker's seminal essay, "Zunahme."

88. Georg Gradnauer, *RT*, 11/I/90, 13 May 1904, 2893–2903; Georg Gradnauer, *Das Elend des Strafvollzugs* (Berlin, 1905), esp. 3–4, 56-80; see the collection of news accounts in Liebknecht, *Reden*, 1, 132–151. This kind of prison scandal with subsequent trial was not atypical. Hall, 78.

89. "Königsberg und Plötzensee," *Die Neue Gesellschaft* 1 (1905), 135.

90. "Resolution Haase," in *Protokoll über die Verhandlungen des Parteitags der Sozialdemokratischen Partei Deutschlands, abgehalten zu Mannheim vom 23. bis 29. September 1906* (Berlin, 1906), 140–142; Hugo Haase, "Strafrecht, Strafprozeß und Strafvollzug," in *Protokoll Parteitag der SPD 1906*, 360–377.

91. *Protokoll Parteitag der SPD 1906*, 378; Ernst Haase, *Hugo Haase: Sein Leben und Wirken* (Berlin-Frohnau [1929]), 16, 94.

92. "Laienbemerkungen zur Reform des Strafrechts," *SM* 10 (1906), 487–492; "Über das Strafrecht der Zukunft," *SM* 15 (1909), 157–165; "Die Wanderer," *SM* 20 (1914), 308–314.

93. Fischer, "Lumpenproletariat," 1138–1139. Compare Wetzell, *Inventing*, 100–105.

94. Juliusburger, 22. The Swiss psychiatrist, radical opponent of alcohol, and criminal anthropologist August Forel, writing in *SM*, could even raise the question of euthanizing certain criminals. "Todesstrafe und Sozialismus: Zum Fall Grete Beier," *SM* 12 (1908), 1048. On Forel, see Spode, 137–138, 221–223, 235–237.

95. See, for example, Karl Liebknecht, "Gegen Klassenstaat und Klassenjustiz," (1907), in *Reden*, 2, 17–42; Erich Kuttner, *Klassenjustiz!* (Berlin, 1913). Compare Klaus Saul, *Staat, Industrie, Arbeiterbewegung im Kaiserreich: Zur Innen- und Außenpolitik des Wilhelminischen Deutschland 1903–1914* (Düsseldorf, 1974), 188–210; Hall, 72–88.

96. S. Weinberg, "Die Strafrechtswissenschaft gegen die Arbeiterklasse," *NZ* 30 (1911–1912), 405–412, quote 406; idem, "Der Strafrechtsentwurf," *NZ* 31 (1912–1913), 490–495; idem, *Die Arbeiterklasse und der Strafgesetzentwurf* (Stuttgart, 1910); Heine, "Reform," 29–30; Michael Sursky, "Sozialdemokratische Randbemerkungen zu den Vorarbeiten der Strafrechtsreform," *NZ* 27 (1907–1908), 33–38, 67–74, 95–106; Otto Lang, "Die grosse Strafrechtsreform," *SM* 13 (1909), 1591–1592, 1595–1596.

97. "Der neue Strafgesetzentwurf," *NZ* 28 (1909–1910), 721–722 (emphasis in the original).

98. Heinrich Wetzker, "Das Elend des Strafvollzuges," *Die Neue Gesellschaft* 1 (1905), 346.

99. Karl Liebknecht, *HdA*, 21/V/61, 1 May 1912, 5025. Here Liebknecht is already developing the thoughts that he formulated in his famous draft "Gegen die Freiheitsstrafe" (1918), in part employing identical language. In *Reden*, 9, 391–396, there is also the formulation "struggle for existence" (ibid., 393). Thus this can hardly be classified as an outstanding and trend-setting document among socialist proposals for reform. See Berger, 263–265; Heinz Cornel, "Resozialisierung—Klärung des Begriffs, seines Inhalts und seiner Verwendung," in *Handbuch der Resozialisierung*, ed. Heinz Cornel, Bernd Maelicke, and Bernd Rüdeger Sonnen (Baden-Baden, 1995), 18.

100. Gradnauer, 44–52, 86–92; Siegfried Weinberg, *Soziales Strafrecht* (Gautzsch, 1908), 29–30; Karl Liebknecht, *HdA*, 21/III/23, 18 February 1910, 1811–1813; *HdA*, 21/IV/20, 6 February 1911, 1411–1424; *HdA*, 21/IV/30, 18 February 1911, 2296–2304; *HdA*, 22/II/33, 21 February 1914, 2706–2711. See note 99. See Oborniker, 222–235. Clearly the SPD's program of penal reform was less constrained by anachronistic world views than by justified mistrust of the class state. Compare Thomas Welskopp, "Im Bann des 19. Jahrhunderts: Die deutsche Arbeiterbewegung und ihre Zukunftsvorstellungen zu Gesellschaftspolitik und 'sozialer Frage,'" in *Das neue Jahrhundert: Europäische Zeitdiagnosen und Zukunftsentwürfe um 1900*, ed. Ute Frevert (Göttingen, 2000), 21–26.

101. Siegfrieda, "Die bisherigen Resultate der bedingten Verurteilung," *NZ* 23 (1904–1905), 455–456; Wolfgang Heine, *RT*, 10/II/274, 5 March 1903, 8409; Karl Liebknecht, *HdA*, 21/V/20, 22 February 1912, 1439–1440; compare Oborniker, 220–221.

102. Wolfgang Heine, "Weniger Strafen" and "Replik," *Vorwärts*, 9 January 1910; quoted according to Weinberg, *Arbeiterklasse*, 26, with further references there; also, Wolfgang Heine, "Gegen den Anklagezwang," *SM* 13 (1909), 481–489; Kuttner, 27–34; Karl Liebknecht, *HdA*, 21/IV/30, 18 February 1911, 2296.

103. Hirsch, 72; 2nd ed. (Berlin, 1907), 122–130, quote 184. Compare Hans Fehlinger, "Über Rassenhygiene," *SM* 14 (1910), 965–970; Schwartz, *Eugenik*, 62–66.

104. Eduard Bernstein, "Die Menge und das Verbrechen," *NZ* 16 (1897–1898), 229–237. Ingrid Gilcher-Holtey has noted that Bernstein's discussion of the work of Italian criminologist Scipio Sighele in this article sparked internal party criticism of Bernstein. See Gilcher-Holtey, *Das Mandat des Intellektuellen: Karl Kautsky und die Sozialdemokratie* (Berlin, 1986), 122–123, 127.

105. Erving Goffman, *Stigma: Notes on the Management of Spoiled Identity* (1963; New York, 1986), 107, quote 114.

106. Foucault, *Discipline and Punish*, 297.

Chapter 3

REFORMING WOMEN'S PRISONS IN IMPERIAL GERMANY

Sandra Leukel

Beginning in the late 1860s, Germany witnessed a growing interest in the issues of female criminality and women's penal institutions.[1] Between 1871 and 1914, the number of publications devoted to this subject substantially increased. The standard works of criminology, then gradually establishing itself as a science, usually devoted separate chapters to female criminality, even though these did not occupy a central position. By the turn of the century, however, an increasing number of publications focused exclusively on female criminality and the treatment of women in penal institutions. This increasing interest cannot be explained by a rise in female criminality. On the contrary, contemporary crime statistics showed that "the crime rates of women are consistently much lower than those of men."[2] In absolute numbers, occasional slight increases in female crime rates could be discerned, but by comparison to the development of male crime rates, these were negligible. In the standard German work on criminology, published in 1903, the criminologist Gustav Aschaffenburg therefore assessed the development of female criminality in optimistic terms: "Happily, the number of women sentenced has only slightly increased. In comparison to men, it has even decreased by 20 percent since 1882."[3] Quantitatively speaking, only male crime seemed to pose a threat to public order. Nevertheless, the subject of female criminality drew a great deal of attention. This chapter will begin by outlining why the treatment of women in penal institutions became the subject of public interest in Imperial Germany and why the female gender played an increasingly important role in the general discussions of the penal system. We will then examine the debates on female criminality and the treatment of women in prison and, finally, conclude by discussing the actual reforms that were implemented regarding women's treatment in penal institutions in response to the calls for reform.

The starting point for the debate about female criminality was the assumption that the increase in female employment would inevitably cause a rise in the number of women committing crimes. This assumption was logically deduced from the generally accepted explanation for the low female crime rate, which argued that because women did not participate in economic and public life to the same extent as did men—instead focusing their lives on their families and close social relations—they had fewer opportunities to commit crimes. Though the proportion of offenders who were female was not yet seen as a threat, contemporaries predicted that female criminality would reach parity with that of males in the future. Thus, in 1903, the prison cleric Reinhold Stade wrote: "Regardless of the outcome of the woman question, it cannot be ruled out that in our turbulent times this change will happen faster than rational minds think possible. One thing is certain: the currently positive figures regarding female criminality will inevitably worsen." There was no discernible reason, Stade continued, "why the woman of the future, independent and in every way equal in the eyes of the public in the realms of business and in trade, would not also become men's equal in the realm of crime."[4] Almost all publications on the topic linked the phenomenon of female criminality to the changing social position of women. This is why direct references were frequently made to the demands of the bourgeois women's movement. In light of the linkage that was being created between female employment and female criminality, the women's movement found it necessary to take a position on the matter. Its publications—including *Die Frau* and the *Centralblatt des Deutschen Frauenbundes*—regularly included articles on crime statistics that attempted to disprove the thesis that women's emancipation and female criminality were correlated. Their authors did not need to carry out their own statistical research, but could rely on the official crime statistics that the Reich government was publishing since 1882 as well as analyses of these statistics that appeared in academic journals. The majority of the articles published in the journals of the women's movement were dedicated to this question: "Have the last decades, with their unleashing of female powers in the public sphere, had a damaging moral effect on women in Germany?"[5] Such an association was vigorously disputed by reference to statistical studies, which for the time period from 1882 to 1899 clearly showed that rates of female criminality had actually declined.[6] Anna Waldeck, for instance, was able to cite an article by Chief District Court Judge (Landgerichtspräsident) Lindenberg in the *Deutsche Juristenzeitung*, which answered the question "Does women's employment influence women's criminality?" with a resounding no. She particularly emphasized Lindenberg's statement "that despite women's increased employment in the public sector, even the proportion of women sentenced for crimes committed in office has declined."[7] As these examples demonstrate, the discussion of female criminality was about much more than the problematization of a marginal group: the subject of female criminality provided an opportunity to discuss the role of women in general and to reflect on the social change that was taking place. The debates about female criminality must therefore, first of all, be understood as reflections on the impact of modernization processes on gender relations. All of the contributions to the debate made a connection between the phenomenon of female criminality and the key words *public sphere, employment,* and *emancipation.*

The symbolic functions of discourses on criminality have been the subjects of numerous studies. In the words of historian Daniel Pick, "[c]rime, hysteria, superstition, parasitism, insanity, atavism, prostitution, crowds, peasantry, and brigands became the circulating figures of disorder."[8] The sociologist Carmen Gransee has argued that every narrative regarding behavior defined as deviant or criminal contains a surplus of normativity that reaches beyond the validation of legal norms and encompasses the demonstration of hegemonic values and the symbolic reproduction of lifestyles. Therefore every narrative about deviance contains not only information on what is prohibited but also on what is permitted and how one ought to behave.[9] In her study of the late-nineteenth-century French discourse on crime, the historian Anne-Louise Shapiro employed this interpretation and also incorporated the category of gender. Drawing on newspaper reports of court proceedings, Shapiro analyzed the symbolic functions of the discussions of female criminals, which met with increasing public interest in France during this time. According to Shapiro, the position of women in society was negotiated through the use of stereotypes like the "husband killer" or the "murderess from passion." This discourse, she argues, indicates that hegemonic norms and values were up for negotiation. Depictions of criminal women gave contemporaries a chance to communicate their conceptions of good and bad women, natural and unnatural mothers, and of the ill and the criminal, thus enabling them to comment on the rules for social relations and the spectrum of proper behavior for the female gender.[10]

Perceptions of female criminality during the Kaiserreich, too, indicate that contemporaries noticed a challenge to the hegemonic social functions assigned to women that threatened the entire gender order. As women entered the public sphere and as their presence there was perceived, society felt called upon to define the range of acceptable behavior for women to assign them their proper place in the bourgeois social order. In the debates on the penal system, these subjects were encapsulated in the question of how to deal with female criminality.

The main actors in this debate were prison officials. This chapter will trace why the previously neglected subject of female criminals and prisoners attracted their attention, which reform demands they made, and what influence they had in shaping and bringing innovation to the treatment of women in penal institutions in Imperial Germany. Since a comprehensive analysis of the debate is beyond the scope of this chapter, I will focus on the most influential publications in order to reconstruct the central line of argumentation.

Penal Reform, Criminology, and the Prison as a Site of Scientific Discovery

There can be no doubt that prison officials who contributed to the boom in publications on the issue of female criminality and female prisoners were, at least in part, motivated by the desire to make a name for themselves and to professionalize their discipline. To lend the subject importance, they argued not only that the "entry of women into public life" would lead to an increase in the female crime rate. They claimed that female criminality represented a threat to society. For this reason, debates on women and the penal system also reflected the idealization of motherhood within the bourgeois family ideal. Thus the prison doctor Abraham Baer noted: "With a family upbringing by a mother who has been released from prison teaching morality, piety, and a commitment to order and work, an upbringing in no way improved by a father with the same mindset, it is no wonder that waywardness and crime will befall the next generation."[11] Prison officials also drew on notions of population policy to direct greater attention to the issue of women's treatment in the penal system. As the director of the Delitzsch prison, Hermann von Valentini, explained: "It must not be overlooked that here, in the prison for women, the number of future criminals is growing far more than in prisons for men. With male convicts, we are dealing with the men themselves, and with the present. With women prisoners, we are dealing with the next generation and the future."[12] This argument thus assigned greater importance to combatting criminality among women than among men. Even if female criminality did not seem problematic in terms of overall numbers, criminal women were viewed as multipliers of crime, exponentially increasing the danger female criminality posed. Prison officials' belief that they would be able to make a name for themselves through the discussion of the proper treatment of women in prison turned out to be thoroughly justified. For the issue could be connected to several debates and contemporary political issues: first, to the discussions regarding the creation of a unified prison system for the entire German Reich; second, to the penal reform movement that sought to change the penal code; and third, closely related, to the establishment of criminology as a scientific discipline.

A central part of the founding of the Kaiserreich in 1871 was the ambition to establish a uniform legal system throughout the German Reich, which manifested itself in the passage of a Reich Penal Code (Reichsstrafgesetzbuch, 1871), a Reich Law on the Organization of the Courts (Gerichtsverfassungsgesetz, 1877), and a Reich Code of Criminal Procedure (Strafprozessordnung, 1877), but which also included the goal of establishing a unified prison system through a Reich Law on Penitentiary Institutions (Reichsstrafvollzugsgesetz). After the proposal for a Reichsstrafvollzugsgesetz failed in the Bundesrat, which represented the different German states, in 1879, efforts turned to using the administrative path to achieve a unified regulation of the prisons, which were administered by the states. On 28 October 1897, the governments of the individual states agreed on "fundamental principles which shall be applied in the administration of legally imposed prison sentences until the passage of further general regulations."[13] Despite the existence of these "fundamental principles," the call for a national law regulating prisons throughout Germany continued. Therefore the organization of penal institutions remained a controversial issue throughout this period, which was continually discussed in professional circles and sometimes even affected political life in parliament and the general public through the daily press.

The second impulse driving the debate on the treatment of women in the penal system arose from the penal reform movement that took shape in the course of the 1880s and was associated with the criminal law professor Franz von Liszt.[14] Its reform agenda derived from the observation that the existing criminal justice system was ineffective, as demonstrated by the high crime rate and, especially, the high rate of recidivism. According to Liszt, the primary purpose of punishment was "to protect society from crime." Criminal sanctions should vary according to the personality of the perpetrator, with the severity and type of punishment determined by the degree to which the individual perpetrator posed a future danger for society. Liszt and his followers sought to determine the motivation for criminal behavior, thereby establishing a new position in the evaluation of crime. Whereas the so-called classical school of criminal law emphasized the free will of the perpetrator, representatives of the modern school made individual predisposition as well as social factors responsible for an individual's criminal behavior. Liszt distinguished between three groups of offenders, for which he postulated different effects of punishment: "criminals of the moment" (*Augenblicksverbrecher*), who would be prevented from further violations of the law through "deterrence"; "constitutional criminals [*Zustandsverbrecher*] capable of and requiring rehabilitation," who could be rehabilitated through appropriate measures; and, finally, "incorrigible constitutional criminals," who should be rendered "harmless" (*unschädlich*) through lifelong or indefinite detention. To classify convicts into one of these groups, Liszt argued, authorities required exact knowledge of the perpetrators' motives, social origins, education, character, and so on. In the process of thus classifying offenders the findings of both anthropological and sociological studies were to be applied. Under this approach, an effective penal policy necessarily required criminological knowledge. While Liszt was not personally engaged in research on criminal behavior, he could rely on numerous contemporary studies.

There is a consensus among scholars that criminology established itself as an independent academic field in the last third of the nineteenth century. Numerous studies trace the rise of this academic discipline in multiple European countries.[15] Two aspects of this development are crucial to understanding the arguments advanced here. First, gender-specific assumptions played an essential role in perceptions, definitions, and explanations of criminal behavior. The explanations of lower female crime rates and the characterizations of "specifically female crimes" offered by the representatives of the anthropological, psychological, and sociological varieties of criminology all rested on constructions of a specific femininity.[16] In describing criminality and its causes, criminologists established male criminality as the universal norm from which "special" or "specific" female criminality deviated. In other words, the gender factor became visible in constructions of criminality only when experts reflected on female criminality. Second, it is important to note that criminologists viewed their field as an empirical science. In Germany the criminological debates were dominated by psychiatrists, especially those who regularly testified in court, and prison doctors, all of whom based their criminological research on empirical, clinical studies of prison inmates. Thus the inmates of prisons and psychiatric wards became important objects of scientific interest. This close relationship between penal institutions and the accumulation of knowledge about criminality was noted by Michel Foucault, when he identified the prison as a "place of observation": "The prison, the place where the penalty is carried out, is also the place of observation of punished individuals. This takes two forms: surveillance, of course, but also knowledge of each inmate, of his behaviors, his deeper states of mind, his gradual improvement; the prisons must be conceived as places for the formation of clinical knowledge about the convicts."[17] The penal institutions must therefore be viewed as a kind of laboratory for the contemporary discourse on criminality. Their inmates provided the empirical material for contemporary constructions of criminality.[18]

But penal institution not only increased in relevance because they were places of scientific discovery. They also gained additional importance through Liszt's call to rehabilitate those offenders who could be rehabilitated. If prisons were to do more than merely incapacitate and deter criminals, the organization of prisons as places of rehabilitation would become one of the most important instruments for combatting crime.[19]

All of these factors provided the basis and background for the reformist discussions among prison officials working in women's prisons, who could finally hope that their area of expertise, ignored for years, would at last gain public recognition. Prison officials repeatedly pointed to the close connection between knowledge about criminality and their work in penal institutions, explicitly deriving their authority to contribute to penal and prison reform from their many years of experience in the penal system. As Josef Lenhard, director of the Bruchsal prison, put it: "Interaction with the incarcerated women and girls offers many opportunities to study women's psychological peculiarities, the laws of their fundamental difference from men, and the roots of criminality."[20]

Prison officials sought to implement their conceptions on several levels. First, they attempted to classify the female inmates. In the process, they often relied on psychological theories even when they lacked any prior knowledge of medicine or psychology. Thus the prison cleric Reinhold Stade, who had no training in psychology, gave his 1903 book *Types of Women from Prison Life* the subtitle *Contributions to a Psychology of the Female Criminal*.[21] Though not everyone developed their own categories, as Stade did, they still viewed themselves as experts who were qualified to confirm or refute the opinions of established criminal psychologists. In doing so, they did not wish to enter into competition with the experts, but to assist in laying the groundwork for more comprehensive research on female criminality in the future.

At a second level, prison officials took positions regarding those aspects of the penal reform agenda that concerned the treatment of women in court, arguing that female offenders' "true" motives usually did not come to light in court, but could only be determined by observing the female criminal in prison. Thus Prison Director Lenhard, for instance, noted that his conversations with female prisoners and his examination of their correspondence had taught him that extenuating circumstances were often not considered in the trials because the women were too ashamed to speak of personal matters before an exclusively male court. In addition, Lenhard asserted that "sexual factors," which according to his observations negatively influenced women's soundness of mind, received too little attention in court proceedings. Based on these "experiences," Lenhard explicitly supported calls made by criminologists Hans Gross and Gustav Aschaffenburg that court proceedings take into consideration the "gender-specific particularities" of women.[22]

On a third level, prison officials drew on their ideas about specifically female causes of crime to develop new measures to prevent crime. Finally, on a fourth level, they demanded that prisons treat women in a manner that was "appropriate to their female nature" (*dem weiblichen Wesen angemessen*). In the debates on the effects of the prison system on women, penal officials portrayed themselves as the sole experts on the matter. Likewise regarding the issue of how best to organize penal institutions in a way that would foster rehabilitation: here, too, prison directors, prison clerics, and prison physicians claimed a unique expertise that lent them authority in professional publications or conferences. In the following section, we will briefly sketch the content of these debates, focusing on the calls for a gender-specific approach to preventing crime and the gender-specific treatment of prisoners.

Opposing Equal Treatment in the Prison System

In their publications, prison officials consistently called for the prison system to incorporate the specific needs of women. The aspiration to organize penal institutions according to "female needs" was not limited to Germany. Indeed, the issue was featured on the agenda of the International Prison Congress in Paris in 1895.[23] After extensive deliberations, that Congress passed the following resolution: "I. For physical as well as moral and intellectual considerations, it is just and necessary to establish different prison regulations for men and women. II. It is necessary to construct special facilities or wards for mothers. III. It is necessary to provide dispositions in the regulations that will ease the severity of the prison system for women and that will improve their food."[24]

In the debates taking place in Imperial Germany, suggestions for the gender-specific treatment of women in prisons concentrated on two areas: first, on the conditions of imprisonment, and second, on measures of rehabilitation. In addition, nearly all writings reflected on the question of what preventive measures society should take to counteract female criminality. All of the suggestions rested on the assumption that men and women were of "completely different natures." Prison director Josef Lenhard, who in 1909 published an essay on the proper organization of women's prisons, based the authority and relevance of his arguments on a quote from the well-known criminologist and judge Hans Gross:

> One of the most difficult tasks for criminologists with regard to psychology remains the evaluation of woman; not only because she is physically and psychologically something completely different than man, but also because men can never fully understand the nature [*Wesen*] of a woman. . . . Woman is different from man: The anatomist and the physician tell us this, as do the historian and the littérateur, the theologian and the philosopher; every layman sees it for himself. Woman is different in her appearance, her perception, her judgment, her feeling, her desire, and her achievements. Only we jurists punish a man's deeds in the same way as a woman's, and treat a man's testimony the same as a woman's.[25]

Prison officials extended this conclusion to the prison system itself: Just as in sentencing, they claimed that women and men were currently receiving "equal treatment" in the prisons.

Gender-Specific Effects of Punishment

"How do women experience punishments compared to men, given the same working hours, the same food, the same amount of exercise, and the other usual conditions of imprisonment?" This was the question that the aforementioned Josef Lenhard, director of the Bruchsal prison, used to introduce the first section of his call for reforming the treatment of women in the prison system.[26] He, too, used the common legitimating topos of "experience." As he put it: "My nearly twenty-five years of experience working in penal institutions for women must be seen as enough time to have gained the necessary information to answer the question posed."[27] Summing up, he noted: "The negative effects of imprisonment on female convicts, especially in cases of longer terms of imprisonment, are apparent even to the layman. We see a reduction in the freshness of appearance and in body weight, as well as readily apparent signs of exhaustion."[28] In addition, he perceived significantly different effects of imprisonment on women versus men: "According to my observations, a period of imprisonment lasting several months usually has a more severe effect on women's health and morals than on men's."[29] The prison doctor Abraham Baer also noted: "Experience shows that prison life, with its negative influences on health, holds more dangers for females than for males."[30] As evidence of the more severe effect of punishment on women, commentators regularly pointed to female prisoners' higher rates of mortality and illness. Leonore Seutter, for instance, noted that in some years the rates of illness among women prisoners in Alsace-Lorraine were twice those of men, while in other years they were only 1 or 2 percent higher.[31] Josef Lenhard, too, offered quantitative data by reporting on the rates of mortality and illness in the local women's prison and the men's prison. According to his figures, the annual mortality rate among male prisoners averaged 11.59 per 1,000, whereas among female prisoners it was 23.38 per 1,000. He also found a higher rate of illness among female prisoners: in the period from 1891 to 1894, the rate of illness was 30.3 male prisoners per 1,000 versus 44.5 female prisoners per 1,000.[32]

Prison officials offered two explanations for these findings. First, they pointed to the fact that the health of the women who entered prison was generally already worse than that of male prisoners.[33] Second, it was claimed that the food given to female prisoners had a negative impact on their health. It was too heavy and hard to digest for the female inmates because they performed their work primarily while seated.[34] In addition, women in prison allegedly faced a psychological disadvantage. As Lenhard put it: "According to my observations, the majority of the women, whose family bonds are severed by their imprisonment, demonstrate their inborn needs for attachment, their more tender sensitivity, and their care for others, above all for their . . . children, to a much greater degree in prison than in freedom, and also differ entirely from male prisoners in this regard."[35] Seutter pointed to the "anomalies in menstruation and pregnancy" that frequently occurred in prison and lead to psychological "conditions of mania and depression."[36] Based on these arguments, reformist prison officials demanded that the future national law on prisons should reduce the amount of prison work required for women. In addition, they advocated adopting longer sleep periods and different dietary standards for female prisoners.[37]

Rehabilitation

In the debates on reforming women's treatment in prison, prison officials generally emphasized rehabilitation (*Besserung*) as the main purpose of punishment. As Josef Lenhard noted in the introduction to his study, "We may safely assume that the ultimate purpose of the prison sentence, provided for by law and imposed by the judge, is primarily to rehabilitate lawbreakers, to train them to lead a free life in the proper way in the future."[38] Lenhard did make some concessions to the findings of criminologists:

> [N]ot all prisoners can be protected from recidivism. There will always be a certain percentage who, due to recklessness, faulty upbringing, or an inborn or pathological desire, end up breaking the law [again] rather than taking the hand that offers to save them, or who are unworthy of protection because they have repeatedly abused it, rejected it and prefer the dark paths of the criminal.[39]

Nevertheless, Lenhard held that the majority of prisoners were capable of being rehabilitated: "The vast majority of the convicted are victims who can still be saved."[40] That said, he stressed that women and girls were generally more receptive to rehabilitative measures than were men. As evidence he pointed to the steadily declining number of female inmates at the women's prison of Bruchsal and to the high ratio of women who had been released early or paroled for good behavior.[41]

Furthermore, reformers demanded that rehabilitative measures not be applied wholesale but adapted to the special conditions of each individual case; a demand that was raised not only regarding women but for the prison system as a whole. In other words, prison officials were calling for the so-called individualization of the rehabilitative measures imposed in prison, which required exact knowledge of each inmate and the individual causes of their offenses.[42] The proper treatment of prisoners thus required criminological knowledge. The reformist officials who participated in these debates clearly viewed the female gender of an inmate as an important factor that justified, even necessitated, a specific kind of treatment.

Constructions of Female Criminality

The period from 1871 to 1914 witnessed the appearance of numerous publications on the specific nature of female criminality. These issues also comprised a significant proportion of the publications of prison officials. Although this is not the place for a comprehensive survey of gender-specific conceptions of criminality,[43] some brief remarks are necessary because some of these constructions played a key role in prison officials' proposals for rehabilitation measures and the prevention of women's criminality.

As a rule, crime statistics focused on certain differences between the genders: the relatively small proportion of female prisoners; gender-specific offenses;

dissimilar age distribution; differences in the influence of marital status; and finally, different motives.[44] Regarding age distribution, statisticians determined that men's criminality peaked between the ages of twenty-one and twenty-five, whereas women's criminality peaked between the ages of thirty and forty. Likewise, researchers detected a difference in the influence of marriage on criminal behavior: whereas the majority of convicted men were single, most of the female convicts were married, so that, in moral terms, marriage was said to have an elevating effect for men, but a lowering effect for women.[45] With regard to the division of the sexes by the kind of offense, researchers noted the high proportion of men's involvement in violent crimes such as assault, coercion, and robbery accompanied by murder. The fact that—aside from sexual offenses like prostitution and procuring—women were disproportionately involved in theft, fraud, embezzlement, and libel prompted the criminologist Gustav Aschaffenburg to conclude that "female criminality carries the characteristic of dishonesty, male crime that of brutality."[46]

A relatively high proportion of women were found to have committed murder and offenses against property. But criminologists emphasized that men's and women's motives for these crimes clearly differed. The majority of women convicted of murder were accused of infanticide. The next-largest group was comprised of those who murdered their husbands. Thus the violent crimes of women took place within their immediate social sphere and, hence, clearly differed from murders by men, which were primarily committed against persons unknown to the perpetrator.[47] Criminologists also assigned two specifically female motives to crimes against property committed by women: first, so-called altruistic reasons for theft and fraud and second, vanity.[48] The explanations offered for these peculiarities were inseparably bound up with gender-specific assumptions about the supposed physical and psychological characteristics of the "female sex in general." Explaining the relatively high rate of women involved in thefts and receipt of stolen goods, Aschaffenburg asserted that these offenses suited women's nature and way of life because women lacked the physical agility and courage for burglary.[49] Women's lower participation in violent crime was also attributed to women's lesser average physical strength. According to these sorts of observations, women committed especially those crimes that reflected their nature (*Wesen*) and thus demanded a lesser expenditure of energy. As a result of the medicalization of the discourse on crime, experts also connected women's propensity for crime to their sexual functions. Criminal psychologists and physicians regarded the "psychological consequences" of menstruation, pregnancy, or menopause as causes of criminal behavior and emphasized that these factors could considerably impair women's soundness of mind.[50]

The combination of heredity and milieu as causal factors in the explanation of crime also characterized the search for the causes of female criminality. Since the low crime rates of women were understood as a result of their broad exclusion from employment and the public sphere, women's increased participation in public life around the end of the nineteenth century was seen as an indicator of potential criminal behavior. How participants in this discourse connected the public sphere, employment, and female criminality depended largely on their interests and positions. As a characteristic example of the lines of argument on this issue I will examine the writings of Josef Lenhard, who was one of the most forceful advocates for the reform of women's penal institutions.

Offenders Become Victims: Lenhard's Typology of Female Inmates

Lenhard divided the prisoners in the Weiberstrafanstalt Bruchsal, the women's prison in Bruchsal, into three categories. The criteria he used demonstrate his proximity to the modern school of criminal law. The assignment of a female prisoner to a category was not based on her criminal offense, but on her social background and on the supposed causes of her criminal behavior.[51] The first category of female perpetrators consisted of young, single women who came from the lower classes and lived in large cities. Among these, he distinguished between those who belonged to the urban proletariat and those who had come from the countryside to the city as servant girls. As the decisive cause of the legal offenses of these women he cited the "dangers" of big-city life. Formative for the women of the "proletarian" class, according to Lenhard, were early sexual relationships, entered into "under the influence of modern-day entertainments and the unaccustomed enjoyment of alcohol, abetted also by the casual view of such sexual relationships that are, regrettably, found in broad segments of society." The resulting pregnancies and births drove the women to social distress until the "desperate women" saw abortion or infanticide as the only way out of their situation. The same was true of women who came to the city from rural areas, who were also led to illegal acts by the "seductions of the large city." To be able to afford "modern clothing," for example, they robbed or defrauded their employers or colleagues.

Lenhard's second category of female offenders was also comprised of single women. Representatives of this group, however, did not come from the lower classes but from somewhat more elevated strata of society. They were shop assistants and office clerks who had decided to pursue "the difficult path of independence." Because these women often failed and then found themselves in the cities with no family, shelter, or means of making a living, they saw crime as their only remaining possibility.

The third category consisted of married women who, in addition to their marital and maternal duties, were also responsible for the financial support of their families. These women typically lived in so-called mismarriages, in which the husband did not carry out his family duties; beatings by a drunken husband were part of their everyday lives. Because their husbands did not provide for the material needs of the family, female perpetrators in this category had primarily altruistic motives for the "specifically female crime" of theft.

The central explanatory trope in Lenhard's writings on women's criminality is the connection between urban life and crime. The women he described all moved freely in the city's public sphere without parental protection or oversight. To be sure, the themes of pleasure seeking, the consumption of alcohol, group living quarters, bed-renting, and urban masses surfaced in discussions of male criminality as well. But the dangers of the large city were assessed differently for men than for women. In explanations of male criminality, the large city served as a synonym for the threats of alcohol and socialist agitation. For women, by contrast, the big city meant primarily "moral and ethical decline."[52] Of central importance to Lenhard's further argumentation was the fact that he described female offenders as victims, calling them "seduced," "lost," "stranded," or "failed."[53] For him, free, unbounded life in the big city posed a greater danger to women than to men because women's weaker physical and mental constitutions were not equal to the seductions of city life or the challenges of the independence that women themselves desired.

Specifically Female Measures of Rehabilitation

Lenhard used his typology of female offenders to demand gender-specific rehabilitation measures as well as gender-specific crime prevention measures for women. His primary demand was to make use of the positive "moral influence" of women by hiring female prison staff and encouraging visits from women in prisoner's aid societies. The advisability of employing female prison staff was discussed at the 1898 and 1901 meetings of the Kongress deutscher Strafanstaltsbeamter (Congress of German Prison Officials).[54] At these conventions, at which women were absent, the importance of female staff for the rehabilitation of female inmates was consistently emphasized. The largely positive response of prison officials derived primarily from the assumption that only women could recognize and comprehend the "inner life" of their imprisoned fellow women and that only they could win their trust.[55] Although there was agreement that female staff was absolutely necessary for women's prisons, there were divided opinions regarding the positions that women should occupy. Prison director Gennat even advocated giving women positions as directors.[56] The majority, however, voted for a resolution that called for filling all lower-level and only some upper-level prison staff positions with women, reserving the position of director for a man.[57]

Prison staff members, however, were not to be the only ones who should have influence on the female prisoners. Women from prisoners' aid societies and private welfare associations were also to be given rights of visitation. It was hoped that such visits would enable the prisons to use the influence of women from "better circles of society" to obtain offers of assistance to prisoners even before they were released.[58] In addition, intensive counseling of female prisoners by prison clergy would serve the important goal of providing a positive moral influence.[59] Furthermore, the prison director was to arrange for the welfare of the prisoner after her release. Single women especially were to be reintegrated into their families. During the female prisoner's detention, the prison staff should establish communication between the prisoner and her family and where applicable seek to achieve family reconciliation.[60]

The establishment of a prison work program occupied only a secondary position in Lenhard's essay. Other authors, however, emphasized this aspect, which played a central part in structuring everyday prison life. Although prison work was defined as compulsory labor, it was generally viewed as one of the most important means of education of the inmates. The goal of prison work should be to enable a prisoner, whether male or female, "to find in honest work a means of making one's living. Three key phrases sum up the program of prison work: Prisoners should become accustomed to steady work; they must be rendered capable of hard work; and they must be taught to find joy in their work."[61] As was the case for male prisoners, the debate on reforming women's prisons included the demand that prison officials find jobs for released prisoners, whether as servant girls or as seamstresses in the textile industry. Leonore Seutter, who in 1912 published a study of work in women's prisons, demanded that prison work must "counter the flood of women into unskilled labor by providing training in an occupation."[62] But even Seutter, who wanted women to gain work qualifications while serving their prison sentences, advocated that women's prison work involved the prisoners' instruction in "specifically female" basic skills like home economics, knitting, sewing, and embroidery, the usefulness of which was assumed to be apparent for all female prisoners regardless of their social origins, background, or age. By favoring these work activities, the author concluded, women's prisons could be transformed into "true educational institutions," thereby "giving valuable assistance to the healing of our family life, which suffers, among other ailments, from the poor education of our women as housewives and mothers."[63]

The view that the causes of female criminality were gender-specific was not only used to justify the special treatment of women in prison but also to promote certain preventive measures for fighting crime. The central measure that was proposed to counteract female criminality was to restrict women's activities to the "domestic sphere." Thus Lenhard noted: "The concern that should take precedence over all other measures is to free women, especially mothers, from the necessity of earning money and to win them again for the performance of their natural duties: caring for the household and raising children."[64]

In sum, prison officials emphasized the gender-specific causes of female criminality. On this basis, they proposed crime prevention measures specifically for women. Their proposals concerning the treatment of women in penal institutions

can be divided into five main points: a strict separation of the sexes in penal institutions; the supervision of female inmates by female staff; special consideration
for the moral influence of staff and prison clergy; the adaptation of the regulations regarding food, discipline, and work hours to women's physical constitutions; and a preference for domestic work in establishing prison work programs.
All of these aspects were to be included in the future law that was to impose
uniformity on penal institutions throughout the German Reich. Moreover, since
female prisoners were labeled "victims," these suggestions could be presented as
measures of protection and welfare. Thus it is no wonder that Lenhard remarked:
"In the end, all of these efforts aim to give incarcerated women the special protection they deserve."[65]

The Treatment of Women in Imperial Germany's Prison Regulations

How did these calls for reform relate to actual state measures affecting the treatment of women in penal institutions in Imperial Germany? According to Article
4, no. 13, of the German Reich constitution, the Reich had the right to pass a
law relating to the penal system. As previously mentioned, however, while the
Kaiserreich witnessed the passage of the Reich Penal Code, a Reich Law on the
Organization of the Courts, and a Reich Code of Criminal Procedure, no agreement was reached on a law that would unify the prison system across the Reich.
To be sure, the above-mentioned laws contained sections that directly related to
the prison system: the Penal Code defined the different types of punishment, the
Law on the Organization of Courts determined the place of punishment, and the
Code of Criminal Procedure determined the beginning and end of punishment.
Nevertheless, the concrete configuration of the prison system remained within
the purview of the individual states.

The only regulations that applied throughout the Reich were the so-called
"Bundesrat Guidelines" of 1897, which were to be "applied in the administration of legally imposed prison sentences until the passage of further general
regulations."[66] These guidelines provided for the separation of prisoners serving
sentences from prisoners awaiting trial; the separation of prisoners sentenced to
compulsory labor (*Zuchthaus*), prison (*Gefängnis*), and jail (*Haft*); the separation of men from women; and the separation of juveniles from adults. Wherever
possible, separate facilities or at least separate wards were to be constructed for
each of these groups. Moreover, regulations were agreed upon regarding the use
of single-cell versus communal imprisonment (§§ 11-16). The guidelines also
addressed the issues of prison labor (§§ 17-22), food (§§ 23-24), disciplinary
action (§§ 34-35), spiritual welfare (§ 28), class instruction (§ 29), and prisoner
complaints (§ 39). It must be noted, however, that these guidelines possessed no

binding legal force. Instead, they must be understood as minimal demands for the penal system, and they essentially represented the least common denominator of the individual states. In addition, the Bundesrat Guidelines allowed considerable leeway for implementation, so that calls for the unification of the penal system throughout the Reich continued unabated.

The importance of these guidelines for Imperial Germany's prisons must therefore not be overestimated. Nevertheless, they demonstrate that the detention of women in separate institutions as well as the supervision of female inmates by exclusively female staff were among the aspects of the penal system that met with a general consensus. The guidelines' section on "Accommodation" stipulated: "As a rule, female prisoners are housed in special institutions (wards). Where this is not possible, the necessary measures shall be taken to prevent any contact between female and male prisoners. For the supervision of female prisoners, large institutions shall use female guards exclusively, smaller institutions shall use female guards as much as possible."[67]

As noted above, the concrete configuration and administration of the prisons remained the affair of the individual states. Therefore, between 1871 and 1914, German prisons were governed by more than sixty different sets of regulations.[68] As the regulations for Prussia demonstrate, the policies of separate facilities for women and the use of female staff to supervise female inmates were indeed implemented at the state level.[69] In 1902 the Prussian Interior Ministry issued a unified set of regulations for the prisons under its administration.[70] They, too, stipulated the detention of women in separate institutions. Moreover, Article 82 of these regulations required the construction of separate wards in those institutions to which both male and female prisoners were admitted and mandated that "every interaction between prisoners of the opposite sex" was to be prevented.[71] Regarding the hiring of staff, Article 42 noted: "For guarding and supervising female prisoners, only female staff—house mothers, supervisors, forewomen, and attendants—may be used."[72]

The separation of the sexes was not an innovative provision, but had been considered essential from the initial institutionalization of modern prisons at the turn from the eighteenth to the nineteenth century.[73] As early as the end of the eighteenth century, the prison reformers John Howard, Eberhard Waechter, Heinrich Balthasar Wagnitz, and Albrecht H. von Arnim had called for separate accommodations for men and women in their writings.[74] Though these authors still favored the construction of gender-segregated wards within a single institution, in 1829 Nikolaus Heinrich Julius advocated the option of constructing separate institutions for each sex.[75] And by the 1840s, the single-sex penal institution was considered the only advisable option.[76] Women's prisons did not remain theoretical constructs in programmatic writings. In Baden as well as in Prussia, the first women-only penal institutions were established in the late 1830s. While the women's prison in Bruchsal remained the only women's prison in Baden until the end of the nineteenth century, in Prussia a whole series of new women's prisons were established, especially between 1850 and 1860.[77] The women's prison was therefore not a new phenomenon of the late nineteenth century. Neither was the employment of female staff in women's prisons, which can also be traced back to the early nineteenth century. In Baden, the exclusive supervision of female prisoners by female staff was decreed in 1838. Prussia followed in 1842.[78]

Thus the content of the 1897 Bundesrat Guidelines regarding the treatment of women in prisons was not new, but could be taken from older regulations. Nevertheless, a clear change can be seen in the time period between 1871 and 1914. The increasing importance of the issue of women's treatment in the penal system was reflected not only in the reform debates but also in the actions of state administrations, which began to criticize its past neglect, which had meant that in Prussia, for instance, the official guidelines had been implemented only to a very limited extent. This was the case, first and foremost, for the hiring of female staff. Looking back in 1901, Karl Krohne, the division head responsible for the prison system in the Prussian Ministry of the Interior, described the situation of women's prisons in the 1860s thus: "All that was accomplished was that, when the number of prisons was increased, a complete separation of female from male prisoners was achieved by means of the construction of special women's prisons. The requirement that in female institutions, except for the warden, only female staff should be used for supervision, was not implemented. Upper- and even lower-level male staff were hired."[79] Between 1871 and 1914, prison officials sought to change this state of affairs and pushed the hiring of female staff very hard. The new women-only hiring effort affected not only the lower-level positions, but also higher-level prison staff positions such as teachers and accountants. Around the turn of the century, Prussia was the first state in the German Reich to try out the appointment of "female supervisors" (*Oberinnen*) to head women's institutions, whose functions were equivalent to those of the prison directors (*Strafanstaltsdirektoren*) of male prisons.[80]

Although reformist prison officials could feel vindicated by these measures introduced not only in Prussia but also in other German states, they also observed dangerous tendencies to be resisted. With the exception of the detention of female inmates in separate women's prisons and the hiring of female staff, they discerned a tendency to equalize the treatment of male and female inmates, which ran counter to their own desire for a penal system that was adapted to supposedly gender-specific traits. As we shall see, there were some indications that their assessment was correct and that the measures introduced by the Prussian Ministry of the Interior, for instance, were indeed moving in the direction of equal treatment of women and men.

The reform of the Prussian prison system did result in the sexes being separated for the most part, at least in the larger institutions. However, by the turn of the century, women's prisons still did not meet contemporary standards of a "modern penal system." Karl Krohne summed up the situation in 1901: "Unfortunately, we have neglected the facilities for female prisoners in a most irresponsible manner. We have the best cellular prisons for men, but have locked up all the women—young and old, rotten to the core and less bad—together without any consideration for their individuality, and have therefore let them morally corrupt one another."[81] From the turn of the century, the increasing importance ascribed to the treatment of women convinced the Prussian Ministry of the Interior to construct new buildings for women's prisons. These new facilities were identical to men's prisons both in their construction and in their system of imprisonment.[82] The same was true for the prison regulations that structured daily life in the institution. In the course of imposing uniformity on the Prussian prison system, the Interior Ministry decided that the new prison regulations (*Hausordnung*) of the Moabit prison in Berlin should serve as the model to be followed in revising the regulations of the other prisons. The Moabit prison was designated exclusively for men, and its regulations therefore conceived for a men's prison, which was clear from their very first sentence: "You are now an imprisoned man!" What was a women's prison to do with this text? The women's prison Siegburg-Brückberg rendered the introduction as follows: "You are now imprisoned!" The daily routine laid out in regulations of the women's prisons was identical to that of men's prisons.[83] Variations in the texts of these regulations were almost exclusively linguistic ones, involving the adaptation of the grammatical gender to the gender of the delinquents.

The inclusion of women's prisons in the process of state reform amounted to an adaptation of women's prisons to the standards and norms of the men's penal system. Prison officials therefore saw their demands for a reform of women's prisons system only partially met. Nevertheless, the significance of their demands should not be underestimated. Although prison officials' reformist publications contained little potential for innovation in the way of concrete suggestions for the organization of women's prisons, they did offer a new sense of meaning for these measures. In the Kaiserreich, therefore, it was not the content of the proposals— for example, for separate women's prisons and female staff—that was new, but the fact that these concrete proposals were connected to a general demand that female prisoners be treated in a manner consistent with "female needs."

In the early prison reform publications around 1800 and in the German *Gefängniskunde* (penology) literature of the first half of the nineteenth century, the separation of the sexes and the exclusive supervision of female prisoners by women were understood primarily as disciplinary strategies. These measures were considered necessary to maintain order and discipline in the institutions, which included establishing the prisons as a sphere free of sexuality.[84] The decision-making of the state administrations that constructed the first women's prisons in the 1830s reveals that the crucial impetus had nothing to with creating a gender-specific women's penal system. Up to the 1850s, the establishment of women's prisons consistently served the goal of maintaining separate men's prisons. The creation of women's prisons was considered an appropriate strategy for implementing the separation of the sexes for both men's and women's penal institutions. In addition, the removal of female prisoners was designed to relieve the overcrowding of existing prisons. Moreover, the responsible ministries viewed separate prisons for the two sexes as an effective means of making the prison system more effective and more economical. Whereas the establishment of gender-specific wards within a single institution meant doubling the amount of space required—for example, due to the necessity of providing separate classrooms, dining rooms, work areas, and so on for male and female prisoners—it was possible to avoid this by having only one sex present in the institution. Thus the establishment of separate women's prisons in the first half of the nineteenth century was not at all connected to the notion that women should receive gender-specific treatment in the penal system. Thus the Badenese state councilor Lamey, for example, commented on the creation of the Women's Prison at Bruchsal in 1838 with the words: "There is no reason to follow special principles in the punishment of women."[85]

In this regard, the Kaiserreich's reform debate reflected a clear change in how the proper treatment of women in the penal system was viewed. The reformist prison officials' demands rested on the conviction that the penal system's treatment of women required specificity and must take "special female needs" into account. They insisted that the penal system's treatment of women must follow special principles, which, moreover, ought to be set down in a federal law on prisons that would make them visible to the public. Programmatic demands, such as detaining women in separate penal institutions and employing female staff to supervise them, which were as old as the penal institutions themselves, were given new meanings. Now, these demands were no longer exclusively seen as disciplinary strategies and pragmatic structural measures used to streamline the penal system, but as the necessary preconditions to meeting the supposed "special needs" of the female sex. The success of this new set of meanings can be seen in numerous handbooks and other works on the prison system published long into the twentieth century.

Conclusion

In Imperial Germany, the proper organization of the penal system became a topic that received attention from many quarters. The discussions regarding a Reichsstrafvollzugsgesetz that would create uniform standards for prisons throughout the Reich, the establishment of criminology as a field of research, and the formation of a powerful penal reform movement all made prisons more important as sites of "scientific discovery" and tools in the "fight against crime." In the course of these developments, the treatment of women in the penal system also attracted more interest. The resulting calls for reform were primarily articulated by prison officials. This chapter has examined the arguments advanced by a group of prisons officials who were significant participants in the debate and were closely associated with the "modern school" of criminal law.

The starting point for their reform arguments was the assumption that women and men were "completely different in nature" (*wesensverschieden*). The contemporary organization of penal institutions, they maintained, did not take account of this fact at all. On the contrary, the organization of men's and women's prisons was described as identical, which reformers interpreted as leading to a clear disadvantage for women. Instead, reformist prison officials demanded that the conditions of women's detention must take into account the physical and psychological "pecularities" of women and that rehabilitation measures, too, must reflect "specifically female" needs. They emphasized rehabilitation as the primary purpose of punishment and assumed that "criminological knowledge" was essential to achieving this goal. Their demands were based on typologies of "female criminality" or of the female inmates of their institutions.

As we saw, the concrete reform demands contained little that was innovative. Some of the measures that were demanded had been recognized as pillars of an effective penal system since modern prisons were established in the late eighteenth and early nineteenth century; others had already been implemented during the Kaiserreich in the form of valid normative guidelines. The transformation reflected in Imperial Germany's reform debates has less to do with the organization of women's penal institutions than with the meaning that was ascribed to the penal system's treatment of women. Thus, what was new was not the content of the demands but their connection to a treatment of women that would reflect "special female needs." We should note that the question whether the actual conditions of imprisonment for men and women were in fact as similar as the reformers claimed can only be answered by detailed comparative research on men's and women's prisons that falls outside the scope of this chapter.[86]

I would like to close with the question of what symbolic function the demand to inscribe special considerations for women in a Reich law on prisons fulfilled. Here we should note the descriptions of female offenders as victims, which formed a considerable component of the reformist argumentation. The characterization of reforms as "measures of protection and welfare" was consistently justified by reference to the physically and psychologically weaker constitution of women, which made them seem less suited for public life and employment than were men. For the same reason, the return of women to the domestic sphere was repeatedly advocated as a central means of preventing crime. At the same time, it should not be overlooked that the reformers viewed the employment of women as necessary in certain cases. Likewise, many demands of the women's movement were recognized as justified; and its calls for the professionalization of female occupations were in fact promoted by the demand for female supervisory staff in women's prisons. However, the argumentation also clearly reveals that there were to be limits to women's changing position in society. Changes were acceptable only as long as they did not endanger the gender order itself. The demand for the special treatment of women in criminal law and in the prison system can thus also be interpreted as a means of normalizing and stabilizing the gender hierarchy.[87]

Notes

Translated by Keith D. Alexander and Richard F. Wetzell. Research for this chapter was completed as part of the author's dissertation research, which was supported by the Deutsche Forschungsgemeinschaft as part of the University of Bielefeld's Graduiertenkolleg "Sozialgeschichte von Gruppen, Schichten, Klassen und Eliten." The author's dissertation has been published as Sandra Leukel, *Strafanstalt und Geschlecht: Geschichte des Frauenstrafvollzug im 19. Jahrhundert (Baden und Preussen)* (Leipzig: Leipziger Universitätsverlag, 2010).

1. By the phrases "female criminality" and "women's criminality," I mean only the legal violations committed by women that were legally defined and sanctioned in penal codes. The concept thus refers to the entire spectrum of the punishable acts of women and does not refer to "woman-specific" or "woman-like" crimes.
2. See among others *Kriminalstatistik für das Jahr 1892*, Dritter Abschnitt: Die Verurtheilten nach Alter und Geschlecht insbesondere, bearb. im Reichs-Justizamt und im Kaiserlichen Statistischen Amt (Berlin, 1894). On the share of female criminality in the Reich's crime statistics, see Eric A. Johnson, *Urbanization and Crime: Germany 1871–1914* (Cambridge, 1995), 184–191.
3. Gustav Aschaffenburg, *Das Verbrechen und seine Bekämpfung: Kriminalpsychologie für Mediziner, Juristen und Soziologen, ein Beitrag zur Reform der Strafgesetzgebung* (Heidelberg, 1903), 129–130.
4. Reinhold Stade, *Frauentypen aus dem Gefängnisleben: Beiträge zu einer Psychologie der Verbrecherin* (Leipzig, 1903), 48.
5. See for example Marie Mellien, "Die weibliche Kriminalität im Deutschen Reiche," *Die Frau* 9 (1902), 499–500.
6. Mellien, "Weibliche Kriminalität," 500. See also Anna Ernst, "Zur Kriminalität der Geschlechter," *Die Frau* 8 (1901), 641–643.
7. Anna Waldeck, "Die Berufstätigkeit der Frauen und die Kriminalität," *Centralblatt des Bundes Deutscher Frauenvereine* 14 (1912), 5.
8. Daniel Pick, *Faces of Degeneration* (Cambridge, 1989).
9. Carmen Gransee, "Zur Reproduktion von Normalitätsvorstellungen von Weiblichkeit durch Kriminalisierungsprozesse—Eine Rekonstruktion der Medienwirklichkeiten," in Detlev Frehsee, ed., *Konstruktion der Wirklichkeit durch Kriminalität und Strafe* (Baden-Baden, 1997), 436–437.
10. Anne-Louise Shapiro, *Breaking the Codes: Female Criminality in Fin-de-Siècle Paris* (Stanford, 1996), 5.
11. Abraham Baer, *Die Gefängnisse, Strafanstalten und Strafsysteme, ihre Einrichtung und Wirkung in hygienischer Beziehung* (Berlin, 1871), 334.
12. Hermann von Valentini, *Das Verbrecherthum im preußischen Staate, Nebst Vorschlägen zu seiner Bekämpfung durch die Gesellschaft und durch die Reform der Strafvollstreckung* (Leipzig, 1869), 246.

13. Hans Dietrich Quedenfeld, *Der Strafvollzug in der Gesetzgebung des Reiches, des Bundes und der Länder: Eine Untersuchung über die normative Grundlage des Strafvollzugs* (Tübingen, 1971), 2–8; Erwin Bumke, "Die Freiheitsstrafe als Problem der Gesetzgebung," in Erwin Bumke, ed., *Deutsches Gefängniswesen: Ein Handbuch* (Berlin, 1928), 16–32. Christina Schenk, *Bestrebungen zur einheitlichen Regelung des Strafvollzugs in Deutschland von 1870 bis 1923: Mit einem Ausblick auf die Strafvollzugsgesetzentwürfe von 1927* (Frankfurt am Main, 2001).

14. On the penal reform movement see: Monika Frommel, "Internationale Reformbewegung zwischen 1880 und 1920," in *Erzählte Kriminalität: Zur Typologie und Funktion von narrativen Darstellungen der Strafrechtspflege, Publizisitik und Literatur*, ed. Jörg Schönert (Tübingen, 1991), 467–495; Richard F. Wetzell, "From Retributive Justice to Social Defense: Penal Reform in Fin-de-Siècle Germany," in *Germany at the Fin de Siècle: Culture, Politics, and Ideas*, ed. Suzanne Marchand and David Lindenfeld (Baton Rouge: 2004), 59–77; Richard F. Wetzell, *Criminal Law Reform in Imperial Germany* (Ph.D. diss., Stanford University, 1991); Richard F. Wetzell, *Inventing the Criminal: A History of German Criminology 1880–1945* (Chapel Hill, 2000), 31–38, 73–105; Eberhard Schmidt, *Einführung in die Geschichte der deutschen Strafrechtspflege*, 2nd ed. (Göttingen, 1951), 350–386.

15. Peter Becker and Richard F. Wetzell, eds., *Criminals and Their Scientists: The History of Criminology in International Perspective* (Cambridge, 2006); Pick, "Faces of Degeneration"; Nicole Hahn Rafter, *Creating Born Criminals* (Chicago, 1997); Robert Nye, *Crime, Madness, and Politics in Modern France* (Princeton, N.J., 1984). On developments in Germany see: Wetzell, *Inventing the Criminal*; Silviana Galassi, *Kriminologie im Deutschen Kaiserreich: Geschichte einer gebrochenen Verwissenschaftlichung* (Stuttgart, 2004). Peter Becker, *Verderbnis und Entartung: Eine Geschichte der Kriminologie des 19. Jahrhunderts als Diskurs und Praxis* (Göttingen, 2002); Christian Müller, *Verbrechensbekämpfung im Anstaltsstaat: Psychiatrie, Kriminologie und Strafrechtsreform in Deutschland 1871–1933* (Göttingen, 2004).

16. This already becomes clear in the title of Cesare Lombroso's work, *Das Weib als Verbrecherin und Prostituirte: Anthropologische Studien, gegründet auf eine Darstellung der Biologie und Psychologie des normalen Weibes* (Hamburg, 1894). See also Mary S. Gibson, "The 'Female Offender' and the Italian School of Criminal Anthropology," *European Studies* 12 (1982), 155–165; Nicole Hahn Rafter and Mary Gibson, eds., *Criminal Woman, the Prostitute, and the Normal Woman: Cesare Lombroso and Guglielmo Ferrero* (Durham, 2004); Karsten Uhl, *Das "verbrecherische Weib": Geschlecht, Verbrechen und Strafen im kriminologischen Diskurs 1800–1945* (Münster, 2003).

17. Michel Foucault, *Discipline and Punish: The Birth of the Prison* (New York, 1979), 249.

18. Thus Cesare Lombroso was a physician in a psychiatric facility and carried out his research and measurements on numerous prisoners. The major figures in German criminology also worked in penal and mental institutions: Gustav Aschaffenburg headed the observation ward for mentally ill criminals at the prison in Halle for a while, and Paul Näcke was staff physician at the Hubertusburg insane asylum. Mariacarla Gadebusch Bondio, *Die Rezeption der kriminalanthropologischen Theorien von Cesare Lombroso in Deutschland von 1880–1914* (Husum,1995); Gibson, "The 'Female Offender,'" 159.

19. Lombroso himself assumed that the category of the born criminal represented only a minority of those sentenced. Gibson, "The 'Female Offender,'" 159.

20. Josef Lenhard, "Psychologische Betrachtungen über Frauen und Mädchen im Strafvollzuge," *Blätter für Gefängniskunde* 43 (1909), 435–92, esp. 439–40.

21. Stade, *Frauentypen*. The same author has published additional works on this subject: *Aus der Gefängnißseelsorge. Erinnerungen aus vierzehnjährigem Gefängnißdienst* (Leipzig, 1901); *Durch eigene und fremde Schuld: Kriminalistische Lebensbilder* (Leipzig, 1904).

22. Lenhard, "Psychologische Betrachtungen," 445.

23. The discussion focused on the question, "Is it advisable to make special regulations for women's prisons that are very different from those for men's prisons, regarding work as well as

the disciplinary system and the provisions? Would it not be advisable to employ a special system for women?" Lothar Frede and Rudolf Sieverts, eds., *Die Beschlüsse der Internationalen Gefängnis-Kongresse 1872–1930* (Jena, 1932), 48.

24. Frede and Sieverts, *Beschlüsse.*
25. Lenhard, "Psychologische Betrachtungen," 437–438. Here he cites Hanns Gross, *Criminalpsychologie* (Graz, 1898)
26. Lenhard, "Psychologische Betrachtungen," 437.
27. Lenhard, "Psychologische Betrachtungen," 437.
28. Lenhard, "Psychologische Betrachtungen," 447.
29. Lenhard, "Psychologische Betrachtungen," 449.
30. Baer, "Die Gefängnisse," 335. On the pages that follow he provides substantial statistical material.
31. Leonore Seutter, *Die Gefängnisarbeit in Deutschland mit besonderer Berücksichtigung der Frauen-Gefängnisse* (Tübingen, 1912), 95.
32. Lenhard, "Psychologische Betrachtungen," 446. See also Lenhard's essay, "Einiges über Körperwägungen und über die Sterblichkeit einer Strafanstalt," *Monatsschrift für Kriminalpsychologie und Strafrechtsreform* 4 (1907/08), 289ff., in which he confirms the much greater weight loss among women prisoners compared to men.
33. Lenhard identified the following reasons for this: For one thing, the female organism had already suffered severely due to "unsupervised" births. For another, however, he blamed women's changing social conditions: the increased occupation of women outside the home in the last decades had brought significant disadvantages to women's general health. See Lenhard, "Psychologische Betrachtungen," 440. Seutter, on the other hand, noted that these women "durch ein ausschweifendes Leben, durch Armut, durch schlechte Ernährung und Körperpflege, durch unhygienische Wohnungen geschwächte Körper mit in die Anstalt bringen" (Seutter, "Gefängnisarbeit," 94).
34. Lenhard, "Psychologische Betrachtungen," 448.
35. Lenhard, "Psychologische Betrachtungen," 440.
36. Seutter here relied on the testimonies of prison officials as well as on her own observations. Seutter, "Gefängnisarbeit," 100.
37. Lenhard, "Psychologische Betrachtungen," 449–450. See also Abraham Baer's remarks on women's physical and psychological constitution in Abraham Baer, *Hygiene des Gefängniswesens: Der Vollzug der Freiheitsstrafe in hygienischer Beziehung* (Jena, 1897), 216–217.
38. Lenhard, "Psychologische Betrachtungen," 436. In addition he called for this determination of purpose to be taken up in any future penal code. Lenhard, "Psychologische Betrachtungen," 455.
39. Lenhard, "Psychologische Betrachtungen," 456.
40. Lenhard, "Psychologische Betrachtungen," 437.
41. Lenhard, "Psychologische Betrachtungen," 453 and 474–475.
42. See for example Hermann Kriegsmann, *Einführung in die Gefängniskunde* (Heidelberg, 1912), 310–331.
43. See Uhl, *Das "verbrecherische Weib"* for an extensive treatment of this issue.
44. See for example Hugo Högel, "Die Straffälligkeit des Weibes," *Archiv für Kriminal-Anthropologie und Kriminalstatistik* 5 (1900), 231–289.
45. Friedrich Prinzing, "Der Einfluss der Ehe auf die Kriminalität des Mannes," *Zeitschrift für Socialwissenschaft* 2 (1899), 109–126; Prinzing, "Die Erhöhung der Kriminalität des Weibes durch die Ehe," *Zeitschrift für Socialwissenschaft* 2 (1899), 433–450.
46. Aschaffenburg, "Das Verbrechen und seine Bekämpfung," 129.
47. Hoegel, "Straffälligkeit des Weibes," 260–269.
48. Seutter, "Gefängnisarbeit," 85.

49. Aschaffenburg, "Das Verbrechen und seine Bekämpfung," 129.

50. For example Gross, "Criminalpsychologie," 413–490.

51. The following descriptions of the different categories are found in Lenhard, "Psychologische Betrachtungen," 458–460.

52. On the contemporary linkage between criminality and the large city, see Becker, *Verderbnis und Entartung*, 324f.; Martin Dinges and Fritz Sack, eds., *Unsichere Großstädte? Vom Mittelalter bis zur Postmoderne* (Konstanz, 2000); Johnson, *Urbanization*.

53. The description of female offenders as victims can also be found in the works of other authors. See, for example, Stade, "Frauentypen," 214.

54. The Darmstadt (1898) and Nuremberg (1901) meetings discussed the question: "Would it be advisable to hire only female staff (physicians and clerics excepted) in women's prisons, and to give a male higher-level prison official only supervisory authority?" See: "Bericht über die XI. Versammlung des Vereins der deutschen Strafanstaltsbeamten in Darmstadt vom 24. Mai bis 27. Mai. Nach stenographischen Aufzeichnungen," *Blätter für Gefängniskunde* 32 (1898), 341–464, esp. 444–462; "Bericht über die XII. Versammlung der deutschen Strafanstaltsbeamten in Nürnberg vom 29. Mai bis 1. Juni 1901. Nach stenographischen Aufzeichnungen," *Blätter für Gefängniskunde* 35 (1901), 1–210, esp. 132–161.

55. See, for instance, the comments of prison director Bässler in H. Bässler, "Gutachten," *Blätter für Gefängniskunde* 32 (1898), 109–114, quote 111.

56. Alice Salomon, "Die Frauenfrage auf dem Kongreß deutscher Strafanstaltsbeamter," *Die Frau* 8 (1901), 623–626, here 625.

57. The exact wording of the resolution was the following: "In Weiberstrafanstalten sind die Stellen a) der Werkführer, Aufseher und Oberaufseher unbedingt mit weiblichen Beamten, b) der Expeditions-, Kassen- und Wirtschaftsbeamten, des Lehrers und des Arztes thunlichst mit weiblichen Beamten, c) der Wächter, Boten, Handwerker, des Geistlichen und des Direktors dagegen nur mit männlichen Beamten zu besetzen."

58. Lenhard, "Psychologische Betrachtungen," 484.

59. Lenhard, "Psychologische Betrachtungen," 460.

60. Lenhard, "Psychologische Betrachtungen," 460. Lenhard viewed it as necessary to assign women who had been released from prison a chaperone to accompany them to their families.

61. Kriegsmann, "Einführung," 207.

62. Seutter, "Gefängnisarbeit," 148.

63. Seutter, "Gefängnisarbeit," 125.

64. Lenhard, "Psychologische Betrachtungen," 460. For similar arguments, see Stade, "Frauentypen," 289.

65. Lenhard, "Psychologische Betrachtungen," 486.

66. Printed, among other places, in *Blätter für Gefängniskunde* 30 (1898), 467–476.

67. Except for one further paragraph, the guidelines lacked any further gender-specific content. That paragraph, whose symbolic meaning should not be underestimated, recommended that female prisoners should not have their hair cut, in contrast to male prisoners, unless for hygienic reasons.

68. Schmidt, "Einführung," 345.

69. The decisions named here were also part of the Badenese official regulations (*Dienstordnung*). *Dienst- und Hausordnung für die Zentralstrafanstalten des Großherzogtums Baden mit Ausschluß des Festungsbaugefängnisses Rastatt vom 15. Dezember 1890* (Karlsruhe, 1891). On the Badenese prison system: Julius Appel, *Der Vollzug der Freiheitsstrafen in Baden: Allgemeine Gesichtspunkte* (Karlsruhe, 1905).

70. *Dienstordnung für die dem Ministerium des Innern unterstellten Strafanstalten und größeren Gefängnissen vom 14. November 1902* (Berlin, 1902). The responsibility for the Prussian prison system was on the one hand under the Ministry of the Interior (workhouses, penal

institutions) (*Zuchthäuser, Strafanstalten*) and on the other under the Ministry of Justice. On this, see P. Jakobs, *Der Dualismus im preußischen Gefängniswesen* (Bonn, 1906); Thomas Berger, *Die konstante Repression: Zur Geschichte des Strafvollzugs in Preußen nach 1850* (Frankfurt am Main, 1974).

71. "Dienstordnung Preußen," 35.

72. "Dienstordnung Preußen," 19.

73. The beginning of the institutionalization of prisons in the modern juridical sense, as facilities where legally imposed prison terms are served, is universally dated to the transition from the eighteenth to the nineteenth century. On the formation of prisons, see Pieter Spierenburg, "The Body and the State: Early Modern Europe," in Norval Morris and David J. Rothman, eds., *The Oxford History of the Prison: The Practice of Punishment in Western Society* (Oxford, 1995), 49–77; Norbert Finzsch, "'Comparing Apples and Oranges?' The History of Early Prisons in Germany and the United States, 1800–1860," in Norbert Finzsch and Robert Jütte, eds., *Institutions of Confinement: Hospitals, Asylums, and Prisons in Western Europe and North America, 1500–1950* (Cambridge, 1996), 213–233. Thomas Nutz, *Strafanstalt als Besserungsmaschine: Gefängnisreformdiskurs und Gefängniswissenschaft 1775–1848* (Munich, 2001).

74. John Howard, *The State of Prisons in England and Wales* (London, 1777); Eberhard Waechter, *Ueber Zuchthaus und Zuchthausstrafen, wie jene zweckmäßig einzurichten, und diese solcher Einrichtung gemäs zu bestimmen und anzuwenden seyen?* (Stuttgart, 1786); Heinrich Balthasar Wagnitz, *Historische Nachrichten und Bemerkungen über die merkwürdigsten Zuchthäuser in Deutschland*, 2 vols. (Halle, 1791); Albrecht H. von Arnim, *Bruchstücke über Verbrechen und Strafen, oder Gedanken über die in den Preußischen Staaten bemerkte Vermehrung der Verbrechen gegen die Sicherheit des Eigentums* (Jena, 1803).

75. Nikolaus Heinrich Julius, *Vorlesungen über die Gefängniß-Kunde, oder über die Verbesserung der Gefängnisse und sittliche Besserung der Gefangenen, entlassene Sträflinge u.s.w., gehalten im Frühlinge 1827 zu Berlin. Erweitert herausgegeben, nebst einer Einleitung über Zahlen, Arten und Ursachen der Verbrechen in verschiedenen europäischen Staaten* (Berlin, 1828), 120–122.

76. See for example the article entitled "Classification," in *Criminallexikon. Nach dem neuesten Stand der Gesetzgebung in Deutschland*, ed. Ludwig von Jagemann, 1854 (Reprint: Leipzig, 1975), 159–161.

77. Karl Krohne, "Der Gefängnißbau in der Verwaltung des königlich preußischen Ministeriums des Innern," in Krone, ed., *Die Strafanstalten und Gefängnisse in Preußen, Bd. 1: Anstalten in der Verwaltung des Ministeriums des Innern* (Berlin, 1901), vii–xlviii, here xxii.

78. Edict of 11 April 1842. See *Reglement für die Strafanstalt zu Rawicz, vom 4. November 1835, durch spätere Bestimmungen auch auf die übrigen Strafanstalten ausgedehnt, nebst den dazu nachträglich ergangenen ergänzenden Bestimmungen* (Berlin, 1868), 97–99. GLA Karlsruhe 234/10394, Staatsrat Lamey, 19. Mai 1838. Gudrun Kling, "Die rechtliche Konstruktion des 'weiblichen Beamten.' Frauen im öffentlichen Dienst des Großherzogthums Baden im 19. und frühen 20. Jahrhundert," in Ute Gerhard, ed., *Frauen in der Geschichte des Rechts: Von der frühen Neuzeit bis zur Gegenwart* (Munich, 1997), 600–616.

79. Krohne, "Gefängnißbau," xxii.

80. Karl Krohne reported extensively regarding the female supervisors at the gathering of prison officials in 1901: "Bericht über die XII. Versammlung des Vereins der deutschen Strafanstaltsbeamten in Nürnberg am 29. Mai bis 1. Juni 1901. Nach stenographischen Aufzeichnungen," *Blätter für Gefängniskunde* 35 (1901), 1–210, here 157–158.

81. Krohne, "Bericht," 157.

82. Krohne, "Gefängnißbau," xxxiv–v. They differ only in size. A women's prison should not admit more than 300 inmates, while a men's prison should not exceed 550 inmates.

83. Hauptstaatsarchiv Düsseldorf, Regierung Düsseldorf, Nr. 11201, Hausordnung für Strafanstalten, vol. 5, 1898–1901, Ministerium des Innern, Berlin den 30. Januar 1899.

84. See for example Carl August Diez, "Ueber den Einfluss der Gefangenschaft auf die Gesundheit," *Annalen der Staatsarzneikunde* 8 (1843), 419–498, esp. 448–450.

85. Generallandesarchiv Karlsruhe, 234/10394, Errichtung einer Zentralstrafanstalt—modo Erbauung eines Weiberzuchthauses—in specie—dessen Einrichtung hinsichtlich der Behandlung der Sträflinge, Staatsrat Lamey, 19 May 1838.

86. For a detailed analysis of a women's prison in Imperial Germany, the Weiberstrafanstalt Bruchsal, see Leukel, *Strafanstalt und Geschlecht*, 187–266.

87. See Lenhard, "Psychologische Betrachtungen," 449.

Part II

PENAL REFORM IN THE WEIMAR REPUBLIC

Chapter 4

BETWEEN REFORM AND REPRESSION
Imprisonment in Weimar Germany

Nikolaus Wachsmann

The prison, at least as we know it today, is a rather recent invention. It was only in the course of the late eighteenth and nineteenth century that institutions designated solely for locking up criminal offenders, dominated by rigid discipline and hidden from the gaze of the public, became key means of punishment in the Western world. This birth (or, more accurately, rebirth) of the prison has caught the eye of historians and social scientists and has been the subject of several celebrated studies dealing with France, Britain, and the United States, among other states.[1] The focus on the late eighteenth and nineteenth century is also reflected in scholarship on the German prison.[2] By contrast, the German prison in the twentieth century had long been ignored. The landscape has only begun to change very recently. But research has generally been limited to the Nazi years and the period immediately after World War II.[3] The prison in the Weimar Republic (1918–1933), by contrast, has remained uncharted territory, and many thousands of files on the prison service are still waiting to be discovered in archives all over Germany. This article presents the first overview of the history of the Weimar prison.[4] Such an examination has obvious relevance for historians interested in crime and punishment and contributes to the still meager literature on the operation of the criminal justice system in the turbulent and short life of the Weimar Republic. But it also has a wider bearing on debates about German history.

Historians have been aware for some time that the study of the treatment of those excluded from society because of their non-normative behavior can give important insights into the often unclearly stated values of society itself. One of

Notes from this chapter begin on page 132.

the most important works on marginal groups in 1920s Germany has been the study of deviant youths by the late Detlev Peukert. Here, and in his general work on Weimar and Nazi Germany, Peukert presented highly original arguments, which continue to stimulate historians of German social and penal policy.[5] Peukert claimed that the study of Weimar was vital because Weimar saw "the emergence of the world we inhabit today." "In less than a decade and a half," Peukert noted, "virtually every social and intellectual initiative we think of as modern was formulated or put into practice. And yet . . . no sooner had modern ideas been put into effect than they came under attack, were revoked or began to collapse." Looking at modern social policy, Peukert argued, the human sciences and the emerging social professions held out the promise that state intervention based on scientific advances in criminology and pedagogy would help to eradicate "social illnesses" such as deviance, just like modern medicine had made immense progress in the cure and prevention of physical illnesses. This modern social policy, Peukert claimed, had a Janus-face: "care for the reformables and exclusion of the incorrigibles." However, Peukert suggested that during the 1920s the question of selection and exclusion had still been marginal. Instead, this period was characterized by "pedagogical dreams of omnipotence." The reigning paradigm was that of the "universality of provision and correction." It was only during the disastrous crisis in the last years of Weimar, according to Peukert, that this utopian vision was reconceptualized in negative terms, "identifying, segregating, and disposing of those individuals who were 'abnormal' and 'sick.'" This paradigm of selection and eradication, Peukert concluded, then shaped the approach toward social outsiders in Nazi Germany, where it gained "unprecedented operational licence."[6] This paper will evaluate to what extent the development of the German prison system fits into this general picture of social policy in the Weimar Republic drawn by Detlev Peukert.

Prisons and Prison Reform in the Early Weimar Republic

The German prison system emerged from World War I in a dire state. Inmate mortality in the 1,700 or so penal institutions had increased in the last years of the war, and many prisoners were ravaged by disease. In some institutions, more than one in ten inmates had died in the last twelve months of the war, often due to malnutrition.[7] But there was no time to take stock after the German defeat as the prison system was immediately plunged into a succession of unprecedented crises. Following the collapse of the imperial order in November 1918, life in Germany was dominated for five years by dramatic political, economic, and social upheaval. This had a direct impact on penal institutions, not least due to the blatant bias of the largely anti-Republican German judiciary. Judges often cracked down with extreme vigor on radical left-wing activists. At the same time, right-wing counterrevolutionaries were let off very lightly.[8] Penal institutions filled up with left-wing radicals, and the Weimar prison soon became a political battleground. Inside, highly politicized inmates were pitched against reactionary governors and warders. And in the public arena, the prison became a symbol for what communists and socialists called class justice. Attacks on penal institutions by activists from the outside, and riots by the inmates on the inside, became familiar events. Officials in fifteen larger penal institutions recorded no fewer than fifty-one riots and serious attacks on guards between 1919 and 1924. Thousands of inmates escaped or were freed. Most local prison officials reacted to the unrest in the only way they knew: even minor disturbances were answered with extreme brutality. Many inmates were severely injured or killed during such incidents. Thousands more were sentenced to further terms of imprisonment for rioting.[9]

The tensions inside penal institutions were intensified by the very poor living conditions. The food supply was particularly bad, sparking off further unrest. For instance, on 28 March 1920, most of the inmates of the Brandenburg penitentiary fled. Several were shot dead, and the recaptured prisoners were tried in June 1920. Asked about his motives, one prisoner replied: "The food was appalling. For weeks, we got no potatoes and the fish that was dished up all the time stank seven miles up wind."[10] Nutritional standards only started to improve in the early 1920s. By that time, penal institutions were already engulfed in another crisis: massive overcrowding. During the war, prisoner numbers had remained rather low. This soon changed, as the catastrophic hyperinflation triggered a wave of crime. The desperate circumstances that led many Germans to break the law are all too manifest in the state in which they arrived in the penal institutions: the Social Democrat newspaper *Vorwärts* reported that of one hundred men committed to the Plötzensee prison in Berlin in 1921, fifty arrived without shirts, sixty without shoes, and eighty without socks.[11] By 1923, crime figures for theft were three times higher than before the war.[12] The dramatic rise in recorded crime resulted in a rapid increase of state prisoners. From 1920, penal institutions all over Germany were reporting lack of space, and by 1923, the daily number of state prisoners in all probability exceeded one hundred thousand. Overcrowding, with five or more inmates forced into a single cell, further aggravated the poor hygienic conditions inside penal institutions, which often lacked running water, proper heating, or sewer systems. One penitentiary inmate complained in 1921 that he had not had a bath for over a year. "The underpants are only changed every eight weeks," he added.[13]

But unrest and chaos were not the only features of the postwar prison. This period also saw far-reaching reform impulses. During the German empire, prison regulations had often remained unchanged for years. This contrasts sharply with the flurry of activity in the individual German states (the prison service was run by the federated states until 1935) in the early Weimar years. Some measures, such as the abolition of corporal punishment for male penitentiary inmates in

Prussia in late 1918, concluded long-term trends that had begun in the second half of the nineteenth century.[14] But such piecemeal measures no longer seemed enough. Most leading legal officials agreed that a more decisive shakeup of the prison system was necessary. While they disagreed about the extent to which they wanted to break with the prewar prison (largely based on uniform retribution and military discipline), the officials did accept that a new approach was called for. Their main impetus was the dramatic crime wave in postwar Germany, which clearly demonstrated that the old-style prison failed to deter criminal behavior. The call for prison reform was part of a much wider search for innovative social policies during the postwar crisis. New solutions were needed, many observers argued, to deal with the plethora of real and imagined problems which appeared to threaten Germany, including the increase in sexual promiscuity, venereal disease, youth delinquency, "trashy literature," divorce rates, and illegitimate births.[15]

The postwar proposals to reform penal policy were influenced by the ideas of the so-called modern school of criminal law, which had emerged during the German empire under the leadership of the liberal law professor Franz von Liszt. Famously, Liszt had rejected the established system of criminal law based on general deterrence and uniform punishment. Instead, he argued that criminal justice should aim at the protection of society and the future prevention of crime. Following Liszt, different types of offenders required different treatment, depending on their future danger. He summarized his demand for special prevention as the "incapacitation of incorrigibles, reformation of reformables." According to Liszt, "reformable" offenders should be rehabilitated. By contrast, "incorrigible habitual criminals" had to be isolated indefinitely, in most cases until their death. It was madness, Liszt exclaimed, ever again to let such an offender "loose on the public like a wild beast." This dual approach of reform and repression already left its mark on German penal policy during the empire and later had a significant impact on the various Weimar drafts for a new criminal code.[16] It also influenced prison regulations in the Weimar years.

The principle of rehabilitation, rather marginal in the prewar prison, was emphasized for young offenders in the Reich Juvenile Justice Act (16 February 1923). Soon, it was extended to adult prisoners, enshrined in the national prison guidelines agreed upon by the individual German states (7 June 1923). The prison regime based on silence and excessive military discipline, still popular before the war, was rejected in these new guidelines, and particularly cruel disciplinary punishment such as detention in a dark cell was also abolished. The aim of imprisonment was that "the prisoner, as far as necessary, is accustomed to order and work and morally strengthened in such a way that he does not reoffend." The introduction of the so-called progressive stages system was encouraged to aid the inmate's "moral advancement." The stages system rewarded individual inmates for their "progress" by transferring them to a higher stage, where they enjoyed more privileges. Some states had already introduced the stages system in the early 1920s. (It had been experimented with before in Germany, most notably in the Wittlich prison for juvenile delinquents just before the war, as part of a wider reform catalogue which had a lasting influence on the debate in the 1920s). By 1926, it had been introduced in all the German states; only inmates with longer sentences, generally one year or more, were eligible for the stages system.[17]

But many officials did not regard the stages system only as a tool of rehabilitation. Rather, they believed that it helped to institutionalize the distinction between reformable and incorrigible offenders, the fundamental principle of Liszt's modern school of criminal law. At the beginning of their sentence, all prisoners would be held on the strict conditions of the lowest stage (stage one). Once the reformable inmates had demonstrated their "inner change," they advanced to the higher stages (two and three). The incorrigibles, by contrast, remained on the lowest stage. The Bavarian directive that had introduced the progressive system for adult prisoners in 1921 urged that against "incorrigible prisoners . . . the greatest sternness is called for; during their treatment the aim of retribution and deterrence in punishment cannot be stressed enough."[18] In the long run, most prison officials and criminologists agreed, it was not enough to merely treat these incorrigibles more harshly than others during their sentence. After all, this would not stop them from reoffending once they were released. What was needed, following Franz von Liszt, was the indefinite detention of dangerous incorrigibles in security confinement, a measure that had already commanded significant support before the war and was included in all the Weimar drafts for a criminal code, starting in 1919.

It should be noted at this point that the division of offenders into reformable and incorrigible was not peculiar to Germany. It was very much an international phenomenon of the late nineteenth and early twentieth century. A number of officials in Europe and the United States experimented with policies that tried to turn the prison into a rehabilitative institution. At the same time, there was widespread agreement that protective measures were necessary against habitual criminals, and states such as Australia and New Zealand actually introduced indefinite confinement. Similarly, harsh treatment inside penal institutions was not unique to Germany. Indeed, disciplinary punishment was often harsher elsewhere, as several Western states continued to practice corporal punishment long after it had been abolished in Germany.[19]

Until now, the focus in this article has been on the general attempts to reform the prison in the early years of the Weimar Republic. But how did this affect the lives of individual inmates inside prisons and penitentiaries? This question will be addressed in the following sections, which examine the reality of policies directed at reformables and incorrigibles in German penal institutions between 1923 and 1930.

Policies and Reforms Directed at
Reformable Prisoners, 1923–1930

Conditions in German penal institutions in the second half of the 1920s were often still poor. But they were better than before, largely as a result of the improving economic climate. Following the end of hyperinflation, criminal convictions declined sharply and judges also passed somewhat more lenient sentences. As a result, prisoner numbers fell drastically. By 1929, the average number of prisoners in the whole of Germany had fallen to about fifty thousand—about half as many as six years earlier. Much less space was now needed for locking up offenders, and a number of dilapidated penal institutions were shut down. Also, more resources could be distributed among the remaining prisoners. The daily amount of money spent by the Prussian authorities on food for each penitentiary inmate increased by half between 1924 and 1929. There were also improvements in the health care of prisoners, and some penal institutions set up specially equipped cells for women giving birth behind bars. It was partly thanks to these developments that the death rate in penal institutions declined.[20]

Life in many penal institutions in the second half of the 1920s was also influenced, to some extent, by the concept of the prison as an educational institution. The most coherent proposals for rehabilitation were put forward by the Study Group for Prison Reform, formed in 1923 by university teachers, prison officials, and civil servants. Their political background was rather diverse, including supporters of the liberal and Catholic parties, as well as Social Democrats and socialists. What united many of them was their belief in the ideals of the German youth movement and in the new approaches to education pioneered in reform pedagogy before World War I—ideas that also influenced schools, social work, reformatories, asylums, and adult education in the 1920s. Thus, the Study Group demanded that character-building exercises and creative stimulation by inspirational teachers were to take the place of purely mechanical and military forms of discipline. Only by awarding prison inmates more freedom and personal responsibility, it was argued, could they become law-abiding citizens after their release. One leading figure of the Study Group was Lothar Frede, who had been appointed by the progressive left-wing government in Thuringia in 1922 as head of the prison service, a position he retained even after power shifted to the right two years later. Thuringia soon became one of the centers of prison reform in Germany. A case study of the Untermassfeld penitentiary, the second-largest Thuringian penal institution for men that was often singled out in the 1920s as a so-called model institution, will highlight the aims and achievements of the Study Group.

The Untermassfeld penitentiary, still in use today, lies on the edge of a small village in the Werra valley. Originally a medieval castle, Untermassfeld was rebuilt after 1813 as a penal institution, resulting in a convoluted construction quite removed from the nineteenth-century ideal of rational prison architecture, the

panopticon. Many of the policies championed by the Study Group were introduced here. Following the demand by the Study Group that trained pedagogues
be recruited, the Untermassfeld prison chaplain was removed and replaced by
three social workers (one for each of the three stages of the new progressive system). They were subordinated to the newly appointed, reform-minded governor.
On arrival, inmates were put on stage one, which also contained those demoted
from higher stages for disciplinary offenses, and those who, in the officials' eyes,
had not yet responded to the educational measures. Over one-third of inmates
were held at this stage. They spent their spare time in solitude in single cells
and did not qualify for any privileges. As Lothar Frede put it, they had to feel
"the full sternness of the penalty." Once promoted to stage two, the prisoners
acquired greater freedom and responsibility. Stage two was open to most prisoners, as the criteria for promotion were not applied very strictly. About half of the
inmate population were held at stage two, including prisoners who had lengthy
disciplinary records because of disobedience and physical violence. At stage
two, school lessons were conducted by the social worker in small groups, and
the inmates spent some of their spare time unsupervised, playing board games,
singing in the choir or orchestra, listening to the radio, or performing plays.
Sports were also popular, and the inmates sometimes played local teams from
the outside. The prisoners were also actively involved in writing and producing
the prison newspaper, a unique innovation in Germany. At stage three, seen as a
preparation for life in liberty, inmates were given an even larger degree of autonomy. Their leisure time was unsupervised, their cells were unlocked and had no
iron bars. Among the most controversial innovations were the walks of prisoners
in the woods outside the prison walls, accompanied only by the unarmed governor (and sometimes a social worker).

Life in Untermassfeld changed in many other ways too. The Study Group
argued that prisoners were imprisoned citizens and should be awarded legal status, a demand that had been championed before World War I by the Frankfurt law professor Berthold Freudenthal, a leading figure in the Study Group.
Before the war, inmates were almost entirely subjected to the whims of the prison
administration. To redress this problem, disciplinary tribunals were set up in
Untermassfeld, consisting of prison officials and inmate representatives (elected
by prisoners at stage two and three). Previously, the governor had not even been
required to hear the inmate's side of the story in disciplinary cases. Now, the court
listened to witness statements by the accused, other prisoners, and the warders.
True, the final decision still rested with the governor. But he often appears to
have followed the views of the other members of the court. The leading prison
officials in Thuringia also opposed the military atmosphere, which still characterized most German penal institutions. Lothar Frede ordered that inmates should
no longer jump up, click their heels, and place their hands on the trouser seam
when he entered a cell or a workshop. Finally, the Study Group demanded that

compulsory prison labor, around which the inmates' day was structured, had to be transformed. Most inmates were employed in their cells with repetitive and dirty labor or in workshops where they used outdated equipment. The Study Group demanded that this approach to prison labor should be replaced with measures aimed at helping the largely untrained prisoners to develop skills useful on the labor market after their release. To realize this aim, a limited company was set up in Untermassfeld, with the governor acting as company director. Modern machines were introduced into agricultural production and some workshops, supervised by trained craftsmen. Some inmates could now learn a trade.[21]

The reform project in Untermassfeld was never uncontested. It came under immediate attack from some local politicians and journalists, who charged that the inmates were being pampered. More worryingly, a number of Untermassfeld guards systematically tried to derail the project. Repeatedly, guards attempted to engineer a crisis by encouraging prisoners to escape or start a riot. This, they hoped, would prove that the reforms undermined the safety in the institution. The motives for the guards' opposition were complex. To start with, the guards had often worked in Untermassfeld for decades. Largely, they were former soldiers, used to enforcing and obeying strict military discipline. Almost overnight, the inmates were now to be treated as individuals with specific educational needs, a task for which many warders had neither sympathy nor training. In addition, the warders felt threatened by the change of the prisoners' status and resented being held accountable in prison tribunals. Also, the reforms increased their workload. Under the old system, prisoners could be treated by the rulebook. But individualization was labor intensive, and the warders, who were poorly paid and overworked, were now expected to take on further duties. Finally, the experienced warders deeply resented the influence of the much younger social workers, fresh out of university. The Thuringian branch of the Association of Prison Warders insisted in 1925 that the battle-scarred warders had more to offer than the young social workers: "Knowledge gained from experience alone is decisive for the practice of the prison service." In the Thuringian prison Ichtershausen, the harassment campaign against the young reformers by veteran prison officials contributed in 1925 to the dramatic suicide of the twenty-four-year-old social worker, Dr. Otto Zirker.[22] The prison administration in Thuringia was not passive in the face of this opposition. The most disruptive Untermassfeld warder was transferred to a small local jail, training courses for the other warders were set up and it was decided that new applicants were to be judged in part according to their ability to treat inmates. By the late 1920s, a number of Untermassfeld warders had been won over and public criticism also became more muted.

For many years, the history of the prison was written as a success story, progressing from primitive cruelty to enlightened benevolence. Only in the 1970s did authors like Michel Foucault, David Rothman, and Michael Ignatieff challenge this narrative.[23] This critique has to be taken into account when evaluating the reforms in Untermassfeld in the 1920s. Untermassfeld should certainly not be depicted as an unmitigated triumph of humane policies. Disciplinary punishment often remained strict, and the general living conditions were still poor. Half of the cells lacked heating. In winter, prisoners went to bed fully clothed and often could not wash in the morning, as the water in their bowls had turned to ice. The inmates also still used worn-out buckets as toilets. The characteristic smell of Untermassfeld continued to be that of urine and excrement.[24] Nevertheless, the impact of the reforms was impressive and transformed the lives of many inmates, who enjoyed previously unheard-of privileges and rights.

The Untermassfeld experience was not typical for imprisonment in the rest of Germany. Not many leading prison officials proved to be as adventurous as Lothar Frede in Thuringia. And a large number of local prison officials—governors, chaplains, teachers, and warders—remained sceptical about the aims of the Study Group. Occasionally, they used progressive language to present their policies as modern, but they often clung to the traditional prison regime based on strict punishment, military discipline, and moralizing lectures. Finally, at least in the case of Prussia, size also mattered. In 1927, there were over one thousand penal institutions in Prussia, compared with only sixty-nine in Thuringia. The size of the Prussian prison service posed serious administrative problems, one of the reasons why Prussia was slow to implement new policies. When the Prussian prison administration did try to introduce an extensive reform package in 1929, it quickly ran into trouble. The measures included the election of prisoner representatives and prisoner leave on the higher stages. Inmates on stage three could even be allowed to take up ordinary jobs in the free economy for normal pay, introducing the so-called half-open principle already in place in some reformatories. However, the impact of these regulations was very limited. The regulations were only introduced fully in the Berlin district, and even here they were never properly put into practice. One problem was timing, as the new regulations were introduced only months before the start of the collapse of the Weimar Republic in the early 1930s. In addition, the regulations were undermined by open criticism from local prison officials, who dismissed them as impractical.[25]

As a result, changes in many German penal institutions in the second half of the 1920s were significantly less pronounced than in the Untermassfeld penitentiary. To be sure, the stages system offered more privileges. Some institutions also introduced more innovative measures such as sports, theater, music, and radio rooms. But the Study Group's call for more prisoner autonomy, prisoner representatives, and prison tribunals was not widely realized. The same was true for the educational thrust of the stages system. In practice, it became nothing but a disciplinary tool, as governors realized that promoting an inmate to a higher stage as a reward for conforming, and the threat of demotion for breaking the rules, functioned as an effective control mechanism. Finally, only limited attempts were made to recruit reform-minded officials. In 1927, the reform strongholds of

Thuringia, Saxony and Hamburg, which together only held some 12 percent of all German state prisoners, employed fifty-five of all the fifty-eight social workers in German penal institutions. By contrast, Prussia, which held well over half of all German prisoners, engaged only one social worker. Instead, the Prussian authorities continued to put their faith in the traditional guardians of the inmates' spiritual guidance: more than seven hundred chaplains were still working in Prussian penal institutions in 1927.[26] Open and sustained opposition to new policies by local prison officials remained limited to the states like Thuringia, which had introduced more extensive changes. Elsewhere, internal criticism was largely limited to individual aspects of prison policy. Most of this grumbling by local officials centered around their claims that inmates were treated too leniently. Among the most controversial issues were prisoner complaints. Before the war, senior civil servants had generally dismissed complaints passed on by the governors. But in the Weimar Republic, they were reviewed more conscientiously, resulting in an increase of prisoner complaints, as more and more inmates believed that it was worth raising their voices.[27]

This development was closely linked to the growing influence of the public sphere. Weimar was obsessed with crime and criminals, and this fixation was reflected in newspaper articles, novels, plays, and films about imprisonment, which mostly painted a bleak picture of life inside penal institutions. Publishers rushed more prisoner memoirs into print than ever before, often penned by former left-wing inmates who were also active in pressure groups such as the German League for Human Rights.[28] There can be no doubt that the public spotlight on the prison had some impact on the civil servants in the prison administration, who ultimately decided about inmate complaints. This was deeply resented by many local prison officials. According to the radical left-wing prisoner Max Hoelz, the governor in the Gross-Strehlitz penitentiary "went completely berserk" as soon as anyone as much as mentioned the League for Human Rights.[29] However, the public sphere did not function exclusively as a check on the disciplining power of officials. To start with, a number of articles in right-wing newspapers pictured penal institutions as five-star hotels, an image which was to feature heavily in the attacks on German prisons in the early 1930s. In addition, a number of articles raised the specter of the incorrigible prisoner. This issue was not confined to the right-wing press, but occupied a central place in the Weimar discourse about crime and punishment.

Policies and Reforms Directed at
Incorrigible Prisoners, 1923–1930

Most Weimar prison officials and criminologists were convinced that some individuals were destined to reoffend, and that biological factors played an important role in creating these incorrigibles. To be sure, not everybody agreed. Some members of the Study Group argued that it was absurd to speak of incorrigibles as long as no real attempts were made to rehabilitate inmates. When explaining persistent criminal behavior, they pointed instead to poor social and economic circumstances on the outside and the widespread prejudice that ex-convicts faced from the population.[30] But most commentators dismissed these arguments as the delusions of naive theoreticians and attacked them for ignoring the demand for the "incapacitation of incorrigibles," one of the core principles of Franz von Liszt and the modern school of criminal law. "Let's return to Liszt!" one leading criminologist exclaimed in 1927.[31] Although there was never an agreed definition of the incorrigible, German criminologists constructed two types of offenders who were often described as incorrigible. The first were the habitual (or asocial) criminals, characterized as drifting into small-time criminality such as theft and begging because they were supposedly weak and driven by primitive urges. Their frequent recidivism was often taken as a sign of their incorrigibility. The second type associated with the incorrigible was the professional (or antisocial) criminal, a construction that was popularized in numerous books and films, such as Fritz Lang's 1931 masterpiece *M*. "Professional criminals," the criminologist Robert Heindl claimed in his lurid book on the subject, did not drift into crime, but actively pursued it as their chosen profession. Between photos of gruesome crime scenes and public executions, which no doubt contributed to the book's popularity, Heindl presented his particularly unrefined typology of dangerous, trained, and highly specialized criminals.[32]

Most commentators believed that many incorrigibles had to be interned in security confinement after their prison or penitentiary sentence to protect society. They would have to be held either until they died or until they posed no more risk to society, for example because their health had seriously deteriorated. It was not clear how many offenders would be targeted by security confinement. The various drafts for a criminal code described it vaguely as a measure against "dangerous habitual criminals," and much would depend on what was considered dangerous. Robert Heindl argued that only about one thousand or so professional criminals should be locked up.[33] But most observers showed less restraint, arguing (in line with Franz von Liszt) that security confinement should target not only the supposed criminal elite, but also a number of habitual criminals, including small-time thieves. German prison officials largely supported this more repressive approach.

Security confinement was never realized in the Weimar Republic, because the parties in the *Reichstag*, increasingly paralyzed in the early 1930s, failed to push through the new criminal code. Nevertheless, the heated debates about the incorrigible did influence the lives of criminal offenders in Weimar Germany. Many prison officials agreed that, as long as security confinement had not become law, incorrigible inmates should at least be excluded from most benefits. As we have seen, the stages system was ideally suited to fulfill this demand. Incorrigibles could be left on the harsh conditions of stage one, and reformables could be promoted. This meant that prison officials had to distinguish between these two criminological types. Apparently, most officials relied on their gut feeling. But in July 1923, the hard-line Bavarian prison administration announced that a "scientifically reliable basis" was required for the classifications. Prison doctors were asked to conduct detailed examinations of inmates, which soon became known as criminal-biological investigations—a mix of various scientific theories popular at the time, including criminal anthropology, psychiatry, criminal psychology, genetics, and racial hygiene (rather similar examinations were carried out in Saxony too). At the center of the examinations stood the question whether the inmate was reformable or not. Those prisoners regarded as incorrigible often faced the harsh conditions of stage one during their entire sentence. It is hardly surprising, then, that some of them tried to undermine the examinations by lying about their family background, keeping silent when asked whether they came from broken homes or whether their parents were alcoholics.[34]

By the late 1920s, criminal-biological investigations had spread to other German states. In Prussia, they were introduced in the context of the new prison regulations of 1929, which are a good example of the connection between reform and repression in Weimar penal policy. Although the regulations introduced policies intended to rehabilitate prisoners, such as prisoner leave, they also stipulated that new institutions for incorrigibles be set up. A wing of the Plötzensee prison was set aside "for the most antisocial elements, with a particularly bleak social prognosis," as they were described by the progressive head of the Berlin prison administration, a member of the Study Group.[35] The formal criteria for transfer to Plötzensee was that the prisoner was older than twenty-three, had been sentenced to at least three months, and had three or more previous convictions of at least one year. Additionally, experts had to confirm the inmate's lack of reformability. For this purpose, prisoners were taken to the Moabit prison, where they were examined by warders, chaplains, and teachers. The final decision was made by the prison doctor, who carried out a criminal-biological investigation.

The examinations of prisoners in Moabit and in the Bavarian penal institutions give an important insight into the construction of the incorrigible in the Weimar Republic. The authority of the examinations derived from the claim that they were based on neutral, scientific observation. But under the veneer of scientific objectivity, the examinations were largely determined by unproven allegations, moralizing assumptions, and the reduction of deviant behavior to biological determinants. Prison officials were particularly inclined to write off those inmates who had most manifestly failed to conform to the moral, political, and social values of bourgeois society. Most of the inmates judged incorrigible had grown up in unstable families in urban centers, which had long been regarded by prison officials as cesspools of depravity and degeneration. The officials highlighted the offenders' unsettled lifestyle and their purportedly abnormal sexual appetite. One prisoner, a Moabit official complained in 1930, talked with "almost cynical openness of his marriage to a prostitute who . . . continued to pursue her trade even after the wedding." The classifications were also strongly influenced by the offense committed. Property offenders were much more likely than any others to be judged incorrigible. They were seen as dangerous threats to the established social order, part of the asocial and degenerate subproletariat. Their offenses were often petty, consisting of minor thefts rather than white-collar crimes. As these offenders received comparatively short sentences of imprisonment, they had accumulated many convictions. On average, each inmate examined in Moabit had fourteen previous convictions. With recidivism often seen as one of the signs of the incorrigible, petty property offenders were thus particularly vulnerable to be singled out. By contrast, prison officials showed greater consideration for sex offenders or violent criminals.[36]

The classification as an incorrigible could not only influence the treatment of prisoners during their sentence. The label also stuck after their release. First of all, help for ex-convicts was restricted to those regarded as reformable. For example, the Lichtenau institution in Bavaria (founded in 1927) provided a temporary home for ex-convicts. But it was open only to deserving offenders. The authorities reassured potential private donors that the assumption that resources were "squandered on the unworthy, habitual, and professional criminals, incorrigibles and dangers to security, is completely false." These ex-convicts did not deserve support but security confinement.[37] Secondly, many incorrigible ex-convicts in Germany were put under strict police supervision. Continual checks by police officials often resulted in the dismissal of former inmates from their jobs or the eviction from their lodgings, leading some ex-convicts to commit further offenses that were then taken by police officials and judges as further proof of their incorrigibility.[38] Thirdly, some incorrigible inmates were detained even after the end of their sentence of imprisonment. In 1926, the Bavarian diet passed the "Law for the fight against Gypsies, travellers, and the work-shy." Article 10 introduced "correctional postdetention" for up to two years in a workhouse for "incorrigible habitual criminals." The Bavarian prison administration welcomed this measure and instructed governors to provide the police with statements about incorrigible offenders who were coming to the end of their sentence.[39] Most Bavarian prison officials were happy to comply, as can be illustrated by the case of Johann W., an unskilled laborer with numerous convictions for property offenses. In 1929, when W. reached the end of his most recent sentence in the Straubing penitentiary, the Munich police asked the Straubing officials for an assessment of W. In response, the Straubing officials compiled a detailed report, concluding that W. was an "incorrigible habitual criminal . . . who leads a parasitic existence."

Following this devastating assessment, Johann W. was interned by the police for sixteen months in the workhouse in Rebdorf, even though he was not guilty of any new offenses.[40]

Prisons and Prison Reform in the Final Years of the Republic

Germany was hit harder than any other Western state by the dramatic global economic crisis following the New York stock exchange crash of 29 October 1929. The economic collapse exposed the frailty of a political system that had lacked legitimacy even during the preceding brief period of relative stability. It also led to the dismantling of the Weimar welfare state: unemployment benefits, pensions, welfare payments, and expenditure on deviant groups were all reduced. The prison service was also immediately affected. Living conditions for inmates deteriorated once more, as the budget for food, clothing, electricity, and health care was cut. Furthermore, just as during the inflation of the early 1920s, the economic collapse contributed to an increase in property crime, with recorded figures for "serious theft" almost doubling between 1928 and 1932. Combined with the fact that German courts at the height of the depression passed almost as many prison sentences as fines, reversing the long-term trend toward more fines of the previous decades, inmate numbers began to rise again. The average number of inmates in Germany increased to about sixty-three thousand in 1932.[41] Many of these prisoners were recidivist property offenders, as former convicts found it harder than most to find subsistence. As Maria B., a prisoner in the Aichach penal institution with numerous convictions for pickpocketing, told the prison officials in August 1930: "I don't yet know how I shall avoid my offenses in future, as I don't yet know what I shall live on." She was released in July 1931 and recommitted to Aichach only four months later, following another sentence for theft.[42]

The economic crisis brought about a strong attack on the Weimar prison. But this backlash was not just a reaction to the economic hardship. Just as the crisis served as a pretext for political and economic elites to abolish innovations that conflicted with their interests, prison officials used the cover of economic arguments to attack some of the new policies they had opposed in the past. What united the attacks on the prison service was the claim that prisoners were pampered and that precious resources were being squandered on incorrigibles, who should instead be locked away indefinitely under harsh conditions. Already in 1930, the head of the Bavarian prison administration announced that he would restructure the stages system to prevent the waste of time, effort, and energy on "unnecessary ballast."[43] Soon, the vast majority of Bavarian inmates were held at stage one, where penitentiary inmates were banned from buying extra rations and from talking to one another during work and could only write one letter every two months. The shift in Bavaria was profoundly influenced by the prison doctor Theodor Viernstein, a key figure in the criminal-biological movement and a fanatical racial-hygienist. Viernstein claimed in 1930 in several high-profile lectures that half of all inmates were incorrigible, mostly on hereditary grounds. This signified a dramatic turnaround, for Viernstein had previously declared that at least two-thirds of all inmates were reformable. What had led him to revise his figures was not any more refined methodology, but the crisis which had begun to engulf Germany: "The state in its present financial and political situation can and must deal, in terms of education and welfare, unreservedly only with those elements . . . who really offer hope for re-socialization . . . There is absolutely no room today for sentimentality! Strictest selection is a duty to state and community."[44] Viernstein was not the only local prison official who demanded a change of direction. Many others claimed that "exaggerated and dangerous humanity" (such as walks outside the prison walls and theater productions) had to be rooted out to be replaced by a renewed emphasis on discipline, obedience, and religion. The officials also hoped that restrictions of the right to complain would restore their total power over inmates.[45] The attack on the prison system went far beyond the prison officials and involved right-wing journalists and politicians, as well as judges and state prosecutors, who joined in the call for cuts in prisoner provisions and a "limitation of exaggerated measures of education and reform."[46]

The Study Group was too weak to put up any meaningful resistance. To start with, the attacks coincided with growing doubts by the reformers regarding their own methods. Social workers in Thuringia acknowledged that they were still "very much at sea" regarding the best way to treat prisoners. They also faced occasional resistance from the prisoners themselves against some measures that had been introduced. The officials became painfully aware that some prisoners did not agree with the aims and methods used to reform them. In addition, the reformers badly missed their two most influential supporters, Moritz Liepmann (a liberal professor for criminal law in Hamburg) and Berthold Freudenthal, who had died in 1928 and 1929, respectively. Finally, the political and economic upheaval undermined many of the principles the reformers stood for. Prison labor, seen by the reformers as central for rehabilitation, was in deep crisis as unemployment quickly spread to penal institutions during the depression. In some states, well over half the inmates were without work by 1932. The aim to rehabilitate convicts by training them in productive work methods became completely unrealistic.[47] The members of the Study Group knew that the tide had turned against them and were weighed down by pessimism and despair.

The backlash was also influenced by the changing political climate in Germany. The sharp turn to the far right, with the Nazis (NSDAP) becoming the largest party in the July 1932 national elections, was accompanied by demands for a more authoritarian approach to punishment.[48] The NSDAP had no coherent program for prison policy, but remarks by the party leadership left no doubt about its general outlook. "Marxism," Hitler charged in 1929, "had made its baleful influence felt in the German judicial system in that humanitarianism was misused and blindly applied to penal policy."[49] The party attacked all "weakness" and "sentimental humanitarianism" toward common criminals, employing terminology popular among the critics of the Weimar penal system.[50] The Nazis aimed to turn back some of the recent prison reforms, which had actually benefited some of their own supporters. For example, Rudolf Höss, later the first commandant of Auschwitz, had profited from new regulations favouring "delinquents motivated by conviction." According to his own testimony, Höss, committed to the Brandenburg penitentiary in 1924 for his part in a gruesome sectarian killing, was the first inmate in the penitentiary to reach the coveted third stage. The light in his cell was kept on until 10:00 P.M., he was allowed to write a letter every two weeks and got an easy job in the administration of the institution.[51]

The Nazi call for a stricter prison service was more than rhetoric. This became clear even before 1933. Following their victory in the Thuringian state elections of 31 July 1932, the Nazis took over the prison administration in the state that for a decade had been dominated by the Study Group. The Nazis quickly dismantled the Thuringian prison service. As one Nazi deputy argued, the prison reformers had to "disappear."[52] It only took the Nazis six months to get rid of the three senior officials in Thuringia associated with the Study Group. By mid-January 1933, the governors in Untermassfeld and Eisenach (Albert Krebs and Curt Bondy) had been removed and the architect of the Thuringian prison service, Lothar Frede, had been transferred to a different position in the judiciary. Events in Thuringia were soon replicated in other German states, after the Nazis had taken control of the whole of Germany in 1933. Those penal institutions that still pursued progressive policies were quickly transformed: prison tribunals and social workers were abolished, the right of inmates to complain was cut back, and the stages system was effectively abandoned. It took several decades before some of the measures championed by the Study Group and pioneered in states like Thuringia were reintroduced into German penal institutions.

Conclusion

The picture that has emerged of imprisonment in the Weimar period is a complex and dynamic one. Carceral institutions have sometimes been described as "total institutions," virtually divorced from the outside world.[53] While this perspective offers valuable insights into the institutional life of the inmates, it is not really concerned with the way in which these institutions were shaped by wider social forces. Looking at the Weimar prison, the life of inmates was profoundly influenced by social, economic, and political developments on the outside, such as the revolution of 1918, the hyperinflation, the expansion of the welfare state, the depression, and the rise of the Nazis. The experience of imprisonment depended on many different factors, such as when the prisoner was held. Location was also crucial, as the ability and willingness of senior officials to introduce new policies differed from state to state. The life of an inmate in Thuringia in 1929 was different in many ways from that of a Bavarian prisoner three years later. There was no typical Weimar prison.

Some aspects of the general development of imprisonment in the Weimar Republic fit well into the evolution of Weimar social policy as sketched by Detlev Peukert. The measures introduced in institutions such as Untermassfeld did contain many of the seeds of the contemporary prison. This is evident in the gradual relaxation of strict military discipline, the introduction of more prisoner autonomy, the emphasis on sport and recreation, the growing recognition of the legal status of the prisoner, the influx of social workers at the expense of chaplains, and the attempts to ease the inmates' transition into society by teaching them practical skills in workshops and in school. In the last years of Weimar, progressive penal institutions like Untermassfeld were hit by a backlash, which can be seen as part of what Peukert described as the "crisis of classical modernity," when policies that had only just been introduced were attacked and started to crumble. Similar developments occurred in other carceral institutions at the same time. In workhouses, policies pioneered in the 1920s, including the employment of social workers, were abolished, and new measures in mental asylums, such as outpatient care and "active therapy," were also scaled down.[54]

However, the history of the Weimar prison also runs counter to some of Peukert's claims. The Weimar prison was certainly never dominated by the optimistic belief that new educational measures could rehabilitate the inmates. Few prison officials had "pedagogical dreams of omnipotence." On the contrary, many officials continued to put their trust largely into the traditional and authoritarian prison regime based on military discipline and retribution. These officials cannot be described simply as conservatives, for they strongly supported the persecution of the incorrigible—the repressive side of the dual policy advanced by the modern school of criminal law. True, this dark side of modern penal policy was pursued with more vigor than ever before during the depression. But it had not been hidden in the shadows in the previous years, as Peukert has suggested in his work on social policy. It was out in the open and played a central role in the 1920s, both in the drafts for a new criminal code and inside penal institutions.

The support for the "incapacitation of the incorrigible" was one of the most important legacies for the Nazi prison. Security confinement for "dangerous habitual criminals" was introduced less than one year after the Nazi "seizure of power," drawing heavily on the criminological debates of the Weimar years. The Nazi prison was influenced above all by the prison policy that had emerged in the early 1930s, just like the backlash against the Weimar welfare state during the depression laid the ground for the Nazi racial state.[55] Thus, from 1933, measures against incorrigible prisoners went hand in hand with the stricter treatment of most other inmates, while the call for the rehabilitation of reformable prisoners was largely ignored. This approach was very much in line with the wishes of many local prison officials. It comes as no surprise that there was a strong continuity among local officials from Weimar to the Third Reich. There was simply no need for the Nazis to purge the prison service.

Notes

This chapter was originally published in the *Historical Journal* 45 (2002). It is republished here by permission, with minor revisions.

1. Among others, see David J. Rothman, *The Discovery of the Asylum: Social Order and Disorder in the New Republic* (Boston, 1971); Michel Foucault, *Surveiller et punir: naissance de la prison* (Paris, 1975); Michael Ignatieff, *A Just Measure of Pain: The Penitentiary in the Industrial Revolution, 1750–1850* (New York, 1978). The term *rebirth* of the prison is introduced in Norbert Finzsch, "Elias, Foucault, Oestreich: On a Historical Theory of Confinement," in Norbert Finzsch and Robert Jütte, eds., *Institutions of Confinement* (Cambridge, 1996), 3–16.

2. Thomas Berger, *Die konstante Repression: Zur Geschichte des Strafvollzugs in Preussen nach 1850* (Frankfurt/Main, 1974); Frank Mecklenburg, *Die Ordnung der Gefängnisse: Grundlinien der Gefängnisreform und Gefängniswissenschaft in der ersten Hälfte des 19. Jahrhunderts in Deutschland* (Berlin, 1983); Paul Sauer, *Im Namen des Königs: Strafgesetzgebung und Strafvollzug im Königreich Württemberg von 1806 bis 1871* (Stuttgart, 1984); Richard J. Evans, *Szenen aus der deutschen Unterwelt: Verbrechen und Strafe, 1800–1914* (Reinbek, 1997); Helmut Berding, Diethelm Klippel, and Günther Lottes, eds., *Kriminalität und abweichendes Verhalten: Deutschland im 18. und 19. Jahrhundert* (Göttingen, 1999); Thomas Nutz, *Strafanstalt als Besserungsmaschine. Reformdiskurs und Gefängiswissenschaft 1775–1848* (Munich, 2001).

3. For an overview of the literature, see Nikolaus Wachsmann, *Hitler's Prisons: Legal Terror in Nazi Germany* (New Haven and London, 2004), 1–13, and Wachsmann, "Reform and Repression: Prisons and Penal Policy in Germany, 1918–1939" (Ph.D. diss., University of London, 2001), 6–23. I have dealt with aspects of the Nazi prison service in two articles, "From Indefinite Confinement to Extermination: 'Habitual Criminals' in the Third Reich," in Robert Gellately and Nathan Stoltzfus, eds., *Social outsiders in Nazi Germany* (Princeton, 2001), 165–91; "'Annihilation through Labor': The Killing of State Prisoners in the Third Reich," *Journal of Modern History* 71 (1999), 624–659.

4. The great majority of penal institutions in Germany were small local jails for fifty or fewer inmates, which generally held offenders serving sentences of three months or less. The focus in this article is on larger penal institutions, where longer sentences were served.

5. Detlev J.K. Peukert, *Grenzen der Sozialdisziplinierung: Aufstieg und Krise der deutschen Jugendfürsorge von 1878 bis 1932* (Cologne, 1986); Peukert, *The Weimar Republic* (London, 1993); Peukert, *Inside Nazi Germany* (London, 1993). For Peukert's influence, see Patrick Wagner, *Volksgemeinschaft ohne Verbrecher: Konzeptionen und Praxis der Kriminalpolizei in der Zeit der Weimarer Republik und des Nationalsozialismus* (Hamburg, 1996); Young-Sun Hong, *Welfare, modernity and the Weimar state, 1919–1933* (Princeton, 1998); David F. Crew, *Germans on*

Welfare: From Weimar to Hitler (New York, 1998); Edward R. Dickinson, *The Politics of German Child Welfare from the Empire to the Federal Republic* (Cambridge, Mass., 1996).

6. Quotes in Peukert, *Weimar*, 276, 282; Peukert, *Sozialdisziplinierung*, 259, 307; Peukert, "The Genesis of the 'Final Solution' from the Spirit of Science," in David F. Crew, ed., *Nazism and German Society* (London, 1994), 289.

7. See, for example, Untermassfeld penitentiary to state ministry, 31 December 1918, Thüringisches Staatsarchiv Meiningen (ThSTA Mgn.), HSM Staatsministerium, Abteilung Justiz, Nr. 990.

8. Heinrich Hannover and Elisabeth Hannover-Druck, *Politische Justiz, 1918–33* (Frankfurt/Main, 1966).

9. Bund der Gefängnisbeamten Deutschlands, ed., *Der Aufsichtsbeamte im Strafvollzuge* (n.p., n.d.), 32–34. In 1921 alone, 649 state prisoners were sentenced to further imprisonment of three months or more for their participation in riots; Reichsjustizministerium and Statistisches Reichsamt, eds., *Kriminalstatistik für das Jahr 1921* (Berlin, 1924).

10. "Revolte im Zuchthaus," *Berliner Tageblatt*, 29 March 1920, Bundesarchiv Berlin (BA Berlin), 61 Re 1/1527, fo. 163; "Das Schwurgericht im Zuchthaus," *Berliner Tageblatt*, 19 June 1920, ibid., fo. 167.

11. "Das Elend der Strafgefangenen," *Vorwärts*, 17 April 1923, BA Berlin, R 3001/5606.

12. Wagner, *Volksgemeinschaft*, 31.

13. Complaints by inmates of the Untermassfeld penitentiary, 15–16 December 1921, ThSTA Mgn., HSM Staatsministerium, Abteilung Justiz, Nr. 985, fo. 187–200.

14. For corporal punishment in nineteenth-century Germany, see Evans, *Szenen*, 141–198.

15. For the wider context, see Richard Bessel, *Germany after the First World War* (Oxford, 1995), 220–253; Peukert, *Weimar*, 129–144, 263–273.

16. Franz von Liszt, "Der Zweckgedanke im Strafrecht," in Liszt, *Strafrechtliche Aufsätze und Vorträge*, 2 vols. (Berlin, 1905), 1, 126–179, here 169, 173. See also Richard F. Wetzell, "From Retributive Justice to Social Defense: Penal Reform in Fin-de-Siècle Germany," in *Germany at the Fin de Siècle: Culture, Politics, and Ideas*, ed. Suzanne Marchand and David Lindenfeld, (Baton Rouge, 2004), 59–77; Wetzell, *Inventing the Criminal: A History of German Criminology, 1880–1945* (Chapel Hill, 2000), 33–38, 75–90; Max Grünhut, *The Development of the German Penal System 1920–32* (Cambridge, 1944), 28.

17. For the general background, see "Grundsätze für den Vollzug von Freiheitsstrafen vom 7. Juni 1923," *Reichsgesetzblatt*, part II; Herbert Schattke, *Die Geschichte der Progression im Strafvollzug und der damit zusammenhängenden Vollzugsziele in Deutschland* (Frankfurt/Main, 1979), 150–157. For experiments with the progressive stages system in nineteenth-century Germany, see Rudolf Plischke, "Historische Rückblicke ins 18. und 19. Jahrhundert zum Stufenstrafvollzug," *Monatsschrift für Kriminalpsychologie und Strafrechtsreform* (MSchriftKrim) 19 (1928), 417–429.

18. Ministerial decision Nr. 57911, 3 November 1921, in Bayerisches Staatsministerium der Justiz, ed., *Der Stufenstrafvollzug und die kriminalbiologischen Untersuchungen der Gefangenen in den bayerischen Strafanstalten* (Munich, 1926), 10–18, here 15.

19. For a good introduction to the history of the prison, see Norval Morris and David J. Rothman, eds., *The Oxford History of the Prison* (New York, 1995).

20. "Statistik des Gefängniswesens"; *Statistik über die Gefangenenanstalten der Justizverwaltung in Preussen 1924* (Berlin, 1927); *Statistik über die Gefangenenanstalten der Justizverwaltung in Preussen 1929* (Berlin, 1931); Hermann Stepenhorst, *Die Entwicklung des Verhältnisses von Geldstrafe zu Freiheitsstrafe seit 1882* (Berlin, 1993), 41–57; Claudia von Gélieu, *Frauen in Haft* (Berlin, 1994), 68. The estimate of prisoner numbers is based on the Prussian statistics for 1929. Prussia held about 60 percent of all German inmates.

21. For the Study Group and Untermassfeld, see *Gefängnisse in Thüringen. Berichte über die Reform des Strafvollzugs* (Weimar, 1930); Albert Krebs, "Die Selbstverwaltung Gefangener in der Strafanstalt," *MSchriftKrim* 19 (1928), 152–164; Krebs, "Die GmbH als Betriebsform der

Arbeit in der Strafanstalt," in Heinz Müller-Dietz, ed., *Freiheitsentzug: Entwicklung von Praxis und Theorie seit der Aufklärung* (Berlin, 1978), 498–508; Lothar Frede, "Der Strafvollzug in Stufen," in Lothar Frede and Max Grünhut, eds., *Reform des Strafvollzuges* (Berlin, 1927), 102–136; Frede, "Der Strafvollzug in Stufen in Thüringen," *Zeitschrift für die gesamte Strafrechtswissenschaft* (ZStW) 46 (1925), 233–248, quote 236. For archival material on Untermassfeld, see the files of the Thuringian Ministry of Justice in the Thüringisches Hauptstaatsarchiv Weimar (= ThHStAW). Secondary sources include Ursula Sagaster, *Die thüringische Landesstrafanstalt Untermassfeld in den Jahren 1923–33* (Frankfurt/Main, 1980); Katharina Witter, "Funktion und Organisation der Zuchthäuser im kapitalistischen Deutschland, dargelegt am Beispiel des Zuchthauses Untermassfeld" (Diplomarbeit, East Berlin, 1982). For prison labor in general, see Philipp Borchers, "Die Gefangenenarbeit in den deutschen Strafanstalten," *Blätter für Gefängniskunde* (BlGefK) 54 (1921), 7–146.

22. Association of prison officials in Thuringia to state ministry, 14 February 1925, ThHStAW, Thüringisches Justizministerium Nr. 423, fo. 4–5. See also disciplinary procedure against the inmate Alfred S., 10 November 1925, ThHStAW, Thüringisches Justizministerium Nr. 1719, fo. 76–78; memorandum by Lothar Frede, 15 June 1931, ThHStAW, Thüringisches Justizministerium Nr. 1683, fo. 167; Association of prison officials in Thuringia to ministry of justice, 16 April 1928, ThHStAW, Thüringisches Justizministerium Nr. 423, fo. 45–46; Untermassfeld penitentiary to ministry of justice, 7 June 1933, ThHStAW, Personalakte Dr. Albert Krebs; memorandum by Lothar Frede, 5 February 1925, ThHStAW, Personalakte Dr. Otto Zirker.

23. See note 1.

24. Untermassfeld penitentiary to ministry of justice, 8 December 1927, ThHStAW, Thüringisches Justizministerium Nr. 1339, fo. 129–130; Untermassfeld penitentiary to ministry of justice, 20 November 1924, ThHStAW, Thüringisches Justizministerium Nr. 1683, fo. 30–35.

25. Rudolf Sieverts, "Die preussische Verordnung über den Strafvollzug in Stufen vom 7. Juni 1929," *MSchriftKrim*, Beiheft 3 (Heidelberg, 1930), 129–151; Bernd Koch, "Das System des Stufenstrafvollzugs in Deutschland" (Ph.D. diss., Freiburg University, 1972), 63–71; "20. Mitgliederversammlung des Vereins der deutschen Strafanstaltsbeamten," *BlGefK* 62 (1931), 1–332, here 201, 229, 293–296.

26. "Statistik des Gefängniswesens." For the role of prison chaplains, see Brigitte Oleschinski, "'Ein letzter stärkender Gottesdienst . . .': Die deutsche Gefängnisseelsorge zwischen Republik und Diktatur 1918–45" (Ph.D. diss., Free University Berlin, 1993).

27. In 1924, one in every fifteen penitentiary inmates submitted a written complaint. By 1929, this figure was down to one in every eleven inmates; *Gefangenenanstalten der Justizverwaltung 1924*; *Gefangenenanstalten der Justizverwaltung 1929*.

28. Memoirs include Felix Fechenbach, *Im Haus der Freudlosen* (Berlin, 1925); Ernst Toller, *Justiz* (Berlin, 1927); Max Hoelz, *Vom "Weissen Kreuz" zur Roten Fahne* (Frankfurt/Main, 1969 edition); Karl Plättner, *Eros im Zuchthaus* (Berlin, 1929).

29. Hoelz, "Vom *Weissen Kreuz*," 362.

30. See, for example, Berthold Freudenthal, "Massregeln der Sicherung und Besserung," in P. F. Aschrott and Eduard Kohlrausch, eds., *Reform des Strafrechts* (Berlin, 1926), 153–172; Curt Bondy, "Zur Frage der Erziehbarkeit," *ZStW* 48 (1928), 329–334; Liepmann, *Krieg*.

31. Franz Exner, "Der Vollzug der bessernden und sichernden Massnahmen," in Lothar Frede and Max Grünhut, eds., *Reform des Strafvollzuges* (Berlin, 1927), 244–260, here 257.

32. Rorbert Heindl, *Der Berufsverbrecher* (Berlin, 1926).

33. Ibid., 191–195.

34. Ministerial decision Nr. 32222, 7 July 1923, in Bayerisches Staatsministerium der Justiz, ed., *Stufenstrafvollzug*, 26–38. For criminal biology in Bavaria, see Wolfgang Burgmair, Nikolaus Wachsmann, and Matthias M. Weber, "'Die soziale Prognose wird damit sehr trübe . . . ':

Theodor Viernstein und die Kriminalbiologische Sammelstelle in Bayern," in Michael Farin, ed., *Polizeireport München* (Munich, 1999), 250–287.

35. "Die einschneidenste Gefängnisreform West-Europas," *Berliner Tageblatt*, 11 July 1929, BA Berlin, R 3001/5631, fo. 139.

36. I have examined the investigations carried out in Moabit between 1 May 1930 and 29 December 1930, collected in Landesarchiv Berlin, Rep 5 Acc 2863, Nr. 97 (for the quote, see the examination of the inmate Erich B., 12 November 1930, ibid., fo. 134). For Bavaria, see Oliver Liang, "Criminal-Biological Theory, Discourse, and Practice in Germany, 1918–45" (Ph.D. diss., Johns Hopkins University Baltimore, 1999), 141–157. For contemporary criticism of the Bavarian examinations, see Werner Petrzilka, *Persönlichkeitsforschung und Differenzierung im Strafvollzug* (Hamburg, 1930).

37. Bayerisches Obsorge Amt, ed., *Die Gefangenenobsorge* (Lichtenau, 1928), 18.

38. Walter Luz, *Ursachen und Bekämpfung des Verbrechens im Urteil des Verbrechers* (Heidelberg, 1928), 243–246; Wagner, *Volksgemeinschaft*, 146–148.

39. Law for the fight against Gypsies, travellers and the work-shy, Bayerisches Hauptstaatsarchiv (BayHStA), MInn 71579; ministerial decision regarding the implementation of the law for Gypsies and the work-shy, BayHStA, MInn 71579; ministry of justice to penal institutions, 16 February 1927, BayHStA, MJu 22525.

40. Straubing penitentiary to Munich police, 24 May 1929, BayHStA, MInn 71560.

41. Wagner, *Volksgemeinschaft*, 215; Stepenhorst, *Entwicklung*, 42; Edgar Schmidt, "Aus der Statistik der preussischen Gefangenenanstalten," *Deutsche Justiz* 96 (1934), 1023–1026; Schmidt, "Die Kosten des Strafvollzuges," *Deutsche Justiz* 96 (1934), 1346–1347. The estimate of prisoner numbers is based on the Prussian statistics for 1932.

42. Curriculum vitae of the inmate Maria B., 22 August 1930, Staatsarchiv München, Justizvollzugsanstalten Nr. 1820.

43. Conference of the Federal Officials Responsible for the Prison Service on 18 January 1930, ThHStAW, Thüringisches Justizministerium Nr. 1337.

44. Report by Dr. Viernstein and Dr. Trunk, 4 February 1930, BayHStA, MJu 22507; Statistical Material of the Report, 3 February 1930. For Viernstein, see Burgmair et al., "'Die soziale Prognose.'"

45. For the quote, see Heinrich Seyfarth, "Der Humanitätsgedanke im Strafvollzug," *Monatsblätter des deutschen Reichszusammenschlusses für Gerichtshilfe* 5 (1930), 67–82.

46. "Ersparnisvorschläge des Preussischen Richtervereins," *Juristische Wochenschrift* 61 (1932), 916–917; "Anregungen der Vereinigung der Preussischen Staatsanwälte zu Ersparnissen auf dem Gebiet der Justizverwaltung und Rechtsprechung," ibid., 917–918.

47. Heinz Brandstätter, "Zur Situation der Strafvollzugsreform," *MSchriftKrim* 23 (1932), 431–432; Eduard Hapke, "Landesstrafanstalt Untermassfeld: Die Behandlung in der Gemeinschaft der II. Stufe," in *Gefängnisse in Thüringen* (Weimar, 1930), 96–105. See also Curt Bondy, "Fortschritte und Hemmungen in der Strafvollzugsreform," *MSchriftKrim*, Beiheft 3 (Heidelberg, 1930), 90–102.

48. See Klaus Marxen, *Der Kampf gegen das liberale Strafrecht: Eine Studie zum Antiliberalismus in der Strafrechtswissenschaft der zwanziger und dreissiger Jahre* (Berlin, 1975).

49. Cit. in Richard J. Evans, *Rituals of Retribution* (London, 1996), 625.

50. Janus, "Rückblick—Ausblick," *Der Strafvollzug* 22 (1932), 169–175.

51. See Höss' prisoner file in Landeshauptarchiv Brandenburg, Pr. Br. Rep. 29, Zuchthaus Brandenburg Nr. 691. See also Martin Broszat, ed., *Kommandant in Auschwitz: Autobiographische Aufzeichnungen des Rudolf Höss* (Munich, 1963).

52. Karl Rompel to Dr. Weber, 13 November 1932, ThHStAW, Thüringisches Justizministerium Nr. 1707, fo. 32–35.

53. See Erving Goffman, *Asylums: Essays on the Social Situation of Mental Patients and Other Inmates* (London, 1971).

54. Wolfgang Ayass, *Das Arbeitshaus Breitenau* (Kassel, 1992), 253–258; Michael Burleigh, *Death and Deliverance: "Euthanasia" in Germany 1900–45* (Cambridge, 1994), 33–34.

55. See Crew, *Germans*, 208.

Chapter 5

THE MEDICALIZATION OF WILHELMINE AND WEIMAR JUVENILE JUSTICE RECONSIDERED

Gabriel N. Finder

> Because of the great import of the juvenile court decisions, the author-
> itative collaboration of the jurist is indispensable, according to German
> legal conceptions, so that attempts to entrust the treatment of punishable
> juveniles to . . . physicians, with an exclusion of jurists, have never been
> able to win ground in Germany.[1]
>
> Herbert Francke, 1932

This statement by Herbert Francke, Weimar Germany's preeminent juvenile
court judge, gives a picture of the development of juvenile justice that is quite
different from Foucault's image of the insidious corrosion of law by a medicalized
version of discipline and from the abiding historiographical inclination to locate
the repressive turn in German criminal justice after 1933 in its Wilhelmine and
Weimar prehistory. This chapter will argue that Francke's assessment is a useful
corrective that has a great deal of validity. First and foremost, historians should be
careful not to overemphasize the mantra of the Wilhelmine and Weimar German
juvenile justice movement, repeated *ad nauseum* since its inception in the 1890s:
"(re)education in lieu of punishment" (*Erziehung statt Strafe*). Although it was
undergirded by a vision of social progress, juvenile justice in Germany, especially
after World War I, represented a historically contingent compromise between a
modest degree of penal experimentation and penal conservatism.[2] To borrow a
phrase from David Crew in a related context, this compromise was forged in the
spirit of "damage control."[3] The erosion of authoritative prescriptions in German criminal law prior to World War I and then their disintegration during and
after the war, which precipitated what cultural critic Siegfried Kracauer labeled a

Notes from this chapter begin on page 153.

"confusion of standards" and an "exceptional degree of insecurity," led desperate Germans to search for an expedient solution to an apparently irrepressible rise in crime, especially juvenile delinquency.[4] This exercise in damage control resulted in the passage of the rather elastic Jugendgerichtsgesetz of 1923 (Juvenile Justice Act; JGG).

To be sure, the act promoted its fair share of eclectic experimentalism in the name of "(re)education," exemplifying the fundamental tension between law and discipline in modern penal reform. In this spirit, it provided for resort to the expertise of forensic psychiatrists in the juvenile courtroom. Already before passage of the JGG, the entrenchment of certain trends in juvenile justice reform indicated the establishment of a niche in juvenile court for forensic psychiatry. These trends included the transformation of juvenile delinquency from a moral into a medical condition, the deemphasis in penal reform of the offense in favor of the personality of the offender, and the abridgment of normal judicial procedures. Furthermore, since many of its pioneers were wont to stress the paradigmatic potential of juvenile justice, with the expectation that innovations successfully tested in the crucible of juvenile justice would then be applied to adult criminals, forensic psychiatrists hoped that their investment of professional capital in the juvenile justice system would reap dividends in the form of extended influence throughout the entire criminal justice system.[5] Nevertheless, in the final analysis, the 1923 act—and by implication all of pre-1933 juvenile justice in Germany—remained, in the words of a highly respected contemporary commentary, "incorporated into the philosophy of criminal law."[6] In juvenile justice of all places, a hallmark of the modern therapeutic approach to social deviance, the impact of forensic psychiatry, I would argue, was limited; to borrow from Jan Goldstein, discipline remained framed by law.[7] The challenge is to explain this unexpected turn of events.

Forensic Psychiatry and the Juvenile Delinquent

In line with German psychiatry's burgeoning social orientation, which entailed its ambition to intervene in the diagnosis and treatment of offending behaviors, including criminal behavior, from the 1890s onward, forensic psychiatrists established their credentials in juvenile court first by promoting their discursive message and then by encouraging its practical social application.[8] Borrowing a phrase from Richard Wetzell's study of German criminology, forensic psychiatry took pains to invent the juvenile delinquent.[9] It recast the existence of juvenile deviance and then toiled indefatigably to identify, explain, and prevent it. While nineteenth-century notions of juvenile delinquency generally ascribed adolescent criminal behavior to the morally debilitating effects of neglect and poverty, the burgeoning endorsement of a socially engineered vision of the social order from the last third of the nineteenth century onward prompted the transformation of this personal deficiency from a moral to a medical condition. Being medical, it was now deemed amenable in principle to diagnosis and treatment. The pathologization of juvenile delinquency suited the welfarist orientation of juvenile justice because the creation of a special nosological category of juvenile offenders promised to expand the power of the state to curb offensive behavior that was not formally proscribed by criminal law.[10]

Prewar studies in forensic psychiatry of juvenile delinquency continued to deemphasize biological factors in favor of environmental ones, but by the end of World War I a biological concept of juvenile deviance established itself in the firmament of German juvenile justice with the landmark publication in 1918 of *Die Verwahrlosung: Ihre klinisch-psychologische Bewertung und ihre Bekämpfung* (Waywardness: Its Assessment in Clinical Psychology and Combating It) by Adalbert Gregor and Else Voigtländer. The authors, who examined fifteen hundred male and female juvenile reformatory inmates, of whom they described one hundred male and one hundred female inmates in detail, stressed the role of a "psychopathic personality" (*Psychopathie*) in the formation of juvenile delinquency. The change in terminology from what these authors considered the "vague concept" of *Verwahrlosung* to the ostensibly more scientifically rigorous *Psychopathie* paralleled a similar usage of the term throughout forensic psychiatry in the discussion of adult criminals. As Richard Wetzell has explained, the German term *Psychopathie* and its derivatives refer to the broad area of mental abnormalities or personality disorders.[11] In Gregor's own words, *Psychopathie* signified a "pathological predisposition (constitution)" that was either "congenital or acquired" and manifested itself "in deviations in relations between psychological functions, in an abnormal way of reacting, and in a conspicuous variation of behavioral patterns."[12]

The correlation of juvenile deviance with mental disorders had already played a minor role in earlier influential studies of juvenile delinquency, which had strained to explicate the interaction of environmental and individual factors in the creation of the deviant personality. But Gregor and Voigtländer drastically minimized the role of environment in favor of a biological etiology of delinquency. According to their findings, which far exceeded those of previous studies, about 90 percent of the juvenile inmates in their study, males and females alike, were "hereditarily burdened" (*erblich belastet*).[13] They hesitated to equate a psychopathic personality with criminal behavior, but in their view most juveniles with psychopathic disorders became criminals because the domination of the intellect by instinctual drives was bound to bring them into conflict with the law.[14] The authors did not entirely dismiss the impact of social factors on delinquent behavior, especially deficient childrearing, and they also noted the baleful effect of World War I on the spiraling rate of juvenile delinquency. In the final analysis, however, "deviance," they concluded, "is determined as a rule not by external factors but rather by the constitution of the individual."[15] After Gregor and Voigtländer's work, biological explanations of juvenile deviance came to overshadow, albeit not totally eclipse, social ones. As a result of the palpable impact of their work, a large percentage of adolescents in juvenile justice would be considered to have a diagnosable mental disorder.

In the aftermath of Gregor and Voigtländer's study, German forensic psychiatrists almost invariably incorporated a highly mutable concept of the psychopathic personality into their own typologies of the juvenile deviant, and precisely because the notion was so mutable, the juvenile delinquent with a psychopathic disorder seemed to assume almost pandemic proportions. The potential consequences of being so classified were clearly articulated by Gregor and Voigtländer. To be considered mentally ill might entail ominous repercussions because "a rehabilitative program [*Erziehung*] operating with intellectual resources, logic, and conviction would be meaningless [in such cases] and a rote form of training [*Dressur*] must take its place, whereby the premises of correctional education dissolve."[16] In this regard, the authors helped spawn the concept of the "uneducable" or, literally, "difficult to educate" (*schwer erziehbar*) juvenile who should be excluded from therapy.[17] The medicalized approach to juvenile delinquency thus came to imply not only endangerment of the individual offender but also dangerousness to society. In line with the approach of Kurt Schneider, a prominent psychiatrist whose work on the psychopathic personality left an indelible mark on criminal biology, a juvenile delinquent came to signify someone who suffers from an illness because of which society suffers, with the accent on social dangerousness.[18] Juvenile delinquency now represented a medical condition of individuals whose way of life was incompatible with a normative vision of social progress. Indeed, before the end of the 1920s, Gregor would consider the rehabilitation of the "uneducable" impracticable and would advocate their exclusion from correctional education because their presence could jeopardize the reformation of other inmates.[19] It would become the function of forensic psychiatry in the juvenile prison and in correctional education to determine who should be excluded from an institution's rehabilitative program. A significant circle of forensic psychiatrists in the Weimar Republic who operated in the juvenile justice system came to share this approach to juvenile delinquency.

Forensic Psychiatry in the Juvenile Courts

What further consolidated the position of forensic psychiatry in late Wilhelmine and Weimar juvenile justice was the era's blueprint for the future of the German criminal justice system. In classical German penal jurisprudence since Feuerbach, guilt was predicated exclusively on the commission of a criminal act, whereas the criminal's internal motivation, not to mention his personality, was irrelevant to a determination of his culpability and punishment. Juvenile justice was poised to throw the old notion of criminal responsibility overboard and become a preemptive instrument of crime prevention, addressing not what one had done but who one was. This prospect of de-legalization tantalized the practitioners of forensic psychiatry. In such a medicalized penal order, the psychiatric profession would have the potential to wield enormous disciplinary power; forensic psychiatrists would be able to significantly influence the verdict, determine an eventual place of incarceration, and shape—or even preclude—carceral therapy.

Moreover, by relaxing or abridging formal procedural requirements in pursuit of creating a nonadversarial environment in juvenile court, which was to be attained in large part through the expansion of judicial discretion, juvenile justice threatened to undermine the very foundation of the rule-of-law state (*Rechtsstaat*), where the promise of law is secured by the guarantee of procedural rights.[20] Thanks to the creation of this collegial atmosphere, forensic psychiatrists could expect to intervene in the system in ample measure during the process of investigation and trial. Through an alliance with the coercive power of the state, forensic psychiatrists hoped to expand their area of authority from narrow medical diagnoses of the mental state of juvenile offenders by seizing opportunities to examine their entire life—whatever may have contributed to shaping their personality—and to design individualized regimens for their future. From the vantage point of forensic psychiatrists, it would be optimal to expand the examination of individual juvenile offenders to include examinations of their relatives because only then would it be possible to draw a "total picture" of their lives.[21]

Forensic psychiatrists had ingratiated themselves with the juvenile court system already from its inception in 1908. An early enthusiastic supporter of forensic psychiatry in the juvenile court was Paul Köhne, a prominent Wilhelmine juvenile court judge who presided over the juvenile court in the central district of Berlin (Berlin-Mitte). Köhne was deeply dissatisfied with the standard superficial judicial assessment of the mental competence of juvenile defendants based on the presence of conspicuous physical handicaps and their familiarity with the Ten Commandments. Köhne firmly believed that this unsophisticated procedure did not satisfy the legal requirement of the criminal code (*Strafgesetzbuch*; StGB) to determine specifically whether a juvenile defendant who was not legally insane should still be excused from criminal responsibility on account of a defective intelligence (§ 56).[22] For this reason he started using forensic psychiatrists immediately after the creation of the juvenile court in central Berlin in 1908.[23] By 1910 he had institutionalized the practice of psychiatric examinations in his court. Although the initial employment of forensic psychiatry in juvenile court generated predictable resistance to the practice in traditional circles, Köhne was able to deflect a lot of this criticism because the new practice did not lead to wholesale acquittals of juvenile offenders on the grounds of mental incompetence. On the contrary, he endorsed the procedure precisely not only because it "impedes the unjust conviction of people whose mental illness without a medical examination is unrecognizable even to the trained eye [of the judge]," but also because "in individual cases the judge needs medical assistance to expose those who feign mental illness."[24] In addition, he supported psychiatric examinations because they helped identify defendants inhabiting the borderland between mental health and mental illness who would benefit from state intervention, especially removal from their current criminogenic environments. He credited psychiatric advice to the court with "saving many a youth from illness and crime."[25] Köhne was pleased with the psychiatrization of his juvenile court. "This procedure," he boasted, "has proved itself very beneficial."[26] Indeed, he was in favor of subjecting most juvenile defendants to a psychiatric examination.

The rate of psychiatric examinations performed for the juvenile court of central Berlin bore witness to the increasing influence of forensic psychiatry in the Berlin juvenile court system. Between the end of 1909 and the end of 1912, roughly 2,300 psychiatric examinations were conducted for that court, an average of 767 examinations a year.[27] By the fall of 1917, 6,745 examinations had been conducted since 1909, an average of 834 per year.[28] An average of 889 examinations per year were conducted in the five-year period between 1912 and 1917. The prominent forensic psychiatrist Jacobsohn estimated that he alone had performed about 2,000 psychiatric examinations for the juvenile court of Central Berlin between 1909 and 1917.[29]

The introduction of forensic psychiatry into the juvenile justice system was not limited to Berlin. From the outset, psychiatrists were authorized by the administrative regulations of several German states to consult the fledgling juvenile courts.[30] Frankfurt is illustrative of this trend. The juvenile court prosecutor routinely solicited an evaluation of a defendant's mental competence, which ensured the engagement of a psychiatrist. Karl Allmenröder, Germany's legendary first juvenile court judge, made it a practice to be consulted by a psychiatrist along with an official from the youth welfare association before each hearing.[31] The municipal Juvenile Observation Center (Jugendsichtungsstelle) established by the forensic psychiatrist Wilhelm Fürstenheim in 1916 worked closely with the juvenile court in Frankfurt. When the impression made by a juvenile offender warranted it, the Juvenile Observation Center would relay its diagnostic findings via the local youth welfare organization to the juvenile court. If deemed necessary, the court then summoned the institution's director to testify. The court issued such summonses in approximately ten percent of its cases.[32]

The alliance between forensic psychiatry and the youth welfare bureaucracy, which was entrusted by the juvenile courts with the task not only of supervising probation but also of assessing juvenile offenders' personalities on the basis of rather intrusive investigations into their lives, was mutually beneficial. In line with the individualizing approach to juvenile deviance, private and semi-public charitable organizations naturally turned to forensic psychiatrists because of their touted expert insight into personality disorders. Collaboration between youth welfare officials and psychiatrists active in juvenile justice was intimate in several cities, including Berlin, Frankfurt, Hamburg, and Nuremberg. As Heinrich Vogt, the first forensic psychiatrist assigned to cases in the Frankfurt juvenile court, observed, "without the investigations [of the Frankfurt youth welfare association] my activity would hardly be possible."[33] Psychiatric observation was no less important to the investigative function of youth welfare associations on account of the suspicion that relatives' frequently tendentious descriptions of juvenile offenders' personalities were unreliable.[34]

In spite of its expanding influence in the juvenile justice system forensic psychiatry was not immune, however, to disappointment. Although forensic psychiatrists continued to insist on the psychiatric examination of all juvenile defendants, the juvenile justice system only partially acceded to this demand. In 1914, of the approximately 550 German juvenile courts in operation, only 10 authorized the psychiatric examination of every juvenile defendant. These juvenile courts were located exclusively in metropolitan areas, including Hamburg, Leipzig, and Central Berlin.[35] This demand never infiltrated the provinces. And even in cities it proved impracticable to continue this practice, even in Berlin. There, in 1917, an exasperated Prussian justice minister was compelled to reissue his previous directive that juvenile court judges could order psychiatric examinations of juvenile defendants only in the presence of compelling reasons because psychiatric examinations had become the rule for the panel of juvenile court judges in central Berlin, who defiantly urged juvenile court judges elsewhere to follow suit. Notwithstanding the practice in central Berlin, in other juvenile courts in Prussia psychiatric examinations were the exception rather than the rule in accordance with the justice minister's concern that superfluous psychiatric examinations in juvenile courts could lead to innumerable unjustifiable acquittals. The cost of this practice did not escape his attention either.[36]

The vulnerability of forensic psychiatry in juvenile justice was also driven home by the reaction of Frankfurt juvenile court judge Paul Levi to that court's cooperation with the Frankfurt Juvenile Observation Center. Levi found that the center's reports were "especially useful to investigate juveniles' personality and manner of acting" and that "they [formed] a good foundation for adjudication and the selection of judicial remedies." But he punctuated his description of his juvenile court's interaction with the center with a caveat: "It is nevertheless self-understood that the juvenile court decided the extent to which it ought to follow the expert opinion and the recommendation of the juvenile observation center only on the basis of the totality of the circumstances."[37]

Seeking to bolster their role in juvenile justice, forensic psychiatrists mobilized in support of revisions of the law. Fürstenheim and others lectured frequently in favor of expanding the law to allow more psychiatric intervention.[38] Forensic psychiatrists also formed the Vereinigung ärztlicher Sachverständiger am

Jugendgericht Berlin-Mitte (Union of Medical Experts at the Juvenile Court of Central Berlin). During legislative debates in 1912 and 1913 on a juvenile justice act, this organization petitioned the Reichstag to broaden the role of forensic psychiatry in juvenile court. It asked legislators not only to provide for the psychiatric examination of every juvenile defendant but also to mandate psychiatric consultation in sentencing and to assess the costs of these practices to the judicial system. It justified these demands by reference to the high proportion of mentally ill juvenile offenders, which, it argued, a juvenile court judge could not be expected to manage competently without the benefit of psychiatric expertise.[39] To the psychiatrists' chagrin, their petition was ignored.

They continued their quest to consolidate their presence in juvenile court when debate on a juvenile justice act resumed after World War I. In 1920, a subcommittee of the Deutscher Jugendgerichtstag (Conference of German Juvenile Courts; DJGT) under the rubric of "Jugendgericht und Arzt" (Juvenile Court and Physician) proposed a resolution, which was adopted by the entire assembly, calling for the psychiatric examination of all juvenile defendants who raised suspicion of a mental abnormality, had committed a serious offense, or demonstrated conspicuous antisocial or deviant behavior.[40] In 1927, when the Reichstag considered the motions of Socialists and Communists to raise the absolute age of criminal responsibility from fourteen to sixteen and the age of limited criminal responsibility from eighteen to twenty or twenty-one, its judiciary committee heard the testimony of half a dozen psychiatrists.[41]

In the end, however, these efforts bore only modest fruit, as the 1923 Juvenile Justice Act provided for psychiatric examinations of juvenile defendants only "in appropriate cases" (§ 31). Juvenile court judges would determine which youth would be referred to a psychiatrist. In the minds of the ministerial framers of the act, the judge's determination whether educative measures were appropriate was to depend on what effect they would have on the juvenile offender's personality; but the juvenile court judge was also to consider what impact an order to replace punishment with nonpenal remedies would have both on the public and on the claim of the victim to redress.[42] The reaction of many forensic psychiatrists to the 1923 act's restrictions on their authority was anything but conciliatory.[43] This reaction was on the mark: the psychiatric profession's self-mobilization during the legislative evolution of the Juvenile Justice Act since the eve of World War I was, in the end, only a partial success and arguably demonstrated the limited character of its disciplinary authority in the judicial system of the German welfare state.

The increasing restriction of psychiatric examinations to demonstrable cases of mental instability, which found legislative expression in the 1923 act, was due to many factors. In addition to budgetary constraints, the influence of psychiatry in juvenile justice was limited by the desire of juvenile court judges to protect the hard-won expansion of judicial discretion in juvenile court. Even so, many juvenile court judges seem to have been sensitive to the dangers of intoxication with their own expanded power. During a seminar for juvenile court judges in 1926, one of their own number admonished his colleagues not to abuse their judicial discretion: "We have to admit that great freedom becomes arbitrariness in the hand of the judge. But we cannot vanquish this danger if our freedom as judges is abridged, but rather only if one educates judges who understand how to use their freedom."[44]

To be sure, their relatively large degree of judicial discretion was in part a form of professional compensation. The German legal profession was highly stratified, and the permanent assignment of juvenile court judges to local courts (*Amtsgerichte*), of which the juvenile court constituted a division, paled in professional status with judgeships in district courts (*Landgerichte*), which were more prestigious and lucrative. However, the majority of Wilhelmine and Weimar juvenile court judges seem not to have resented the superior status of their colleagues in higher courts; service in the gestating juvenile justice system seemed to provide sufficient reward for most of them.

Without a doubt, not all juvenile court judges were sympathetic to the plight of juvenile offenders, many of whom were driven to law-breaking by economic distress. Such juveniles could expect no quarter from older juvenile court judges in particular. But which other judge in the German criminal justice system but a juvenile court judge could have conceived of defining his judicial role in terms of compassion? Thus Herbert Francke could unabashedly urge his colleagues on the juvenile court bench to cultivate a "love of youth."[45]

The Tenacity of Rule-of-Law Habits

Indeed, juvenile court judges had another, more substantive motive not to concede too much ground to doctors: From their perspective, the introduction of a medicalized approach into criminal justice threatened to lead to the progressive moral disarmament of the law. For the most part, juvenile court judges were liberal-minded jurists who supported reform of the current judicial treatment of juvenile offenders, but they also believed in imposing limits on the contents of reform. In particular, the majority of juvenile court judges, with the support of other legal practitioners in the juvenile court system, remained committed to the notion of criminal responsibility. Regardless of how entrenched forensic psychiatry eventually became in the German state's mechanisms of control before 1933, not only in criminal justice but also in various forms of social welfare, in juvenile justice the stubborn survival of old rule-of-law habits limited the latitude of forensic psychiatry.

This tenacity of rule-of-law habits in juvenile justice is illustrated in contemporary commentaries to the law. Even though the 1923 Juvenile Justice Act vested broad discretionary authority in the juvenile court "to refrain from punishment" and in its place to order "educative remedies" (*Erziehungsmaßregeln*) from an ample catalogue of such remedial measures (§§ 5-7), interpretation of this novelty was unsettled. Albert Hellwig, a judge and then, during the Weimar Republic, an official in the Prussian Justice Ministry who helped shape juvenile justice legislation, interpreted the discretionary use of educative measures restrictively; he would have subordinated the act's promotion of behavior modification to the need for deterrence.[46] Herbert Francke's construction of the Juvenile Justice Act was only somewhat less restrictive. In his view, the act contemplated judicial approval of educative remedies only "if they of themselves suffice to produce the success intended [otherwise] by punishment." And he restricted their use even further by adding that "there are cases in which consideration of the general public makes the imposition of punishment appear unavoidable."[47] On the other hand, the commentary of Wilhelm Kiesow, a high official in the Reich Justice Ministry who participated in framing the act, stressed the educative objective of the law: "The reaction of the state," he argued, "is now certainly directed . . . in the first place at the [juvenile] offender; he ought to be rehabilitated, to be kept away from future violations of the law. Education forms one means to this end." Yet Kiesow, too, added a caveat: "It would be to fully misconstrue the state of affairs if one meant to exclude [the] retributive idea from penal law."[48] The act's educative measures, then, represented a significant innovation, but there was palpable reluctance to cede too much traditional ground to an alternative vision of criminal responsibility.

The modus operandi of Bruno Müller, chief judge of the Hamburg magistrate court and juvenile court during the Weimar Republic, illustrates the extent to which law framed discipline in German juvenile justice. Müller brought a substantial degree of rationalization to the Hamburg juvenile justice system by reducing the number of cases brought to the juvenile courts, terminating some proceedings before they reached a verdict, and preferring educative alternatives to incarceration. Nevertheless, he was inclined to order punishment when the "gravity of the offense" (*Schwere der Straftat*) dictated it, even if the juvenile was a first-time offender.[49] He employed this terminology, which did not appear in the Juvenile Justice Act, deliberately because he felt compelled to establish doctrinal grounds for the incarceration of juvenile offenders. Such grounds were missing from the 1923 act, which vaguely authorized juvenile court judges to refrain from ordering punishment if rehabilitative measures were "adequate" (§ 6).

Müller's formulation speaks to the ambiguous character of late Imperial and Weimar juvenile justice. It was in society's interest to minimize the social dissonance of juvenile crime, especially juvenile recidivism. Juvenile justice largely promoted conformity to a minimal consensus about normative behavior, and in this respect operated no differently from any other form of penal law. What distinguished juvenile justice was that its partial disengagement from traditional criminal law through "(re)education" imparted an essential elasticity to it. Although the rehabilitative ideal could serve to minimize punitive reactions to venial and first-time offenses, under certain circumstances, especially if the offense was grave or the offender was a recidivist, it could also serve to maximize the punitive reactions to juvenile wrongdoing. To borrow from Franz Streng, offenders came to assume a "contingent position" in German juvenile justice: "On the one hand, they [could] count on extensive consideration of their developmental prerequisites. The well-intentioned attitude of their fellow citizens [had] limits, however, when the offense [entailed] an all too obstinate or all too massive calling into question of social values."[50] Francke made the same point in a speech to juvenile court professionals in 1927, in which he articulated his commitment to criminal responsibility and punishment when the preservation of the sanctity of generally accepted norms dictated punishment because the offense, even if caused by negligence, was serious:

> In my opinion, on the basis of the [Juvenile Justice Act] there is absolutely no question that the educational ideal is not sole sovereign, but that the general concept of punishment, as realized in criminal justice against adults, must not be totally disregarded. . . . [In section 9 of the Juvenile Justice Act] we find the stipulation that punishment of up to ten years can be imposed on juveniles. No one will pretend to assert that such punishment can be justified purely on grounds of the educative ideal. . . . If the law has . . . adopted such rules, these provisions can be explained only on the basis of the fact that the legislator's position was that under [certain] circumstances the legal order must be preserved against juveniles, even at the price of the educational objective, which must then retreat.[51]

Notwithstanding the rationalization of juvenile justice, the judicial philosophies of Bruno Müller and Herbert Francke, perhaps the two most influential juvenile court judges in the Weimar Republic, look a lot like an attempt to reinscribe, albeit with limitations, the old-fashioned concept of guilt in juvenile justice.

The persistence of old rule-of-law habits affected the resort to educative remedies in general. An instructive example is the fate of administrative "juvenile arrest" (*Jugendarrest*)—the committal of juvenile status offenders to solitary confinement for varying lengths of time in a public institution like a school or a jail. This measure was already proposed in 1911, and the spiraling juvenile crime rate during World War I generated support for it. But although it won the endorsement of the juvenile justice movement in the 1920s, juvenile arrest never became law in the Weimar Republic. For his part, Bruno Müller, who went to great lengths to improvise alternatives to incarceration, refused to order juvenile arrest even though he approved of it in principle—if implemented properly, it could lend "inner support" to a juvenile offender—because it was not specifically enumerated in the Juvenile Justice Act's catalogue of educational remedies and was too intrusive to be considered implicitly sanctioned by the 1923 act. Juvenile arrest was later enacted under the Third Reich. If a disciplinary measure like juvenile arrest was not incorporated systematically into German juvenile justice, it was, I would suggest, because late Wilhelmine and Weimar juvenile justice lacked a single-minded ideological agenda to replace Germany's existing legal system with the normative power of an administrative legality, which the enthronement of forensic psychiatry in the courtroom would have epitomized. Rather, German juvenile justice before 1933 demonstrated considerable sensitivity to liberal principles of penal jurisprudence. Juvenile justice was not merely an alibi to redescribe punitive sanctions in the vocabulary of reform. The medicalization of juvenile justice was limited precisely because of the prevalence of this commitment to the liberal principle of the rule of law.

Judges as Lay Psychologists

Sensitive to the incursion of forensic psychiatry into their courtrooms but only partially able to check its momentum, juvenile court judges mobilized to co-opt it by transforming themselves into lay psychologists.[52] They rationalized their strategy by pointing to their expanded judicial discretion, which, they asserted, empowered them to evaluate not only the legal dimensions of an offense but also the soul of the offender. In this enterprise, they found support in the increasing promotion of a judge's "intuitive grasp of the psychological life of the criminal," which delegates to the 1925 meeting of the German chapter of the Internationale Kriminalistische Vereinigung (International Penal Association; IKV), for instance, endorsed.[53] In the 1920s, several members of the second generation of juvenile court judges who were now entering professional maturity developed expertise in adolescent psychology. One juvenile court judge, Walter Hoffmann of Leipzig, even made a significant contribution to the field with the publication of a book in 1922.[54]

The formation of a consensus that juvenile court judges should possess expertise of this type generated an effort to institutionalize the systematic specialized training of prospective and sitting juvenile court judges. In 1924 and 1927, the Deutscher Jugendgerichtstag (DJGT), the institutional voice of the juvenile justice reform movement, passed resolutions calling for the specialized training of juvenile court judges and other juvenile court professionals.[55] In 1928, the Deutsche Vereinigung für Jugendgerichte und Jugendgerichtshilfen (German Association for Juvenile Courts and Juvenile Court Assistance; DVJJ) convened thirty experts, including Herbert Francke, to discuss the training of juvenile court judges. They unanimously endorsed the integration of the study of psychology, along with sociology, the organization of welfare, and education, into the curriculum of law students who intended to become juvenile court judges. To this end, in 1929 the DVJJ proposed the creation of a practical and theoretical training course of six to nine months for prospective juvenile court judges.

The majority of juvenile court judges attended one or more seminars conducted by the DVJJ in the second half of the 1920s. The first such seminar, held in Berlin in June 1925, was representative of the others. It addressed both the theoretical and practical aspects of juvenile justice. Twelve lecture hours were allotted to the psychological and psychiatric causes of juvenile delinquency and eight to the pedagogical approach to problem adolescents. The Berlin seminar included observations of a juvenile prison and reformatories in the region. Most seminars also featured a lecture by a respected juvenile court judge who discussed both the practical application of the 1923 Juvenile Justice Act and the judicial philosophy of juvenile justice. Seminars of this sort were organized not only in Berlin but also in Hamburg, Bonn, Kassel, Frankfurt, and Dresden.[56] Several shorter conferences for juvenile court judges were also organized in the late 1920s.[57]

Although the Depression frustrated the DVJJ's plan to establish a regular nine-month course for future juvenile court judges, the organization's plea inspired circuit court officials in Berlin to sponsor a special one-month regional course for a dozen prospective and fledgling juvenile court judges and prosecutors in 1929 and 1930. In the first and third weeks of the course, participants divided their time evenly between lectures on psychology, sociology, and welfare policy and visiting local youth welfare offices, where they observed social workers in action, even accompanying them on home visits. The course's second week was solely devoted to lectures. During its last week each participant resided in a different reformatory. This immersion in the daily rhythm of a reformatory created a deep appreciation for the complexity of resocializing problem adolescents. According to the reports of participants, not all who attended were sympathetic to psychiatric and psychological explanations of delinquency, but the lecturers seem to have persuaded the majority of them to pay as much attention to the juvenile offender as to his offense and to study the adolescent personality with the help of psychology. Most participants left the course inspired to apply what they had learned.[58]

A prominent lecturer on this circuit was Herman Nohl, an acclaimed professor of education in Göttingen. A perusal of his 1926 lectures in Hamburg and Göttingen imparts a sense of the message being conveyed to juvenile court judges.[59] Nohl explained theoretical concepts in the psychological sciences for his listeners and suggested to them how they could employ these concepts in the creation of a "pedagogical relationship" (*pädagogischer Bezug*) with juvenile offenders—which they might achieve in large measure with the aid of psychoanalytic techniques, especially transference—because "the first task" of the juvenile court judge was winning the juvenile offender's confidence and trust.[60] If the juvenile court judge hoped to modify the behavior of a juvenile offender, he would have to understand him. Judicial assessment of the facts of the case alone would be inadequate because the relevant facts lay primarily "in the soul of the offender."[61] In this vein, "if he thinks pedagogically, the judge sees the offender and not merely the offense."[62] Nohl urged juvenile court judges to use the diagnostic categories of psychology, psychiatry, and especially psychoanalysis. He traced many acts of juvenile delinquency to the instinctual reactions of juveniles to enticement; the juvenile's perception of a desired object motivated him instinctively without malice or forethought to acquire it. More serious criminal offenses ensued from a "psychopathic"—that is to say, abnormal—overreaction to a physiological weakness created by puberty. Such weaknesses occurred in all youngsters, but some had a more pronounced disposition to a labile temperament, which caused psychological "short-circuits" during the maturation process. Suppression of physical urges might induce the defective development of especially weak adolescents. Finally, adolescents were frequently not equal to the expectations of parents, and to flee the intense pressure to succeed they often escaped into private fantasies and led a double life, frequently descending into youth gangs. This was especially true of adolescents from proletarian backgrounds, who went to work at age fourteen but were unprepared for the demands of employment and thrown prematurely into the company of cynical adults.[63] But Nohl warned his listeners that however enlightening the psychological sciences may be, they were still in their infancy, and, in the final analysis, juvenile court judges "stand again every time before the individual with his singular history. . . . The child must . . . always feel that it is not merely a case and a type but a you!"[64]

Although Nohl urged juvenile court judges to be sensitive to the emotional life of juvenile offenders, he adamantly defended the role of punishment in juvenile justice. He was of the conviction that punishment was tantamount to an "authoritative expression of ethical life." In punishment, the juvenile offender perceived the "reality of the authority of [a] higher [form of life]." In the final analysis, "punishment is certainly not the first thing in education, but ever and again the last, truly the famous *ultima ratio* . . . It is . . . indispensable because through it and it alone the authority of a higher existence proves itself [superior] to the authority of the [individual] ego."[65]

What lessons did juvenile court judges, especially novices, draw from Nohl's lecture? The published report of a judge in training who attended the 1926 seminar in Hamburg describes what he derived from Nohl's presentation:

> The exposition certainly does not have the objective of making juvenile court judges into psychiatrists, but it will certainly make it easy for judges to recognize whether a psychiatric opinion should be requested and how it should be used in reaching judgment. Certainly in some cases deep understanding will hardly make the decision of the judge easy, e.g. in a case of arson motivated by homesickness, for it can hardly be disposed of without punishment.[66]

This reaction of a student training to become a juvenile court judge attests to the inculcation of a certain judicial style in juvenile justice: juvenile court judges were expected to be solicitous of the emotional weaknesses and handicaps of problem adolescents and to cooperate in their courtrooms with psychiatrists, but when confronted with serious criminal offenses, whatever the cause, they remained committed to the traditional notion of criminal responsibility.

Forensic Psychiatrists and the Suasion of the Rule of Law

In spite of their initial hostility to the 1923 Juvenile Justice Act's limit on their influence, forensic psychiatrists came to reconcile themselves partially to the resistance of juvenile court judges. This attitude was dictated in large part by professional interest. To remain relevant in the juvenile courtroom, it was not unusual for psychiatrists to formulate their roles in juvenile court in a restrictive manner. Heinrich Vogt, who conducted the first psychiatric examinations in the Frankfurt juvenile court system, expressed his respect for the "free discretion of the judge" to heed or reject his medical opinion and emphatically confined the role of the psychiatrist to that of "advisor" (*Ratgeber*) to the juvenile court judge.[67] Many other psychiatrists who were active in juvenile court proceedings made similar public professions of deference to judicial authority.[68] Moreover, co-optation of forensic medicine was not all that difficult. For all of its pretensions to scientific rigor, it clothed bourgeois moral values in scientific terms. Indeed, what I find rather remarkable is the dispassionate approach of these forensic psychiatrists to healing. Although they never disavowed interest in healing, it was never at the center of their concerns. In my research, I have found only one psychiatrist who expressed the task of forensic psychiatry in humanitarian terms—in this specific instance, to serve the "humanization of adjudication."[69] Thus it is not surprising that forensic psychiatry tended to generate outcomes that were acceptable to the judiciary of the juvenile justice system. In cases involving serious offenses such as homicide or even automobile theft, forensic psychiatrists often negated any suspicion of mental incompetence on the part of juvenile defendants, even if they showed serious signs of personality disorder. This made it easy for juvenile court judges to endorse their opinions.[70] In line with the philosophy of modern criminal law reform, with its emphasis on "social defense," forensic psychiatry essentially defended conventional norms against socially unacceptable transgressions. Forensic psychiatrists were able to accommodate this subordination of their role in the juvenile courtroom by focusing their activity increasingly on the juvenile prison.

Finally, without wanting to indulge in overstatement, I would suggest that an influential circle of psychiatrists started to have second thoughts about two issues: the wholesale pathologization of the juvenile delinquent and the role of the forensic psychiatrist in the juvenile courtroom. In the first place, the resuscitation in some circles of the so-called born criminal caused unease among many participants in juvenile justice. Herbert Francke, the preeminent juvenile court judge in the Weimar Republic, emphatically dismissed the notion in his 1926 study of juvenile deviance.[71] The challenge posed by this redirection in approach to juvenile delinquency prompted a special commission of the DVJJ calling itself "Juvenile Court and Physician" (not to be confused with the 1920 subcommittee of the DJGT under the same name) to convene two meetings of experts in Berlin in March 1928 and in Dresden in June 1930 to discuss the "significance of predisposition in crime"—in shorthand, the question of the born criminal. Several of the most important figures in German juvenile justice debated the existence of hereditary juvenile criminality. Without a doubt, the lawyers among them were uncomfortable with this trend, but they were not alone. The vast majority of the psychiatrists who attended these sessions, including Eduard Hapke, who opened the first meeting and closed the second, and Franz Kramer, a distinguished forensic psychiatrist active in the juvenile justice system, cast doubt on the validity of the born criminal and, notwithstanding the undisputed significance of the role of personality in criminality, still considered the nature of the interaction of personal traits and environmental influences in the formation of juvenile deviance unsettled. After two meetings the conferees failed to clarify the causes of juvenile criminality, but one implicit outcome of the proceedings was to marginalize the idea of the born criminal.[72]

The suasion of rule-of-law habits on forensic psychiatry is compellingly illustrated in a report by Kramer that was prepared for his appearance in 1927 before the Reichstag judiciary commission that was conducting hearings on the joint proposal by the Socialists and the Communists to raise the age of criminal responsibility and the age of limited criminal liability. Kramer wrote:

> There are . . . without a doubt many offenses that do not suggest a danger of future delinquency at all, but must be confronted nonetheless. If we have only rehabilitative remedies at our disposal in combating these offenses, there could, in my opinion, exist the danger that rehabilitative measures overshoot the mark of what is necessary in an individual case. . . . The following point appears significant to me as well: Criminal proceedings afford the juvenile rights that he does not possess in rehabilitative proceedings [in civil guardianship court]. The clarification of questionable facts is significantly enhanced by the formalities of criminal proceedings.[73]

He later concluded his actual testimony to the commission with an exhortation to maintain "sufficient optimism to introduce a legislative epoch."[74] This remarkable testimony by a leading forensic psychiatrist was tantamount to an admonition to the parliamentary guardians of the *Rechtsstaat* to resist the pressure—or the temptation—to pathologize juvenile justice lest it forfeit its rule-of-law heritage altogether.

Conclusion

In the final analysis, the narrative of the alliance between forensic psychiatry and Wilhelmine and Weimar juvenile justice is a contrapuntal one of integration and fragmentation: forensic psychiatry made significant inroads into the juvenile justice system, but its aspirations to centrality were constrained by the competing claim of judicial authority. Juvenile court judges were encouraged to cooperate with doctors, but they were averse to relinquishing their authority to them in wholesale fashion because of their commitment to the idea of criminal responsibility and—this is what is unexpected—to the autonomous integrity of the individual, even when that individual, in this case the juvenile offender, was a member of a socially marginal group. Without a doubt, the law made important concessions to forensic psychiatry, but it still held sufficient sway to circumscribe the psychiatric profession's more ominous and promiscuous potentialities, in large part by appropriating the tools of psychiatric professionalism.

This unexpected fate of forensic psychiatry in Wilhelmine and Weimar juvenile justice has implications for the historiographical treatment of pre-1933 German criminal justice in general. Richard Wetzell has argued that the readiness of penal reformers around Franz von Liszt to curtail the legal rights of defendants in the interests of social defense paved the way for an alliance of forensic medicine and state power that "made possible the transformation of the traditionally antagonistic relationship between law and psychiatry into the symbiotic one that came to be the hallmark of criminal justice in the age of criminology."[75] Although Wetzell's argument should apply to German juvenile justice, I have tried to show that German juvenile justice before 1933, with all of its contradictions, ultimately becomes intelligible only if we take into account not only the convergence but also the collision of forensic psychiatry and a liberal commitment to the rule-of-law tradition. Although forensic psychiatry, with its ominously imaginative theories and diagnoses, insinuated itself into juvenile justice and was sustained by the hygienic vision of German society endorsed by penal reform, it was nonetheless forced in the juvenile justice system to contend with and accommodate different holdover habits and values in support of certain guarantees promised by law, even if the implementation of these habits and values was increasingly threatened by erosion.

Notes

1. Herbert Francke, "Juvenile Courts in Germany," *Sociology and Social Research* 16 (1932), 408.
2. See Jörg Wolff and Christine Dörner, "Jugendstrafrecht zwischen Weimar und Nationalsozialismus," *Recht der Jugend und des Bildungswesens* 38 (1990), 55.

3. David Crew, "The Ambiguities of Modernity: Welfare and the German State from Wilhelm to Hitler," in *Society, Culture, and the State in Germany, 1870–1930*, ed. Geoff Eley (Ann Arbor, 1996), 326.

4. Siegfried Kracauer, "The Murder Trial and Society," in *The Weimar Republic Sourcebook*, ed. Anton Kies, Martin Jay, and Edward Dimendberg (Berkeley, 1994), 741.

5. For articulation of this aspiration by a forensic psychiatrist, see W[ilhelm] Fürstenheim to Frankfurt Juvenile Court, 18 August 1926, Geheimes Staatsarchiv Preußischer Kulturbesitz, Berlin-Dahlem (GStA) Rep. 84a, no. 1032, 109.

6. Wilhelm Kiesow, *Das Jugendgerichts-Gesetz vom 16. Februar 1923* (Mannheim, Berlin, and Leipzig, 1923), xxxiii.

7. Jan Goldstein, "Framing Discipline with Law: Problems and Promises of the Liberal State," *American Historical Review* 98 (1993), 364–381.

8. On the development of social prophylaxis in German psychiatry, see Eric J. Engstrom, *Clinical Psychiatry in Imperial Germany: A History of Psychiatric Practice* (Ithaca and London, 2003), chap. 7.

9. Richard F. Wetzell, *Inventing the Criminal: A History of German Criminology, 1880–1945* (Chapel Hill, 2000).

10. On the co-production of scientific knowledge and normative prescriptions, see Sheila Jasanoff, ed., *States of Knowledge: The Co-Production of Science and Social Order* (London and New York, 2004).

11. Wetzell, *Inventing the Criminal*, 145.

12. Adalbert Gregor and Else Voigtländer, *Die Verwahrlosung: Ihre klinisch-psychologische Bewertung und ihre Bekämpfung* (Berlin, 1918), 61, 153.

13. Ibid., 218–219, 475–476

14. Ibid., 194–212.

15. Ibid., 231.

16. Ibid., 4–5.

17. Ibid., 146–149.

18. See Wetzell, *Inventing the Criminal*, 147.

19. A[dalbert] Gregor, "Wie ist die Erziehung Schwersterziehbarer zu gestalten in bezug auf Fürsorgeerziehung?" *Zeitschrift für Kinderforschung* (*ZKF*) 37 (1930), 153–161.

20. On the integral function of procedural rules in the Imperial *Rechtsstaat*, see Kenneth F. Ledford, "Lawyers, Liberalism, and Procedure: The German Imperial Justice Laws of 1877–79," *Central European History* 26 (1993), 171–172.

21. See the remarks of Franz Kramer in *Kreistagung der Deutschen Jugendgerichtshilfen (4. Deutscher Jugendgerichtstag) am 12., 13., und 14. April 1917 zu Berlin* (Berlin, 1918), 116–117.

22. Paul Köhne, "Das Strafverfahren gegen Jugendliche," in *Reform des Strafprozesses: Kritische Besprechungen der von der Kommission für die Reform des Strafprozesses gemachten Vorschlägen*, ed. P[aul] F[elix] Aschrott (Berlin, 1906), 627.

23. Idem, "Über Jugendgerichte," speech to the twelfth Landesversammlung der Landesgruppe Deutsches Reich at Posen in 1908, *Mitteilungen der internationalen kriminalistischen Vereinigung* (*MIKV*) 15 (1908), 545.

24. Idem, "Die Tätigkeit des Jugendgerichts Berlin-Mitte im Jahre 1910," *Deutsche Juristenzeitung* 16 (1911), 627–628; see also idem, "Die Mitwirkung der Ärzte bei den Jugendgerichten," *Zentralblatt für Vormundschaftswesen, Jugendgerichte und Fürsorgeerziehung* (*ZblVorm*) 4 (1912–1913), 212.

25. Idem, "Mitwirkung der Ärzte," 212.

26. Idem, "Tätigkeit des Jugendgerichts Berlin-Mitte," 627. For the expression of similar sentiments by another early Berlin juvenile court judge, see L. Fischer, speech, *Verhandlungen des 1. Deutschen Jugendgerichtstages 15. bis 17. März 1909* (Berlin and Leipzig, 1909), 34; idem,

"Die Tätigkeit des Jugendgerichts vor, in und nach der Hauptverhandlung," *Monatsschrift für Kriminalpsychologie und Strafrechtsreform* (*MKPStR*) 6 (1909–1910), 326–327.

27. This figure is available in the petition of the Union of Medical Experts at the Juvenile Court of Central Berlin (Vereinigung ärztlicher Sachverständiger am Jugendgericht Berlin-Mitte) to the Reichstag, January 1913, Bundesarchiv Berlin-Lichterfelde (BABrlL) Rep. 30.01, no. 5573, 95.

28. Kammergerichtspräsident und Oberstaatsanwalt bei dem Königslichen Kammergericht to Prussian Justice Minister, 22 November 1917, GStA Rep. 84a, no. 1030, 219.

29. L. Jacobsohn to Prussian Justice Ministry, no date [October 1917], GStA Rep. 84a, no. 1030, 217.

30. See, e.g., the regulations of the Bavarian and Saxon justice ministries in the appendix to "Bericht der 13. Kommission über den Entwurf eines Gesetzes über das Verfahren gegen Jugendliche," in *Stenographische Berichte über die Verhandlungen des Reichstags*, 13. Legislaturperiode, 1. Session, vol. 302, Aktenstück Nr. 1054, 1800, 1803.

31. Karl Allmenröder, "Die Tätigkeit des Frankfurter Jugendrichters," in *Das Jugendgericht in Frankfurt a. M.*, ed. Berthold Freudenthal (Berlin, 1912), 9; Ludwig Becker, "Die Tätigkeit des Staatsanwaltes," in ibid., 25; H[einrich] Vogt, "Die Tätigkeit des ärztlichen Gutachters beim Jugendgericht," in ibid., 87.

32. Amtsgerichtsrat [Paul] Levi via Amtsgerichtsdirektor to Landesgerichtspräsident in Frankfurt am Main, 19 August 1926, GStA Rep. 84a, no. 1032, 103; Wilhelm Fürstenheim to the Frankfurt Juvenile Court, 18 August 1926, GStA Rep. 84a, no. 1032, 108–109.

33. Vogt, "Die Tätigkeit des ärztlichen Gutachters," 94.

34. On the collaboration between forensic psychiatry and the youth welfare bureaucracy in juvenile court, see Anna Schultz, "Aus der Praxis der Jugendgerichte und der privaten Jugendgerichtshilfe," *MKPStR* 6 (1909–1910), 574–577; Immanuel Fischer, "Die erzieherische Tätigkeit des Jugendgerichtshelfers," in *Die erzieherische Beeinflussung straffälliger Jugendlicher: Referate der Tagung der Vereinigung für Jugendgerichte und Jugendgerichtshilfen am 11. und 12. Juni 1926 zu Göttingen* (Berlin, 1927), 46–47; Franz Kramer, *Die Mitwirkung des Psychiaters im Vormundschafts- und Jugendgerichtsverfahren* (Berlin, 1931); Karl Tilman Winkler, "Reformers United: The American and German Juvenile Court, 1882–1923," in *Institutions of Confinement: Hospitals and Prisons in Western Europe and North America, 1500–1950*, ed. Norbert Finzsch and Robert Jütte (Cambridge, 1996), 270.

35. Stein, "Ueber Jugendgerichte," speech, "Verhandlungen der 9. Tagung der Deutschen Gesellschaft für gerichtliche Medizin," in *Vierteljahresschrift für gerichtliche Medizin und öffentliches Sanitätswesen* (3. Folge) 47 (Supplement-Heft) (1914), 298.

36. See the series of exchanges in Amtsgerichtspräsident to Kammergerichtspräsident, 24 April 1917, Rep. 84a, no. 1030, 204; Prussian Justice Minister to Kammergerichtspräsident und Oberstaatsanwalt beim Kammergericht, 22 June 1917, Rep. 84a, no. 1030, 212; Prussian Justice Minister to Kammergerichtspräsident und Oberstaatsanwalt beim Kammergericht, 31 December 1917, Rep. 84a, no. 1030, 225; juvenile court judges Lindhorst, Karwinkel, Herr, and Langer to Amtsgerichtspräsident, 14 June 1918, GStA Rep. 84a, no. 1030, 223; Kammergerichtspräsident and Oberstaatsanwalt beim Kammergericht to Prussian Justice Minister, 15 August 1918, GStA Rep. 84a, no. 1030, 231–232.

37. Amtsgerichtsrat [Paul] Levy via Amtsgerichtsdirektor to Landesgerichtspräsident in Frankfurt am Main, 19 August 1926, GStA Rep. 84a, no. 1032, 103.

38. See press reports of such lectures in "Die Jugend auf der Anklagebank," *Der Tag*, 5 November 1909, GStA Rep. 84a, no. 10724, n.p.; "Die sittliche Reife jugendlicher Angeklagter," *Der Tag*, 16 February 1912, GStA Rep. 84a, no. 10724, n.p.

39. Petition of the Union of Medical Experts at the Juvenile Court of Central Berlin to the Reichstag, January 1913, BABrlL Rep. 30.01, no. 5573, 94–97. For a psychiatrist's public advocacy

of the petition, see L. Jacobsohn, "Zum Strafverfahren gegen Jugendliche," *Vossische Zeitung*, 20 December 1912, GStA Rep. 84a, no. 10724, n.p.

40. *Die Verhandlungen des 5. Jugendgerichtstages in Jena 1920* (Berlin, 1922), 63, 75.
41. Unpublished transcript of the fourth session of the 21. Ausschuß (Reichsstrafgesetzbuch), 11 October 1928, GStA Rep. 84a, no. 8445, 29.
42. "Begründung zum Entwurf eines Jugendgerichtsgesetzes," 24 October 1922, in *Stenographische Berichte über die Verhandlungen des Reichstags*, vol. 375, Drucksache Nr. 5171, 10–11 (§§ 5, 6).
43. See, e.g., the criticism of the dean of German forensic psychiatry, Gustav Aschaffenburg, "Der Jugendgerichtsarzt," speech, in *Die Durchführung des Jugendgerichtsgesetzes als Personenfrage: Bericht über die Verhandlungen des 7. Deutschen Jugendgerichtstages* (Berlin, 1928), 107–108.
44. Dürhen, "Die erzieherische Tätigkeit des Jugendrichters," in *Die erzieherische Beeinflussung straffälliger Jugendlicher*, 42.
45. Herbert Francke, "Erziehungsgedanke im Jugendgerichtsgesetz," in *Der Erziehungsgedanke im modernen Jugendrecht: Vorträge des 1. Rheinischen Fortbildungskursus für Jugend- und Vormundschaftsrichter, Jugendstaatsanwälte und Jugendstrafvollzugsbeamte*, ed. Ludwig Clostermann (Düsseldorf, 1927), 41.
46. Albert Hellwig, *Jugendgerichtsgesetz* (Berlin, 1923), 29.
47. Herbert Francke, *Das Jugendgerichtsgesetz von 16. Februar 1923*, 2nd ed. (Berlin and Munich, 1926), 42–43.
48. Kiesow, *Jugendgerichts-Gesetz*, 54.
49. Bruno Müller, "Die praktische Handhabung des deutschen Jugendgerichtsgesetzes," speech, in *Verhandlungen des 6. Deutschen Jugendgerichtstages Heidelberg 17.-19. September 1924* (Berlin, 1925), 15; see also idem, "Das Jugendgerichtsgesetz in der Praxis des Hamburger Jugendgerichts" (unpublished manuscript), BABrlL Rep. 30.01, no. 5568, 83 (19). For a similar contemporary gloss on the act by Herbert Francke using the terminology "gravity of the case" (*Schwere des Falles*), see Herbert Francke, "Denkschrift zum § 4 des Entwurfes eines Jugendgerichtsgesetzes," 25 September 1922, GStA Rep. 84a, no. 1031, 35–36.
50. Franz Streng, "Erziehungsgedanke im Jugendstrafrecht: Überlegungen zum Ideologiecharakter und zu den Perspektiven eines multifunktionalen Systembegriffs," *Zeitschrift für die gesamte Strafrechtswissenschaft* (*ZStW*) 106 (1994), 76–78.
51. Francke, "Erziehungsgedanke im Jugendstrafrecht," 39–40.
52. This concerted effort to co-opt psychiatry in juvenile court is reminiscent of the contemporaneous demand by the Prussian Judges Association to assume control over *Gerichtshilfe* (court assistance), which Warren Rosenblum describes in his chapter in this volume.
53. See the speeches by Linz, Mittermaier, Schulze, and Liepmann in *MIKV* (Neue Folge) 1 (1926), 22, 34, 45, 50.
54. Walter Hoffmann, *Die Reifezeit: Probleme der Entwicklungspsychologie und Sozialpädagogik* (Leipzig, 1922).
55. "Entschließung I," in *Verhandlungen des 6. Deutschen Jugendgerichtstages*, 57; "Entschließung I," in *Die Durchführung des Jugendgerichtsgesetzes als Personenfrage: Bericht über die Verhandlungen des 7. Deutschen Jugendgerichtstages*, 127–128.
56. Reports from many of these seminars were published in *Zentralblatt für Jugendrecht und Jugendwohlfahrt* (*ZblJugR*). See, e.g., Herbert Francke, "Psychologisch-pädagogische Fortbildung von Richtern und Staatsanwälten in Jugendsachen: Sonderkursus der Vereinigung für Jugendgerichtshilfen in Berlin," *ZblJugR* 17 (1925–1926), 113–114; Bahnson, "Jugendrichtertag in Hamburg," *ZblJugR* 18 (1926–1927),133–134; Ludwig Clostermann und Stoffregen, "Zwei Fortbildungskurse für Jugendrichter und Jugendstaatsanwälte," *ZblJugR* 19 (1927–1928), 76–79; Daus, "Fortbildungskurs für Jugendrichter und Jugendstaatsanwälte," *ZblJugR* 20 (1928–1929), 77–78. The Bonn lectures were published in *Der Erziehungsgedanke im modernen Jugendrecht: Vorträge des ersten Rheinischen Fortbildungskursus für Jugend- und*

Vormundschaftrichter, Jugendstaatsanwälte und Jugendstrafvollzugsbeamte, ed. Ludwig Clostermann (Düsseldorf, 1927).

57. Lectures from two of these conferences were published. See *Die erzieherische Beeinflussung straffälliger Jugendlicher: Referate der Tagung der Vereinigung für Jugendgerichte und Jugendgerichtshilfen am 11. und 12. Juni 1926 zu Göttingen* (Berlin, 1927); Max Grünhut and Bruno Müller, *Zwei Vorträge über Jugendgerichtsbarkeit vor thüringischen Jugendrichtern und Jugendstaatsanwälten in Eisenach am 21. März 1927* (n.p., n.d. [1927]).

58. On the 1929 course, see Hans Steinlitz, "Ein Sonderlehrgang für Jugendrichter and Jugendstaatsanwälte," *ZblJugR* 22 (1930–1931), 317–320; on the 1930 course, see Lührse, "Der zweite Jugendrichter-Kursus in Berlin," *ZblJugR* 23 (1931–1932), 69–73.

59. Both lectures were published. His Hamburg lecture appears in Herman Nohl, "Zum psychologischen Verständnis der Tat," in *Jugendwohlfahrt* (Leipzig, 1927), 55–70; the Göttingen lecture appears in "Gedanken für die Erziehungstätigkeit mit besonderen Berücksichtigung der Erfahrungen von Freud und Adler," ibid., 71–83. A summary of his Hamburg lecture is available in Bahnson, "Jugendrichtertag in Hamburg," 133. The Göttingen lecture appeared originally in *Die erzieherische Beeinflussung straffälliger Jugendlicher*, 3–16. References to these lectures here are from *Jugendwohlfahrt*.

60. Nohl, "Gedanken für die Erziehungstätigkeit," 74.

61. Idem, "Zum psychologischen Verständnis der Tat," 56.

62. Idem, "Gedanken für die Erziehungstätigkeit," 73.

63. Idem, "Zum psychologischen Verständnis der Tat," 58–69.

64. Ibid., 57.

65. Idem, "Gedanken für die Erziehungstätigkeit," 82–83.

66. Bahnson, "Jugendrichtertag in Hamburg," 133.

67. Vogt, "Die Tätigkeit des ärztlichen Gutachters," 91, 125, 128.

68. See the speeches of Anton and Dühring, respectively, in *Kriegstagung der Deutschen Jugendgerichtshilfen*, 122, 125.

69. Düring, speech, in *Kriegstagung der Deutschen Jugendgerichtshilfen*, 126.

70. See the printed judgments of Weimar juvenile court judges in "Psychiatrische Gutachten über kriminelle Jugendliche (Minderjährige) und jugendliche Zeugen," *ZKF* 38 (1931), 390–391, 402–403, 408–409; Ludwig Closterman, "Urteil des Jugendgerichts N.," *ZKF* 39 (1932), 171–175; Werner Villinger, "Psychiatrische Begutachtung zweier jugendlicher Mörder," *ZKF* 42 (1934), 415–418.

71. Herbert Francke, *Jugendverwahrlosung und ihre Bekämpfung* (Berlin, 1926), 14–15. See also idem, "Der Erziehungsgedanke im Jugendstrafrecht," 50–51.

72. Reports of the two meetings are available in "Bericht über die Sachverständigenkonferenz der Deutschen Vereinigung für Jugendgerichte und Jugendgerichtshilfen," *ZKF* 34 (1928), 631–645 and "Sachverständigen-Konferenzen des Deutchen Vereins zur Fürsorge für jugendliche Psychopathen und der Vereinigung für Jugendgerichte und Jugendgerichtshilfen, Dresden, 6./7. Juni 1930" *ZKF* 37 (1930), 112–130. For papers delivered at the Dresden conference, see ibid., 131–412.

73. Franz Kramer, "Jugendzeit und Strafmündigkeit," *ZblJugR* 19 (1927–1928), 3, 230–231.

74. See the unpublished transcript of the fourth session of the 21. Ausschuss (Reichsstrafgesetzbuch), 11 October 1928, GStA Rep. 84a, no. 8445, 30.

75. Richard F. Wetzell, "The Medicalization of Criminal Law Reform in Imperial Germany," in *Institutions of Confinement*, ed. Finzsch and Jütte, 282–283.

Chapter 6

WELFARE AND JUSTICE
The Battle over *Gerichtshilfe* in the Weimar Republic

Warren Rosenblum

Soziale Gerichtshilfe was a pivotal institution in Weimar visions of criminal policy reform. Started in Bielefeld by a coalition of reformers, *Gerichtshilfe* was a vehicle for introducing social knowledge and technologies into criminal justice. Under *Gerichtshilfe*, welfare auxiliaries known as "court assistants" (*Gerichtshelfer*) produced a "comprehensive portrait" of accused offenders and their milieux. Their sources included interviews with the accused and his or her family, friends, employers, teachers, and clergy. The court assistants might also examine records and files from welfare associations, government agencies, and perhaps medical and psychological examinations. This material was then distilled into a social diagnosis and prognosis that could be used for sentencing and pardoning decisions and provided the guidelines for probation or parole. In some cases, the court assistants themselves supervised the offenders after their return to society.

Promising to build a bridge between the worlds of justice and welfare, *Gerichtshilfe* caught the imagination of reformers in both realms. The enthusiasm for this institution reflected a broad consensus in the early Weimar Republic that criminal policy must do more than simply enforce the law and protect society: it must actively contribute to producing disciplined and productive citizens. Justice, it was argued, required an apparatus to evaluate and sort the varieties of "human material" in relation to their social context. As one reformer wrote, "treating the criminal according to his type" was now recognized as the "essential task [of criminal justice], beginning with the first investigation of a crime and ending only when the criminal—so far as possible—is placed into ordered society."[1]

The success of *Gerichtshilfe*, however, opened up a set of difficult questions about who should control the social investigation of criminals and how social knowledge should be used in criminal justice. Judges and states' attorneys argued

---

Notes from this chapter begin on page 177.

that *Gerichtshilfe* should be placed under the authority of the prosecutor's office. The function of the court assistants, in their view, was to provide raw data to the prosecutors about the social world of the accused. They stressed that *Gerichtshilfe* was not about advice or aid to the accused, but first and foremost about assistance *to the court*. This vision of *Gerichtshilfe* was emphatically rejected by the proponents of public welfare. Thus Prussian state welfare officials argued that *Gerichtshilfe* should perform a wide range of independent welfare tasks under the administration of city welfare offices. For some members of the left, even for some within the Prussian government, *Gerichtshilfe* raised hopes of a fundamental transformation of justice: piercing and eventually dismantling the walls that separated justice from social policy. A third perspective on *Gerichtshilfe* was represented by private prison societies and associations for prisoner and ex-prisoner welfare. In the early years of the Republic, these charitable associations sought a compromise position between the judges and the public welfare officials. Although they recognized many of their own traditional ideals in the demands of public welfare advocates, the advocates of private charity feared the consequences of state control over penal welfare, especially with the socialists in control of the Prussian state government.

Eventually, the concerns of the judges and the charitable associations converged around the fear that state-controlled *Gerichtshilfe* would undermine the integrity and the severity of justice. Welfare assistance, it was feared, would become a *right* for all criminals, rather than a *privilege* reserved for the repentant and morally deserving minority of offenders. The possibility that justice could be submerged in social policy—that punishment could be dissolved into welfare—seemed very real to conservatives at the end of the Republic. For Prussian judges and Protestant charities, *Gerichtshilfe* was a battleground in the struggle to rein in and contain a dangerous trend in reform.

This essay tells the story of *Gerichtshilfe*, from its origins in the Bielefeld System during World War I to the crisis that engulfed it in the latter years of the Weimar Republic. Following the trajectory of this institution, one can track both interwar Germany's consensus in favor of a social approach to criminal justice and the origins of a conflict, as a domain of social intervention was mapped out and brought into practice. In the last years of the Weimar Republic, disagreements over *Gerichtshilfe* animated the leading law and welfare reform societies, political parties, and the press. Ultimately the debate over this once-obscure institution helped define two irreconcilable visions of social order.

"Justice and Charity Kiss": The Origins of the Bielefeld System during World War I

The origins of *Gerichtshilfe* lay at the confluence of diverse streams in German social reform. Christian charitable organizations, progressive jurists, socialists, and feminists all contributed to the making of *Gerichtshilfe*. The Weimar officials who promoted the institution were usually students of the so-called modern school of criminal law reform, which emerged under the leadership of legal scholar Franz von Liszt in the last decades of the previous century. By contrast, the men and women who established *Gerichtshilfe* agencies in towns and cities across Germany were more likely to be disciples of the Christian social reform movement or professional welfare workers, committed to the expansion of social rights to the underclass. So many groups put their stamp on *Gerichtshilfe*, it is perhaps not surprising that ownership of the institution would soon be a subject of lively dispute.[2]

The father of *Gerichtshilfe*, Judge Alfred Bozi, was a reformer with wide-ranging interests and an extraordinarily large network of contacts. Bozi was the scion of a leading Westphalian textile family and the author of numerous essays on civil law, legal reform, and the role of the judiciary in Imperial Germany. During World War I, Bozi formed a Committee for the Discussion of Social Issues, along with his fellow Bielefelder and friend, socialist leader Carl Severing. The committee included employers and union leaders, teachers, and doctors, and also representatives from the nearby Bethel Asylum, a famous facility led until 1911 by the great Christian social reformer Pastor Friedrich von Bodelschwingh and thereafter administered by his son. While the Bielefeld Committee addressed issues such as labor relations, crime, and prostitution on a local level, Bozi worked on questions of national reform with the Society for Social Law, an organization that he had helped to establish a few years before the war.[3]

In 1915, the Bielefeld Committee spawned the forerunner to *Gerichtshilfe*, the Bielefeld System for the regulation of vagrants and beggars. According to the penal code, such "vagabonds" were sentenced to a few months in prison and then transferred to the state police at the discretion of the presiding judge. The police then incarcerated the offenders for up to two years in a workhouse or placed them under police supervision, in which case they were required to accept certain conditions for their freedom, including possible police visits at their home or workplace.

The Bielefeld System introduced alternative measures for these offenders. It was essentially an arrangement between the Bielefeld City Court, the Bielefeld Prison Association, and the Bethel Asylum. Members of the prison association were called to the court whenever defendants stood accused of vagabondage. These volunteers then investigated whether particular vagabonds could be deemed adult children, that is, persons "incapable of supporting themselves through consistent, orderly labor, because of their weakness of will." The so-called adult children were then given the option of placing themselves under protective supervision (*Schutzaufsicht*) at the worker colony at Bethel, rather than being transferred to the custody of the police. The offenders were required to stay at Bethel for a defined period, not to exceed two years, with the threat of the police workhouse looming over them if they transgressed the asylum's rules and regulations.[4]

The worker colony at Bethel was considered a more humane environment than the police workhouse, but it would be wrong to see this reform principally as an attempt to ameliorate the condition of the vagabonds. The Bielefelders turned to Bethel because of the Christian reformers' supposed expertise in categorizing and treating socially marginal, criminally at-risk individuals. "Father Bodelschwingh" had created the worker colony as a "port of security for all of those small crafts damaged on the high seas . . . who needed long and basic repairs."[5] The colony offered hot meals, a structured environment, and hard, physical, productive labor, usually outdoors. Such work, according to Bodelschwingh, was both the "ancient touchstone" of men's character and a lever for moral improvement. Those who survived two years in the colony had supposedly proven themselves ready and deserving of full participation in society.

Since its inception in 1884, the worker colony primarily took in wayfarers who came of their own accord. The Bielefeld System gave Bethel a new form of coercive power over some of its charges. The individuals convicted of vagrancy or begging still officially entered the worker colony by choice, but the threat of the police workhouse was obviously a strong incentive. Once they arrived at Bethel, the possibility of being cited for rule-breaking—and therefore being sent to the police—was a Sword of Damocles hanging over the offenders' heads. If they were transferred to police custody, they could be subject to the full two-year workhouse sentence, regardless of how much time they had already spent under protective supervision at Bethel. According to Bozi, the Bielefeld System actually expanded the net of social control in Bielefeld. Due to the notoriety of the workhouses, the courts had previously been reluctant to transfer any but the most hardened offenders to the police. Under the Bielefeld System, scores of petty offenders who would previously have been freed after a few weeks in prison were now essentially placed under the authority of a welfare organization for up to two years.[6]

The Bielefeld System was embraced by the wartime Prussian state government as a way to modernize the fight against vagabondage. German officials believed that the coming peace (and peace was always "around the corner") would bring a flood of vagrants comparable to previous postwar demobilizations. Meanwhile, as the Great War dragged on, there was increasing public dissatisfaction with the workhouse. Critics pointed to the high cost of incarceration and the wasted labor power at a time when workers and soldiers were desperately needed for the war effort. The director of the Prussian Department of Prisons, Karl Finkelnburg, told the head of Bethel that he "welcomed any measure leading to limitations upon corrective custody."[7]

Late in 1916, the Bielefeld reformers adapted the principles of their system to aid in the fight against "sexual immorality." The city's female police assistant recruited female volunteers to investigate women accused of unlicensed prostitution or violations of the police codes on venal sex. These welfare advisers helped determine whether the accused would benefit from protective supervision. As with vagrants and beggars, the judge could then force women offenders to accept protective supervision as a condition for avoiding the workhouse. In this case, however, protective supervision included a range of possible measures. Only the most "depraved" women were sent to enclosed institutions comparable to the worker colonies. Most were sent to urban halfway houses or were supervised at home and encouraged to seek employment in industry or domestic labor. Others were allowed to live with their own families, but remained subject to visits by supervisors and restrictions on their lifestyle. Overall, as was the case with the vagabonds, the Bielefeld System helped increase the number of women subjected to supervision, even as fewer women were sent to the workhouse. Welfare again offered a gentler form of supervision, but cast a far wider net—and the police power was still there, in case women offenders failed to meet the demands of their welfare overseers.[8]

For Bozi, the most significant result of these measures was mobilizing a diverse group of individuals and organizations to work with the courts in regulating women's behavior. In implementing the Bielefeld System and propagating its spread, Bozi collaborated with prominent moral reformers such as Pastor Friedrich Onnasch of Berlin and Pastor Walter Thieme of Frankfurt, as well as advocates of women's social and political equality such as Anna Pappritz and Margarethe Bennewitz.[9] At the end of 1918, Bozi brought together a remarkably diverse group of reformers in a movement to harness women's "particular sensibilities" on behalf of criminal justice. For a brief moment, radical feminists and arch-conservatives were united in an effort to make women's special skills and knowledge available to judges. In Bozi's view, such participation was key to his larger vision of constructing a bridge "between the social and the juridical."[10]

In the long run, Bozi's reform coalitions in the city of Bielefeld and across the Reich could not be sustained.[11] Nevertheless, the energies that produced the Bielefeld System inspired the belief that the "New Germany" emerging from the crucible of war could and should develop new forms of social control. Left, right, and center agreed that welfare supervision, built upon the broadest possible forms of popular participation, was vital to establishing domestic security and maximizing the productive labor power that resided in the *Volk*.[12]

The next logical step for Bozi was to expand the Bielefeld System to all categories of criminals, including felons. He wanted welfare organizations to advise the courts on whether to recommend a conditional pardon for convicted offenders and to arrange protective supervision for the period of their probation. The ultimate decision on the pardon would be made by the state penal authorities. The worker colony at Bethel was expected to play a key role in housing the offenders and in guaranteeing the integrity and reliability of the system.

The war seemed an opportune time for such reform. State administrators were using the pardon power liberally but unsystematically to address a pair of dilemmas. First, the state needed laborers and, of course, soldiers for the war effort. According to German law, however, anyone who served time in a penitentiary (*Zuchthaus*) was stripped of the privilege of serving in the Emperor's army. If a sentence could be reduced from the penitentiary to prison (*Gefängnis*) or, better yet, suspended in its entirety, then a potential soldier was saved. Meanwhile, the state could deflect mounting public criticism concerning the cost of incarceration and the shirkers who allegedly enjoyed warm rooms and hot meals while the best and bravest fought and suffered at the front. Another source of headaches for the Prussian state involved the thousands of ordinary, otherwise law-abiding Germans who faced prison terms due to the growing number of "war-related offenses" added to the books. The pardons given to such "normal" citizens had become important for addressing the popular sense of fairness and the public's support for the legal system.[13]

Bozi's reform promised to rationalize the granting of pardons—a "horribly ceremonious process" of dubious juridical legitimacy. An element of arbitrariness clung to the pardon almost by definition. The pardon (*Gnade*) was an act of mercy in which the sovereign power intervened in the machinery of justice. Historically, mercy might arrive for no reason beyond the king's celebration of a birthday or wedding, and it could be denied without any explanation at all. In more recent times, mercy was bureaucratized and, at least in principle, dispensed with an eye toward individual justice and public concerns with fairness. Bozi and others sought to give the pardon a social meaning and justification and a firmer legal foundation.[14]

In trying to expand the Bielefeld System to ordinary criminals, Bozi faced new obstacles. Pastor Bodelschwingh of Bethel worried that taking in large numbers of convicted felons would transform the character of his worker colony. His fellow directors from other colonies were even more skeptical toward Bozi's proposal. They had no trouble seeing vagabonds and prostitutes as hybrid penal-welfare subjects, as these groups were traditionally objects of both juridical regulation and administrative measures, including police, medical, and welfare intervention. By definition, the so-called adult children were not taken to be fully responsible for their actions. Felons, on the other hand, were presumed to be fully responsible for their crimes and thus subject to retributive measures that were the exclusive task of the state. It was asked whether welfare had *any* role to play in treating criminals until after the punishment was finished.

Bozi's most significant obstacle, however, was the law itself and the German tradition of granting judges relatively little discretion in sentencing. Bozi believed that judges should be "bound by the law, but only as a natural scientist works with received principles which are constantly extended and refined on the basis of methodical experience."[15] The dominant school of jurisprudence in Imperial Germany started with very different assumptions. Judges were taught to ignore the social particularities of a criminal case and to follow "the naked letter of the law." That law was built essentially upon principles of retribution and deterrence: the judge's first and essential duty was to uphold the majesty of justice by punishing the criminal act. There was no place for cost-benefit analysis or other pragmatic considerations based on empirical observation. The war was an ally for pragmatists like Bozi, who argued that criminal justice must change to meet the desperate need for manpower. But even in the last years of the war, the Reichstag blocked initiatives by socialist and left-liberal deputies to give the courts the power of conditional sentencing.[16]

Bozi's experiment in Bielefeld nevertheless moved forward during the last year of the war and the chaotic first months of 1919. He found new allies in the campaign to expand judicial discretion and to empower welfare organizations on both sides of the political divide. Socialist jurists like Wolfgang Heine and Hugo Heinemann, who would each serve briefly as Prussian Justice Minister in 1919, made the case for the Bielefeld reforms and conditional sentencing to the National Assembly in Weimar and to the new government. At the same time, politically arch-conservative clergymen involved in charitable associations for released prison inmates worked with Bozi to develop institutions modeled on Bielefeld's. Pastor Heinrich Seyfarth, the Director of the Deutscher Hilfsverein in Hamburg, played an important role in mobilizing interest among prison societies nationwide. Seyfarth was a disciple of Father Bodelschwingh who had become known as an advocate of bold, experimental approaches to welfare for criminal offenders, including the organized resettlement of German criminals overseas and in rural communities at home. Seyfarth told Bozi that the "only difficulties" in his own charitable efforts were that former offenders "could *not be forced* to make use of [the] welfare institutions." Pastor Hermann Hage, the head of the venerable Prison Society of Sachsen-Anhalt, worked with Bozi to establish a system of welfare advisers for the city courts in Halle, as well as a halfway house for offenders on protective supervision.[17] Although socialists like Heine and Heinemann and conservatives like Seyfarth and Hage did not necessarily work together after 1919, they remained—thanks to Bozi—strange bedfellows in the movement to transform criminal court practice.

Critique from the Left: The Crisis of Trust in Justice

In the heady months following the collapse of the Imperial government, the dominant call of reformers was to increase popular participation in justice. Max Alsberg, a celebrated author and defense attorney, argued that "we can no longer do without the lay element in criminal justice." He saw opportunities for a new era of popular participation in justice resulting from the fact that so many otherwise respectable Germans were prosecuted under wartime black-market laws. "The sphere of those touched by the punishing power of the state has moved closer to the general consciousness," he wrote.[18] Hugo Heinemann and others associated with the new Prussian state government promised prison advisory boards, a jury system, and expanded use of lay judges (*Schöffen*). Journalist and activist Hans Hyan argued that greater public involvement would create a scientific foundation for penal policy. Only those who knew and understood the "life experiences" of the people, he wrote, could gather social data from the private sphere and adapt it effectively to criminal justice.[19] In its historic Görlitzer Program of 1921, the Social Democratic Party (SPD) distilled such populist assumptions about justice into an agenda for moderate reform.[20]

Much of this impulse for reform in the early Weimar Republic was a reaction to the so-called crisis of trust in justice (*Vertrauenskrise der Justiz*). Since the *fin de siècle*, the Prussian judiciary—once a great symbol of modernization and the rule of law—was increasingly perceived as an obstacle to progress. Critics accused judges of being *lebensfremd*, distant, from the *Volk* and trapped in a "dry and bloodless" formalism. Even Judge Bozi, a fierce defender of the judiciary, routinely invoked such images to describe the majority of his colleagues. Judges, he wrote in 1896, were overly specialized and ignorant of the important changes in society, economics, and ideas. In 1917, he suggested there were good reasons why so many Germans "perceived the law as an alien mechanism of coercion."[21]

In the postwar era, it was on the left—but by no means only on the left—that this discourse was articulated most forcefully. The moderate socialist Gustav Radbruch warned the Reichstag in 1920 that "there is deep mistrust, deep exasperation among the people, among the working class, against our justice system."[22] In his inaugural address as Reich Minister of Justice, he referred to a "state of war" between the people and their courts. The very qualities that had once made German judges into heroes of the left now made them into subjects of ridicule and contempt. "Our judges are utterly and completely incorruptible," declares Herr Peachum in Brecht's *Three-Penny Opera* (1928). "No amount of money could corrupt them into doing justice."[23] By the late 1920s, conservatives were infuriated by such assertions, but in the early Weimar years they implicitly and even sometimes explicitly acknowledged the *Vertrauenskrise* as a real and pressing issue.

From 1919 to 1923, the sense of urgency and opportunity kept jurists and welfare activists working on a common reform project, even as politics increasingly tugged them apart. The new Prussian state government first enacted sweeping reforms of the prisons and penitentiaries.[24] In 1920, Hugo am Zehnhoff, a conservative lawyer from the Catholic Center Party, joined the government as Minister of Justice. Zehnhoff, whom one subordinate remembers as "especially pardon-happy," focused the Ministry's attention on how to integrate the pardon process into ordinary court practice and give it a strong social component.[25] The result was a series of government decrees giving judges the authority to suspend sentences in certain cases where offenders promised to place themselves under welfare supervision. If the offenders made "an actual demonstration of overall satisfactory behavior" during probation, then judges would arrange for a total pardon. [26] The duration of the probationary period was set by the judge and did not depend upon the seriousness of the crime. In many cases, supervision could last longer than the original sentence, and once it was over, there was no guarantee that the sentence would be forgiven. Simply staying out of trouble, the Ministry made clear, was not enough. [27]

To provide a foundation for the successful use of the pardon, the Ministry turned to Bozi. Working with the Prison Society of Silesia, Bozi had developed general principles for the role of welfare advisers in the criminal court and rechristened the "Bielefeld System" *Soziale Gerichtshilfe*, or Social Court Assistance. The name harkened back to a similar institution developed for the investigation of juvenile offenders and thus underscored the fact that criminals would be treated less as independent, fully responsible legal subjects possessed of free will and more as products of their social environments, broadly defined. [28] Prussian officials hoped that *Gerichtshilfe* would help judges determine the precise contours of protective supervision, insure the "educational" character of these measures, and, perhaps more importantly, screen out dangerous individuals and others who should not be considered for pardon.

In announcing state support for *Gerichtshilfe*, Minister am Zehnhoff praised the institution as an antidote to the crisis of trust in justice. He noted the "conviction among wide sectors of the working class that the judiciary cannot properly judge their circumstances and their struggles, because they are cut off from the people and therefore do not possess sufficient knowledge of their life conditions." Although the Minister defended the judges, he declared it was "nevertheless vitally necessary that we prove to the public that the state is doing everything in its power to provide for the insight of judges into all social conditions." [29] This sentiment would be echoed repeatedly over the next several years. In the words of the legal scholar Wolfgang Mittermaier, *Gerichtshilfe* had the same purpose as that of the lay judges: its "popular perspective" supplemented the one-sided, routinized perspective of the professional judge. [30]

The Spread of *Gerichtshilfe*

Over the next three years, dozens of *Gerichtshilfe* agencies were founded across Prussia, while the Ministry continually extended the terms under which judges could exercise their new power of discretion. While the state helped fund *Gerichtshilfe*, the initiative for the agencies always came from below. Bozi insisted that *Gerichtshilfe* should be "adapted to the conditions of local welfare organizations." [31] As a result, the institution took on different forms, depending upon the configuration of local forces. Many cities followed the Bielefeld model, creating independent offices to mediate between the courts and welfare associations.

Towns with especially strong prison societies tended to follow the example of Halle, which established *Gerichtshilfe* under the auspices of the Prison Society for Sachsen-Anhalt. Finally, a number of larger cities, starting with Berlin, set up *Gerichtshilfe* as a part of the public welfare office.

Both the Halle model and the Berlin model differed from Bielefeld *Gerichtshilfe* in that the court assistants did not simply investigate cases and arrange for welfare intervention, but actually practiced welfare themselves. Their goal, in fact, was "continuous welfare," which meant that one welfare adviser was assigned to an individual from the first moment of conflict with the law, through the trial and imprisonment, and into the period of conditional freedom and protective supervision. In Halle, *Gerichtshilfe's* court assistants helped accused offenders spiritually and even financially, visited prisoners and advised their families, and helped released prisoners to find jobs and housing. Having moved beyond mere investigation and mediation, as one social worker argued, the purpose of *Gerichtshilfe* in Halle was to pursue "every art of binding the individual to his environment."[32]

In Berlin, *Gerichtshilfe* was closely associated with juvenile justice and welfare for sexually at-risk girls.[33] The court assistants in Berlin were principally female police assistants, who worked under the direction of Else von Liszt, the director of welfare for youth offenders and the daughter of the great legal reformer.[34] In a sense, Berlin's *Gerichtshilfe* piggybacked on the legitimacy and prestige of the juvenile justice movement, promising to inject pedagogical rhetoric into the discourse of adult punishment. Indeed, the female police assistants were principally trained in welfare for children and sexually "endangered" girls.[35] In the words of one reformer, Berlin *Gerichtshilfe* embodied an ideal of the judge as "people's educator." There was no real difference between youth and adult supervision, another Berliner claimed, except that juvenile institutions aimed to transform the offender's underlying character (*Bildung*), while adult institutions focused upon the more modest goal of adjusting a person's behavior to real existing conditions, especially to the demands of modern working life.[36]

The spread of *Gerichtshilfe* accelerated after 1926 when another ordinance of the Prussian Justice Ministry called for the social diagnosis of *all* defendants in criminal prosecutions—even in cases where a pardon was unlikely. The Ministry ordered judges and prosecutors to consider the relationship of a criminal act to the personality of the offender. They were to determine "to what extent the act was based upon a reprehensible mentality [*verwerfliche Gesinnung*] or inclination of the will, and to what extent it rested upon causes which cannot be blamed upon the offender." This ordinance obligated the courts to assess the offender's early life and personal and economic relations at the time of the criminal act; the impact of mental disease or disturbance; the motive, incentive, and purpose of the act; the level of remorse; and the offender's present condition and the likely impact of punishment upon the offender and any family relations.[37] Judges were required to marshal the special knowledge of welfare organizations and reach into the everyday lives of offenders and their milieux. *Soziale Gerichtshilfe*, or some equivalent, was henceforth indispensable to the regular Prussian judicial process.

Gerichtshilfe and Municipal Welfare

In the wake of the Prussian ordinance of 1926, government officials and reformers began to address the question of how to formalize the place of *Gerichtshilfe* in law and administration. In particular, there was concern that the Prussian state must choose a single *Gerichtshilfe* model. For many, the increasing scope and complexity of *Gerichtshilfe*'s tasks was a clear argument in favor of putting the institution under the authority of the municipal government, as in the Berlin model, rather than depending on relatively unschooled and often inexperienced volunteers. Civil servants, under the administration of the cities' welfare authorities, would be accountable to the public and would have easy access to the welfare, police, and medical histories of individual clients. Advocates of placing *Gerichtshilfe* under the authority of the municipal welfare offices (*Kommunalisierung*) also pointed to the so-called Frankfurt numbers which indicated that 65 percent of the offenders who came before one *Gerichtshilfe* agency were previously clients of the city's regular welfare office. If "continuous welfare" was the goal, then the state seemed best positioned to unify the various existing forms of welfare oversight.[38]

Moreover, socialist and progressive reformers increasingly hoped and expected that protective supervision would become a responsibility of the state rather than private associations. To be sure, as late as 1926, Werner Gentz, a prominent reformer and SPD official in Kiel, declared that charitable organizations were necessary to "supplement and animate" state welfare. To bureaucratize charity work [*Liebesarbeit*]," he wrote at that time, "is to remove the love [*Liebe*]. Welfare without love is control."[39] Within two years, however, Gentz, like many SPD officials, was insisting that the state must oversee penal welfare to insure that it protected both the security of the public and the rights of offenders.[40] As the Reich government became increasingly interested in protective supervision, national leaders seemed to agree. In 1927, the Reich Minister of Justice declared that "it can no longer be doubted that a well-ordered and thorough welfare for released prisoners is the most successful means for the battle against criminality." He called for the Reich government to develop its own institutions to supervise ex-offenders and, in the meantime, to gain a "determinative influence" over the prison societies.[41]

In the late 1920s, many on the left came to see the communalization of *Gerichtshilfe* as a first step in fundamentally revising the relationship between justice and welfare. It became customary to argue that welfare and justice had essentially the same function. Both were concerned, as Gustav Radbruch argued, with the individual "embedded in society, with all his intellectual and social constraints, with his total class-determined character." [42] Reformers wanted to see the courts take true cognizance of their social task, and this was only possible, they argued, if welfare experts were given a more prominent role in the analysis and determination of cases. As Werner Gentz argued,

> [T]he criminal act is not a social phenomenon sui generis but rather only a special case of asocial behavior more generally. . . . One cannot pull the individual who has manifested this onto two different tracks: to attack the social distress by means of welfare . . . and the criminal act by means which are utterly indifferent to these matters. The conceptual distinction between these modes of procedure must not be allowed to grow into a discrepancy between the measures. *It concerns one and the same individual 'person.'* He is not separable into an object of criminal justice and one of welfare. [43]

The only way to insure that criminal policy operated, as it were, on a single track was to build *Gerichtshilfe* into an institution that independently, forcefully, and systematically brought social perspectives into the courtroom. Clearly, such an outcome could only be realized with state backing for *Gerichtshilfe*. In describing the courtroom of the future, Socialist reformers even envisioned a "working group" (*Arbeitsgemeinschaft*) or round table at which judges, welfare-officials, doctors, and prison wardens would discuss criminal cases as equals. "The judge," Wolfgang Mittermaier argued, "will thereby climb down from his somewhat elevated seat," whereas the remaining contributors will "climb up from the position of consultants." [44]

Critique from the Right: The Weakening of Justice

From its beginnings, *Gerichtshilfe* faced an ambivalent, if not actually hostile, reception from many Prussian judges. Individual judges rarely stated their feelings openly, but public and private *Gerichtshilfe* agencies complained of passive resistance from the bench. In cities where *Gerichtshilfe* investigated cases on its own initiative, conservative judges simply ignored the welfare reports or refused to allow the agencies to participate in the main proceedings. In some other locales, *Gerichtshilfe* was simply underutilized, as the judges rarely asked for the agencies' intervention. Tensions between judges and the *Gerichtshilfe's* court assistants could be especially acute in cities like Berlin, where the agencies were administered by the municipal authorities. [45]

The principal reason for judicial resistance to *Gerichtshilfe* was the judges' concern with the so-called *Verweichlichung* of justice—the softening or weakening of justice—which was blamed upon the penetration of alien ideas and the politicization of criminal policy. *Verweichlichung* referenced both the courts' diminished institutional integrity and the decline in the severity of punishment.

Trained to see themselves as agents of retribution and deterrence, many judges were inherently mistrustful of the effort to force social concepts into legal reasoning. The very notion of judicial discretion, in some views, was a Trojan horse for nonjuridical (welfare, medical) institutions to infiltrate and eventually co-opt criminal justice.

The judges' underlying fear of foreign elements within legal discourse was exacerbated by growing evidence of a trend toward mildness in German justice since before the First World War. Two studies published in 1926 argued that the courts had become excessively lenient. Law professor Franz Exner offered a statistical analysis of long-term patterns in sentencing practices, arguing that serious felons were increasingly spared the *Zuchthaus* (penitentiary) and sent to regular prison for shorter terms instead. The trend toward reduced sentences, he argued, began in the late nineteenth century, but accelerated in the postwar era, even as the frequency of many offenses increased. Part of the reason for this, Exner noted, was that the courts took postwar deprivation and the effects of hyper-inflation into account when sentencing offenders. He rejected the idea, however, that social trauma was sufficient to explain or to justify this change in practice. He noted that multiple recidivists also received lighter sentences and that the trend toward mildness continued even after economic conditions improved.[46]

In a more polemical attack on sentencing practices, the criminologist Robert Heindl argued that justice institutions were increasingly infected by a "meaningless, exaggerated sentimentality." Heindl originally rose to prominence as a critic of Wilhelmine schemes to rehabilitate German criminals through resettlement in colonial environments. In the Weimar era, he again attacked the so-called utopian belief in corrigibility. Rejecting the welfarist conception of criminals as weak-willed, vulnerable individuals who could be transformed through supervision, he insisted that a substantial percentage of offenders were professionals— that is, individuals who were committed to crime as a vocation and thoroughly socialized into a criminal lifestyle. The increase in pardons and the reduction in sentences, Heindl charged, simply consolidated the position of a powerful criminal underworld.[47]

The evidence of more lenient sentencing produced a simmering discomfort with reform among many judges and prosecutors. During the era of "relative stability" in the mid-twenties, conservatives complained of a steady decrease in conviction rates, the increased use of monetary fines in lieu of prison terms, and the increasing neglect of police supervision for released prisoners.[48] Advocates for the judiciary were particularly caustic in regard to the perceived meddling of state administrative bodies in judicial affairs. Even after the momentous reforms in the practice of suspended sentencing based on conditional pardons, it was still up to the state judicial authorities to make the final, official decision of whether to grant a pardon. Critics accused the Prussian state of "politicizing" justice through its interest in the outcome of individual cases. Alongside these administrative pressures, judges complained about more diffuse cultural pressures, the "softness of the times," which subtly but consistently pushed them toward mildness. Even criminologist Gustav Aschaffenburg, a longtime advocate of flexible sentencing, argued in 1926 that the courts now "yielded too much to popular sensibilities."[49]

The discourse of *Verweichlichung* also reflected intense skepticism concerning protective supervision as a model of social control. In truth, protective supervision remained a poorly defined and chronically neglected institution throughout the Weimar years. To be sure, the Prussian state periodically considered upgrading welfare for released prisoners and establishing specialized asylums and halfway houses (*Übergangsheime*) for former offenders.[50] Welfare associations likewise explored the possibility of developing closed facilities specifically for ex-offenders or of getting the worker colonies to supervise more offenders on probation. The directors of many asylums, however, resisted segregating ex-offenders from the larger population of persons in need of welfare. In their view, the essential task of welfare for released prisoners was to bring them into the mainstream and shelter them from social stigma.[51]

The persistence of high unemployment in the 1920s undermined both the moral and the practical arguments in favor of welfare for criminal offenders. Critics asked why ex-criminals should receive special benefits and job assistance while millions of ordinary, law-abiding Germans were forced to fend for themselves. Underlying the growing discomfort with protective supervision was the dilemma known as the "principle of less eligibility": for punishment to maintain its deterrent effect, it must always be more unpleasant than ordinary living conditions of the law-abiding poor. If punishment, in its overall effect, improved the condition of the poor, then people would have an incentive to commit crimes.[52] With the onset of a new economic crisis after 1929, prison societies became increasingly focused on restricting the pool of offenders who were eligible for protective supervision. "The burning question is that of selection," wrote the prison association in Berlin in an annual report that boasted of a drop in clients. Not surprisingly, many associations looked to criminal biology in hopes of finding a scientific method for excluding the unwanted.[53]

In Bozi's original plan for *Gerichtshilfe*, the growth of welfare supervision was supposed to offset the inevitable decline in incarceration. With the failure to expand or even sustain the work of the prison societies, state welfare offices or worker colonies, a generation of released criminals now allegedly went unsupervised. Critics claimed to see the disintegration of traditional social controls, pointing to such developments as a piece of Weimar legislation that limited the length of time during which information about offenders could be maintained in the criminal register. They also pointed to state and local decrees that restricted the scope of police supervision in such ways that the authorities could no longer banish ex-convicts from certain locales or even visit them at their homes or their places of employment. The 1927 draft of the penal code envisioned abolishing police supervision entirely.[54]

Critics of reform claimed that criminal offenders who were granted a conditional pardon or early release had few obligations beyond filling out forms and dropping by the police station now and then. Unless they sought direct financial assistance, the welfare agencies allegedly lost sight of them. Professional criminals were said to have become mocking and contemptuous of the Weimar justice system. A well-known saying of the Berlin underworld, according to Theodor Noetzel, was "[E]*rst klau' ick, dann bewähr' ick mir*" [[F]irst I heist somethin', then supervise meself]."[55] Critics claimed that offenders now saw a sentence of protective supervision as equivalent to an acquittal. "I was acquitted for three years," was another supposed saying from Berlin. Since first offenses rarely led to prison terms, criminals believed that the first offense, in essence, "did not count."[56] By the late 1920s, the softening (*Verweichlichung*) of justice was as much a keyword of right wing politics as "crisis of trust" *(Vertrauenskrise)* in justice was for the left. When Prussia appointed a new justice minister in 1928, even the liberal *Berliner Tageblatt* urged the minister to treat the question of *Verweichlichung* as the first topic of discussion during his introductory press conference.[57]

Controlling *Gerichtshilfe:* Judiciary versus Welfare Authorities

To contain the threat of *Verweichlichung* and protect the integrity of the courts, judges and prosecutors sought to assert control over *Gerichtshilfe*. A leading force in mobilizing the judiciary in this respect was Theodor Noetzel, the chief prosecutor in Kassel as well as founder and director of one of the first *Gerichtshilfe* agencies. Kassel's *Gerichtshilfe* was created on the Bielefeld model, whereby an independent association, dominated by jurists, oversaw the institution. Noetzel, however, went further than the Bielefelders in subjecting *Gerichtshilfe* to the direct control of the court. Not only did Prosecutor Noetzel personally select and train the *Gerichtshelfer*, but, in contrast to its Bielefeld counterpart, the Kassel *Gerichtshilfe* could intervene in criminal cases only if specifically authorized by Noetzel's office. Its reports were submitted directly to the prosecutors, who summarized them for the judges and assessed their implications for a given case. In sum, the Kassel *Gerichtshilfe* reports were shaped to correspond to the interests and concerns of the prosecution.[58]

In many ways, Noetzel was a more compelling advocate for reform among Prussian judges than Bozi. In contrast to his Bielefeld colleague, Noetzel had never been a critic of the judiciary, nor had he ever worked closely with questionable allies such as socialists and feminists. Even though he urged judges to embrace *Gerichtshilfe*, he was solicitous regarding judges' misgivings toward the penal reform movement. Noetzel was also sharply critical of welfare organizations, citing their mistrust of the judiciary and their tendency to empathize too much with the accused. In a speech at a gathering of Christian reformers, Noetzel began by summarizing the arguments of *Gerichtshilfe*'s critics. He asked rhetorically:

> In a time of the deepest moral decline [and] extraordinary indifference to justice and law do you want to support the criminal against the suffering, innocent national comrade [*unbestrafter Volksgenosse*]? Do you want to take away the last vestige of the criminal's sense of responsibility through the punctilious investigation of the intellectual, spiritual, and economic foundations of a crime? Can you answer for the progressive weakening of criminal justice and, resulting from that, the reduction and the effacement of the internal restraints upon those national comrades with an asocial predisposition?

Noetzel responded that "correctly practiced" *Gerichtshilfe* would not constitute aid and support for criminal offenders *against the court*, but rather assistance *to* the court against criminals. This approach, he argued, was consistent with Bozi's original vision of *Gerichtshilfe*, and it was the only form in which the institution would not undermine justice and public security.[59] *Gerichtshilfe*, he declared, must provide facts and descriptive information "unclouded" by one-sided concern for the criminal's "well-being." The *Gerichtshilfe*'s court assistants were to serve as the eyes and ears of the prosecutors and judges within the social realm. Their principal concern had to be the purpose of the punishment.[60]

Noetzel thus offered Prussian judges a vision of *Gerichtshilfe* in which romantic, utopian ideals of popular justice were contained by the steadying hand of the prosecutor. The court assistants in the Kassel *Gerichtshilfe* included a factory director, two factory workers, an artisan, "ladies" from the Jewish, Catholic, and Protestant welfare associations, and one woman from the public welfare office. These voices of the people, however, along with the voice of the criminal were introduced into the court record only after being analyzed, interpreted, and reformulated by the prosecutor's office. They impacted the proceedings only within the context of the prosecutor's case.[61] Over and over, Noetzel argued that *soziale Gerichtshilfe* was *not* a welfare institution, but a mediating institution working on behalf of the court. To avoid any confusion about the purpose of *Gerichtshilfe*, he even argued that its official name should be changed, dropping the modifier *soziale* (social) and calling the institution adult *Gerichtshilfe* or, better, simply *Gerichtshilfe*. At best, he asserted, referring to *Gerichtshilfe* as a social institution was redundant or obvious. More often, he asserted, the name encouraged the misconception that *Gerichtshilfe*'s principal loyalties were to the social realm.

Largely owing to his leadership, Prussian judges soon mobilized around the issue of *Gerichtshilfe*, encouraging its growth, but insisting that it serve "the interests of the court" and "not the interests of the accused." The symbolic valence of the *Gerichtshilfe* issue was such that it reinvigorated a largely moribund organization called the Prussian Judges Association (Preussischer Richterverein, PRV) after 1927.[62] In that year the PRV established principles on *Gerichtshilfe* and, one year later, proposed legislation authored by Noetzel to formally establish the institution as an arm of the prosecutor's office. This intervention, in turn, became the centerpiece of fierce controversies over the future of German penal policy.

Charitable Prison Societies: Between Welfare and Justice

The debates over *Gerichtshilfe* were also significantly shaped by the charitable prison societies. The very concept of *Gerichtshilfe* as welfare owed a great deal to the Christian social tradition. The Prison Society of Sachsen-Anhalt had basically invented the idea of *Gerichtshilfe* as the fulcrum for an all-encompassing welfare system, whereas other local charitable associations had continued to play often leading roles in shaping this combination of investigatory, custodial, and spiritual functions.

The close connection between *Gerichtshilfe* and welfare was also reflected in the title of the Weimar Republic's new umbrella organization for prison societies, the Deutscher Reichsverband für Gerichtshilfe, Gefangenen- und Entlassenenfürsorge (National Association for Gerichtshilfe, Prison Welfare and Welfare for Released Prisoners). The Reichsverband was formed in 1926 under the leadership of Pastor Seyfarth of the Deutscher Hilfsverein, who had insisted that a new organization was necessary to represent the expanding role of charitable societies in Weimar criminal justice. This new organization replaced the National Association of Prison Charitable Societies (Verband der deutschen Schutzvereine für entlassene Gefangene) founded in 1892. Criticizing the older association as inextricably tied to the outdated notion that "welfare . . . starts only after the punishment has ceased," Seyfarth argued that the new Reichsverband would "take a position on all problems encompassed by guilt and atonement . . . [and] stimulate changes . . . through which the entire penal system will be saturated with welfare ideals."[63] A key element of the multipronged social agenda of the Reichsverband was the establishment of *Gerichtshilfe* agencies across Prussia. As a first step, Seyfarth founded and edited a new journal, the *Monatsblätter für Gerichtshilfe, Gefangenen- und Entlassenenfürsorge*, which served as a forum for the discussion of practical issues in the border areas between punishment and welfare.

As an advocate of the prison societies, Seyfarth's Reichsverband should have been a natural ally of the public welfare advocates in their effort to establish *Gerichtshilfe* as a welfare institution. Whereas the Prussian Judges Association insisted that *Gerichtshilfe* must not provide "aid and comfort" to the accused, the prison societies had traditionally stressed compassion and empathy for offenders. For Seyfarth, a disciple of Father Bodelschwingh, the essential purpose of protective supervision was to create "a connection between the criminal and the circles of people constituted as religious, professional or social communities." In the inaugural issue of the *Monatsblätter*, Seyfarth described accused offenders as persons "torn suddenly from their professional and family life." A key goal of prison welfare, he argued, was to help respectable society overcome its natural prejudice against and revulsion toward criminals.[64] Another pastor echoed this theme at a Reichsverband conference. Penal welfare, he declared, was essentially "care of the community [*Gemeinschaftspflege*] . . . an effort to awaken the sense of co-responsibility among the public." Its purpose was to "anchor the consciousness of responsibility for offenders in public life."[65]

Many rank-and-file Protestants active in local prison societies also clung to an image of *Gerichtshilfe* embedded in this tradition of custodial care and oversight. Sharing this outlook, the leaders of the Innere Mission searched for a synthesis between Noetzel's insistently juridical viewpoint and the extreme social perspective of the proponents of public welfare.[66] Some charitable organizations feared compromising the traditional ideals of the prison societies by becoming too closely associated with the court's prosecutorial apparatus.[67] Of particular concern was how prison societies could build and maintain the trust of criminal defendants if they were to become tools of the court. Paradoxically, however, the Inner Mission argued that the defendants' trust in the court-assistants was endangered when criminal defendants had access to the *Gerichtshilfe* reports—something that was required by law once *Gerichtshilfe* reports were placed among the prosecutor's evidentiary materials. In some German towns, *Gerichtshilfe* court assistants faced harassment and threats of retaliation from the families of defendants subjected to negative reports. A certain Pastor Oehlert of Rinteln vividly described a mother's anger over his role in her son's *Gerichtshilfe* report. The woman cursed him as "black police" and allegedly rallied support from "radical political elements."[68] The Inner Mission feared that under the judges' plan for *Gerichtshilfe*, the helpers themselves would be subject to more such confrontations, and indeed, could even be called as witnesses to testify against the accused.[69]

Despite such reservations about judicial control of *Gerichtshilfe*, however, Christian charitable associations chose to ally themselves with the judges and mobilized against the welfarist interpretation of *Gerichtshilfe*. Seyfarth and the Reichsverband stood firmly alongside Noetzel, and the *Monatsblätter* increasingly adopted the tone of the Prussian Judges Association. Prison societies boasted of their efforts to purge excessive sentimentality from their ranks and to train welfare advisers to be coolly detached and skeptical toward the claims of their charges.[70]

The charitable associations' retreat into the arms of conservative judges derived from fears that public welfare advocates were set to make suspended sentences coupled with protective supervision into a *right* for all criminals, rather than a *privilege* reserved for the deserving few. By rejecting the very principle of retribution, socialist and progressive reformers had allegedly decoupled punishment from its moral purpose. Once punishment became just another aspect of social policy, the decision to suspend sentences through a conditional pardon was based purely upon the criminal's capacity to be socialized, to live peaceably and labor productively in the future. Criminals would be let loose upon society without showing remorse, performing restitution or being subject to the "knowing eye" of Christian love.[71]

Noetzel's and Seyfarth's most important recruit to their cause was Alfred Bozi, who was given a seat of honor as the "father of *Gerichtshilfe*" at Reichsverband functions. Bozi had originally supported communalization in Bielefeld and only grew disillusioned with municipal control after socialists on the welfare council objected to the use of public funds to support private charities.[72] Throughout his most active years as a reformer, Bozi had refused to take sides in the debate between proponents of public welfare and the private charities, and in fact had encouraged experimentation at the local level. It thus marked a rather abrupt change of position in 1928, when the physically ailing and retired judge endorsed Noetzel's view that *Gerichtshilfe* was "assistance to the court, but not a welfare measure."[73] In explaining his views, Bozi expressed alarm at the politicization of justice, which, he claimed, inevitably resulted from the municipal administration of *Gerichtshilfe*. As was generally the case with such accusations, the charge was vague and unsubstantiated. To him it seemed self-evident, and even a decade later he would cite the "politicization of justice" as a key experience that drove him to embrace Hitler's promise of "national renewal."[74]

Conclusion

Over time, the debate over *Gerichtshilfe* became a proxy for a more fundamental conflict about the nature of punishment and the locus of authority in criminal justice. "Perhaps hardly an area of the penal sciences is as controversial as *soziale Gerichtshilfe*," declared the *Berlin Börsen-Courier* in 1929.[75] The Congress of German Municipalities and the Association of German Juvenile Courts helped mobilize indignation against the Prussian Judges Association's proposal to subordinate *Gerichtshilfe* to the judiciary. The Reich Conference of Socialist Jurists accused the judges of "an attempted coup against the social state."[76] Judges and prosecutors fought back at professional meetings and in the press, accusing welfare proponents of trying to make *Gerichtshilfe* a Trojan horse with which to infiltrate and manipulate court procedure.[77] "Between the judges and the representatives of public welfare," observed a participant at the Internationale Kriminalistische Vereinigung (IKV) in 1929, "there were utterly divergent viewpoints concerning the relationship between welfare and punishment."[78]

The jurist Wolfgang Mittermaier noted wearily that there was something "typically German" in having allowed an institution to develop informally without ever agreeing upon who would participate, what it would do, or even what it would be called. Such haphazard, grassroots development was possible and perhaps necessary in the context of postwar Germany, where the essential appeal of *Gerichtshilfe* was precisely in its organic roots and its populist character. By the late 1920s, however, *Gerichtshilfe* had matured, and control of its stake had become a central issue in two rival and apparently irreconcilable visions of penal policy.

Notes

This chapter, written especially for this volume, draws on material from the author's *Beyond the Prisons Gates: Punishment and Welfare in Germany, 1850–1933* (Chapel Hill: University of North Carolina Press, 2008).

1. Wolfgang Mittermaier, "Grundgedanken der Gerichtshilfe," *Die Justiz* 6, 1 (October, 1930), 7.
2. On the modern school of criminal reform, see Richard F. Wetzell, "From Retributive Justice to Social Defense: Penal Reform in Fin-de-Siècle Germany," in *Germany at the Fin de Siècle: Culture, Politics, and Ideas,* ed. Suzanne Marchand and David Lindenfeld (Baton Rouge, 2004), 59–77; idem, *Inventing the Criminal: A History of German Criminology 1880–1945* (Chapel Hill, 2000), 33–38. There has been surprisingly little historical work on the private prison societies. See Andrew Lees, *Cities, Sin, and Social Reform in Imperial Germany* (Ann Arbor, 2002), 182–185.
3. Stadtarchiv Bielefeld, Nachlass Bozi, A. Bozi, *Lebenserinnerungen,* unpublished manuscript (1937), 145–147; and Nachlass Bozi, Nr. 37.
4. Hauptarchiv der von Bodelschwingschen Anstalten Bethel, Entwurf. 2/12-16, Entwurf. F. 705. Minister of the Interior von Loebell to Regierungspräsidenten and Polizeipräsidenten, 23 November 1916.
5. Friedrich von Bodelschwingh, "Die Arbeiterkolonien und Verpflegungsstationen," *Die Arbeiter-Kolonie* 1, 3 (1884), 85; and "Bericht über die erste Hauptversammlung des Deutschen Herbergsvereins," ibid., 170.
6. Geheimes Staatsarchiv Preussischer Kulturbesitz, Rep. 77, Tit. 1104, Nr. 18, Adh. III. Fürsorge für die willenschwachen Wanderarmen und ihre Unterbringung in Arbeiterkolonien, 1916–1919.
7. Nachlass Bozi, Nr. 37, Bodelschwingh to Bozi, 15 May 1915. On the actual decline of the workhouse during the war, see Wolfgang Ayass, *Das Arbeitshaus Breitenau* (Kassel, 1992), 241–243.
8. Georg Steigerthal, *Grundriss der Anstaltsfürsorge* (Berlin, 1933), 147, 157–158.
9. Onnasch and Thieme were disciples of Adolph Stoecker who were active in the morality movement. Correspondence in Nachlass Bozi, no. 23.
10. Nachlass Bozi, no. 23, Bozi to Professor W. Mittermaier, 5 November 1918.
11. The women's committee fell apart in the spring of 1919 after the feminist members started publicly advocating for the admission of women into the judiciary. A little later, reformers in Bielefeld divided along political lines over a dispute concerning funding for private welfare. Nachlass Bozi, no. 23. Bozi to Leyen, 11 July 1919.
12. Alfred Bozi, ed., *Recht, Verwaltung, und Politik im neuen Deutschland* (Stuttgart, 1916). On the role of the war in forging new reform coalitions, see Ursula Ratz, *Zwischen Arbeitsgemeinschaft*

und Koalition: Bürgerliche Sozialreformer und Gewerkschaften im Ersten Weltkrieg, (Munich, 1994).

13. "Neue Gnadenerweise für Kriegsteilnehmer," *Deutsche Strafrechtszeitung* 2 (1915); *Stenographische Berichte über die Verhandlungen des Reichstages*, 164. Sitzung, 13 May 1918; ibid., 82. Sitzung, 23 February 1917, Anfrage no. 107.

14. Nachlass Bozi, no. 34. Bozi to Schiffer, 24 April 1918. On pardons, see James Q. Whitman, *Harsh Justice: Criminal Punishment and the Widening Gap Between America and Europe* (Oxford, 2003).

15. Bozi's thinking was often aligned with the "free law movement," though he did not consider himself to be a part of any school. See Alfred Bozi, *Die Weltanschauung der Jurisprudenz* (Hannover, 1907); idem, *Lebendes Recht: Ein Ausblick in den Probleme der Justizreform* (Hannover, 1915); idem, "Das Rechtsgesetz als Naturgesetz," *Monatsschrift für Kriminalpsychologie und Strafrechtsreform* 15 (1924), 166–169. On criminal justice and the free law movement, see Benjamin Carter Hett, *Death in the Tiergarten: Murder and Criminal Justice in the Kaiser's Berlin* (Cambridge, 2004), 20, 170–171.

16. *Stenographische Berichte über die Verhandlungen des Reichstages*, 164. Sitzung, 13 May 1918. On conditional sentencing, see Eberhard Schmidt, *Einführung in die Geschichte der deutschen Strafrechtspflege* (Göttingen, 1947).

17. Nachlass Bozi, no. 38, Seyfarth to Bozi, 19 August 1919, emphasis in the original; Hage, "Die Übergangsstation im Dienste der Fürsorge an den entlassenen Gefangenen," in *Jahrbuch der Gefängnis Gesellschaft für die Provinz Sachsen und Anhalt* 32, 41–52.

18. Max Alsberg, "Vorwort," in *Berliner Gefängnisse*, ed. Hans Hyan (Berlin, 1920), 11–12. Alsberg was apparently much less enthusiastic about popular participation prior to World War I; see Hett, *Death in the Tiergarten*, 161–178.

19. Hans Hyan, *Verbrechen und Strafe im neuen Deutschland: Flugschriften der Revolution, Nr. 4.* (Wiesbaden, 1919), 23.

20. Behrle, *Stellung*, 57; Klaus Marxen, *Der Kampf gegen das liberale Strafrecht* (Berlin, 1975), 76–77.

21. Alfred Bozi, *Die Angriffe gegen den Richterstand* (Breslau, 1896); idem, *Soziale Rechtseinrichtungen in Bielefeld* (Stuttgart, 1917), 32.

22. Quoted in Robert Kuhn, *Die Vertrauenskrise der Justiz (1926–1928): Der Kampf um die "Republikanisierung" der Rechtspflege in der Weimarer Republik* (Cologne, 1983), 44.

23. Bertolt Brecht, *Die Dreigroschenoper* (orig. 1928, Suhrkamp, 1982), 71. Weimar playwrights and novelists made an important contribution to the negative image of judges and prosecutors. See Jakob Wassermann, *Der Fall Maurizius* (orig. 1928, Munich, 1988), and Ricarda Huch, *Der Fall Deruga*, (orig. 1917, 1992).

24. "Allgemeine Verfügung über Milderungen im Strafvollzuge vom 19. Dez. 1918," in Alfred Behrle, *Die Stellung der deutschen Sozialisten zum Strafvollzug von 1870 bis zur Gegenwart* (Leipzig and Berlin, 1931), 25–27; Nikolaus Wachsmann, "Between Reform and Repression: Prisons in Weimar Germany," *Historical Journal* 45 (2002), 413–414.

25. Fritz Hartung, *Jurist unter Vier Reichen* (Cologne, 1971), 34–40.

26. Bundesarchiv, Rep. 30.01, no. 6109. Staatsmin.-Erlaß, 2 August 1920; and Allgemeine Verfügung, 19 Oct. 1920; Theodor Noetzel, "Bewährungsfrist," in *Handwörterbuch der Kriminologie*, ed. Alexander Elster and Heinrich Lingemann (Berlin and Leipzig, 1933), 160. The original decree limited use of the pardon to criminals facing a sentence of six months or less.

27. Hartung, *Jurist*, 38–39.

28. Nothing in the 1920s understanding of "the social" precluded the consideration of imminent, biological factors as influences upon individual behavior. In fact, such factors were presumed an essential part of the social fabric.

29. Geheimes Staatsarchiv, Rep. 84a, no. 8511. Am Zehnhoff to Minister of Finance, 30 June 1922.

30. Mittermaier, "Grundgedanken," 7.

31. Else Bozi, *Gerichtshilfe für Erwachsene* (Stuttgart, 1925), 19.

32. Magdalene Deimling-Triebel, *Die Eingliederung von Rechtsbrechern in Wirtschaft und Gesellschaft als Aufgabe der Gerichtshilfe* (Durlach, 1932), 127.

33. Brandenburgisches Landeshauptstaatsarchiv, Potsdam, Rep. 12A. Neuruppin, "Erklärung" von M. Neumann, 15 July 1925, Bericht über die Tagung der Gerichtshilfe für Erwachsene in Halle Mai 1925. See also, E. Bozi, *Gerichtshilfe*, 22–26.

34. Eventually, Gerichtshilfe work in Berlin would constitute over 50 percent of the female police assistants' activities. See Patrick Wagner, *Volksgemeinschaft ohne Verbrecher* (Hamburg, 1996), 107–109.

35. Ursula Nienhaus, "Einsatz für die 'Sittlichkeit': Die Anfänge der Weiblichen Polizei im Wilhelminischen Kaiserreich und in der Weimarer Republik," in *"Sicherheit" und "Wohlfahrt": Polizei, Gesellschaft und Herrschaft im 19. und 20. Jahrhundert*, ed. Alf Lüdtke (Frankfurt, 1992).

36. Brandenburgisches Landeshauptstaatsarchiv, no. 1338, Vortrag von Herrn Obermagistratsrat Knaut, gehalten am 17. Juni 1926.

37. Geheimes Staatsarchiv, no. 8512, "Allgemeine Verfügung des Preussischen Justizministers vom 8. März 1926 über die Strafzumessung"; Böhmert, "Rechtliche Grundlagen," 26–27.

38. Gröschner, "Die Frankfurter Gerichtshilfe," *Monatsblätter des deutschen Reichsverbandes für Gerichtshilfe, Gefangenen- und Entlassenenfürsorge* (hereafter *Monatsblätter*) 2, 11/12 (November/December 1927); *Mitteilungen der Internationalen Kriminalistischen Vereinigung* (hereafter *Mitteilungen der IKV*), (1930), 33–34; Bundesarchiv, no. 5726, Bericht an Preuss. Just. Min., 1929; Archiv des Diakonischen Werkes der Evangelischen Kirche (hereafter: ADW), no. 1308. Fritze, "Abschrift," 19 October 1926.

39. Werner Gentz, "Der Fürsorgeanspruch des entlassenen Gefangenen," *Monatsblätter* 1, 3 (March 1926); and "Gefangenenfürsorge als wirtschaftliches Problem," *Monatsblätter* 1, 4 (June/July 1926).

40. See also Otto Krebs, *Straffälligenfürsorge*; Karl Finkelnburg, *Berliner Tageblatt*, 27 October 1928; Magdalene Deimling-Triebel, *Die Eingliederung von Rechtsbrechern in Wirtschaft und Gesellschaft als Aufgabe der Gerichtshilfe* (Durlach, 1932); criticism in Max Grünhut and Hugo Pfefferkorn, *Die Gerichtshilfe*, (Heymann, 1930).

41. Bundesarchiv 5683, Reichsministerium des Innern to Reichsjustizministerium (RJM), 12 June 1926; RJM to Reich Minister der Finanzen, Aus Haushalt 2/1 (1927); Abschrift zu RJM no. VW. aus den Akten Haushalt 2/1 (1927).

42. Gustav Radbruch, "Sozialismus und Strafrechtsreform," *Sozialistische Monatshefte* (1927); also Muthesius in *Mitteilungen der IKV* (1930), 27.

43. Werner Gentz, "Die Gerichtshilfe: Wohlfahrt im Strafrecht," *Vossische Zeitung*, 23 May 1929, original emphasis. See also the review of Buerschaper, *Soziale Strafrechtspflege* in *Vossische Zeitung*, 8 August 1929.

44. Mittermaier, "Grundgedanken," 8; *Mitteilungen der IKV* (1930), 36–37. The debate over the communalization of Gerichtshilfe paralleled a more widely known debate over the communalization of welfare; see Young Sun Hong, *Welfare, Modernity, and the Weimar State* (Princeton, 1998).

45. Brandenburgisches Landeshauptstaatsarchiv, 1338, "Vortrag"; Charlotte Meyer, "Entwicklung und Probleme der Berliner Sozialen Gerichtshilfe," *Berliner Wohlfahrtsblatt* 5, no. 24; Geheimes Staatsarchiv no. 8511, Vortrag, Oberlandesgerichtspräsident Köln, 30 April 1923; E. Bozi, *Gerichtshilfe*, 11; extensive evidence for the Province of Brandenburg in Brandenburgisches Landeshauptstaatsarchiv, no. 1338.

46. Exner, "Zur Praxis der Strafzumessung," 372. For a detailed discussion of Exner's larger impact on German criminology, see Wetzell, *Inventing*, 107–124.

47. Robert Heindl, *Der Berufsverbrecher: Ein Beitrag zur Strafrechtsreform* (Berlin, 1926). On Heindl's influence, see *Mitteilungen der IKV* Neue Folge 3 (1928), 38.

48. Monika Frommel, *Präventionsmodelle in der deutschen Strafzwecksdiskussion: Beziehungen zwischen Rechtsphilosophie, Dogmatik, Rechtspolitik und Erfahrungswissenschaften* (Berlin, 1987), 19; Adeline Rintelen, *Die Polizeiaufsicht und ihre Ersatzmittel im Entwurf 1928* (Würzburg, 1929).

49. Aschaffenburg in the discussion at the 1926 meeting of the IKV, in *Mitteilungen der IKV*, Neue Folge 2 (1927), 100–101.

50. Frede, "Richtlinien für die Ausübung von Schutzaufsicht über Volljährige," *Monatsblätter* 4, 10/11 (October/November 1929).

51. The Inner Mission conducted a survey of worker colonies in 1924–1925 concerning whether they would be willing to admit larger numbers of former prison inmates, particularly cases requiring formal, i.e., "protective," supervision. Responses collected in ADW, no. 325.

52. Georg Rusche and Otto Kirchheimer, *Punishment and Social Structure* (New York, 1939); see David Garland, *Punishment and Modern Society* (Chicago, 1990), 83–110.

53. *Tätigkeitsbericht der Berliner Gefangenenfürsorge für die Zeit vom 1. Januar 1928 bis 31. März 1929.* See also Hans Hein, "Gefangenen-Fürsorge am Ende: Berliner Gefangenen-Fürsorge erklärt sich selbst bankrott," *Welt am Abend* (24 September 1932).

54. The number of cases in which judges authorized police supervision of released offenders fell with remarkable consistency over the course of the Kaiserreich and the Weimar Republic. There were 8,238 cases in 1882. By 1928, there were only 791. *Kriminalstatistik für das Jahr 1932,* (Berlin, 1933), 69.

55. Cited in Noetzel, "*Gerichtshilfe*," 33; "Bewährungsfrist," 162; and Baumbach, "Das Bankrott der Strafjustiz," *Deutsche Juristenzeitung* (1928).

56. Biesenthal, "Der Zusammenbruch des Strafvollzuges," *Archiv für Kriminalanthropologie* (1926), 139–40; Albert Hellwig, "Kriminalbiologie und Strafzumessung," in *Mitteilungen der Kriminalbiologischen Gesellschaft* 2 (1928), 92–99; Exner, *Studien über die Strafzumessungspraxis der deutschen Gerichte* (Leipzig, 1931).

57. Geheimes Staatsarchiv, no. 3994, untitled document, with questions and themes submitted in advance for conference with the press, 22 September 1928.

58. The role of the German state's attorney is very different from the English or American prosecutor. In contrast to the adversarial system, German criminal procedure calls upon the prosecutor "to investigate not merely the circumstances incriminating, but also those exonerating the accused." In spite of his accusatory function, he was technically a neutral, objective arbiter of interests among the defendant, victim, and the public. Peter Badura et al., eds., *Das Fischer Lexikon: Recht* (Frankfurt, 1987), 216–231.

59. "Tagung des Deutschen Reichsverbandes für Gerichtshilfe, usw., in Düsseldorf am 16. und 17. Juni 1926," *Monatsblätter* 1, 8/9 (August/September 1926).

60. Theodor Noetzel, "Gerichtshilfe," *Monatsblätter* 1, 1 (January 1926).

61. Noetzel, "Über den derzeitigen Stand der Gerichtshilfefrage," *Monatsblätter* 3 (June 1928), 114.

62. The PRV met for the first time since the war in October 1926, with a relatively diffuse agenda, *Deutsche Juristenzeitung*, 31, 19 (1926).

63. Seyfarth, "Aufgaben und Ziele des Deutschen Reichsverbandes für Gerichtshilfe, Gefangenen- und Entlassenenfürsorge," *Monatsblätter* 1, 1 (January 1926).

64. Archiv des Diakonischen Werkes der Evangelischen Kirche (hereafter ADW), no. 1329/5, Seyfarth, untitled manuscript.

65. ADW, no. 1329/5, Bericht, Tagung, "Rechtspflege und Fürsorge," 18 October 1927. The first quote is from D. Mahling's speech at the conference.
66. ADW, no. 1308, Bäcker to D. Ulrich. Bäcker noted that Catholic penal reformers in Caritas were quicker to support the judges' standpoint. Bäcker, "Bericht."
67. ADW, no. 1308, Bericht des Leiters der Magdeburger *Gerichtshilfe*, Müller. (1928); Hermeline Bäcker, Bericht, "Über die evangelische Mitarbeit in der Sozialen Gerichtshilfe," (1931) H. Bäcker to D. Ulrich, 19 June 1931.
68. ADW, no. 1308, Elli Proebsting (Westfällischer Provinzialverband für Inneren Mission) to Evangelische Konferenz Für Straffälligenpflege, 12 April 1932, Pfarrer Oehlert to Evangelische Konferenz Für Straffälligenpflege, 24 December 1932.
69. ADW, no. 1308, Aktenmäßige Behandlung der Gerichtshilfe Auskünfte," 26 April 1928.
70. Geheimes Staatsarchiv, 84a, Nr. 8517, Gerichtshilfe, Sammelberichte.
71. Bundesarchiv, no. 5683, Entschliessung des 26. Deutschen Caritastages 1925.
72. Nachlass Bozi, no. 38.
73. ADW, no. 1329/5, Bericht, Tagung, "Rechtspflege und Fürsorge," 18 October 1927, Brandenburgisches Landeshauptstaatsarchiv, no. 1338; Bozi, "Richtlinien." Bozi played only an intermittent part in the reform movement after 1926 because of poor health, especially eye disease. Bozi, "Lebenserinnerungen."
74. Bozi, "Die soziale Gerichtshilfe als Rechtseinrichtung," *Monatsschrift für Krimalpsychologie und Strafrechtsreform* 19 (1928), 658–662. Nachlass Bozi, Bozi, "Deutschlands Erneuerung," (1938), unpublished manuscript.
75. Werner Peifer, *Berlin Börsen Courier*, 18 July 1929.
76. "Konferenz sozialdemokratischer Juristen: Beratung über Soziale Gerichtshilfe," *Vorwärts*, 28 May 1929. Albert Hellwig, "Soziale Gerichtshilfe und Strafrechtsreform," *Königsburg: Hartungsche Zeitung*, 2 June 1929; Gentz, "Gerichtshilfe."
77. Richard Messerer, "Soziale Gerichtshilfe," *Münchener Zeitung*, 29 April 1930.
78. Dr. Böhmert, in *Mitteilungen der IKV* Neue Folge 4 (1930).

Part III

CONSTRUCTIONS OF CRIME IN THE WEIMAR COURTS, MEDIA, AND LITERATURE

Chapter 7

PROSTITUTES, RESPECTABLE WOMEN, AND WOMEN FROM "OUTSIDE"

The Carl Grossmann Sexual Murder Case in Postwar Berlin

Sace Elder

Few of Weimar Germany's notorious criminals epitomize the sexual and moral decadence often associated with the period better than the "sexual murderer" Karl (who went by Carl) Friedrich Wilhelm Grossmann. Known popularly as the Blue Beard or the Beast of the Silesian train station district of Berlin, Grossmann won infamy in August 1921, when he was discovered in his one-room apartment in one of the poorest of Berlin's proletarian districts, standing blood-soaked over the lifeless body of young Marie Nitsche. After many weeks of interrogation, Grossmann admitted to the murders of two other women. Officials, however, became convinced that he was in fact responsible for the violent deaths of many more women, some of whom had never been identified.[1] The most horrifying aspect of the murders was the brutal dismemberment of the bodies, which had been tossed into the canals and channels of eastern Berlin. Grossmann's motive, officials and medical examiners believed, had been sexual: Grossmann was, they argued, a classic sexual murderer who achieved sexual satisfaction through killing his victim during sexual intercourse. Like the period's other notorious sexual predators, Fritz Haarmann and Peter Kürten, Grossmann's story has become iconic as a symbol of the criminality and gender anxiety of the 1920s. The Grossmann case in particular provided a set of visual themes for artists such as George Grosz and Otto Dix. Scholarly literature on the subject of sexual violence in Weimar culture has demonstrated the prevalence of representations of violated female bodies in avant-garde art and literature and has suggested that the images of mutilated breasts, ripped wombs, and slashed vaginas were indicative of a male psychological trauma stemming from the war and the disruption of prewar bourgeois gender norms.[2]

Grossmann thus perpetrated his crimes in a society that was very much concerned with sexual and criminal deviance.[3] Historian Kerstin Brückweh has explained the twentieth-century fascination with sexual murder in terms of "an ambivalent emotion defined by attraction and interest" that is conditioned in part by feelings and also by fantasy.[4] Perhaps this fascination is why the story of Grossmann and his victims became as elastic and mythologized as any urban legend, even in criminological literature. Already before the trial, rumors circulated that Grossmann, who had worked as a butcher's apprentice earlier in life, had sold the flesh of his victims to unsuspecting neighbors.[5] Later descriptions fictionalized the case to fit certain notions of criminality. In a treatise on the "professional criminal," the criminologist Robert Heindl, for example, described Grossmann as a dangerous criminal who profited from his crimes by selling the flesh and clothing of his victims to unwitting neighbors. According to Heindl, Grossmann's motives were purely economic and Grossmann was therefore a professional or habitual criminal who needed to be removed from society.[6] By contrast, in his 1930 work *Sex and Crime* (*Geschlecht und Verbrechen*), sexologist Magnus Hirschfeld regarded Grossmann as a typical *sexual* murderer who, far from selling anything, ate the flesh and drank the blood of his victims.[7] According to Curt Elwenspoek's 1930 book on the criminal police (intended to popularize police work), Grossmann was an anonymous urban killer whom no one suspected until it was too late.[8]

Grossmann's crimes became the stuff of legend even before his trial was held. During the months-long investigation and his abbreviated trial, the press, crime experts, and local citizens all sought to make sense of Grossmann and his crimes. The case captured the public imagination in 1921–1922 precisely because it touched on the themes most relevant to the topsy-turvy world of postwar and postrevolutionary Germany. Whereas Grossmann may have represented the pathology of urban anonymity, his victims represented the social and cultural crises feared by many observers: rural-urban migration increased by privation in the countryside, the "surplus of women" produced by wartime mobilization, the alleged decline in morality among women and juveniles, and the increased criminality in the city. In the end, the Grossmann case was about sex in the way that sex is always about everything else, and in this instance, it was about the state of German gender and class relations.

The Carl Grossmann case was thus quintessentially "Weimar" because it reflected the contested nature of social and gender relations in the immediate postwar period. It is therefore important to interrogate the specific historical context in which the narratives were first formulated and understand what they might have meant for the construction of lower-class sexuality and gender roles in the postwar years.[9] Crime reporting in the metropolitan press had been a crucial component in the *reading* and *writing* of urban space in the prewar years, and it would likewise help shape perceptions of social reality in the postwar period.[10] The Grossmann case thus provides a useful vantage point from which to observe the public anxieties about sexuality, the family, and womanhood, while also providing clues as to how these were being culturally reconstituted in the postwar era.[11]

The extensive and sensationalized press coverage associated with the criminal investigation and trial placed Grossmann, his victims, and his proletarian neighborhood under close public scrutiny. In addition, countless women from Grossmann's milieu revealed to investigators and court officials that they, too, had experienced Grossmann's violence. The copious court records generated by the investigation reveal a set of social relations in the poorest parts of proletarian Berlin that was at odds with the often salacious and sensational public narratives written about the perpetrator and his victims. It is in the space between the public narratives told about Grossmann's victims and their milieu and the stories that the women of the Silesian train station neighborhood told about themselves that the significance of the Grossmann case for early Weimar class and gender relations can be found.

Grossmann's Victims and Their Milieu

The area surrounding the Silesian train station in the eastern part of the Berlin was one of Berlin's most economically depressed neighborhoods and a reputed crime district (*Verbrecherviertel*). The economic and social conditions of the postwar period created a mixed population of permanent residents and transients passing through the city on their way to and from the eastern provinces. Factory workers, day laborers, seasonal workers, prostitutes, the unemployed, peddlers, shopkeepers, wives, and mothers called this district home. Police found it difficult to maintain their accustomed control over such a population. Registration of domicile with the local police precinct was the chief means by which police could control and identify individuals, yet migrants and runaways tended to live unregistered, moving from one temporary housing situation to another.

Despite the clandestine activities, life in the district was extremely public. As in all working-class districts of Berlin, many of life's daily activities were carried out in the streets, especially in the summertime, when the narrow and poorly ventilated tenement houses were particularly uncomfortable. The local pubs, the market, and the train station itself were favorite meeting places for lonely-hearts, as well as prostitutes and their clients. Hans Ostwald, in his prewar study of prostitution in Berlin, described the scene in this corner of the city: "In the sooty Koppenstraße at the Silesian train station poor, weathered, and wrecked creatures walk around nightly, especially on Saturdays, without head-covering and with blue kitchen aprons. They count on the drunken workers returning home, to whom they can offer themselves for one to two Marks."[12] In this public life of the streets and parks, Grossmann, who had moved to the neighborhood from a cabin in a suburban garden colony in 1919, made the acquaintance of many women. As Grossmann well knew, the neighborhood's close proximity to the train station as well as the openness of the street facilitated encounters with the residents and migrants in the neighborhood, many of whom were unemployed. Among the area residents' favorite gathering and resting places was the Andreasplatz, a small park just one block north of Grossmann's apartment building in Lange Straße; it was in this park that Grossmann met many of his female acquaintances. One resident of the area who had known Grossmann for two years and frequently went to Andreasplatz "on doctor's orders" for fresh air reported that Grossmann was a "well known personality" in the park because "he was there almost daily and always had a different friend with him."[13]

To the women he met who were in dire economic circumstances, Grossmann would often offer food, shelter, money or, in many cases, employment as a house-keeper. Many residents of the neighborhood availed themselves of Grossmann's financial assistance. As a relatively successful street peddler in this economically depressed neighborhood, Grossmann was an employer of women, a customer of prostitutes and local drinking establishments, a moneylender to neighbors, and to a few, a drinking companion. Grossmann certainly performed these roles with an eye to his own interests, exploiting the economic, physical, and sexual vulnerabilities of his would-be beneficiaries. His economic position, although marginal by middle-class standards, afforded him in this neighborhood the status of benefactor of last resort.[14] The very neighbors who reported Grossmann to the authorities, for example, also owed him money and were known to have social-ized with Grossmann in local drinking establishments and amusement parks. A married woman who lived on Grossmann's floor admitted to police in her first interview that she and her husband owed Grossmann 58 Marks.[15]

In his neighborhood, then, Grossmann was no anonymous urban predator like the Ripper of Whitechapel, with whom he would later be compared. He was, on the contrary, quite well-known, if not universally liked. He participated in the open sociability of the neighborhood inhabited by both transients and long-term residents. The women who accepted work, food, or clothing from Grossmann in exchange for labor or sexual favors were all very poor, but came from a range of occupational backgrounds and family situations. One resident of Grossmann's building told police that the women he had seen trafficking in Grossmann's apartment had been "mostly prostitutes, partly also respectable [*anständige*] women. . . . Partly he also had women from outside [Berlin] in his apartment."[16] We know quite a bit about the women who made Grossmann's acquaintance in this way because many of them came forward to give testimony regarding Grossmann's sexual behavior and social connections. The stories some of these women told of sexual abuse at the hands of Grossmann were used as evidence of his propensity to sexual violence. According to their statements and testimonies, many of the women who had accepted Grossmann's offers were single women with no social networks, whether they had recently arrived in the city or had lived there for some time. Although some of his "guests" were registered prostitutes, others were mothers living in the neighborhood. One woman told police that she had met Grossmann through a friend and, after leaving her six-year-old son at home, went to Grossmann's apartment. In return for sleeping with him she received some used clothing.[17] Another woman who lived in the building next door to Grossmann's had met him in the summer of 1920 on Andreasplatz and had agreed to have sex with him in exchange for food for herself and her child.[18] An unemployed worker, who was married when she gave her statement in August 1921, told officials she had lived briefly with Grossmann under similar circumstances in his cabin in 1918.[19]

In 1921, these women of the Silesian train station district were still feeling the economic and social effects of the war and postwar demobilization. They were the women that historian Belinda Davis has identified as the "women of lesser means" whose marginal existences during the war drew considerable public attention and produced widespread criticism of the Imperial government's wartime policies. In fact, the neighborhood was the site of two butter riots in October 1915.[20] For many of these women, the war effort had meant bearing the double burden of running the household while the men of the family were away, only to end up unemployed at the end of the war. Even in the fall of 1920, when unemployment had begun to abate elsewhere in Germany, Berlin, along with Saxony and Hamburg, still had one of the highest rates of unemployment in the immediate postwar years. Part of the reason for the high unemployment rate in Berlin was the high level of immigration to the city. Unemployment among women was particularly high in Berlin, where women made up 47 percent of those looking for jobs.[21] Even with the return to full employment in 1922, the labor market was not favorable to women seeking heavy industrial jobs, as demobilization policies carried out by employers tended to displace women back into traditional jobs of cooking, cleaning, and textiles.[22]

That many women in this area of Berlin, whether recent arrivals or long-term residents, had turned to domestic labor or prostitution to make ends meet was not unusual for women of their milieu. In fact, the biographical profiles of the women who had turned to Grossmann for material aid were very much typical of the profiles of prostitutes in general, who were usually women of marginal social status who resorted to prostitution as a transitional strategy to cope with changed economic circumstances. Often these women later returned to other forms of employment, although the regulation of prostitution, which included compulsory registration, could make this return to so-called respectability difficult.[23] Hans Ostwald categorized such women with gainful employment who occasionally exchanged sex for money, gifts, or food as "casual prostitutes" (*Gele-genheitsdirnen*), whose numbers he estimated at five to ten times the number of registered prostitutes. Prostitution such as this was casual because it did not constitute an occupation or a complete lifestyle. Unlike many critics of prostitution at the time, Ostwald saw this kind of pecuniary sexual activity as an economic strategy rather than the result of sexual perversity or innate moral depravity.[24]

Although Ostwald admitted that it was often difficult to tell the difference between casual prostitution and a love affair, it is clear that many of the women who came into contact with Grossmann fit Ostwald's description of occasional prostitutes. To be sure, some of Grossmann's guests were registered prostitutes, but most did not practice prostitution as a sole means of support. Among those women interviewed by officials, some indicated that they had understood from the beginning that Grossmann had expected sexual favors in return for his beneficence. Others indicated that they had accepted Grossmann's invitation as a legitimate offer of employment or aid. One unemployed industrial worker, for example, accepted Grossmann's offer of employment as a housekeeper in August 1921. After she had worked for a day performing household tasks for Grossmann, he drugged and raped her.[25] Most of the women who had had remunerative sexual relations with Grossmann had a range of occupational experience, although virtually all were unemployed.

Most of the women who had visited Grossmann's apartment had worked for him or had exchanged sexual relations for food or money and could therefore not be categorized as *Straßendirnen* (streetwalkers) or *Kontrollmädchen* (registered prostitutes) who sustained themselves through illicit sexual behavior. Significantly, in some cases it was precisely those women who had the most experience in such situations who avoided the fate of Grossmann's victims. Prostitute Erika, for example, found Grossmann's residence and his demeanor too "creepy" to complete the sexual transaction to which she had agreed, [26] while Johanna, a recent migrant to the city, gladly and perhaps naively accepted Grossmann's invitation to dinner. But neither were these women who had never run into trouble with the law. Nitsche, Grossmann's final murder victim, had been enjoying her first day of freedom after a month-long stay at Moabit prison when she made Grossmann's acquaintance on the street. After an evening of drinking in the local pubs, Grossmann and Nitsche retired to Grossmann's apartment, where he laced her coffee with cyanide, bound her hands and feet, and beat her head until she was dead.[27]

In sum, the women of Grossmann's milieu shared a marginal subsistence-level existence conditioned by the adverse conditions of urban migration, postwar mobilization, and economic destabilization; and they all faced employment and residential options circumscribed by the exigencies of official and unofficial gender politics. But in terms of their family status, their relationship to their community, their occupational and residential histories, the community of women that the Grossmann case revealed was fairly diverse. The women's testimonies suggested, in fact, that marriage and motherhood had not protected women from the dangers of Grossmann's apartment.

What the women did share was an aversion to state authority that dissuaded them from seeking the aid or protection of the police. Although not all of the women who admitted having had sexual intercourse with Grossmann had had violent experiences with him, many of the women told harrowing stories of sexual abuse. One woman told police that Grossmann had laced her coffee with a sedative that made her unconscious, and when she awoke she found herself bound to the bed and experienced pain in her genitalia. She suspected he had inflicted some kind of "perversity" on her.[28] When another woman visited Grossmann's apartment, he bound her to his bed and brutally thrust his hand into her vagina so that she bled profusely.[29] That none of the women had made an official complaint to the police was due to several interrelated factors. Helene B. admitted in her second interview with detectives that she had been so ashamed of what Grossmann had done to her she had initially lied to them about her relationship with him. That the damage he had done to her vagina had resulted from initially consensual intercourse had no doubt led her to avoid police rather than seek their protection.[30]

There was no space in the judicial system to redress the grievances of these women because of their compromised relationship with the police. If suspected of solicitation, a woman would have been registered as a prostitute with the morals police and subjected to the regular medical examinations of prostitutes provided for in the German criminal code. Although the registration of prostitutes did not stigmatize them within working-class communities in Germany to the degree that it did in France, Britain, and Italy, the practice did limit their ability to move freely about the city and made it more difficult for women to find adequate housing or to return to other forms of employment.[31] Even if they did not fear being suspected of prostitution, some of the women probably worried about being cited for living unregistered in Grossmann's apartment, as all city residents were (and are) required by law to register their addresses with the local police. The women thus had reason to see the police not as protectors, but as persecutors. Furthermore, the police saw these women's stories as evidence in a murder case, not as evidence of violent crimes committed on their persons.[32]

Grossmann was able to use the antagonistic relationship between the authorities and the women of the neighborhood to his advantage. He became notorious at the local police station for accusing his female housekeepers of stealing money from him; at least until the police grew tired of his frequent visits. By the time the police questioned Emma B. about Grossmann's accusations, they were more inclined to believe her because Grossmann had become something of a nuisance with his frequent visits to the police station.[33] Frieda T., however, did not escape so easily. Charges against her were dropped only after Grossmann was apprehended and she agreed to testify against him at trial.[34]

On the surface, Carl Grossmann's life history looked very much like those of other members of Germany's lower classes in the period of rapid industrialization. He was born in 1863 as one of seven children of a merchant in Neuruppin where he attended school until he was fourteen years old, when he went to work in a textile factory to help support his family. At age sixteen he left Neuruppin with a friend for Berlin, where he hoped to find work. In Berlin he held many jobs, including an apprenticeship at a butcher's shop. At age nineteen he was drafted into the military, but was released due to a hernia. After his release he returned to Berlin, and later Pomerania, Mecklenburg, and other rural areas, where he worked as an agricultural laborer, always returning to Berlin in between. In the ten years before his capture, Grossmann had been a permanent resident of the capital city, in various apartments in the eastern part of the city and in a cabin in an allotment garden (*Laubenkolonie*), which he left in 1919, when he took up permanent residence at Lange Straße 88/89.[35] In light of his crimes, Grossmann's wanderings may have been attributed to a shiftless and criminal nature. In fact, however, his geographic and occupational mobility was quite characteristic of the rural-urban migrants who, in the last phases of urbanization before the war, slowly began to settle permanently in urban areas.[36]

Where Grossmann stood out from his milieu was in both the length and the nature of his criminal history. His criminal record began at age twenty, when he was sentenced to three days in jail for begging. After that, Grossmann spent much of his life serving short sentences for begging, theft, vagrancy, and crimes against decency. Such petty crimes, of course, were common both in Berlin and in the countryside. In 1896, however, he was convicted of "unnatural sexual assault" on a sheep in Mannheim; in 1897 for sexual assault against a twelve-year-old girl in Nuremberg; and in 1899 he was sentenced to fifteen years hard labor in the penitentiary for the rape of two small girls, one of whom was badly injured in the assault.[37]

At the time of his apprehension in August 1921, Grossmann had been a member of the Silesian train station neighborhood for about two years. He was a frequent if unwelcome guest at the local police station with his fallacious reporting of missing and felonious housekeepers. He was also well-known in his tenement house at Lange Straße: quite notorious, in fact, for returning home to his one-room apartment very late in the evenings with one or more women, creating quite a racket as they ascended the numerous flights to the top-story apartment. Strange noises and noxious odors emanated from his apartment, prompting residents to wonder aloud what went on there so late in the evenings.

A crowded apartment building, open streets, familiar bars—how did Grossmann manage to rape, murder, and dismember the bodies of his victims? Based on their statements to investigators, the reaction of Grossmann's neighbors was indicative of a broad cultural acceptance of violence against women, which was regarded as an essentially private matter. Domestic abuse was pervasive in the working-class communities of the Weimar era (and indeed, earlier) and was one of the most insidious ways in which male authority in the working-class household was maintained. Very seldom did neighbors intervene on behalf of a battered wife. The informal mutual-help networks of women that were such an integral part of female working-class life were usually only able to provide solace after the fact.[38] Grossmann's womanizing became most bothersome to his neighbors when it became noisy and invaded their private space, but even then their interventions were limited. The frustrated demand of a neighbor one evening that Grossmann desist from abusing his female visitor, whose screams could be heard throughout the floor, was met with an angry "Shut your face!" ("Halt die Schnauze!") from Grossmann's side of his closed apartment door.[39] No one made sure that the woman in Grossmann's apartment was safe; they were only concerned that the noise stop. Max Neumann, also on Grossmann's corridor, tried to defend this behavior by telling police that the cries they heard had not been cries for help (*Hilferufe*) but rather cries of pain (*Wehrufe*).[40] Whether this distinction was his own or prompted by police, the fact that a distinction was made at all indicates that investigators and witnesses were seeking to explain why no one had intervened more forcefully on behalf of Grossmann's victims.[41]

Grossmann's neighbors thus confessed that they had known that he had abused his many female visitors. And although they occasionally demanded that he desist from that abuse, this was done only when the violence caused enough noise to disturb the neighbors in their own apartments. Although Grossmann's behavior was bothersome, it was not so far out of the ordinary as to be considered criminal. Not until police posted public notices of the latest crimes in early August 1921 and made it known that they suspected that the murderer lived in the Silesian train station district did his neighbors suspect that Grossmann could be involved in the crimes. Helene and Mannheim Itzig, corridor neighbors of Grossmann's, admitted to having bored a hole through Grossmann's door in order to better observe his activities, having noticed how roughly he treated women. The wanted posters regarding the murdered women in the neighborhood led them to think "instinctively" of Grossmann. "As a consequence, he was closely observed by us."[42] It is impossible to know whether they were observing Grossmann out of a sense of civic responsibility, a hope for reward, or to blackmail him. Perhaps it was a combination of all three. Whatever their motivations, the Itzigs did on a certain level behave exactly as the police expected them to: They carefully observed the suspicious activities of a neighbor and eventually brought these activities to the attention of the authorities.

Aside from the commotion created by the cries of pain coming from Grossmann's apartment, the malodorous smell emanating from the bloody body parts also drew the attention of his neighbors. But when Grossmann was asked about the foul stench emanating from his apartment, he answered simply that chicken meat had spoiled, an explanation readily accepted by neighbors living in the same crowded and poorly ventilated apartment building in the stifling July and August heat. Although the smell was unpleasant, only in retrospect did it become criminal.

In view of the physical features of Grossmann's living situation, the brutal elements of his crimes appear to have had a practical aspect as well. In this crowded apartment building, removing the body from the fourth floor would have been most difficult without attracting attention. By dismembering the bodies, Grossmann was able to remove them from his apartment in inconspicuously small paper packages and burn some of the pieces in his apartment oven. To dispose of not just one but several human corpses in such a way surely required a certain amount of sadism and psychopathic misogyny. At the same time, however, the elements of the crime that most aroused the morbid fascination of the public and most attested to Grossmann's sadistic perversity were also practical (criminal) responses to the challenges presented by the urban environment.

The Silesian train station neighborhood was a marginal community whose economic conditions facilitated Grossmann's violence against women. Far from being the innocuous neighbor described by Elwenspoek, Grossmann was a familiar, although to many unpopular, figure in the neighborhood. His somewhat better economic position (however attained) made him a significant if unsavory resource not only for single women, but also for established residents of the community. Grossmann was able to carry out his violent abuse of women not simply because of their economic situation, but because of the prevailing codes of behavior in urban tenement houses, which reinforced the boundaries between public and private, and because of a system of regulation that discouraged women from discussing their experiences with the authorities. The social identities of these women cannot be reduced to that of prostitute because mothers, wives, and women with previous occupational experience could be counted among the visitors to Grossmann's apartment. If anything, the testimonies of the witnesses in the Grossmann trial revealed that traditional family roles—motherhood, marriage, domestic work—had not provided protection from the sexual danger Grossmann presented. All this is especially significant because the ways in which the press and crime professionals sought to make sense of the crimes only served to mask these complex social identities and reinforce the power relations that made Grossmann's crimes possible in the first place.

Public Narratives of the Crime

Grossmann was apprehended in August 1921. His trial was held in early July 1922 and was cut short after three days by his jail-cell suicide. In the intervening months, the primary detectives in the case, Werneburg and Riemann, as well as the state attorney's office sought to establish the full extent of Grossmann's crimes. As the investigation wore on, the press, police, and other criminological experts tried to reconstruct Grossmann's crimes by establishing just who Grossmann's victims were. The social and moral identities of Grossmann's victims were of singular importance to the investigation for two reasons. First, the police had been investigating the unsolved murders of many young women since 1919, some of whom had been dismembered and found in the Luisenstadt Canal and the Engelbecken reservoir. Officials had been unable to put names to some of the corpses, so that the identities of these victims remained a mystery. Second, as in many murder cases, the identity of the victims held the key to the degree of the perpetrator's guilt. This was particularly important in the Grossmann case because Grossmann claimed that his victims had provoked his violence by stealing from him, but it was also true with respect to the public's perception of Grossmann's criminality: a killer of innocents seemed more horrifying and less explicable than a killer of prostitutes. As Judith Walkowitz has argued with regard to the Jack the Ripper case, the moral status of the victims taught newspaper readers important lessons about the dangers of the city.[43] Although the Social-Democratic newspaper *Vorwärts* reported that the Grossmann case excited a "great furor" and "has caused primarily the feminine population of Berlin understandable anxiety and excitement,"[44] most of the reporting on the Grossmann case separated the identities of the victims from so-called respectable society, reassuring the reader of (her) safety. The German detective and criminologist Robert Heindl would point out later, with regard to Jack the Ripper, that most Londoners were, in fact, as safe as ever in 1888 when the Ripper was prowling Whitechapel.[45] Press reports, forensic experts, and crime professionals established essentially two sets of identities for Grossmann's victims: prostitutes and innocent young girls from the countryside. Both groups of women fell outside the protective confines of family and community and placed themselves in danger.

There were many reasons why the Grossmann murders became a public sensation. In the heady years of the immediate postwar period, bloated, water-logged bodies—dismembered or otherwise—frequently surfaced in the city's numerous waterways. Victims of political violence, such as Karl Blau, of domestic violence, such as Anselm Hemberger, or of neighborly disputes found their penultimate resting places in the Landwehr Canal, the Luisienstadt Canal, the river Spree, or the lakes on the outskirts of town, to be found by unsuspecting citizens.[46] In the context of postwar disruptions and urban migration, unidentified victims of murder or suicide were especially disconcerting for a public already distressed by the high number of persons who seemed to have disappeared into the anonymity of metropolitan life. On 7 August 1921, Egon Jacobsohn published an article in the *Berliner Morgenpost* titled "Persons who Disappear," in which he reported that 3,425 people had been reported missing in Prussia and other German states in 1919, and that the number climbed to 4,280 in 1921. Many of these were young runaways, Jacobsohn wrote, especially attractive young women seeking fame on the stage or film.[47] Just two days later, *Morgenpost* readers would have found evidence of the dire consequences of the missing-persons epidemic when the paper reported the discovery in the Luisenstadt Canal of the lower leg and spinal cord of an unidentified woman in her early twenties.[48]

Particularly sensational was Grossmann's official designation as a sexual offender. Already two weeks before Grossmann was apprehended, newspapers were reporting that the murdered women whose dismembered bodies had been found in the city's waterways in previous months had fallen victim to a *Lustmörder* (sexual murderer).[49] Grossmann initially insisted that the three murders to which he confessed had been acts of passion (*Affekthandlungen*), that the women had tried to steal money from him, and that he had killed them in a rage. He further contended that he had dismembered his victims' bodies only to dispose of the corpses—a strategy other murderers had used in the crowded tenements of Berlin in the very months when Grossmann had committed his crimes.[50] Nevertheless, there was no doubt in the minds of investigators and medical experts that Grossmann was a sexual murderer. By 1921, sexual murder was a well-documented and well-defined phenomenon, which experts understood as a pathological manifestation of psychosexual dysfunction. According to one of the period's most prolific authors on the subject, the jurist Erich Wulffen, true sexual murder was related to rape and was one in which the motive was the "manifestation of a degenerate sexual urge."[51] Criminalists associated the mutilation of corpses with sexual perversions that resulted in particularly gruesome violent acts. According to jurists and criminologists, *Lustmörder* were sexually aroused by extreme violence to the victim's body, by the sight of blood, or by sexual intercourse with a corpse; such crimes did not necessarily require the completion of the sexual act on the part of the murderer. Murders committed after sexual contact but for different motives, such as from fear of discovery, were generally not considered true sexual murders. The criminal psychology of sexual murder became such an important factor in the determination of criminal indictments (murder versus manslaughter) that by 1941 the motive of sexual desire, along with greed and the drive to kill, was added to the German penal code as a prerequisite for first-degree murder.[52]

But the sexual perversion of the murderer alone did not suffice to make the murders morally and culturally legible. Even before the identities of the murderer and his victims were known, the social geography of the city played a key role in the investigation of the crimes. The location of the discovery of the unidentified bodies not far from the Silesian train station gave them a moral and social identity and also indirectly confirmed the assumption that the murders had been sexual. Following the profile of the sexual criminal that had been most influentially articulated by Erich Wulffen, the police assumed that the women, given the location of their bodies, had been prostitutes. Wulffen and others had maintained that most sexual murders involved prostitutes because they supposedly exposed themselves to male sexual perversion more than did respectable women. Pursuing this line of argument, a newspaper article in the *Berliner Morgenpost* published shortly after Grossmann was arrested reassured readers that although Grossmann could be counted among such notable serial killers as Jack the Ripper, most such murderers victimized prostitutes. As if to further reassure respectable female readers of their safety, the article continued: "In Berlin the murders of women have been carried out in rather considerable numbers. Most of these are isolated crimes." [53]

Murders of prostitutes tended to receive less attention from police and the public than did murders of innocent children and "morally upstanding" women.[54] The violent demise of a prostitute seemed explicable because she exposed herself to aggressive male sexuality and cheapened her own life through the commodification of her body. This popular attitude was evident in October 1920 when newspapers reported the murder of prostitute Frieda Schubert, whose death was later attributed to Grossmann. On 16 October the *Berliner Morgenpost* related the gory details of the crime, explaining that the murder appeared to have been the work of a sadist, who "sawed the bones apart with unbelievable brutality and tore the heart from the ribcage and the right arm from the shoulder."[55] The horror of the story was alleviated, however, by its incongruous juxtaposition on the page with an unrelated market report with the byline "Meat is Getting Cheaper" ("*Das Fleisch wird billiger*"). Whether the alignment of these two stories was the result of newsroom humor or editorial oversight is not clear. However, a callous attitude toward the brutal death of the young woman was clearly evident in an article the following day, which reported that the Identification Service of the Berlin Police had identified the victim through fingerprint records. Thirty-three year-old "street girl" Frieda Schubert, born in Dresden, "was not particularly well liked in her neighborhood because of her impudent behavior [*freches Auftreten*]." On the day of her disappearance, the story continued, Schubert had approached several men on the street until one unidentified man (supposedly the murderer) accepted her services.[56] The implication of the article was clear: Schubert's lifestyle, which her cheeky behavior indicated was chosen rather than forced upon her, had led to her ultimate demise; in the end, she was responsible for her own death. The descriptions of Schubert's character in the press were in keeping with the ways in which crime professionals characterized the women of Grossmann's milieu, to whom they attributed low-level criminality and social and mental inferiority. According to Peter Becker, as criminal science became medicalized in the latter part of the nineteenth century, German criminological discourse characterized the prostitute as both a victim and a vehicle of social degeneration; her mental and physical development were supposedly hindered by inherent physiological conditions or by the environment. Under this paradigm, according to Becker, prostitutes were seen as psychologically and physically weak, unable to protect themselves from moral depravity or to live in respectable society.[57]

Once the identity of Berlin's serial sexual murderer was discovered, the Berlin newspapers' treatment of the murder victims masked the social identities and experiences of Grossmann's victims in a variety of ways. The rather conservative *Berliner Lokal-Anzeiger*, for instance, was much more interested in the criminal than in his victims. Grossmann was a "degenerate" (*Wüstling*), a "homely, ugly man" (*unscheinbarer, häßlicher Mensch*), who preyed on women who "suffered from need and hunger."[58] The newspaper was only interested in the identity of the victims insofar as they could prove the number of women Grossmann had killed. "The homicide squad has conclusive evidence that Grossmann's victim's number at least 15 to 20 who were murdered not just in Berlin but also outside of the city," the newspaper reported on 4 September.[59]

By contrast, in the pages of the liberal Ullstein newspapers, the portrayals of Grossmann as a morally aberrant sexual predator featured characterizations of his victims as weak and vulnerable. Although most of the information about Grossmann's sexual exploits came from women who had experienced this first-hand, the newspapers' descriptions of the unidentified murder victims differed from the identities and experiences of these female witnesses. The *Morgenpost* characterized Grossmann's murder victims as young, single migrants from the countryside. The women were thus made out to be, as Grossmann's defense attorney later described them, "poor girls from the provinces."[60] In a report on the case a day after Grossmann's capture, the *Berliner Morgenpost* dramatized for its readers what a meeting between the murderer and his victim might have been like:

[He] goes searching the streets. There stands a girl looking greedily into a grocery store. "Well, little one, do you want to eat?" inquires Grossmann. "Yes, but I have no money!" is the unhappy answer. That is his cup of tea. He seeks out the hungry. They are the most submissive. "Would you like to be my housekeeper?" he asks and pulls from his coat pocket his wallet with numerous hundreds. Overjoyed the suffering one seizes the opportunity. [She] goes with the old one. Fearless. What can this weak fellow do to her? He stands there, says a witness later, before his deathbed. [She] receives, of course, not one penny in wages. Only plenty to eat. And that is the most important thing.[61]

The vignette, written in the style of crime fiction, contrasts the street-smart and calculating urban male predator against the naive, weak, and trusting female victim, whose sexual exploitation is made possible by her material destitution. The young woman is apparently oblivious to the sexual intentions of her host, who dupes her with the promise of legitimate employment. The reader already knows how the scenario ends: the young woman's desperation ends in her violent death.

The *BZ am Mittag* similarly reconstructed for its readers how one missing person and alleged murder victim, Melanie Sommer, might have met Grossmann in a restaurant one day in December 1920. "She shuddered with disgust as she saw this old, unclean and repulsive man before her but, after a long resistance, followed him despite this because in her great need she preferred staying with him to dying of hunger."[62] The fictional description of Sommer's reaction to Grossmann's appearance morally separated the criminal from his victim by emphasizing his advanced age, his unpleasant physical attributes, and the victim's negative reaction to his presence. The physical presence of the victim, on the other hand, is only signified through her physiological need for food. Her decision to follow him, in spite of her revulsion, is portrayed as an act of desperation.[63]

These images of the female murder victims served as a foil for Grossmann's characterization as a sexual predator. According to these images, the murder victims' behavior arose from their economic desperation, while the murderer's behavior was based on malevolent calculation for the satisfaction of his perverse sexual appetite. This did not mean, however, that the victims were morally innocent. Grossmann's victims supposedly represented the young, single women newly arrived in Berlin with no family, no social network, and no job, who were at the mercy of the impersonal forces of the urban terrain and the market. In other words, they stood outside the protective confines of conventional gender roles of marriage, motherhood, and family. According to the *Berliner Morgenpost*, one missing person and possible murder victim, Emma Baumann, came from a "good family" in Mecklenburg. After a fight with her father—a landed proprietor, the newspaper helpfully detailed—she ran away to Berlin "without money and without protection." The police found her name and vital information in a list made by the morals police (*Sittlichkeitspolizei*) during a hotel raid in December 1920.[64] According to the *BZ am Mittag*, Emma was a "picture-pretty, nineteen year-old girl" who had run away on foot and, in her doubtful circumstances, ran into Grossmann on her first day in Berlin.[65] Implicit in the reporting was the fate of the wayward daughter: her fractiousness led to a life of prostitution and later murder. The women were thus not merely victims of circumstance; they were also partly to blame for the violence committed against them because they lived outside the protective confines of family and community.

By presenting the women as victims of circumstance rather than as whores (as with Frieda Schubert), the liberal Ullstein Press's narratives of Grossmann's crimes magnified Grossmann's social, sexual, and moral depravity. Clearly, these characterizations of Grossmann's victims were rather more sympathetic in their appreciation of the dire material circumstances that would have led young women into Grossmann's apartment. Nevertheless, the moral status of the victims was not unequivocal. The narratives of the crimes were tragic because the victim's own waywardness had led them into desperate situations and thus made them vulnerable to the sinister sexual criminal Grossmann. By living away from family and social networks, the young women had exposed themselves to the predatory male realm of the city. Neither the *Morgenpost* nor the other popular newspapers examined the broader economic and social circumstances that shaped these women's experiences and made Grossmann an alternative to "dying of hunger." The fatal result of the victims' transgressions eliminated the possibility of redemption and reconciliation with respectable society.

The public fascination with Grossmann's self-titled "housekeeper system"—luring women into his apartment with an offer of employment as his cleaning woman—showed that the public was struggling to make sense of the social and moral ambiguity of the victims. "Residents [of Grossmann's apartment building] speak of at least 150 [housekeepers]!" was one exclamatory report in the *Morgenpost*. The press routinely referred to Grossmann's victims and the women involved in the case as "housekeepers," using quotation marks to expose Grossmann's intentions and the sexual nature of the relationship, which even the most sensational reports never explicitly discussed. When the press referred to Grossmann's victims as "housekeepers," the quotation marks implicated the women in the crimes committed against them by exposing the attempt to legitimate illicit sexual relations through an employer-employee relationship. The image of the household servant or "domestic" would have been a complicated one for the *Morgenpost*'s readers. Middle-class concerns about morality among young girls and within the family had long connected domestic service with sexual license and prostitution. Since the turn of the century, socialists and social reformers alike had been drawing public attention to the psychological impact of domestic service, which supposedly rendered young girls submissive, lacking in self-awareness, and easily turned toward sexual impropriety. Such reformers maintained that domestic servants were statistically far more likely to become prostitutes, produce illegitimate children, and commit infanticide.[66]

Grossmann and his "housekeepers" were clearly engaging in what Hans Ostwald called casual, or "occasional," prostitution. During the war, such exchanges were characterized as "secret prostitution"—that is, prostitution not registered with the police. Secret prostitution became a grave concern to policymakers worried about low birth rates and morale at the war front, who saw it not as a strategy for economic survival but rather as the frivolous deviance of married and unmarried women who had forgotten their familial and social responsibilities while their men were away at war.[67] Officials' concern with secret prostitution reflected wartime anxieties about the erosion of the family and women's purported resistance to rational mobilization. After the war, reformers used casual prostitution as evidence for the failure of regulation to put an end to prostitution altogether. In the years following the 1918–1919 Revolution and the extension of the franchise to women, anti-regulationists campaigned for the limitation of the powers of the morals police.[68]

The press and crime experts also made morally legible the women on whom the police depended for information about Grossmann's victims and violent proclivities. A psychiatrist commenting on the Grossmann trial spoke of Grossmann's victims in the Social-Darwinist terms of being "not fit for the struggle for survival." The "indolence" and "emotional apathy of th[e] low social sphere" these women inhabited explained why no one interfered in Grossmann's activities before his capture.[69] In his view, Grossmann's milieu bore part of the blame for the crimes because of its alleged passivity and moral turpitude. Another forensic psychiatrist warned prosecutors that "the girls whom he [Grossmann] took in came mostly from completely depraved and evil social circles, and certainly many exaggerate and lie."[70] Similarly, the *Berliner Lokal-Anzeiger*, perhaps the least sympathetic to the women in the Grossmann case of all the Berlin dailies, declared that "about half of the female witnesses [in the case] are homeless, belong in part to the offscouring [*Hefe*] of the population, and can only be located and brought forward by a detective" when they are needed.[71] Those who believed in the fundamental depravity of the women and their milieu found evidence for their convictions when Grossmann's neighbor was arrested for allegedly having blackmailed Grossmann before his arrest. The *Berliner Volkszeitung* dramatized for its readers a fictitious scene between Grossmann and the neighbor, putting in her mouth the words "Now hand over fifty Marks, or I'll turn you in!"[72]

The *Berliner Morgenpost* was the only newspaper to address the issue of the regulation of prostitution as a deterrent to the female witnesses against coming forward with their experiences sooner. The daily paper explained, correctly, that the female witnesses "never would have wanted to make an official complaint to police because they feared that they would have been held responsible because they lived with him unregistered [with police]."[73] But the implication of the report was also that although the women were performing their civic duty by offering their knowledge to investigators, it was not to be forgotten that this knowledge was gained through illicit activity. Furthermore, the report was misleading in suggesting that it was not registration as prostitutes that the women feared but being caught without proper residential documentation.

Just as in Victorian London, the public narratives of Grossmann's crimes also held lessons for women about the consequences of living outside the parameters of moral and social respectability in the city. Ignoring the experiences of Grossmann's known victims—both living and dead—the press's narratives concealed the extent to which family, motherhood, and social connections within the city had failed to protect Grossmann's victims against economic deprivation and sexual exploitation. Instead, the press identified migration to the city and the economic and social independence of working-class women as the source of the victims' downfall. Two narrative strategies explained the women's situations: The first characterized them as fallen women of a criminal milieu; the second saw them as atomized victims of male sexual aggression whose desperation and vulnerability resulted from tragic individual choices. Yet even where they focused on the victims, the public narratives were ultimately about Grossmann and his crimes; the vulnerability and fear of the female victim only served to distance the murderer morally from the newspaper-reading public.[74]

Conclusion

The public narratives constructed to explain Grossmann's crimes offered no clear villains, victims, or heroes and diverged on several key points. Grossmann was either a cunning scoundrel clever enough to evade police or an imbecile with no control over his baser instincts. His victims were either hapless innocents or depraved women. Their milieu was either a community of virtuous citizens or an assembly of apathetic and callous denizens of iniquity. In sum, the press reporting on the Grossmann case revealed a tension between two narrative themes. In one, the killer was a faceless psychopath, whose predatory activities were made possible by the anonymity of the city, which hid both his identity and those of his victims. Only with the watchfulness of attentive citizens cooperating with the authorities was such an urban monster brought to justice. In the other version of the story, the killer was a product of his milieu, which existed on the social and moral margins of the city. The criminality of the milieu thus explained the depravity of the criminal, the fate of his victims, and the inattention of his community. Neither version bore much resemblance to the social reality in which the crimes took place.

The Grossmann case touched a variety of raw nerves in postwar Berlin. The elusiveness of the victim's identities was a testament to the anonymity of city life and the inadequacy of bureaucratic attempts to police the movements of individuals in the confusion of postwar demobilization. It was especially disturbing for lower-class citizens who had lost track of loved ones in the rural-urban migration that followed the war. For left-liberal observers, the case was a reminder that the poverty and class divisions that urbanization had brought about had not disappeared but been exacerbated by the war. For conservative observers, Grossmann's crimes brought to light the immorality and criminality that lurked in Berlin's marginal neighborhoods.

Public narratives of the Grossmann case did not, then, make the city "legible," but imposed particular identities on the perpetrator and his victims: social and moral identities that served to make sense of the social and gender relations of the immediate postwar years. The experiences of the witnesses and victims as well as the public narratives that were told about them suggest that criminal stories were a powerful tool for re-stabilizing prewar gender relations in the postwar period.

Notes

This chapter, written especially for this volume, draws on material from the author's *Murder Scenes: Normality, Deviance, and Criminal Violence in Weimar Berlin* (Ann Arbor: University of Michigan Press, 2010). Research for the article was supported by the Berlin Program for Research in the Humanities of the Freie Universität Berlin and the Social Science Research Council.

1. The exact number of Grossmann's victims is unknown. Although he was (and is) widely rumored to have killed fifty, police in 1921 hoped to pin as many as twenty-seven on Grossmann, but a more conservative number of six was mentioned in an undated police report (Landesarchiv Berlin (hereafter: LAB) A Rep. 358-01 Generalstaatsanwaltschaft bei dem Landgericht Berlin 1919–1933, Nr. 1522, Bd. 1 (Reel 741), Bl. 60–66.

2. Maria Tatar, *Lustmord: Sexual Murder in Weimar Germany* (Princeton, 1995); Beth Irwin Lewis, "Lustmord: Inside the Windows of the Metropolis," in Charles W. Haxthausen and Heidrun Suhr, eds., *Berlin: Culture and Metropolis* (Minneapolis and Oxford, 1990), 111–140; Martin Lindner, "Der Mythos 'Lustmord.' Serienmörder in der deutschen Literatur, dem Film und der bildenden Kunst zwischen 1892 und 1932," in Joachim Linder et al., eds., *Verbrechen-Justiz-Medien. Konstellationen in Deutschland von 1900 bis zur Gegenwart* (Tübingen, 1999), 273–305; Sabine Smith, *Sexual Violence in German Culture: Rereading and Rewriting the Tradition* (New York and Frankfurt/Main, 1998). On sexual violence and sexual crimes in Imperial Germany, see Tanja Hommen, *Sittlichkeitsverbrechen: Sexuelle Gewalt im Kaiserreich* (Frankfurt /Main and New York, 1998).

3. For recent retellings of the Grossmann case intended for a popular audience, see Kathrin Kompisch and Frank Otto, *Bestien des Boulevards: Die Deutschen und ihre Serienmörder* (Leipzig, 2003), 58–76; Jan Feustel, *Raub und Mord im Kiez. Historische Friedrichshainer Kriminalfälle. Begleitmaterial zur Ausstellung* (Berlin, 1996); Horst Bosetzky, *Die Bestie vom Schlesischen Bahnhof* (Berlin, 2005).

4. Kerstin Brückweh, *Mordlust: Serienmorde, Gewalt und Emotionen im 20. Jahrhundert* (Frankfurt/Main and New York, 2006), 14. Translation mine. Brückweh offers an analysis of four serial murder cases involving male perpetrators and male victims: Fritz Haarmann, Adolf Seefeld, Erwin Hagedorn, and Jürgen Bartsch.

5. *Berliner Lokal-Anzeiger* (BLA), n. 412, 1. September 1921.

6. Robert Heindl, *Der Berufsverbrecher. Ein Beitrag zur Strafrechtsreform* (Berlin, 1926), 141.

7. Magnus Hirschfeld, *Geschlecht und Verbrechen* (Leipzig, 1930), 209–211.

8. Curt Elwenspoek, *Mord und Totschlag: "Polizei greift ein!" So kämpft die Kriminalpolizei!* (Stuttgart, 1930), 16–18.

9. On the historicizing of narratives of sexual violence, see Judith R. Walkowitz, "Jack the Ripper and the Myth of Male Violence," *Feminist Studies* 8, 3 (1982), 541–574.

10. Peter Fritzsche, *Reading Berlin, 1900* (Cambridge, Mass., and London, 1996), 59, 83–86.

11. That the First World War had disrupted prewar marital and family relations and gender roles more generally is clear. What is less clear is whether those prewar gender relations were reconstituted or altered. A provocative if inconclusive essay in this regard is Elisabeth Domansky, "Militarization and Reproduction in World War I Germany," in *Society, Culture, and the State in Germany, 1870–1930*, Geoff Eley, ed. (Ann Arbor, 1997), 427–463. For a tentative revision of the view that Weimar was characterized by gender anxiety see Birthe Kundrus, "The First World War and the Construction of Gender Relations in the Weimar Republic," in Karen Hagemann and Stefanie Schüler-Springorum, *Home/Front: The Military, War and Gender in Twentieth-Century Germany* (Oxford and New York, 2002), 159–179.

12. Hans Ostwald, *Das Berliner Dirnentum*, Hans Ostwald, ed., vol. 6, *Großstadtdokumente* (Berlin, 1905), vol. 1, 20.

13. LAB A Rep. 358-01, Nr. 1522, Bd. 4 (reel 742), Bl. 134.

14. Brückweh has observed that Fritz Haarmann, the serial murderer of Hannover apprehended in 1924, also used "bait" to secure his victims. Brückweh, *Mordlust*, 59.

15. LAB A Rep.358-01, Bd. 1 (reel 741), Bl. 21–22. Grossmann actually implicated Helene as an accomplice, saying that she had known about the murders and had used this knowledge to blackmail him. Police took these charges seriously enough to take her into custody, but

without corroborating evidence released her, assuming Grossmann's accusation was an act of revenge toward those who had turned him in. Ibid., 31–38.

16. Ibid., Bl. 19.

17. Ibid., Bd. 3, Bl. 42.

18. Ibid., Bd. 3, Bl. 92–93.

19. Ibid., Bd. 3, Bl. 61–62.

20. Belinda Davis, *Home Fires Burning: Food, Politics, and Everyday Life in World War I Berlin* (Chapel Hill and London, 2000), map p. 84.

21. Richard Bessel, *Germany after the First World War* (Oxford and New York, 1993), 154 –160.

22. Ibid., 163–164.

23. Regina Schulte, *Sperrbezirke: Tugendhaftigkeit und Prostitution in der bürgerlichen Welt* (Frankfurt/Main, 1979); Lynn Abrams, "Prostitutes in Imperial Germany, 1870–1918: Working Girls or Social Outcasts?" in *The German Underworld: Deviants and Outcasts in German History*, Richard J. Evans, ed. (London and New York, 1988), 189–209.

24. Hans Ostwald, *Das Berliner Dirnentum*, vol. 8, Hans Ostwald, ed., vol. 6, *Großstadtdokumente* (Berlin: 1905), 3.

25. LAB A Rep. 328-01, Nr. 1522, Bd. 3, Bl. 89-91 (Reel 742).

26. Ibid., Bd. 3, Bl. 3.

27. Ibid., Bd. 1, Bl. 8, 34–37 (reel 741).

28. LAB A Rep. 358-1, A Rep. 358-01, Nr. 1522, Bd. 3, Bl. 1–3 (reel 742).

29. Ibid., Bl. 4-6; LAB A Rep. 358-01, Nr. 1522, Bd. 6, Bl. 26, (reel 743).

30. LAB A Rep. 358-01, Nr. 1522, Bd. 3, Bl. 29–30.

31. Lynn Abrams, "Prostitutes in Imperial Germany," 193. See also Richard Evans, "Prostitution, State, and Society in Imperial Germany," *Past and Present* 70 (1976), 106–129; Evans, *Tales from the German Underground: Crime and Punishment in the Nineteenth Century* (New Haven, 1998). For comparison, see Judith Walkowitz, *Prostitution and Victorian Society: Women, Class, and the State* (Cambridge and New York, 1980); Mary Gibson, *Prostitution and the State in Italy, 1860–1910* (New Brunswick, 1986); Jill Harsin, *Policing and Prostitution in Nineteenth-Century Paris* (Princeton, 1985); Alain Corbin, *Women for Hire: Prostitution and Sexuality in France after 1850*, trans. Alan Sheridan (Cambridge, Mass. and London, 1990 [1978]).

32. Brückweh finds this treatment of the surviving victims as witnesses rather than as victims of violent crime in the four cases of serial murder she analyzes, all of which involved male victims and homosexual murderers. She also observes that women were more likely to be perceived as victims than were men. Brückweh, *Mordlust*, 42–49.

33. LAB A Rep. 358-01, Nr. 1522, Bd. 4, Bl. 128–130 (reel 742).

34. LAB A Rep. 358-01, Nr. 1522, Bd 3., Bl. 205–210 (reel 742).

35. LAB A Rep. 358-01, Nr. 1522, Bd. 1, Bl. 31–38, (reel 741).

36. Stephan Bleek, "Mobilität und Seßhaftigkeit in deutschen Großstädten während der Urbanisierung," *Geschichte und Gesellschaft* 15, 1 (1989), 5–33.

37. LAB A Rep. 358-01, Nr. 1522, Bd. 10 (reel 744), Personalakten; LAB A Rep. 358-01, Nr. 1522, Bd. 4, Bl. 247–249 (reel 743).

38. Eva Brücker, "'Und ich bin da 'rausgekommen': Gewalt und Sexualität in einer Berliner Arbeiternachbarschaft zwischen 1916/17 und 1958," in *Physische Gewalt: Studien zur Geschichte der Neuzeit*, Thomas Lindenberger and Alf Lüdtke, eds. (Frankfurt/Main, 1995), 337–365. On domestic violence in imperial Germany, see Lynn Abrams, Martyrs or Matriarchs? Working-Class Women's Experience of Marriage in Germany before the First World War," *Women's History Review* 1, 3 (1992), 357–376, and Abrams, "Companionship and Conflict: the Negotiation of Marriage Relations in the Nineteenth Century," in *Gender Relations in German History: Power, Agency and Experience from the Sixteenth to the Twentieth Century*, Lynn Abrams

and Elizabeth Harvey, eds. (Durham, 1996). On the normalization of domestic violence in the Weimar period, see Sace Elder, *Murder Scenes: Normality, Deviance, and Criminal Violence in Weimar Berlin* (Ann Arbor, 2010), 157–189.

39. LAB A Rep. 358-01, Nr. 1522, Bd. 1, Bl. 20 (reel 741).

40. LAB A Rep. 358-01, Nr. 1522, Bd. 3, Bl. 65 (reel 742).

41. Equally bothersome to neighbors as the cries, and in retrospect equally as significant, was the stench that emanated from Grossmann's apartment. Several neighbors questioned Grossmann about the strong smell of rotting meat that clearly came from his room, but willingly accepted the explanation that that he had forgotten to remove a chicken that had spoiled in the summer heat.

42. LAB A Rep. 358-01, Nr. 1522, Bd. 1, Bl. 21 (reel 741).

43. Judith Walkowitz, *City of Dreadful Delight: Narratives of Sexual Danger in Late-Victorian London* (Chicago, 1992). See also Marie-Christine Leps, *Apprehending the Criminal: The Production of Deviance in Nineteenth-Century Discourse* (Durham and London, 1992), 112–134.

44. *Vorwärts* (VW) n. 427, 10 September 1921.

45. Heindl, *Der Berufsverbrecher*, 197;

46. *Berliner Morgenpost* (BMP), 26 February 1920; BLA, 2 July 1921. On the Blau case, see LAB A Rep. 358-01, Nr. 386 (reel A463).

47. "Menschen, die verschwinden," BMP, n. 186, 7 August 1921, 1. Beilage. Jacobsohn admonished all missing persons to report to the police missing person's center.

48. BMP, n. 188, 9 August 1921, 1. Beilage.

49. VW, n. 374, 10 August 1921.

50. See, for example, BLA 4 July 1921(Morgenausgabe).

51. Erich Wulffen, *Der Sexualverbrecher. Ein Handbuch für Juristen, Verwaltunsbeamte und Ärzte,*Encyklopädie der modernen Kriminalistik (Berlin, 1910), 454. Richard Krafft-Ebing, *Psychopathia sexualis. Mit besonderer Berücksichtigung der conträren Sexualempfindung* (Stuttgart, 1903), 47ff. See Maren Hoffmeister, "Lustmord: Widerständige Körper im Deutungssystem Justiz," in *Körper und Recht. Anthropologische Dimensionen der Rechtsphilophie,* Ludger Schwarte and Christoph Wulf, eds. (Munich, 2003), 339–355. On German criminology, see Richard Wetzell, *Inventing the Crimnal: A History of German Criminology, 1880–1945* (Chapel Hill and London, 2000).

52. Swen Thomas, *Geschichte des Mordparagraphens—eine normalgenetische Untersuchung bis in der Gegenwart* (Bochum, 1985), 255–265; Michael Schetsche, "Der Wille, der Trieb und das Deutungsmuster vom Lustmord," in *Sexuelle Sozialisation: Sechs Annäherungen,* Renate Berenike Schmidt and Michael Schetsche, eds. (Berlin, 2009). On criminal biology and the prosecution and punishment of murder, see Richard Evans, *Rituals of Retribution: Capital Punishment in Germany, 1600–1987* (Oxford, 1996), 528–533.

53. *Berliner Morgenpost* (hereafter: BMP), no. 200, 24 August 1921, 1. Beilage.

54. Tatar, *Lustmord,* 53–54.

55. BMP, no. 266, 16. October 1920, 1. Beilage.

56. BMP, no. 267, 17. October 1920.

57. Peter Becker, "Weak Bodies? Prostitutes and the Role of Gender in the Criminological Writings of 19th-Century German Detectives and Magistrates," *Crime, Histoire and Societies* 3, 1 (1999), 45–69. See also Becker, *Verderbnis und Entartung. Eine Geschichte der Kriminologie des 19. Jahrhunderts als Diskurs und Praxis* (Göttingen, 2002), 117–175.

58. *Berliner Lokal-Anzeiger* (hereafter: BLA) 23 August 1921 (Morgenausgabe).

59. BLA, 4 September 1921 (Sonntagsausgabe).

60. Erich Frey, *Ich beantrage Freispruch* (Hamburg, 1959), 44.

61. BMP, no. 199, 23 August 1921, 1. Beilage.

62. *BZ am Mittag,* no. 199, 26. August 1921.

63. Many observers, including Magnus Hirschfeld almost ten years later, expressed surprise that the wizened, unattractive, slovenly-looking man could lure so many women into his apartment. In his *Geschlecht und Verbrechen*, Hirschfeld placed a caption under a photograph of Grossmann that read, "Grossmann, the bluebeard of the Silesian train station who despite his appearance always found women." Hirschfeld, *Geschlecht und Verbrechen*, 215.

64. BMP, no. 296, 14. December 1921, 1. Beilage.

65. *BZ am Mittag*, no. 197, 24. August 1921.

66. Gertraud Zull, *Das Bild vom Dienstmädchen um die Jahrhundertwende. Eine Untersuchung der stereotypen Vorstellungen über den Charakter und soziale Lage des städtischen weiblichen Hauspersonals* Reihe Kulturwissenschaften (Munich, 1984), 175–186; Karin Walser, *Dienstmädchen. Frauenarbeit und Weiblichkeitsbilder um 1900* (Frankfurt/Main, 1985); Dorthee Wierling, *Mädchen für Alles. Arbeitsalltag und Lebensgeschichte städtischer Dienstmädchen um der Jahrhundertwende* (Berlin, 1987).

67. Ute Daniel, *The War from Within: German Working-Class Women in the First World War*, trans. Margaret Ries (Oxford and New York, 1997; orig. 1989), 138–147.

68. Julia Roos, *Weimar Through the Lens of Gender: Prostitution Reform, Women's Emancipation, and German Democracy, 1919–1933* (Ann Arbor, 2010), esp. 97–136; Julia Roos, "Backlash against Prostitutes' Right: Origins and Dynamics of Nazi Prostitution Policies," *Journal of the History of Sexuality* 1, 1/2 (2002), 67–94; and Elisabeth Meyer-Renschenhausen, "The Bremen Morality Scandal," in *When Biology Became Destiny: Women in Weimar and Nazi Germany*, Renate Bridenthal, Atina Grossmann, and Marion Kaplan, eds. (New York, 1984), 87–108. On prostitution in the Kaiserreich, see Nancy Reagin, "A True Woman Can Take Care of Herself: The Debate over Prostitution in Hanover, 1906," *Central European History* 24, 4 (1991), 347–380.

69. Arthur Kronfeld, "Bemerkungen zum Prozeß gegen Karl Großmann," Zeitschrift für Sexualwissenschaft 9, 5 (1922), 138–139. Arthur Kronfeld, "Bemerkungen zum Prozeß gegen Karl Großmann," *Zeitschrift für Sexualwissenschaft* 9, 5 (1922), 137–149. Robert Heindl would later echo such sentiments when he wrote, "In the area around the Silesian train station one did not like to interfere in the love affairs of his fellow men." See "Das Berufsverbrechertum der Großstadt," in *Unser Berlin: Ein Jahrbuch von Berliner Art und Arbeit* (Berlin, 1928). For Heindl, this observation served to demonstrate the essential depravity of this *Kriminalviertel*.

70. LAB A Rep. 358-01, Nr. 1522, Bd. 4, Bl. 227 (reel 743).

71. BLA 20 Sept. 1921, 1. Beiblatt (Morgenausgabe).

72. *Berliner Volkszeitung* (hereafter: BVZ), no. 437, 16 September 1921.

73. BMP 30. August 1921, 1. Beilage.

74. Karen Halttunen has described how in the early American context, Enlightenment notions of human nature and free will necessitated the alienation of the murderer from so-called normal citizens, in contrast to colonial murder narratives that emphasized the sinfulness of all humans as an invocation to repentance on the part of all members of a community. Karen Halttunen, *Murder Most Foul: The Killer in the American Gothic Imagination* (Cambridge, Mass., 1998).

Chapter 8

CLASS, YOUTH, AND SEXUALITY IN THE CONSTRUCTION OF THE *LUSTMÖRDER*
The 1928 Murder Trial of Karl Hussmann

Eva Bischoff and Daniel Siemens

In the early morning of 23 March 1928, two workers who were on their way to their shift discovered a body in front of the house at Schultenstrasse 11 in Gladbeck, a small town in the northern part of the industrial district of the Ruhr.[1] The men woke the physician Dr. Lutter, who lived close by. Dr. Lutter, after realizing that the person in question was beyond his help, went to his friend Adolf Daube, headmaster [*Rektor*] of the local *Lutherschule*, a protestant primary school, who lived at Schultenstrasse 11, and called the police. When Lutter and Daube stepped out to have a look at the body, Adolf Daube suddenly exclaimed, "But, this is my boy!"[2] The corpse was indeed that of Helmut Daube, Adolf Daube's nineteen-year-old son. Police from Gladbeck's criminal investigation department arrived twenty minutes later.[3] Daube's father knew that the night before his son had been out drinking with Karl Hussmann, a friend and former classmate. They had attended a recruiting evening [*Keilabend*] of the local branch of the right-wing student fraternity *Alte Burschenschaftler* in Buer, an hour's walk from Gladbeck. After Lutter found out that Hussmann and Daube had left the pub and headed back home together, he called Hussmann.

Karl Hussmann answered the call rather quickly, given that he had been drinking the night before. Born in Guatemala in 1908, he was a half-orphan: his father had died on a journey from Guatemala to Germany in 1921. Therefore, Hussmann lived with foster parents, the family of the headmaster of a protestant school in Gladbeck-Rentfort, the Kleiböhmers. Hussmann considered himself Daube's closest friend.[4] Both young men had participated in a bible-reading circle for several years, together with Ilse Kleiböhmer, the daughter of Hussmann's foster parents. About a year before the events discussed here, Daube had fallen in love with Ilse, but their relationship had remained platonic and did not last long. Just a few weeks before the crime took place, Daube and Hussmann had graduated from high school together.

When Hussmann arrived at the crime scene, everyone who was present recognized that he reacted to Helmut's death in a surprisingly "cold" and indifferent manner.[5] Detective superintendent Klingelhöller of Gladbeck's criminal investigation department discovered small drops of blood on Hussmann's shoes and questioned the young man about them.[6] Hussmann replied that he had killed a cat a few days earlier and that the cat's blood must have soiled his shoes.[7] But this explanation did not satisfy Klingelhöller, who decided to keep the shoes as potential evidence against Hussmann.[8]

By 7:30 A.M., Gladbeck's investigating judge, Dr. Meyer, arrived. When he examined the corpse, he discovered that someone had cut the victim's throat and removed his genitals. Up to this point, the police had assumed that Daube had committed suicide, although no knife was found near him.[9] Klingelhöller had asked Hussmann whether he had witnessed Daube's suicide and run away in panic. When the mutilation was discovered, however, it was thought most likely that a murder had occurred, and Hussmann became the primary suspect. Detective Klingelhöller searched Hussmann's rooms and found bloodstained clothes and a coat that definitely had been cleaned very recently to remove some sort of spot. The police also discovered a sheath from which the knife was missing.[10]

When Dr. Neef, the public prosecutor, arrived, he decided that the shoes should be sent to a chemical institute in Recklinghausen and ordered an examination to determine whether the blood was of human or animal origin.[11] Hussmann was taken into custody for interrogation. At 5:00 P.M., he was to be questioned by the investigating judge, Dr. Meyer. Prior to the interrogation, all investigating personnel—Public Prosecutor Neef, Judge Meyer, and the police officers Klingelhöller and Pest gathered for a meeting. When Klingelhöller informed Neef of the circumstantial evidence that made him believe that Karl Hussmann had killed Daube, Prosecutor Neef replied:

> If a worker would be under such suspicion, he would be arrested on the basis of these suspicious facts. However, as Hussmann is well-known around here. . . . Well, Mr. Meyer, it is up to you to decide on the warrant of arrest.[12]

Hussmann was released after the interrogation. A few days later, the results of the chemical test came in and showed that the blood on Hussmann's shoes belonged to a human being. Moreover, a second laboratory test, which verified this result, proved that the blood belonged to Daube's blood group, not Hussmann's.[13] As soon as the first result became known, the local press called for the investigation to be taken over by the Berlin homicide department, which had a strong reputation, thanks at least in part to successful public relations efforts.[14] On 30 March, the prosecutor's office of the district of Essen-Ruhr gave in to this public pressure and asked for help from the Berlin specialists.[15] The Berlin criminal police quickly discovered that the local police forces had done a poor job.[16] Nevertheless, they shared Detective Klingelhöller's initial assumption that Helmut Daube had most likely been murdered by Hussmann. The investigating detectives learned from several witnesses that Hussmann might have engaged in mutual masturbation with classmates. They also found letters written by Hussmann that could be interpreted as evidence of a homosexual attraction to Daube. According to the Berlin police, all this suggested that Hussmann was a *Lustmörder* (sexual murderer).[17] The prosecutor's office shared this assessment and formally charged Hussmann with Daube's murder.[18] Hussmann's trial, which was based exclusively on circumstantial evidence, took place from 16 to 30 October 1928. The prosecution summoned 110 witnesses and six experts, which were interrogated during the eleven days allotted to the trial.[19] In the end, the judges were not convinced of the innocence of the defendant, but because his guilt could not be proven beyond a reasonable doubt, their verdict was not guilty.[20]

Although this outcome suggests that one could frame the story of the Hussmann trial as a success story demonstrating that the German legal system could operate quite effectively even under great political and public pressure, we intend to pursue a different line of argument. By examining how the judges' nagging doubts came into existence, we will tell a story of converging strategies and interests, class prejudice, and homophobic anxieties. We will analyze the practices and discourses that unfolded in the context of the Hussmann case to reconstruct the role of intersecting categories of difference such as class, sexuality, and age in the construction of criminality in general and of the *Lustmörder* in Weimar Germany in particular. From this perspective, the main question becomes: Why was Karl Hussmann *not* considered to be a homosexual psychopath?

Of Trials and Rituals: On the Performativity of Criminality

To Hussmann's contemporaries, criminal trials were much more than legal procedures of reconstructing a chain of events and determining a sentence for unlawful behavior. As the famous Berlin court reporter Gabriele Tergit put it, criminal trials were increasingly regarded as "sources for the understanding of our times."[21] Taking up this notion, we consider trials to be performances, confined to a particular point in time and space, yet reiterable, in which "social relations are displayed and renewed and the hierarchical forms underlying social relations [are] confirmed and strengthened."[22] In other words, we will treat criminal trials as social rituals.

The performative character of human activities has been the focus of grow-ing attention in the field of German cultural studies. This includes all sorts of activities, such as the "performance of identity, gender, a social or theatrical role, ethnicity, religious belief, a text or a film script."[23] Performances are not restricted to an enactment of what existed before but are considered to be productive: As "performative acts" they continuously create social categories and meaning.[24] Yet these acts and the resulting identities are not arbitary, but structured along exist-ing "axes of differentiation such as class, race, ethnicity, gender, age."[25] Therefore, recent work in Gender and Queer Studies has emphasized the intersectionality of all identities as performative, social constructions.[26] Relying on this conceptual framework, we will consider criminal trials as social rituals and performative acts in which interdependent categories such as sexuality, class, and criminality are (re)produced.[27]

To answer the question why Karl Hussmann was not considered a *Lustmörder*, we will focus our analysis on three central characteristics of criminal trials as social rituals. First, as social rituals, trials are enacted by a group of people that includes not only the persons in court but also the audience. As anthropologists have demonstrated, the audience plays a constitutive role in the performance of rituals, which have to be enacted in front of the social group to which they convey social meaning. In fact, by witnessing a performance, the audience lit-erally participates in it.[28] In modern, complex societies, audience participation is not necessarily restricted to physical participation in the ritual event, but can take place in a mediated form, that is, through mass media.[29] Second, all social rituals follow a fixed set of rules; in the case of criminal trials, the most import-ant rules specify how the truth of what happened is to be determined. After all, reconstructing the chain of events and determining an appropriate sentence for the person identified as the perpetrator is considered to be the most important task of a criminal trial. This goal, however, is continuously undermined by the conflicting interests and strategies of the persons involved. The truth is of deli-cate nature.[30] Moreover, as Michel Foucault has demonstrated, every process of determining the truth is structured along the lines of power: each society has its own "regime of truth."[31] In the Hussmann trial, scientific knowledge in the form of medico-psychiatric expert opinions played a key role in this "regime of truth" as they were considered to reveal the true nature of the defendant.[32] Third, social rituals have an ambivalent character: They operate simultaneously in an affirmative and a subversive manner.[33] Every time a ritual is performed, it is interpreted by different actors, often with conflicting interests and interpreta-tions of their role.

On the basis of these general considerations, we will focus our analysis on the role of the audience (the press coverage of the trial) and of expert knowledge (the psychiatric evaluations of Hussmann) to reconstruct the strategies and interests involved in the Hussmann trial. As we shall see, it was precisely these interests that prevented Hussmann from being seen as a sexual psychopath who had killed and mutilated his schoolmate to satisfy his deviant sexuality.

The Malady of Youth: The Hussmann Trial and the Media

The trial against Karl Hussmann received great attention in the local as well as in the national press. Throughout the 1920s, criminal trials were closely followed in the press and seen to represent society's moral condition.[34] As the philosopher Theodor Lessing wrote after the Hussmann trial, beyond the legal problems, such trials "highlight[ed] education and soul, economy and society."[35] Journalists examined Hussmann's case with great enthusiasm. One topic was of special interest to them: the "malady of youth." This expression, which was borrowed from Ferdinand Bruckner's play *Krankheit der Jugend*, performed with great success in the spring of 1928,[36] became a slogan denoting a general distrust in middle-class youth.

This point of view was especially popular after the public had extensively discussed the famous Krantz trial, which took place in Berlin in February 1928. Teenage sexual experimentation and jealousy, mixed with alcohol and adolescent melancholia, led to a catastrophe for a group of youngsters in Berlin-Steglitz. The morning after a *nuit blanche*, two of them, Günther Scheller and Hans Stephan, were found in the bedroom of Scheller's parents, killed by bullets fired from a gun belonging to Krantz, who owned the weapon illegally. Like Hussmann, the nineteen-year-old Paul Krantz was accused of murder. According to the prosecution, he had—just after his first sexual experiences with Günther's sister Hilde—shot to death Hans Stephan, his rival for the affection of the young girl.[37]

The subsequent trial was a sensation. Here was a capital crime among young middle-class high-school graduates from a respectable Berlin neighborhood, and—what made it even more attractive to the press—the opportunity to discuss juvenile sexuality in public. To boost sales figures, reporters published as many details as possible about the sexual life of these urban teenagers, aged from fifteen to eighteen years at the time of the incident. Class also played a role, although a comparatively minor one: in contrast to the Scheller family and most of his classmates, the defendant Paul Krantz was of proletarian background and only had access to the *Gymnasium* thanks to the fact that the obligatory school fees were waived in his case. Some of the contemporary commentators established a link between his social background and the fact that he was accused of murder. In contrast to the well-to-do parents of Günther and Hilde Scheller, who lobbied for a harsh punishment of the alleged murderer, Krantz' parents were not in a position to influence the authorities or to agitate for public support.[38]

The extensive press coverage, which lasted for several weeks, was also of great interest to teachers and other "experts of youth," who used the trial as a starting point for discussing "dangerous tendencies" among German youth.[39] This topic was very much *en vogue*: not only was it the major concern of the new field of adolescent psychology, which had been established about a decade earlier,[40] but it was also addressed in contemporary theater and art—the most famous example being Frank Wedekind's drama *Frühlings Erwachen*, first performed in 1906. In the spring of 1928, this play was seen as the fictional model of the "tragedy of Steglitz" that gave rise to the Krantz trial.[41] In Gladbeck, the Krantz trial had been a topic of intense debate as well. Hussmann, Daube, and their peers had discussed it more than once.[42] During his police interrogation, Hussmann said:

> We [Daube and Hussmann] talked about sexual perversions and homosexual intercourse. I remember that we mentioned diverse problems in this respect in our conversations on the occasion of the Krantz trial.[43]

Considering this context, it is not surprising that the press saw the opportunity to tell the story of a "new Krantz." Major analogies between the two cases made such an approach look promising. In both cases, a recent high-school graduate was accused of murder, probably driven by sexual motives. Likewise, both cases featured homosexuality as one of the central issues, with a ménage à trois lurking in the background.[44] Journalists reported extensively on a daily basis from the courthouse in Essen; some of them were specially assigned to the trial.

There was, however, one important difference in the press coverage between the two trials: the press reports on the Hussmann trial were much more cautious than those on the Krantz trial had been and spoke less openly about sensational details. In the light of recent debates on the Krantz trial in the German Reichstag, which had examined the conflict between the freedom of the press and the need to safeguard public morality,[45] the court in Gladbeck and the journalists opted for a cooperative strategy. Their collaboration was designed to effectively balance the economic interests of the press with the interests of the state, which disapproved of the widespread criticism of its judiciary. On the day before the trial started, the court's newly established press bureau invited journalists, lawyers, and judges to an improvised press conference, at which it explained the central legal proceedings and the special problems of the trial, and in return for this service asked for moderate and decent coverage.[46] The authorities' carrot-and-stick policy proved highly successful: whereas on other occasions, the press and the judiciary had bitterly confronted and even insulted one another—contemporary liberal and socialist writers spoke of a fundamental "crisis of confidence" in the Weimar legal system[47]—in Gladbeck, press and court cooperated quite well with each other. One can argue that both sides were willing to learn: the judiciary started to understand that great media interest in a particular trial was not necessarily a sign of sensationalism, but also reflected broader, legitimate concerns on behalf of the general public, while the journalists realized that certain forms of sensationalist press coverage cast doubt on their self-declared role of informing and educating the public for the benefit of all.

The results of this cooperation clearly did not satisfy all sections of civil society. The catholic youth organization in Groß-Essen, for example, wrote to the presiding judge in October 1928 to demand stricter censorship:

> Thanks to the way the press is reporting, the attention of all parts of the population is focused on the trial. It has to be recognized that our youth is highly interested. Hence a large percentage of them became aware of the true nature of the accusation, the perverted sexuality, for the first time. It would be disastrous if an unpedagogical coverage spread harmful information on these matters in all parts of the population. Because of the way the Hussmann trial has been presented so far, we do not trust all journalists to report in a pedagogically [*volkserziehlich*] faultless manner.[48]

Despite this criticism, the cooperative strategy with which the legal system handled the delicate case was generally successful. Although the representatives of the press were excluded from the courtroom from time to time, especially when sexual matters were at stake, this practice did not result in negative press reports. On the contrary, the journalists displayed unusual sympathy with the judges and the prosecutor. They even wrote positively about the Prussian legal system itself, a rarity in the troubled Weimar years. Thus Moritz Goldstein, the correspondent for Berlin's liberal *Vossische Zeitung*, for instance, noted:

> [The court] can be certified to have worked on solving the mystery of Gladbeck with relentless assiduity and admirable patience. . . . One could notice a gentleman-like, amicable understanding between the prosecutor and the defense lawyer, and because the defendant knew how to behave himself, the whole trial reflected the best conventional proprieties.[49]

Instead of criticizing the court, the press picked mostly on Gladbeck's criminal police. More importantly, many reporters demonstrated remarkable sympathy with the defendant, mostly for two reasons. First, the press, especially the liberal press, generally regarded criminals not as callous perpetrators but as "victims of society."[50] Second, in this particular case, journalists sympathized with a defendant who had been subjected not only to an investigation filled with absurdities, but also to gossip and prejudices circulating in Gladbeck that created a stifling atmosphere of suspicion. A typical critique, such as that offered by August Hermann Zeiz in the liberal *Berliner Tageblatt*, read:

> In this nest of overheated brains of [Gladbeck's] Philistines, the suspicion against the defendant became a fact and everybody "came clean." The detectives wrote down everything they had been informed of, embroidered it, and in Essen prosecutors were found who built an impossible accusation on the basis of impossible evidence.[51]

The newspapers rarely mentioned that Hussmann himself belonged to the protestant middle class in Gladbeck, a town predominantly inhabited by Catholics, and that he was connected to a right-wing student fraternity. Only the communist press claimed that his foster father served as president of the local branch of the right-wing *Stahlhelm*.[52] During his pretrial detention Hussmann wrote letters to his friends in which he spoke pejoratively about *Republikaner* (supporters of the Weimar Republic) and *Reichsbannerhelden* (members of the Social-Democratic paramilitary organization), thus sharing a common attitude among middle-class schoolboys and university students of that time, who often cultivated an "anti-bourgeois" habitus and were easily attracted by illiberal, "revolutionary" political parties.[53] Only communist newspapers explicitly made the connection between the conduct of the trial and class differences. Thus the *Rote Fahne* wrote:

> [E]stablished bourgeois society, and with it the investigating judge, are of the same opinion that a high-school graduate, . . . member of the *Stahlhelm* and of a right-wing student fraternity, cannot commit a sexual murder of his friend. During the first days following the murder, these circles even launched a relief attack for Hussmann in the press.[54]

An analysis of the trial's press coverage reveals that two main factors protected Hussmann against conviction. First, he was defended by a middle-class milieu that marked criminal behavior as "alien." Consequently, the well-established Hussmann, who was from a "good family," simply *could not* be guilty. Second, the newspapers prevented a possible demonization of the defendant both because of their general skepticism towards Weimar's police and legal system and because of their temporary sensitivity regarding juvenile sexual deviance and its public representation.

"Nothing More than the Normal Phenomenon": The Medical Expert Opinions

As the local police physician, Dr. Marcks, noted in his autopsy report, the removal of Helmut Daube's genitals and his cut throat indicated a "murder because of sadistic tendencies, a so-called *Lustmord*." Yet, to be certain, he elaborated, a confession and a "psychiatric exploration" of the offender were necessary.[55] Hussmann, however, never confessed. Nevertheless, three medico-psychiatric expert opinions were prepared. In contrast to other spectacular *Lustmord* cases of the Weimar Republic, in which the delinquents (Carl Grossmann,[56] Friedrich Haarmann,[57] and Peter Kürten[58]) had confessed after their arrest, in the Hussmann case the experts did not try to determine the suspect's mental condition at the time of the crime, but his general psychiatric profile to answer the question whether or not Hussmann could possibly have murdered for sexual reasons.[59] To clarify this point, the experts discussed two questions: Was Hussmann a sadist? And was he a homosexual?

In the scientific literature of the 1920s, *Lustmord* was defined as a murder for the satisfaction of deviant sexual desires. Legal and medical experts distinguished four major deviations of the sexual drive: sadism, masochism, fetishism, and homosexuality.[60] Sadism was thought to be the expression of pathologically enhanced aggression, which was otherwise considered a natural part of male sexuality. The physician and psychiatrist Richard von Krafft-Ebing was the first to describe this pattern under this label, referring to the writings of Donatien Alphonse François de Sade, better known as Marquis de Sade.[61] According to Krafft-Ebing, sadism was caused by an "inherited diseased condition of the central nervous system (functional signs of degeneration),"[62] which, according to the opinions of leading sexologists, were hereditary and resulted in a neurological weakness, also called neurasthenia.[63] This weakness destroyed the willpower of the afflicted, who followed their aggressive instincts instead of restraining them as so-called healthy men would do. *Health*, in this context, was used synonymously with *civilization* by Krafft-Ebing and his fellow scientists. To them, civilization was the final stage of an evolutionary process in which male aggressive impulses were restrained and restructured, resulting in modern, that is, bourgeois moral norms and attitudes.[64] Krafft-Ebing and his colleagues thus endorsed the notion of a linear evolutionary process, in which so-called natives as well as members of the lower classes embodied earlier stages of human evolution.[65]

In this context, it should be noted that the prosecutor as well as the medical experts knew that Hussmann's mother and one of her brothers were considered mentally inferior (*geistig minderwertig*) by the authorities.[66] Netty Hussmann was thought to be a "singularly simple-minded" person, and her brother had been placed in an asylum for "heredity imbecility" and "harmless insanity with delusions."[67] Hussmann himself stressed his birth in Guatemala and suggested that his parental line might have included indigenous ancestors. According to racist theories of descent, this implied that Hussmann could have inherited the strong sexual desires of his alleged native relatives as well as their weaker willpower, which made it almost impossible for him to withstand his bodily instincts.[68]

However, the medical experts were unprepared to envision the possibility that a member of their own social group could be prone to heredity degenerative defects. As the medical expert witness Dr. Teudt wrote:

> The hereditary material which is incorporated in Husmann [sic] is not totally immaculate, because there is proof of cases of mental disorder within the mother's family. . . . However, often too much emphasis is placed on such heriditary factors, as if an offspring of such a family necessarily had to be impaired.[69]

Ignoring the possibility of a racial degeneration by heredity, the medical experts stressed the variation in the heritability of degenerative signs.[70] Strikingly, this was a line of argument that does not appear in any of the medical expert opinions on the prominent *Lustmörder* who were found guilty during the Weimar Republic, which, in fact, were partially written by the same experts.[71] Peter Kürten, for example, known as the Vampire of Düsseldorf, was depicted as a "psychopath with a distinctly sadistic sexual drive, incriminated by heredity and impaired by his milieu from childhood on," who had been "unrestrained in the choice of the means to satisfy his sadistic desire."[72] Carl Grossmann was described as "burdened by serious hereditary defects" (*erblich stark belastet*), "completely degenerated,"[73] and having "strong sexual urges with pronounced sadistic elements."[74] Friedrich Haarmann, nicknamed the Werewolf of Hannover, was simply classified as a "pathological personality."[75] All of them came from a proletarian milieu in which petty criminality was commonplace. This focus on members of the *classes dangereuses* concurred with the descriptions in scientific literature. Here, too, men who were presented as typical *Lustmörder* came from the lower classes and often had an extensive criminal background. They most definitely were not high-school graduates on their way to pursuing university studies.[76]

The medical expert opinions also invalidated those elements of Hussmann's behavior that, according to criminological authorities such as Erich Wulffen, should have been interpreted as indicators of sadistic tendencies:[77] most prominently, Hussmann's killing, exhibiting, and photographing a cat or the violence he exerted on his schoolmates. Instead, all the medical expert opinions stressed that cruelties and fisticuffs were part of the normal development of young males and that Hussmann only killed the cat by order of his foster parents who wanted to protect the singing birds (ignoring the fact that the parents surely never said a word about exhibiting the cat's corpse or taking photographs of it).[78]

Declaring Hussmann's attitudes and behavior to be part of normal male juvenile behavior was also central to the medico-psychiatric experts' arguments on the question whether or not he was to be considered a homosexual. They emphasized that Hussmann was still an adolescent and that, therefore, it would not be reasonable to measure his acts by the standards of adult sexuality:

> Experience teaches us that because of the capriciousness of the activity during puberty youngsters often have homosexual emotions and act upon them, yet find the right and normal path by the end of the crisis. Therefore, such an activity is only a transitional phenomenon.[79]

Instead of claiming that Hussmann's homosexual practices were an expression of a so-called degenerative hereditary predisposition, which was one of the prevalent contemporary theories on homosexuality,[80] the experts interpreted his behavior against the background of Eduard Spranger's study on the psychology of adolescents (*Psychologie des Jugendalters*).[81] Spranger distinguished between *eroticism* and *sexuality* and claimed that boys (as well as girls) had little or to no interest in physical sexuality. Instead, he argued, they practiced a "predominantly spiritual form of love," which aimed at "empathy and becoming a unity with the other soul."[82] In Spranger's model, homosexual acts were not necessarily excluded, but they were seen as harmless aberrations and derailments into the realm of the physical.[83] Finally, the medical experts concluded that in their examinations as well as in their studies of his schoolmates' testimonies, they could find "nothing more than the normal phenomenon"[84] among male adolescents. This assessment reflected one of the two psychiatric models on the development of homosexuality prevailing in the 1920s. Whereas other suspects, such as Fritz Haarmann, were considered hereditarily tainted and their homosexuality explained as a result of their degeneracy, Hussmann was described in the terms of a model that emphasized the dynamic character of the development of sexual identities from a psychological point of view.

Conclusion: The Impossible *Lustmörder*

Our analysis of the trial of Karl Hussmann has demonstrated a central ambiguity. On the one hand, the press and the investigating authorities pursued the established strategies in dealing with delinquents who were considered abnormal. Thus the murder and the subsequent trial were embedded in the context of contemporary discussions on the relationship between the press and the legal system, scientific models of deviance, and debates on the "malady of the youth." On the other hand, despite the circumstantial evidence indicating a sadistic sexual murder, Hussmann was not constructed as a *Lustmörder* either in the press or in the medical expert opinions. This is all the more remarkable because it would not have been difficult to label him a degenerate other, by reference either to his birth in Guatemala or to degeneration theory.

The medical experts' and the court's emphasis on the impact of Hussmann's socialization and juvenile development, instead of interpreting his ancestry from a racist and hereditarian perspective, was only possible in a unique situation in which three mutually reinforcing elements came together. The first factor was the cooperation of the local legal authorities and the press, which was a reaction to the public backlash against the voyeuristic press coverage of the trial of Paul Krantz eight months earlier. In the Hussmann case, the court provided the press with a continuous flow of information in exchange for the press's promise of moderation in its reporting of the trial. Although the parallels to the Krantz trial would have made a similarly sensationalist coverage financially attractive, the journalists kept speculation on the murderer's sexual motives to a minimum. The second factor in the trial's unique constellation was that Hussmann was middle class and a member of the local educational elite, most prominently indicated by his participation in the bible movement and his contacts to a right-wing student fraternity. The third and final factor that prevented his being viewed as a *Lustmörder* was his youth. By referring to his age, the psychiatric experts could render the accusations of homosexuality and sadism harmless, thus normalizing behavior generally marked as perverse and criminal. All three elements created a situation that was exceptional, especially compared with the cases of Haarmann, Grossmann, and Kürten, all middle-aged men from the lower classes. Considering this exception on a more general level indicates that most historical analyses of the construction of criminality and of the *Lustmörder* in particular have disregarded the role of two major, intersecting categories: class and age.

Epilogue

Daube's murderer was never apprehended. Unsolved spectacular cases such as the one at hand pique the curiosity of contemporaries and historians alike. Nevertheless, we have deliberately not considered the question whether or not the defendant was rightfully acquitted.

Hussmann, however, commented on this very question a few years later, at least indirectly. After having studied law at the universities of Göttingen, Munich, Berlin, Hamburg, and Kiel, he received his Ph.D. from the University of Bonn in 1935. His advisor was Hans von Hentig, a well-known law professor and an expert in criminology, who advocated a "biologistic crime policy."[85] In the concluding chapter of his thesis, titled "The False Confession," Hussman wrote:

> There is no doubt that many crimes can only be solved by a confession from the perpetrator. The more his psychic structure is revealed, the more clearly the crime will be understood. In this respect, the confession seems to be indispensable for legal reasoning.[86]

Given Hussmann's own experiences with the German legal system, it is difficult to interpret such a statement as anything other than a deliberation on his own case. Yet, it is ambiguous. On the one hand, Hussmann gives a possible explanation of why Daube's case was never solved: it lacked the confession of the perpetrator. That a man who had been the prime suspect of a spectacular murder trial could exploit his personal insights for an academic career underlines the importance of class in post–World War I Germany. On the other hand, Hussmann's commentary raises the question whether he perceived his own trial as a telling example of a lack of confession. Either way, Hussmann's remark serves as an unusual punch line to one of the most spectacular murder trials of the Weimar Republic—a trial that left the case unsolved but allows historians to reconstruct the paradigmatic way class, youth, and sexuality were interconnected in modern Germany.

Notes

1. "Hussmann, Karl, Abiturient, wegen Ermordung des Abiturienten Helmut Daube in Gladbeck (Sexualmord) 11 Js 312/28," Landesarchiv Nordrhein-Westfalen, Abteilung Rheinland, Standort Düsseldorf, formerly Hauptstaatsarchiv Düsseldorf (hereafter, HSA Düsseldorf) 299/822–833; "Zeitungsveröffentlichungen über den Mordprozeß gegen den Abiturienten Karl Hußmann (Angeklagt des Sexualmordes an seinem Mitabiturienten Helmut Daube in Gladbeck), "HSA Düsseldorf 6/755; "Lustmord in Gladbeck, Opfer: Helmut Daube, Abiturient, 22 March 1928," Landesarchiv Berlin (hereafter LAB) A Pr. Br. 030 Berlin C Tit. 198 B/1755.
2. Interrogation of Adolf Daube, 10 April 1928, HSA Düsseldorf 299/825, 35–36.
3. For more detail, see the popular but sensationalist book on the murder of Helmut Daube by Sabine Kettler, Eva-Maria Stuckel, and Franz Wegener, *Wer tötete Helmut Daube? Der bestialische Sexualmord an dem Schüler Helmut Daube im Ruhrgebiet 1928* (Gladbeck, 2001).
4. HSA Düsseldorf 299/822, 8–11.
5. HSA Düsseldorf 299/829, 155.
6. HSA Düsseldorf 299/822, 4–5.
7. Ibid.; Report of the Gladbeck criminal police officer Pest, 5 November 1928, HSA Düsseldorf 6/755, 89–97, here, 91.
8. As Klingelhöller remarked in his report, the shoes were quite wet—more than they should have been, considering that the night before only light rain had fallen. HSA Düsseldorf 299/822, 80–82; LAB A Pr. Br. 030 Berlin C Tit. 198 B/1755, 25.
9. HSA Düsseldorf 299/829, 155; Report Pest, 5 November 1928, HSA Düsseldorf 6/755, 89–97, here, 90.
10. Report Pest, 5 November 1928, HSA Düsseldorf 6/755, 89–97, here, 91.
11. On the importance of this trial in context of the forensic establishment of blood group serology in the 1920s, see Myriam Spörri, *Reines und gemischtes Blut: Zur Kulturgeschichte der Blutgruppenforschung*, chapter 7 (Bielefeld, 2013).
12. Ibid. A similar quotation is cited in "Bindungen in Gladbeck," *Vossische Zeitung* 14 November 1928 (also in HSA Düsseldorf 6/755 [newspaper clippings]: 99).
13. LAB A Pr. Br. 030 Berlin C Tit. 198 B/1755, 80–81; Ludwig Werneburg, "Die praktische Bedeutung der Blutgruppenuntersuchung. Im Anschluß an den Gladbecker Mordfall Daube," in: *Kriminalistische Monatshefte. Zeitschrift für die gesamte kriminalistische Wissenschaft und Praxis* 2, 9 (1928), 180–181, esp. 181.
14. The Berlin criminal police enjoyed a good reputation since the Kaiserreich and was regularly sent to other cities for special investigations. See, for instance, Helmut Walser Smith, *The Butcher's Tale: Murder and Anti-Semitism in a German Town* (New York, 2002), and Philipp Müller, *Auf der Suche nach dem Täter: Die öffentliche Dramatisierung von Verbrechen im Berlin des Kaiserreichs* (Frankfurt a. M., 2005).
15. LAB A Pr. Br.030 Berlin C Tit. 198 B/1755, 21–26.
16. LAB A Pr. Br. 030 Berlin C Tit. 198 B/1755. The public criticism became so intense that the head of the police department in the Prussian ministry of Justice felt obliged to counter them in detail, see Erich Klausener, "Der Fall Hußmann und die Kriminalpolizei," *Kriminalistische Monatshefte: Zeitschrift für die gesamte kriminalistische Wissenschaft und Praxis* 2, 12 (1928), 265–269.
17. LAB A Pr. Br. 030 Berlin C Tit. 198 B/1755, 21–26.
18. Bill of indictment against Hussmann, 3 September 1928, HSA Düsseldorf 299/829, 1–18.
19. Ibid., 2–3.
20. HSA Düsseldorf 299/829, 164–165.

21. Gabriele Tergit, "Gestalten aus dem Femeprozeß. Gespenster," *Berliner Tageblatt*, 25 March 1927.
22. Nicholas B. Dirks, "Ritual and Resistance: Subversion as a Social Fact," in *Culture/ Power/ History. A Reader in Contemporary Social Theory*, Nicholas B. Dirks and Geoff Eley et al., eds. (Princeton, NJ, 1992), 483–503, here, 483.
23. Carolin Duttlinger and Lucia Ruprecht, "Introduction," in *Performance and Performativity in German Cultural Studies*, Carolin Duttlinger and Lucia Ruprecht et al., eds. (Oxford, 2003), 9–19, here, 11. See also Jürgen Martschukat and Steffen Patzold, "Geschichtswissenschaft und 'performative turn'. Eine Einführung in Fragestellung, Konzepte und Literatur," in *Geschichtswissenschaft und "performative turn": Ritual, Inszenierung und Performanz vom Mittelalter bis zur Neuzeit*, ed. Jürgen Martschukat and Steffen Patzold (Köln, 2003), 1–31, here, 8.
24. This perspective has been strongly influenced by Gender Studies, most prominently by the work of Judith Butler; see Duttlinger and Ruprecht, "Introduction," 12; as well as Martschukat and Patzold, "Geschichtswissenschaft und 'performative turn,'" 8. For an application of the concept of performativity in masculinity studies see Olaf Stieglitz and Jürgen Martschukat, *"Es ist ein Junge!" Einführung in die Geschichte der Männlichkeiten in der Neuzeit* (Tübingen, 2005), 67–93.
25. Rosi Braidotti, *Nomadic Subjects. Embodiment and Sexual Difference in Contemporary Feminist Theory* (New York, 1994), 4.
26. See, for instance, Katharina Walgenbach and Gabriele Dietze et al., eds., *Gender als interdependente Kategorie: Neue Perspektiven auf Intersektionalität Diversität und Heterogenität* (Opladen, 2007); Cornelia Klinger and Gudrun-Axeli Knapp, eds., *Über-Kreuzungen. Fremdheit, Ungleichheit, Differenz* (Münster, 2008); Gabriele Winker and Nina Degele, *Intersektionalität: Zur Analyse sozialer Ungleichheiten* (Bielefeld, 2009).
27. For recent appropriations of theories on the performativity of categories of identity in the context of criminology, see, for instance, Susanne Krasmann, *Die Kriminalität der Gesellschaft: Zur Gouvernementalität der Gegenwart* (Konstanz, 2003), 153–155.
28. Erika Fischer-Lichte, "Performance, Inszenierung, Ritual. Zur Klärung kulturwissenschaftlicher Schlüsselbegriffe," in *Geschichtswissenschaft und "performative turn": Ritual, Inszenierung und Performanz vom Mittelalter bis zur Neuzeit*, ed. Jürgen Martschukat and Steffen Patzold (Köln, 2003), 33–54, here, 34–35, and 47–52. On the performativity of trials, see Henning Grunwald, "Justice as Performance? The Historiography of Legal Procedure and Polictical Criminal Justice in Weimar Germany," *InterDisciplines. Journal of History and Sociology* 3 (2012), 2, 46–78.
29. On the interaction between criminal justice and mass media, see Peter Fritzsche, "Talk of the Town. The Murder of Lucie Berlin and the Production of Local Knowledge," in *Criminals and their Scientists. The History of Criminology in International Perspective*, Peter Becker and Richard F. Wetzell, eds. (Cambridge, 2005), 377–398; Harald Kania Michael and Hans-Jörg Albrecht, eds., *Alltagsvorstellungen von Kriminalität: Individuelle und gesellschaftliche Bedeutung von Kriminalitätsbildern für die Lebensgestaltung* (Münster, 2004); Müller, *Auf der Suche nach dem Täter*, 73–91.
30. See Ludger Hoffmann, "Vom Ereignis zum Fall. Sprachliche Muster zur Darstellung und Überprüfung von Sachverhalten vor Gericht," in *Erzählte Kriminalität: Zur Typologie und Funktion von narrativen Darstellungen in Strafrechtspflege, Publizistik und Literatur zwischen 1770 und 1920. Vorträge zu einem interdisziplinären Kolloquium, Hamburg, 10–12. April 1985*, ed., Jörg Schönert (Tübingen, 1991), 87–113.
31. Michel Foucault, "Truth and Power," in *The Foucault Reader*, ed., Paul Rabinow (New York, 1984), 51–75, here, 73.

32. For a broader perspective, see Michel Foucault, "Lecture on 8 January 1975," in *Abnormal. Lectures at the Collège de France 1974–1975*, eds. Valerio Marchetti and Antonella Salomoni, trans. by Graham Burchell (London, 2003), 1–30.
33. See Dirks, "Ritual and Resistance," 488.
34. For a transnational perspective, see Daniel Siemens, *Metropole und Verbrechen. Die Gerichtsreportage in Berlin, Paris und Chicago 1919–1933* (Stuttgart, 2007).
35. Theodor Lessing, "Die Schüler und ihre Lehrer," *Prager Tageblatt*, 1 November 1928, in: Theodor Lessing, *Haarmann. Die Geschichte eines Werwolfs*, ed. Rainer Warwedel (Frankfurt a. M., 1989), 240–244, here, 244.
36. Ferdinand Bruckner, *Krankheit der Jugend. Schauspiel in drei Akten* (Berlin, 1928). See also Doris Engelhardt, "Ferdinand Bruckner als Kritiker seiner Zeit. Standortsuche eines Autors" (Ph.D. dissertation, RHTW Aachen, 1984), 56–86.
37. This theory was invalidated during the trial, which revealed that Günther Scheller had shot Hans and afterward killed himself.
38. For further details, see Siemens, *Metropole und Verbrechen*, 269–290; Heidi Sack, "'Wir werden lächend aus dem Leben scheiden'. Faszination Selbstmord in der Steglitzer Schülertragödie und in Diskursen der Weimarer Zeit," in: *Historical Social Research / Historische Sozialforschung* 34 (2009), 4, 259–272; Wolfgang Schild, "Berühmte Berliner Kriminalprozesse der Zwanziger Jahre," in *Rechtsentwicklungen in Berlin. Acht Vorträge, gehalten anläßlich der 750-Jahrfeier Berlins*, Friedrich Ebel and Albrecht Randelzhofer, eds. (Berlin, 1988),163–187; Thomas Lange, "Der Steglitzer Schülermordprozeß 1928," in *"Mit uns zieht die neue Zeit"—Der Mythos Jugend*, Thomas Koebner and Rolf-Peter Janz et al., eds. (Frankfurt a. M., 1985), 412–437; Ernst Erich Noth, *Erinnerungen eines Deutschen* (Hamburg, 1971), 93–111.
39. Siemens, *Metropole und Verbrechen*, 272–282.
40. See, for example, Eduard Spranger, *Die Psychologie des Jugendalters* (Leipzig, 1924); Charlotte Bühler, *Über das Seelenleben der Jugendlichen. Versuch einer Analyse und Theorie der psychischen Pubertät* (Jena, 1922); Walter Hoffmann, *Die Reifezeit. Probleme der Entwicklungspsychologie und Sozialpädagogik* (Leipzig, 1921).
41. "Mordprozeß gegen den Primaner Krantz. Erotik und Revolverschüsse," *Berliner Gerichts-Zeitung*, 2 December 1927.
42. Statement of Hussmann's schoolmate Erich Quaden, HSA Düsseldorf 299/822, 83.
43. Hearing of Karl Ernst August Hussmann, 23 February 1928, HSA Düsseldorf 299/822, 8–11.
44. Even more analogies could be found, which were seen and discussed by the contemporaries. See, e.g., the great number of letters written to the court included in HSA Düsseldorf 299/831.
45. Verhandlungen des Reichstages, III. Wahlperiode 1924, vol. 395, Stenographische Berichte (Berlin 1928), 12737, 12779–12780.
46. HSA Düsseldorf 6/755, 2–4.
47. See Robert Kuhn, *Die Vertrauenskrise der Justiz (1926–1928). Der Kampf um die "Republikanisierung" der Rechtspflege in der Weimarer Republik* (Köln, 1983); Daniel Siemens, "Die 'Vertrauenskrise' der Justiz," in *Die "Krise" der Weimarer Republik. Zur Kritik eines Deutungsmusters*, Moritz Föllmer and Rüdiger Graf, eds. (Frankfurt a. M., 2005), 139–163.
48. HSA Düsseldorf 299/831, 166–167.
49. Moritz Goldstein, "Vor dem Urteilsspruch," *Vossische Zeitung*, 28 October 1928 (HSA Düsseldorf 6/755 [newspaper clippings]).
50. See Daniel Siemens, "Explaining Crime. Berlin Newspapers and the Construction of the Criminal in Weimar Germany," *Journal of European Studies* 39 (2009), 336–352.
51. August Hermann Zeiz, "Belastungszeugen widerrufen," *Berliner Tageblatt*, 26 October 1928 (HSA Düsseldorf 6/755 [newspaper clippings]).

52. "Mordprozeß Hussmann," *Ruhr-Echo*, 16 October 1928 (HSA Düsseldorf 6/755, 29). For details concerning the *Stahlhelm*, see Volker R. Berghahn, *Der Stahlhelm. Bund der Frontsoldaten, 1918–1935* (Düsseldorf, 1966).

53. Report from police district superintendent Mikfeld, HSA Düsseldorf 6/755, 87–89, here, 87. On the attitudes and political standpoints of Weimar juveniles, see the contributions in Wolfgang R. Krabbe (Ed.), *Politische Jugend in der Weimarer Republik* (Bochum, 1993); on the habitus' of young right-wing activists see Peter Fritzsche, "On Being the Subjects of History: Nazis as Twentieth-Century Revolutionaries," in *Language and Revolution. Making Modern Political Identities*, ed., Igal Halfin (London, 2002), 161–183.

54. "Der Bibelkreis," *Rote Fahne*, 23 October 1928 (HSA Düsseldorf 6/755 [newspaper clippings]).

55. Report on the autopsy of the corpse of Helmut Daube by Dr. Marcks, 23 March 1928, HSA Düsseldorf 299/826, 38–45, here, 41. The German term *Lustmord* stresses a murder's alleged sexual motive, whereas the English term usually used for this category of crime—"serial killer"—refers to the repetitive character of the criminal acts. The German term as such cannot be rendered in English without a significant loss of meaning. (See Maria Tatar, *Lustmord: Sexual Murder in Weimar Germany*. 2nd ed. [Princeton, 1997], 7–8). Therefore, *Lustmord* will not be translated in this text.

56. Carl Grossmann, born in 1863 in Neuruppin, was arrested on 21 August 1921 in Berlin and was suspected of having killed several women who came to Berlin looking for jobs to support themselves in the economically difficult years after World War I. He committed suicide just before the end of the trial on 5 June 1922. For further details, see Sace Elder's chapter in this volume as well as Matthias Blazek, *Karl Großmann und Friedrich Schumann. Zwei Serienmörder in den zwanziger Jahren* (Stuttgart, 2009).

57. Friedrich (Fritz) Haarmann, who was born in Hannover in 1879, was found guilty of murdering twenty-four young men in a homosexual frenzy and sentenced to death on 19 December 1924. The death penalty was carried out on 16 April 1925. For further details, see Kathrin Kompisch, "Der Fall Fritz Haarmann (1924)," *Hannoversche Geschichtsblätter* 55/56 (2001/02), 97–116, and Thomas Kailer, "Werwölfe, Triebtäter, minderwertige Psychopathen. Bedingungen der Wissenspopularisierung: Der Fall Haarmann," in *Wissenspopularisierung. Konzepte der Wissensverbreitung im Wandel*, ed., Carsten Kretschmann (Berlin, 2003), 323–359.

58. Kürten was born in 1883 in Mühlheim (today a municipal district of Cologne) and was arrested in Düsseldorf on 24 May 1930. He was sentenced to death for murder in nine and of attempted murder in seven cases (women, girls, and one man) on 22 April 1931 and was executed on 2 July 1931. The case of Peter Kürten inspired Fritz Lang's famous film *M—Eine Stadt sucht einen Mörder* (Germany 1931, English title: *M. (Murderer Among Us)*. For further details, see Karl Berg, *Der Sadist. Gerichtsärztliches und Kriminalpsychologisches zu den Taten des Düsseldorfer Mörders Peter Kürten. Mit zwei Artikelserien des Kriminal-Polizeirats Ernst Gennat und der Verteidigungsrede von Dr. Alex Wehner*, ed. Michael Farin (München, 2004); Elisabeth Lenk and Roswitha Kaever, eds., *Leben und Wirken des Peter Kürten, genannt der Vampir von Düsseldorf* (München, 1974).

59. The German penal code (*Reichsstrafgesetzbuch*, 1871) exempted the accused from full legal responsibility under the condition that he or she had been unable to exert his or her free will by mental disturbances (§ 51). The court could rely on expert opinions to determine the mental state of the person in question. See Ernst Traugott Rubo, *Kommentar über das Strafgesetz für das deutsche Reich und das Einführungsgesetz vom 31. Mai 1870 sowie die Ergänzungsgesetze vom 10. Dezember 1871 und 26. Februar 1876. Nach amtlichen Quellen*. Berlin 1879, reprint, ed., and intro., Werner Schubert [Frankfurt a.M., 1991], 114). The expert statements were prepared by the local forensic physician Dr. Teudt and dated 31 June 1928 (HSA Düsseldorf 299/826, 58–74), Prof. Hübner, director of the mental asylum in Bonn and professor of psychiatric medicine at the University of Bonn and Prof. Müller-Heß, member of the Committee

of Forensic Medicine of the Rhine Province ("Gerichtsärztliche Ausschuß der Rheinprovinz"). The written opinions of Hübner and Müller-Heß unfortunately are not included in the archival materials. Yet, their statements are extensively quoted in the verdict against Hussmann, which enabled us to reconstruct their positions (Verdict against Karl Hussmann, 30 October 1928, HSA Düsseldorf 299/829, 130–165).

60. See, for instance, Erich Wulffen's seminal work on the sexual criminal (*Der Sexualverbrecher: Ein Handbuch für Juristen, Polizei- und Verwaltungsbeamte, Mediziner und Pädagogen. Mit zahlreichen kriminalistischen Originalaufnahmen.* 11th ed. [Berlin 1928], 305 and 454). According to the report of officer Pest, the criminal police in Gladbeck had an edition of Wulffen's manual at hand (5 November 1928, HSA Düsseldorf 6/755, 89–97, here, 96). For the influence of the *Lustmord* on the construction of an aggressive and potentially dangerous male sexuality, see Hania Siebenpfeiffer, "Kreatur und Kalter Killer. Der Lustmörder als Paradigma männlicher Gewalt in der Moderne," in *Gewalt und Geschlecht. Bilder, Literatur und Diskurse im 20. Jahrhundert*, Hanno Ehrlicher and Hania Siebenpfeiffer, eds. (Köln, 2002), 109–130; Michael Schetsche, "Der Wille, der Trieb und das Deutungsmuster vom Lustmord," in *Serienmord. Kriminologische und kulturwissenschaftliche Skizzierungen eines ungeheuerlichen Phänomens*, Frank J. Robertz and Alexandra Thomas, eds. (München, 2004), 346–364.

61. Richard von Krafft-Ebing, *Psychopathia Sexualis. With Especial Reference to the Antipathic Sexual Instinct. A Medico-Forensic Study.* trans. Franklin S. Klaf (New York, 1998), 53. In contemporary scientific literature, Krafft-Ebings explanatory model and terminology was not undisputed. Iwan Bloch and Caspar von Schreck-Notzing, for example, promoted the term "active algolagny" in contrast to "passive algolagny" (masochism) to emphasize that they believed the infliction and the experience of intense pain to be the motive of these activities, not, as suggested by Krafft-Ebing, the exertion of unlimited power (Iwan Bloch, *Das Sexualleben unserer Zeit in seinen Beziehungen zur modernen Kultur*, 2nd and 3rd expanded ed. [Berlin, 1907], 616, and Caspar von Schrenck-Notzing, "Beiträge zur forensischen Beurtheilung von Sittlichkeitsvergehen mit besonderer Berücksichtigung der Pathogenese psychosexueller Anomalien," *Archiv für Kriminologie und Anthropologie* 1 [1889], 5–25, here, 25).

62. Krafft-Ebing, *Psychopathia Sexualis*, 32.

63. See, e.g., Schrenck-Notzing, "Beiträge zur forensischen Beurtheilung," 18–19.

64. Krafft-Ebing, *Psychopathia Sexualis*, 1–3, 56–57.

65. See Anne McClintock, *Imperial Leather. Race, Gender and Sexuality in the Colonial Contest* (London, 1995), 36–41, and Sander L. Gilman, "Sexology, Psychoanalysis, and Degeneration: From a Theory of Race to a Race to Theory," in *Degeneration. The Dark Side of Progress*, Edward J. Chamberlain and Sander L. Gilman, eds. (New York, 1985), 72–100, here, 73–75. For the influence of colonial racist thinking on the construction of the *Lustmörder*, see Eva Bischoff *Kannibale-Werden. Eine postkoloniale Geschichte deutscher Männlichkeit um 1900* (Bielefeld, 2011), 186–194, 200–210.

66. See the correspondence between the inquisitor and the police in Baden (HSA Düssseldorf 299/826, 53–54) and Teudt's medical opinion on Hussmann, 31 June 1928, HSA Düsseldorf 299/826, 58–74, here, 58.

67. Medical opinion of Dr. Teudt, 31 June 1928, HSA Düsseldorf 299/826, 58–74, here, 58.

68. As referred to by the prosecution in its bill of indictment against Hussmann, HSA Düsseldorf 299/829, 1–18, here, 17. For the interdependency of nationalist and racist thinking, see Christian Geulen, *Wahlverwandte. Rassendiskurs und Nationalismus im späten 19. Jahrhundert* (Hamburg, 2004), and for the discussion on the degenerative effect of "inter-racial" marriages in Germany, see Fatima El-Tayeb, *Schwarze Deutsche. Der Diskurs um "Rasse" und nationale Identität 1890–1933* (Frankfurt a. M./New York, 2001).

69. Medical opinion of Dr. Teudt, 31 June 1928 [sic], HSA Düsseldorf 299/826, 58–74, here, 67.

70. Ibid., 67–68.

71. Hübner's expertise for example is called upon not only in the trial against Hussmann but also in that against Peter Kürten. (See Hübner's medical opinion on Kürten, 26 March 1931, HSA Düsseldorf 17/730). Prof. Strauch (Berlin), who prepared a psychiatric expertise on Carl Grossmann (see Medical opinion on Carl Grossmann by Prof. Strauch, 26 April 1922, LAB A 358-01/1522, vol. 4, 210–245), was involved in the Hussmann trial as well: the Berlin homicide squad asked his opinion on the question of how much blood would have been spilled on the murderer of Helmut Daube. In his answer, Störmer included speculations on the possible motive of the murderer. According to him, it most likely was jealousy, homosexual desire, or sadism. (HSA Düsseldorf 299/826, 49–52).

72. Medical opinion on Peter Kürten by Dr. Raether, 2 January 1931, HSA Düsseldorf 17/731, 269.

73. Medical opinion on Carl Grossmann by Dr. Störmer, 20 May 1922, LAB A 358-01/1522, vol. 4, 246–266, here, 261–262.

74. Medical opinion on Carl Grossmann by Prof. Strauch, 26 April 1922, LAB A 358-01/1522, vol. 4, 210–245, here, 230.

75. Medical opinion on Friedrich Haarmann by Dr. Schultze, 1 October 1924, HSA Hannover Hann 155 Göttingen 864a: 106–130, here, 130.

76. See the description Wulffen gives of the "typcial" *Lustmörder* "J." (*Der Sexualverbrecher*, 478–482).

77. Wulffen, *Der Sexualverbrecher*, 341–342, 348–349. In medical opinions on convicted *Lustmörder*, however, these juvenile acts of aggression are explicitly stressed. See, e.g., the expert opinion on Peter Kürten by Prof. Sioli, in which Kürten's questionable accounts of his cruelties to dogs and his murder of a playmate at an early age were taken at face value. Moreover, Sioli referred to them to demonstrate that Kürten's perversion was already developed at an early age (14 November 1930, HSA Düsseldorf 17/728, 11 and 277).

78. See the expertise by Hübner and Müller-Heß as included in the verdict against Hussmann, 30 October 1928, HSA Düsseldorf 299/829, 130–165, here, 143.

79. Medical opinion on Hussmann by Dr. Teudt, 31 June 1928 [sic], HSA Düsseldorf 299/826, 58–74, here, 70. Müller-Heß concurred with this assessment (see the verdict against Hussmann, 30 October 1928, HSA Düsseldorf 299/829, 130–165, here, 144) whereas Hübner distinguished between "normal" behavior and some single acts, which were unusual for pubertal sexuality (ibid., 143).

80. For the construction of the "homosexual body," see John C. Fout, "Sexual Politics in Wilhelmine Germany: The Male Gender Crisis, Moral Purity, and Homophobia," *Journal of the History of Sexuality* 2, 3 (1992), 388–421; Siobhan Somerville, "Scientific Racism and the Emergence of the Homosexual Body," *Journal of the History of Sexuality* 5, 2 (1994), 243–266; Jennifer Terry, "Anxious Slippages Between 'Us' and 'Them.' A Brief History of the Scientific Search for Homosexual Bodies," in *Deviant Bodies. Critical Perspectives on Difference in Science and Popular Culture*, Jennifer Terry and Jacqueline Urla, eds. (Bloomington 1995), 129–169. For views of homosexual male prostitution in the 1920s, see Martin Lücke, *Männlichkeit in Unordnung. Homosexualität und männliche Prostitution in Kaiserreich und Weimarer Republik* (Frankfurt a.M., 2008).

81. Eduard Spranger, *Psychologie des Jugendalters* (Leipzig, 1924, here quoted according to the 28th edition 1966). Spranger's book was considered the seminal study on the topic of adolescent psychology until the 1970s.

82. Medical opinion of Dr. Teudt, 31 June 1928 [sic], HSA Düsseldorf 299/826, 58–74, here, 69. See also Spranger, *Psychologie des Jugendalters*, 90–92, 94–97.

83. For Spranger, the "sound development of the soul" was at risk predominantly by the "repression of the sexual instinct" (*Psychologie des Jugendalters*, 128). Concerning male homosexuality,

he considered "enthusiastic and idealistic tendencies among young men to be a necessary phenomenon of growing up" (ibid., 115).

84. Verdict against Hussmann, 30 October 1928, HSA Düsseldorf 299/829, 130–165, here, 145.

85. See Christian Müller, *Verbrechensbekämpfung im Anstaltsstaat. Psychiatrie, Kriminologie und Strafrechtsreform in Deutschland 1871–1933* (Göttingen, 2004), 156–158.

86. Karl Hussmann, *Das falsche Geständnis* (Kiel, 1935), 63.

Chapter 9

CRIME AND LITERATURE IN THE WEIMAR REPUBLIC AND BEYOND
Telling the Tale of the Poisoners Ella Klein and Margarete Nebbe

Todd Herzog

At the end of Don DeLillo's novel *Libra*, a fictional account of the case of Lee Harvey Oswald and the Kennedy assassination, Oswald's mother Marguerite testifies in court about her son, explaining why she cannot offer a straightforward account of the events leading up to the assassination:

> Your honor, I cannot state the truth of this case with a simple yes and no. I have to tell a story. . . . There are stories within stories, judge. . . . I intend to research this case and present my findings. But I cannot pin it down to a simple statement. . . . It takes stories to fill out a life.[1]

Marguerite Oswald's testimony attests to an inherent conflict within the notion of the criminal case. On the one hand, whether the case is related in a court trial or a traditional detective novel, it needs to reach a conclusion—guilty or not guilty? Whodunit? On the other hand, both forms of the criminal case are typically structured as narratives. Cases are a narrative form of knowledge; they need to tell a story. And yet these stories can ultimately preclude precisely that which the case seeks to reach: a definitive answer, a concrete judgment. DeLillo's fictional narrative is able to weave this tension throughout the novel: Marguerite Oswald's testimony makes up one strand of DeLillo's historical novel; the other strand narrates the work of Nicholas Branch, a former CIA agent who is given access to all documents pertaining to the case and is charged with the task of writing an authoritative history of it. Eventually, the fact-based investigator Branch comes around to Marguerite Oswald's position, proclaiming that "it is premature to make a serious effort to turn these notes into coherent history. Maybe it will always be premature."[2]

By the 1980s, when DeLillo was writing *Libra*, the concept of narrative uncertainty and the genre of true-crime fiction were both well established. In this chapter, I want to return to the period when these concepts were being developed. If narrative is a primary means to distinguish between types, reach judgments, and explain causes, what happens when the belief in narrative coherence goes into crisis, as it does in the early twentieth century? To address this question, I will examine a case from 1922–1923 that has attracted an enormous amount of attention to this day: the case of Ella Klein and Margarete Nebbe, who were convicted of the murder of one of their husbands and the attempted murder of the other.

I will first examine the events surrounding the case and then turn to a remarkable monograph on the case, Alfred Döblin's *Die beiden Freundinnen und ihr Giftmord* (*The Two Girlfriends and their Murder by Poisoning*), which seeks to probe the issues at the center of the genre of the case study—the very conflicts addressed in *Libra*. I will conclude by briefly considering three post–World War II re-workings of the case. By examining several different accounts of the case spanning eight decades (from the 1920s to the 1990s) and four different media (press, literature, theater, and film), I hope to bring to light the complex relationship between crimes and crime stories—between events and actions and narrative accounts of these events and actions—and investigate the role that narrative plays in establishing notions of causality. To return to the language of Marguerite Oswald's fictional testimony, I wish to delve into these "stories within stories" and examine how they work and what they do as they go about attempting to "fill out a life."

"So Typical . . . That It Could Have Been Taken from a Scientific Treatise": The Case of Ella Klein and Margarete Nebbe

When, in 1922, two women were arrested in Berlin for the murder of one of their husbands and the attempted murder of the other, the ensuing trial, which revealed their lesbian relationship and contained all of the major traditional stereotypes of female criminality—hysteria, childlike behavior, hypersexuality—created quite a sensation.[3] The facts of the case were never much in dispute and are, on one level at least, fairly straightforward. In 1918, nineteen-year-old Ella Thieme, a hairdresser from Braunschweig, moved to Berlin; two years later, she married a carpenter named Klein. Klein, an alcoholic, brutally mistreated Ella, who continually rebuffed his sexual advances, leading her to leave him and seek a divorce after spending only a few weeks together. Her family, however, convinced her to return to her husband, and the mistreatment continued.

Ella soon met another unhappily married woman, Margarete Nebbe, a neighbor in the working-class district of Berlin-Lichterfeld. The two quickly developed an intense emotional and sexual relationship. Over the next several months, they exchanged nearly six hundred letters in which they fantasized about liberating themselves from their husbands so that the two of them could be free to be together. To facilitate this liberation, they concocted a plan to poison their husbands by applying arsenic to their food. Ella began the process in February 1922; two months later, on 1 April, Klein was pronounced dead of alcohol poisoning in a Berlin hospital.

Klein's mother quickly grew suspicious of Ella's odd behavior and the mysterious circumstances surrounding her son's death. She launched an investigation into the cause of Klein's death, which an autopsy revealed to be arsenic poisoning. On 22 May 1922, Ella Klein was arrested and charged with the murder of her husband. One week later, Margarete Nebbe was also arrested on charges of aiding Ella in her murder and attempting to poison her own husband as well. Nebbe's mother, Marie Riemer, was also implicated in the plan, but was later pronounced innocent.

Over the course of the five-day trial, which began on 12 March 1923, the story of the two women became a topic of widespread public discussion. All six hundred letters that Klein and Nebbe had exchanged were read aloud in court, and their often racy content was reproduced in the press. A series of medical experts, including the noted sexologist Magnus Hirschfeld, offered testimony in the case. Though the public was not admitted to the courtroom, the papers reported large crowds gathering outside each day to catch a glimpse of the participants and to hear the latest developments.[4] On 16 March, both women were found guilty by the jury and given jail sentences that most commentators on the trial found to be shockingly light.[5]

The guilt of the two women was never really in doubt. Yet the case clearly struck a nerve. Surely the sensational elements of the trial—especially the homosexual relationship between the defendants—had much to do with the grip it had on the public. But it was ultimately something else about the case that captured the attention of a number of interested observers: not its uniqueness, but rather its *typicality*. The typicality of the case was noted by two prominent writers who closely followed the proceedings, Joseph Roth and Robert Musil, both of whom wrote short pieces about it immediately following the trial. As Roth noted in an article that appeared in the *Berliner Börsen-Courier* on the day following the decision: "As unusual as this 'sensational trial' is and as odd as these two women are—their marriages and their lives are typical for women of petty bourgeois circles, from which Nebbe and Klein come. It is through this typicality that the trial gains its special social and psychological significance."[6] Though he does not retreat from his initial class-oriented observation, Roth does extend the implications of the case beyond the milieu of working-class women:

> The murderers are psychologically interesting in that they supply evidence that in these primitive women, whom one thinks one knows so well because one encounters

them in the subway, on the streets and in stores, the most complicated processes are being played out: perversion and refinement, mysteries and inextricabilities are not only the consequences of a luxurious spiritual decadence. They are not the outcome of well-bred sensitive nerves, but rather natural-unnatural psychological storms whose preconditions are everywhere, in every person—in the "simple" souls of regular people and in the "refined" organisms of intellectuals.[7]

This universality was, for Roth, the real ground for interest in the case, though, he argued, this was precisely what was lost on the curious public, who were not "mature enough to ignore the excitement and lasciviousness of the events" and instead pay attention to the lesson of the case, which lay in the fact that the "unnatural predisposition" that came to light over the course of the trial was not limited to these two women, nor to others of their class or gender. It was, rather, perhaps present in all of us. Mentioning the widespread disapproval of divorce and homosexuality, Roth also pointed out that it was social strictures that were ultimately responsible for prompting these women's actions.

Writing three days later, Robert Musil made an observation similar to Roth's, pronouncing the case "so typical . . . that it could have been taken from a scientific treatise."[8] For Musil, as for Roth, it was the case's very typicality that made it interesting. He went a step further than Roth, however, in that he saw this typicality as not explaining the events, but rather lending an air of uncertainty and mystery to the case.[9] The difficulty of the case, for Musil, lay in the uncertainty as to where to locate guilt: "One should ask in crimes of this type what portion of the blame should lie with society for allowing it to get so far. A resolute criminal has indeed more bad in him or her than a good, but weak, person, but also more seeds of goodness, says John Stuart Mill."[10] For Musil, the murky cause of the crime was not to be found in feelings of hatred or revenge, but rather in the nature of love itself: "Not only do noble feelings of love transform themselves into crimes, but at the same time outwardly criminal thoughts are internally perceived as indistinguishable from a noble feeling of love."[11] Musil seems to be pointing here not to asocial or antisocial behavior as the cause of the women's crimes, but rather to an overidentification, an oversocialization—not distance, but closeness. I will return to this notion and discuss it further in my consideration of Döblin's case study.

This uncertainty about where to locate the ultimate cause of the crime played itself out both among expert witnesses and public commentators in the Klein-Nebbe case. Whereas many argued, along with Roth and Musil, that the cause of the crime (and therefore at least part of the guilt) lay in social relations, others argued just as forcefully that the cause of the crime must be sought in the physical or psychological make-up of the defendants. For many commentators, the events had to be viewed primarily within the context of sexual perversity: "Everything in this trial breathed sexuality," wrote Arthur Brandt, the defense attorney for Klein and Nebbe, in the *BZ am Mittag*.[12] In this view, the crime therefore had to be seen as a "sex crime."[13] The socialist *Vorwärts*, too, argued that "the decisive word in this case belongs not to the field of psychiatry, but to sexual pathology."[14] "In any event," the report continued, "the expert witnesses were in agreement that both of the defendants display[ed] congenital psychological defects" and Klein in particular suffered from "limitations in mental and physical development that extend even to the internal sexual organs."[15] The experts were also in agreement about "the presence of a homosexual tendency in both defendants."[16] In other words, the medical experts called in to testify in the trial all agreed that the women suffered from a sexual pathology that lay in their physical constitution and their sexual orientation. In this reading of the case, the cause of the crimes lay not in the social repression that Roth and Musil cited, but in the physical and psychological conditions of the individual women who were guilty of them. They had committed the crimes because they, unlike the rest of society, suffered from a sexual pathology.

Other commentators took a different stance, viewing the murder not as the manifestation of the two women's sexual pathology, but of the perversity of social conditions. A commentator for *Vorwärts* summed up this position:

> The artificially cultivated ignorance and mental complacency of women, the position of marital servitude that has been sanctified by tradition and law, the lack of understanding by the parents, the brutality of the "Lord of the creation," the husband in married life, make up the social background of this drama. The women were thus "innocently guilty."[17]

To prevent the further occurrence of such crimes, argued those who located guilt in Weimar society, one must concentrate not on curing or incarcerating the individual criminals but on altering social conditions. In contrast, those who located guilt in a psychological or physical abnormality in the two women argued in favor of treating the women.

The arguments that came to the fore in the case of Klein and Nebbe were not, of course, new or particular to the crime under question here. Rather, they revolved around an ongoing debate in criminology since its beginnings: the question of what produces criminal behavior. The development of the modern science of criminology since the end of the nineteenth century saw the emergence of three competing schools of thought on what makes a criminal. The anthropological school, which argued that the source of criminality lay in biological factors; the sociological school, which argued in favor of social factors in determining criminality; and the psychological school, which sought to tie criminality to psychic factors.[18] The debates among (and within) these three general schools as to whether criminality was ultimately inner-determined (psychological or physical) or outer-determined (sociological) was still heated in the 1920s and, indeed, continues to this day.[19] This debate, which, as we have seen, played itself out in the Klein-Nebbe case, also figured prominently in Alfred Döblin's investigation into the case. Indeed, his investigation of the case was, in fact, primarily an investigation into the arguments about where to locate the cause of criminality. Is criminality primarily inner-determined or outer-determined? Do these distinctions make sense in this case—or in any case? In answering these questions, Döblin incorporated the various voices—expert and otherwise—that surrounded the case, not to decide on which was most compelling, but rather to figure out how they went about reaching their conclusions—to analyze what it meant to have "stories within stories" and figure out how to narrate this condition.

"We Understand It, on a Certain Level": Alfred Döblin's *Die beiden Freundinnen und ihr Giftmord*

In his re-telling of the story of Klein and Nebbe published in 1924, just a year after the trial had ended, Döblin changed the characters' names to Elli Link and Grete Bende, but otherwise made no attempt to obscure the connection to the real case, which had attracted considerable attention throughout Germany and would have been obvious to any informed contemporary reader. Indeed, the links and breaks between the real case and Döblin's re-telling of it stand at the center of his investigation, which sought to address the genre of the case study and the ways in which it serves to placate its audience by locating guilt in an individual and thus preserve the social order.

That Döblin saw his case study as an intervention in the traditional form of the genre becomes quite clear in his remarkable epilogue to the volume, in which he argued that the reasons behind this crime could never be known: "I wanted to demonstrate the difficulty of the case, to question the impression that one could understand everything or even most things about such a large chunk of life. We understand it, on a certain level."[20] Döblin had already exhibited this narrative skepticism a decade earlier in his programmatic essay "An Romanautoren und ihre Kritiker" ("To Novelists and their Critics"), in which he argued that the psychological novel is "a purely abstract phantasmagoria" and that "the analyses and attempts at differentiation have nothing to do with the process of an actual psyche."[21] To avoid such myths of causality and individuality, Döblin advocated a turn away from psychology and toward psychiatry as the basis of literary production:

> We can learn from psychiatry, the one science that captures the whole psychic life of the individual. It has long recognized the naïveté of psychology and confines itself to noting the products and movements of the psyche—and shrugs its shoulders at anything further, the "whys" and "hows."[22]

Döblin's position in this early essay is certainly consistent with the epilogue of *Die beiden Freundinnen und ihr Giftmord*, in which he seeks to question not just the notion of causality implied by a coherent narrative of a life, but also the effects of its imposition in turning a person and an event into a case:

> We know nothing about psychic continuity, causality, the psyche and its concentrations of elements. We must accept the facts of this case, the letters and actions, and programmatically refuse to truly explain them. Not even if we were to delve here and there more deeply into events, would anything have happened (112).

As a theoretician, Döblin was remarkably consistent. Yet, these musings on the nature of the case study in the epilogue come as a shock to the reader because they follow a story of over one hundred pages in which this complex case is related as a crisp, exciting, and smoothly flowing narrative. In retrospect, it becomes clear that this narrative could be kept intact only because the narrator's presence was elided throughout the entire story. In the first line of the epilogue the narrator made his first, sudden appearance: "When I attempt an overview of the entire course of events, it is just like in the story: 'a wind came and uprooted the tree'" (112). The introduction of the first person coincides with the mention of a story. Clearly the initial semblance of narrative order functioned as a necessary step in Döblin's argument. Indeed, Döblin admitted his own need to establish the very narrative order about which he would, in the epilogue, exhibit such skepticism— his need to understand the mysteries of the case:

> When I reflected on the three, four people involved in this affair, I had the impulse to travel the streets that they routinely traveled. I also sat in the pubs in which the two women got to know one another, I visited the apartment of one of them, spoke with her personally, spoke with others involved and observed them (114).

The story Döblin tells, which incorporates newspaper reports, trial records, medical testimony, and statements from those involved in the case, is, in fact, full of "whys" and "hows." Indeed, the question of *whether* Elli was guilty of murdering her husband (along with the question of whether Bende served as her accomplice) was never really an issue either in the case or in Döblin's re-telling of it. [23] What was at stake in the courtroom, as Döblin points out, was something that took the jury well beyond questions of guilt and innocence. The question concerned not the crime itself, but rather the constitutions of the criminals that led them to the crime:

> A small group of learned men studied the physical and mental constitutions of the women and attempted to form an image on the basis of extensive experience. The prosecuting and defending attorneys both shed light on the lives of these women. In every case it was not the act that stood in the center, the poisoning itself, but rather practically

the opposite of an act: namely how this course of events came to be, how it was possible. Indeed, they set out to demonstrate how this event was unavoidable (100).

These various expert voices were incorporated into Döblin's account of the case and the trial. Döblin's case history devoted the bulk of its attention to detailing the arguments and positions presented at the trial, which, as we have seen, broke into two main schools: those experts who saw the crimes as arising from certain physical or psychological abnormalities in the two women (childhood trauma, malformed organs, and an innate homosexual "drive") and those experts who argued that the causes lay in social conditions (abusive spouses, economic hardship, and a society unaccepting of homosexuality).

Döblin ultimately did not, of course, decide between these competing explanations. Indeed, at times he seemed to take sides with each. Elli's "female organs," he tells us, "were not properly developed," thus presenting the jury with the task of "pronouncing a uterus guilty" (100–101). But, at the same time, Döblin argued, the jury ought to have, but could not, consider other possible locations of guilt, such as her father, who forced Elli to return to her abusive husband.[24] At one moment the source of Elli's criminality seemed to lie in her body; at another moment, it seemed to lie in her society. What Döblin offers us is not a mystery that lacks a coherent explanation, as the epilogue seems to announce, but rather an abundance of explanations—plenty of "whys" and "hows."

The first part of the story and the epilogue, in short, simply do not hold together. Nor, I would argue, did Döblin intend them to. His experiment with the narrative form of the case study attempts to overcome the fixation on guilt and the artificial separation of the criminal from noncriminal society by allowing the different parts of his text to come into conflict with one another. In other words, not only does he detail a battle among representations in the trial, he also sets up a battle among his own representations. His narrative thus not only exposes the conflicts and contradictions among various accounts of the case; it turns on itself and maps the conflicts and contradictions within itself. It is at once a record of the conflicts inherent in the criminal case study and a self-aware example of those conflicts.

In addition to the story and the epilogue, Döblin appended two sections to his study: the first is a series of charts that are supposed to serve as "a visual overview of the main phases of the case" (110). Though it initially seems that Döblin might have intended these charts to offer a final explanation of the case, they, too, fall short of describing the course of events. Döblin's various attempts to explain the "how" and "why" of the case are, by his own admission, inadequate; he remarks of the charts that the stress lies less on theoretical truth than on their vivid graphic quality: "The main thrust here lies not on theoretical truth, but rather on the graphic demonstration, the possibility of simply communicating at least the most important elements" (111). The second section appended to the study is a series of handwriting samples, along with character analyses based on Elli's and Grete's writing styles. Even after the publication of the volume, Döblin continued to be interested in this graphological evidence, writing to the noted graphologist Ludwig Klages and asking his opinion on the case.[25] One sees clearly here that Döblin is not interested simply in throwing his hands up and declaring the ultimate truth behind the case to be unattainable. Rather, he wants to uncover that truth—by journalistic investigation, by interpreting the expert testimony, by analyzing the two women's handwriting and psychological states. But at the same time he is aware that this truth is indeed confused by the "stories within stories."

The need to explain, situate, separate, and—at the same time—to avoid the reductions that come with this very act of explanation, situation, separation are simultaneously present in Döblin's study. He summarized his presentation thus:

> The whole thing is a tapestry made up of many individual scraps—cloth, silk, even pieces of metal and clumps of clay. It is stuffed with straw, wire and yarn and in many places the pieces are not bound together. Many tears are bound together with glue or glass. Then everything is seamless and bears the stamp of the truth. It has been thrust into our customary processes of thinking and feeling. It happened that way—even the participants believe that. But it also didn't happen that way (112).

It happened that way, and it did not happen that way. What Döblin emphasizes here is the mythical nature of the criminal case history: a crime cannot adequately be explained and hence contained by giving it narrative form, for the narrative necessarily becomes a myth. But Döblin also recognizes the need to construct such myths: A crime must be explained and irrational behavior must be given a cause to keep our worlds in order. Even as he insists on—and demonstrates—the impossibility of narrating a life, he insists just as forcefully on the need to tell stories, the need for narrative rescue from uncertainty.

Indeed, one of the few moments in which Elli seems to find a way out of her tormented life is when she is able to tell her own story: "Then Elli narrated what she was able to—spasmodically, abruptly. . . . Elli achieved something. . . . It was a formal change, a liberation" (23). The narrator and his subject here are both driven by the need to tell a story, and there is a certain pathos around this drive for a narrative that is at once impossible and necessary. And the narrative in each of these cases revolves around the same questions of causality, questions for which Döblin insists there are ultimately no clear answers.

Refusing to believe in causality, Döblin adopts instead the notion of mysterious motors that drive events beyond the logic of causality: "Zoology has uncovered actual motors of our actions. The greatest mass of our psyches is driven by instincts. The uncovering and dissection of these instincts brings to light quite decisive motors of our actions" (117). Throughout his study, Döblin turns to various figures to represent these motors, and he never seems able to settle upon one appropriate metaphor. In the passage quoted above, for example, it is the wind ripping out a tree. Most notably, the motor figures as a bullet: "Invisible bullets come out of nowhere and strike us, they change us and we notice only the change, not the actual motor, the agent, the bullet. Everything then proceeds within us in a causal manner" (117).

This wind, this bullet, can hit anybody, and hence we cannot be assured that "I am not a criminal because I am not like her" and prove this through a case study that shows *her* to be different from *me* and shows *them* to be different from *us*. Döblin's study of this borderline case puts this very border—that between criminal and noncriminal, sane and insane, those violently struck by the bullet and those not struck by the bullet—into question. "We were no longer on the terrain of 'guilt and innocence,'" Döblin writes, "but rather on another, terribly uncertain terrain—that of connections, recognition, insight" (100). The legal system, of course, does not permit the judge or the jury to enter into this uncertain territory, and the traditional case history also avoids such considerations. But Döblin's case study, which takes the modernist crisis of narrative as its starting point to depict a larger crisis of faith in the legal and social order, insists that we must venture into this territory, that in the seeming aberration of criminal conduct the otherwise hidden, normal workings of society suddenly become evident. Criminality, Döblin argues, cannot be traced to an understandable cause—neither in the individual nor in society. The criminal justice system, like the criminal case study, seeks to construct a narrative that traces an event back to such a cause. And in so doing, both fall into mythologizing and thereby lose sight of—indeed, even work to obscure—the uncertain motors and bullets that prompt our actions.

Not only can experts not point to a cause of criminality, criminals themselves are deceived about the cause of their own actions. In the opening sentences of his narrative, Döblin plays with this uncertainty of agency: "The pretty blond Elli Link arrived in Berlin in 1918. She was 19 years old. She had previously worked as a beautician in Braunschweig, where her parents were carpenters. A minor act of juvenile delinquency happened to her: She took five Marks from the wallet of a customer." After beginning what seems like a straightforward story about a young woman, Döblin inserts a structurally odd sentence that plays a trick on the reader: Elli initially seems to be the victim of a crime (it "happened to her"), but in fact the elaboration of this statement after the colon reveals Elli to have *committed* the crime ("she took five Marks"). Döblin's narrative thus takes the reader by surprise, and in so doing clouds the notion of agency.[26]

In a traditional crime narrative, this small juvenile delinquency would foreshadow and to some extent foreordain and serve to explain the later, larger crime. But Döblin subtly turns this process on its head. At work here is an interesting notion of trauma that provides an alternative to the more common location of trauma in individual (usually childhood) experiences. As Mark Seltzer notes in his study of serial killers, our tendency to locate trauma in childhood amounts to a privatization of trauma.[27] Döblin's language of an anonymous, impersonal violence hitting one like a bullet from the outside amounts to a publicization of criminality. "Insofar as we react to this blow in our own way," he writes, "we believe that we are in touch with 'ourselves'" (117). What Döblin tries to show here can be characterized by paraphrasing a Monty Python sketch: "This trauma that I have—that is to say, which is mine—is mine."[28] But, in Döblin's view, one cannot claim possession of one's own trauma or even one's own crimes—you don't commit them; they happen to you. It is, of course, a commonplace in criminology that there are imitative types who suffer from a breakdown of boundaries and overly identify with others. However, Döblin argues that it is not simply imitative types who are susceptible to a breakdown of borders between self and society; rather, this dissolution of borders is precisely the normal condition of the individual in modernity—the individual in a state of shock.

The implications for the very notion of individuality that lies at the center of the notion of the case study are enormous. In Elli Link, we are no longer dealing with an individual, with a subject, but much more with the breakdown of the border between the individual and society, between public and private, between inside and outside. This study of what Döblin repeatedly refers to as a "border-line case" (*Grenzfall*), which constantly attempts to locate and transgress borders, turns out to be about the very permeability of borders in modernity—especially the border between self and society. Döblin insists that Elli Link is not antisocial or even asocial, but rather *overly* socialized. Döblin writes of Elli's time alone in jail—a situation of the most intense isolation—as precisely a moment in which social forces seem to do battle within her:

> While in prison, Elli was often confronted in dreams and day-dreams with people and events blown up to violent proportions. . . . Elli was deeply impacted by the events, the imprisonment, the interrogations. . . . From this source now flowed overly-large masses of social impulses. While she seemed happy during the day and behaved calmly, at night and in her dreams she was the object of bourgeois impulses that were fiercely flaming up (80–82).

Elli becomes here nothing more than an object under attack by social impulses. The language clearly does not depict an individual, but rather a site of conflicting drives. The charts appended to the end of the volume, which purport to present a "Spatial Presentation of the Psychic Developments," similarly depict Elli as an object under attack, as circles representing differing impulses move in and out of the permeable borders that make up the site called "Elli."

The traditional case history—like the psychological novel—fails to explain the cause of criminality precisely because its emphasis on the individual fails to look beyond the borders of individuality. Döblin's crucial point is that if one follows the general modernist tendency to view shock as the individual's normal experience of modernity, then it is no longer accurate to argue about psychological versus sociological motivations and determinations. Rather, as Seltzer has noted in a different context, "it's not a matter either of equating inside and outside (the 'psychological' and the 'sociological') or a matter of choosing between them, since it's precisely the boundaries between inside and outside that are violently transgressed, renegotiated, reaffirmed in these cases."[29] Döblin's case study attempts to find a way to write this nonborder, to think both individual and society—and the violent exchanges between the two—together at the same time:

> I didn't set out to write a cheap milieu study. The only thing that was clear to me was that the life—or a portion of the life—of an individual cannot be understood in itself. People stand in a symbiotic relationship with other people and other things. . . . This is in itself a reality: the symbiosis with others and with apartments, houses, streets, places. This is a certain, if murky, truth. If I pull out an individual person, it is as if I were to look at a leaf or a thumb and attempt thereby to describe nature and development. But they cannot be described in that way; the branch, the tree and the animal must also be described (114).

Döblin clearly states here that his narrative stands in opposition to more traditional case studies: he wishes to avoid both writing a "cheap milieu study" and following individual clues in the manner of a detective. Indeed, the reference to thumbs is not incidental—recall how important body parts are to Sherlock Holmes's investigations, most notably in "The Adventure of the Engineer's Thumb."[30] Against such narratives, Döblin opposes his own innovative form of crime story that seeks to narrate individuals and their society at the same time and detail the mysterious and traumatic forces of causality that traditional crime narratives obscure. Prompted by a difficult case that seemed to defy explanation, Döblin found himself confronted with the problems and uncertainties of narrating a life. His experimental narrative attempts to tell "stories within stories" and allow stories to stand in conflict with one another. He refuses to settle upon a single explanation or to tell a coherent story, but at the same time insists on the need to tell stories. He thus found in this narrative crisis a productive position from which to write. Later authors and filmmakers would also turn to this case as a source for their stories. I will now to turn to these later versions of the story of these two women and their crime, each of which views the case primarily through Döblin's account of it and wrestles with the issues that he raises. Each of these later narratives, however, also takes the case in a different direction and offers a different version of the story.

Postwar Re-Tellings of the Case of Klein and Nebbe

The case of Klein and Nebbe and Döblin's account of it received little attention throughout the middle of the twentieth century. However, the republication of

Die beiden Freundinnen in the 1970s sparked a resurgence of interest in both the text and the case it depicts. The *Bild-Zeitung* ran a series devoted to the original case, and new critical examinations of Döblin's work arose, as well as a number of literary and cinematic re-workings of the text. In the remainder of this chapter, I focus on three adaptations of *Die beiden Freundinnen*, produced in three different media—theater, film, and literature—to examine how they go about narrating the case and wrestling with the issues that it prompts.

During the 1976–1977 theatrical season, Döblin's tale was adapted for the stage by Peer Raben and produced for the *Kammerspiele* in Bochum. Issues of authority and freedom come to the fore in this stage version, and the murder is presented as an emancipatory gesture carried out against a repressive patriarchal order. The heavy-handed staging cast one area of the stage in darkness, featuring sparse and oppressive surroundings, contrasting starkly with a second area bathed in light and set with flowers and a gurgling fountain. The former area was occupied by despotic fathers and husbands, while the paradisiacal setting of the second was reserved for Grete and her mother.

The production was received poorly in the press and frequently compared unfavorably to the Döblin text. One reviewer had high praise for the extraordinarily rich material of Döblin's work, pronouncing it "differentiated, complex and psychologically and sociologically illuminating."[31] The reviewer lamented, however, that the stage production effected an oversimplification of the work that rendered it "noticeably flat, simplified, indeed uninteresting."[32] Döblin's nuanced psychological portrait appears to have been sacrificed in the production's politicization of the text. Contemporary reviewers did credit the play with an interesting innovation in the addition of a character called "the Stettiner" (Döblin's birthplace), cast as a reporter figure who reads from Döblin's theoretical works. This device gave expression to Döblin's psychological analysis, even as the play centered primarily on issues of gender. This production illustrates the difficulty of offering a multiperspective, yet coherent narrative. Although it tries to preserve the conflict between story and theory in the dramatization of Döblin as a character, it is unable to preserve the psychological ambiguity of the characters and their actions. Instead, the case is understood within the discourse of patriarchy and feminism—a valid interpretation, and one buttressed by parts of Döblin's account, but only one of the many nested stories that need to be considered.

In the following year, Axel Corti directed a film version of the work for television, in a joint Austrian-German production. *Die beiden Freundinnen: Ein Plädoyer* (*The Two Girlfriends: A Plea*) aired on 10 April 1978 on the German television network ZDF, receiving a significant 33 percent share of television viewership. The film does not depict the sensational murder trial—which forms the center of Döblin's text—opting instead for a more subtle treatment of the relationship between the social environment in which the principal figures lived and the psychological developments leading up to the murder. Corti was intent on presenting the social relations of working-class Berlin in the 1920s, which appears without the glamour of more recent filmic depictions of the Weimar era.

As in the Bochum stage production, space is the primary metaphor of the film. As the actors move through the dark, cramped spaces of the urban working class, this environment appears to circumscribe not only their movements and actions, but their thoughts as well. Corti favors tight shots, providing no overview or distance from the actors and sets in front of the camera. Objects and set design assume a leading role in the film, sharing more or less equal billing with the actors. In adopting this interesting dual focus, Corti followed a theoretical tenet important to Döblin's work, for Döblin sought to explain the relationship between people and objects as a means of exploring human psychology. In the cinematic medium, Corti availed himself of a form better equipped to depict this symbiosis than the written word. As Matthias Prangel has suggested, on film Corti was able to express visually what Döblin had to explain, giving the viewer an immediate and direct experience of Elli's psychological immobility. Döblin's program is thus taken further in Corti's cinematic reading than in the original work.[33]

Whereas the stage adaptation viewed the case through the lens of gender, Corti clearly assigned primary importance to the role of class. If the Bochum production staged the two women's lesbian relationship as a means of escape from a repressive patriarchal society, the Corti film relegated the relationship to a space of less significance. In Grete's apartment, Elli finds a welcome respite from life with Karl and his mother, turning to Grete for safety and comfort, as well as joy in an otherwise difficult life. This, however, is not the paradise removed from the pressures of daily existence as in the stage version, for Grete and her mother also belong to the working poor, and Corti does not depart from the realism of his portrayal of this milieu in depicting their lives. Moreover, it is not the relationship with Grete that dominates Elli's psyche, but her troubled and violent relationship with Karl. Karl and Elli are clearly at the center of this account, and it is through the development—and deterioration—of their relationship that Corti conveys the psychological damage that a meager, narrow existence may inflict.

Elfriede Czurda also delivers powerful psychological analysis in her novel *Die Giftmörderinnen* (*The Poisoners*), published in 1991 as the first work in a planned trilogy on the topic of violence and aggression titled *Three Double Lives*. Here it is not the narrowness of her life that drives Else to murder; rather, in turning to poison Else seeks to marshal a new weapon in a psychological battle that is gradually defeating her. In this reworking of the case, Else is simply overwhelmed by the more powerful people in her life. The two separate relationships of the stage and film versions, in which Else turns to Grete essentially to escape from Hans, are here replaced by a distinctly triangular relationship, in which Else is exploited from both sides, by her lover as well as her husband.

Czurda's novel reads like an extended prose poem, as she draws on a heavily stylized language to present the subjective experience of her characters. In

Czurda's writing, language is transformed through radical play, enacted through both the breaking down of compound words and the compression of series of words into new forms. Critics have differed in their interpretations of this use of language. Whereas Kristie Foell has emphasized the creative and playful, near musical quality of the language alongside Czurda's critical impulses, Geoffrey Howes and Kathleen Thorpe each emphasize its fragmented quality as a way of expressing the fragmented experience of the central character.[34] Thorpe insightfully discusses Czurda's concern with the relationship between language and violence, describing her dismembering of common compounds as an attempt to destroy the language of oppression: *Ehe Mann* (husband); *Einzel Zelle* (solitary cell); *Scheide Weg* (crossroads).[35] Thorpe does not elaborate, however, on the constructive use of language, in which Czurda creates single words from expected and unexpected series of words: constellations constructed sometimes by Hans, *Elsespatzschönbistdu* (Elsesparrowyouarebeautiful), and sometimes by Else, *Hansderwolf, Hanshyäne, Hannsderkanns* (Hansthewolf, Hanshyena, Hanshecandoit) or her names for Erika (the Grete Bende character in the novel), such as *Austernlenkrad* (Oystersteeringwheel). These innovations are creative, rather than destructive, and we may ask whether they constitute an alternative to the language Czurda dismantles. Yet while they may represent an attempt at a new language, Else's nonsensical constructions in particular do not foster communication, as Erika repeatedly rejects them and tries to draw Else back into conventional speech.

Indeed, Else is continually cast in the novel as being at a linguistic disadvantage vis-à-vis Hans and Erika. Having power over language, Hans is the word and Else, wordless, is also powerless. She sees herself as he sees her: a mere receptacle, not only for Hans's poetics but also for the flood of sentiment that Erika unleashes as soon as their relationship begins. In this respect, she resembles Döblin's Elli under attack by people, things, and impulses—rendered in Czurda's account as an attack of words. Else's attraction to Erika, as to Hans, stems in part from admiration for Erika's mastery of the language.[36] The inequality in their communication becomes strikingly evident as they begin a daily correspondence (which also plays a significant role in Döblin's text), in which Erika writes a veritable flood of passionate, lyrical love letters and admonishes Else for the paucity of her replies. Later, alone in her prison cell, Else remembers the events that brought her there. Her isolation is now total. Hans is dead and Erika is no longer in her life, but both of them continue to occupy her mind. She laments that the thick prison walls offer her no protection against thoughts of them. Because they dominated her with language, their power over her persists as she is unable to forget the way they spoke and what they said to her.[37]

Whereas narrative is the crucial element in Döblin's story and objects are central to Corti's story, Czurda's Else is plagued by a combination of the two: words themselves become objects that attack Else from all sides. She returns again and again to Hans's and Erika's language, perceiving it as a fresh assault each time that she remembers.[38] After the murder, Else bitterly reproaches herself for her vulnerability to Hans's and Erika's language. She is filled with fury at the *Wort Macher* (Word Makers) who sought to cut away the best part of her with their words. Her attempted suicide attests to the potency of the verbal attacks she experienced. At the conclusion, she finds herself surrounded by "a ruin of words," still struggling.[39]

Czurda's novel shares with the Corti film the central tenet that Else's individual unhappiness and psychological problems are symptomatic of wider societal dysfunction. For Corti, Else's difficulties are reflective of the repression of the working class as a whole. In contrast, Czurda is often seen as making an argument about gender. Kathleen Thorpe's exploration of the relationship between violence and language traces the roots of oppressive language to male-dominated society. Kristie Foell sees the novel as "a programmatically feminist work," taking aim at the patriarchal social structures that reinforce the oppression of women.[40] While these gender-based readings certainly address a significant aspect of the text, I would argue that this focus is not sufficiently broad to encompass Czurda's social criticism. Czurda may indeed provide an "uncompromisingly feminist analysis of marriage," as Foell suggests, but Else's marriage to Hans is far from her only troubled relationship. Foell's identification of patriarchal social structures as the central villain in the novel fails to account, for example, for the deeply problematic relations among women in the text. Here, too, Foell locates the source of conflict in a patriarchal system that pits women against one another. This may be helpful in interpreting Else's antagonistic relationship with her mother-in-law, as the two women are at war over Hans, but this argument is less satisfying as an explanation for Else's relationship to Erika, whose manipulation and exploitation is as devastating as Hans's abuse. Like Raben's stage version and (to a lesser extent) Corti's film version, such interpretations do what Döblin's text, and Czurda's rereading of it, attempt to explode: "solving the case" by locating a single, easily defined problem.

Conclusion

Each of the writers and filmmakers considered here initially approach this case with a similar intent: to solve its mysteries and answer the seemingly straightforward question, What prompted Klein's decision to murder her husband? Yet, each author is ultimately led to a different question: (how) can I tell this story? This is the question that, in their most illuminating moments, these texts make the true object of their investigations. Taken as a whole, they attest to the paradox at the heart of the genre of the case study: the need to tell a story is countered by the retarding effect that narrative has on reaching a conclusion, rendering a judgment, tracing an effect to a cause. Each text concludes not with the triumphal explanation that one expects from a detective in the final pages of a classic detective novel, but rather on a note of ambiguity and inconclusiveness. Döblin's study ends with the confession that "we understand it, on a certain level."[41] Czurda's novel leaves its reader with an empty and suicidal Else standing among "a ruin of words."[42] Corti's film freezes on a close-up of Elli following the murder and holds it for an uncomfortably extended period of time, inviting the viewer to attempt to read the inscrutable expression on her face: Is it an expression of liberation? Horror? Regret? Fear? We can never know. This uncertainty is precisely what the modernist and postmodernist crime narrative learns from the study of cases such as that of Klein and Nebbe. The case is not closed—indeed, the case is never closed. And in this crisis of narrative and impossibility of closure, these artists have found a productive position from which to write.

Notes

Parts of this chapter, written especially for this volume, draw on material from the author's *Crime Stories: Criminalistic Fantasy and the Culture of Crisis in Weimar Germany* (New York and Oxford, 2009).

1. Don DeLillo, *Libra* (New York, 1988), 449–453. James Chandler discusses *Libra* and its interrogation of the form of the case in *England in 1819: The Politics of Literary Culture and the Case of Romantic Historicism* (Chicago, 1998), 209–211.
2. DeLillo, *Libra*, 301.
3. For a discussion of the trial and the attention it received in the daily press, see Isabella Claßen, *Darstellung von Kriminalität in der deutschen Literatur, Presse und Wissenschaft 1900–1930* (Frankfurt/Main, 1988), 158–198. See also Inge Weiler, *Giftmordwissen und Giftmörderinnen. Eine diskursgeschichtliche Studie* (Tübingen, 1998), 131–148.
4. See Claßen, *Darstellung von Kriminalität*, 177.
5. Klein was sentenced to four years of prison (*Gefängnis*); Nebbe was sentenced to one and a half years of hard labor (*Zuchthaus*).
6. Joseph Roth, "Die Frauen Nebbe und Klein," in *Werke*, Klaus Westermann, ed. (Köln, 1989), I: 952. All translations, unless otherwise noted, are my own.
7. Roth, "Die Frauen Nebbe und Klein," 952.
8. Robert Musil, "Das verbrecherische Liebespaar: Die Geschichte zweier unglücklicher Ehen," in *Gesammelte Werke*, Adolf Frisé, ed. (Reinbeck bei Hamburg, 1978), II: 670.
9. Musil, "Das verbrecherische Liebespaar," 669.
10. Musil, "Das verbrecherische Liebespaar," 671.
11. Musil, "Das verbrecherische Liebespaar," 671.
12. Rechtsanwalt Dr. Arthur Brandt, "Das Urteil im Mordprozeß Klein," *BZ am Mittag* 46 (17 March 1923).
13. "Giftmörderinnen vor Gericht," *Berliner Tageblatt* 129 (12 March 1923).
14. "Der Prozess der Giftmischerinnen," *Vorwärts* 40 (15 March 1923, Morgenausgabe).
15. "Die Gutachten über die Giftmischerinnen," *Vorwärts* 40 (16 March 1923, Morgenausgabe).

16. "Die Gutachten über die Giftmischerinnen."

17. "Der Prozess der Giftmischerinnen."

18. For a history of criminology in Germany from the end of the nineteenth century until the end of World War II, see Richard F. Wetzell's *Inventing the Criminal: A History of German Criminology, 1880–1945* (Chapel Hill, 2000). As Wetzell's history demonstrates, the relationships between the different schools are complex and the divisions quite permeable.

19. Over the course of the twentieth century, investigations into the causes of criminal behavior have become increasingly specific. However, they continue to break down into the same three main areas: biological, psychological, and sociological explanations—though most commentators tend to emphasize a so-called mixed bag of causes. For a biological approach, see James Q. Wilson and Richard J. Hernstein, *Crime and Human Nature* (New York, 1985), in which even those old somatotype images pop up once again. A sociological theory of criminality can be found in Elliot Currie, "Confronting Crime: New Directions," in *Crime and Society*, Robert Crutchfield, George S. Brides, and Joseph G. Weis, eds. (Thousand Oaks, CA, 1996). For a psychological approach, see Christopher Bollas, *Cracking Up* (New York, 1995). For a recent attempt at an integrated theory of violent behavior in general, see *Biosocial Bases of Violence*, Adrian Raine, Patricia A. Brennan, and David P. Farrington, eds. (New York, 1997).

20. Alfred Döblin, *Die beiden Freundinnen und ihr Giftmord*, Außenseiter der Gesellschaft, vol. 1, Rudolf Leonhard, ed. (Berlin, 1924), 117. Page numbers given in parentheses in the main text refer to this work.

21. Alfred Döblin, "An Romanautoren und ihre Kritiker," *Schriften zu Ästhetik, Poetik und Literatur*, Erich Kleinschmidt, ed. (Olten und Freiburg i.B., 1989), 120. See Georg Reuchlein's excellent study of the relationships among literature, psychology, and psychopathology in Döblin's early short story, "Die Ermordung einer Butterblume: 'Man lerne von der Psychiatrie,'" *Jahrbuch für internationale Germanistik* 23, 1 (1991), 10–68.

22. Döblin, "An Romanautoren und ihre Kritiker," 120–121.

23. For the sake of consistency, I will use Döblin's version of the characters' names.

24. "Sie sollten auch eigentlich Recht sprechen über den Vater, der Elli wieder ihrem Mann zugeführt hatte—und dieser Vater war der Inbegriff einwandfreier bürgerlicher Gesinnung . . . Das Gericht fragte nicht nach der Beteiligung, 'Schuld', Kleins, des Vaters, der Mutter Kleins" (101). It is interesting to note that for the first and only time in this study, Döblin here uses the victim's real name (Klein) rather than the name he is given elsewhere (Link). Though this error is corrected in a later edition (see Alfred Döblin, *Die beiden Freundinnen und ihr Giftmord* [Olten, 1992], 95) it strikes me that this use of Klein rather than Link in precisely the paragraph where Döblin insists on looking beyond "was innerhalb des Kreises, der Grenzen geschah" is not coincidental.

25. Döblin wrote to Klages: "Der Fall selbst ist in einer bestimmten Hinsicht dunkel . . . Ich wollte Sie fragen: mögen Sie einmal das kleine Buch durchblättern, seine Fakten zur Kenntnis nehmen und alsdann mir sagen, wie Sie über die Handschriften denken oder: was sich, in dem gesamten festgestellten Ensemble, über die beiden Personen sagen läßt; wie sie graphologisch über den—psychiatrisch sehr verschiedenen beurteilten—Fall denken." The letter is dated 23 December 1924. (See *Alfred Döblin 1878–1978: Eine Ausstellung des Deutschen Literaturarchivs im Schiller-Nationalmuseum Marbach am Neckar*, Bernhard Zeller, ed. [München, 1978], 171–172).

26. I am grateful to Thomas Kovach for bringing this odd turn of phrase to my attention.

27. See Mark Seltzer, *Serial Killers: Death and Life in America's Wound Culture* (New York, 1998), 257–258. Interestingly, childhood plays an important role in few of the case studies in the *Außenseiter* series.

28. In the classic Monty Python sketch, a dinosaur expert is being interviewed about her latest theory concerning the brontosaurus. As she avoids presenting her theory, she continually claims it

as her own: "Well, this theory that I have—that is to say, which is mine—is mine." Her theory, incidentally, turns out to be that brontosaurus was thin at both ends and thick in the middle.

29. Seltzer, *Serial Killers*, 100.

30. See "The Adventure of the Engineer's Thumb" in Sir Arthur Conan Doyle, *Sherlock Holmes: The Complete Novels and Stories* (New York, 1986), vol. 1, 369–388.

31. Hans Schwab-Felisch, "Mit Arsen gegen das Patriarchat: Döblin, 'Die beiden Freundinnen und ihr Giftmord' in Bochum," *Theater Heute* (1. Januar 1977), 55.

32. Schwab-Felisch, 55.

33. See Matthias Prangel, "Die Döblinisierung Döblins. Zur Adaptation von 'Die beiden Freundinnen und ihr Giftmord' durch den Film," *Internationales Alfred-Döblin-Kolloquium, Leipzig 1977*, Ira Lorf and Gabriele Sander, eds. (Berne, 1999), 80.

34. See Kristie Foell, "Elfriede Czurda: Poison and Play," in *Out From the Shadows: Essays on Contemporary Austrian Women Writers and Filmmakers*, Margarete Lamb-Faffelberger, ed. (Riverside, CA, 1997), 158–171; Geoffrey Howes, "Therapeutic Murder in Elfriede Czurda and Lilian Faschinger," *Modern Austrian Literature* 32, 2 (1999), 79–93; Kathleen Thorpe, "Aggression and Self-Realization in Elfriede Czurda's Novel *Die Giftmörderinnen*," *Modern Austrian Literature* 31, 3/4 (1998), 175–187.

35. Thorpe, 175, 180.

36. Elfriede Czurda, *Die Giftmörderinnen* (Reinbek, 1991), 89.

37. Czurda, 14.

38. Czurda, 13.

39. Czurda, 174.

40. Foell, 159.

41. Döblin, 117.

42. Czurda, 174. Compare Thorpe, 184.

Part IV

CRIMINAL JUSTICE IN NAZI AND POSTWAR GERMANY

Chapter 10

Serious Juvenile Crime in Nazi Germany

Robert G. Waite

With the outbreak of World War II in 1939, German law enforcement professionals grew increasingly concerned that the patterns of World War I and some prewar trends in juvenile delinquency would intensify and that they might witness an overall rise in all types of crime, from minor property offenses to serious and violent crime. Indeed, after the outbreak of the war, police and court officials from a number of communities observed significant jumps in the incidence of crime.[1] Political leaders shared these concerns, and as early as 1 February 1940, Hermann Göring called a meeting to discuss the challenges facing German youth during the war.[2] The relationship between war and the mounting seriousness of teenage crime continued to be a topic of discussion over the next several years as the data compiled by the Reich Statistical Agency revealed a steady increase.

Police, court officials, and some political leaders were not the only observers to notice a disturbing trend in crime among juveniles. In 1941, Edith Roper, a young reporter who had covered the criminal courts in Berlin, published a book on her experiences, devoting a chapter to "young murderers." Written in American exile, Roper's exposé shed considerable light on the operation of the Nazi justice system and the impact of Nazism on German society and particularly its youth. Roper stated that "since 1937 the number of youthful murderers has risen steadily and rapidly," and she held the violence that permeated Nazi Germany responsible.[3]

When Nazi officials took notice of and focused on the issue of serious teenage crime, their response was swift and severe. On 4 October 1939, the Ministerrat für die Reichsverteidigung (Ministerial Council for the Defense of the Reich), chaired by Hermann Göring, issued the Decree for the Protection against Juvenile Serious Offenders, which took effect immediately.[4] While the Nazi regime

---

Notes from this chapter begin on page 264.

had long taken pride in the effectiveness of its response to crime, this decree was an admission that the policies for dealing with serious teenage offenders had not worked. Under the decree, youngsters over sixteen years of age and identified by the courts as sufficiently mature to be prosecuted as an adult were subject to adult punishments, including lengthy prison terms and even the death penalty.[5] The decree embodied a number of contemporary legal tendencies, some long established in German criminology, others fundamental to Nazi jurisprudence. Under its provisions, most of the responsibility in deciding whether to prosecute a teen under the terms of the decree was left to the district attorney and the court, thus giving prosecutors and judges greater flexibility and discretion in determining the fate of an accused youngster. Thus the trend toward eliminating "community aliens," "asocials," and others who did not fit neatly into Nazi society, as well as draconian sentencing practices, were now extended to juveniles.[6]

In practice, the number of prosecutions under the terms of the decree remained low during the first two years of the war.[7] The rise in the incidence of violent crime among juveniles was not halted, however, and its persistence caused grave concern within the Ministry of Justice. The problem became so acute that Martin Bormann, head of the Nazi Party Office (Chef der Parteikanzlei) and Hitler's closest confidant, contacted the Minister of Justice, demanding new and more drastic actions. In spite of the severity of the problem and the sensitivity toward it among the political leaders, change came only in November 1943, when, as part of a revision of the criminal code, the age of legal responsibility was lowered to fourteen. Draconian sentences—and even capital punishment—could now be imposed on these youngsters.[8] This too proved ineffective.

Clearly, both law enforcement professionals and political leaders were concerned about the problem of serious and violent crime among teenagers. How extensive was it? Do the statistical data and reports collected throughout the Reich indicate a rising incidence of such offenses among youth? What measures were taken by the regime? How effective were they?

The Problem: Serious Teenage Crime

"The participation of juveniles in severe and brutal offenses began rising long before the war," wrote a Hitler Youth official in his 1940 report on juvenile delinquency. Although the overall trend for the 1930s had been a drop in the incidence of violent offenses, caused in part by the easing of political tensions and the stabilization of the economy, convictions began to rise in the middle of the decade. It took several years, however, for this trend to show up in the official statistics.[9]

Serious and violent crimes committed by teenagers remained a problem throughout the decade. Although in fact quite rare, such crimes attracted public attention and, consequently, the concern of political leaders largely because of their seemingly inexplicable nature. The brutal murder of a restaurant owner in a Bavarian village in July 1933, for example, carried out by three adolescents, generated considerable local interest. A year later, a thirteen-year-old boy murdered a classmate. After his arrest, he described his crime to the police and told them that he had coveted the victim's Hitler Youth uniform. The only way he thought he could have it was by murdering the boy, and after several days of planning, he carried out the crime. Police arrested him the next day as he walked through the village wearing his victim's uniform.[10]

A contemporary analysis of the increase in serious juvenile crime came from former Berlin court reporter Edith Roper who attributed it to the "general contempt for human life" that pervaded the Third Reich.[11] In most of the cases that Roper observed in the juvenile courts of Berlin, the circumstances were remarkably similar: the young defendant, brought before a judge, was unable to explain or justify the violent act he had carefully planned and carried out. These youngsters, she wrote, neither demonstrated nor felt any remorse for their crimes. Characteristically, they had not even tried to evade the police. Most sat through the court hearings showing no emotion, no concern for themselves or their victim, and made no effort to defend themselves. For Roper, who had fled Nazi Germany, this behavior confirmed the moral bankruptcy of Nazi Germany and its pernicious influence on youth.[12]

Roper's observation of an increase in serious juvenile crime was supported by official data. Material collected and statistics compiled by the Reich Criminal Police for the years 1936–1939 confirm that violent and serious teenage crime was on the rise, and its surge in the latter part of the decade began to attract considerable attention. Reports of alarming crimes came from all parts of the Reich. In Chemnitz, for example, a sixteen-year-old girl killed her newborn child, and an eighteen-year-old boy severely injured two girls during a break-in.[13] The arrest of a sixteen-year-old boy in Offenbach in 1939 halted a wave of break-ins and robberies that he had carried out with some friends, two of whom were under the age of fourteen.[14] In Bockheim, two teenagers were arrested for assaulting a worker and stealing his money. In Hamburg, police arrested a seventeen-year-old and his companion on charges of car theft, thus stopping a crime wave that had already resulted in the theft of more than a dozen vehicles. The teens had used the stolen vehicles to commit other offenses, such as break-ins and robberies, crimes that were sufficient to have them identified as serious offenders. A local police officer commented that these crimes were not unusual, and "every other week during 1939 shows a similar picture." In fact, robberies involving use of a stolen car rose sharply as teens mimicked the criminal exploits of the Brothers Sass, who terrorized sections of Berlin with their brazen thefts.[15] In Hamburg, a fourteen-year-old boy stabbed his father to death in early July 1939. The indictment noted that "the relationship between the accused and his father was nothing special."

When his father returned home drunk and started an argument, the teen got his knife and stabbed him. The father died of wounds to the neck. The boy was prosecuted, convicted of manslaughter, and sentenced to eight years in prison.[16]

The incidence of serious teen crime jumped during the first quarter of 1939. Compared with the previous three months, based on incomplete data from the Reich Criminal Police Agency, the number of murders or attempted murders by teenagers rose by 45 percent. Robberies shot up by 59 percent. Serious moral offenses increased by 26 percent.[17] Anecdotal reports and the number of arrests and prosecutions corroborated the official data. With most officials expecting an initial drop in the crime rate with the outbreak of war, the continuing increase in serious crime among teens caused a great deal of concern.[18]

The Nazi regime had long believed that its efforts to stabilize political life, stimulate economic recovery, and organize the youth would have a positive effect, particularly on teenagers. By the end of the decade, however, it became apparent that the problem of teenage crime was grave.[19] There was widespread agreement that the Nazi regime had to take whatever steps necessary to curb adolescent crime, especially serious and violent offenses. Although Germany's Juvenile Justice Act (Jugendgerichtsgesetz), originally passed in 1923, stipulated that everyone under the age of eighteen be prosecuted as a minor, after the Nazi seizure of power jurists began to discuss new measures for dealing with hardened juvenile criminals. Thus the Academy for German Law, a Nazi-sponsored organization that worked on revising the German criminal code, strongly recommended that several measures used to combat serious adult offenders, including the 1933 Law against Dangerous Habitual Criminals, which authorized preventive detention (*Sicherungsverwahrung*), be extended to minors. These new measures, it was believed, would weed out serious and violent teenage offenders and thereby protect society.[20] These discussions also renewed interest in teenage offenders among German criminologists, who had long maintained that the crimes of those aged sixteen to eighteen typically resulted from the young offender's immaturity and insecurity. Adolescence, they argued, was a time of probing, testing, and experimenting: years when the desire for stimulus and excitement could easily overwhelm a youngster's sense of judgment and responsibility. These factors, however, did little to explain the *rise* in serious teenage crime. Other explanations, such as the demographic increase in the number of youths reaching the age of sixteen, the intensified investigation and prosecution of offenders regardless of age, or the enactment of new laws, also failed to offer a plausible answer.[21]

There were increasing calls for more stringent punishment of juveniles convicted of violent or serious offenses, and criminologists and jurists concluded that new preventive measures were necessary. In November 1938, for example, a Berlin judge suggested that the age of legal responsibility, a criterion for determining competency to stand trial, be lowered so that more youngsters would face adult punishments for their offenses. A case tried in his Berlin courtroom involved a teenager charged with the assault of twenty-two women, one of whom he had allegedly raped and killed. After convicting the boy the judge wrote that "the defendant deserved the death penalty and would have been sentenced to death if the law had permitted it." Another case from the same court involved a seventeen-year-old boy convicted of robbery and murder. The judge complained that the ten-year sentence, the maximum allowed under the Juvenile Justice Act, did not fit the crime and commented, "The case invites the question: Do the penalties of the juvenile court, created under the influence of liberal legal structure, require a change?"[22]

Similar complaints came from other members of the judiciary, who strongly advocated a wider range of sentencing options to be imposed on teenagers convicted of serious offenses.[23] Once war broke out in September 1939, confronting this issue could no longer be postponed; the war also served as a catalyst for the implementation of long-discussed changes. An increase in teenage violent crime had already been detected in the figures compiled by the Reich Statistical Agency and in reports from local officials.[24] It was believed that only prompt, decisive action could prevent a recurrence of the problems experienced during World War I. Efforts to explain the latest crime wave were largely based on the experiences of the previous war, and most criminologists and Nazi officials still relied on the standard explanations: fathers were now serving in the military or working longer hours in war-related industries, supervision at home was lax because the mothers were now working, time spent at school was reduced as some teachers were drafted into the armed forces, many youngsters worked night shifts, large numbers of soldiers were quartered nearby, increased blackouts; all of these factors, it was argued, contributed to increasing juvenile delinquency.[25]

Some criminologists offered more sophisticated interpretations of serious juvenile crime that included a variety of other factors, such as some teenagers' desire to get the money needed to live a more independent lifestyle or to impress friends, which might prompt them to commit robberies or break-ins. Other explanations focused on the teen offender's personality and home environment. A criminologist who studied the problem for the Hitler Youth organization, for example, suggested that closer cooperation between the Hitler Youth and parents was imperative and would yield favorable results in combating juvenile delinquency.[26] Still other theories of teenage crime stressed the young offender's biological development, and several criminologists emphasized the need to examine these factors to evaluate juvenile offenders properly. A number of Nazi jurists and criminologists argued that some teenager offenders' crimes expressed an inability to function as a normal citizen in Nazi society and concluded that, due to inherited traits that destined them to lead lives of crime, such youths would never be worthy members of the *Volksgemeinschaft*. A few criminologists suggested that such biologically abnormal youths, essentially born criminals, be sterilized and/or incarcerated to protect society.[27]

What appeared to be a rise in serious teenage crime, coupled with the expectation that the problem would only worsen, precipitated the swift enactment of the Decree for the Protection against Juvenile Serious Offenders (Verordnung zum Schutz gegen jugendliche Schwerverbrecher) of October 1939. The decree reflected the demand for tougher measures, which was justified with the argument that not all juvenile offenders could be reintegrated into society. Some, it was argued, were already beyond rehabilitation, destined to a life of serious crime and, in fact, "racially defective." Hence, it was best to remove them from society as soon as possible.[28] The decree addressed these concerns directly. Previously, the legal treatment of teenage offenders had been governed by the Juvenile Justice Act of 1923, which stipulated that all offenders between the ages of fourteen and eighteen must be treated differently from adults even if they were arraigned on the same charges.[29] While the act was still regarded as adequate for dealing with the typical juvenile offender, the crimes of some teenagers were now viewed as so serious that their perpetrators should no longer be exempted from adult punishments. Criminologists saw this as one of the "most difficult and urgent criminal/ political issues of the day."[30]

The Response: The Decree for the Protection Against Juvenile Serious Offenders

The Decree for the Protection against Serious Juvenile Offenders was issued by the Ministerial Council for the Defense of the Reich on 4 October 1939 and took effect with its publication in the *Reichsgesetzblatt* on 9 October (Nr. 199, 2000). The reaction of judges and criminologists to the new law was immediately favorable, tempered only by surprise at the speed with which "one of the most significant criminological problems of the day" had been tackled. Only five weeks after the outbreak of war, a major new law, and a key element of legal reform, was enacted. Many judges welcomed the opportunity to impose more severe sentences on serious teen offenders.[31] The 1939 decree targeted juvenile offenders who had committed a serious crime and were between sixteen and eighteen years of age at the time of their offense. In general, the prosecution of juvenile offenders who fell under the decree took place in an adult court and in accordance with the rules of that court. However, if the district attorney initiated the prosecution of a minor in a juvenile court and the defendant was later characterized as a serious criminal, the trial had to continue in the juvenile court.[32] Moreover, in some jurisdictions, cases of extreme violence were not handled under this law.[33]

The first two paragraphs of Article I of the decree read: "The district attorney can issue an indictment against a juvenile who at the time of the criminal act was over 16 years of age before a court that is also responsible for adult trials and decisions. In these cases the thus delegated court imposes those punishments and precautionary measures that are used against adults if the [juvenile's] mental and moral development is on the level of a person over 18 years of age, and if, in light of the criminal act or an especially reprehensible criminal character, the protection of the *Volk* demands such penalties."[34] This provision established the criteria that had to be met before a teenager could be prosecuted as an adult. First, the youngster had to be older than sixteen years of age at the time of the crime. This also applied to an offender who committed a series of crimes even though the offender might not have been sixteen when the string of crimes began.[35] Second, the juvenile had to be criminally responsible in accordance with Article III of the 1923 Juvenile Justice Act, which stated that a juvenile could be prosecuted only if he or she was sufficiently mature to recognize the illegality of his or her act at the time it was committed.[36] Third, the maturity of the juvenile offender at the time of the offense had to, in fact, exceed the minimum stipulated by the Juvenile Justice Act: to be prosecuted in an adult court, the juvenile must have reached a level of maturity equivalent to that of an eighteen-year-old.

Whether a teenager had the necessary experiences in life, the understanding, and the moral values of an average eighteen-year-old was difficult to determine. Criminologists and psychologists pointed out that there was no readily identifiable boundary in a youngster's development at the eighteenth birthday, that early maturity among teens was the exception, and that the process of maturation was generally completed only at about twenty to twenty-two years of age.[37] To be prosecuted as an adult, the development of a juvenile's intelligence, sensitivity, character, and physical growth had to demonstrate adulthood, no longer exhibiting the characteristic naïveté of childhood.[38] A careful examination of the individual was necessary to establish the youngster's maturity at the time of the offense. Simply proving the offender's maturity at the time of the trial was not sufficient; the court had to be convinced that this level of maturity had been achieved before the offense was committed. The proof of this development, criminologists argued, could be found in the circumstances of the criminal act.[39]

Even if a youth had reached maturity before the age of eighteen, this did not mean that he could be prosecuted under the new decree; in addition, he also had to be a serious offender (*Schwerverbrecher*).[40] The decree targeted teenagers who were seen as having embarked on the path to a lifetime of crime and were therefore viewed as posing the greatest threat to society. The courts, however, faced a major problem in determining which youngsters were, as one criminologist wrote, "the future serious criminal[s]." In general, youngsters with long criminal records and years spent in remand homes and who showed "an unfavorable prognosis" despite numerous attempts at rehabilitation were most likely to be considered targets of the new decree. Legal and criminological commentators interpreted the decree to be concerned with removing "developing habitual criminals" from German society while they were still minors. As criminologist Sigmund Silbereisen wrote: "Now that the ranks of the old habitual criminals had been thinned out, it was necessary to prevent new ones from replacing them. This, in turn, would eventually lead to success in battling serious criminality."[41] The focus became the criminal and not the crime.

Judges and criminologists identified some problems with the new law. Because physical maturity often proceeded at a rate different from mental and social growth, it proved difficult for the courts to evaluate correctly the maturity of a suspected serious adolescent offender and thus appraise his or her competency to stand trial. Moreover, some of the most serious cases involved teens who were developmentally impaired and could never be expected to reach the mental and social maturity of an adult. Even at the age of eighteen or nineteen, such individuals would remain on the maturity level equivalent to a young adolescent.[42] Although this issue generated much discussion among criminologists, in judicial practice such youngsters were often subjected to more severe punishments than regular juvenile offenders despite the decree's provisions regarding maturity. In one such case, a seventeen-year-old boy who had already been sterilized because of feeble-mindedness was charged with robbery. Even though his level of maturity and understanding were clearly well below that of an adult, he was prosecuted and convicted as a juvenile serious offender and received the relatively harsh sentence of five years in prison. In Rostock, a court indicted a sixteen-year-old who was described as "of average mental development" but of a "degenerate and psychopathic character" for a brutal murder. A court-appointed expert classified the youngster as a "textbook case of an egotistical disposition who in spite of his primitiveness cannot be categorized as retarded but rather as cunning and shrewd." Although his social and moral development was not that of an eighteen-year-old, the court found him guilty, treated him as an adult, and sentenced him to death.[43]

Even though such teens clearly did not fit within the letter of the decree, criminologists and judges advanced a broad interpretation that sought to justify their being tried as adults. Arguing that the most dangerous juvenile offenders were often precisely those "whose mental and social values would never reach those of an adult," Franz Exner, one of Germany's leading law professors, insisted such offenders must be prosecuted under the new law.[44] To justify the application of the law to juveniles who did not, in fact, have the maturity of an average adult, Exner resorted to a subjective rather than objective definition of maturity and competency: The question before the court, he contended, was whether the juvenile offender aged sixteen to eighteen had reached "the maturity *he* would have at the age of 19."[45] Even if his development was impaired, as long as no change in his development could be expected by age nineteen, he could be treated as an adult. Exner justified this de facto expansion of the decree by arguing that teen psychopaths who did not mature along typical lines formed the core of juvenile offenders and would later swell the ranks of habitual offenders. In fact, he wrote,

"[T]his is perhaps the only case where a reliable prognosis of the hardcore criminal can be made."[46]

In addition to the juvenile offender's maturity, the decree stipulated that the offender qualify as a so-called serious criminal. Adult punishment could be imposed only if "a particularly reprehensible criminal character [was] demonstrated when committing the offense" and the "protection of the *Volk*" therefore demanded severe punishment. In practice, only one of these criteria needed to apply to the young defendant. Still, jurists debated the legal application of these two clauses and their meaning. Franz Exner viewed the two clauses of the second paragraph as being roughly equal in importance. For Exner, the clause required both a certain kind of individual guilt and a need for protection.[47] Another group of jurists, however, whose most prominent spokesman was the committed National-Socialist Graf von Gleispach, argued that because the central task of criminal justice was the protection of the *Volk*, the offense need not, in fact, be serious for a juvenile offender to come under the terms of the decree: threatening individuals of any age should be interned and dealt with to "protect the *Volk*."[48]

In practice, the courts experienced considerable difficulty in deciding when a teenagers' disposition was "particularly reprehensible and criminal." Judges looked to several aspects of a defendant's personality and the actual crime for verification, including motives, behavior of the offender, and the context of the crime. A particularly reprehensible criminal disposition was generally ascribed to juveniles whose offenses were characterized by extremely brutal and senseless violence, a lack of emotion, "a violation of trust against the *Volk* community," or a vicious attack on a family member or their employer.[49] Although these personality traits provided the basis for prosecution, they need not be demonstrated by a single criminal act. A series of offenses might confirm a "particularly reprehensible criminal disposition," even though the crimes themselves were minor. In one case, a seventeen-year-old boy "earned a living by approaching, in most cases, drunken men and engaging in sexual intercourse with them for payment. His purpose was to rob them." The youngster used the money to support what was described as a comfortable and extravagant lifestyle while wandering throughout Germany, instead of earning a living through honest means, "which he often had opportunity to do." This string of crimes, and the way in which they were carried out, provided enough justification to prosecute him as a serious offender (*Schwerverbrecher*).[50]

The second clause of the decree called for the "protection of the *Volk*" and was designed to protect what the Nazis called the *Volksgemeinschaft* from serious crime committed by adolescent offenders. In contrast to the subjective nature of a criminal disposition, this clause was concerned with objective circumstances and the conditions surrounding a crime. Its intention was to protect society as a whole. In evaluating whether this section applied, officials reviewed the offender's criminal record, his or her behavior, the damage caused by the crime, and the danger resulting from the crimes. The protection of the *Volk* also demanded the prosecution of those youngsters who showed "no inhibitions in committing a crime," whose prospect of rehabilitation remained slight, who came from a "degenerate, asocial manner of living, or who demonstrate a considerable amount of bad discipline in connection with and indestructible tendency toward committing crimes."[51]

The remaining articles of the decree covered procedural matters. Article II dealt with the prosecution of juvenile offenders by the military. Article III changed several of the penalties that could be imposed on teenage criminals in Austria. Article IV permitted the retroactive application of the decree to defendants whose crimes took place before the decree became law; this did, in fact, occur: a sixteen-year-old boy who had brutally murdered a ten-year-old schoolgirl at a children's fair in June 1939 was prosecuted in a widely publicized case. The court found the youngster guilty of murder and sentenced him to death. He was beheaded on 23 April 1940. Article V stated that the decree was also valid for the Reich Protectorate of Bohemia and Moravia as long as "the offender is subject to German court jurisdiction."[52]

Judges and criminologists never arrived at a precise definition of what a juvenile serious offender (*jugendlicher Schwerverbrecher*) was. Although most jurists agreed that Article I contained the legal definition that would be binding in court, in the Third Reich law became malleable, subject to interpretations in line with Nazi ideology. As Franz Exner put it: "The concept of a 'serious criminal' [*Schwerverbrecher*] is not a simple summation of the two cases cited in the decree. On the contrary, the introduction of this concept has an independent significance. We may and should use this concept for a more precise definition and thereby convert the alleged legal definition."[53]

Judicial Practice

Franz Exner doubted that a strict interpretation of the decree could be agreed upon. "Are those whose criminal act indicates a particularly reprehensible disposition really serious criminals?" he asked. "And are all those whose incapacitation the protection of the *Volksgemeinschaft* demands serious criminals?" In many cases they were clearly not, and the responsibility for deciding this rested with the judge. In every case to which the criteria of Article I applied, the judge had to determine if the defendant represented the criminal type identified as a serious offender. Exner maintained that the *Volk*, as the "the source of all law," must provide the definition, meaning that the definition would remain deliberately vague. "For only through the view of the *Volk* can the legal definition be arrived at in accordance with the living legal consciousness." Exner wondered aloud who, in the popular view, would be branded a serious criminal: certainly not a recidivist pickpocket or a marriage swindler, but probably "a burglar who does not shirk from the use of violence." Exner also believed that the general public would not consider "someone who in a unique, one-time situation [was found] guilty of manslaughter" a serious criminal; there would, he argued, be sufficient understanding of the individual and his circumstances to prevent this.[54]

Others held different opinions. Criminal law professor Edmund Mezger, a colleague of Exner's on the law faculty of the University of Munich, conceived of the serious offender as an "objective criminal type"—one with readily identifiable characteristics.[55] Roland Freisler, a high-ranking official in the Reich Justice Ministry, who would later (1942–1945) become infamous as the chief judge of the People's Court, argued that the framers of the decree had in mind "those youngsters whose hereditary structure already pointed to the criminal path as the most probable." Freisler later wrote that "this decree applied to the early-maturing serious criminal whose personality, as already reflected in his offenses, and as is already written in the stars, is on the way to becoming outright asocial."[56] According to this view, the decree was intended "to lead a preventive fight against all hopeless individuals whose grim future makes them" a threat to society.[57]

The lack of a clear definition of the serious juvenile offender—whether it be a juvenile who simply committed a serious crime, one whose criminal career could not be checked, or a person whose personality fit the criminal type, or any combination of these—placed most of the burden on the courts. The judges relied on expert opinions from specialists, including youth welfare workers and psychiatrists. During pretrial detention, defendants underwent interrogations, evaluations, and psychiatric exams in one of the criminal-biological offices at the juvenile detention center. Such investigations sometimes lasted for several months and provided much of the basis for the prosecution and trial. The results of these evaluations were supposed to aid the courts in deciding whether the defendant did, in fact, have the maturity of an adult at the time of the offense and how his or her behavior might change in the future.[58]

The determination of a young offender's maturity proved to be a difficult task. How to handle those who would never reach mental and social maturity remained a dilemma. The courts called upon parents, teachers, employers, Hitler Youth officials, and the local youth welfare office to offer insight into a juvenile offender's character and prospects. Coming from the youth's immediate environment, the testimony of these individuals served as an important supplement to the psychiatric evaluation. The broadest possible spectrum of opinion was necessary and desirable because the penalties for youths treated as adults were so severe. Most criminologists, in fact, urged caution and restraint and reminded the courts of the exceptional nature of those covered by the decree.[59] In practice, however, many courts paid little attention to a juvenile offender's precise level of maturity; and they often placed greater weight on the impression made by the defendant during the trial than on outside evaluations. It was not unusual to read about a youngster being convicted because he "was clearly aware" of the seriousness of the offense or because he was a "leader." Court-appointed physicians serving as expert witnesses frequently concurred and supported the prosecution of marginally responsible defendants. Often the trial began long after the crime had been committed, and maturity at the time of the offense was thereby virtually impossible to determine. In one case, the hearing took place fourteen months after an arrest.[60]

Numerous trials illustrate how problematic the courts' application of the criteria of the decree often was. In August 1941, for example, the *Reichsgericht* reviewed the decision of a Special Court against a seventeen-year-old girl convicted under the provisions of Article IV of the People's Enemy Decree (*Volksschädlingsverordnung*). Clearly guilty of fraud and falsification of documents, the girl was determined by the court to be a juvenile serious offender because of the severity of the crimes and her adult-like maturity, even though she had no previous criminal record. Of foremost importance in the application of the decree on juvenile serious offenders, the high court decided, was not "whether the defendant possessed the maturity of an 18-year-old when the offense was committed," but "whether the early maturity of the youth was apparent in a strongly developed moral depravity and a particularly reprehensible criminal disposition." Moreover, judicial guidelines published in the *Richterbriefe* advised judges that a youth could be prosecuted under the decree if he had reached his final level of maturity, regardless of his actual age.[61]

While the exact trends in serious juvenile crime after the passage of the October 1939 Decree for Protection against Juvenile Serious Offenders are difficult to establish, one fact remains clear: serious teenage crime persisted as a major problem for law enforcement officials and the courts. Robberies, brutal beatings, assaults, and murders continued to be reported, and prosecutions rose. In May 1940, for example, the district attorney in Rastadt complained about a "noticeable rise in serious crime among juveniles." Similar expressions of concern came from Ludwigshafen, where teenagers were implicated in numerous shootings and sexual assaults throughout the spring of 1940. The same year reports from Darmstadt noted a "remarkable rise" in crime committed by youngsters aged fifteen to eighteen years, including robbery, burglary, and manslaughter. In late 1941, officials in Königsberg noted a "striking increase in serious offenses, especially among male adolescents." Police reports from Nuremberg also complained about the number of serious crimes carried out by teens.[62] In a summary of juvenile delinquency in late 1941, a Ministry of Justice official summarized the impact of the decree. "On the basis of the Decree for the Protection against Juvenile Serious Offenders of October 4, 1939, three juveniles were sentenced to death in 1939, six in 1940, five during the first quarter of 1941, and two in the second quarter of 1941," he reported. The figures continued to rise. In 1942 eight juveniles were convicted of murder, seven of manslaughter, and seventy-five on charges of robbery. The number of those sentenced to death rose to eighteen, and for just the first six months of 1943 that figure went to eighteen.[63]

Particularly alarming was the fact that many of the worst offenders were under fourteen years of age. The police in Brunn, for example, arrested a thirteen-year-old student in July 1942 for assault with intent to commit murder. Under the pretext of picking up his mother, the youngster hired a taxi and directed the driver to an area outside of Brunn. There, he hit the driver on the head nine times with a hatchet. The boy later told the court that he had simply intended to "make the driver unconscious" and steal the two *Reichsmarks* that he needed to take care of library fines.[64] In a letter to the Reich Minister of Justice, the district attorney of Zweibrücken described the case of a thirteen-year-old who, during a June 1942 attempted robbery, stabbed the store owner repeatedly in the head and neck. After his arrest, the teen admitted to ten additional thefts, all carried out since 1940. No legal action could be taken against this youth because of his age.[65] In Berlin, two youngsters, aged thirteen and fourteen, broke into the apartment of a seventy-six-year-old pensioner in search of money. When the woman surprised them, the youngsters tried to strangle her, hit her with a coal shovel, and finally stabbed her to death. In another case, two brothers, one only thirteen, stole three cars at gunpoint and twice shot passengers in the vehicles. While being pursued by an SA patrol, a gunfight broke out during which two SA men and one of the brothers were shot dead. The surviving boy was not prosecuted because of his age.[66] In Strickhausen, a fifteen-year-old housegirl working for a teacher devised a scheme to leave her service and return to the city: when the initial plan to poison the teacher by putting Lysol in her coffee failed, the girl strangled her with a clothesline.[67]

Plans for Further Legislation

Crimes such as these soon led to calls for additional measures against younger juvenile offenders. In July 1942, the Reich Ministry of Justice responded with draft legislation that would lower the age of legal responsibility and competency further. As an official pointed out, "[I]t has been repeatedly demonstrated during the war that the age limit of the Juvenile Justice Act and for criminal responsibility in general does not insure the protection of the *Volksgemeinschaft*."[68] As noted above, juvenile offenders had to be at least fourteen to be prosecuted at all and at least sixteen to be tried as an adult under the 1939 Juvenile Serious Criminal Decree. Citing several particularly reprehensible cases, the Reich Ministry of Justice submitted a draft for a "Second Decree for the Protection against Juvenile Serious Offenders . . . 1942," which read:

The *Volksgemeinschaft* demands for justified retribution mean that serious juvenile offenders be determined not in accordance with age but rather on the basis of their moral, social, and mental development. The Ministerial Council for the Defense of the Reich thereby orders with the force of law:

Article I: The regulations for the protection against juvenile serious offenders can, with the agreement of the Reich Minister of Justice, also be used against youngsters who at the time of the offense are not yet 16 years old. In the area of Wehrmacht jurisdiction, the agreement of the chief of the OKW is needed.

Article II: (1) Persons who are not yet 14 years of age but who can be considered equivalent to a juvenile [i.e., age fourteen to eighteen] in their social and mental development will be held responsible as a juvenile when the protection of the *Volk* or the particularly reprehensible criminal personality of the offender, as manifested in the crime, require criminal prosecution. (2) Prosecution requires approval of the Reich Ministry of Justice.

Article III: (1) The decree applies to the entire Reich territory. It is applicable in the Protectorate of Bohemia and Moravia in so far as the offender is covered by German legal jurisdiction. (2) The decree can be used against those offenders committed before it took effect.[69]

In short, the draft decree proposed not just to lower but to eliminate the age limit for prosecution in juvenile court (fourteen years) as well as the age limit for prosecution as a juvenile serious offender and therefore as an adult (sixteen years); in both cases, no new, lower age limit was set, but the age limits could simply be disregarded if, in the case of juvenile court prosecutions, the "protection of the *Volk*" or the juvenile's "reprehensible criminal personality" demanded it or if, regarding adult prosecutions of juveniles, the Reich Minister of Justice approved.

Martin Bormann, head of the Nazi Party Office (Reichskanzlei) and Hitler's closest adviser, wrote to the Reich Minister of Justice that he approved of the proposed measure, but expressed reservations about publishing the new law and about using the harsher measures to serve as a warning. This legislative action might suggest, he wrote, that the "present wartime situation has led to a brutalization of youth and that the number of capital offenses committed by youngsters has risen to unexpected heights." Bormann was also worried that "enemy propaganda could in this way get some welcome material." He therefore suggested that these proposals be incorporated into a more comprehensive reform of the 1923 Juvenile Justice Act. "In this manner the included articles would not be too noticeable, nor would they give reason for excessive comments."[70] Bormann was not the only official fearful of calling attention to Nazi Germany's troubled dealings with violent youths. The Reich Minister of Justice concluded a July 1942 letter by advocating changes in the age of legal responsibility, but he, too, was concerned with the response from abroad: "For reasons of foreign policy, I have composed the draft in such a way that the goals and the affected age levels are less noticeable." A Ministry of Justice official concurred: "It is impossible at this time to present such regulations, because it would give the impression that crime among those 14 to 16 years of age rose so much as to make such a measure necessary."[71]

While Bormann and Ministry of Justice officials were cautious, the demands for broadening the jurisdiction for juvenile offenders grew as teenage violent and serious crimes continued to worry Party officials. In a letter of 22 April 1943, an official in the Nazi Party Central Office (Parteikanzlei) wrote to the Minister of Justice complaining about the "alarming number of the most serious crimes committed by youngsters," and included summaries of thirteen cases—most of which were property crimes—from the first several months of 1943. Some of the offenders were only twelve or thirteen years old and had already carried out multiple burglaries. In Dessau, for example, four pupils between the ages of nine and thirteen stole purses from more than thirty women. Police in Breslau arrested eight teenagers who had burglarized sixteen stores in a single month. Their loot included twenty thousand cigarettes as well as other items that could readily be sold on the black market. Other youngsters targeted unguarded air raid shelters and cellars.[72] Juveniles were also involved in violent crimes of great brutality. In one case, a fifteen year-old boy poisoned his sixty-five-year-old grandfather to steal his life savings.[73]

Another fifteen-year-old boy stabbed his best friend "in a horrible manner" because the youth had wanted to eliminate a small debt he owed. In spite of the seriousness of the offense, the court determined that he did not possess the maturity of an adult. As a court appointed expert stated, "[T]he defendant is no further developed than any of his cohorts." He was therefore not prosecuted under the 1939 juvenile serious offender decree. In its judgment the court ruled: "It is very possible that the defendant is so morally corrupt that he cannot be rehabilitated. But that does not change the fact that he cannot be punished as an adult." The court found the youth guilty of attempted murder and sentenced him to ten years' imprisonment, the maximum penalty allowed for juveniles under existing law. The Minister of Justice was not pleased with the verdict and sent a circular to all judicial offices using this case as an example of the difficulty in prosecuting young defendants as juvenile serious offenders who could be tried as adults. The circular also noted that because the offender—in the view of the court appointed expert—would probably not be any more mature at the age of eighteen, the decree should, in fact, have been applied. The perceived need for additional legislation was increasing.[74]

In spite of legal ambiguities, convictions of juveniles under the 1939 Juvenile Serious Offender Decree continued to climb. In 1942 the number rose sharply to 107, which surpassed the total number of convictions for the previous three years. The figure suggests both an increase in the number of serious crimes and an increased willingness on the part of prosecutors and judges to apply the decree. Among the offenders convicted in 1942, sixteen were arraigned on charges of murder or manslaughter, a figure much higher than previous years. Still, property crimes remained the most common offenses, amounting to half of all convictions. The courts did not hesitate to hand down severe punishments. Of the 107 youths convicted in 1942, 24 received death sentences and 83 received prison terms of one year or more. During the first two years of the war, capital punishment had been imposed in only nine juvenile cases.[75]

The incidence of serious teenage offenses continued to climb in spite of the draconian sentences. During the first half of 1943, the courts convicted 73 juveniles as "serious offenders," a rise of 38 percent over the last six months of 1942. One postwar analyst of this development concluded that the courts were dealing more severely with the youths because "human nature cannot undergo such far-reaching changes in six months. It is, therefore, to be assumed that the courts had fewer hesitations about using the decree."[76] A Rostock judicial official writing in July 1944 concluded that the overall rise in the number of convictions—and in particular the tougher sentencing—"stand out because the police are more rigorous in their enforcement of the law." The use of capital punishment went up by 17 percent during the first half of 1943, and more long-term prison sentences were imposed.[77] Calls for even tougher sentences and a further extension of the death penalty in these cases became more common. Nazi officials, however, continued to fear the adverse publicity, a fact that made them more cautious, for they wanted to keep the extent of the problem secret. Nothing was done until 1943, when the Juvenile Justice Act was revised. Placed where it would attract little outside attention, one of its articles provided for broader use of capital punishment.[78]

The November 1943 Decree on the Simplification and Standardization of Juvenile Criminal Justice (Verordnung über die Vereinfachung und Vereinheitlichung des Jugendstrafrechts) effected a complete revision of the Juvenile Justice Act of 1923. The new Reich Juvenile Justice Law (Reichsjugendgerichtsgesetz) took effect on 1 January 1944 and marked the culmination of the Nazi regime's efforts to change the treatment of minors in the criminal justice system. Its Article 20 went significantly beyond the 1939 Juvenile Serious Offender Decree in expanding the courts' ability to try juvenile offenders as adults. It stated:

> The judge can order the use of the general [i.e., adult] criminal code if [the juvenile offender is] morally and intellectually as developed as an 18-year-old or if the healthy feelings of the *Volk* [*das gesunde Volksempfinden*] demands it because of his/her serious criminal intentions or because of the seriousness of the crime.
>
> (2) The same applies if the juvenile's moral and intellectual development at the time of the crime is not equal to that of an adult but the assessment of his total personality and the offense show that he is a serious criminal with an abnormal character [*charakterlich abartiger Schwerverbrecher*] and that the protection of the Volk demand this action.[79]

As soon as the law was published, jurists applauded it as a major reform. Article 20 received attention and praise for more specific reasons. The prominent criminal law professor Edmund Mezger accurately pointed out that it greatly expanded the option of prosecuting juvenile offenders as adults and thus addressed some of the criticisms that had been leveled at the 1939 decree by those eager to impose harsher punishments on juvenile offenders. Under the new law, a youngster no longer needed to be as mature as an adult to be prosecuted to the full extent of the general criminal code. Regardless of a juvenile offender's age or level of maturity, he or she could now be prosecuted as an adult if he or she was a "serious criminal with an abnormal character" and the "protection of the *Volk*" required severe punishment. According to Mezger, the new provision applied to juvenile offenders who had experienced "serious inborn character changes which lead one to call such an individual 'psychopathic.'" His endorsement of the law did not mince words and revealed its draconian intentions: "Practical experience has shown the need for lowering the age of responsibility. A series of cases has proven it necessary to use the death penalty against those under 16 who previously were subject to sentences of up to ten years."[80]

Conclusion

The problem of juvenile crime had long preoccupied German penal reformers, criminologists, and law enforcement officials. The majority of penal reformers in the Imperial and Weimar periods held the view that juvenile offenders must be treated differently from adults: they should be tried in special juvenile courts; be exempt from adult punishments; and, whenever it seemed appropriate, should be sentenced to correctional education in homes for wayward youth rather than a prison sentence. This reformist consensus found its legislative expression in the Juvenile Justice Act of 1923, which stipulated that juvenile offenders between the ages of fourteen and eighteen must be tried in juvenile court. When, in the late 1930s, prosecutors, judges, Nazi party officials, and police and local officials became alarmed by what they perceived as a growing incidence of serious juvenile crime, they decided that it was time to roll back the special treatment that the Juvenile Justice Act had guaranteed youth offenders. The October 1939 Decree for the Protection against Juvenile Serious Offenders therefore allowed some juvenile offenders to be tried as adults so that harsher sanctions could be imposed. But even though Nazi jurists were reversing the pre-1933 reform movement's special treatment of all juvenile offenders, in defining which juvenile offenders could be tried as adults they drew on the penal reform movement's key strategies of categorizing offenders and individualizing punishment: the new criminal type of the *jugendlicher Schwerverbrecher* was essentially a juvenile version of the so-called dangerous habitual criminal. In doing so, they were shifting the boundary between reformable and incorrigible criminals in ways that circumscribed the scope of rehabilitation and expanded that of repression. Over the course of the Nazi regime, and especially during the war, this boundary kept shifting in the direction of repression and draconian punishment for more and more categories of offenders.

The courts welcomed the 1939 decree and responded by prosecuting increasing numbers of juveniles as adults and issuing harsh sentences including the death penalty. The definition of *jugendlicher Schwerverbrecher* proved malleable. Initially, only juveniles over sixteen who were of adult maturity could be tried as adults. Then the courts decided that even juveniles whose development was impaired but who were as mature as they were ever going to be as adults could be subject to adult punishments. Later, the 1943 decree removed the lower age limit of sixteen as well as the maturity requirement. From now on, juveniles of any age could receive adult punishments (including the death penalty) not only if they possessed adult maturity but also if they were *charakterlich abartige Schwerverbrecher* or if an adult punishment was demanded by "healthy popular feeling" (*gesundes Volksempfinden*). In short, who could be tried as an adult depended not just on the subjective characteristics and alleged competency of the juvenile but also on the supposed attitudes of the "national community" toward the crime and the criminal in question. Thus ambiguous terms such as *Schutz des Volkes* (protection of the *Volk*) or *gesundes Volksempfinden* became legal principles that basically allowed any juvenile to be punished as an adult and condemned to death if the court wished. In this way, criminal justice became a tool in the hands of judges whose main concern were the demands of society as defined by Nazi leaders and Nazi ideology, which became ever more draconian as the wartime situation worsened.

Notes

1. Reichsführer SS, "Bericht zur innerpolitischen Lage, 20 November 1939, National Archives, microfilm T-175, roll 258, frame 750290; "Meldungen aus dem Reich," January 26, 1940, National Archives, microfilm T-175, roll 2, frame 750700; Reichsminister der Justiz Dr. Thierack, "Die Jugendkriminalität im Kriege," Bundesarchiv Koblenz, R22/5016; Oberstaatsanwalt München I, "Betrifft: Die Kriminalität der Jugendlichen," Bundesarchiv Koblenz, R22/1189, Bl. 9–10; "Anzeigestatistik in den Jahren 1939 bis 1942 gegenüber Stafunmündige," Bundesarchiv Zwischenarchiv Dahlwitz-Hoppegarten, 30.01 9843, Bl. 20–23; Herbert Vornefeld, "Jugendführung gegen Jugendkriminalität: Was lehren die Erfahrungen des Weltkrieges?," *Das Junge Deutschland* 33 (1 December 1939), 475–479.
2. "Niederschrift über die Besprechung vom 1.2.1940 über Fragen der Jugendbetreuung," Bundesarchiv Koblenz, R22/1189, Bl. 84–92.

3. Edith Roper and Clara Leiser, *Skeleton of Justice* (New York, 1941), 246–285; quote 248. Roper attributed the rise in teenage violent crime to the social context, viewing crime as learned behavior, much as argued by a contemporary criminologist Edwin A. Sutherland in his *Principals of Criminology*, 3rd ed. (Chicago, 1939).

4. "Verordnung zum Schutz gegen jugendliche Schwerverbrecher vom 4.10.1939," *Reichsgesetzblatt*, Teil I (1939), 2000; Franz Exner, "Die Verordnung zum Schutz gegen jugendliche Schwerverbrecher," *Zeitschrift für die gesamte Strafrechtswissenschaft* 60 (1941), 335–337; W. Knopp, *Kriminalität und Gefährdung der Jugend: Lagebericht bis zum Stande vom 1. Januar 1941* (Berlin, 1941), 77, 85; Frank Kebbedies, *Außer Kontrolle: Jugendkriminalität in der NS-Zeit und der frühen Nachkriegszeit* (Essen, 2000), 189–196.

5. "Verordnung zum Schutz gegen jugendliche Schwerverbrecher vom 4.10.1939," and Dr. Otto Schwarz, *Srafgesetzbuch: Nebengesetze, Verordnungen, Kriegsstrafrecht* 12th ed. (Munich, 1943), 1041–1042; On adult offenders, see Christian Müller, "Das Gewohnheitsverbrechergesetz vom 24. November 1933, NS-Strafrecht zwischen Reformtradition und rassistischer Neubestimmung," *Zeitschrift für Geschichtswissenschaft* 47 (1999), 965–979.

6. These topics have received much attention in recent years; see Müller, "Das Gewohnheitsverbrechergesetz vom 24. November 1933, 965–979; Dieter Dölling, "Kriminologie im 'Dritten Reich,'" in *Recht und Justiz im 'Dritten Reich,'* Ralf Dreier and Wolfgang Sellert, eds. (Frankfurt am Main, 1989), 194–220; Nikolaus Wachsmann, "'Annihilation through Labor': The Killing of State Prisoners in the Third Reich," *Journal of Modern History* 71(September 1999), 626–635, 658–659; Wachsmann, *Hitler's Prisons* (New Haven and London, 2004); Wolfgang Ayaß, *Gemeinschaftsfremde": Quellen zur Verfolgung von Asozialen, 1933–1945* (Koblenz: Bundesarchiv, 1998), xi–xx; Patrick Wagner, *Volksgemeinschaft ohne Verbrecher: Konzeptionen und Praxis der Kriminalpolizei in der Zeit der Weimarer Republik und des Nationalsozialismus* (Hamburg, 1996); Richard F. Wetzell, *Inventing the Criminal: A History of German Criminology, 1880–1945* (Chapel Hill, 2000), especially 209–231; Kebbedies, *Außer Kontrolle*, 187–189; and Thomas Roth, *"Verbrechensbekämpfung" und soziale Ausgrenzung im nationalisozialistischen Köln* (Cologne, 2010), 44–47, 157–159.

7. "Tabelle 11: Verurteilungen auf Grund der VP vom 4.X.39," Bundesarchiv Koblenz, R22/1158; "Entwicklung der Jugendkriminalität auf Grund der vorläufigen Ergebnisse der Reichskriminalstatistik für das 1. Vierteljahr 1941," Bundesarchiv Koblenz, R22/1158, Bl. 60; Roper, *Skeleton of Justice*, 270–273.

8. Mezger, "Die jugendliche Schwerverbrecher," in *Zum neuen Jugendstrafrecht* (Berlin, 1944), 87–89; NSDAP Partei-Kanzlei, "Betrifft: Entwurf einer Verordnung über Erweiterungen der Strafmündigkeit," 26 October 1942, Bundesarchiv Koblenz, R22/1177.

9. Knopp, *Kriminalität und Gefährdung der Jugend*, 81; Karl-Heinz Behm, "Die Kriminalität der Jugend im Spiegel der Kriminalstatistik (1914–1939)," (Diss., University of Heidelberg, 1943), 46, 54, 56; Karl-Heinz Huber, *Jugend unterm Hakenkreuz* (Frankfurt am Main, 1986), 214–223.

10. "Schwere Bluttat in Niederbayern," *Münchener Neuste Nachrichten*, July 29, 1933; Fritz Weber, "Raubmord eines dreizehnjahrigen an einem dreizehnjährigen und seine Aufklärung," *Kriminalistische Monatshefte* 10 (1936), 59–61.

11. Roper, *Skeleton of Justice*, 246–250, 277–279; the quote is from page 281.

12. Ibid.; Oellermann, "Todesurteil 48 Stunden nach der Mordtat," *Kriminalistik* 15(1941), 104–105. See the discussion of the impact of Nazi rule on the brutalization of society in Cologne in Roth, *Verbrecherungsbekämpfung*, 527ff.

13. Knopp, *Kriminalität und Gefährdung der Jugend*, 78–79.

14. "Offenbach, 4. Februar 1939," Hessisches Hauptstaatsarchiv, Wiesbaden, 4833790.

15. Ursula Uetzmann, "Jugendliche Schwerverbrecher: Eine Untersuchung im Anschluss an die VO zum Schutze gegen jugendliche Schwerverbrecher vom 4. Oktober 1939," (diss.,

University of Hamburg, 1940), 4–79; "Raubüberfall am hellen Tag," *Berliner Lokal-Anzeiger*, 10 August 1938; Fabisch, "Die Straftaten der Gebrüder Sass," *Kriminalistik* 14 (1940), 85; Kupfer, "Zur Bekämpfung der Autobanditen," *Kriminalistische Monatshefte* 11 (1937), 65.

16. Oberstaatsanwalt bei dem Landgericht, Hamburg . . . gegen Heinz R, Staatsanwaltschaft Hamburg, 2 Kls 198/39, Rep Nr. 532/1940.

17. "Entwicklung der Jugendkriminalität," Bundesarchiv Koblenz, R22/1158, B. 47–50; Knopp, *Kriminalität und Gefährdung der Jugend*, 81.

18. "Ausrottung des Verbrechertum: Starker Rückgang der Kriminalität im neuen Deutschland," *Stuttgarter NS-Kurier*, 80, 16 February 1935; Knopp, *Kriminalität und Gefährdung der Jugend*, 49–52.

19. F. Schaffstein, "Die Bewahrung asozialer Minderjähriger," *Akademie für Deutsches Recht* 5 (Jahrbuch 1938), 64–69.

20. "Jugendgerichtsetz. Vom 16. Februar 1923," *Reichsgesetzblatt*, Teil I (27 February 1923), 135; and Otto Grube, "Das Jugendgerichtsgesetz vom 16.II.1923 und die allgemeinen Verbrechensleben" (diss., University of Kiel, 1928), 2–4, 12–16. Vornefeld, "Jugendführung gegen Jugendkriminalität," 476. For the case of one youngster who attracted local police attention, see "Das Verhalten der _____, Tochter des Haupm. d. Schupo beim Polizeiamt in Friedberg," 13 May 1936, Hessisches Staatsarchiv Darmstadt, G15 Friedberg XIX/2 Kono. 3. A. Gregor, "Minderjähriger Schwerverbrecher und ihre strafrechtliche und sozial-padagogische Behandlung," *Allgemeine Zeitschrift für Psychiatrie und ihr Grenzgebiete* 114 (1940), 330–336.

21. Knopp, *Kriminalität und Gefährdung der Jugend*, 80; "Anzeigestatistik in den Jahren 1939 bis 1942 gegenüber Strafunmündige," Bundesarchiv Zwischen Archiv Dahlwitz-Hoppegarten, 30.01 9843; Behm, "Kriminalität der Jugend," 49–50, 68–70.

22. Landgerichtspräsident, "Betrifft: Vorschlag einer Änderung strafrechtlicher Vorschriften," Berlin, 21 November 1938, Bundesarchiv Koblenz, R22/1178. For a discussion of competency see Grube, "Das Jugendgerichtsgesetz vom 16.II.1923, 24–27, and Wolfgang Mittermaier, " Zurechnungsfähigkeit," in *Handwörterbuch der Rechswissenschaft*, vol. 6 (Berlin and Leipzig, 1929), 1052–1057.

23. Ibid.

24. Vornefeld, "Jugendführung gegen Jugendkriminalität," 476–479.

25. E. Roesner, "Krieg und Kriminalität im Spiegel der Statistik," *Blätter für Gefängniskunde* 73 (1942); Exner, "Verordnung," 335–336; "Anzeigestatistik in den Jahren 1939 bis 1942."

26. Oberstaatsanwalt München I, "Betrifft: Die Kriminalität der Jugendlichen"; "Niederschrift über die Besprechung vom 1.2.1940," Bl. 84–87; Knopp, *Kriminalität und Gefährdung der Jugend*, 80, 82–84.

27. Exner, "Verordnung," 335; Karl Heinz Nüse, *Das Kriegsstrafrecht und Kriegsstrafverfahren* (Berlin-Leipzig, 1940), 28–29; Knopp, *Kriminalität und Gefährdung der Jugend*, 84; Graf von Gleispach, "Die Verordnung zum Schutz gegen jugendliche Schwerverbrecher," *Deutsches Recht* 9 (1939), 1964; Oberstaatsanwalt München, "Kriminalität der Jugendlichen," 7 December 1939.

28. Edmund Mezger, *Kriminalpolitik*, 2nd ed. (Stuttgart, 1942), 264–265, the quote is from 265. Dr. Paul Bockelmann, "II. Aussprache," *Zeitschrift für die gesamte Strafrechtswissenschaft* 60 (1940), 351–352.

29. Gleispach, "Verordnung," 1964.

30. Edmund Mezger, "Kriegsstrafrecht und Kriegsstrafverfahrensrecht," *Zeitschrift der Akademie für deutsches Recht* 7 (1940), 61; Nagler, "Die jugendliche Schwerverbrecher," *Gerichtssaal* 115 (1941), 1.

31. Nagler, "Jugendliche Schwerverbrecher," 1; Hotes, "Jugendliche Schwerverbrecher," 9; Nüse, *Das Kriegsstrafrecht und Kriegsstrafverfahren*, 28–29; Reichsfhrer SS und Chef der deutschen Polizei, "Bericht zur innere politische Lage," Berlin, 19 November 1939, National Archives,

microfilm T-175, roll 285, frame 2750234; "Lageberichterstattung," Berlin, October 16, 1939, NA, T-175 roll 285 frame 2750089; Dr. Annaliese Ohland, "Todesstrafe—auch für eine Jugendlichen," *Wohlfahrts-Woche*, 14 (Feburary 1940), 103–105; Manuela Neugebauer, *Der Weg in das Jugendschutzlager Moringen: Eine entwicklungspolitische Analyse nationalsozialistishcer Jugendpolitik* (Mönchengladbach, 1997), 106–107.

32. Grau, *Deutsches Strafrecht*, 2nd ed., 451–452.

33. See, for example, Oberstaatsanwalt bei dem Landgericht in Hamburg . . . Günther K. . . . wegen Mordes, Staatsanwaltschaft Hamburg, 2 Js/426/40, Rep Nr. 5191/1940.

34. "Verordnung zum Schutz gegen jugendliche Schwerverbrecher vom 4.10.1939"; Freisler, Grau, Krug, Rietzsch, *Deutsches Strafrecht*, vol. I, (Berlin, 1941), 259–260; Gleispach, "Verordnung," 1966; Nüse, *Das Kriegsstrafrecht und Kriegsstrafverfahren*, 28–29; Grau, Krug, Rietasch, *Deutsches Strafrecht*, 2nd ed. (Berlin, 1943), 452. Excluded were juveniles whose cases had opened in a Special Court, a district court, the People's Court, or in the Special Criminal Senate of the Reich Court.

35. Freisler, *Deutsches Strafrecht*, 260–261.

36. Ibid.

37. Exner, "Verordnung," 338–339; Fritz Schulz, "Der jugendliche Schwerverbrecher," (diss., University of Munich, 1943), 4–20; Wolfgang Lemme, "Der Begriff des jugendlichen Schwerverbrechers in der Verordnung zum Schutz gegen jugendliche Schwerverbrecher vom 4. Oktober 1939," (diss., University of Göttingen, 1943), 7–10.

38. Freisler, *Deutsches Strafrecht*, 261; Schulz, "Der jugendliche Schwerverbrecher," 10–15, 22–23; Nagler, "Der jugendliche Schwerverbrecher," 8.

39. Freisler, *Deutsches Strafrecht*, 261; Exner, "Verordnung," 339; Gleispach, "Verordnung," 1965.

40. Freisler, *Deutsches Strafrecht*, 262; Dr. Keßler, "Für die Frage, ob es sich um einen jugendlichen Schwerverbrecher i. S. der VO vom 4.10.1939 handelt . . . ," *Zeitschrift der Akademie für deutsches Recht* 8 (1941), 86–87.

41. Lemme, "Der Begriff des jugendlichen Schwerverbrechers," 2, 3, 32–35, 44–45; Sigmund Silbereisen, *Die spätere Straffälligkeit jugendlicher Rechtsbrecher: Eine Nachuntersuchung uber die im Jahre 1928 in München verurteilten Jugendlichen* (Leipzig, 1940), 7–8, 57–64.

42. Exner, "Verordnung," 340–341.

43. Ibid.

44. On Exner, see Walter Fuchs, *Franz Exner (1881–1947) und das Gemeinschaftsfremdengesetz: Zum Barbarisierungspotenzial moderner Kriminalwissenschaft* (Münster, 2008), and Wetzell, *Inventing the Criminal*, 109–110, 213–219.

45. Exner, "Verordnung," 341.

46. Ibid.; Lemme, "Der Begriff des jugendlichen Schwerverbrechers," 44, 46; Nagler, "Der jugendliche Schwerverbrecher," 2–6; Schulz, "Der jugendliche Schwerverbrecher," 12–16.

47. Exner, "Verordnung," 340–341.

48. Gleispach, "Verordnung," 1965–1966; Nagler, "Der jugendliche Schwerverbrecher," 11–16; Lemme, "Der Begriff des jugendlichen Schwerverbrechers," 45; Schulz, "Der jugendliche Schwerverbrecher," 88–89.

49. Lemme, "Der Begriff des jugendlichen Schwerverbrechers," 21–23; Schulz, "Der jugendliche Schwerverbrecher," cases 3, 4, 5, 7, 9, 10, 15, 16, 26, and 31.

50. Gleispach, "Verordnung," 1966; Freisler, *Deutsches Strafrecht*, 263.

51. Freisler, *Deutsches Strafrecht*, 263; Lemme, "Der Begriff des jugendlichen Schwerverbrechers," 24–27. See Richard J. Evans, *Rituals of Retribution: Capital Punishment in Germany, 1600–1987* (Oxford, 1996), 691, 696, 702.

52. Nüse, *Das Kriegsstrafrecht und Kriegsstrafverfahren*, 29; Freisler, *Deutsches Strafrecht*, 267; Alfred Kögler, "Über jugendliche Mörder," *Monatsschrift für Kriminalbiologie* 32 (1941), 73–85; Gleispach, "Verordnung," 1967.

53. Exner, "Verordnung," 343.

54. Exner, "Verordnung," 343–345; Lemme, "Der Begriff des jugendlichen Schwerverbrechers," 18–19.

55. On Mezger see Gerit Thulfaut, *Kriminalpolitik und Strafrechtslehre bei Edmund Mezger (1883–1962)* (Baden-Baden, 2000), and Wetzell, *Inventing the Criminal*, 209–213.

56. Mezger, "Der jugendliche Schwerverbrecher," in *Zum neuen Jugendstrafrecht*, 83, 89; Freisler, *Deutsche Justiz* (1940), 53.

57. Freisler, *Deutsche Justiz*; Exner, "Verordnung," 345.

58. Dr. E. Mezger, "Strafrecht," *Deutsches Recht* 11(1941), 1721–1722; A. Gregor, "Zur Frage der Beurteilung jugendliche Schwerverbrecher," *Monatsschrift für Kriminalbiologie* 32 (1941), 282–283.

59. Ibid. For a summary of such investigations, see Gregor, "Minderjähriger Schwerverbrecher," 316ff, and Hotes "Der jugendliche Schwerverbrecher," 8. The best discussion of court practices is in Schulz, "Der jugendliche Schwerverbrecher," 108–125.

60. Schulz, "Der jugendliche Schwerverbrecher," 109–112; Gregor, "Beurteilung jugendlicher Schwerverbrecher," 265–283.

61. See Boldt's comments on the decision in *Deutsches Recht* 11(1941), 44–45; *Zeitschrift der Akademie für deutsches Recht* 8 (1941), 86–87; *Deutsches Recht* 11 (1941), 1722–1726; "Richterbrief" Nr. 14 vom 1. November 1943, 112–113, BAK, R22/1177; Johannes Schottky, "Über den Mordversuch eines Jugendlichen bei geplantem Selbstmord," *Monatsschrift für Kriminalbiologie* 32 (1941), 1.

62. Oberlandesgerichtspräsident, "Betrifft: Bericht über die allgemeine Lage," Darmstadt, 10 May 1940, Bundesarchiv Koblenz, R22/3361; Generalstaatsanwalt, "Betrifft: Zweimonatlicher Lagebericht," Zweibrücken, 4 April 1940, Bundesarchiv Koblenz, R22/3389; "Schnellbrief," Kripostelle Ludwigshafen am Rhein, 7 May 1940, Bayerisches Hauptstaatsarchiv, Abt. II, Reichsstatthalter 377; Oberlandesgerichtspräsident, "Betrifft: Bericht über die allgemeine Lage," Darmstadt, 6 September 1941, Bundesarchiv Koblenz, R22/3361. Generalstaatsanwalt bei dem Oberlandesgericht Königsberg, 12 December 1941, Bundesarchiv Koblenz, R22/3375; Nuremberg, 18 September 1941, 27 November 1941, 13 November 1942, Bayerisches Hauptstaatsarchiv, Abt. II, Reichsstatthalter 378.

63. "Herrn Staatssekretär Dr. Freisler. Die Gesamtbewegung der Jugendkriminalität . . . ," BAK, R22/1158. Deutsches Reichsamt, "Die Jugendkriminalität im Großdeutschen Reich I Jahre 1942 und 1. Halbjahr 1943," BAK Koblenz, R22/1159, 4, 6, 9.

64. Reichssicherheitshauptamt, Amt V, Berlin, 14 July 1942, Bundesarchiv Koblenz, R22/1179.

65. Der Oberstaatsanwalt, Saarbrücken, 23 July 1942, Bundesarchiv Koblenz, R22/1178.

66. See "Fälle strafunmündiger junger Schwerverbrecher," and "I. Fälle, in denen sich die Anwendung der VO zum Schutz gegen jugendliche Schwerverbrecher beim fünfzehnjährigen als erforderlich erwiesen hat," Bundesarchiv Koblenz, R22/1178, Bl. 190, 240.

67. Ibid.; "Fälle 14 und 15 jähriger Schwerverbrecher, bei den die Schwerverbrecher VO keine Anwendung finden konnte," Bundesarchiv Koblenz, R22/1178, Bl. 191.

68. Reichsminister der Justiz, "Betr. Entwurf einer Verordnung über Erweiterungen der Strafmündigkeit," 3 July 1942, Bundesarchiv Koblenz, R22/1177, Bl. 565.

69. Ibid.; "Zweite Verordnung zum Schutz gegen junge Schwerverbrecher, vom . . . 1942," Bundesarchiv Koblenz, R22/1178, Bl. 190 See also the proposed "Verordnung über Erweiterungen der Strafmündigkeit, vom . . . 1942," Bundesarchiv Koblenz, R22/1177, Bl. 566.

70. NSDAP Partei-Kanzlei, "Entwurf einer Verordnung."

71. Reichsminister der Justiz, "Entwurf einer Verordnung"; "Abschrift: Der Chef der Reichskriminalpolizeiamtes . . . ," Bundesarchiv Koblenz, R22/1177.

72. Mezger, "Der jugendliche Schwerverbrecher," in *Zum neuen Jugendstrafrecht*, 83, 89; Hotes, "Der jugendliche Schwerverbrecher," 20, 32, 60.

73. "Richterbriefe," Nr. 14, 1. November 1943, Bundesarchiv Koblenz, R22/1177, Bl. 112–113, 119.

74. Ibid.

75. Statistisches Reichsamt, "Die Jugendkriminalität im Grossdeutschen Reich im Jahre 1942 und im 1. Halbjahr 1943," Bundesarchiv Koblenz, R22/1159, Bl. 14; Mezger, "Der jugendliche Schwerverbrecher," 88–89; Bruno Blau, "Die Kriminalität in Deutschland während des zweiten Weltkrieges," *Zeitschrift für die gesamte Strafrechtswissenschaft* 64 (1952), 71.

76. Blau, "Kriminalität während des Weltkrieges," 71; "Jugendkriminalität im Jahre 1942 und im 1. Halbjahr 1943," 14.

77. "Auszug aus dem Bericht des Oberlandesgerichtspräsidenten und des Generalstaatsanwaltes bei dem Oberlandesgericht Rostock, z. Zt. in Schwerin, vom 29.7.1944," Bundesarchiv Koblenz, R22/1176; "Jugendkriminalität im Grossdeutschen Reich im 1942 und 1. Halbjahr 1943."

78. Heinz Kummerlein, "Reichsjugendgerichtsgesetz vom 6. November 1943," (Munich-Berlin, 1944), 162.

79. Ibid.

80. Mezger, "Der jugendliche Schwerverbrecher," 83, 89; Hotes, "Jugendliche Schwerverbrecher," 20, 32, 60.

Chapter 11

CRIMINAL LAW AFTER NATIONAL SOCIALISM
The Renaissance of Natural Law and the Beginnings of Penal Reform in West Germany

Petra Gödecke

The effort to achieve a comprehensive revision of the penal code had occupied German professors and practitioners of criminal law since the *Kaiserreich*.[1] But the penal reform movement and the official reform commissions, which continued all the way up to the Nazi regime's penal reform commission under Justice Minister Franz Gürtner, remained unsuccessful. This chapter investigates when penal reform reappeared on the agenda of German criminal law professors after 1945 and what shape this new penal reform discourse took. The early postwar phase of the reform discourse had little influence on the comprehensive penal reform that was eventually passed in 1969 or on the revisions of laws on sexual offenses that took place from 1969 to 1973. But this early phase is of considerable interest because it reveals the complex mix of continuity and change in a particular discipline at a moment of political rupture and because it reconstructs how a new reform discourse emerged under the influence of the experiences of the Nazi period and the social and cultural upheavals of the postwar era.

This chapter begins with a brief overview of the penal code and of the situation of academic criminal law at the universities around 1945. The next two sections examine the debates on natural law and the question of why there were no efforts to completely revise the criminal code immediately after 1945. This issue leads into the following two sections, which explore the work situation, publication venues, and professional meetings of legal academics in the field of criminal law after 1945. The final two sections trace which professors participated in the reform debates and examine the two basic positions in the reform discourse:

---

retribution versus behavorial prevention (*Spezialprävention*). The conclusion seeks to explain why retributivism prevailed in the postwar reform discourse.

The Penal Code

The German penal code that was in force after 1945 was a product of the nineteenth century. Aside from a few amendments, it was identical to the Reich Penal Code of 1871.[2] The criminal law focused on the criminal offense; the purpose of punishment was retribution for this offense. The offender, the individual perpetrator, played no role in this conception of criminal law. The criminal code's system of punishments included *Zuchthaus* (imprisonment with hard labor), *Gefängnis* (regular prison), *Haft* (jail), *Einschliessung* (*custodia honesta*, a special form of detention for prisoners of conscience), and fines. Fines were the exclusive punishment for some offenses; for other offenses they could be imposed either instead of or in addition to a prison sentence. Despite the failure of a complete reform of the penal code, the code was significantly altered through individual amendments in the Kaiserreich and in the Weimar Republic.[3] In addition to changes resulting from particular political, economic, or sociocultural events and developments,[4] these alterations of the penal code included a 1912 amendment that reduced punishments for many offenses, the Juvenile Justice Act of 1923,[5] as well as the expansion of the use of monetary fines in 1923–1924,[6] which already by 1911 accounted for more than half of all punishments. Around the turn of the century, suspended sentencing was introduced through administrative ordinances in Prussia and several other German states in the form of a "conditional pardon" based on the right of pardon of each state's ruler.[7] (Suspended sentencing was not integrated into the penal code until 1953.)[8] Shortly after the National Socialists came to power, a further amendment introduced "Preventive and Corrective Measures" including indefinite detention for "habitual criminals," internment in an asylum for mentally abnormal offenders or in a workhouse for asocial offenders[9] as well as castration for sex offenders, which was removed from the penal code after 1945 by the Allies.[10]

In terms of penal theory, the Reich Penal Code was based on a combination of retributive justice and general deterrence: general deterrence through just retribution.[11] Since the late nineteenth century, the debates about reforming the criminal code centered around three elements of punishment: retribution, general deterrence (*Generalprävention*), and specific (i.e., individual) deterrence (*Spezialprävention*). In the discourse on criminal law, the concept of retribution was usually derived from Kant and Hegel's theories of absolute punishment.[12] But whereas authors who have studied Kant and Hegel's philosophies of law have offered nuanced interpretations,[13] in the mainstream retributivist criminal law discourse Kant and Hegel were simply placeholders for absolute theories of punishment, at the center of which stood retribution.[14]

The Situation of Academic Criminal Law in 1945

The situation of the German legal profession after the National Socialist regime was extremely difficult. The profession's adaptation to the Nazi state without any resistance, its compliant support of the regime through judicial verdicts that flouted the rule of law, the willing exclusion of Jewish jurists, and many other misdeeds had utterly compromised the entire profession. This was especially true of criminal law, which of all the areas of the law was capable of the greatest interference in citizens' lives.[15] The most infamous example here was the People's Court (*Volksgerichtshof*), which can only be described as an "instrument of terror."[16] The criminal law professor and legal historian Eberhard Schmidt therefore characterized the situation in drastic terms: "With the collapse of 1945, what remained of the field criminal law was spiritual rubble."[17]

After 1945 both professors and practitioners of criminal law faced the difficulty of simultaneously dealing with the violent crimes of the National Socialists in criminal trials, reflecting on the Nazi regime's instrumentalization of criminal justice and searching for a new foundation for their discipline. Their debates on these topics took place not only in the journals of the legal profession, which started to appear again or were newly founded, but also in general-circulation newspapers and magazines, which were appearing in unprecedented numbers in the early postwar years.[18] In 1947, for example, journals such as *Forum* and *Die Kirche in der Welt* published articles on "Criminal Law and Culture" and "Justice and Legal Certainty"; an essay on the "Removal of National Socialist Interference in Criminal Justice" appeared in *Geist und Tat*, a Hamburg monthly for "Law, Freedom, and Culture"; and a key text by Gustav Radbruch on the "Renewal of Law" was published in the renowned journal *Die Wandlung*.[19] Such articles were sometimes supplemented by autobiographically inspired pieces on the desolate situation of the prison system.[20] These articles and their dissemination in prominent periodicals reveal the widespread interest in the problems of criminal law and the penal system after 1945. The discourse among jurists took place in the newly founded professional journals, initially the *Süddeutsche Juristenzeitung* (*SJZ*) and the *Deutsche Rechts-Zeitschrift* (*DRZ*). The *SJZ* was licensed for the American zone of occupation in 1946, and the *DRZ* for the French zone.[21]

The Critique of Legal Positivism and the Renaissance of Natural Law

One of the first professors of criminal law to address the issue of law under National Socialism after 1945 was Gustav Radbruch, who had been a Reich Justice Minister and prominent penal reformer during the Weimar Republic.[22] In a much-cited article with the programmatic title "Legal Injustice and Supra-legal

Justice," Radbruch assigned the primary blame for judicial compliance with Nazism to legal positivism (*Gesetzespositivismus*). Legal positivism, Radbruch argued, "with its conviction that 'law is law' rendered the German legal profession defenseless against laws of arbitrary and criminal content."[23] Although a comprehensive analysis and critique of Radbruch's "positivism thesis" cannot be pursued here, it should be noted that legal-historical studies have identified numerous cases in which judges handed down sentences that went beyond the National Socialist laws and many instances of legal academics interpreting the existing laws very broadly, thus demonstrating that legal positivism actually played little role in Nazi jurisprudence.[24] In the postwar era, however, Radbruch's thesis had considerable appeal because it offered "easy exoneration" for both legal practitioners and legal academics.[25] After all, a legal theory could hardly be put in the dock for criminal prosecution; and blaming a theory also conveniently obviated questions about personal responsibility for legal verdicts during the Nazi era. The exoneration was made still more effective by the fact that Radbruch himself could not be accused of wanting to exculpate Nazi justice. As a staunch democrat Radbruch was above suspicion politically and in no way tainted by National Socialism. He had lost his university chair immediately after the Nazi seizure of power. In addition, Radbruch himself had been considered a representative of legal positivism during the Weimar Republic, which gave his critique special validity.[26]

Radbruch thought that "overcoming positivism"[27] could represent a new beginning even though, unlike other jurists, he shied away from a simple endorsement of natural law and timeless legal norms.[28] Instead, he situated law in a field of tension between legal certainty (*Rechtssicherheit*), justice (*Gerechtigkeit*), and expedience (*Zweckmäßigkeit*), with an emphasis on the first two aspects:

> The conflict between justice and legal certainty [*Rechtssicherheit*] should be resolved by granting priority to the existing positive law that is secured by statutes and power even when its content is unjust and inexpedient [*unzweckmäßig*], unless the contradiction between the positive law and justice reaches such an unbearable extent that the law, as "incorrect law" [*unrichtiges Recht*] must give way to justice. It is impossible to draw a sharper line between cases of legal injustice [*gesetzlichen Unrechts*] and laws that remain valid despite their incorrect content. Another boundary, however, can be drawn quite sharply: Where justice is not even striven for, where equality, which constitutes the core of justice, is intentionally denied in the establishment of positive laws, in those cases the law is not only "incorrect law" but lacks the character of a legal norm [*Rechtsnatur*] altogether. For law, even positive law, cannot be defined as anything other than an order and statute whose very purpose is to serve justice.[29]

Despite his skepticism regarding natural law,[30] Radbruch stood at the beginning of the "renaissance of natural law" that took place after 1945; many authors explicitly referred to his arguments.[31] The early postwar years saw the publication of numerous essays and books on natural law that resolved the conflict of legal positivism versus natural law in favor of the latter. Participants in this discussion included jurists—not only from the field of criminal law—as well as theologians and philosophers.[32] Although natural law was not always discussed with reference to a Christian canon of values—Radbruch himself did not make such references—religious arguments were common. The reference to Christian values was appealing given the prominent postwar role of both the Protestant and Catholic Churches as allegedly untainted institutions.[33] The influence of Christian traditions, especially Catholic natural law, steered the postwar jurisprudence that was based on natural law arguments in a conservative direction, which was especially apparent in the decisions of the *Bundesgerichtshof,* the highest German court, in the 1950s.[34]

In the immediate postwar years, natural law arguments served to condemn and reverse Nazi injustice. In contrast to many esoteric discussions in the realm of criminal jurisprudence (*Strafrechtsdogmatik*), the natural law debate was not without practical relevance. Legal arguments referencing natural law played an important role in the judicial practice of German criminal courts, especially in court decisions regarding Nazi justice and Nazi crimes. As the West German legal historian Winfried Hassemer has written, in the postwar years "criminal law jurists faced a problem of natural law that could not to be evaded: . . . [during the Nazi period] judges had applied the criminal laws, which had been established in a formally valid manner, and the result was a mockery of proportionality, fairness, and human dignity."[35] A legal reckoning with National Socialism—however inadequate it may be considered in retrospect—probably could not have taken place without resorting to standards based on natural law. This was not only true of the Nuremberg Trials, but also for many smaller trials, for example, trials in denunciation or desertion cases, and was reflected in the judgments of many German courts.

Among professors of criminal law, however, not everyone drew on natural law arguments. At one of the first postwar meetings of German jurists, in 1947, for instance, Hellmuth von Weber of the University of Bonn opposed the idea that individual judges should check criminal laws against a natural law standard.[36] Even Karl Peters, one of very few Catholic professors of criminal law, who was closely associated with Catholic moral teachings, represented more of a legal positivist view, arguing that the only time to refuse to obey a law was when "an overt, grave violation of natural law or the supernatural order is present" or "when the law is consciously driven by considerations that are foreign to the law."[37] Radbruch had supported a similar position, even if both differed in their terminology.

In evaluating the postwar years, one would have to agree with Dieter Simon's assessment that both the law faculties and the courts "made their way back to natural law."[38] With the exception of the jurisprudence of the Bundesgerichtshof, however, it is not clear how long the sway of natural law over legal academics and legal practitioners lasted. The contemporary evidence is contradictory. Whereas as late as 1955 criminal law professor Thomas Würtenberger still claimed that "after overcoming legal positivist inhibitions and prejudices, natural law presently dominates not only the theory of criminal law but also its practice,"[39] two years earlier his colleague Hans Welzel had already argued the contrary: "A relatively rapid disenchantment has spread. The enthusiasm for natural law has been replaced by a renewed turn toward positive law." Although he himself was a critic of natural law, Welzel warned: "Seven years after the collapse, we find ourselves . . . in severe danger of sliding back into an extreme legal positivism [*Gesetzespositivismus*]."[40]

These differing judgments regarding the duration of the postwar natural law renaissance may be explained by the differing sources used to support the two arguments. Whereas Würtenberger's thesis is supported by a wealth of monographs and essays on the subject of natural law and legal positivism published in this period, Welzel's statement referred to a decision by the Oberlandesgericht (Superior District Court) Hamburg and to a decree of the British military government, both of which asserted the validity of a law even when it contradicted supra-legal principles.[41] Even the Bundesgerichtshof decision of 1954 regarding *Verlobten-Kuppelei*, which declared sexual intercourse between adults who were engaged to be indecent, raises doubts about the long-term effects of the renaissance of natural law. [42] For although the ruling's natural law argumentation appears to support Würtenberger's position, the decision met with massive criticism among professors of criminal law; only the Catholic Karl Peters praised the decision.[43]

"Purging" Criminal Law of Nazi Provisions or Comprehensive Reform?

Parallel to the natural law debate, the immediate postwar period faced the issue of removing the specifically National Socialist influences and formulations in criminal law. The issues involved ranged from the removal of specific Nazi terms such as *gesundes Volksempfinden* (healthy popular sentiment)[44] and the repeal of clearly National Socialist penal laws such as those regarding *Rassenschande* (race defilement) to the removal of newly introduced penal sanctions such as castration[45] and some highly controversial subjects. The latter included the question of whether the 1935 changes made to the penal code's article 175, which aggravated the prosecution and punishment of male homosexuality, were National Socialist in nature or well within the scope of similar pre-1933 legislation.[46]

The initial legal basis for changes of the penal code was provided by the laws issued by the Allied Control Council and by the decrees of the military governments in the individual zones of occupation.[47] The basic principles for this process had been laid down by the Potsdam Conference, which had decreed "that the legal system shall be purified in accordance with the basic principles of democracy, equality before the law, and equal rights for all citizens, without regard to race, nationality, or religion."[48] Implementing this decision, the military governments restricted the imposition of the death penalty and made major changes in the penal code in several comprehensive laws.[49] In West Germany, this process continued with the permanent repeal of the death penalty in the Grundgesetz (Basic Law) and further far-reaching modifications of the criminal law in a series of laws amending the criminal code, the so-called *Strafrechtsänderungsgesetze (StrÄG)*, starting in 1951. These laws, however, were not limited to purging the penal code of Nazi elements. Through new definitions of political offenses (1. StrÄG of 30 August 1951) the new laws already reflected the influence of the Cold War, and by introducing suspended sentences on probation (3. StrÄG of 4 August 1953), they embarked on new paths in penal policy.[50]

Given the numerous attempts at penal reform from the Kaiserreich through the Nazi era and the considerable number of changes to the penal code that were needed in the postwar period, the question arises of why a fundamental reform of criminal law was not attempted early on after the war. There were, however, good arguments against such an approach, including the division of the country into different zones of occupation, the lack of a sovereign lawmaker, as well as the chaotic economic and social conditions of the postwar years. In 1946, criminal law professor Eberhard Schmidt regarded the "revision of the penal system" as "irrefutably necessary," but doubted whether this could be realized at that time:

Here we see quite clearly that a penal reform that strives for justice and effectiveness in penal policy requires orderly state, social, and moral conditions. . . . Only when we emerge from the current chaos, when we live in orderly social conditions, and when, last but not least, the individual is given back his moral center [*sittliche Selbstbestimmung*], and a fundamental recognition of human dignity and human rights has finally taken place, can we make an attempt at a just and rational penal reform with any hope of success.[51]

Especially Germany's division into zones of occupation and their later transformation into two states appeared to be detrimental to a fundamental penal reform. Richard Lange, one of the first professors of criminal law to address the issue of penal reform after 1945, formulated this clearly in 1949: "In the interest of the unity of the Reich, one will certainly refrain from intervening in the criminal code. Our present situation does not call for comprehensive legislation in this area."[52] Despite Lange's rejection of a comprehensive reform, he was not satisfied with the status quo and did not content himself with simply purging the criminal code of Nazi influences. In his revision of the criminal code for Thuringia in 1945, he had called for major changes by introducing "indefinite sentencing" for "dangerous habitual offenders" instead of increased penalties or preventive detention.[53] By changing the order of the "Maßregeln zur Sicherung und Besserung" (Measures for Prevention and Correction) of the 1933 Law on Habitual Criminals to "Maßregeln der Besserung und Sicherung," he sought to give the idea of rehabilitation priority over the protection of society.[54]

The legal academics who viewed the chances of fundamental penal reform with skepticism in the postwar years had one dissenter, Karl Peters. Already in 1947, Peters anticipated that work on reforms would soon begin and called for the formulation of Catholic interests for this project: "It is our task to grapple with the numerous problems early enough so that we can make our contribution to the revision of criminal law when the time comes."[55]

The Situation of the Criminal Law Professors after 1945

The question of why only a few professors of criminal law tackled the issue of a comprehensive reform of criminal law in the immediate postwar years requires an examination of their circumstances of work and life, a classic approach in the sociology of knowledge. In 1946 Eberhard Schmidt had spoken of "orderly social circumstances" and the overcoming of the "present chaos" as preconditions for taking up the project of reforming the penal code. The circumstances of the professors, by contrast, were characterized by uncertainties in many respects, in some cases into the 1950s. Leaving aside the precarious socioeconomic conditions of the postwar era (regarding food and housing), which were shared by the majority of the population,[56] I will focus on the specific situation of the legal academics regarding their opportunities and conditions of work. University professors are members of an extremely specialized profession who can practice their profession only in a few places. In 1937, these were the twenty-three universities in the territory of the old Reich, as well as the German University in Prague, to which after 1938 the three Austrian universities in Graz, Innsbruck, and Vienna were added. As a result of Nazi occupations, the universities in Posen and Strasbourg also fell under German authority, so that the "German University Guide" of 1941 counted a total of twenty-nine universities with law faculties.[57]

After 1945 the number of work opportunities was drastically reduced.[58] Prague, Breslau, Königsberg, Posen, and Strasbourg returned to the formerly occupied countries or ended up as part of other nations in the wake of the reorganization of Europe. In Austria, the German university teachers had to vacate their positions. In the territory occupied by the Soviets (SBZ) and the later German Democratic Republic (GDR), the law faculties in Greifswald [59] and Rostock[60] were closed, and many law professors from the other universities emigrated to the western zones. All in all, the universities in the western zones of occupation absorbed nearly all of the professors of criminal law from the rest of the universities listed in 1941. These included the universities of East Berlin, Greifswald,

Halle, Jena, Leipzig, and Rostock; the Austrian universities of Graz, Innsbruck, and Vienna; and the universities of Königsberg, Breslau, Posen, Strasbourg, and the German University in Prague.

For professors of criminal law, this meant that the number of potential employers was reduced from twenty-nine to initially fourteen.[61] Through the founding of new universities, the University of Mainz in 1946 and the Free University of Berlin in 1948, the number of universities in West Germany and West Berlin increased to a total of sixteen.[62] German university professors also taught at the University of Saarbrücken, founded in 1948, which until the incorporation of the Saar into the Federal Republic in 1957 was situated on French territory.

Most of the universities in the three western zones of occupation were affected by war damage.[63] Only the universities of Heidelberg[64] and Tübingen[65] made it through the war nearly unscathed; the universities in Erlangen[66] and Göttingen suffered only minor damage. In the last months of the war and the immediate postwar period, the University of Göttingen became the gathering place for professors from the eastern universities,[67] while Strasbourg University and the law, political science, and economics faculties from Freiburg and Heidelberg were moved to Tübingen.[68] All other universities had suffered severe damage.[69] Despite the damage and the cuts in personnel, the universities returned to teaching relatively quickly, some as soon as the Fall of 1945.[70]

But another factor added to the uncertainty of professors: denazification. The military defeat of Nazi Germany and the division of the country into four zones of occupation resulted in denazification procedures that obliged university teachers to undergo individual examinations of their past during the Third Reich. Nearly all professors had to submit to this scrutiny of their political and academic careers during National Socialism. The guidelines for these procedures, however, showed significant differences between the occupation zones;[71] moreover, they varied from university to university within the same zone, and, in fact, depended largely on the local military government and even the individual university officer (*Universitätsoffizier*).[72] In general, it can be said that the purges of the university teaching corps were most radical in the Soviet zone of occupation, followed by those in the American zone. In the British and the French zones, the approach of the occupation authorities was more moderate and more strongly shaped by pragmatic considerations.[73]

For one criminal law professor, Karl Siegert, the end of the Nazi regime spelled the end of his career.[74] For the majority of the professors of criminal law, however, denazification meant only a short interruption in their career. While many could return to their positions after a few months, for others the denazification procedure lasted between one and three years. For professors like Edmund Mezger (Munich) and Gotthold Bohne (Cologne), denazification brought only relatively short interruptions of their university teaching; Mezger, for example, was reinstated in 1948. Hamburg criminal law professor Rudolf

Sieverts was detained by the British occupation authority in 1945,[75] but soon returned to his position. A few professors had to wait longer until they were able to return to the universities in the wake of the so-called "131-er" Law of April 1951, which facilitated the reinstatement of former civil servants: among these were Georg Dahm and Friedrich Schaffstein (both of whom had been militant National Socialists from the very beginning of the Third Reich), as well as Heinrich Henkel and Hans-Jürgen Bruns.[76]

Other professors, such as Thomas Würtenberger, changed universities when their denazification did not go well for them; Würtenberger moved from Erlangen to Mainz.[77] These professors exploited the varying intensity with which the occupying powers pursued denazification. Whereas the Americans, in whose zone Erlangen was located, carried out the purges with great seriousness, the French were more lenient. Würtenberger was not the only one to find a haven in the French zone of occupation after 1945; Ulrich Stock, who was dismissed from his Marburg post in 1945, joined the Saarbrücken faculty in 1948.[78]

If one looks at specific universities and the biographies of individual professors, it becomes clear that denazification certainly had a share in producing discontinuities in university faculties. For the early postwar period, the high fluctuation of this group is particularly apparent. Their lives, like those of the population as a whole, were characterized by a high degree of mobility.[79] Only a few biographies show no change of university in the immediate postwar years. And in contrast to "normal" times, these moves to a different university were not motivated by offers of a famous university chair or a prestigious university.[80] Such career moves become apparent again only in the mid-1950s at the earliest, when, to take Thomas Würtenberger as an example, he left his professorship in Mainz to take up a university chair in Freiburg, which he retained for the next eighteen years until he was granted emeritus status.[81]

The tight employment market for law professors was somewhat improved by the establishment of new universities, retirements, and the dismissal or suspension of a number of professors in the denazification process. We should also note that the number of law professors had declined in the Nazi era, and that in the last years of the war law faculties had further contracted as professors were drafted into military service, died, or became prisoners of war. After the war, there was therefore increased demand for law professors, especially at the universities in the western zones.

Nevertheless, from the perspective of the criminal law professors, the postwar years were a time of extreme uncertainty and high mobility under difficult conditions. Professors who arrived in the western zones of occupation from universities that ended up in the Soviet zone or fell to other states in the wake of territorial reorganization could not usually hope for a seamless continuation of their careers. To be sure, Eberhard Schmidt, who left Leipzig, immediately received a professorship in Göttingen because the dismissal of Karl Siegert left one of the two chairs in criminal law vacant.[82] But Schmidt lived in rather makeshift conditions in Göttingen, while his family remained in the Soviet zone.[83] His colleague Paul Bockelmann, formerly a full professor in Königsberg, had to be content with adjunct teaching in Göttingen from 1946 to 1949, until he was appointed to a full professorship there after Eberhard Schmidt's move to Heidelberg.[84] A similar trajectory was shared by Friedrich Schaffstein, who had much greater difficulties with the denazification process (for good reason) and therefore did not get an adjunct appointment at Göttingen until 1952; within two years, however, he succeeded Hans Welzel as full professor after Welzel had moved to Bonn.[85]

Although university professors were certainly no worse off than the rest of the population in terms of their living and working conditions, postwar conditions were subjectively experienced as particularly difficult by this highly privileged social group, most of whom, certainly among the law professors, had been born into the propertied and educated middle classes. These social-psychological circumstances were, of course, not conducive to a return to penal reform debates. The top priorities for most law professors, aside from surviving the immediate postwar period, were the continuation of their careers, the restoration of their former workplaces, the replacement of the law libraries and teaching materials, and the building of new university structures.

Denazification and the control exercised by the occupying powers also led to a depoliticization of university professors in the early postwar years. Especially for jurists the early postwar motto was: "Whatever you do, don't stand out!" Concerned about uncertain career prospects, handicapped by denazification proceedings, and limited by precarious institutional settings, most did not consider it advisable to attract attention through bold pronouncements on fundamental policy matters such as the shaping of the future criminal law. Those who did so were usually among those who were not compromised by association with the Nazi regime (at least in the postwar judgment of their colleagues), such as Richard Lange and Eberhard Schmidt, or convinced democrats who had passed through the Nazi period completely untainted, such as Gustav Radbruch. Despite these exceptions, the work of criminal law professors after 1945 was generally characterized by a retreat from politics and a turn to "pure" scholarship. This was true, of course, not only for the academic field of criminal law, but for professors and the universities in general. After years of the "political university" and politicized scholarship under the Nazi regime, this turn away from politics in the academic field of criminal law was reflected in a preference for issues of jurisprudence and legal philosophy over questions of penal policy. This escapism often took the form of philosophical meditations on the meaning of punishment, justice, or the gap between *ought* and *is*, all conducted in the academic style of humanist education. Work in this vein was complemented by legal-historical studies, through which politically compromised professors of criminal law reentered the academic conversation and sought to rehabilitate themselves; witness, for example, Friedrich

Schaffstein's 1952 study of Wilhelm von Humboldt and his 1954 study "The European Academic Field of Criminal Law [*europäische Strafrechtswissenschaft*] in the Age of Enlightenment."

Publication Venues and Professional Meetings After 1945

In addition to the changes in the working and living conditions after 1945, the resumption of a discourse of penal reform was hampered by the scarcity of professional journals and the initial lack of opportunities for meeting at conferences. There were few professional venues at which the isolation of the individual scholar could be overcome and opinions shaped. Moreover, the first postwar meetings of German jurists were held under the aegis of the occupying powers.

Thematically, the professional meetings of jurists after 1945—held mostly for the individual zones—primarily discussed problems of judicial practice and the organization of the courts.[86] After the Association of German Jurists (Deutscher Juristentag) assembled again in 1949, the first meeting of its criminal law section, in 1950, addressed offenses related to the protection of the state. Not until the following year was the revision of the criminal code placed on the Juristentag's agenda.[87] The professors of criminal law did not resume their own professional meetings until 1952.[88]

The most important media for the criminal law professors' reform discourse were the legal journals. After the end of the occupying powers' licensing policy, the number of legal periodicals increased in the late 1940s and the early 1950s. The *Süddeutsche Juristenzeitung* (*SJZ*) and the *Deutsche Rechts-Zeitschrift* (*DRZ*),[89] licensed in 1946 for the American and French zones, respectively, fused in 1951 to become the *Juristen-Zeitung* (*JZ*).[90] In the same year, the venerable *Zeitschrift für die gesamte Strafrechtswissenschaft* (*ZStW*), founded by Franz von Liszt in 1881, began appearing again. *Goltdammer's Archiv für Strafrecht* (*GA*) appeared again in 1953.[91] The *Neue Juristische Wochenschrift* (*NJW*) and the *Monatsschrift für Deutsches Recht* (*MDR*)[92] had been on the market since 1947. The *Juristische Rundschau* (*JR*) also began publication in 1947, and the *Deutsche Richterzeitung* (*DRiZ*) since 1949. The *Monatsschrift für Kriminologie und Strafrechtsreform* (*MschrKrim*), whose changing name reflected the shifting priorities of criminological thought—from 1904 to 1936 it was titled *Monatsschrift für Kriminalpsychologie und Strafrechtsreform*, from 1936 to 1945 *Monatsschrift für Kriminalbiologie und Strafrechtsreform*—resumed publication in 1951; *Kriminalistik* resumed publication already in 1946, and the *Archiv für Kriminologie* in 1955.[93] The *Zeitschrift für Strafvollzug*, a newly created periodical that did not pick up the tradition of the *Blätter für Gefängniskunde*,[94] appeared for the first time in 1950.

Criminal law professors published mainly in the *Zeitschrift für die gesamte Strafrechtswissenschaft*, which always printed the papers presented at their annual meetings, in *Goltdammer's Archiv*, the *Juristen-Zeitung*, and the *Neue Juristische Wochenschrift*. Occasionally, articles on criminal law appeared in the *Juristische Rundschau*, the *Monatsschrift für Deutsches Recht*, and the *Deutsche Richterzeitung*. The *Zeitschrift für Strafvollzug* and the *Monatsschrift für Kriminologie und Strafrechtsreform* were specialized publications that published the work of criminal law professors interested in prison reform (*Zeitschrift für Strafvollzug*) or engaged with criminological research (*Monatsschrift*).[95] Essays or short contributions also appeared in general-interest magazines or church-affiliated publications such as the Catholic *Caritas* or the Protestant *Radius*.

Who published in which journal had to do with the composition of editorial boards or agreements to serve as a regular contributor for a certain journal. In 1955, for example, almost all of the criminal law professors who served on the official Commission on Criminal Law were members of the editorial board of the *Zeitschrift für die gesamte Strafrechtswissenschaft*: Paul Bockelmann, Wilhelm Gallas, Hans-Heinrich Jescheck, Richard Lange, Eberhard Schmidt, and Hans Welzel all served on both capacities; only commission members Rudolf Sieverts and Edmund Mezger were missing from the editorial board. Sieverts served as co-editor of the *Monatsschrift für Kriminologie und Strafrechtsreform*, and Mezger headed the reconstituted Kriminalbiologische Gesellschaft (Criminal-Biological Society.)[96] In addition to the German periodicals, German legal academics also used the journals of other German-speaking countries for their publications. In Austria, these consisted of the *Österreichische Juristenzeitung* and the *Juristische Blätter*. In Switzerland, the most important was the *Schweizerische Zeitschrift für Strafrecht*, which in the Nazi era had given emigrated German law professors Gustav Radbruch and Wolfgang Mittermaier the opportunity to publish.

The *Monatsschrift für Kriminologie und Strafrechtsreform*, the only journal whose title included the words "penal reform," was neither a preferred forum for professors of criminal law, nor were its articles primarily focused on penal reform. During the 1950s, the *Monatsschrift* featured only a handful essays by professors of criminal law. Even Rudolf Sieverts, who co-edited the journal together with Hans Gruhle, professor for psychiatry in Bonn, published only one article and an obituary (1959) there. Of the fifty articles published in the *Monatsschrift* from 1954 to 1957 only 10 percent were written by professors of criminal law; a further 16 percent by other jurists (including judges and junior scholars); and 18 percent by prison psychologists, prison clerics, and other prison staff. The largest share, 56 percent, was comprised of contributions from medical doctors, especially psychiatrists (twenty-eight articles).[97] Only a few of the contributions addressed the issue of penal reform; the overwhelming majority of articles were devoted to issues of criminology and criminal psychology, the prison system, and juvenile justice. This analysis therefore confirms how little interest criminal law professors showed in criminological issues compared to their interest in jurisprudence and legal philosophy.

The Participants in the Postwar Discourse on Penal Reform

From the 1880s through the Nazi regime, penal reform had been a central topic for German professors of criminal law. Although one might have thought that, after the initial restrictions of the postwar era had passed, criminal law professors would have been eager to resume the debate in the 1950s, in fact very few did so. Of the about thirty-five professors of criminal law who taught at West German universities (or continued to publish as emeriti), only a tiny minority published articles that addressed central issues of penal reform. If the others made any contributions at all, they only addressed partial aspects of reform.[98] The minority of professors who took an active part in the reform discourse included some members of the official Commission on Criminal Law which began its work in 1954 (Hans-Heinrich Jescheck, Richard Lange, Eberhard Schmidt), but also Karl Peters, whose contributions appeared in legal journals as well as publications associated with the Catholic Church, and Thomas Würtenberger, whose articles often focused on the system of penal sanctions and the prison system. Paul Bockelmann, Karl Alfred Hall, Wilhelm Sauer, and Walter Sax also made some contributions; Karl Engisch and Wilhelm Gallas published the reports they prepared for the Commission on Criminal Law.

Those professors of criminal law who experienced a longer interruption in their careers as a result of denazification made almost no contributions regarding penal reform. Ulrich Stock published a single essay on reform in 1952,[99] and Hans-Jürgen Bruns commented on suspended sentencing in 1956 and on "measures of correction" in 1959.[100] Georg Dahm, a prominent voice for an explicitly National-Socialist approach to penal reform during the Third Reich, did not publish anything on penal reform after the war, whereas his comrade-in-arms Friedrich Schaffstein wrote primarily on juvenile justice after the war; not until 1963 did Schaffstein publish a piece on penal reform.[101] Karl Siegert, the only criminal law professor not to receive a professorship after 1945, published nothing on penal reform; neither did Heinrich Henkel or Erich Schwinge.

The enumeration of professors with a significant Nazi past who kept out of the postwar penal reform debate should not give the impression that those who actively participated in the debate after the war had escaped the Nazi period politically untainted. Rather, the Nazi pasts of those who participated in the debate were characterized by two traits: first, they had not been among the regime's favorites who were appointed to professorships in 1933–1934; second, their behavior during the Third Reich had been at least somewhat ambivalent— in other words, political conformity in one area (for example, university politics) had coexisted with nonconformist behavior in another area (such as publications or private contacts with expelled colleagues).

The discussions in the academic field of criminal law did not, of course, center exclusively on penal reform. Professors of criminal law commented on amendments to the penal code and published monographs and articles on general and specialized topics in criminal law, textbooks, and commentaries on judicial decisions. In the area of criminal jurisprudence, the 1950s and 1960s were dominated by the debate about the "finale Handlungslehre" formulated by Hans Welzel, which offered a new approach to analyzing and judging the criminal act and the degree of guilt associated with it.[102] The discussion regarding natural law versus legal positivism was another area of emphasis.

The Penal Reform Debate: Retribution versus Individualized Prevention

The criminal law professors' discourse on penal reform was characterized by two competing positions. The first position saw the primary purpose of criminal justice in retribution (*Vergeltung*), to which all other functions of punishment were subordinated. The opposing position stressed *Spezialprävention*, individualized behavioral prevention, that is, preventing the individual perpetrator from offending again in the future. This position focused on rehabilitation, the system of penal sanctions, and the prison system. To be sure, the developments examined in this chapter so far—the post-1945 debate on natural law, the turn toward issues of legal philosophy, and the depoliticization of the university teachers—were all more suitable to defending the first position. Nevertheless, it should be noted that at least initially, the postwar penal reform discourse was fairly open regarding the future direction of reform.

The academic community's uncertainty about the future direction of criminal law reform can be illustrated by a lecture on the system of penal sanctions delivered by Karl Alfred Hall, professor of criminal law at Marburg, at the 1952 meeting of criminal law professors. In it Hall posed a number of central questions, including:[103] Should criminal law place more emphasis on retribution, general deterrence, or individualized behavioral prevention? How should the system of penal sanctions be reformed? Should the *Zuchthausstrafe* (imprisonment with hard labor) be retained as a distinct sanction, or should it be merged with the regular prison sentence (*Gefängnisstrafe*) in a unified prison sentence? How should the problem of short-term punishments be addressed in the future? Hall's answers to these questions were contradictory and logically inconsistent, as though he sought to keep open as many options as possible. The distinction between *Zuchthaus* and *Gefängnis*, for instance, was strongly criticized by proponents of individualized behavioral prevention because they regarded the *Zuchthausstrafe* as stigmatizing and hence hostile to rehabilitation.[104] But Hall's position on this issue was contradictory: even though he argued that the administration of both kinds of prison sentences should be unified, he also insisted that the distinction between *Zuchthaus* and *Gefängnis* should be legally maintained "for reasons of general deterrence."[105]

Regarding short-term prison sentences, Hall suggested setting three months as a minimum.[106] Prison terms under three months, he argued, should be replaced by fines, suspended sentences with probation (*Strafaussetzung zur Bewährung*), or special penalties such as suspending a driver's license or banning someone from a profession.[107] But although the replacement of short prison terms by alternative sanctions was a key demand of those who championed *Spezialprävention*, Hall's argumentation was mainly retributivist:

> Adult penal law is focused on the criminal offense [*Tatstrafrecht*]. Punishment is first and foremost retribution [*Vergeltung*], atonement [*Sühne*]. Justice takes priority over purposiveness [*Zweckmäßigkeit*]. . . . A purpose is externally ascribed to punishment. The purposes of deterrence, rehabilitation, and prevention can be achieved or not achieved. They do not affect the essence [*Wesen*] of punishment. . . . From the perspective of the legal community the punishment is retribution. From the perspective of the perpetrator the punishment is atonement.[108]

Even in his legitimation of probationary sentences, Hall referred to the retributivist idea of atonement (*Sühne*). "Atonement through probation" was the motto.[109] "The perpetrator atones for his deed by proving himself on the front of life."[110] Failure to prove himself did not necessarily mean committing another crime: "It suffices, for example, if he continues to be refractory [*renitent*], if he violates the ban on visits to the tavern, seeks out bad company, and so on."[111] Here, the metaphysical idea of retribution was joined by an agenda of regulating behavior that was not limited to legal violations but sought to impose discipline. The proposed bans on tavern visits and "bad company" were indicative of anachronistic ideas about the "dangerous classes." Thus even though the content of Hall's proposals seemed to point in the direction of individualized behavioral prevention, the terminology he used showed his proximity to retributivism. In sum, his 1952 lecture marked the beginning of the retributivist discourse of penal reform that would characterize the official Commission on Criminal Law (*Große Strafrechtskommission*) convened in 1954.[112]

The general discourse on penal reform as well as the official Commission on Criminal Law were dominated by the proponents of retributive justice. This assessment is supported not only by the predominance of retributivist publications, but also by the lack of opposition from the silent majority of criminal law professors who did not take part in the reform discourse. Retributive justice was based on the idea of nondeterminism, in other words, the notion of an individual free will that is not determined by genetics, environment, or upbringing. Central concepts for this position were justice, retribution, atonement, and value system (*Wertordnung*). Its proponents drew connections to the values of freedom and human dignity enshrined in the West German Basic Law (*Grundgesetz*) and to the rule of law (*Rechtsstaatsidee*).

One of the most active proponents of retributivism in the postwar penal reform debate was Richard Lange, professor of criminal law in Cologne, who was well positioned to influence the debate through his dual role as a member of the official Commission on Criminal Law and editor-in-chief (*Schriftleiter*) of Germany's premier criminal law journal, the *Zeitschrift für die gesamte Strafrechtswissenschaft*, from 1953 to 1968. Lange claimed that the ideal of retributive justice could be justified empirically, based on criminological studies, "historical experiences," and the reception of work in other disciplines such as psychology.[113] His reception of psychological research was, however, highly selective: Lange did not draw on the Freudian positions that would have contradicted his arguments, but on the Austrian psychologist Viktor Frankl, whose works, he argued, proved the indeterminate nature of man. Despite these limitations, Lange demonstrated a certain openness to other disciplines and to criminological research, which was highly unusual among his colleagues.

The arguments of the proponents of the retribution paradigm were characterized by a tendency to appeal to higher philosophical principles and to issue categorical statements, for example, regarding anthropological definitions of the "image of man" (*Menschenbild*) that supposedly lay at the root of criminal justice and penal reform. By the early 1960s, at least three studies by criminal law professors had appeared that were exclusively devoted to the image of man, not including numerous considerations of this issue in other essays and monographs.[114] In lectures, too, "the image of man and penal reform" was a popular subject, as demonstrated by a lecture with this title that Richard Lange delivered to the Society of Hamburg Jurists (Gesellschaft Hamburger Juristen) in 1962.[115] The image of man that was expounded in these lectures and publications was explicitly based on the West German constitution, the Grundgesetz (Basic Law). The Basic Law, it was argued, saw man as free and self-determined; therefore, it was deduced, man possessed free will and was morally and legally responsible for his actions; there was no room for determinism. For the retributivists, the Basic Law's injunction to respect and protect "human dignity" was evidence that the Basic Law rejected a criminal justice system based on either *Spezialprävention* or *Generalprevention*. Individual preventive measures such as rehabilitation, correctional education, and psychiatric treatment were rejected as excessive interventions in the life of the individual, while general deterrence was rejected as reducing the individual to a mere object in the deterrence of the general public. Characteristically, Hans-Heinrich Jescheck ended his essay on the "image of man and penal reform" with a reference to Hegel:

> The image of man of our time [must] be determined by the great postulates of freedom and personal dignity, which form the supporting pillars of our state. In criminal law,

the notion of [human] freedom must be understood in the sense that man, despite determining factors like drives, body-type, mental state, hereditary traits, and environment, is a being founded on individual responsibility. . . . Therefore punishment means that man is "held responsible" for his rebellion against a system of values that he, too, desires; and in this sense, Hegel's dictum that through punishment "the criminal is honored as a rational being" remains valid. [116]

The retributivist contributions to the penal reform discourse were notable for their focus on ethical-philosophical questions, especially the "meaning" (*Sinn*) and "essence" (*Wesen*) of punishment and the "system of values" (*Wertordnung*) on which criminal law was supposed to rest. As Jescheck wrote: "Our time must give itself laws that reflect its own best nature in order to show the rest of the world its true purpose [*Bestimmung*]. . . . The spiritual situation of our time must be mastered through legislative achievements."[117]

Such philosophically inclined texts obscured the political content of the positions; more generally, the contributions of retributivist criminal law professors to the penal reform debate were characterized by an avoidance of political references. This reflected the silence with which National Socialism was being treated in many areas of social and intellectual life. Although National Socialism was omnipresent, it was rarely referred to explicitly. Approaches favoring individual behavorial prevention (*Spezialprävention*) were denounced with vague references to Nazi criminal law and the omnipotent intervention of the Nazi state in the life of the individual citizen. This line of argument linked *Spezialprävention* and *Zweckstrafe* (a utilitarian, as opposed to retributive, conception to punishment) to a totalitarian criminal justice system that was hostile to freedom, as Wilhelm Gallas formulated it in the Commission on Criminal Law:

> The *Zweckgedanke* [i.e., the notion that punishment should serve a preventive purpose] contains something hostile to freedom. To be sure, often, as in Nazi criminal law, the ideas of atonement and retribution [*Sühne und Vergeltung*] have been used to veil the *Zweckgedanke*. . . . The concern that *das reine Zweckdenken* can lead to totalitarian criminal justice forces us to hold fast to the notion of the *Schuldstrafe* [i.e., retributive punishment based on guilt].[118]

This strategy of discrediting the position that punishment primarily ought to serve the purpose of individualized behavioral prevention (rather than retributive justice)—which was the position of Franz von Liszt and the "modern school of criminal law" that dominated the penal reform movement in the Kaiserreich and the Weimar Republic—by associating it with Nazism and totalitarianism was characteristic of other retributivists as well. Thus, during the deliberations of the Commission on Criminal Law, Edmund Mezger justified his support for retributive justice by claiming that the "*Zweckstrafe* leads to a totalitarian criminal law."[119] These arguments allowed the commission to justify both the retention of the highly stigmatizing *Zuchthausstrafe* (imprisonment with hard labor) and the retention of short-term prison sentences (as opposed to alternative sanctions).

Before the official Commission on Criminal Law made these decisions, the direction that postwar penal reform would take had still been an open question. In a 1955 lecture in Vienna, Richard Lange contrasted the Commission's recent decisions with international developments and the penal reform trajectory of the Weimar Republic, concluding that the Commission had taken a "surprising" direction:

> It must appear surprising that already in the first meetings to lay the foundations of its work, the German commission on criminal law has taken a different, almost opposite approach. The new direction is characterized by a conscious return to a commitment to material justice. . . . The commission has quite consciously tried to establish a firm structure of values between the absolute and the relative purposes and meanings of punishment.[120]

Despite holding on to a retributive model of criminal justice, nearly all professors of criminal law who tended in this direction—and this was the overwhelming majority—tried to integrate some elements of individualized prevention into the criminal law. More far-reaching ideas for reform, however, were blocked by the fundamental decision in favor of a retributive system of criminal justice. In the draft code produced by the official Commission on Criminal Law between 1954 and 1959, the retributivists were able to impose their notions on the system of penal sanctions. Although they agreed, for example, to limit the *Zuchthausstrafe* to serious crimes, they prevented its elimination, arguing that the "social-ethical condemnation," which differed for criminal acts of varying gravity, had to be reflected in different types of punishment. Similarly, even though short-term prison sentences were viewed as problematic, nothing was done aside from a name change: prison terms of one week to one month were going to be called *Strafhaft* rather than *Gefängnisstrafen*. The minimum term for *Zuchthausstrafen* should be two years. Suspended sentences with probation were to be an option for prison sentences up to nine months' duration.[121] Fines should be imposed along the lines of the Scandinavian system of *dagsböter*, fines levied in proportion to the offender's daily wages and ability to pay.[122]

The criminal law professors' reluctance to revise the system of penal sanctions thoroughly as well as their divergence from international developments can be explained by their endorsement of retributive justice (and, to some extent, general deterrence) rather than individualized prevention as the primary purpose of criminal justice. This should not, however, leave the impression that the discourse of the retributivists was entirely homogeneous. Even professors of criminal law who endorsed the idea of retribution could oppose the *Zuchthausstrafe* and short-term prison sentences, as Hans-Heinrich Jescheck and Paul Bockelmann, both members of the Commission on Criminal Law, did.[123] According to Jescheck, making punishments match an offender's guilt by no means required that every punishment must be executed (rather than suspended).[124]

Such distinctions, however, faded before the fundamental decision in favor of a criminal justice system based on retribution. This point was driven home by critics such as Thomas Würtenberger, who began the published version of his 1955 inaugural lecture, "The Intellectual Situation of German Academic Criminal Law,"[125] with an attack on the current state of criminal law at the law faculties:

> Behind the mask of tough adherence to a criminal law based on guilt and retribution, which is certainly justified at its core, a deplorable "doctrinarianism" has spread. All this leads to the result that a true breakthrough to a social criminal justice system [*soziale Strafrechtsordnung*] has eluded German academic criminal law [*Strafrechtswissenschaft*]. Opinions regarding the meaning and purpose of punishment are—not least in the effort to achieve a reform of criminal law—mostly characterized by a fear of genuine penal policy decisions. This is most noticeable in a pronounced mistrust of individualization and *Spezialprävention* as key penal policy concepts of our time.[126]

Those professors of criminal law who, like Würtenberger, wished to reform the criminal justice system in the direction of individualized prevention were in the minority. Their reform agenda had no place for the *Zuchthausstrafe* or for short-term prison sentences. Instead, they called for replacing short prison terms with other sanctions such as fines, alternative punishments such as the suspension of driver's licenses, or suspended sentence with probation. Moreover, the prison system (*Strafvollzug*) played an important role in their argumentation.[127] After the decisions of the Commission on Criminal Law had brought a victory for retributive justice, some of the proponents of individualized prevention, such as Eberhard Schmidt, sought to shift priority from the reform of criminal law to a reform of the prison system. "Would it not be perhaps more important to use all of the energy for reform and all the means available to achieve a thorough reform of our prison system [*Strafvollzug*]?" he asked in 1957[128] and criticized the retributivists' fixation on jurisprudence and theory:

> In my view, the revival of the idea of retribution is to blame for the fact that the fundamental conceptions of punishment, its purpose, and sentencing have been derived entirely from the realm of theory, and that the hard realities that actually determine the fate of those convicted in the prison system remain completely unexamined.[129]

It is also quite possible that Schmidt's shift from the subject of criminal law reform to the subject of prison reform was primarily strategic because he had been unable to prevail against the proponents of retributive justice in the first arena. Schmidt placed himself within the tradition of the "modern school of criminal law" of Franz von Liszt, with whom he had studied, whereas the retributivists oriented themselves toward Kant and Hegel—at least partly in an effort to overcome the stain of the Nazi past through recourse to leading lights of German philosophy.[130]

By contrast, Eberhard Schmidt, Rudolf Sieverts, and others embraced a more pragmatic approach and focused on the so-called hard realities of the prison system. While the discourse of the retributivists was primarily normative, based on a formulaic equivalence of offense and punishment, the discourse of those favoring individualized prevention was characterized by frequent references to the actual administration of punishment. Thus it should come as no surprise that most of the criminal law professors who championed individualized prevention were active participants in the Working Group for the Reform of the Prison System (*Arbeitsgemeinschaft für die Reform des Strafvollzugs*). The *Arbeitsgemeinschaft*, founded in the 1923,[131] met again for the first time after the war in 1948. It included practitioners who worked in the prison system or dealt with prison matters in the bureaucracy as well as professors of criminal law who were interested in the prison system, often quite consciously continuing discussions of the Weimar years.[132] Its inner circle was composed of Eberhard Schmidt (chairman) and Rudolf Sieverts (secretary), both also members of the Commission on Criminal Law, as well as criminal law professors Wolfgang Mittermaier and Thomas Würtenberger.[133] The *Arbeitsgemeinschaft*'s first resolution in 1948 simply called for the implementation of an educational approach in the penal system, the training and hiring of prison personnel educated in *Sozialpädagogik*, and unified regulations for the penal system.[134] At its second meeting in 1950, the *Arbeitsgemeinschaft* supplemented these demands with calls to restrict the imposition of prison sentences and to abolish the distinction between *Zuchthaus* and *Gefängnis*. The group thus explicitly picked up where the Weimar reform movement had left off and established clear positions on key issues before the beginning of the later work on reform.[135]

Conclusion

What was the attraction of a retributivist conception of criminal justice for the majority of criminal law professors in the 1950s? The question can only be answered by reference to a complex of reasons ranging from psychological and social factors to individual preferences to the historical situation of the postwar period and the legacy of the Nazi past. Many of them have been suggested in the course of this chapter.

First, the sociologist Hans Braun has used the phrase "the pursuit of security" (*Streben nach Sicherheit*) to characterize the collective social-psychological state of German society in the 1950s.[136] If we compare the competing positions in the penal reform debate, the concept of retributive criminal justice undoubtedly conveyed a greater degree of security. First, existing criminal law was already oriented in this direction. Second, one could draw on the politically unproblematic "classical" era of German history around 1800 with its important figureheads Kant and Hegel. Third, retributivists could remain within the security of the "ivory tower" of ideas and philosophical meditations on the meaning and purpose of punishment without exposing themselves to the uncertainties of empiricism and a pragmatic penal policy, an orientation that also reflected the trend toward depoliticization and an apolitical academy.

Second, the inclination toward retributive criminal law was at least partially prepared by the renaissance of natural law. In the postwar era, natural law was important for coming to terms with and prosecuting Nazi injustice, but also pushed the penal reform discourse toward legal philosophy, that is, grounding criminal law on a metaphysical rather than a pragmatic foundation. As law professor Walter Sax put it in 1957: "Every legal policy must . . . transcend the narrow realm of utility to the state; that is, taking full consideration of the factual needs of community life, it must derive its fundamental aims from realms that lie beyond the state [*staatsjenseitigen Bereichen*]."[137]

Third, the expulsion of Jewish and left-wing professors of criminal law during the Nazi regime had severely weakened certain reform traditions. As the sociologist M. Rainer Lepsius wrote, "[T]he emigration is . . . more than the sum of persecuted individuals, it also represents traditions and ideas, academic paradigms and ways of looking at problems, artistic styles and programs."[138] The casualties of emigration included criminal law professors who had been active in the prison reform in the Weimar era (such as Max Grünhut) as well as some who were criminologically oriented (such as Hermann Mannheim). In the 1950s, German criminology was primarily the domain of psychiatrists, as our analysis of the *Monatsschrift für Kriminologie und Strafrechtsreform* demonstrated. For the proponents of a retributivist criminal law, criminological knowledge was not necessary because absolute theories of punishment derive from norms rather than empirical data. For the proponents of *Spezialprävention*, however, the lack of an interest in criminology among most criminal law professors was an additional handicap.

Fourth, on the few occasions when Nazi criminal justice was discussed after 1945, the majority of criminal law professors portrayed it as *Präventionsstrafrecht*, that is, a criminal justice system based on *Generalprävention* (general deterrence) and *Spezialprävention* (individualized prevention), rather than retribution; given the prominence of retributivist arguments and rhetoric in Nazi criminal justice, this was at the least a one-sided interpretation. Nevertheless, it resulted in placing postwar reform proposals that emphasized prevention under general suspicion of either running roughshod over the perpetrator in the service of general deterrence or, more importantly, going too far in intervening in the life of the individual perpetrator through individualized preventive measures.

Fifth, the proponents of retributive criminal law succeeded in linking their theory of punishment to the West German Basic Law. The Basic Law's concept of the rule of law and its image of man both offered openings for legitimating a retributivist moral foundation of criminal law.

Finally, the retributivist direction of penal reform was also determined by the Justice Ministry's selection of the members of the official Commission on Criminal Law. The views of potential members were relatively easily to identify through publications and personal contacts. The published proceedings of the commission demonstrate how frequently Eberhard Schmidt found himself defending a minority position against the retributivists. The decisions of the commission then sent a message to the larger community of criminal law professors.

Notes

Translated by Keith D. Alexander and Richard F. Wetzell.

1. See Richard F. Wetzell, "From Retributive Justice to Social Defense: Penal Reform in Fin-de-Siècle Germany," in *Germany at the Fin de Siècle: Culture, Politics, and Ideas*, Suzanne Marchand and David Lindenfeld, eds. (Baton Rouge, 2004), 59–77; Christian Müller, *Verbrechensbekämpfung im Anstaltsstaat: Psychiatrie, Kriminologie und Strafrechtsreform in Deutschland 1871–1933* (Göttingen, 2004), 125–169; Wetzell, *Inventing the Criminal: A History of German Criminology, 1880–1945* (Chapel Hill, 2000), 31–38; Monika Frommel, "Internationale Reformbewegung zwischen 1880 und 1920," *Erzählte Kriminalität: Zur Typologie und Funktion von narrativen Darstellungen in Strafrechtspflege, Publizistik und Literatur zwischen 1770 und 1920*, Jörg Schönert, ed. (Tübingen, 1991), 467–495; Eberhard Schmidt, *Einführung in die Geschichte der deutschen Strafrechtspflege*, 3rd ed. (Göttingen, 1983; orig. 1947), 394–399, 405–413.

2. On the 1871 German penal code (*Reichsstrafgesetzbuch*) and its origins, see Sylvia Kesper-Biermann, *Einheit und Recht: Strafgesetzgebung und Kriminalrechtsexperten in Deutschland vom Beginn des 19. Jahrhunderts bis zum Reichsstrafgesetzbuch 1871* (Frankfurt, 2009), 270–371; Werner Schubert and Thomas Vormbaum, eds., *Entstehung des Strafgesetzbuchs*, 2 vols. (Baden-Baden, 2002; Berlin, 2004); Werner Schubert, "Der Ausbau der Rechtseinheit unter dem Norddeutschen Bund: Zur Entstehung des Strafgesetzbuchs von 1870 unter besonderer Berücksichtigung des Strafensystems," in *Festschrift für Rudolf Gmür zum 70. Geburtstag, 28. Juli 1983*, Arno Buschmann et al., eds. (Bielefeld, 1983), 149–189; Schmidt, *Einführung*, 344; Karl Kroeschell, *Rechtsgeschichte Deutschlands im 20. Jahrhundert* (Göttingen, 1992), 32; Thomas Nipperdey, *Deutsche Geschichte 1866–1918*, vol. 2, *Machtstaat vor der Demokratie* (Munich, 1992), 184.

3. On changes in criminal law during the Kaiserreich and Weimar Republic, see Thomas Vormbaum, *Einführung in die moderne Strafrechtsgeschichte* (Berlin, 2009), 117–183, esp. 142–152, 163–169; Wolfgang Sellert and Hinrich Rüping, *Studien- und Quellenbuch zur Geschichte der deutschen Strafrechtspflege*, vol. 2, *Von der Aufklärung bis zur doppelten Staatsgründung* (Aalen, 1994), 107–122, 177–187; Thomas Vormbaum and Jürgen Welp, eds., *Das Strafgesetzbuch: Sammlung der Änderungsgesetze und Neubekanntmachungen*, vol. 1, *1870 bis 1953* (Baden-Baden, 2000).

4. Schmidt, *Einführung*, 399.

5. See Christine Dörner, *Erziehung durch Strafe: Die Geschichte des Jugendstrafvollzugs von 1871–1945* (Weinheim/Munich, 1991), 59–73; Frank Kebbedies, *Außer Kontrolle: Jugendkriminalpolitik in der NS-Zeit und der frühen Nachkriegszeit* (Essen, 2000), 69–73.

6. On the reform of fines, see Hans-Heinrich Jescheck, "Der Einfluß der IKV und der AIDP auf die internationale Entwicklung der modernen Kriminalpolitik. Festvortrag auf dem XII. Internationalen Strafrechtskongreß in Hamburg am 17. September 1979," *Zeitschrift für die gesamte Strafrechtswissenschaft* [herafter, *ZStW*] 92 (1980), 997–1020, esp. 1002.

7. Schmidt, *Einführung*, 401.

8. Hans-Heinrich Jescheck, *Lehrbuch des Strafrechts. Allgemeiner Teil* (Berlin, 1969), 69.

9. In general regarding the workhouse: Andrea Rudolph, *Die Kooperation von Strafrecht und Sozialhilferecht bei der Disziplinierung von Armen mittels Arbeit: Vom Arbeitshaus bis zur gemeinnützigen Arbeit* (Frankfurt am Main, 1995), 31ff.

10. On the 1933 law, see: Christian Müller, *Das Gewohnheitsverbrechergesetz vom 24. November 1933* (Baden-Baden, 1997). On the Allied invalidation of the law, see Matthias Etzel, *Die Aufhebung von nationalsozialistischen Gesetzen durch den Alliierten Kontrollrat 1945–1948* (Tübingen, 1992).

11. Jescheck, *Lehrbuch*, 50.

12. Schmidt, *Einführung*, 232; Arthur Kaufmann, "Problemgeschichte der Rechtsphilosophie," in *Einführung in Rechtsphilosophie und Rechtstheorie der Gegenwart,* ed. Arthur Kaufmann and Winfried Hassemer (Heidelberg, 1985), 23–123, esp. 61.

13. On Hegel, see Jens-Christian Müller-Tuckfeld, *Integrationsprävention: Studien zu einer Theorie der gesellschaftlichen Funktion des Strafrechts* (Frankfurt am Main, 1998), 281–287 and passim; on Kant see Wolfgang Schild, "Anmerkungen zur Straf- und Verbrechensphilosophie Immanuel Kants," in *Festschrift für Wolfgang Gitter zum 65. Geburtstag am 30. Mai 1995,* ed. Meinhard Heinze and Jochem Schmitt (Wiesbaden, 1995), 831–846, esp. 833 note 17.

14. See, for example, Franz von Liszt, *Lehrbuch des Deutschen Strafrechts* (Berlin, 1894), 39f.

15. Dieter Grimm, "Die 'Neue Rechtswissenschaft'—Über Funktion und Formation nationalsozialistischer Jurisprudenz," in Grimm, *Recht und Staat der bürgerlichen Gesellschaft* (Frankfurt am Main, 1987), 373–395, esp. 382.

16. This term was used in a unanimous declaration of the German Bundestag in 1985, Bundestags-Drucksache 10/2368, cited in Klaus Marxen, *Das Volk und sein Gerichtshof: Eine Studie zum nationalsozialistischen Volksgerichtshof* (Frankfurt am Main, 1994), 24.

17. Eberhard Schmidt, "Probleme staatlichen Strafens in der Gegenwart," *Süddeutsche Juristenzeitung* 1 (1946), 204–209, quote 205. Schmidt (1891–1977) was one of the last living students of Franz von Liszt, the Kaiserreich's leading penal reformer. He had received his first professorship in 1921 in Breslau. At the end of World War II he was a professor in Leipzig, but was immediately offered a professorship in Göttingen. In 1948 he moved to the University of Heidelberg, where he became emeritus in 1959. In 1948 he became chairman of the Frankfurt Committee for Economic Criminal Law (*Wirtschaftsstrafrecht*). In the 1950s he was a member of the official Commission on Criminal Law. On Eberhard Schmidt, see Karl Engisch, "Eberhard Schmidt," *Jahrbuch der Heidelberger Akademie der Wissenschaften* (1979), 80–83.

18. Dietrich Thränhardt, *Geschichte der Bundesrepublik Deutschland* (Frankfurt am Main, 1986), 42.

19. Richard Lange, "Strafrecht und Kultur," *Forum. Zeitschrift für das geistige Leben an den deutschen Hochschulen* 1 (1947), 10; Karl Peters, "Gerechtigkeit und Rechtssicherheit," *Die Kirche in der Welt* III. Lfg. 76 (1947–1948), 379–386; Hans Lüttger, "Beseitigung nationalsozialistischer Eingriffe in die Strafrechtspflege," *Geist und Tat: Monatsschrift für Recht, Freiheit und Kultur,* Hamburg, 2 (1947), 8, 28; Gustav Radbruch, "Die Erneuerung des Rechts," *Die Wandlung* 2 (1947), 8–16.

20. Herbert Blank, "Hinter dem Gitter . . . schmeckt der Honig bitter," *Nordwestdeutsche Hefte* 1 (1946), 9, 17–22; "Heutiger Strafvollzug," *Union-Pressedienst,* Hamburg (1948), 5–6; Ernst Schwaiger, "Eine deutsche Strafanstalt. Die Lebensbedingungen der Gefangenen," *Rheinischer Merkur,* 7 February 1948, 3–4; "Verhaftet . . . ," *Benjamin. Zeitschrift für junge Menschen,*

Hamburg 2 (1948), 4, 16–17; Heinz Scholl, "Strafvollzug reformbedürftig," *Begegnung. Zeitschrift für Kultur und Geistesleben* 4 (1949), 11–12.

21. On the origins of the *Deutsche Rechts-Zeitschrift*, see Karl S. Bader, "Walter Mallmann und die Gründung der 'Deutschen Rechts-Zeitschrift'," in *Festschrift für Walter Mallmann zum 70. Geburtstag*, Otto Triffterer and Friedrich von Zezschwitz, eds. (Baden-Baden, 1978), 17–31; as well as his journal entries: Karl Siegfried Bader, "Der Wiederaufbau. Tagebuch Juli 1945 bis Juni 1946" (with an introduction and comments by Ulrich Weber), in *Gelb-rot-gelbe Regierungsjahre. Badische Politik nach 1945: Gedenkschrift zum 100. Geburtstag Leo Wohlebs (1888–1955)*, Paul-Ludwig Weinacht, ed. (Sigmaringendorf, 1988), 33–88. Bader, later legal historian at the University of Zurich, participated in the founding of the *Deutsche Rechts-Zeitschrift* in his capacity as the Badenese Attorney General.

22. Gustav Radbruch (1878–1949) was among the most important German professors of criminal law in the twentieth century. During his short term as Social Democratic Minister of Justice he produced a draft penal code in 1922. A law professor in Heidelberg, he was dismissed by the Nazis in 1933, but got his professorship back in 1945 before becoming emeritus in 1948. On Radbruch, see Arthur Kaufmann, "Gustav Radbruch—Leben und Werk," in Gustav Radbruch, *Rechtsphilosophie I*, Arthur Kaufmann, ed. *Gustav Radbruch Gesamtausgabe* (GRGA), vol. 1 (Heidelberg, 1987), 7–88.

23. Gustav Radbruch, "Gesetzliches Unrecht und übergesetzliches Recht," *Süddeutsche Juristenzeitung* [hereafter, *SJZ*] 1 (1946), 5, 105–108 (107).

24. See Dieter Simon's analysis of legal positivism in the Nazi era in Dieter Simon, "Zäsuren im Rechtsdenken," in *Zäsuren nach 1945: Essays zur Periodisierung der deutschen Nachkriegsgeschichte*, Martin Broszat, ed. (Munich, 1990), 153–167, esp. 154. For an example of a very broad interpretation of the penal code, see a 1942 article by Richard Lange, who conceded that "a deed that does not make a German a sex offender cannot be used to qualify a Pole as a sex offender" but continued with the remark: "but in the case of [a Polish offender] the need for just retribution will more often require the death penalty." Richard Lange, "Täterschuld und Todesstrafe," *ZStW* 62 (1942), 175–232, quote 179. On the broad interpretation of the "Volksschädlingsverordnung" in the administration of justice see Helmut Kühn et al., "32 Strafurteile der Hamburger Justiz 1933–1934. Mit Erläuterungen zum juristischen, zeitgeschichtlichen und biographischen Hintergrund. Fall 25: Schwerer Diebstahl 1943," in *"Von Gewohnheitsverbrechern, Volksschädlingen und Asozialen. . . ." Hamburger Justizurteile im Nationalsozialismus*, Justizbehörde Hamburg, ed. (Hamburg, 1995), 310–329, esp. 321. Helmut Kramer reached a similar judgment regarding the Nazi administration of justice. He notes that in "zahlreiche[n] Entscheidungen . . . Richter dem nationalsozialistischen Gesetzgeber vorauseilten." Helmut Kramer, "Die Aufarbeitung des Faschismus durch die Nachkriegsjustiz in der Bundesrepublik Deutschland," in *Recht, Justiz und Faschismus—nach 1933 und heute*, Helmut D. Fangmann and Norman Paech, eds. (Cologne, 1984), 75–93, quote 85.

25. Simon, "Zäsuren," 154.

26. See Radbruch's comments on "Geltung des Rechts" in Gustav Radbruch, *Rechtsphilosophie* (Stuttgart, 1973, unaltered reprint of the 1932 original), 178.

27. "Grundsätzliche Überwindung des Positivismus"; Radbruch, "Gesetzliches Unrecht," 107.

28. On this point, Arthur Kaufmann (the foremost expert on Radbruch's legal philosophy and the editor of Radbruch's complete works) has noted: "Radbruch's notion of law cannot be equated with natural law since for him 'correct law' is not an absolute value . . . For Radbruch 'correct law' can only be approximated. " Kaufmann, "Gustav Radbruch," 72.

29. Radbruch, "Gesetzliches Unrecht," 107. On this concept, see Björn Schumacher, "Rezeption und Kritik der Radbruchschen Formel" (Ph.D. diss., Universität Göttingen, 1985); Frank Saliger, *Radbruchsche Formel und Rechtsstaat* (Heidelberg, 1995).

30. Radbruch, "Gesetzliches Unrecht," 107: "Es darf nicht verkannt werden—gerade nach den Erlebnissen jener zwölf Jahre—, welche furchtbaren Gefahren für die Rechtssicherheit der Begriff des 'gesetzlichen Unrechts' für die Leugnung der Rechtsnatur positiver Gesetze mit sich bringen kann." A nuanced introduction to Radbruch's legal philosophy is offered by Winfried Hassemer in Gustav Radbruch, *Rechtsphilosophie III* (GRGA Bd. 3), (Heidelberg, 1990), 1–16, who draws on Radbruch's texts from the Nazi era and after 1945.

31. See, for example, Helmut Coing, "Zur Frage der strafrechtlichen Haftung der Richter für die Anwendung naturrechtswidriger Gesetze," *SJZ* 2 (1947), 61–64 (64); Adolf Arndt, "Die Krise des Rechts," *Die Wandlung* 3 (1948), 421–440, esp. 421.

32. See Arthur Kaufmann, "Die Naturrechtsrenaissance der ersten Nachkriegsjahre—und was daraus geworden ist," in *Die Bedeutung der Wörter: Studien zur europäischen Rechtsgeschichte. Festschrift für Sten Gagnér zum 70. Geburtstag*, Michael Stolleis et al., eds. (Munich, 1991), 105–132, esp. 109ff. and 117ff.

33. Christoph Kleßmann, *Die doppelte Staatsgründung: Deutsche Geschichte 1945–1955* (Göttingen,1991), 59–63; Thränhardt, *Geschichte*, 38–39.

34. Ulfried Neumann, "Rechtsphilosophie in Deutschland seit 1945," in *Rechtswissenschaft in der Bonner Republik: Studien zur Wissenschaftsgeschichte der Jurisprudenz,* ed. Dieter Simon (Frankfurt am Main, 1994), 145–187, esp. 148.

35. Winfried Hassemer, "Strafrechtswissenschaft in der Bundesrepublik Deutschland," in *Rechtswissenschaft,* ed. Simon, 259–310, quote 264.

36. Hellmuth von Weber gave a presentation at the meeting of German jurists held in Bad Godesberg from 30 September—1 October 1947 on "Recht und Pflicht des Richters zur Prüfung der Gültigkeit des Strafgesetzes." *SJZ* 2 (1947), 567–570 (569). Hellmuth von Weber (1893–1970) became a professor extraordinarius at the German University in Prague, then moved to a professorship in Jena and in 1937 to Bonn. While the Commission on Criminal Law was being convened, he was a frequent contact for the ministerial bureaucracy, but he declined to serve on the commission and rejected a comprehensive reform of criminal law, advocating instead for amending it through legislation. This can be seen in a note by Ministerialrat Eduard Dreher, who played a large role in organizing the commission: Vermerk von Dreher, 2.2.1954, 4. Bundesarchiv (BA) B 141-17229. On the biography of von Weber: Hans-Heinrich Jescheck, "Hellmuth von Weber zum Gedächtnis," *JZ* (1970), 517–518.

37. Karl Peters, "Gerechtigkeit und Rechtssicherheit," 380. Peters (1904–1998) completed his *Habilitation* in Cologne in 1931, assumed a professorship in 1942 in Greifswald, moving to Münster in 1946. In 1962 he moved to Tübingen, where he became emeritus in 1972. Karl Peters participated in the penal reform discourse with many articles, but due to his Catholic orientation played an outsider role in the legal academic community, which was dominated by Protestants. He was one of the few professors of criminal law who welcomed the controversial Bundesgerichtshof decision on so-called *Verlobten-Kuppelei* (see below). A large number of his texts did not appear in the usual legal journals, but in publications close to Catholicism, such as *Caritas, Hochland, Stimmen der Zeit, Michael,* and *Die Kirche in der Welt.* On Karl Peters, see Jürgen Baumann, "Karl Peters 70 Jahre," *Juristische Zeitung* 2 (1974), 66–67.

38. Simon, "Zäsuren," 154.

39. Thomas Würtenberger, *Die geistige Situation der deutschen Strafrechtswissenschaft* (Karlsruhe, 1959), 19.

40. Hans Welzel, "Naturrecht und Rechtspositivismus," in *Naturrecht oder Rechtspositivismus,* Werner Maihofer, ed. (Darmstadt, 1966), 322–338, quote 325 [Originally published 1953]. As early as 1951, Welzel had formulated his criticism of natural law arguments: "All natural law arguments prove only as much as their substantive arguments; reference to nature does not add to their plausibility but, on the contrary, is likely to expose them to the suspicion

of being ideological." Hans Welzel, *Naturrecht und materiale Gerechtigkeit* (Göttingen, 1962), 249.

41. Welzel, "Naturrecht und Rechtspositivismus," 325.

42. The court ruled: "The moral order demands that the intercourse of the sexes take place in a monogamous marriage because the meaning and result of intercourse is the child." *Entscheidungen des Bundesgerichtshofes in Strafsachen (BGHSt)* vol. 6, Mitglieder des Bundesgerichtshofes und der Bundesanwaltschaft, ed. (Berlin, 1954), 46ff., cited in Hermann Weinkauff, "Der Naturrechtsgedanke in der Rechtsprechung des Bundesgerichtshofes," *NJW* 38 (1960), 1689–1696, quote 1694.

43. Karl Peters, "Kuppelei bei Verlobten," *Ehe und Familie im privaten und öffentlichen Raum. Zeitschrift für das gesamte Familienrecht* 1 (1954), 96–99; Paul Bockelmann, "Zur Strafbarkeit der Kuppelei. Bemerkungen zu dem Beschluß des Großen Senats für Strafsachen vom 17. Februar 1954," *JR* 10(1954), 361–364; Hans-Heinrich Jescheck, "Zur Frage der Kuppelei gegenüber Verlobten," *MDR* 8 (1954), 11, 645–649; Walter Sax, "Zur Frage der Kuppelei bei Geschlechtsverkehr unter Verlobten," *JZ* 9 (1954), 15/16, 474–477. Comments on the ruling: *NJW* 20 (1954), 766–768; *JZ* 15/16 (1954), 508–511.

44. A decision by the Supreme Court of the British Zone of 7 June 1949 decreed that all penal laws "that use the term 'gesundes Volksempfinden' [healthy popular feeling] in reference to the application of penal laws have lost their validity." *SJZ* 4 (1949), 10, 711–713.

45. Control Council Law no. 11 of 30 January 1946.

46. The Supreme Court of the British zone took the latter view and therefore upheld the 1935 version of §§ 175, 175a. See *SJZ* 4 (1949), 278–282. Specifics regarding additional court decisions in *Das Strafgesetzbuch an Hand der höchstrichterlichen Rechtsprechung für die Praxis*, with explanations by Erich Mühlmann and Gert Bommel (Regensburg, 1949), 388f.

47. In general, see Etzel, *Aufhebung*.

48. Cited in Albert Krebs, "Zur Erneuerung des Gefängniswesens (insbesondere in der amerikanischen Besatzungszone Deutschlands)," *SJZ* 1 (1946), 209–231, quote 209.

49. Law no. 1 of the military governments, Art. IV Ziff. 8. *Das Strafgesetzbuch an Hand der höchstrichterlichen Rechtsprechung für die Praxis*, footnote 466.

50. The second Strafrechtsänderungsgesetz (StRÄG) of 6 March 1953 only added § 141, which criminalized the recruitment of Germans into foreign military service. See Hans Welzel, *Das deutsche Strafrecht: Eine systematische Darstellung* (Berlin, 1956), 401.

51. Eberhard Schmidt, "Probleme," 208.

52. Richard Lange, "Zur Strafrechtsreform," *NJW* 18 (1949), 695–698, 696. Richard Lange (1906–1995) became professor extraordinarius in Jena in 1940, where he received a professorship in 1943. In 1949 he moved to the Free University of Berlin and in 1951 to Cologne, where he taught until he received emeritus status. In 1946 he was president (without party affiliation) of the consulting state assembly in Thuringia, which drafted Thuringia's constitution. In the 1950s he was a member of the official Commission on Criminal Law. On Lange see Hans-Heinrich Jescheck, "Richard Lange zum Gedächtnis," *ZStW* (1996), 1–8.

53. *Das Strafgesetzbuch für das Deutsche Reich in der Fassung des Thüringischen Anwendungsgesetzes vom 1. November 1945 mit strafrechtlichen Einzelgesetzen*, Richard Lange, ed. (Weimar, 1946), 44f. § 20, par. I.

54. In 1947 Lange called the Nazi version a "reversal of the system of values." Lange, "Zu neuen Ufern im Strafrecht," 10.

55. Karl Peters, "Caritas und Strafrecht," *Caritas: Zeitschrift für Caritasarbeit und Caritaswissenschaft* (1947), 73–75.

56. See the chapter on the "Zusammenbruchgesellschaft" in Kleßmann, *Staatsgründung*, 37–65; relevant eyewitness reports can be found in Alexander von Plato and Almut Leh, *"Ein unglaublicher Frühling": Erfahrene Geschichte im Nachkriegsdeutschland 1945–1948* (Bonn, 1997).

57. The figures are from the entries in the German University Guide of 1941. Reichsstudentenwerk, ed., *Der Deutsche Hochschulführer: Lebens- und Studienverhältnisse an den deutschen Hochschulen*, vol. 23 (Berlin, 1941), 44f.

58. A brief view of the universities after 1945 is given in Hans-Werner Prahl, *Sozialgeschichte des Hochschulwesens* (Munich, 1978), 326–330; Axel Schildt, "Im Kern gesund? Die deutschen Hochschulen 1945," in *Vertuschte Vergangenheit: Der Fall Schwerte und die NS-Vergangenheit der deutschen Hochschulen*, Helmut König et al., eds. (Munich, 1997), 223–240.

59. Friedrich Schubel, *Universität Greifswald* (Frankfurt am Main, 1960), 98f.; *Universität Greifswald 525 Jahre*. Im Auftrage des Rektors verfaßt von Wolfgang Wilhelmus et al. ([East] Berlin, 1982), 59.

60. Christiane Drawz, "Die Schließung der Juristischen Fakultät 1950," *Beiträge zur Geschichte der Universität Rostock* 19 (Rostock, 1994), 33–43.

61. In Gießen, which was two-thirds destroyed in the war, the university was reduced to only three faculties and remained without a law faculty for twenty years. See Markus Bernhardt, *Gießener Professoren zwischen Drittem Reich und Bundesrepublik: Ein Beitrag zur hessischen Hochschulgeschichte 1945–1957* (Gießen, 1990), 9ff.

62. Boehm/Müller, *Universitäten und Hochschulen*, 256f.; 64.

63. David Phillips, "Die Wiedereröffnung der Universitäten in der britischen Zone. Nationalistische Gesinnung, Entnazifizierung und das Problem der Zulassung zum Studium," *Bildung und Erziehung* 36 (1983), 1, 35–53 (35).

64. Eike Wolgast, *Die Universität Heidelberg 1386–1986* (Berlin, 1986), 167.

65. Otto Herding, "Bericht der Universität Tübingen," *Studium Generale* 1 (1948), 3, 185–188.

66. Kurt Stangl, "Bericht der Universität Erlangen," *Studium Generale* 1 (1948), 7, 440–443; Hans Liermann, *Erlebte Rechtsgeschichte* (Neustadt an d. Aisch, 1976), 152–167 on the period 1945–1948 in Erlangen.

67. Günther Meinhardt, *Die Universität Göttingen. Ihre Entwicklung und Geschichte von 1734–1974* (Göttingen, 1977), 114.

68. Wilfried Setzler, "Die Tübinger Studentenfrequenz im Dritten Reich. Ein Kurzüberblick zur zahlenmäßigen Entwicklung des Universitätsbesuchs und deren Ursachen," in Uwe Dietrich Adam, *Hochschule und Nationalsozialismus. Die Universität Tübingen im Dritten Reich* (Tübingen, 1977), 217–227 (222).

69. On the situation at the universities, see: for Bonn, Gernot Rath, "Bericht der Universität Bonn," *Studium Generale* 1 (1948), 383–388; *Einweihung des Fakultätsgebäudes der Rechts- und Staatswissenschaftlichen Fakultät der Rheinischen Friedrich-Wilhelms-Universität am 21. November 1967* (Bonn, 1970), 6f.; for Frankfurt, Edelgard Timm, "Bericht der Universität Frankfurt," *Studium Generale* 2 (1949), 62–66, and Notker Hammerstein, *Die Johann Wolfgang Goethe-Universität Frankfurt am Main. Von der Stiftungsuniversität zur staatlichen Hochschule*, vol. 1, *1914 bis 1950* (Neuwied, 1989), 550; for Freiburg, Gerd Tellenbach, "Bericht der Universität Freiburg," *Studium Generale* 3 (1950), 326–330; for Hamburg, Jürgen Lafrenz, "Die Universität in Hamburg als Problem der Stadtplanung 1919 bis 1945," in Eckart Krause, ed., *Hochschulalltag im Dritten Reich. Die Hamburger Universität 1933–1945*, vol. 1 (Berlin, 1991), 327–366 (360); for Cologne, Bernd Heimbüchel, "Die neue Universität. Selbstverständnis—Idee und Verwirklichung," in Heimbüchel and Klaus Pabst, *Kölner Universitätsgeschichte*, vol. 2, *Das 19. und 20. Jahrhundert* (Cologne/Vienna, 1988), 101–692 (600); for Münster, Peter Respondek, "Der Wiederaufbau der Universität Münster in den Jahren 1945–1952 auf dem Hintergrund der britischen Besatzungspolitik" (Ph.D. diss., University of Münster, 1992), 43; for Würzburg, Jürgen Aschoff, "Bericht der Universität Würzburg," *Studium Generale* 2 (1949), 4/5, 278–284; *Bayerns Hochschulen in der Nachkriegszeit 1945 bis 1952* (Munich, 1953), 11.

70. On the reconstruction phase, see Christoph Oehler, *Hochschulentwicklung in der Bundesrepublik Deutschland seit 1945* (Frankfurt/New York, 1989), 16f.; an overview of the scattered

timing of the reopenings can be found under the title "Neues Leben an den deutschen Universitäten nach dem Zweiten Weltkrieg," in *Wiedergeburt des Geistes: Die Universität Tübingen im Jahre 1945. Eine Dokumentation* (Tübingen, 1985), 118f.

71. Liermann, *Erlebte Rechtsgeschichte*, 164; Hammerstein, *Goethe-Universität*, 585.

72. On the university officer, see the information in Respondek, "Wiederaufbau," 178ff. with further notes.

73. Schildt, "Im Kern gesund?" 230–234.

74. Frank Halfmann, "Eine 'Pflanzstätte bester nationalsozialistischer Rechtsgelehrter': Die Juristische Abteilung der Rechts- und Staatswissenschaftlichen Fakultät," in *Die Universität Göttingen unter dem Nationalsozialismus: Das verdrängte Kapitel ihrer 250-jährigen Geschichte*, Heinrich Becker et al., eds. (Munich, 1987), 88–141, esp. 120.

75. According to Hoimar von Ditfurth, Sieverts was imprisoned by the English occupation authorities in the former KZ Neuengamme but was released in 1946 after the intervention of the former *Oberlandesgerichtsrat* Rée and the first postwar mayor of Hamburg, Petersen. Hoimar von Ditfurth, *Innenansichten eines Artgenossen: Meine Bilanz* (Munich, 1991), 215.

76. On the origins of this law and on the significance of Art. 131 of the Basic Law for the reinstatement of denazified officials, which, of course, included university professors, see Norbert Frei, *Vergangenheitspolitik: Die Anfänge der Bundesrepublik und die NS-Vergangenheit* (Munich, 1997), 69–100.

77. Alfred Wendehorst, *Geschichte der Friedrich-Alexander-Universität Erlangen-Nürnberg* (Munich, 1993), 235.

78. Ulrich Stock (1896–1974). Anne Christine Nagel, ed., *Die Philipps-Universität Marburg im Nationalsozialismus: Dokumente zu ihrer Geschichte* (Stuttgart, 2000), 546. In Saarbrücken, the Austrian criminologist Ernst Seelig also found a refuge. Seelig had lost his professorship at the University of Graz after the war ended and taught as of 1954—after a guest professorship—as a professor at Saarbrücken University. Karlheinz Probst, *Strafrecht—Strafprozessrecht—Kriminologie. Geschichte der Rechtswissenschaftlichen Fakultät der Universität Graz, Teil 3* (Graz, 1987), 61–72; specifically on the postwar era, 68ff. Ernst Seelig was a functionary of the *NS-Dozentenbund*: see Steirische Gesellschaft für Kulturpolitik, eds., *Grenzfeste Deutscher Wissenschaft: Über Faschismus und Vergangenheitsbewältigung an der Universität Graz* (Graz, 1985), 71.

79. In general, see Kleßmann, *Staatsgründung*, 39–44.

80. An exception was Eberhard Schmidt's change from Göttingen to Heidelberg in 1948.

81. Würtenberger taught from 1946 to 1955 in Mainz and from 1955 to 1973 was Professor für Strafrecht, Strafverfahrensrecht, Kriminologie und Rechtsphilosophie in Freiburg. Renate Wittern, ed., *Die Professoren der Friedrich-Alexander-Universität Erlangen 1763–1960. Teil I: Theologische Fakultät, Juristische Fakultät* (Erlangen, 1993), 181.

82. Wilhelm Ebel, ed., *Catalogus Professorum Gottingensium 1734–1962* (Göttingen, 1962), 55.

83. The depiction of living conditions in Göttingen comes from the legal academic Ludwig Raiser. See Ludwig Raiser, "Wiedereröffnung der Hochschulen—Ansätze zum Neubeginn," in *Nationalsozialismus und die deutsche Universität* (Berlin, 1966), 174–188, quote 175.

84. Ebel, *Catalogus*, 56, 61, 72.

85. Meinhardt, *Universität Göttingen*, 114.

86. Only at the interzonal meeting of jurists in 1946 did Eduard Kohlrausch report on the "Revision des Strafgesetzbuches durch Beseitigung der Vorschriften nationalsozialistischen oder militaristischen Ursprungs." "Interzonale Juristentagung 3.–6.12.1946 in Wiesbaden," *SJZ* 2 (1947), 37–40. At the meeting of jurists in Konstanz, held in 1947 for the French occupation zone, the Tübinger professor of criminal law Eduard Kern addressed the "Probleme der Gerichtsverfassung und der Wiedereinführung der Laiengerichtsbarkeit in Deutschland." Militärregierung des französischen Besatzungsgebietes in Deutschland. Generaljustizdirektion,

Der Konstanzer Juristentag (2.–5. Juni 1947). Ansprachen, Vorträge, Diskussionsreden (Tübingen, 1947), compare to the report: "Der Konstanzer Juristentag," *SJZ* 2 (1947), 6, 347–349. At the 1947 meeting of jurists in Bad Godesberg, Hellmuth von Weber spoke about "Recht und Pflicht des Richters zur Prüfung der Gültigkeit des Strafgesetzes," and Eberhard Schmidt addressed the "Unabhängigkeit der Rechtspflege." *Tagung deutscher Juristen Bad Godesberg, 30. September/1. Oktober 1949. Reden und Vorträge*, ed. Zentraljustizamt für die britische Zone (Hamburg, 1947), see the report: "Tagung deutscher Juristen in Bad Godesberg vom 30.9.-1.10.1947," *SJZ* 2 (1947), 10, 567–570. At the 1948 meeting of jurists in Munich, Eberhard Schmidt spoke about "Wirtschaftsstrafrecht." See the report: "Juristentagung in München vom 1.–4. Juni 1948," *SJZ* 3 (1948), 6, 338–342.

87. The agenda item was called "Grundfragen der Bereinigung des Strafgesetzbuches unter besonderer Berücksichtigung der Strafzwecke, der Strafzumessungsnormen und der Tatbestandstechnik." See the chronological overview: "Die Verhandlungen des Deutschen Juristentages 1860 bis 1960," assembled by Jan Albers, in *Hundert Jahre deutsches Rechtsleben. Festschrift zum hundertjährigen Bestehen des Deutschen Juristentages 1860–1960*, vol. 2, Ernst von Caemmerer, Ernst Friesenhahn, and Richard Lange, eds. (Karlsruhe, 1960), 353–387.

88. The reports, lectures, and discussions at the Deutschen Juristentage are available in printed form. The lectures at the Strafrechtslehrertagungen (meetings of the professors of criminal law) are partially reprinted in the *Zeitschrift für die gesamte Strafrechtswissenschaft*, while the discussions at those meetings are only available in conference reports in the professional journals, above all in the *Juristenzeitung*. On the meetings of the professors of criminal law, see Johannes Driendl, "Die deutsche Strafrechtslehrertagung in Geschichte und Gegenwart," *ZStW* 92 (1980), 1–18.

89. Bader, "Wiederaufbau," 33–88; Bader, "Walter Mallmann," 17–31.

90. Karl S. Bader, "Zum 50. Jahrgang der Juristenzeitung," *JZ* 50 (1995), 1. 1.

91. See Hans-Jürgen Bruns et al., "Geleitwort," in *140 Jahre Goltdammer's Archiv für Strafrecht. Eine Würdigung zum 70. Geburtstag von Paul-Günter Pötz*, Jürgen Wolter, ed. (Heidelberg, 1993), v–x.

92. Egon Schneider, "50 Jahre MDR," *MDR* 51 (1997), 4, 305.

93. Starting in 1951, the journal was subtitled "Monatsschrift für naturwissenschaftliche Kriminalistik und Polizeiarchiv." Robert Heindl, "Das 'Archiv für Kriminologie': Ein historischer Rückblick," *Archiv für Kriminologie* 115 (1955), 3–5.

94. Albert Krebs, "Die ersten 25 Jahre der Zeitschrift für Strafvollzug. Zur Geschichte des Gefängniswesens in Deutschland seit 1945," *Zeitschrift für Strafvollzug* 26 (1977), 1–7 (2).

95. On German criminology after 1945 see Imanuel Baumann, *Dem Verbrechen auf der Spur: Eine Geschichte der Kriminologie und Kriminalpolitik in Deutschland 1880–1980* (Göttingen, 2006).

96. Except for the volume on the first working meeting after 1945, the *Mitteilungen der Kriminalbiologischen Gesellschaft* appeared in the series *Kriminalbiologische Gegenwartsfragen* and contained the (sometimes expanded) lectures at the meetings of the society. On Edmund Mezger (1883–1962), who headed the *Kriminalbiologische Gesellschaft* until 1961, see the biography by Gerit Thulfaut, *Kriminalpolitik und Strafrechtslehre bei Edmund Mezger (1883–1962). Eine wissenschaftsgeschichtliche und biographische Untersuchung* (Baden-Baden, 2000), esp. 328–334. Mezger became professor in Marburg in 1925; in 1932 he moved to Munich, where he taught until he retired. He was a member of the Nazi regime's Commission on Criminal Law Reform and the Große Strafrechtskommission that was convened in 1954.

97. This statistical analysis is based on the tables of contents of the *Monatsschrift* from 1954 to 1957. Only the articles in the category "Abhandlungen und Sprechsaal" were considered; the short reports, obituaries, or congratulatory items in the category "Mitteilungen und Besprechungen" were not included.

98. Of the numerous essays, only those by Kern and Sauer are cited here: Eduard Kern, "Das künftige Schicksal der Übertretungen," *Der Rechtspfleger* (1960), 266ff. and Wilhelm Sauer, "Tatbestand, Unrecht, Irrtum und Beweis. Zur Strafrechtsreform," *ZStW* 69 (1957), 1ff.

99. Ulrich Stock, "Zur Strafrechtsreform in Deutschland," *Die Kirche in der Welt* 5 (1952), 2, 195–198.

100. Hans-Jürgen Bruns, "Die Strafaussetzung zur Bewährung. Ein Rückblick auf Rechtsprechung und Lehre seit dem Inkrafttreten der §§ 23ff. StGB (n.F.)," *GA* (1956), 193–240; Bruns, "Die Maßregeln der Besserung und Sicherung im StGB-Entwurf 1956," *ZStW* 71 (1959), 2, 210–251.

101. Friedrich Schaffstein, "Die vorbeugende Verwahrung nach dem StGB-Entwurf 1962," in Hans Welzel, ed., *Festschrift für Hellmuth von Weber zum 70. Geburtstag* (Bonn, 1963), 121ff.

102. See Wolfgang Naucke, *Strafrecht: Eine Einführung* (Neuwied, 1995), 247–258. Hans Welzel (1905–1977) taught in Göttingen from 1937 to 1952, from 1952 up to his retirement in Bonn. On Welzel see Fritz Loos, "Hans Welzel (1904–1977), Die Suche nach dem Überpositiven im Recht," in Loos, ed., *Rechtswissenschaft in Göttingen: Göttinger Juristen aus 250 Jahren* (Göttingen, 1987), 486–509.

103. Karl Alfred Hall, "Die Freiheitsstrafe als kriminalpolitisches Problem," *ZStW* 66 (1954), 1, 77–110. The text contained an expanded version of his lecture of 1952. Hall was appointed professor extraordinarius (adjunct or associate professor) in Gießen in 1936, was a Soviet prisoner of war until 1950, and then taught in Marburg, where he was appointed as full professor (Ordinarius) in 1961 at age fifty-five. On Hall, who is depicted as an eccentric figure, see the biographical sketch by Heinz Holzhauer, "Karl Alfred Hall (1906–1974)—ein Denkmal," in Wilfried Küper et al., eds., *Beiträge zur Rechtswissenschaft: Festschrift für Walter Stree und Johannes Wessels zum 70. Geburtstag* (Heidelberg, 1993), 1263–1279.

104. "Das spezialpräventive Denken . . . fordert die Einheitsstrafe." Eberhard Schmidt, "Vergeltung, Sühne und Spezialprävention," *ZStW* 67 (1955), 2, 177–195 (185).

105. Hall, "Freiheitsstrafe," 80.

106. Hall, "Freiheitsstrafe," 81.

107. Hall, "Freiheitsstrafe," 80–93. The warning with the possibility of punishment sets the penalty simultaneously with the declaration of guilt. A second, oral hearing held after a set probationary period determines whether the perpetrator has reformed. If so, he can be considered not to have a prior conviction because the sentence was set but not pronounced.

108. Hall, "Freiheitsstrafe," 93f.

109. Hall, "Freiheitsstrafe," 95.

110. Hall, "Freiheitsstrafe," 94.

111. Hall, "Freiheitsstrafe," 99.

112. Hall made only one more contribution to the penal reform debate: Karl Alfred Hall, "Sicherungsverwahrung und Sicherungsstrafe," *ZStW* 70 (1958), 41–63.

113. Lange, "Grundfragen," 373–397.

114. Hans-Heinrich Jescheck, *Das Menschenbild unserer Zeit und die Strafrechtsreform* (Tübingen, 1957); Ernst Heinitz, "Das Menschenbild im Strafrecht," *Franz-Lieber-Hefte* (Bad Nauheim) 2 (1960), 4, 7–21; Richard Lange, "Menschenbild und Strafrechtsreform," *Zeitwende. Die neue Furche* (Hamburg) 33 (1962), 582–597.

115. On 23 March 1962, see Lutz Jasper, *Gesellschaft Hamburger Juristen 1885–1985. Erinnerungsschrift anläßlich ihres hundertjährigen Bestehens im Dezember 1985* (Cologne, 1985), 91.

116. Hans-Heinrich Jescheck, "Grundgedanken der deutschen Strafrechtsreform," *Radius. Vierteljahresschrift der Evangelischen Akademikerschaft in Deutschland* 1 (1956), 11–17 (15).

117. Jescheck, "Grundgedanken," 12.

118. Wilhelm Gallas in the official Commission on Criminal Law in *Niederschriften über die Sitzungen der Großen Strafrechtskommission*. 14 Bände, Band 1 (Bonn, 1956), 41.

119. Edmund Mezger in the Commission on Criminal Law in *Niederschriften Band 1*, 43.
120. Richard Lange, "Grundlagen der heutigen deutschen Strafrechtsreform," *Österreichische Juristenzeitung* 10 (1955), 11, 307–308 (307).
121. This was consistent with the existing penal code: *Strafaussetzung zur Bewährung* had been introduced in 1953 through the Third Criminal Law Amendment Act.
122. See the draft code of the Commission on Criminal Law in the first reading (Erste Lesung) in *Niederschriften über die Sitzungen der Großen Strafrechtskommission*, vol. 12 (Bonn, 1959).
123. In the second reading of the draft, however, Bockelmann spoke in favor of *Zuchthausstrafe*.
124. Jescheck, "Grundgedanken," 17.
125. Thomas Würtenberger, *Die geistige Situation der deutschen Strafrechtswissenschaft* (Karlsruhe, 1957). The text is the expanded version of the inaugural speech held by Würtenberger in 1955 at the University of Freiburg.
126. Würtenberger, *Situation*, 8 (quote from the 1959 edition).
127. See, for example, Schmidt, "Vergeltung" and Schmidt, "Kriminalpolitische und strafrechtsdogmatische Probleme in der deutschen Strafrechtsreform," *ZStW* 69 (1957), 359–396.
128. Schmidt, "Kriminalpolitische und strafrechtsdogmatische Probleme," 367.
129. Schmidt, "Kriminalpolitische und strafrechtsdogmatische Probleme," 374.
130. This also stemmed from the love of quotations by Goethe. See Hans Wrobel, *Verurteilt zur Demokratie. Justiz und Justizpolitik in Deutschland 1945–1949* (Heidelberg, 1989), 194–199.
131. On the *Arbeitsgemeinschaft* during the Weimar years, see Nikolaus Wachsmann's chapter in this volume.
132. On postwar prison reform, see Kai Naumann, *Gefängnis und Gesellschaft: Freiheitsentzug in Deutschland in Wissenschaft und Praxis 1920–1960* (Berlin, 2006), esp. 206–213, 228–232.
133. See "Zur Reform des Strafvollzuges," *JZ* 21 (1951), 698–699. Prison officials and other practitioners active in the group included Curt Bondy, Helga Einsele, Walter Herrmann, Albert Krebs, Wilhelm Mollenhauer, Harald Poelchau, and Franz Zeugner.
134. "Resolution der 'Arbeitsgemeinschaft für Reform des Strafvollzugs' vom 4. September 1948," *ZfStrVo* 1 (1950), 6, 57–58.
135. "Reform des Strafvollzuges," *SJZ* 5 (1950), 302–303. "Bericht über die Tagung der AG am 22./23. März 1950; Abdruck der Resolution vom 23. März 1950," *ZfStrVo* 1 (1950), 6, 58–59.
136. Hans Braun: Das Streben nach 'Sicherheit' in den 50er Jahren. Soziale und politische Ursachen und Erscheinungsweisen, in AfS 18 (1978), S. 279–306.
137. Walter Sax, "Kriminalpolitik und Strafrechtsreform," *JZ* 1 (1957), 1–7 (3f.).
138. M. Rainer Lepsius, "Kultur und Wissenschaft in Deutschland unter der Herrschaft des Nationalsozialismus," in Lepsius, *Demokratie in Deutschland: Soziologisch-historische Konstellationsanalysen. Ausgewählte Aufsätze* (Göttingen, 1993), 119–132, quote 122.

Chapter 12

REPRESSIVE REHABILITATION

Crime, Morality, and Delinquency in
Berlin-Brandenburg, 1945–1958

Jennifer V. Evans

Wenn wir einen Bürger erziehen, so erziehen wir damit auch das sexuelle Gefühl.*

—*Anton Makarenko*

In an April 1958 memorandum, an unknown author outlined the current state
of youth criminal policy in the German Democratic Republic. "Unlike in West
Germany," the author wrote, "in the GDR, delinquency is no longer the product
of war and fascism as it was in the years after 1945." Implicitly connected to the
evils of capitalism, juvenile delinquency was less of a problem in East Germany
due to the social character of the workers-and-farmers state. Contemporary cases
of youth endangerment and criminality owed their existence not to the structure
of state socialism, the author suggested, but to the unequal application of youth
policy and educational methods within its borders. Indeed, socialist education
programs were either unknown or "not uniformly applied by those responsible
for instituting policy." As long as this remained the case, the endangerment of
GDR children and teens called into question the work of committed caseworkers
who employed "socialist education methods to agitate for the betterment of East
German youth."[1]

   During the early days of the Cold War, the situation in Berlin and the surrounding region of Brandenburg posed unique challenges for police, court, and
youth welfare workers in dealing with juvenile criminal behavior.[2] Even before
the erection of the Berlin Wall in 1961, the proliferation of petty criminality

---

and crimes of morality following the war's end, together with the economic pressures brought about by the 1949 division of Germany, forced East Berlin authorities to consider a variety of ways to tackle the mounting problem of juvenile delinquency. In a flurry of legal and welfare reform measures, the East German government clarified the conditions under which young offenders could be placed in protective custody and resurrected the use of workhouses and special remand homes (*Jugendwerkhöfe*) to deal with the problem of endangered youth and juvenile criminals. Conceived as the final sites of intervention once youth rehabilitation had exhausted all other avenues, these houses, numbering some thirty facilities by the 1950s, were designed not only to correct malevolent behavior but to inculcate the moral qualities of socialist citizenship and personhood through a program of political education and hard work.[3] Caseworkers provided an education and limited instruction in household management, agricultural production, and industrial labor. They also collaborated with police and the youth courts to devise practical solutions to what they saw as the growing passivity of the nation's youth. Many believed that the best way to guard against a juvenile's full-blown derailment (*Entgleisung*) was to promote and foster an "active, positive upbringing with . . . respect for the ten . . . commandments of the new socialist morality,"[4] based on the model advanced by Walter Ulbricht in 1958 and put into practice in the day-to-day operation of the nation's workhouses and remand homes.[5]

This chapter focuses on the East German state's treatment of those criminal and endangered youth who were deemed unable to conform to the dictates of the new socialist moral code, a code that found informal expression through the regulatory actions of agencies and reformers well before 1958. Caught in the police dragnet for petty crime, vagrancy, prostitution, homosexuality, and general "hanging about" (*herumtreiben*), young offenders posed the ultimate challenge to state authorities intent on substantive ideological refashioning. Youth's involvement in "building" socialism certainly forms a significant part of GDR historiography, one which has received much attention in recent years on both sides of the Atlantic.[6] Indeed, most historians agree that the quest to rehabilitate delinquent youth was anything but apolitical.[7] On the one hand, rehabilitation was a constant reminder of the legacy of the Nazi era. On the other, caseworkers and reformers were forced to reevaluate prewar penal and welfare policy while simultaneously searching for new ways to eradicate the remnants of capitalism during the transition to socialism. And, of course, in the initial years after the war, rehabilitation efforts were deeply concerned with securing social stability by any means available.

Although common assumptions informed social policy in both Germanys after 1949, in resurrecting reformatories for the purposes of behavioral and ideological reorientation East Germany sought to sever its connection to the welfare tradition and heritage it shared with the West. Rehabilitation strategies established in remand homes and workhouses represented a conscious effort to refashion key social reform measures from the Weimar period to achieve a revolutionary transformation of society, which Konrad Jarausch has claimed resulted in the creation of a welfare dictatorship.[8] Despite a full-frontal attack on the *Adenauerstaat* among East German criminologists and legal reformers, the GDR's penal and welfare strategies to combat youth waywardness actually emphasized a vision of delinquency, vice, and moral endangerment that had much more in common with the Christian West than one might imagine. As Günter Grau has argued elsewhere, attempts to promote a radical reorganization of society did not necessarily undercut the valency of bourgeois morality, especially in the area of sexual behavior.[9]

In the GDR, juvenile delinquency and promiscuity, still understood in Lombrosian terms, represented a lapse not just in the social but in the moral development of future citizens, and could only be corrected by state involvement in the familial sphere. In identifying which transgressions merited state intervention, penal and welfare institutions both reflected and refracted gendered notions of delinquency and deviance. Caseworkers designed programs to meet the needs of their charges, deciding how best to integrate them into healthy and productive work and family life. These programs, which stressed household, agricultural, and industrial labor, were pragmatic in providing a trade and livelihood, but nevertheless structured rehabilitation around the promotion of specifically gendered identities. Against the backdrop of the mass exodus of able-bodied citizens to West Germany, a rise in divorces, and continued concerns over the falling birth rate, East German youth policy sought to buttress the faltering family by crafting a particular vision of the roles these young citizens were to fulfill in a budding socialist society. Although youth authorities emphasized civic responsibility, productive labor, and healthy gender roles, the inability to implement policy smoothly into the day-to-day management of juvenile delinquency presented a challenge to the utility of a formal socialist morality. At the same time, it hinted that causes for failure could not be externalized indefinitely.

Criminality and the Moral Endangerment of Youth

Youth criminality and youth endangerment linked three strands of social policy to the emergence of the German welfare state: penal reform, child welfare, and corrective education. From the last third of the nineteenth century onward, reformers, jurists, psychiatrists, and a host of self-proclaimed experts rallied the governments of Imperial Germany to implement provisions guaranteeing the utility and function of public custodianship.[10] While guardianship and welfare initiatives were continually debated in the formulation of the German Civil Code (*Bürgerliches Gesetzbuch* or BGB), adult correctional facilities, reformatories, and workhouses were licensed through the Criminal Code, which, as of 1923, included a separate statute for juvenile offenders, the Reich Juvenile Justice Act (*Reichsjugendgerichtsgesetz* or RJGG).[11] Youth reformatories emerged on the scene at the same time, linking child welfare to penal reform by extending patriarchal authority from the confines of the family to the correctional institution. Reforms to the Imperial Penal Code (Reichsstrafgesetzbuch, or RStGB) allowed German states the option of establishing the criteria for reformatories in the prevention of moral waywardness.[12] The family was no longer out of the reach of the state as a quasi-autonomous domain of unfettered patriarchal authority. In an admixture of custodial and criminal law, the state established *Rettungshäuser* for both criminal and socially endangered youth and in the process laid claim to public guardianship in a manner that had previously been reserved for the heads of households.[13] In fact, according to a prominent penal reformer of the day, correctional facilities were fully capable of inculcating paternal authority and discipline because wayward children could be instructed in the appropriate teachings of traditional society through a surrogate institutional setting.[14]

Although workhouses and reformatories were the product of conflicting visions of social reform, they embodied both a valorization and fear of the family's role in socializing the young. Progressive reformers from all sides of the political and confessional spectrum called for standardized methods for treating social dislocation and minimizing the destructive aspects of modernity's relentless march. *Rettungshäuser*, workhouses, youth courts, jails, municipal youth bureaus (*Jugendämter*), and legal statutes for young offenders all represented a collective strategy for socializing errant youth while integrating them into society as contributors to national, political, and economic life. When, in the 1920s, moral failings, unruliness, and impoverishment were transformed into medically conceived causes of endangerment, child welfare reformers gained unparalleled authority in defining the form and function of corrective intervention.[15] Despite these gains, however, by 1934 private charities and laypeople lost most of their real and imagined authority, as the Nazi consolidation of power gave rise to initiatives like the National Socialist People's Welfare (Nationalsozialistische Volkswohlfahrt, or NSV) and other new institutions designed to underscore the power of the state in structuring social identity.

After World War II, the professional preoccupation with youth formed part of a calibrated response to Nazi policies. Brought into public view by the misery of occupation and defeat, the soaring level of criminality reflected the war-ravaged conditions into which the younger generation had been born. Weaned on a virulent strain of Nazi population policy that tied the Reich's reproductive health to the glory of the nation, many youths had come of age early to serve the nation as soldiers or as dutiful wives and mothers.[16] Placing blame for postwar lawlessness squarely on the shoulders of Hitler and the Nazis, local government, church officials, and social reformers debated ways in which to curb juvenile delinquency to resocialize what they feared was an entire generation of morally decayed youth. Just as before the war, youth issues would reemerge as a contested terrain upon which jurists, child welfare advocates, police, and social workers vied for the authority to help shape social policy in an occupied and divided Germany.

Juvenile Delinquency in Postwar Berlin

Overwhelmed by the situation at war's end, youth advocates in the Soviet Occupation Zone (Sowjetische Besatzungzone or SBZ) likewise linked Nazi population policy to the rise in crime precipitated by the collapse of Hitler's Germany. Although they officially eschewed any connection to National Socialist policy and directives, in the days and weeks after capitulation, SBZ officials had no choice but to uphold several Nazi laws and ordinances to preserve order: maintaining curfews, restricting youth access to adult-oriented nightclubs, and limiting certain forms of employment.[17] To construct a new social order, young men and women had to be educated in the roles they were expected to fulfill upon reaching adulthood.[18] Criminality, especially crimes of a sexual nature, could not be tolerated if the GDR was to compete both morally and economically with its neighbors to the West. Securing a foundation for moral rebuilding became the priority of all public officials, and as early as 1947 Paul Markgraf, the Berlin chief of police, proclaimed the readiness of his East Berlin police force to protect the interests of children, youth, and society.[19]

Putting youth policy into practice on the streets required the work of many different people, institutions, and ministries. Similarly, remand homes and reformatories were governed by a variety of directives, and overseen by a host of professionals from police to caseworkers, physicians to teachers. As in the case of the Struveshof facility in Ludwigsfelde, these facilities often served many purposes in housing wards of the state, orphans, convicts, and *schwererziehbare*, or difficult youth.[20] While the local youth service workers coordinated efforts in Berlin, military government laws gave local authorities license to build and operate similar houses for rehabilitative purposes. Police and health service workers also set up a system of reformatories that targeted not only "asocial persons without permanent living quarters or demonstrable work habits" but also women deemed promiscuous to combat the spread of venereal disease.[21] Youth under the age of eighteen charged with a crime or suspected of general asociality or promiscuity or of leading an itinerant lifestyle could also be sent to homes operated under the auspices of the Ministry of *Volksbildung* (education) which, following Order no. 156 of the Soviet Military Authority, oversaw youth services in East Berlin as of 1947.[22] These *Jugendwerkhöfe* were designed for the most difficult cases and included educational programming intended to "make [difficult juveniles] into worthy citizens of the workers' and farmers' state." After serving a sentence in a youth facility, criminal youth could expect to be sent on to remand homes so that further monitoring of their progress could be guaranteed. Despite the differences on paper, this complicated network of facilities and institutions had one thing in common: above all else, caseworkers and government agreed "the main ingredient for reforming wayward youth . . . was work."[23]

But before reaching remand homes, youth first encountered reform policy in the streets and homes of their communities. Among the most visible agents of youth reform were special police detachments, consisting largely of women, that oversaw the policing of sexual offenses and crimes involving children. These officers, who on occasion worked in tandem with Allied Military Police in conducting sweeps of local bars, moviehouses, and cafés, were the first to encounter promiscuous and endangered youth. Once a crime was committed and an offender identified, the police documented the occurrence in their precinct's ledger and, depending upon the nature of the crime, they might also enter the youth's profile into a general card index like those assembled for other sexual offenses such as prostitution and homosexuality.[24] After the initial round of questions at the station house, police forwarded the teens to a temporary outreach center, the *Jugendhilfestelle*, in the basement of the Dircksenstrasse police headquarters near Alexanderplatz, where, in consultation with the Central Youth Bureau (Hauptjugendamt), they prepared the youth for a possible hearing in court. The *Jugendhilfestelle* was in such demand that it had to be renovated in 1948 because ten thousand youths had passed through its doors since the defeat of the Reich in May 1945. The Dircksenstrasse facility, along with its overflow center on Greifswalder Strasse, contained 145 beds for temporary shelter, and according to a 1948 newspaper report in *Sozialdemokrat*, it hardly kept pace with the influx of detainees.[25]

Gender distinctions impressed themselves from the very moment youth were brought under regulatory control. Unlike male youths, young women and girls rounded up in raids were forcibly sent (*zwanggestellt*) not to the *Jugendhilfestelle*, but to venereal disease clinics run by the Berlin Department of Health, where they could expect to be detained overnight before undergoing mandatory pelvic examinations for gonorrhea and syphilis. If they had a sexually transmitted disease, they were committed by law for the duration of their illness while health officials forwarded their particulars to both the *Jugendamt* and the police, because the willful and wanton spread of disease constituted a misdemeanor according to both occupation health ordinances and the German penal code.[26] Meanwhile, boys and young men who had been picked up were held at the *Jugendhilfestelle* until police and social workers determined the appropriate course of action. Depending on the nature of the crime committed, a youth might be forwarded to one of the city's group homes to await a hearing in a juvenile court. In the meantime, the case came under the jurisdiction of the Youth Court Counseling Services (*Jugendgerichtshilfe*), whose task it was to research the offender's background and family history, and, if deemed necessary, create a psychological profile to help identify the cause and extent of moral endangerment. Social workers then submitted these reports to the judge presiding over the youth's case. A direct carry-over from the Weimar period,[27] the *Jugendgerichtshilfe* attempted to make the court more sensitive to the plight of wayward youth by drawing attention to milieu and family life as indicators of the need for corrective education instead of outright punishment. With careful intervention instead of incarceration, young charges might learn the error of their ways and embrace reform.[28] Far from simply indicating a preexisting criminal predisposition, however, these profiles reinforced widely held notions of asociality, tracing origins and causes of the condition to the broken and overburdened family. But in the early postwar era, such indicators as dirty living quarters and a working mother—frequently mentioned in these evaluations—were more often the rule rather than the exception. If an intact family was a measurement of healthful maturation and social development, many Berliners certainly fell short of this mark.[29]

In a 1948 article in one of the Berlin dailies titled "Mom Threw Me Out! An Afternoon at Social Services—Helping Hands, Healing Words," a reporter documented a day at the municipal department of social services (*Sozialamt*). The mise-en-scène follows the story of a typical parent during her visit to the offices of the local *Sozialamt* because of her teenage son's predicament. Describing him as possessing a "mixture of stupidity and smarts," the mother outlined that Freddy had already spent time in the Fichtebunker youth detention center for breaking and entering, theft, and shirking work responsibilities. Returning to her home with the journalist, Freddy's mother added that "he stole anything that wasn't nailed down to buy cigarettes and chocolate" and even "socialized with known homosexuals." As a result of his most recent crimes, Freddy was sent to the *Jugendhilfestelle* on Dirksenstrasse, where he initially seemed to conduct himself well. Eight days before Christmas, however, he ran away, only to be caught once more by police. This time, a juvenile court judge would decide Freddy's fate after a short psychiatric assessment. Whatever the outcome in court, the reporter suggested that the boy would be best served by a stay in the country, a phrase synonymous with a term in one of the city's workhouses and remand homes.

The reporter's story draws attention to several features of postwar criminality and rehabilitative care. Freddy's crimes are quite typical of the period: his initial charges of petty theft and shirking were representative of the kinds of infractions committed by boys and male teens. In addition to this misbehavior, however, he is also described as being sexually permissive, with the added perceived danger of hanging about with friends of dubious sexual orientation. If Germans perceived a threat from youth in a general sense, the specific acts of stealing, shirking, and sexual promiscuity were the three main causes of alarm among youth service workers and police.

Containing Youth Waywardness

Despite the well-meaning intervention of youth service workers, efforts to effect meaningful change in the lives of endangered youth were hampered by material hardship, administrative chaos, and overlapping spheres of influence. Until the currency reform of 1948, economic hardship was a widespread and well-documented factor in monthly statistical reports that charted increasing rates of property crime and malnutrition.[30] Politically, general uncertainty about the Soviet consolidation of power in the Soviet Occupation Zone caused the flight and dislocation of a new wave of political refugees. By the end of 1949 alone, half a million youth aged fourteen to twenty were registered in newly established West Germany, many now living in temporary camps and shelters among other displaced persons who had fled the former eastern German territories in advance of the Russians at war's end.[31] Since Berlin served as a kind of island in the storm—a Western toehold within the Soviet Occupation Zone—it became home to many transient and disaffected youth, provoking the fears of critics who dreaded the influx of a populace searching for escape, excitement, and leisure among the bright lights of the big city.

To be sure, the decline in living standards, privation, and the breakdown of the family unit caused alarm among police, social service workers, and health authorities in the days and months after the war. The steady stream of transient youths into the city from the surrounding Eastern zone taxed an already overburdened social system. As one health care worker noted in a 1948 health authority report from the West Berlin district of Zehlendorf, delinquent refugees from the Soviet Zone of Occupation (SBZ) were the most difficult to handle since they were "without scruples . . . never ha[d] papers on them, and often use[d] false names."[32] Still, nothing worried the authorities more than the high rates of venereal disease among adolescents. To protect against the moral endangerment of Berlin youth and to curb the spread of disease, a vast network of public and private, short- and long-term care facilities marshaled their meager resources to intervene directly, seeking to stem the tide of deviant behavior through educational and welfare programs. In all too many cases, however, these facilities contributed to the very problems they were designed to prevent.

As in any institutional setting, difficulties arose in the youth facilities due to overcrowding, inadequate supervision, and a lack of resources. The *Jugendhilfestelle* on Dircksenstrasse near Alexanderplatz, to which police sent teenaged boys caught hanging around the train station without identification, had a serious problem with kids running away due to the terrible conditions. One of the facility's coordinators, Frau Hoffmann, described it as a dismal, prison-like structure, with forty-seven beds available for ninety charges. The facility was poorly outfitted and dirty and had no linen outside of what was donated; boys were forced to sleep two to a bed.[33] The situation was so troubling that caseworkers as far away as Struveshof believed it was partially responsible for the rising number of young male hustlers making their way through the system and ultimately landing in their care.[34]

Unable to meet the immediate needs of its wards, the Dircksenstrasse facility instead operated as a kind of clearinghouse where boys would receive short-term evaluations before being forwarded into youth jail or workhouses like Struveshof. Despite the best intentions of youth services and the police, many of these adolescents learned a variety of survival techniques—both good and bad—while in care of the authorities that, in fact, better equipped them for life on the streets. In his 1951 criminology textbook, the criminologist Ernst Seelig argued that shirkers and asocials were forging friendships with other delinquents in group homes, sidestepping all hope for reform.[35] In one episode at Struveshof, two boys escaped the facility and convinced a john that they were interested in selling their bodies before robbing him of his money and possessions.[36] In some cases, wards fell into even deeper peril at the hands of staff, including caseworkers, who abused their authority. In one instance, a caseworker was suspected of having sexual relations with two teenage wards while simultaneously romancing a secretary, prompting the facility's director to alert the police and inform the man's fiancée.[37] In an earlier case from 1945, the director of operations in a youth home on Mittelstrasse reportedly raped young female charges procured by the director of the facility herself. In the Tannenhof correctional facility in Lichtenrade, security was so lax that the girls frequently resorted to locking up their personal effects out of fear that the other wards and staff might steal them.[38]

Despite these setbacks, East German jurists and youth advocates lauded workhouses and remand homes as progressive and humane alternatives to overcrowded prisons and jails.[39] Although these facilities had initially been conceived as stopgap measures, by the 1950s they were invested with the authority to help foster a sense of civic responsibility and socialist morality and to promote healthful gender roles, especially at such a critical time in the personal and political development of the nation's youth. However, given the structural inability of East Berlin's administrative services to implement policy smoothly in the day-to-day management of delinquency, corrective education was not a panacea for rehabilitation.[40] Nevertheless, the remedial programs did at least provide occupational training for the young men and women in custody. In effect, the fledgling East German state was promoting a type of social rehabilitation that was not primarily based on revolutionary theory but on traditional notions of gender and the rudimentary necessities of economic stability.

Engendering Reform

By 1949 in Berlin and Brandenburg, educators working for the Ministry of *Volksbildung* together with the Ministry of Justice sought ways to correct behavior while simultaneously cultivating civic identification through the promotion of work and family values. But this was not the only region employing workhouses and remand homes in this way; in other districts, these facilities were especially important because, as contemporaries put it, many youths "protest[ed] against all community standards as a result of their asocial origins and development." According to one advocate, this was particularly distressing since these youths were not just rebelling against their parents' ways, but fostering generational angst and outright hostility toward the new organization of a socialist society.[41] As head of the East German Central Justice Administration, Dr. Gentz responded to these fears by underscoring that the purpose of rehabilitative justice was to "awaken social consciousness in the youth to such a degree that they undertake socially-useful employment of their own free will." Only through "productive work" could a youth's educational and career path be secured. Of course, these concerns were not simply altruistic but also politically expedient, as Dr. Gentz himself demonstrated when he highlighted the role both the Free German Youth (FDJ) and the Democratic Association of German Women (DFD) would play in these homes.[42]

Workhouses, in other words, represented an important site of social and penal reform while simultaneously instilling overtly political imperatives. Youth penal policy and welfare reform was part of an overarching strategy of differentiating East German jurisprudence from that of the West that came into sharp focus after 1949. At issue was the role of the courts and welfare services in best serving the needs of the day's youth. While some bureaucrats were debating the merits of bypassing the courts in favor of forwarding certain offenders directly to the employment office (*Arbeitsamt*), youth welfare workers continued to operate a network of workhouses and youth facilities that was overburdened by the number of wayward teens in the system.[43] Although they were frequently overextended, these facilities nevertheless played a significant role in the state's strategy to build healthy work and family relationships among a new generation of citizens and workers.[44]

Some workhouses were located in close proximity to the burgeoning number of nationalized factories (*Volkseigene Betriebe*, or *VEB*), making it easier for teenaged boys to participate in industrial production.[45] Indeed, most of the homes for boys involved a program of industrial labor, with the exception of one facility specifically designed to promote agriculture.[46] In learning a trade, these youths were given the skills needed to serve as providers and producers once they left the workhouse. Girls in protective custody for promiscuity and prostitution at the Heidekrug institution in Brandenburg/Havel, on the other hand, busied themselves with domestic chores including cooking, washing, mending, and cleaning. In Werftpfuhl, "healthy behavior and lifestyle" were imparted to female charges through a program based on gardening, sewing, and nursing.[47] Of course, these skills were designed to facilitate the girls' behavioral reform so that they, too, could leave the facility with marketable skills and take their proper social place as morally upstanding wives and mothers.[48]

But reforming behavior required resources that these workhouses and reformatories simply did not have. As with the material hardships faced by the *Jugendhilfestelle* in Berlin, these facilities frequently encountered problems. Although they were designed to reform aberrant behavior and promote socialism, they suffered from core organizational problems that undermined the state's efforts at rehabilitation. In a real sense, these institutions contained the seeds of their own destruction because the desired outcome—moral reform—was inhibited by the very structure and operation of the social program itself. If domesticity and maternal instincts were the markers of young women's successful rehabilitation, then the success of these facilities remained a source of frustration for wards and officials alike.

In Heidekrug, which housed up to three hundred women, most of the guards and workers were members of the communist party, the SED. Although they had the authority of political affiliation, they worked without a proper uniform that would have demarcated the staff from the inmates. Although chores included washing and cleaning, the charges went frequently without soap. Upon visiting Heidekrug, Käthe Kern of the Demokratischer Frauenbund Deutschlands (DFD) concurred with previous reports that the institution was in disrepair, lacking in soap, coal, and basic amenities. The situation was even worse at a reformatory for endangered girls in Thuringia, where guards reportedly begged for food from the inmates because they received better food rations than the staff.[49] Although material hardship threatened to end reform before it began, it was not the only issue hampering these facilities. One report observed that while the young women in Heidekrug spent their afternoons working in the fields, guards took the opportunity to take naps while on duty.[50]

Although these workhouses and reformatories served as the primary tool for building healthy behavior by teaching youth the merits of productive labor, reformers worried that it was impossible to gauge how deeply or genuinely the young men and women in custody internalized this message. This bitter truth was not only debated among professionals and laypeople, but also shaped public perceptions about the success of socialist reeducation. In a newspaper report for *Neue Zeit* published under the sensationalized title "Education with Popular Music: A Visit to a Reformatory for Endangered Girls," Dr. Fuchs-Kamp of the Institute for Psychiatry in Berlin visited a Brandenburg facility to evaluate firsthand the problem of institutionally rehabilitating so-called fallen girls and women. Although all the girls were eighteen and younger, they had already come into contact with the VD hospital, where they had presumably undergone quarantine after contracting gonorrhoea or syphilis. Those sent to the Cottbus facility were most likely repeat offenders or suspected of underage prostitution and therefore placed in custody for a year to ensure that they were "placed on the right path through hard work." Given the depths to which these girls had apparently sunk, rehabilitating them was "no easy task." On one night table, the doctor observed, stood a number of pictures of beautiful men. One desk held three framed photos, all of them of different men, and the same was in evidence on another bedside table. As if to underscore the nature of the girls' depravity, Fuchs-Kamp asked one charge how she came to be institutionalized in the workhouse. She responded that, like so many others of her generation, she just "wanted to have some fun." After all, she asked the doctor, was she expected "to die as an old maid?" Seeking out another example to demonstrate the difficulties educators faced in reforming such girls, the doctor turned to another young girl, who sat crossed legged during the interview and appeared very "ladylike," with painted-on eyebrows, nail polish, and lipstick. When asked what motivated her to put such effort into her appearance while in custody, she answered, with a coquettish glance to the side, that "first of all, sometimes we get the odd visitor here," and secondly, she hardly wanted "to become a wallflower."[51]

The newspaper article's descriptions are significant because they provide insight into the professional and popular visions of sexual delinquency. The girls were portrayed as being "on the make" despite their detention in an institution and therefore apparently beyond the reach of reform efforts. As members of the next generation, these young women served as the canvas upon which Germans, lay or professional, could express their own insecurities about the future and the consequences of their recent past. Although concern with girls' reproductive future contrasted with the concern for boys' productivity, both represented a conjoined problem for citizens and officials. Whether mingling with friends at the *Bahnhof* or staying out late at the cinema, the actions of youth assumed a threatening countenance that consumed considerable resources and defied both scientific management and moral rhetoric.

Socialist Morals and the Family

Despite these difficulties in applying policy uniformly, the rise in youth criminality in postwar Germany forced professionals to engage the question of the origins of juvenile crime anew. Baffled by the rise in crime, caseworkers and policymakers asked: Were certain youths predisposed to criminal behavior because of a *Fehlentwicklung*, that is, a psychological development that went wrong? What role did the environment play in shaping delinquency? Was asocial behavior a result of postwar hardship or, as the director of the Hephata-Treysa institution claimed in 1957 regarding the 80 percent of youth in his facility, due to a variety of neurological afflictions?[52] These contrasting claims continued to animate discussion in the years after the war and, with few changes, remained in circulation at least until the 1960s.

If there was one issue that most youth advocates could agree upon, despite the emerging ideological divide, it was that defeat in war had brought dramatic challenges to reforming wayward youth. "As a result of Hitler's war," stated a 1947 police memorandum on the fight against youth crime, "Germany emerged not simply as a rubble heap in a material sense" but it experienced "an unimaginable lowering of its moral and ethical worth."[53] Capitulation gave rise to "confused families and weakened family ties," and these damaged domestic relationships now "played themselves out at an alarming rate on the situation of the youth."[54] The numerous cases of juvenile delinquency stemmed in large part from the rise of broken homes and so-called half families that confirmed for many Berliners that the world had been turned upside down after defeat.[55] By the time Hanns Eyferth wrote in 1950 that this generation of delinquents "might not be healed of their particular wounds," many people had begun to fear that the youth teetered dangerously on the brink of outright asociality.[56]

If the initial fears concerning youth delinquency transcended the boundaries that separated the emerging socialist state from its capitalist neighbor, these common priorities were increasingly divided by the language and imperatives of reform as the 1950s unfolded.[57] Social policy on crime and juvenile delinquency suddenly became part of the Cold War battle, in which the attitudes and behavior of the younger generation emerged as fundamental in securing economic and political legitimacy. Despite considerable fanfare, the founding of the East German "Workers' and Farmers' State" in October 1949 did not result in social and industrial stabilization, and the number of unregistered youth continued to alarm authorities because they frequently fell into criminal activity and prostitution.[58]

To combat the mounting threat of social and sexual dislocation, the *Jugendamt*, the Department of Health, and the Ministry of *Volksbildung* combined their efforts to reform the way workhouses, reformatories, youth homes, and counseling services functioned with the goal of fundamentally realigning priorities. Although never intended for this purpose, workhouses and reeducation facilities were sometimes used for the detention of hardened criminals or political prisoners. More generally, there was a concerted effort to impart political education via carefully schooled educators. As a volume on GDR legal history from the 1970s put it, workhouses were successful when they operated with the principles of "work and self-discipline [as] the main forms of corrective education" but also paid attention to the "political work of each and every youth and their educators."[59] As was the case in some of the privately run confessional group homes in and around Berlin, a best-case scenario envisioned reformed youth who had been educated by example, and might even return to the institution to hold marriage ceremonies or christenings to share their joy with the caseworkers who helped turn their lives around.[60]

As the 1950s unfolded, the problem of juvenile delinquency and waywardness became subsumed within social policy on the general protection of youth. Part of a sweeping anti-smut and anti-pornography campaign that targeted the corrupt

West as the origin of all forms of immorality, measures to combat unhealthy sexual development linked citizens' physical and sexual health to the overall productivity of the nation. Recidivism, sexual promiscuity, itinerant lifestyles, fears of American cultural exports like rock 'n' roll and jazz, and the flight of many young East Germans to the West all spurred the government to clamp down once and for all on all things counterproductive to the march of socialism.[61] Cliques of youth hanging around Berlin's train stations were especially targeted, since surveys and spot checks confirmed that many of them were uneducated and untrained, representing the loss of an important resource to the East German state. Ideally, every citizen's productive capacity had to be harnessed in support of population growth and industrial renewal.[62]

In practice, East Germany adopted norms that were, at times, hardly distinguishable from "the bourgeois family," although this was never acknowledged. Like their counterparts in the West, officials targeted sexual comportment as a vital link in the transition from postwar chaos to stability. In the end, however, the slow rebuilding of Berlin had to be waged on three fronts—on the streets, in the courts, and in care—that offered no guarantees that aberrant behavior could be successfully modified to fit the new model of morality. Work, both domestic and industrial, held the promise of rehabilitating wayward youth by channeling their attention into productive pursuits. The language of productivity also informed West Berlin juvenile penal policy on asocials and prostitutes, especially in cases where judges had to decide whether to send a repeat offender to youth jail or prison.[63] Whereas workhouses were a sanction contained in the postwar West German Penal Code, in the East they formed part of a large-scale reorganization of the legal and social service system that sought to implement more humanistic alternatives to imprisonment even as the state deprived local authorities of control over these matters. Only in these long-term institutions, which supplemented parallel measures for hardened criminals, could "routine work patterns and socially useful thinking and behavior" be taught.[64]

Just as the family had served as the barometer of successful (or failed) socialization before the Second World War, the ideal of marriage and family continued to set the parameters of the debate for a successful postwar youth policy. In postwar German discourses of renewal and reconstruction, the family emerged as a kind of safe haven in troubled times and the locus of social and political stability. Challenges to the family, such as those that had resulted from National Socialist population policies, engendered the utmost scrutiny and suspicion. As a corrective measure against a totalitarian relapse, the West German constitution enshrined the family as a bulwark against possible future aggression—a liberal democratic private sphere that must be shielded from state intervention. More importantly, the family emerged as the primary site of political power with prescribed roles for husband and wife, forming the basis for what might be viewed as a kind of (re-)productive citizenship.[65]

In the German Democratic Republic, too, the family ideal was strong and similarly situated in party and constitutional discourses of appropriate civic comportment. But the image of the family propagated in the GDR was socialist and self-consciously devoid of the idolatry of the bourgeois *Sittenkodex*. Of course, popular and official discourses could not hide the fact that the family's bourgeois underpinnings remained alive and well despite claims to the contrary. Throughout the 1950s officials attempted to formulate a proletarian moral code, looking to the Soviet Union for inspiration. The Soviet pedagogue Anton Makarenko's (1888–1939) account of the place of law and morality in a socialist society provided a canonical analysis of the role class consciousness and scientific humanism could play in forming a new kind of social relationality within an otherwise traditional family structure.[66] As late as the Fifth Party Congress (1958) of the reigning Socialist Unity Party (SED), Party Chairman Walter Ulbricht initiated a preemptive strike against what he feared was the continued influence of all things bourgeois in the fledgling socialist state. As part of a ten-point policy for the continued Sovietization of morality, Ulbricht outlined the steps East Germans should take to secure the path toward socialist renewal. Not entirely unlike the ten biblical commandments, these socialist strictures instructed citizens to "live a clean and respectable life and respect the family."[67]

Intent on limiting alternative forms of sexual expression, the East and West German states were more similar than distinct in this regard in the 1950s. Despite their opposed ideological orientation, socialist and Christian Democratic visions of the family bore striking resemblance to each other. Nowhere was this more demonstrable than in the concern over the younger generation and its moral upbringing. But each state's safeguarding measures were not aimed simply at resocializing youth and eradicating criminality. Against the backdrop of increasing Cold War polarization, this generation of young citizens would not simply demonstrate to the world the scope of German democratic renewal. As future contributors to the moral, civic, and political reconstruction of the East German state, the youth of the 1950s was an essential element in the state's ideological refashioning. Because family rhetoric united the personal and political spheres and also linked generations of Germans together with shared experiences, fears, and expectations, it functioned as an important site of legitimization for Ulbricht's regime. Because the family represented one of its foundational elements, any threat to its stability had to be addressed by institutionalized disciplinary structures under the careful management of professionals and party officials.

Conclusion

Workhouses and reformatories operated as both welfare and legal institutions involving the most difficult cases of asocial behavior, juvenile delinquency, and promiscuity. Although East German authorities envisioned them as emblematic of education instead of incarceration, the line between welfare and punishment was frequently blurred because workhouses and reformatories often held wards who were just released from jail or seemed likely candidates for future imprisonment. The way in which the state determined who could be sent to workhouses demonstrates the elasticity of the terms *endangerment* and *delinquency* in the postwar years. Although the language of biological determinism had been dropped, the criteria for what constituted deviant behavior necessitating state intervention remained relatively unchanged from those of the Nazi period.[68]

During National Socialism the perils of a biological understanding of deviance had been demonstrated through the forced sterilization of criminals and asocials.[69] Although these policies came to an end with the defeat of the Nazi regime, postwar policy on juvenile delinquency and waywardness was still influenced by medicalized views of deviance. Thus the social policies practiced in curative institutes and workhouses reflected an ongoing preoccupation with identifying and overcoming "unhealthy" sexual practices before they could be transmitted to a new generation. Important distinctions must be drawn, however. In the court counseling service and the juvenile facilities psychiatrists, social workers, and psychologists interviewed family members to ascertain the extent of debasement within a particular family. In other words, the family environment—rather than genetics—was recognized as playing a major role in delinquency. Nevertheless, postwar social workers and medical authorities did not demonstrate a strong resolve to break with eugenics-inspired conceptions of deviance. Beyond that, state policies on sexual deviance highlight the continued insecurity of the East German state in leaving sexual acculturation to the biological family.

East German reformatories and youth services complemented the state's efforts to secure the active participation of the nation's youth in building socialism in the GDR. The transfer of these institutions from the aegis of the Ministry of Social Services (*Sozialwesen*) to that of the Ministry of People's Education (*Volksbildung*) reveals the ideological imperative: remedying deviant behavior was closely bound up with building socialism through (re)productive labor. In this way, reforming wayward youth was also about state-building, since rehabilitative education protected the family while simultaneously harnessing the participation of the youth in strengthening the state in accordance with the 1950 ordinance on the Contribution of Youth to the Building of the GDR.

Despite initial efforts to blame the war and later the West for the ideological waywardness of the younger generation, child welfare workers, police, and members of the East German government quickly recognized the need to look for solutions internally. Petty criminality, delinquency, prostitution, and clique building plagued the divided city of Berlin and therefore attracted the attention of GDR policy makers who feared that asocial young adults were especially susceptible to the influence of American-style cultural capitalism.[70] The persistence of youth criminality in the East underscored the state's inability to meet the challenges of social and economic revitalization. The danger posed by the morally derailed (*entgleist*) younger generation was indeed great, for without rehabilitation it was unclear who would shoulder the burdens of increased industrial productivity to help rebuild the war-torn GDR. As the situation worsened in the 1950s, the state employed a variety of methods to promote preferred socialization. Organized sport and leisure, Free German Youth retreats, and Young Pioneer parades were supplemented by another form of intervention that borrowed from prewar advances in treating juvenile delinquents.[71] Targeting certain young offenders for rehabilitation in workhouses, remand homes, and reformatories, the East German state equated antisocial behavior with antisocialist behavior and sought to impose retributive justice through hard work and austere living conditions. From here, it was but a small step to the inhuman institutionalization of delinquents in the notoriously brutal Torgau facility.[72]

By the 1950s, concerns regarding Nazi-era policies fell by the wayside as the consolidation of East Germany took place in the shadow of American-backed consumer capitalism in the Federal Republic. No longer preoccupied with the fascist past, and having met the challenge of postwar reconstruction at least in theory, GDR social policy found a new foil in Adenauer's Christian Democracy. These stages in the development of East German social policy—engaging the specter of National Socialism, forging a platform for rebuilding, and legitimizing the current regime—were reflected in the treatment of young offenders in the courts, in custody, and in care.

Youth facilities formed an essential part of East German attempts to define and delimit an appropriate civic identity based on proper familial roles, productive labor, and moral reform. As a result, hundreds of East German youths were funneled through institutions designed to leave a distinct impression of what contributions to society were required of them. Just as GDR health policy linked population policy to the self-legitimation of communist East Germany, social policy on the problem of youth criminality reflected similar preoccupations.[73] Bringing wayward teens to an awareness of socialist mores meant imbuing them with the knowledge of, and respect for, Ulbricht's family-based industrial political economy. To educate young offenders about their contribution to the health and prosperity of the nation, the Ministry of *Volksbildung* employed a variety of methods in the management of postwar delinquency. In workhouses and remand homes delinquent youth received careful instruction on how to fulfill their social obligations to state and society. Cloaking social policy in the language of morality and borrowing managerial strategies of containment and prevention from the prewar era, the GDR sought the support of average citizens who were equally invested in eradicating moral dissipation and confusion.

By 1955, the problem of youth waywardness was anything but solved. In fact, a special commission was needed to redirect attention to the issue of youth crime in the city of Berlin. The Committee for the Eradication of Youth Crime, again under the supervision of the Ministry of *Volksbildung*, consisted of members of the East German criminal police, the prosecutor's office, the Ministry of Work and Apprenticeship, the Free German Youth, the Association of German Democratic Women, and the Free German Trade Union. An especially perplexing problem was *Republikflucht*, or defection, since an alarming number of teens found their way to the West. Whereas in the early postwar period juvenile crime and waywardness were attributed to the privations brought about by defeat, by the 1950s these phenomena were regarded as emblematic of a different sort of oppositionality. The fear was that these youth were not simply asocial, or even antisocial, but that they were in fact anti-state. Supposedly influenced by the "smut and dirt" of American cultural imperialism, turning their backs on family and factory, and lured to a life in the West by agents of the *Adenauerstaat*, GDR youth were perceived as a potentially serious impediment to the consolidation of state power and control over the private sphere. In the eyes of the East German officials, the extent of youth endangerment could be measured in the "difficulty in reforming waywardness, in the rise in crime, and also in the number of traitorous acts" committed against the state.[74] Socialist morality was not taking hold, and despite the most coercive attempts to reform aberrant behavior and revise gender roles in support of the industrial economy, this goal remained elusive.

What was the government protecting in sending its youth to workhouses and group homes? In promoting a healthy work ethic, the family, and traditional gender roles, youth policy in the GDR continued to gender delinquency, seeking to harness the supposedly natural capacities of young men and women under the guise of rehabilitation. Far from being a natural result of German socialism, the ideal family required the intrusion of the state to shape behavior and tailor morality to meet the imperatives of socialist comportment and the "public good." Although attempts to impose state control over aberrant behavior resulted in incarceration for many, promiscuity and petty criminality did not disappear, as many East German youths continued to live lives outside of the strictures of appropriate identification.

Notes

This chapter, written especially for this volume, draws on material from the author's *Life among the Ruins: Cityscape and Sexuality in Cold War Berlin* (Houndmills: Palgrave Macmillan, 2011).

* "When we educate a citizen, we also educate [the citizen's] sexual feeling."
1. Bundesarchiv Berlin (hereafter, BArch Berlin), DC 4 Amt für Jugendfragen, Nr. 1401 Bekämpfung der Jugendkriminalität, Konzeption für die Abteilung, Leiter Beratung am 22.4.1958 zur Vorbereitung einer zentralen Konferenz über Jugendschutzarbeit.

2. BArch Berlin, DC 4 Amt für Jugendfragen, Nr. 1401 Bekämpfung der Jugendkriminalität, Thesen für die Bezirksbeauftragten zur Zentralen Arbeitsgemeinschaft für Jugendschutz zur Vorbereitung und Durchführung der Konferenzen über die Fragen des Jugendschutzes in den Bezirken, circa 1958.

3. Gerhard Jörns argues there were thirty-six actual *Jugendwerkhöfe* in the GDR by 1956. For more information see his *Der Jugendwerkhof im Jugendhilfesystem der DDR* (Göttingen, 1995), 66. Aside from these workhouses, between 1945 and 1951 there also existed a variety of remand homes and reformatories in and around Berlin. According to one study conducted by the *Innere Mission*, public, private, and church-based organizations in Berlin oversaw as many as thirty-six youth facilities in all four occupation sectors with 690 spots allocated to boys, and 1,425 to girls under the age of eighteen. These facilities ranged from protective custody facilities where young offenders awaited trial, to foster homes and specialty housing for those who traveled to Berlin to complete apprenticeship training. Fifteen institutions were operated by the city government directly, whereas the *Innere Mission* ran eleven and the catholic welfare organization *Caritas* administered nine. Some of these facilities, like Struveshof, would be renamed *Jugendwerkhöfe* in the early 1950s. Archiv Diakonisches Werk, Gesamtverband der Berliner Inneren Mission (GVB), Nr. 14 Verschiedenes 1945–1951, "Jugendliche in Gefahr, Jugendliche Verbrechen in Berlin."

4. BArch Berlin, DC 4 Amt für Jugendfragen, Nr. 1401 Bekämpfung der Jugendkriminalität, Thesen für die Bezirksbeauftragten zur Zentralen Arbeitsgemeinschaft für Jugendschutz zur Vorbereitung und Durchführung der Konferenzen über die Fragen des Jugendschutzes in den Bezirken, circa 1958.

5. Bundesministerium für gesamtdeutsche Fragen, *Der V. Parteitag der SED (10.—16.7. 1958): Eine Analyse* (Berlin, 1958); also printed in *Neues Deutschland*, 18.7.1958.

6. In addition to Gerhard Jörns' book, recent examples include Gerrit Bratke, *Die Kriminologie in der DDR und ihre Anwendung im Bereich der Jugenddelinquenz: Eine zeitgeschichtlich-kriminologische Untersuchung* (Münster, 1999); Thomas Lindenberger, "Aufklären, Zersetzen, Liquidieren: Policing Juvenile Rowdytum in East Germany, 1956–1968," unpublished paper presented to the annual German Studies Association conference, 4–7 October 2001, Arlington,VA; Dorothy Wierling, "Die Jugend als innerer Feind: Konflikte in der Erziehungsdiktatur der sechziger Jahre," in *Sozialgeschichte der DDR*, Hartmut Kaelble, Jürgen Kocka, Hartmut Zwahr, eds. (Stuttgart, 1994), 404–425; "Der Staat, die Jugend und der Westen: Texte zu Konflikten der 1960er Jahre" in *Akten, Eingaben, Schaufenster: Die DDR und ihre Texte: Erkundungen zu Herrschaft und Alltag*, Alf Lüdtke and Peter Becker, eds. (Berlin, 1997), 223–240; and "The Hitler Youth Generation in the GDR: Insecurities, Ambitions and Dilemmas" in *Dictatorship as Experience: Towards a Socio-Cultural History of the GDR*, Konrad Jarausch, ed. (New York, 1999), 307–324; Molly Wilkinson, *Training Socialist Citizens: Sports and the State in East Germany* (Leiden, 2008). On the treatment of young offenders in West Germany, see Frank Kebbedies, *Außer Kontrolle: Jugendkriminalität und Jugendkriminalpolitik in der NS-Zeit und der frühen Nachkriegszeit* (Essen, 2000).

7. Of course, social policy was never truly devoid of politics. A *Tagesspiegel* article from 25.9.46 documents a strategy adopted in the French zone. The article states that youth under eighteen are not housed in prison, but sent to custodial homes where they receive instruction from experienced anti-fascists under the direction of former French officers who served in the "Maquis," or French Resistance. "These youth," the article makes plain, "demonstrate a fine sense of justice."

8. See Konrad H. Jarausch, "Care and Coercion: the GDR as Welfare Dictatorship," in *Dictatorship as Experience*, 59.

9. Günter Grau, "Return of the Past: The Policy of the SED and the Laws Against Homosexuality in Eastern Germany between 1946 and 1968," *Journal of Homosexuality* 37 (1999), 1–21.

10. Edward Dickinson suggests that during the Weimar Republic, two major pieces of legislation helped standardize a comprehensive, locally centralized child welfare policy, including municipal welfare agencies, the participation of religious charities, in addition to correctional education services and youth courts. See Edward Dickinson, *The Politics of German Child Welfare from the Empire to the Federal Republic* (Cambridge, MA, 1996), 153. On youth policy and penal reform initiatives in the Wilhelmine and Weimar years, see Christine Dörner, *Erziehung durch Strafe: Die Geschichte der Jugendstrafe 1871–1945* (Weinheim and Munich, 1991); Elizabeth Harvey, *Youth and the Welfare State in Weimar Germany* (Oxford, 1993); Derek S. Linton, *"Who Has the Youth Has the Future": The Campaign to Save Young Workers in Imperial Germany* (Cambridge, UK, 1991); Detlev Peukert, *Grenzen der Sozialdisziplinierung: Aufstieg und Krise der deutschen Jugendfürsorge von 1878 bis 1932* (Cologne, 1986).

11. Peukert, *Grenzen der Sozialdisziplinierung*; there were a variety of ways in which adults could be committed to a workhouse, most notably through § 361,5 or § 42d of the Penal Code in addition to corresponding welfare legislation. For more information, see Wolfgang Ayass, *Das Arbeitshaus Breitenau. Bettler, Landstreicher, Prostituierte, Zuhälter und Fürsorgeemppfänger in der Korrektions- und Landarmenanstalt Breitenau (1874–1949)* (Kassel, 1992); Andrea Rudolph, *Die Kooperation von Strafrecht und Sozialhilferecht bei der Disziplinierung von Armen mittels Arbeit: Vom Arbeitshaus bis zur gemeinnützigen Arbeit* (Frankfurt am Main, 1995).

12. See Deputy Wachler's comments advocating reform in *Stenographische Berichte über die Verhandlungen des preussischen Hauses der Abgeordneten* (1878), as cited in Dickinson, 20.

13. These developments resulted from the amendment to the RStGB and gained expression in laws both in Prussia and Baden that allowed for the placement of youth in foster families or reformatories if the child's behavior indicated suitable cause for concern. Dickinson states that a number of other states passed similar legislation in the 1890s. Dickinson, 21.

14. Hugo Appelius, *Die Behandlung jugendlicher Verbrecher und verwahrloster Kinder* (Berlin, 1892), 25.

15. For an analysis of the influence of medicalization on child welfare and penal reform advocates, see Gabriel Finder, "Education Not Punishment: Juvenile Justice in Germany 1890–1930" (Ph.D. diss., University of Chicago, 1997); and Michael Voss, *Jugend ohne Rechte: Entwicklung des Jugendstrafrechts* (Frankfurt, 1986).

16. For an extended discussion of health policy and *Bevölkerungspolitik*, see Annette Timm, "The Legacy of *Bevölkerungspolitik*: Venereal Disease Control and Marriage Counseling in Post-WWII Berlin" *Canadian Journal of History* 18 (August 1998), 173–214.

17. For an overview of the postwar reorganizaiton of youth criminal policy, see Jörg Wolff, Margreth Egelkamp, Tobias Mulot, and Michael Gassert, *Das Jugendstrafrecht zwischen Nationalsozialismus und Demokratie: Die Rückkehr der Normalität* (Baden Baden, 1997). With the founding of the German Democratic Republic in October 1949, these laws were finally rewritten along with a host of other policy directives aimed at purging the remnants of Nazi social engineering while streamlining youth support for state socialism.

18. See especially the 1950 law on youth's role in building socialism in *Gesetz über die Teilnahme der Jugend am Aufbau der GDR*, February 1950. Archiv Diakonisches Werk, Allg. Slg. C61.4 Jugend in der GDR.

19. Landesarchiv Berlin (LAB), C Rep 303/9 Polizeipräsident in Berlin, 1945–1948, Nr. 11. Präsidialabteilung, Schutz der Jugend memo from Markgraf dated 1.2.47 to all the necessary departments, including the Hauptjugendamt.

20. Despite a well-developed network of short-term counseling and care facilities, by 1950 public and private youth homes housed over two thousand boys and girls, and youth courts forwarded an additional two thousand per month to these longer-term institutions. Due to shortages of space and financial backing, young offenders sometimes shared the same quarters as general wards of the state, compromising in the minds of educators the effectiveness of contemporary

youth policy. Archiv Diakonisches Werk (ADW) Gesamtverband der Berliner Inneren Mission (GVB), Nr. 14 Verschiedenes 1945–1951, "Jugendliche in Gefahr. Jugendliche Verbrechen in Berlin" (a forty-five-page report on youth homes in Berlin-Brandenburg, undated but written around 1950).

21. BArch Berlin, DO 1 7.0 Deutsche Verwaltung des Innern (DVdI), Nr. 355 Die Entwicklung der Kriminalpolizei in der SBZ von 1945–1949. Correspondence from 24.12.1947 concerning the work of the Kriminalpolizei in policing sexual crimes.

22. The Ministry of Volksbildung oversaw children's aid and traditional child welfare services (such as adoption and care facilicites), while also coordinating penal policy and directives as they affected children and teens. For information on the SMAD Order, see Deutsche Verwaltung für Volksbildung in der SBZ, ed., *Jugendämter: Aufbau und Aufgaben* (Berlin, 1948), 31.

23. BArch Berlin, DC 4 Amt für Jugendfragen, Nr. 1657 die Arbeit zwischen Jugendklubhäuser und Heimen und soziale Betreuung Jugendlicher 1952–1956, Bericht über die Lage in den Jugendwerkhofen und die Perspektiven im 2. Fünfjahrplan (undated).

24. For a detailed discussion of the process of policing homosexual youth, see Jennifer V. Evans, "*Bahnhof* Boys: Policing Male Prostitution in Post-Nazi Berlin," *Journal of the History of Sexuality* 12 (2003), 605–636.

25. BArch Berlin, DQ 2 Ministerium für Arbeit und Berufsausbildung, Nr. 3772 Zeitungsausschnitte zur Bekämpfung gefährdete Jugendlicher 1946–1948. The newspaper snippet dated 6.2.48 titled "Jugendhilfestelle wird ausgebaut" found in the files of the Ministry for Employment and Apprenticeship states that over ten thousand young boys and girls employed the services of the *Jugendhilfestelle*. This number included those youth removed from difficult family situations as well as criminals.

26. For more information on the laws governing disease transmission and suspected prostitution, see Uta Falck, *VEB Bordell: Prostitution in der DDR* (Berlin, 1998), and Annette Timm, "Guarding the Health of Worker Families in the GDR: Socialist Health Care, *Bevölkerungspolitik*, and Marriage Counselling, 1945–72," in *Arbeiter in der SBZ-DDR*, Peter Hübner and Klaus Tenfelde, eds. (Essen, 1999), 463–495.

27. See Warren Rosenblum's chapter in this volume.

28. Of primary importance to police and social services was the need to convince Berlin's youth that their job was to help the youth navigate a path through the judicial and reformatory system. Understandably, many youths remained wary of any help police sought to provide. See BArch Berlin, DO 1 7.0 Deutsche Verwaltung des Innern (DvdI), Nr. 353 Broschüren zur Verordnung zum Schutz der Jugend 1948, Merkblatt zur Bekämpfung der Jugendkriminalität, Zonenkriminalamt Referat K6, Berlin 28.7.47, no author.

29. For examples of the treatment of young offenders, in this case young men charged with male prostitution, see the court case files from the Amtsgericht Tiergarten in 1947, which include examples of information gathered both by the *Jugendamt* and the *Jugendgerichtshilfe* before the division of municipal services in 1948. LAB B Rep 051 Amtsgericht Tiergarten.

30. In the first few years after capitulation, property crimes in Berlin had risen 885 percent from the 1937 figures. See Richard Bessel, "Grenzen des Polizeistaates. Polizei und Gesellschaft in der SBZ und frühen DDR, 1945–1953" in *Die Grenzen der Diktatur: Staat und Gesellschaft in der DDR*, Richard Bessel and Ralph Jessen, eds. (Göttingen, 1996), 225. But violent crime also climbed in the postwar period. For statistics governing violent criminal infractions see LAB C Rep 303/9 Polizeipräsident in Berlin 1945–1948, Nr. 246 Statistiken der Kriminalpolizei 1945–1948.

31. Hermann Glaser, *Kleine Kulturgeschichte der Bundesrepublik Deutschland* (Bonn, 1991), 72–73.

32. LAB, B Rep 210 Bezirksamt Zehlendorf, Acc. 840, Nr. 91/3 Tätigkeitsberichte des Gesundheitsamts vom 1. Januar bis 31. Dezember 1948. Report for the period of 1 January to 31 March 1948 signed by a caseworker identified only as S.E.

33. Frau Hoffmann describes the Dircksenstrasse facility in the Diakonisches Werk report on youth services. See Archiv Diakonisches Werk, Gesamtverband der Berliner Inneren Mission (GVB), Nr. 14 Verschiedenes 1945–1951, "Jugendliche in Gefahr: Jugendliche Verbrechen in Berlin." See also the article in *Sozialdemokrat* from 6.2.48 "Jugendhilfsstelle wird ausgebaut" regarding the desperately needed renovations to the facility.

34. LAB C Rep 120 Magistrat der Stadt Berlin, Hauptabteilung Volksbildung. Nr. 2710 Geschäftstätigkeit des Jugendwerkhöfes Struveshof 1948–1960, Paedagogisches Referent, Konferenz mit Heimleitern und Erziehern in Struveshof über Weglaufen, Schwarzurlaub, Schwarzmarkt, Heimdiebstaehle, Arbeitsverweigerung, und Strafen, am Mittwoch den 16.2.1949, 283.

35. Ernst Seelig, *Lehrbuch der Kriminologie* (Dusseldorf, 1951), 48. Selig suggests that "shirking career criminals take to a life of crime while teens, often remarking later in life that they couldn't find work as young adults. In reformatories (homes for wayward youth or similar institutions) they aren't cured, but instead learn from more established career criminals and refine their skills . . . once on the outside they continue to seek out established criminals and form small bands of grifters." Interestingly, Seelig suggests that no form of state intervention will prevent these youths from re-offending. However, he notes that in a few cases marriage brings about resocialization.

36. LAB C Rep 303/9 Polizeipräsident in Berlin, Nr. 248, Tätigkeitsbuch MII/I—Aussendienst—, 8. Mai 1948–23 April 1949.

37. See the letter from the Director of the Jugendhilfestelle Herr Weimann to the head of the Kriminalpolizei from 28.9.48 in LAB C Rep 303/9 Polizeipräsident in Berlin 1945–1948, Nr. 259 Weibliche Kriminalpolizei 1945–1949.

38. See the weekly reports in LAB C Rep 303/9 Polizeipräsident in Berlin 1945–1948.

39. BArch Berlin, DP 1 Ministerium der Justiz, Hauptabteilung Strafvollzug II-42 Jugendstrafvollzug 1949–1952. For information concerning the East and West German debates concerning the reform of the Young Offenders Act in general and education in lieu of incarceration, see especially *Unsere Jugend* 1949, Nr. 10, 30; *Unsere Jugend* (1950), 10, *Unsere Jugend* (1949), 21. A series of warm reflections from one caseworker were published in 1961 based on his experiences at one GDR facility. Hans Joachim Mahlberg, Man Muss Nur den Schlüssel Finden. Erzählung aus einem Jugendwerkhof. (Rudolstadt, 1961).

40. Despite efforts to promote education instead of incarceration for teenaged youth, in special circumstances charges could be kept in custody beyond their eighteenth birthday if the situation warranted continued supervision. BArch Berlin, DC 4 Amt für Jugendfragen, Nr. 1657 die Arbeit zwischen Jugendklubhäuser und Heimen und soziale Betreuung Jugendlicher 1952–1956, Bericht über die Lage in den Jugendwerkhofen und die Perspektiven im 2. Fünfjahrplan (undated).

41. BArch Berlin, DP 1 Ministerium der Justiz, Hauptabteilung Strafvollzug II-42 Jugendstrafvollzug 1949–1952. Report from 30.09.50 Ministerium für Volksbildung des Landes Sachsen, Jugendhilfe, und Heimerziehung titled "Unsere kommenden Aufgaben in Jugendwerkhöfen."

42. BArch Berlin, DP 1 Ministerium der Justiz, Hauptabteilung Strafvollzug II-42 Jugendstrafvollzug 1949–1952. Working plan for the amelioration of youth workhouses as drafted by Dr. Gentz and submitted to the Ministerium der Justiz upon receipt of the 30.09.50 report from Saxony.

43. The problems affecting East Berlin and the emerging GDR were not necessarily specific to the East. Overcrowding of youth facilities, including the mixing of simple offenders and more advanced criminals, raised the ire of many youth advocates in the West as well. See the article "Jugend protestieren" in *Juna* from 12.09.1950 regarding the deplorable conditions in the Plötzensee youth facility. In an article in *Telegraf* from 15.06.48 titled "Sommersonntag hinter Gefängnismauern: als Chorsänger im Jugendgefängnis Plötzensee—Gespräche mit Häftlingen—Kriminelle, Gefährdete, Gestrauchelte," the author reports how the young prisoners eat

their rations out of empty cans that have been cleaned with sand because there were no available dishes.

44. In the Treuenbrietzen facility, boys lived in small groups with a single caseworker in what were deliberately designed as family-like environments. See Horning, "Die Arbeit des Jugendwerkhofes Treuenbrietzen an straffällig gewordenen und erziehungsgefährdeten Jugendlichen," *Neue Justiz* 3 (1949), 38–39.

45. For an example from Saxony, see the article by an Amtsgericht judge in Aue, "Erfahrungen mit dem produktiven Arbeitseinsatz Strafgefangener," *Neue Justiz* 4 (1950), 57–58.

46. At Struveshof in Ludwigsfelde, boys could learn a variety of trades in the facility's workshops including roofing, carpentry, and electrical work. Generally, youths did not enjoy agricultural work because the hours were long and the work hard. They were rarely embraced by local farmers, who often saw them as difficult city youths with poor attitudes and a lack of respect. See C Rep 120 Magistrat von Berlin, Abteilung Volksbildung, Nr. 2710 Geschäftstätigkeit des Jugendwerkhofes Struveshof, 1948–1960.

47. LAB C Rep 120 Magistrat von Berlin, Abteilung Volksbildung, Nr. 2976 Tätigkeit der Berliner Heime und Jugendwerkhöfe. Die gegenwartige Situation in den Berliner Jugendwerkhöfen— no date but from 1956, 194–201 (undated but ca. 1956).

48. The persistence of traditional gender roles despite the language of equality has been emphasized in a variety of studies. For an example, see Ina Merkel, "Leitbilder und Lebensweisen von Frauen in der DDR" in *Sozialgeschichte der DDR*.

49. See "Die Errichtung eines Fürsorge-Erziehungsheimes für gefährdete Mädchen ist im Schloss Friedrichswert Friedrichswerth,"*Abendpost*, 16 August1947.

50. Brandenburgisches Landeshauptarchiv—Abteilung Bornim, Rep 212 Ministerium der Justiz Hauptabteilung Justiz, Nr. 1266 Haftlager Heidekrug für Frauen 1947–1949. Report from Gerda Konrad and Helene Wosniak from 23.06.1950. Conditions were also deplorable in the Landesmädchenheim Schenkendorf near Königs Wusterhausen. See Nr. 1366, Unterbringung weiblicher Jugendlicher im Landesmädchenheim Schenkendorf bei Königs Wusterhausen 1951.

51. "Erziehung mit Schlagermusik: Ein Besuch im Erziehungsheim für gefährdete Mädchen," *Neue Zeit*, 28 May 1948.

52. Dr. Schimmelpfeng, "Die Betreuung von Kindern, Jugendlichen und Heranwachsenden in Heimen und Anstalten" in *Bekämpfung der Jugendkriminalität: Arbeitstagung im Bundeskriminalamt Wiesbaden vom 1. November bis 6. November über die Jugendlichen und Heranwachsenden* (Wiesbaden, 1955), 231.

53. Merkblatt zur Bekämpfung der Jugendkriminalität, Zonenkriminalamt Referat K6, Berlin dated 28.5.47, author unknown. BArch Berlin, DO 1 7.0 Deutsche Verwaltung des Innern (DvdI), Nr. 353 Broschüren Materialien zur Verordnung zum Schutz der Jugend 1948.

54. Merkblatt zur Bekämpfung der Jugendkriminalität, Zonenkriminalamt Referat K6, Berlin dated 28.5.47. BArch Berlin, DO 1 7.0 Deutsche Verwaltung des Innern (DvdI), Nr. 353 Broschüren Materialien zur Verordnung zum Schutz der Jugend 1948.

55. For more information and statistics from the early postwar situation in Berlin see Heide Thurnwald, *Gegenwartsprobleme Berliner Familien: Eine soziologische Untersuchung an 498 Familien* (Berlin, 1948).

56. Hans Eyferth, *Gefährdete Jugend: Erziehungshilfe bei Fehlentwicklung* (Hannover, 1950), 4.

57. On cross-fertilization and sharing of resources: Uta Poiger points to the paradoxes provided by postwar Berlin. In the sensational court proceedings against gang member Werner Gladow held in East Berlin in 1950, the prosecution actually called for the expert testimony of a West Berlin psychiatrist. Despite the entrenched battle lines between the two states, this court case demonstrates the continued sharing of resources until the early 1950s. See Poiger's discussion

of the case in *Jazz, Rock and Rebels: Cold War Politics and American Culture in a Divided Germany* (Berkeley, 1999), 48–51.

58. Even as late as 1955, East Berlin health authorities continued to lament the influx of itinerant youth that lounged about in unsavory circles and frequently fell into prostitution. See LAB C Rep 118 Magistrat des Gesundheits- und Sozialwesens, Nr. 555 Beratung zur Bekämpfung der Prostitution, Dezember 1955. Meeting on 6.12.1955 in the Headquarters of the Committee to Fight the Spread of Venereal Disease. Responses to report by a representative of the district of Mitte on the importance of working together with the police and social services to combat the spread of disease in the East. According to the Director of the East Berlin Department of Health, Dr. Gross, each police precinct recorded between eight hundred and one thousand unregistered and homeless people, many of them youths. See his letter from 2.12.1954 to the representative of the mayor of Berlin, Frau Johanna Kuzia in LAB C Rep 118 Magistrat des Gesundheits- und Sozialwesens, Nr. 668 Maßnahmen zur Bekämpfung der Geschlechtskrankheiten besonders bei Jugendlichen 1954–1955.

59. Text by law student Gerda Grube in *Zur Geschichte der Rechtspflege der DDR 1945–1949*, which was purportedly written by a collective of authors under the direction of Hilde Benjamin (Berlin, 1976), 277.

60. See the individual cases listed in Archiv Diakonisches Werk (ADW), Gesamtverband der Berliner Inneren Mission (GVB), Nr. 14, Verschiedenes 1945–1951, "Jugendliche in Gefahr. Jugendliche Verbrechen in Berlin," a forty-five-page report on youth homes in Berlin-Brandenburg, undated but written around 1950.

61. See Uta Poiger, "Rock 'n' roll, Kalter Krieg und deutsche Identität" in *Amerikanisierung und Sowjetisierung in Deutschland 1945–1970*, edited by Konrad H. Jarausch and Hannes Siegrist (Frankfurt, 1997), 275–289; in addition to her article "A New, "Western" Hero? Reconstructing German Masculinity in the 1950s" *Signs: Journal of Women in Culture and Society* 24 (1998), 147–162.

62. See the letter from the head of the East Berlin department of health dated 3.5.1955. LAB C Rep 118 Magistrat des Gesundheits- und Sozialwesens, Nr. 668 Maßnahmen zur Bekämpfung der Geschlechtskrankheiten besonders bei Jugendlichen 1954–1955.

63. See the psychological assessment and case file of the underage Erhard S. charged with homosexual prostitution in 1958 in LAB B Rep 069, Jugendstrafanstalt Plötzensee, Acc. 4202, Nr. 1032.

64. See the article "Jugend protestiert" in *Juna* from 12.09.1950.

65. This argument was made in reference to West Germany in Robert Moeller, *Protecting Motherhood: Women and the Family in the Politics of Postwar Germany* (Berkeley, 1993).

66. Makarenko was highly regarded among pedagogues and his writings were frequently cited in the documents. He represents the Soviet state's efforts to deal with the growing problem of homeless children and juvenile crime after 1917. For one of his key contributions to juvenile delinquency, see A. S. Makarenko, *Problems of Soviet School Education* (Moscow, 1965). Makarenko was especially lauded for his work with the *besprizornyi* or delinquents of the early post revolutionary era. Wendy Goldman suggests that in Soviet Russia by 1924, the state viewed young criminals as a distinct subculture that was "stubbornly entrenched and inimical to the ideals of the state." To deal with the problem posed by young offenders, the state sought new ways to channel their energy towards respect for the family and key social institutions. See Wendy Z. Goldman, *Women, the State, and Revolution: Soviet Family Policy and Social Life, 1917–36* (Cambridge, 1993), 89. For additional information on the problem of child welfare and juvenile delinquency in post-1917 Soviet Russia, see Alan M. Ball, *And Now My Soul Is Hardened: Abandoned Children in Soviet Russia, 1918–1930* (Berkeley, 1994); Laurie Bernstein, "Fostering the Next Generation of Socialists: *Patronirovanie* in the Fledgling Soviet

State," *Journal of Family History* 26 (2001), 66–89; Margaret K. Stolee, "Homeless Children in the USSR, 1917–1957," *Soviet Studies* 40 (1988); and Jennie A. Stevens, "Children of the Revolution: Soviet Russia's Homeless Children (Besprizorniki) in the 1920s," *Russian History/Histoire Russe* 9 (1982), 250–252.

67. Presse- und Informationsstelle Berlin, Bundesministerium für gesamtdeutsche Fragen, *Der V. Parteitag der SED (10.—16.7. 1958): Eine Analyse* (Berlin, 1958); also printed in *Neues Deutschland*, 18.7.1958.

68. Elizabeth Heineman includes a short description of the use of workhouses for the work-shy, prostitutes, and asocials during the war. See *What Difference Does a Husband Make? Women and Marital Status in Nazi and Postwar Germany* (Berkeley, 1999), 30.

69. See Richard F. Wetzell, *Inventing the Criminal: A History of German Criminology, 1880–1945* (Chapel Hill, 2000), 233–294.

70. The best analysis of the influence of American culture on postwar German youth can be found in Uta G. Poiger, *Jazz, Rock, and Rebels*.

71. Much work has been done on the Free German Youth movement in English and in Germany. Wilkinson, *Training Socialist Citizens* examines the role of sport in East Germany's quest to mould and shape healthy and active socialist citizens.

72. The closed workhouse of Torgau was regarded as the most heinous juvenile facility in the GDR. For information on its history see Gerhard Jörns, 149–178, and especially Norbert Haase, Brigitte Oleschinski, eds., *Das Torgau-Tabu: Wehrmachtsstrafsystem, NKWD-Speziallager, DDR-Strafvollzug* (Leipzig, 1993).

73. Annette Timm argues that the ongoing importance of population politics in Berlin health policy suggests that the family occupied a primary role in shaping socialist citizenship. See "Guarding the Health of Worker Families in the GDR: Socialist Health Care, *Bevölkerungspolitik*, and Marriage Counselling, 1945–72."

74. BArch Berlin, DC 4 Amt für Jugendfragen, Nr. 1401, Bekämpfung der Jugendkriminalität, Thesen für die Bezirksbeauftragten zur Zentralen Arbeitsgemeinschaft für Jugendschutz zur Vorbereitung und Durchführung der Konferenzen über die Fragen des Jugendschutzes in den Bezirken, circa 1958.

CONTRIBUTORS

Eva Bischoff is assistant professor of international history at the University of Trier. She is the author of *Kannibale-Werden. Eine postkoloniale Geschichte deutscher Männlichkeit um 1900* (transcript, 2011) and the coeditor, with Elisabeth Engel, of *Colonialism and Beyond: Race and Migration from a Postcolonial Perspective* (Lit, 2012). She is currently working on a history of Quaker settler families in Australasia, exploring how they negotiated religious beliefs, humanitarian activism, and the everyday violence of the frontier.

Sace Elder is associate professor of history at Eastern Illinois University. Her publications include *Murder Scenes: Normality, Deviance, and Criminal Violence in Weimar Berlin* (University of Michigan Press, 2010). Her current research examines corporal punishment, child abuse, and the anti-cruelty movement in late nineteenth- and early twentieth-century Germany.

Jennifer V. Evans is associate professor of history at Carleton University. She has published articles on the history of violence and postwar rebuilding in *Social History, Feminist Studies, German History,* and the *Journal of the History of Sexuality.* Her book *Life Among the Ruins: Cityscape and Sexuality in Cold War Berlin* (Palgrave Macmillan, 2011) explores the rebirth of the city's various subcultures in the aftermath of World War II. She has coedited a volume with Matt Cook titled *Queer Cities, Queer Cultures: Europe since 1945* (Continuum, forthcoming 2014) and is working on a new project that analyzes social media and everyday activism for its usefulness in combating the far right.

Gabriel N. Finder is associate professor of Germanic languages and literatures and director of the Jewish Studies Program at the University of Virginia. His current research on trials of Nazi criminals in postwar Poland is incorporated into a book he is writing on Jewish and Polish memories of the Holocaust during the Cold War. He is also coediting a volume on postwar Jewish honor courts.

Andreas Fleiter is a Ph.D. candidate at Ruhr University Bochum. He is currently preparing his dissertation on "Prison and Penal Reforms in Germany and the United States of America: Prussia and Maryland, 1870–1935." He has published on prisoners' letters as historical sources, the history of crime statistics, and concepts of recidivism. His most recent publication is "Schreiben hinter Gittern: Briefe, Kassiber und Beschwerden von Strafgefangenen als historische Quellen," in *Hinter Gittern*, Silke Klewin, Herbert Reinke, and Gerhard Sälter, eds. (Leipzig, 2010).

Petra Gödecke studied history at the University of Bielefeld and is an independent scholar.

Todd Herzog is associate professor and Chair of German Studies at the University of Cincinnati. He is coeditor of the *Journal of Austrian Studies*. His books include *Crime Stories* (Berghahn, 2009), *Rebirth of a Culture* (Berghahn, 2008, with Hillary Hope Herzog and Benjamin Lapp), and *A New Germany in a New Europe* (Routledge, 2001, with Sander Gilman). Recent articles include studies of Quentin Tarantino's *Inglourious Basterds* and Michael Haneke's *Caché*.

Benjamin Carter Hett, professor of history at Hunter College and the Graduate Center, CUNY, received his Ph.D. from Harvard in 2001. He is the author of *Death in the Tiergarten* (Harvard UP, 2004), *Crossing Hitler* (Oxford UP, 2008), which was awarded the Fraenkel Prize, and a forthcoming book on the controversy over the Reichstag fire. He has been the recipient of the Hans Rosenberg article prize and fellowships from the Guggenheim Foundation and the ACLS.

Sandra Leukel earned her doctorate as part of the DFG-Graduiertenkolleg "Sozialgeschichte von Gruppen, Schichten, Klassen und Eliten" at the University of Bielefeld. She is the author of *Strafanstalt und Geschlecht: Geschichte des Frauenstrafvollzugs im 19. Jahrhundert (Baden und Preußen)* (Leipziger Universitätsverlag, 2010). Her research interests focus on women's history and gender history. She is currently working on a double biography of Fanny and Mentona Moser.

Warren Rosenblum is associate professor of history and director of the European studies program at Webster University in St. Louis. His book *Beyond the Prison Gates: Punishment and Welfare in Germany, 1850–1933* (University of North Carolina Press, 2008) won the Baker-Burton Award of the European History Section of the Southern Historical Association. He is currently writing a book about the case of Rudolf Haas, a Jewish industrialist in the Weimar Republic who was falsely accused of murder.

Daniel Siemens is DAAD Francis L. Carsten Lecturer for Modern German History at University College London, School of Slavonic and East European Studies, and assistant professor for History of Modern Societies at Bielefeld University (currently on leave). His most recent books are *The Making of a Nazi Hero:*

The Murder and Myth of Horst Wessel (London 2012) and *"Hass und Begeisterung bilden Spalier": Horst Wessels politische Autobiographie* (Berlin 2011, coedited with Manfred Gailus). His research focuses on the history of Europe and the United States between 1848 and 1968, with particular emphasis on the cultural history of the interwar years and Nazi Germany.

Nikolaus Wachsmann is reader in modern European history at Birkbeck College, University of London. He is the author of *Hitler's Prisons: Legal Terror in Nazi Germany* (Yale, 2004), which won the Royal Historical Society Gladstone Prize and the Longman-History Today Book of the Year Award. He is also the coeditor, together with Jane Caplan, of *Concentration Camps in Nazi Germany: The New Histories* (Routledge, 2010).

Robert G. Waite is a research historian at the Forschungsstelle Widerstandsgeschichte of the Gedenkstätte Deutscher Widerstand and the Freie Universität Berlin. Recent publications include "'Ish bin ein Bearleener.' JFK's 26 June 1963 Visit to Berlin: The Views from East Germany," *Journal of Contemporary History* 45 (2010); "'The Most Model Prison of the World.' The Albany County Penitenitary and 19th Century Prison Reform," *New York History Review* (2011); and "'Das Beste, was passieren konnte.' Amerikanische Reaktionen auf den deutschen Angriff auf die Sowjetunion," in *Vor 70 Jahren: Der Überfall Hitlerdeutschlands auf die Sowjetunion* (Berlin, 2011).

Richard F. Wetzell is a research fellow at the German Historical Institute in Washington, D.C. and the editor of the *Bulletin of the German Historical Institute*. Trained at Stanford University, he was a postdoctoral fellow at Harvard University and has taught at the University of Maryland, Georgetown University, and the Catholic University of America. He is the author of *Inventing the Criminal: A History of German Criminology, 1880–1945* (University of North Carolina Press, 2000) and coeditor of *Engineering Society: The Role of the Human and Social Sciences in Modern Societies, 1880–1980* (Palgrave, 2012) and *Criminals and Their Scientists: The History of Criminology in International Perspective* (Cambridge UP, 2006). He is currently writing a legal and political history of penal reform in modern Germany from 1870 to 1970.

BIBLIOGRAPHY

Abrams, Lynn. "Prostitutes in Imperial Germany, 1870–1918: Working Girls or Social Outcasts?" In *The German Underworld: Deviants and Outcasts in German History*, ed. Richard J. Evans, 189–209. London, 1988.

———. "Martyrs or Matriarchs? Working-Class Women's Experience of Marriage in Germany before the First World War." *Women's History Review* 1, no. 3 (1992): 357–376.

———. "Companionship and Conflict: the Negotiation of Marriage Relations in the Nineteenth Century." In *Gender Relations in German History: Power, Agency and Experience from the Sixteenth to the Twentieth Century*, ed. Lynn Abrams and Elizabeth Harvey, 101–120. Durham, 1996.

Anderson, Margaret Lavinia. *Practicing Democracy: Elections and Political Culture in Imperial Germany*. Princeton, 2000.

Andriopoulos, Stefan. "Die Zirkulation von Figuren und Begriffen in kriminologischen, juristischen und literarischen Darstellungen von 'Unfall' und 'Verbrechen'." *Internationales Archiv für Sozialgeschichte der deutschen Literatur* 21 (1996): 113–142.

Angermund, Ralph. *Deutsche Richterschaft 1919–1945*. Frankfurt/Main, 1990.

Aragon-Yoshida, Amber Marie. "*Lustmord* and Loving the Other: A History of Sexual Murder in Modern Germany and Austria (1873–1932)." Ph.D. diss., Washington University in St. Louis, 2011.

Aschheim, Steven E. *The Nietzsche Legacy in Germany, 1890–1990*. Berkeley, 1992.

Ayass, Wolfgang. *Das Arbeitshaus Breitenau*. Kassel, 1992.

———. *'Asoziale' im Nationalsozialismus*. Stuttgart, 1995.

———. "*Gemeinschaftsfremde*": Quellen zur Verfolgung von Asozialen, 1933–1945. Koblenz, 1998.

Bader, Karl Siegfried. "Walter Mallmann und die Gründung der 'Deutschen Rechts-Zeitschrift.'" In *Festschrift für Walter Mallmann zum 70. Geburtstag*, ed. Otto Triffterer and Friedrich von Zezschwitz, 17–31. Baden-Baden, 1978.

———. "Der Wiederaufbau. Tagebuch Juli 1945 bis Juni 1946." In *Gelb-rot-gelbe Regierungsjahre. Badische Politik nach 1945: Gedenkschrift zum 100. Geburtstag Leo Wohlebs (1888–1955)*, ed. Paul-Ludwig Weinacht, 33–88. Sigmaringendorf, 1988.

———. "Zum 50. Jahrgang der Juristenzeitung." *JuristenZeitung* 50, no. 1 (1995): 1.

Badura, Peter, Erwin Deutsch, and Claus Roxin, eds. *Das Fischer Lexikon: Recht*. Frankfurt/Main, 1987.

Ball, Alan M. *And Now My Soul Is Hardened: Abandoned Children in Soviet Russia, 1918–1930*. Berkeley, 1994.

Bareither, Christoph, and Urs Büttner, eds. *Fritz Lang: "M-Eine Stadt sucht einen Mörder": Texte und Kontexte*. Würzburg, 2010.

Barrows, Susanna. *Distorting Mirrors: Visions of the Crowd in Late Nineteenth Century France*. New Haven, 1981.

Baumann, Imanuel. *Dem Verbrechen auf der Spur: Eine Geschichte der Kriminologie und Kriminalpolitik in Deutschland 1880 bis 1980.* Göttingen, 2006.

Baumann, Jürgen. "Karl Peters 70 Jahre." *JuristenZeitung* 2 (1974): 66–67.

Bayertz, Kurt. "Naturwissenschaft und Sozialismus: Tendenzen der Naturwissenschafts-Rezeption in der deutschen Arbeiterbewegung des 19. Jahrhunderts." *Social Studies of Science* 13 (1983): 362–367.

Becker, Peter. "Kriminelle Identitäten im 19. Jahrhundert: Neue Entwicklungen in der historischen Kriminalitätsforschung." *Historische Anthropologie* 2 (1994): 142–157.

———. "'Gefallene Engel' und 'verwahrloste Menschen': Über 'Erzählmuster,' Prostituierte und die Kriminalistik des vorigen Jahrhunderts." In *Konstruktion der Wirklichkeit durch Kriminalität und Strafe,* edited by Detlev Frehsee, Gabi Löschper, and Gerlinda Smaus, 340–346. Baden-Baden, 1997.

———. "Weak Bodies? Prostitutes and the Role of Gender in the Criminological Writings of 19th-Century German Detectives and Magistrates." *Crime, Histoire and Societies* 3, no. 1 (1999): 45–69.

———. *Verderbnis und Entartung: Eine Geschichte der Kriminologie des 19. Jahrhunderts als Diskurs und Praxis.* Göttingen, 2002.

Becker, Peter, and Richard F. Wetzell, eds. *Criminals and Their Scientists: The History of Criminology in International Perspective.* New York, 2006.

Behrle, Alfred. *Die Stellung der deutschen Sozialisten zum Strafvollzug von 1870 bis zur Gegenwart.* Berlin, 1931.

Bendix, Ludwig. "Die Rechtsbeugung im künftigen deutschen Strafrecht." *Die Justiz* 2, no. 1 (1926): 42–75.

Benjamin, Hilde, ed. *Zur Geschichte der Rechtspflege der DDR 1945–1949.* Berlin, 1976.

Benton, Ted. "Social Darwinism and Socialist Darwinism in Germany: 1860 to 1900." *Rivista di Filosofia* 73 (1982): 110–120.

Berding, Helmut, Diethelm Klippel, and Günther Lottes, eds. *Kriminalität und abweichendes Verhalten: Deutschland im 18. und 19. Jahrhundert.* Göttingen, 1999.

Berg, Karl. *Der Sadist. Gerichtsärztliches und Kriminalpsychologisches zu den Taten des Düsseldorfer Mörders Peter Kürten. Mit zwei Artikelserien des Kriminal-Polizeirats Ernst Gennat und der Verteidigungsrede von Dr. Alex Wehner,* ed. Michael Farin. München, 2004.

Berger, Thomas. *Die konstante Repression: Zur Geschichte des Strafvollzugs in Preußen nach 1850.* Frankfurt/Main, 1974.

Berghahn, Volker R. *Der Stahlhelm. Bund der Frontsoldaten, 1918–1935.* Düsseldorf, 1966.

Bernhardt, Markus. *Gießener Professoren zwischen Drittem Reich und Bundesrepublik: Ein Beitrag zur hessischen Hochschulgeschichte 1945–1957.* Gießen, 1990.

Bernstein, Laurie. "Fostering the Next Generation of Socialists: *Patronirovanie* in the Fledgling Soviet State." *Journal of Family History* 26 (2001): 66–89.

Bessel, Richard. *Germany after the First World War.* Oxford, 1995.

———. "Grenzen des Polizeistaates. Polizei und Gesellschaft in der SBZ und frühen DDR, 1945–1953." In *Die Grenzen der Diktatur: Staat und Gesellschaft in der DDR,* ed. Richard Bessel and Ralph Jessen, 224–252. Göttingen, 1996.

Bischoff, Eva. *Kannibale-Werden. Eine postkoloniale Geschichte deutscher Männlichkeit um 1900.* Bielefeld, 2011.

Blackbourn, David. *Populists and Patricians: Essays in Modern German History.* London, 1987.

———. *The Long Nineteenth Century: Germany 1780–1918.* London, 1997.

Blackbourn, David, and Geoff Eley. *The Peculiarities of German History: Bourgeois Society and Politics in Nineteenth Century Germany.* Oxford, 1984.

Blasius, Dirk. *Bürgerliche Gesellschaft und Kriminalität: Zur Sozialgeschichte Preußens im Vormärz.* Göttingen, 1976.

———. *Geschichte der politischen Kriminalität in Deutschland, 1800–1980.* Frankfurt/Main, 1983.

Blazek, Matthias. *Karl Großmann und Friedrich Schumann: Zwei Serienmörder in den zwanziger Jahren.* Stuttgart, 2009.

Blau, Bruno. "Die Kriminalität in Deutschland während des zweiten Weltkrieges." *Zeitschrift für die gesamte Strafrechtswissenschaft* 64 (1952): 71.

Bleek, Stephan. "Mobilität und Seßhaftigkeit in deutschen Großstädten während der Urbanisierung." *Geschichte und Gesellschaft* 15, no. 1 (1989): 5–33.

Böhme, Monika. *Die Moralstatistik: Ein Beitrag zur Geschichte der Quantifizierung in der Soziologie, dargestellt an den Werken Adolphe Quetelets und Alexander von Oettingens.* Cologne, 1971.

Bollas, Christopher. *Cracking Up.* New York, 1995.

Bosetzky, Horst. *Die Bestie vom Schlesischen Bahnhof.* Berlin, 2005.

Braidotti, Rosi. *Nomadic Subjects. Embodiment and Sexual Difference in Contemporary Feminist Theory.* New York, 1994.

Bratke, Gerrit. *Die Kriminologie in der DDR und ihre Anwendung im Bereich der Jugenddelinquenz: Eine zeitgeschichtlich-kriminologische Untersuchung.* Münster, 1999.

Braun. Hans. "Das Streben nach 'Sicherheit' in den 50er Jahren. Soziale und politische Ursachen und Erscheinungsweisen." *Archiv für Sozialgeschichte* 18 (1978): 279–306.

Bretschneider, Falk. *Gefangene Gesellschaft: Eine Geschichte der Einsperrung in Sachsen im 18. und 19. Jahrhundert.* Konstanz, 2008.

Broszat, Martin. "Zur Perversion der Strafjustiz im Dritten Reich." *Vierteljahreshefte für Zeitgeschichte* (1958): 390–441.

———, ed. *Kommandant in Auschwitz: Autobiographische Aufzeichnungen des Rudolf Höss.* Munich, 1963.

Brücker, Eva. "'Und ich bin da 'rausgekommen': Gewalt und Sexualität in einer Berliner Arbeiternachbarschaft zwischen 1916/17 und 1958." In *Physische Gewalt: Studien zur Geschichte der Neuzeit*, ed. Thomas Lindenberger and Alf Lüdtke, 337–365. Frankfurt/Main, 1995.

Brückweh, Kerstin. *Mordlust: Serienmorde, Gewalt und Emotionen im 20. Jahrhundert.* Frankfurt/Main, 2006.

Brückweh, Kerstin, et al., eds., *Engineering Society: The Role of the Human and Social Sciences in Modern Societies, 1880–1980.* Houndmills, 2012.

Bruns, Hans-Jürgen. Preface to *140 Jahre Goltdammer's Archiv für Strafrecht. Eine Würdigung zum 70. Geburtstag von Paul-Günter Pötz*, edited by Jürgen Wolter, V-X. Heidelberg, 1993.

Bumke, Erwin. "Die Freiheitsstrafe als Problem der Gesetzgebung." In *Deutsches Gefängniswesen: Ein Handbuch*, ed. Erwin Bumke, 16–32. Berlin, 1928.

Burgmair, Wolfgang, Nikolaus Wachsmann, and Matthias Weber. "'Die soziale Prognose wird damit sehr trübe . . . ' Theodor Viernstein und die kriminalbiologische Sammelstelle in Bayern." In *Polizeireport München*, ed. Michael Farin, 250–287. Munich, 1999.

Burleigh, Michael. *Death and Deliverance: "Euthanasia" in Germany 1900–45.* Cambridge, 1994.

Burleigh, Michael, and Wolfgang Wippermann. *The Racial State: Germany 1933–1945.* Cambridge, 1991.

Bussard, Robert L. "The 'Dangerous Class' of Marx and Engels: The Rise of the Idea of the 'Lumpenproletariat'." *History of European Ideas* 8 (1987): 675–692.

Byer, Doris. *Rassenhygiene und Wohlfahrtspflege: Zur Entstehung eines sozialdemokratischen Machtdispositivs in Österreich bis 1934.* Frankfurt/Main, 1988.

Caplan, Jane, and Nikolaus Wachsmann, eds. *Concentration Camps in Nazi Germany: The New Histories.* London, 2010.

Chandler, James. *England in 1819: The Politics of Literary Culture and the Case of Romantic Historicism.* Chicago, 1998.

Classen, Isabella. *Darstellung von Kriminalität in der deutschen Literatur, Presse und Wissenschaft: 1900 bis 1930.* Frankfurt/Main, 1988.

Conze, Werner. "Proletariat, Pöbel, Pauperismus." *Geschichtliche Grundbegriffe: Historisches Lexikon zur politisch-sozialen Sprache in Deutschland,* ed. Otto Brunner, Werner Conze, and Reinhart Koselleck, vol. 5, 27–68. Stuttgart, 1984.

Conze, Werner, and Dieter Groh. *Die Arbeiterbewegung in der nationalen Bewegung: Die deutsche Sozialdemokratie vor, während und nach der Reichsgründung.* Stuttgart, 1966.

Corbin, Alain. *Women for Hire: Prostitution and Sexuality in France after 1850,* trans. Alan Sheridan, 1978. Cambridge, MA, 1990.

Crew, David F. "The Ambiguities of Modernity: Welfare and the German State from Wilhelm to Hitler." In *Society, Culture, and the State in Germany, 1870–1930,* ed. Geoff Eley, 319–344. Ann Arbor, 1996.

———. *Germans on Welfare: from Weimar to Hitler.* New York, 1998.

Curran, Vivian Grosswald. "Fear of Formalism: Indications from the Fascist Period in France and Germany of Judicial Methodology's Impact." *Cornell International Law Journal* 35 (2001): 101–187.

Currie, Elliot. "Confronting Crime: New Directions." In *Crime and Society,* ed. Robert Crutchfield, George S. Brides, and Joseph G. Weis. Thousand Oaks, CA, 1996.

Daniel, Ute. *The War from Within: German Working-Class Women in the First World War.* Translated by Margaret Ries. Oxford and New York, 1997. Originally published in 1989.

Davis, Belinda. *Home Fires Burning: Food, Politics, and Everyday Life in World War I Berlin.* Chapel Hill, 2000.

Davis, John A. *Conflict and Control: Law and Order in Nineteenth-Century Italy.* Houndmills, 1988.

DeLillo, Don. *Libra.* New York, 1988.

Dickinson, Edward R. *The Politics of German Child Welfare from the Empire to the Federal Republic.* Cambridge, MA, 1996.

Dierl, Florian, et al. *Ordnung und Vernichtung: Die Polizei im NS-Staat.* Dresden, 2011. Catalog of the exhibition shown at Deutsches Historisches Museum, Berlin.

Dinges, Martin, and Fritz Sack, eds. *Unsichere Großstädte? Vom Mittelalter bis zur Postmoderne.* Konstanz, 2000.

Dirks, Nicholas B. "Ritual and Resistance: Subversion as a Social Fact." In *Culture/ Power/ History. A Reader in Contemporary Social Theory,* ed. Nicholas B. Dirks, Geoff Eley, and Sherry B. Ortner, 483–503. Princeton, NJ, 1992.

Ditfurth, Hoimar von. *Innenansichten eines Artgenossen: Meine Bilanz.* Munich, 1991.

Dölling, Dieter. "Kriminologie im 'Dritten Reich.'" In *Recht und Justiz im 'Dritten Reich,'* ed. Ralf Dreier and Wolfgang Sellert, 194–220. Frankfurt/Main, 1989.

Dörner, Christine. *Erziehung durch Strafe: Die Geschichte der Jugendstrafe 1871–1945.* Weinheim, 1991.

Domansky, Elisabeth. "Militarization and Reproduction in World War I Germany." In *Society, Culture, and the State in Germany, 1870–1930,* ed. Geoff Eley, 427–463. Ann Arbor, 1997.

Dowe, Dieter, and Kurt Klotzbach, eds. *Programmatische Dokumente der deutschen Sozialdemokratie*. Berlin, 1973.

Draper, Hal. *Karl Marx's Theory of Revolution*, vol. 2, *The Politics of Social Classes*. New York, 1978.

Drawz, Christiane. "Die Schließung der Juristischen Fakultät 1950." *Beiträge zur Geschichte der Universität Rostock* 19 (1994): 33–43.

Dreßen, Wolfgang. *Die pädagogische Maschine: Zur Geschichte des industrialisierten Bewußtseins in Preußen/Deutschland*. Frankfurt/Main, 1982.

Driendl, Johannes. "Die deutsche Strafrechtslehrertagung in Geschichte und Gegenwart." *Zeitschrift für die gesamte Strafrechtswissenschaft* 92 (1980): 1–18.

Duttlinger, Carolin, and Lucia Ruprecht. Introduction to *Performance and Performativity in German Cultural Studies*, ed. Carolin Duttlinger, Lucia Ruprecht, and Andrew Webber, 9–19. Oxford, 2003.

Dworkin, R. M., ed. *The Philosophy of Law, Oxford Readings in Philosophy*. Oxford, 1977.

Dubber, Markus Dirk. "Judicial Positivism and Hitler's Injustice." Book Review of *Hitler's Justice: The Courts of the Third Reich*, by Ingo Müller. *Columbia Law Review* 93 (1993): 1807–1831.

Elder, Sace. *Murder Scenes: Normality, Deviance, and Criminal Violence in Weimar Berlin*. Ann Arbor, 2010.

Eley, Geoff. *Reshaping the German Right: Radical Nationalism and Political Change after Bismarck*. Ann Arbor, 1991.

El-Tayeb, Fatima. *Schwarze Deutsche. Der Diskurs um "Rasse" und nationale Identität 1890—1933*. Frankfurt/Main, 2001.

Emig, Brigitte. *Die Veredelung des Arbeiters: Sozialdemokratie als Kulturbewegung*. Frankfurt/Main 1980.

Emsley, Clive. *Crime and Society in England 1750–1900*. Harlow, 1987; 2nd ed. 1996.

———. *Crime, Police, and Penal Policy: European Experiences 1750–1940*. Oxford, 2007.

Engelhardt, Doris. "Ferdinand Bruckner als Kritiker seiner Zeit. Standortsuche eines Autors." Ph.D. diss., Rheinisch-Westfälische Technische Hochschule Aachen, 1984.

Engelmann, Bernt. *Die unsichtbare Tradition: Richter zwischen Recht und Macht 1779–1918*. Cologne, 1988.

Engisch, Karl. "Eberhard Schmidt." *Jahrbuch der Heidelberger Akademie der Wissenschaften* (1979): 80–83.

Engstrom, Eric J. *Clinical Psychiatry in Imperial Germany: A History of Psychiatric Practice*. Ithaca, 2003.

Essner, Cornelia. *Die "Nürnberger Gesetze" oder die Verwaltung des Rassenwahns 1933–1945*. Paderborn, 2002.

Etzel, Matthias. *Die Aufhebung von nationalsozialistischen Gesetzen durch den Alliierten Kontrollrat 1945–1948*. Tübingen, 1992.

Evans, Jennifer V. "*Bahnhof* Boys: Policing Male Prostitution in Post-Nazi Berlin." *Journal of the History of Sexuality* 12 (2003): 605–636.

———. *Life among the Ruins: Cityscape and Sexuality in Cold War Berlin*. London and New York, 2011.

Evans, Richard J. "Prostitution, State, and Society in Imperial Germany." *Past and Present* 70 (1976): 106–129.

———. "'Red Wednesday' in Hamburg: Social Democrats, Police and Lumpenproletariat in the Suffrage Disturbances of 17 January 1906." *Social History* 4, no. 1 (1979): 1–31.

---. *Kneipengespräche im Kaiserreich: Stimmungsberichte der Hamburger Politischen Polizei, 1892–1914.* Reinbek, 1989.

---. "The 'Dangerous Classes' in Germany from the Middle Ages to the Twentieth Century." In *Proletarians and Politics: Socialism, Protest and the Working Class in Germany before the First World War*, 1–27. New York, 1990.

---. "Proletarian Mentalities: Pub Conversations in Hamburg." In *Proletarians and Politics: Socialism, Protest and the Working Class in Germany before the First World War*, 124–191. New York, 1990.

---. *Rituals of Retribution: Capital Punishment in Germany, 1600–1987.* Oxford, 1996.

---. *Szenen aus der deutschen Unterwelt: Verbrechen und Strafe, 1800–1914.* Reinbek, 1997.

---. *Tales from the German Underground: Crime and Punishment in the Nineteenth Century.* New Haven, 1998.

Exner, Franz. *Studien über die Strafzumessungspraxis der deutschen Gerichte.* Leipzig, 1931.

Falck, Uta. *VEB Bordell: Prostitution in der DDR.* Berlin, 1998.

Feustel, Jan. *Raub und Mord im Kiez: Historische Friedrichshainer Kriminalfälle. Begleitmaterial zur Ausstellung.* Berlin, 1996.

Finder, Gabriel. "Education Not Punishment: Juvenile Justice in Germany 1890–1930." Ph.D. diss., University of Chicago, 1997.

Finzsch, Norbert. "'Comparing Apples and Oranges?' The History of Early Prisons in Germany and the United States, 1800–1860." In *Institutions of Confinement: Hospitals, Asylums, and Prisons in Western Europe and North America, 1500–1950*, ed. Norbert Finzsch and Robert Jütte, 213–233. New York, 1996.

---. "Elias, Foucault, Oestreich: On a Historical Theory of Confinement." In *Institutions of Confinement: Hospitals, Asylums, and Prisons in Western Europe and North America, 1500–1950*, ed. Norbert Finzsch and Robert Jütte, 3–16. New York, 1996.

Finzsch, Norbert, and Robert Jütte, eds. *Institutions of Confinement: Hospitals, Asylums and Prisons in Western Europe and North America, 1500–1950.* New York, 1996.

Fischer-Lichte, Erika. "Performance, Inszenierung, Ritual. Zur Klärung kulturwissenschaftlicher Schlüsselbegriffe." In *Geschichtswissenschaft und "performative turn": Ritual, Inszenierung und Performanz vom Mittelalter bis zur Neuzeit*, ed. Jürgen Martschukat and Steffen Patzold, 33–54. Cologne, 2003.

Foell, Kristie. "Elfriede Czurda: Poison and Play." In *Out From the Shadows: Essays on Contemporary Austrian Women Writers and Filmmakers*, ed. Margarete Lamb-Faffelberger, 158–171. Riverside, CA, 1997.

Forsythe, W. J. *Penal Discipline, Reformatory Projects and the English Prison Commission 1895–1939.* Exeter, 1990.

Foucault, Michel. *Surveiller et punir: Naissance de la prison.* Paris: Gallimard, 1975; translated as: *Discipline and Punish: The Birth of the Prison.* New York, 1978.

---. "Truth and Power." In *The Foucault Reader*, ed. Paul Rabinow, 51–75. New York, 1984.

---. "Lecture on 8 January 1975." In *Abnormal. Lectures at the Collège de France 1974–1975*, ed. Valerio Marchetti and Antonella Salomoni, trans. Graham Burchell, 1–30. London, 2003.

Fout, John C. "Sexual Politics in Wilhelmine Germany: The Male Gender Crisis, Moral Purity, and Homophobia." *Journal of the History of Sexuality* 2, no. 3 (1992): 388–421.

Frede, Lothar, and Rudolf Sieverts, eds. *Die Beschlüsse der Internationalen Gefängnis-Kongresse 1872–1930.* Jena, 1932.

Frei, Norbert. *Vergangenheitspolitik: Die Anfänge der Bundesrepublik und die NS-Vergangenheit.* Munich, 1997.

Freunde eines Schwulen Museums, ed. *Die Geschichte des §175: Strafrecht gegen Homosexuelle.* Berlin, 1990.

Frigessi, Delia. "Scienza socialista e scienza borghese tra 'Archivio di psichiatria' e 'Critica sociale'." In *Le radici del socialismo italiano*, ed. Lucia Romaniello, 223–234. Milan, 1997.

Fritzsche, Peter. *Reading Berlin, 1900.* Cambridge, MA, 1996.

———. "On Being the Subjects of History: Nazis as Twentieth-Century Revolutionaries." In *Language and Revolution. Making Modern Political Identities*, ed. Igal Halfin, 161–183. London, 2002.

———. "Talk of the Town. The Murder of Lucie Berlin and the Production of Local Knowledge." In *Criminals and their Scientists. The History of Criminology in International Perspective*, ed. Peter Becker and Richard F. Wetzell, 377–398. Cambridge, 2005.

Frommel, Monika. *Präventionsmodelle in der deutschen Strafzweck-Diskussion: Beziehungen zwischen Rechtsphilosophie, Dogmatik, Rechtspolitik und Erfahrungswissenschaften.* Berlin, 1987.

———. "Internationale Reformbewegung zwischen 1880 und 1920." In *Erzählte Kriminalität: Zur Typologie und Funktion von narrativen Darstellungen in Strafrechtspflege, Publizistik und Literatur zwischen 1770 und 1920*, ed. Jörg Schönert, 467–495. Tübingen, 1991.

Fuchs, Walter. *Franz Exner (1881–1947) und das Gemeinschaftsfremdengesetz: Zum Barbarisierungspotenzial moderner Kriminalwissenschaft.* Berlin, 2008.

Fuller, Lon L. *The Morality of Law.* New Haven, 1969.

Gadebusch-Bondio, Mariacarla. *Die Rezeption der kriminalanthropologischen Theorien von Cesare Lombroso in Deutschland von 1880–1914.* Husum, 1995.

Galassi, Silviana. *Kriminologie im Deutschen Kaiserreich: Geschichte einer gebrochenen Verwissenschaftlichung.* Stuttgart, 2004.

Garland, David. *Punishment and Welfare: A History of Penal Strategies.* Aldershot, 1985.

———. *Punishment and Modern Society.* Chicago, 1990.

Gartner, Theodor. "Sozialdemokratische Partei und Strafrecht." Ph.D. diss., Albert-Ludwigs-Universität Freiburg, 1927.

Gélieu, Claudia von. *Frauen in Haft.* Berlin, 1994.

Gellately, Robert, and Nathan Stoltzfus, eds. *Social Outsiders in Nazi Germany.* Princeton, 2001.

Geulen, Christian. *Wahlverwandte. Rassendiskurs und Nationalismus im späten 19. Jahrhundert.* Hamburg, 2004.

Gibson, Mary S. "The 'Female Offender' and the Italian School of Criminal Anthropology." *European Studies* 12 (1982): 155–165.

———. *Prostitution and the State in Italy, 1860–1910.* New Brunswick, 1986.

———. *Born to Crime: Cesare Lombroso and the Origins of Biological Criminology.* Westport, CT, 2002.

Gilman, Sander L. "Sexology, Psychoanalysis, and Degeneration: From a Theory of Race to a Race to Theory." In *Degeneration. The Dark Side of Progress*, ed. Edward J. Chamberlain and Sander L. Gilman, 72–100. New York, 1985.

Glaser, Hermann. *Kleine Kulturgeschichte der Bundesrepublik Deutschland.* Bonn, 1991.

Goffman, Erving. *Asylums: Essays on the Social Situation of Mental Patients and Other Inmates.* London, 1971.

———. *Stigma: Notes on the Management of Spoiled Identity.* 1963. New York, 1986.

Goldberg, Ann. *Honor, Politics, and the Law in Imperial Germany, 1871–1914.* Cambridge, 2010.

Goldman, Wendy Z. *Women, the State, and Revolution: Soviet Family Policy and Social Life, 1917–36.* Cambridge, 1993.

Goldstein, Jan. "Framing Discipline with Law: Problems and Promises of the Liberal State." *American Historical Review* 98 (1993): 364–381.

Goldstein, Moritz. *George Grosz freigesprochen: Gerichtsreportagen aus der Weimarer Republik,* ed. Manfred Voigts, Till Schicketanz, and Martina Flohr. Hamburg, 2005.

Gumbel, Emil Julius. *Vier Jahre politischer Mord.* Berlin, 1922.

Gransee, Carmen. "Zur Reproduktion von Normalitätsvorstellungen von Weiblichkeit durch Kriminalisierungsprozesse: Eine Rekonstruktion der Medienwirklichkeiten." In *Konstruktion der Wirklichkeit durch Kriminalität und Strafe,* ed. Detlev Frehsee, 435–455. Baden-Baden, 1997.

Gräser, Marcus. *Der blockierte Wohlfahrtsstaat: Unterschichtjugend und Jugendfürsorge in der Weimarer Republik.* Göttingen, 1995.

Grau, Günter. "Return of the Past: The Policy of the SED and the Laws Against Homosexuality in Eastern Germany between 1946 and 1968." *Journal of Homosexuality* 37 (1999): 1–21.

Greve, Ylva. *Verbrechen und Krankheit: Die Entdeckung der "Criminalpsychologie" im 19. Jahrhundert.* Cologne, 2004.

Grimm, Dieter. "Die 'Neue Rechtswissenschaft'—Über Funktion und Formation nationalsozialistischer Jurisprudenz." In *Recht und Staat der bürgerlichen Gesellschaft,* 373–395. Frankfurt/Main, 1987.

Gruchmann, Lothar. *Justiz im Dritten Reich 1933–1940: Anpassung und Unterwerfung in der Ära Gürtner.* 1988. Reprint, Munich, 1990.

Grünhut, Max. *The Development of the German Penal System 1920–32.* Cambridge, 1944.

Grunwald, Henning. "Der Gerichtssaal als 'revolutionäre Tribüne': Ideologische Selbst-Inszenierung im Medium politischer Prozesse der Weimarer Republik." *Paragrana* 15 (2006): 211–225.

———. "Die 'Vertrauenskrise der Justiz' in der Weimarer Republik: Justiz als Krisendiagnostik." In *Krisis! Krisenszenarien, Diagnosen und Diskursstrategien,* ed. Henning Grunwald and Manfred Pfister, 177–199. Stuttgart, 2007.

———. "From Courtroom to 'Revolutionary Stage': Performing Ideology in Weimar Political Trials." In *Das Gericht als Tribunal oder: Wie der NS-Vergangenheit der Prozess gemacht wurde,* ed. Georg Wamhof, 41–52. Göttingen, 2009.

———. "Justice as Performance? The Historiography of Legal Procedure and Political Criminal Justice in Weimer Germany." *Inter Disciplines. Journal of History and Sociology* 3, no. 2 (2012), 46–78.

———. *Courtroom to Revolutionary Stage: Performance and Ideology in Weimar Political Trials.* Oxford, 2012.

Grüttner, Michael. "Working-Class Crime and the Labour Movement: Pilfering in the Hamburg Docks, 1888–1923." In *The German Working Class, 1888–1933: The Politics of Everyday Life,* ed. Richard J. Evans, 54–75. London, 1982.

———. "Die Kultur der Armut: Mobile Arbeiter während der Industrialisierung." *Jahrbuch Soziale Bewegungen* 3 (1987): 24–29.

Haase, Norbert, and Brigitte Oleschinski, eds. *Das Torgau-Tabu: Wehrmachtsstrafsystem, NKWD-Speziallager, DDR-Strafvollzug.* Leipzig, 1993.

Habermas, Rebekka. *Diebe vor Gericht: Die Entstehung der modernen Rechtsordnung im 19. Jahrhundert.* Frankfurt/Main, 2008.

————. "Rechts- und Kriminalitätsgeschichte revisited—Ein Plädoyer." In *Verbrechen im Blick: Perspektiven der neuzeitlichen Kriminalitätsgeschichte*, ed. Rebekka Habermas and Gerd Schwerhoff, 19–41. Frankfurt/Main, 2009.

Habermas, Rebekka, and Gerd Schwerhoff. "Vorbemerkung." In *Verbrechen im Blick: Perspektiven der neuzeitlichen Kriminalitätsgeschichte*, ed. Rebekka Habermas and Gerd Schwerhoff, 10–12. Frankfurt/Main, 2009.

Halfmann, Frank. "Eine 'Pflanzstätte bester nationalsozialistischer Rechtsgelehrter': Die Juristische Abteilung der Rechts- und Staatswissenschaftlichen Fakultät." In *Die Universität Göttingen unter dem Nationalsozialismus: Das verdrängte Kapitel ihrer 250-jährigen Geschichte*, ed. Heinrich Becker, Hans-Joachim Dahms, and Cornelia Wegeler, 88–141. Munich, 1987.

Hall, Alex. *Scandal, Sensation and Social Democracy: The SPD Press and Wilhelmine Germany, 1890–1914*. Cambridge, 1977.

Halttunen, Karen. *Murder Most Foul: The Killer in the American Gothic Imagination*. Cambridge, MA, 1998.

Hammerstein, Notker. *Die Johann Wolfgang Goethe-Universität Frankfurt am Main: Von der Stiftungsuniversität zur staatlichen Hochschule*, vol. 1, 1914 bis 1950. Neuwied, 1989.

Hannover, Heinrich, and Elisabeth Hannover-Drück. *Politische Justiz 1918–1933*. Frankfurt/Main, 1966.

————. *Politische Justiz 1918–1933*. Frankfurt/Main, 1966. 2nd ed. Bornheim-Merten, 1987.

Harsin, Jill. *Policing and Prostitution in Nineteenth-Century Paris*. Princeton, 1985.

Hartung, Fritz. *Jurist Unter Vier Reichen*. Cologne, 1971.

Harvey, Elizabeth. *Youth and the Welfare State in Weimar Germany*. Oxford, 1993.

Hassemer, Winfried. "Strafrechtswissenschaft in der Bundesrepublik Deutschland." In *Rechtswissenschaft in der Bonner Republik: Studien zur Wissenschaftsgeschichte der Jurisprudenz*, ed. Dieter Simon, 259–310. Frankfurt/Main, 1994.

Hawkins, Mike. *Social Darwinism in European and American Thought, 1860–1945: Nature as Model and Nature as Threat*. Cambridge, 1997.

Hay, Douglas, et al., eds. *Albion's Fatal Tree: Crime and Society in Eighteenth-Century England*. New York, 1975.

Heimbüchel, Bernd. "Die neue Universität: Selbstverständnis—Idee und Verwirklichung." In Bernd Heimbüchel and Klaus Pabst. *Kölner Universitätsgeschichte*, vol. 2, *Das 19. und 20. Jahrhundert*, 101–692. Cologne and Vienna, 1988.

Heineman, Elizabeth D. *What Difference Does a Husband Make? Women and Marital Status in Nazi and Postwar Germany*. Berkeley, 1999.

Henze, Martina. *Strafvollzugsreformen im 19. Jahrhundert: Gefängniskundlicher Diskurs und staatliche Praxis in Bayern und Hessen-Darmstadt*. Darmstadt, 2003.

Herbe, Daniel. *Hermann Weinkauff (1894–1981): Der erste Präsident des Bundesgerichtshofs*. Tübingen, 2008.

Herzig, Arno. *Unterschichtenprotest in Deutschland, 1790–1870*. Göttingen, 1988.

Herzog, Todd. *Crime Stories: Criminalistic Fantasy and the Culture of Crisis in Weimar Germany*. New York, 2009.

Hett, Benjamin Carter. "The 'Captain of Köpenick' and the Transformation of German Criminal Justice, 1891–1914." *Central European History* 36 (2003): 1–43.

————. *Death in the Tiergarten: Murder and Criminal Justice in the Kaiser's Berlin*. Cambridge, 2004.

————. "Hans Litten and the Politics of Criminal Law in the Weimar Republic." In *Modern Histories of Crime and Punishment*, ed. Darkus Dirk Dubber and Lindsay Farmer, 175–197. Stanford, 2007.

————. *Crossing Hitler: The Man Who Put the Nazis on the Witness Stand*. New York, 2008.

Himmelfarb, Gertrude. *The Idea of Poverty: England in the Industrial Age*. London, 1984.

Hölscher, Lucian. *Weltgericht oder Revolution: Protestantische und sozialistische Zukunftsvorstellungen im deutschen Kaiserreich*. Stuttgart, 1989.

Hoffmann, Ludger. "Vom Ereignis zum Fall. Sprachliche Muster zur Darstellung und Überprüfung von Sachverhalten vor Gericht." In *Erzählte Kriminalität: Zur Typologie und Funktion von narrativen Darstellungen in Strafrechtspflege, Publizistik und Literatur zwischen 1770 und 1920. Vorträge zu einem interdisziplinären Kolloquium, Hamburg, 10.-12. April 1985*, ed. Jörg Schönert, 87–113. Tübingen, 1991.

Hoffmeister, Maren. "Lustmord: Widerständige Körper im Deutungssystem Justiz." In *Körper und Recht. Anthropologische Dimensionen der Rechtsphilophie*, ed. Ludger Schwarte and Christoph Wulf, 339–355. Munich, 2003.

Hofmann, Wolfgang, Kristina Hübener, and Paul Meusinger, eds. *Fürsorge in Brandenburg*. Berlin, 2007.

Holzhauer, Heinz. "Karl Alfred Hall (1906–1974): ein Denkmal." In *Beiträge zur Rechtswissenschaft: Festschrift für Walter Stree und Johannes Wessels zum 70. Geburtstag*, ed. Wilfried Küper, Walter Stree, and Johannes Wessels, 1263–1279. Heidelberg, 1993.

Hommen, Tanja. *Sittlichkeitsverbrechen: Sexuelle Gewalt im Kaiserreich*. Frankfurt/Main, 1998.

Hong, Young-Sun. *Welfare, Modernity, and the Weimar State, 1919 to 1933*. Princeton, 1998.

Howes, Geoffrey. "Therapeutic Murder in Elfriede Czurda and Lilian Faschinger." *Modern Austrian Literature* 32, no. 2 (1999): 79–93.

Huber, Karl-Heinz. *Jugend unterm Hakenkreuz*. Frankfurt/Main, 1986.

Ignatieff, Michael. *A Just Measure of Pain: The Penitentiary in the Industrial Revolution, 1750–1850*. New York, 1978.

Jasanoff, Sheila, ed. *States of Knowledge: The Co-Production of Science and Social Order*. London, 2004.

Jasper, Lutz. *Gesellschaft Hamburger Juristen 1885–1985: Erinnerungsschrift anläßlich ihres hundertjährigen Bestehens im Dezember 1985*. Cologne, 1985.

Jescheck, Hans-Heinrich. "Hellmuth von Weber zum Gedächtnis." *Juristische Zeitung* (1970): 517–518.

————. "Der Einfluß der IKV und der AIDP auf die internationale Entwicklung der modernen Kriminalpolitik. Festvortrag auf dem XII. Internationalen Strafrechtskongreß in Hamburg am 17. September 1979." *Zeitschrift für die gesamte Strafrechtswissenschaft* 92 (1980): 997–1020.

————. "Richard Lange zum Gedächtnis." *Zeitschrift für die gesamte Strafrechtswissenschaf* 108 (1996): 1–8.

Jessen, Ralph. "Gewaltkriminalität im Ruhrgebiet zwischen bürgerlicher Panik und proletarischer Subkultur, 1879–1914." In *Kirmes—Kneipe—Kino: Arbeiterkultur im Ruhrgebiet zwischen Kommerz und Kontrolle 1850–1914*, ed. Dagmar Kift, 226–255. Paderborn, 1992.

John, Michael. *Politics and the Law in Late Nineteenth-Century Germany: The Origins of the Civil Code*. Oxford, 1989.

Johnson, Eric. *Urbanization and Crime: Germany 1871–1914*. New York, 1995.

Jörns, Gerhard. *Der Jugendwerkhof im Jugendhilfesystem der DDR*. Göttingen, 1995.

Joseph, Detlef, ed. *Rechtsstaat und Klassenjustiz: Texte aus der sozialdemokratischen "Neuen Zeit" 1883–1914*. Freiburg, 1996.

Jureit, Ulrike. *Erziehen, Strafen, Vernichten: Jugendkriminalität und Jugendstrafrecht im Nationalsozialismus*. Münster, 1995.

Kaes, Anton. *M*. London, 2000.

Kailer, Thomas. " Werwölfe, Triebtäter, minderwertige Psychopathen. Bedingungen der Wissenspopularisierung: Der Fall Haarmann." In *Wissenspopularisierung. Konzepte der Wissensverbreitung im Wandel*, ed. Carsten Kretschmann, 323–359. Berlin, 2003.

———. *Vermessung des Verbrechers: Die Kriminalbiologische Untersuchung in Bayern, 1923–1945*. Bielefeld, 2011.

Kania, Harald, Michael Walter, and Hans-Jörg Albrecht, eds. *Alltagsvorstellungen von Kriminalität: Individuelle und gesellschaftliche Bedeutung von Kriminalitätsbildern für die Lebensgestaltung*. Münster, 2004.

Kästner, Alexander, and Sylvia Kesper-Biermann, eds. *Experten und Expertenwissen in der Strafjustiz von der Frühen Neuzeit bis zur Moderne*. Leipzig, 2008.

Kaufmann, Arthur. "Problemgeschichte der Rechtsphilosophie." In *Einführung in Rechtsphilosophie und Rechtstheorie der Gegenwart*, ed. Arthur Kaufmann and Winfried Hassemer, 23–123. Heidelberg, 1985.

———. *Gustav Radbruch*. Munich, 1987.

———. "Gustav Radbruch—Leben und Werk." In *Gustav Radbruch Gesamtausgabe* (GRGA).Vol. 1, *Rechtsphilosophie I*, ed. Arthur Kaufmann, 7–88. Heidelberg, 1987.

———. "Die Naturrechtsrenaissance der ersten Nachkriegsjahre—und was daraus geworden ist." In *Die Bedeutung der Wörter: Studien zur europäischen Rechtsgeschichte. Festschrift für Sten Gagnér zum 70. Geburtstag*, ed. Michael Stolleis et al., 105–132. Munich, 1991.

Kebbedies, Frank. *Ausser Kontrolle: Jugendkriminalpolitik in der NS-Zeit und der frühen Nachkriegszeit*. Essen, 2000.

Kesper-Biermann, Sylvia. *Einheit und Recht: Strafgesetzgebung und Kriminalrechtsexperten in Deutschland vom Beginn des 19. Jahrhunderts bis zum Reichsstrafgesetzbuch 1871*. Frankfurt/Main, 2009.

Kesper-Biermann, Sylvia, and Petra Overrath, eds. *Die Internationalisierung von Strafrechtswissenschaft und Kriminalpolitik (1970–1930): Deutschland im Vergleich*. Berlin, 2007.

Kettler, Sabine, Eva-Maria Stuckel, and Franz Wegener. *Wer tötete Helmut Daube? Der bestialische Sexualmord an dem Schüler Helmut Daube im Ruhrgebiet 1928*. Gladbeck, 2001.

Kleßmann, Christoph. *Die doppelte Staatsgründung: Deutsche Geschichte 1945–1955*. Göttingen, 1991.

Klewin, Silke, Herbert Reinke, and Gerhard Sälter, eds. *Hinter Gittern: Zur Geschichte der Inhaftierung zwischen Bestrafung, Besserung und politischem Ausschluss vom 18. Jahrhundert bis zur Gegenwart*. Leipzig, 2010.

Kling, Gudrun. "Die rechtliche Konstruktion des 'weiblichen Beamten': Frauen im öffentlichen Dienst des Großherzogthums Baden im 19. und frühen 20. Jahrhundert." In *Frauen in der Geschichte des Rechts: Von der frühen Neuzeit bis zur Gegenwart*, ed. Ute Gerhard, 600–616. Munich, 1997.

Klinger, Cornelia, and Gudrun-Axeli Knapp, eds. *Über-Kreuzungen. Fremdheit, Ungleichheit, Differenz*. Münster, 2008.

Koch, Bernd. "Das System des Stufenstrafvollzugs in Deutschland." Ph.D. diss., Freiburg University, 1972.

Kolloquien des Instituts für Zeitgeschichte, ed. *NS-Recht in historischer Perspektive*. Munich, 1981.

Kompisch, Kathrin. "Der Fall Fritz Haarmann (1924)." *Hannoversche Geschichtsblätter* 55/56 (2001–2002): 97–116.

———. "Wüstling—Werwolf—Teufel: Medienbilder von Serienmördern in der deutschen Massenpresse 1918–1945." Ph.D. diss., University of Hamburg, 2008.

———. "Gewaltdarstellungen in der Massenpresse der Weimarer Republik am Beispiel des Falles Fritz Haarmann (1924)." In *Repräsentation von Kriminalität und öffentlicher Sicherheit: Bilder, Vorstellungen und Diskurse vom 16. bis zum 20. Jahrhundert*, ed. Karl Härter, Gerhard Sälter, and Eva Wiebel, 487–508. Frankfurt/Main, 2010.

Kompisch, Kathrin, and Frank Otto. *Bestien des Boulevards: Die Deutschen und ihre Serienmörder.* Leipzig, 2003.

Krabbe, Wolfgang R., ed. *Politische Jugend in der Weimarer Republik.* Bochum, 1993.

Krafft, Sybille. *Zucht und Unzucht: Prostitution und Sittenpolizei im München der Jahrhundertwende.* Munich, 1996.

Krafft-Ebing, Richard von. *Psychopathia Sexualis. With Especial Reference to the Antipathic Sexual Instinct. A Medico-Forensic Study*, trans. Franklin S. Klaf. New York, 1998.

Kramer, Helmut. "Die Aufarbeitung des Faschismus durch die Nachkriegsjustiz in der Bundesrepublik Deutschland." In *Recht, Justiz und Faschismus—nach 1933 und heute*, ed. Helmut D. Fangmann and Norman Paech, 75–93. Cologne, 1984.

Krasmann, Susanne. *Die Kriminalität der Gesellschaft: Zur Gouvernementalität der Gegenwart.* Konstanz, 2003.

Krebs, Albert. "Die ersten 25 Jahre der Zeitschrift für Strafvollzug: Zur Geschichte des Gefängniswesens in Deutschland seit 1945." *Zeitschrift für Strafvollzug* 26 (1977): 1–7.

———. "Die GmbH als Betriebsform der Arbeit in der Strafanstalt." In *Freiheitsentzug: Entwicklung von Praxis und Theorie seit der Aufklärung*, ed. Heinz Müller-Dietz, 498–508. Berlin, 1978.

Kreutzahler, Birgit. *Das Bild des Verbrechers in Romanen der Weimarer Republik: Eine Untersuchung vor dem Hintergrund anderer gesellschaftlicher Verbrecherbilder und gesellschaftlicher Grundzüge der Weimarer Republik.* Frankfurt/Main, 1987.

Kroeschell, Karl. *Rechtsgeschichte Deutschlands im 20. Jahrhundert.* Göttingen, 1992.

Kühn, Helmut, et al. "32 Strafurteile der Hamburger Justiz 1933-1934. Mit Erläuterungen zum juristischen, zeitgeschichtlichen und biographischen Hintergrund. Fall 25: Schwerer Diebstahl 1943." In *"Von Gewohnheitsverbrechern, Volksschädlingen und Asozialen . . ." Hamburger Justizurteile im Nationalsozialismus*, ed. Justizbehörde Hamburg, 310–329. Hamburg, 1995.

Kuhn, Robert. *Die Vertrauenskrise der Justiz, 1926–1928: Der Kampf um die "Republikanisierung" der Rechtspflege in der Weimarer Republik.* Cologne, 1983.

Kundrus, Birthe. "The First World War and the Construction of Gender Relations in the Weimar Republic." In *Home/Front: The Military, War and Gender in Twentieth-Century Germany*, ed. Karen Hagemann and Stefanie Schüler-Springorum, 159–179. Oxford and New York, 2002.

Lafrenz, Jürgen. "Die Universität in Hamburg als Problem der Stadtplanung 1919 bis 1945." In *Hochschulalltag im Dritten Reich: Die Hamburger Universität 1933–1945*, ed. Eckart Krause, vol. 1, 327–366. Berlin, 1991.

Landwehr, Achim. *Geschichte des Sagbaren: Einführung in die historische Diskursanalyse.* Tübingen, 2001.

Lange, Thomas. "Der Steglitzer Schülermordprozeß 1928." In *"Mit uns zieht die neue Zeit"— Der Mythos Jugend*, ed. Thomas Koebner, Rolf-Peter Janz, and Frank Trommler, 412–437. Frankfurt/Main, 1985.

Larenz, Karl. *Methodenlehre der Rechtswissenschaft*, 6th ed. Berlin, 1991.

Leps, Marie-Christine. *Apprehending the Criminal: The Production of Deviance in Nineteenth-Century Discourse*. Durham, 1992.

Ledford, Kenneth F. "Lawyers, Liberalism, and Procedure: The German Imperial Justice Laws of 1877–79." *Central European History* 26 (1993):165–193.

———. *From General Estate to Special Interest: German Lawyers 1878–1933*. Cambridge, 1996.

———. "Formalizing the Rule of Law in Prussia: The Supreme Administrative Law Court, 1876–1914." *Central European History* 37 (2004): 203–224.

Lees, Andrew. *Cities, Sin, and Social Reform in Imperial Germany*. Ann Arbor, 2002.

Lepsius, M. Rainer. "Kultur und Wissenschaft in Deutschland unter der Herrschaft des Nationalsozialismus." In *Demokratie in Deutschland: Soziologisch-historische Konstellationsanalysen. Ausgewählte Aufsätze*, 119–132. Göttingen, 1993.

Lenk, Elisabeth, and Roswitha Kaever, eds. *Leben und Wirken des Peter Kürten, genannt der Vampir von Düsseldorf*. München, 1974.

Leukel, Sandra. *Strafanstalt und Geschlecht: Geschichte des Frauenstrafvollzug im 19. Jahrhundert (Baden und Preussen)*. Leipzig, 2010.

Lewis, Beth Irwin. "Lustmord: Inside the Windows of the Metropolis." In *Berlin: Culture and Metropolis*, ed. Charles W. Haxthausen and Heidrun Suhr, 111–140. Minneapolis and Oxford, 1990.

Liang, Oliver. "Criminal-Biological Theory, Discourse and Practice in Germany 1918–1945." Ph.D. diss., Johns Hopkins University, 1999.

———. "The Biology of Morality: Criminal Biology in Bavaria, 1924–1933." In *Criminals and Their Scientists: The History of Criminology in International Perspective*, ed. Peter Becker and Richard F. Wetzell, 425–446. New York, 2006.

Lichtblau, Albert. "Die Debatten über die Ritualmordbeschuldigungen im österreichischen Abgeordnetenhaus am Ende des 19. Jahrhunderts." In *Die Legende vom Ritualmord. Zur Geschichte der Blutbeschuldigung gegen Juden*, ed. Rainer Erb, 267–293. Berlin, 1993.

Lidtke, Vernon. *The Outlawed Party: Social Democracy in Germany, 1878–1890*. Princeton, 1966.

Lindenberger, Thomas. "Aufklären, zersetzen, liquidieren: Policing Juvenile Rowdytum in East Germany, 1956–1968." Unpublished paper presented to the annual German Studies Association conference, Arlington, VA, October 4–7, 2001.

Linder, Joachim, and Claus-Michael Ort, eds. *Verbrechen—Justiz—Medien: Konstellationen in Deutschland von 1900 bis zur Gegenwart*. Tübingen, 1999.

Lindner, Martin. "Der Mythos 'Lustmord.' Serienmörder in der deutschen Literatur, dem Film und der bildenden Kunst zwischen 1892 und 1932." In *Verbrechen-Justiz-Medien. Konstellationen in Deutschland von 1900 bis zur Gegenwart*, edited by Joachim Linder and Claus-Michael Ort, 273–305. Tübingen, 1999.

Linton, Derek S. *"Who Has the Youth Has the Future": The Campaign to Save Young Workers in Imperial Germany*. Cambridge, UK, 1991.

Loos, Fritz. "Hans Welzel (1904–1977): Die Suche nach dem Überpositiven im Recht." In *Rechtswissenschaft in Göttingen: Göttinger Juristen aus 250 Jahren*, ed. Fritz Loos, 486–509. Göttingen, 1987.

Lücke, Martin. *Männlichkeit in Unordnung. Homosexualität und männliche Prostitution in Kaiserreich und Weimarer Republik*. Frankfurt/Main, 2008.

McClintock, Anne. *Imperial Leather. Race, Gender and Sexuality in the Colonial Contest*. London, 1995.

Makarenko, A. S. *Problems of Soviet School Education*. Moscow, 1965.

Marrus, Michael. *The Nuremberg War Crimes Trial 1945–46: A Documentary History*. Boston, 1997.

Martschukat, Jürgen. *Inszeniertes Töten: Eine Geschichte der Todesstrafe vom 17. bis zum 19. Jahrhundert*. Cologne, 2000.

Martschukat, Jürgen, and Steffen Patzold. "Geschichtswissenschaft und 'performative turn'. Eine Einführung in Fragestellung, Konzepte und Literatur." In *Geschichtswissenschaft und "performative turn": Ritual, Inszenierung und Performanz vom Mittelalter bis zur Neuzeit*, ed. Jürgen Martschukat and Steffen Patzold, 1–31. Cologne, 2003.

Marxen, Klaus. *Der Kampf gegen das liberale Strafrecht: Eine Studie zum Antiliberalismus in der Strafrechtswissenschaft der zwanziger und dreißiger Jahre*. Berlin, 1975.

———. *Das Volk und sein Gerichtshof: Eine Studie zum nationalsozialistischen Volksgerichtshof*. Frankfurt/Main, 1994.

Mecklenburg, Frank. *Die Ordnung der Gefängnisse: Grundlinien der Gefängnisreform und Gefängniswissenschaft in der ersten Hälfte des 19. Jahrhunderts in Deutschland*. Berlin, 1983.

Meyer-Renschenhausen, Elisabeth. "The Bremen Morality Scandal." In *When Biology Became Destiny: Women in Weimar and Nazi Germany*, ed. Renate Bridenthal, Atina Grossmann, and Marion Kaplan, 87–108. New York, 1984.

Miller, James Edward. *From Elite to Mass Politics: Italian Socialism in the Giolittian Era 1900–1914*. Kent, OH, 1990.

Miquel, Marc von. "Juristen: Richter in eigener Sache." In *Karrieren im Zwielicht: Hitlers Eliten nach 1945*, ed. Norbert Frei, 181–237. Frankfurt/Main, 2001.

———. *Ahnden oder amnestieren? Westdeutsche Justiz und Vergangenheitspolitik in den sechziger Jahren*. Göttingen, 2004.

Moeller, Robert. *Protecting Motherhood: Women and the Family in the Politics of Postwar Germany*. Berkeley, 1993.

Morris, Douglas G. *Justice Imperiled: The Anti-Nazi Lawyer Max Hirschberg in Weimar Germany*. Ann Arbor, 2005.

Morris, Norval, and David J. Rothman, eds. *The Oxford History of the Prison: The Practice of Punishment in Western Society*. New York, 1995.

Mosse, George L. Introduction to *Degeneration*, by Max Nordau, viii–xxxiii. Lincoln, NE, 1993.

Müller, Christian. *Das Gewohnheitsverbrechergesetz vom 24. November 1933*. Berlin, 1997.

———. "Das Gewohnheitsverbrechergesetz vom 24. November 1933, NS-Strafrecht zwischen Reformtradition und rassistischer Neubestimmung." *Zeitschrift für Geschichtswissenschaft* 47 (1999): 965–979.

———. *Verbrechensbekämpfung im Anstaltsstaat: Psychiatrie, Kriminologie und Strafrechtsreform in Deutschland 1871–1933*. Göttingen, 2004.

Müller, Ingo. *Furchtbare Juristen*. München, 1987, trans. Deborah Lucas Schneider as *Hitler's Justice: The Courts of the Third Reich*. Cambridge, MA, 1991.

Müller, Philipp. *Auf der Suche nach dem Täter: Die öffentliche Dramatisierung von Verbrechen im Berlin des Kaiserreichs*. Frankfurt/Main, 2005.

Müller-Tuckfeld, Jens-Christian. *Integrationsprävention: Studien zu einer Theorie der gesellschaftlichen Funktion des Strafrechts*. Frankfurt/Main, 1998.

Muscheler, Karlheinz. *Hermann Ulrich Kantorowicz. Eine Biographie*. Berlin, 1984.

———. *Relativismus und Freirecht. Ein Versuch über Hermann Kantorowicz*. Heidelberg, 1984.

Nagel, Anne Christine, ed. *Die Philipps-Universität Marburg im Nationalsozialismus: Dokumente zu ihrer Geschichte*. Stuttgart, 2000.

Naucke, Wolfgang. "Die Aufhebung des strafrechtlichen Analogieverbots 1935." In *NS-Recht in historischer Perspektive*, ed. Kolloquien des Instituts für Zeitgeschichte, 71–108. Munich, 1981.

———. "NS-Strafrecht: Perversion oder Anwendungsfall moderner Kriminalpolitik?" *Rechtshistorisches Journal* 11 (1992): 279–292.

———. *Strafrecht: Eine Einführung*. Neuwied, 1995.

———. *Über die Zerbrechlichkeit des rechtsstaatlichen Strafrechts*. Baden-Baden, 2000.

Naumann, Kai. *Gefängnis und Gesellschaft: Freiheitsentzug in Deutschland in Wissenschaft und Praxis 1920–1960*. Münster, 2006.

Neugebauer, Manuela. *Der Weg in das Jugendschutzlager Moringen: Eine entwicklungspolitische Analyse nationalsozialistischer Jugendpolitik*. Mönchengladbach, 1997.

Neumann, Ulfried."Rechtsphilosophie in Deutschland seit 1945." In *Rechtswissenschaft in der Bonner Republik: Studien zur Wissenschaftsgeschichte der Jurisprudenz*, ed. Dieter Simon, 145–187. Frankfurt/Main, 1994.

Nienhaus, Ursula. "Einsatz für die 'Sittlichkeit': Die Anfänge der Weiblichen Polizei im Wilhelminischen Kaiserreich und in der Weimarer Republik." In *"Sicherheit" und "Wohlfahrt": Polizei, Gesellschaft und Herrschaft im 19. und 20. Jahrhundert*, ed. Alf Lüdtke, 243–266. Frankfurt/Main, 1992.

Nipperdey, Thomas. *Deutsche Geschichte 1866–1918*.Vol. 2, *Machtstaat vor der Demokratie*. Munich, 1992.

Nonn, Christoph. "Zwischenfall in Konitz. Anti-Semitismus und Nationalismus im preußischen Osten um 1900." *Historische Zeitschrift* 266 (1998): 387–418.

Nutz, Thomas. *Strafanstalt als Besserungsmaschine: Reformdiskurs und Gefängniswissenschaft 1775–1848*. Munich, 2001.

Nye, Robert. *Crime, Madness, and Politics in Modern France*. Princeton, NJ, 1984.

Oehler, Christoph. *Hochschulentwicklung in der Bundesrepublik Deutschland seit 1945*. Frankfurt/Main, 1989.

Oleschinski, Brigitte. "'Ein letzter stärkender Gottesdienst . . . ': Die deutsche Gefängnisseelsorge zwischen Republik und Diktatur 1918–45." Ph.D. diss., Free University Berlin, 1993.

Petersen, Klaus. *Literatur und Justiz in der Weimarer Republik*. Stuttgart, 1988.

Peukert, Detlev. *Grenzen der Sozialdisziplinierung: Aufstieg und Krise der deutschen Jugendfürsorge von 1878 bis 1932*. Cologne, 1986.

———. *The Weimar Republic*. London, 1993.

———. *Inside Nazi Germany*. London, 1993.

———. "The Genesis of the 'Final Solution' from the Spirit of Science." In *Nazism and German Society*, ed. David F. Crew, 274–299. London, 1994. Originally published as "Die Genesis der Endlösung aus dem Geist der Wissenschaft." In *Max Webers Diagnose der Moderne*, 102–121. Göttingen, 1989.

Phillips, David. "Die Wiedereröffnung der Universitäten in der britischen Zone. Nationalistische Gesinnung, Entnazifizierung und das Problem der Zulassung zum Studium." *Bildung und Erziehung* 36, no. 1 (1983): 35–53.

Pick, Daniel. *Faces of Degeneration: A European Disorder, 1848–1918*. Cambridge, 1989.

Plato, Alexander von, and Almut Leh. *"Ein unglaublicher Frühling": Erfahrene Geschichte im Nachkriegsdeutschland 1945–1948*. Bonn, 1997.

Poiger, Uta. "Rock 'n' Roll, Kalter Krieg und Deutsche Identität." In *Amerikanisierung und Sowjetisierung in Deutschland 1945–1970*, ed. Konrad H. Jarausch and Hannes Siegrist, 275–289. Frankfurt/Main, 1997.

———. "A New, "Western" Hero? Reconstructing German Masculinity in the 1950s." *Signs: Journal of Women in Culture and Society* 24 (1998): 147–162.

———. *Jazz, Rock and Rebels: Cold War Politics and American Culture in a Divided Germany.* Berkeley, 1999.

Prahl, Hans-Werner. *Sozialgeschichte des Hochschulwesens.* Munich, 1978.

Prangel, Matthias. "Die Döblinisierung Döblins. Zur Adaptation von 'Die beiden Freundinnen und ihr Giftmord' durch den Film." In *Internationales Alfred-Döblin-Kolloquium, Leipzig 1977*, edited by Ira Lorf and Gabriele Sander, 80. Berne, 1999.

Probst, Karlheinz. *Strafrecht—Strafprozessrecht—Kriminologie.* In *Geschichte der Rechtswissenschaftlichen Fakultät der Universität Graz*, vol 3. Graz, 1987.

Przyrembel, Alexandra. *"Rassenschande": Reinheitsmythos und Vernichtungslegitimation im Nationalsozialismus.* Göttingen, 2003.

Quedenfeld, Hans Dietrich. *Der Strafvollzug in der Gesetzgebung des Reiches, des Bundes und der Länder: Eine Untersuchung über die normative Grundlage des Strafvollzugs.* Tübingen, 1971.

Radkau, Joachim. *Das Zeitalter der Nervosität. Deutschland zwischen Bismarck und Hitler.* Munich, 2000.

Rafter, Nicole Hahn. *Creating Born Criminals.* Chicago, 1997.

Rafter, Nicole Hahn, and Mary S. Gibson, eds. *Criminal Woman, the Prostitute, and the Normal Woman: Cesare Lombroso and Guglielmo Ferrero.* Durham, 2004.

Raine, Adrian, Patricia A. Brennan, and David P. Farrington, eds. *Biosocial Bases of Violence.* New York, 1997.

Raphael, Lutz. "Die Verwissenschaftlichung des Sozialen als methodische und konzeptionelle Herausforderung für eine Sozialgeschichte des 20. Jahrhundert." *Geschichte und Gesellschaft* 22 (1996): 165–193.

Ratz, Ursula. *Zwischen Arbeitsgemeinschaft und Koalition: Bürgerliche Sozialreformer und Gewerkschaften im Ersten Weltkrieg.* Munich, 1994.

Reagin, Nancy. "A True Woman Can Take Care of Herself: The Debate over Prostitution in Hanover, 1906." *Central European History* 24, no. 4 (1991): 347–380.

Redaktion Kritische Justiz, ed. *Der Unrechtsstaat: Recht und Justiz im Nationalsozialismus.* 2 vols. Frankfurt/Main, 1979–1984.

Reifner, Udo, and Bernd-Rüdeger Sonnen, eds. *Strafjustiz und Polizei im Dritten Reich.* Frankfurt/Main, 1984.

Requate, Jörg. *Der Kampf um die Demokratisierung der Justiz: Richter, Politik und Öffentlichkeit in der Bundesrepublik.* Frankfurt/Main, 2008.

Respondek, Peter. "Der Wiederaufbau der Universität Münster in den Jahren 1945–1952 auf dem Hintergrund der britischen Besatzungspolitik." Ph.D. diss., University of Münster, 1992.

Reuchlein, Georg. "Die Ermordung einer Butterblume: 'Man lerne von der Psychiatrie'." *Jahrbuch für internationale Germanistik* 23 (1991): 10–68.

Ritter, Gerhard A. *Die Arbeiterbewegung im Wilhelminischen Reich: Die sozialdemokratische Partei und die freien Gewerkschaften, 1890–1900.* 2nd ed. Berlin, 1963.

Roos, Julia. "Backlash against Prostitutes' Right: Origins and Dynamics of Nazi Prostitution Policies." *Journal of the History of Sexuality* 1, no. 1/2 (2002): 67–94.

————. *Weimar Through the Lens of Gender: Prostitution Reform, Women's Emancipation, and German Democracy, 1919–1933*. Ann Arbor, 2010.

Rosenblum, Warren. *Beyond the Prison Gates: Punishment and Welfare in Germany, 1850 to 1933*. Chapel Hill, 2008.

Ross Dickinson, Edward. *The Politics of German Child Welfare from the Empire to the Federal Republic*. Cambridge, MA, 1996.

Roth, Thomas. *Verbrechensbekämpfung und soziale Ausgrenzung im nationalsozialistischen Köln: Kriminalpolizei, Strafjustiz und abweichendes Verhalten zwischen Machtübernahme und Kriegsende*. Cologne, 2010.

Rothman, David J. *The Discovery of the Asylum: Social Order and Disorder in the New Republic*. Boston, 1971.

Rückert, Joachim. "Justiz und Nationalsozialismus: Bilanz einer Bilanz." In *Fünfzig Jahre Institut für Zeitgeschichte: Eine Bilanz*, ed. Horst Möller and Udo Wengst, 181–213. Munich, 1999.

Rudolph, Andrea. *Die Kooperation von Strafrecht und Sozialhilferecht bei der Disziplinierung von Armen mittels Arbeit: Vom Arbeitshaus bis zur gemeinnützigen Arbeit*. Frankfurt/Main, 1995.

Rüthers, Bernd. *Entartetes Recht: Rechtslehren und Kronjuristen im Dritten Reich*. Munich, 1988.

Sack, Heidi. "'Wir werden lächelnd aus dem Leben scheiden'. Faszination Selbstmord in der Steglitzer Schülertragödie und in Diskursen der Weimarer Zeit." *Historical Social Research / Historische Sozialforschung* 34, no. 4 (2009), 259–272.

Sagaster, Ursula. *Die thüringische Landesstrafanstalt Untermassfeld in den Jahren 1923–33*. Frankfurt/Main, 1980.

Saldern, Adelheid von. *Auf dem Wege zum Arbeiter-Reformismus: Parteialltag in sozialdemokratischer Provinz Göttingen 1870–1920*. Frankfurt/Main, 1984.

Saliger, Frank. *Radbruchsche Formel und Rechtsstaat*. Heidelberg, 1995.

Sauer, Paul. *Im Namen des Königs: Strafgesetzgebung und Strafvollzug im Königreich Württemberg von 1806 bis 1871*. Stuttgart, 1984.

Schädler, Sarah. *'Justizkrise' und 'Justizreform' im Nationalsozialismus: Das Reichsjustizministerium unter Reichsjustizminister Thierack, 1942–1945*. Tübingen, 2009.

Schattke, Herbert. *Die Geschichte der Progression im Strafvollzug und der damit zusammenhängenden Vollzugsziele in Deutschland*. Frankfurt/Main, 1979.

Schauz, Desiree. *Strafen als moralische Besserung: Eine Geschichte der Straffälligenfürsorge 1777–1933*. Munich, 2008.

Schauz, Desiree, and Sabine Freitag, eds. *Verbrecher im Visier der Experten: Kriminalpolitik zwischen Wissenschaft und Praxis im 19. und frühen 20. Jahrhundert*. Stuttgart, 2007.

Scheerer, Sebastian. "Beyond Confinement? Notes on the History and Possible Future of Solitary Confinement in Germany." In *Institutions of Confinement: Hospitals, Asylums and Prisons in Western Europe and North America, 1500–1950*, ed. Norbert Finzsch and Robert Jütte, 349–359. New York, 1996.

Schenk, Christina. *Bestrebungen zur einheitlichen Regelung des Strafvollzugs in Deutschland von 1870 bis 1923: Mit einem Ausblick auf die Strafvollzugsgesetzentwürfe von 1927*. Frankfurt/Main, 2001.

Schetsche, Michael. "Der Wille, der Trieb und das Deutungsmuster vom Lustmord." In *Serienmord. Kriminologische und kulturwissenschaftliche Skizzierungen eines ungeheuerlichen Phänomens*, ed. Frank J. Robertz and Alexandra Thomas, 346–364. München, 2004.

Schild, Wolfgang. "Berühmte Berliner Kriminalprozesse der Zwanziger Jahre." In *Rechtsentwicklungen in Berlin. Acht Vorträge, gehalten anläßlich der 750-Jahrfeier Berlins*, ed. Friedrich Ebel and Albrecht Randelzhofer, 163–187. Berlin, 1988.

———. "Anmerkungen zur Straf- und Verbrechensphilosophie Immanuel Kants." In *Festschrift für Wolfgang Gitter zum 65. Geburtstag am 30. Mai 1995*, ed. Meinhard Heinze and Jochem Schmitt, 831–846.Wiesbaden, 1995.

Schildt, Axel. "Im Kern gesund? Die deutschen Hochschulen 1945." In *Vertuschte Vergangenheit: Der Fall Schwerte und die NS-Vergangenheit der deutschen Hochschulen*, ed. Helmut König, Klaus Schwabe, and Wolfgang Kuhlmann, 223–240. Munich, 1997.

Schmid, Manfred, and Volker Schäfer. "Neues Leben an den deutschen Universitäten nach dem Zweiten Weltkrieg." In *Wiedergeburt des Geistes: Die Universität Tübingen im Jahre 1945. Eine Dokumentation*, ed. Manfred Schmid and Volker Schäfer, 118f. Tübingen, 1985.

Schmidt, Eberhard. *Einführung in die Geschichte der deutschen Strafrechtspflege*. 1947. 3rd ed. Göttingen, 1995.

Schneider, Egon. "50 Jahre MDR." *MDR* 51, no. 4 (1997): 305.

Schoeps, Julius H. "Ritualmordbeschuldigung und Blutaberglaube. Die Affäre Buschoff im niederrheinischen Xanten." In *Köln und das rheinische Judentum*, ed. Jutta Bohnke-Kollwitz, 286–299. Cologne, 1984.

Schönert, Jörg ed. *Erzählte Kriminalität: Zur Typologie und Funktion von narrativen Darstellungen in Strafrechtspflege, Publizistik und Literatur zwischen 1770 und 1920*. Tübingen, 1991.

Schöningh, Claudia. *"Kontrolliert die Justiz": Die Vertrauenskrise der Weimarer Justiz im Spiegel der Gerichtsreportagen von Weltbühne, Tagebuch und Vossischer Zeitung*. Munich, 2000.

Schorn, Hubert. *Der Richter im Dritten Reich*. Frankfurt/Main, 1959.

Schubel, Friedrich. *Universität Greifswald*. Frankfurt/Main, 1960.

Schubert, Werner. "Der Ausbau der Rechtseinheit unter dem Norddeutschen Bund: Zur Entstehung des Strafgesetzbuchs von 1870 unter besonderer Berücksichtigung des Strafensystems." In *Festschrift für Rudolf Gmür zum 70. Geburtstag, 28. Juli 1983*, ed. Arno Buschmann et al., 149–189. Bielefeld, 1983.

Schubert, Werner, and Thomas Vormbaum, eds. *Entstehung des Strafgesetzbuchs*. 2 vols. Baden-Baden, 2002, Berlin, 2004.

Schulte, Regina.*Sperrbezirke: Tugendhaftigkeit und Prostitution in der bürgerlichen Welt*. Frankfurt/Main, 1979.

Schumacher, Björn." Rezeption und Kritik der Radbruchschen Formel." Ph.D. diss., Universität Göttingen, 1985.

Schwab-Felisch, Hans. "Mit Arsen gegen das Patriarchat: Döblin, 'Die beiden Freundinnen und ihr Giftmord' in Bochum." *Theater Heute* (1 January 1977): 55.

Schwartz, Michael. "'Proletarier' und 'Lumpen': Sozialistische Ursprünge eugenischen Denkens." *Vierteljahreshefte für Zeitgeschichte* 42 (1994): 537–570.

———. *Sozialistische Eugenik: Eugenische Sozialtechnologien in Debatten und Politik der deutschen Sozialdemokratie 1890–1933*. Bonn, 1995.

———. "Kriminalbiologie und Strafrechtsreform: Die 'erbkranken Gewohnheitsverbrecher' im Visier der Weimarer Sozialdemokratie." *Juristische Zeitgeschichte* 6 (1997): 13–68.

Schwerhoff, Gerd. *Historische Kriminalitätsforschung*. Frankfurt/Main, 2011.

Sellert, Wolfgang, and Hinrich Rüping. *Studien- und Quellenbuch zur Geschichte der deutschen Strafrechtspflege*. Vol. 2, *Von der Aufklärung bis zur doppelten Staatsgründung*. Aalen, 1994.

Sellin, Thorsten. "Enrico Ferri (1856–1929). "In *Pioneers in Criminology,* ed. Hermann Mannheim, 277–300. 1958. London, 1960.

Seltzer, Mark. *Serial Killers: Death and Life in America's Wound Culture.* New York, 1998.

Setzler, Wilfried. "Die Tübinger Studentenfrequenz im Dritten Reich: Ein Kurzüberblick zur zahlenmäßigen Entwicklung des Universitätsbesuchs und deren Ursachen." In Uwe Dietrich Adam. *Hochschule und Nationalsozialismus: Die Universität Tübingen im Dritten Reich,* 217–227. Tübingen, 1977.

Shapiro, Anne-Louise. *Breaking the Codes: Female Criminality in Fin-de-Siècle Paris.* Stanford, 1996.

Siebenpfeiffer, Hania. "Kreatur und Kalter Killer. Der Lustmörder als Paradigma männlicher Gewalt in der Moderne." In *Gewalt und Geschlecht. Bilder, Literatur und Diskurse im 20. Jahrhundert,* ed. Hanno Ehrlicher and Hania Siebenpfeiffer, 109–130. Cologne, 2002.

―――. *"Böse Lust": Gewaltverbrechen in Diskursen der Weimarer Republik.* Cologne, 2005.

Siemens, Daniel. "Die 'Vertrauenskrise der Justiz' in der Weimarer Republik." In *Die Krise der Weimarer Republik. Zur Kritik eines Deutungmusters,* ed. Moritz Föllmer and Rüdiger Graf, 139–164. Frankfurt/Main, 2005.

―――. *Metropole und Verbrechen: Die Gerichtsreportage in Berlin, Paris und Chicago, 1919–1933.* Stuttgart, 2007.

―――. "Explaining Crime: Berlin Newspapers and the Construction of the Criminal in Weimar Germany." *Journal of European Studies* 39 (2009): 336–352.

Sighele, Scipio. *Das Mandat des Intellektuellen: Karl Kautsky und die Sozialdemokratie.* Berlin, 1986.

Simon, Dieter. "Zäsuren im Rechtsdenken." In *Zäsuren nach 1945: Essays zur Periodisierung der deutschen Nachkriegsgeschichte,* ed. Martin Broszat, 153–167. Munich, 1990.

Sling [Paul Schlesinger], *Richter und Gerichtete.* Berlin, 1929.

Smith, Helmut Walser. *The Butchers Tale: Murder and Anti-Semitism in a German Town.* New York, 2002.

Smith, Sabine. *Sexual Violence in German Culture: Rereading and Rewriting the Tradition.* New York and Frankfurt/Main, 1998.

Somerville, Siobhan. "Scientific Racism and the Emergence of the Homosexual Body." *Journal of the History of Sexuality* 5, no. 2 (1994): 243–266.

Spierenburg, Pieter. "The Body and the State: Early Modern Europe." In *The Oxford History of the Prison: The Practice of Punishment in Western Society,* ed. Norval Morris and David J. Rothman, 49–77. Oxford, 1995.

Spode, Hasso. *Die Macht der Trunkenheit: Kultur- und Sozialgeschichte des Alkohols in Deutschland.* Opladen, 1993.

Spörri, Myriam. *Reines und gemischtes Blut: Zur Kulturgeschichte der Blutgruppenforschung.* Bielefeld, 2013.

Staff, Ilse, ed. *Justiz im Dritten Reich: Eine Dokumentation.* Frankfurt: Fischer, 1964.

Stark, Gary D. *Banned in Berlin: Literary Censorship in Imperial Germany, 1871–1918.* New York, 2009.

Steinberg, Hans-Josef. *Sozialismus und deutsche Sozialdemokratie: Zur Ideologie der Partei vor dem 1. Weltkrieg.* 5th ed. Berlin, 1979.

Steirische Gesellschaft für Kulturpolitik, eds. *Grenzfeste Deutscher Wissenschaft: Über Faschismus und Vergangenheitsbewältigung an der Universität Graz.* Graz, 1985.

Stepenhorst, Hermann. *Die Entwicklung des Verhältnisses von Geldstrafe zu Freiheitsstrafe seit 1882.* Berlin, 1993.

Stevens, Jennie A. "Children of the Revolution: Soviet Russia's Homeless Children (Besprizorniki) in the 1920s." *Russian History/Histoire Russe* 9 (1982): 250–252.

Stieglitz, Olaf, and Jürgen Martschukat. *"Es ist ein Junge!" Einführung in die Geschichte der Männlichkeiten in der Neuzeit.* Tübingen, 2005.

Stolee, Margaret K. "Homeless Children in the USSR, 1917–1957." *Soviet Studies* 40 (1988): 64–83.

Stolleis, Michael. "Recht im Unrecht." In *Recht im Unrecht: Studien zur Rechtsgeschichte des Nationalsozialismus,* 7–35. Frankfurt/Main, 1994.

———. *The Law under the Swastika: Studies on Legal History in Nazi Germany.* Chicago, 1998.

Stolleis, Michael, and Dieter Simon. "Vorurteile und Werturteile der rechtshistorischen Forschung zum Nationalsozialismus." In *NS-Recht in historischer Perspektive,* 13–51. Munich, 1981.

Streng, Franz. " Erziehungsgedanke im Jugendstrafrecht: Überlegungen zum Ideologiecharakter und zu den Perspektiven eines multifunktionalen Systembegriffs." *Zeitschrift für die gesamte Strafrechtswissenschaft* 106 (1994): 76–78.

Taschke, Jürgen, ed. *Max Alsberg: Ausgewählte Schriften.* Baden-Baden, 1992.

Tatar, Maria. *Lustmord: Sexual Murder in Weimar Germany.* Princeton, 1995.

Tergit, Gabriele. *Wer schießt aus Liebe? Gerichtsreportagen.* Berlin, 1999.

Terry, Jennifer. "Anxious Slippages Between 'Us' and 'Them'. A Brief History of the Scientific Search for Homosexual Bodies." In *Deviant Bodies. Critical Perspectives on Difference in Science and Popular Culture,* ed. Jennifer Terry and Jacqueline Urla, 129–169. Bloomington 1995.

Thomas, Swen. *Geschichte des Mordparagraphens—eine normalgenetische Untersuchung bis in der Gegenwart.* Bochum, 1985.

Thompson, E.P. *Whigs and Hunters: The Origin of the Black Act.* New York, 1975.

Thorpe, Kathleen. "Aggression and Self-Realization in Elfriede Czurda's Novel *Die Giftmörderinnen.*" *Modern Austrian Literature* 31, no. 3/4 (1998): 175–187.

Thränhardt, Dietrich. *Geschichte der Bundesrepublik Deutschland.* Frankfurt/Main, 1986.

Thulfaut, Gerit. *Kriminalpolitik und Strafrechtslehre bei Edmund Mezger (1883–1962). Eine wissenschaftsgeschichtliche und biographische Untersuchung.* Baden-Baden, 2000.

Timm, Annette. "The Legacy of *Bevölkerungspolitik*: Venereal Disease Control and Marriage Counseling in Post-WWII Berlin." *Canadian Journal of History* 18 (1998): 173–214.

———. "Guarding the Health of Worker Families in the GDR: Socialist Health Care, *Bevölkerungspolitik,* and Marriage Counselling, 1945–72." In *Arbeiter in der SBZ-DDR,* edited by Peter Hübner and Klaus Tenfelde, 463–495. Essen, 1999.

Uhl, Karsten. *Das "verbrecherische" Weib: Geschlecht, Verbrechen und Strafen im kriminologischen Diskurs 1800–1945.* Münster, 2003.

———. "Die Gewaltverbrecherin im kriminologischen und literarischen Diskurs des frühen 20. Jahrhunderts." In *Frauen und Gewalt: Interdisziplinäre Untersuchungen zu geschlechtsgebundener Gewalt in Theorie und Praxis,* ed. Antje Hilbig, Claudia Kajatin, and Ingrid Miethe, 91–103. Würzburg, 2003.

Valkhoff, J. "Bongers Werken." In W. A. Bonger. *Verspreide Geschriften.* Vol. 1, *Criminologie en Criminele Statistiek,* xxxvi–xcii. Amsterdam, 1950.

Vogel, Joachim. *Einflüsse des Nationalsozialismus auf das Strafrecht.* Berlin, 2004.

Vormbaum, Thomas. *Einführung in die moderne Strafrechtsgeschichte.* Berlin, 2009.

Vormbaum, Thomas, and Jürgen Welp, eds. *Das Strafgesetzbuch: Sammlung der Änderungsgesetze und Neubekanntmachungen,* vol. 1, *1870 bis 1953.* Baden-Baden, 2000.

Voss, Michael. *Jugend ohne Rechte: Entwicklung des Jugendstrafrechts.* Frankfurt/Main, 1986.

Wachsmann, Nikolaus. "'Annihilation through Labor': The Killing of State Prisoners in the Third Reich." *Journal of Modern History* 71(September 1999): 624–659.

———. "Reform and Repression: Prisons and Penal Policy in Germany, 1918–1939." Ph.D. diss., University of London, 2001.

———. "Between Reform and Repression: Prisons in Weimar Germany." *Historical Journal,* 45 (2002): 413–414.

———. *Hitler's Prisons: Legal Terror in Nazi Germany.* London, 2004.

Wagner, Joachim. *Politischer Terrorismus und Strafrecht im Deutschen Kaiserreich von 1871.* Heidelberg, 1981.

Wagner, Patrick. *Volksgemeinschaft ohne Verbrecher: Konzeptionen und Praxis der Kriminalpolizei in der Zeit der Weimarer Republik und des Nationalsozialismus.* Hamburg, 1996.

———. *Hitlers Kriminalisten.* Munich, 1992.

Wagner, Walter. *Der Volksgerichtshof im nationalsozialistischen Staat.* 1974. Reprinted with a report on recent research by Jürgen Zarusky. Munich, 2011.

Walgenbach, Katharina, et al., eds. *Gender als interdependente Kategorie: Neue Perspektiven auf Intersektionalität Diversität und Heterogenität.* Opladen, 2007.

Walkowitz, Judith. *Prostitution and Victorian Society: Women, Class, and the State.* Cambridge, 1980.

———. "Jack the Ripper and the Myth of Male Violence." *Feminist Studies* 8, no. 3 (1982): 541–574.

———. *City of Dreadful Delight: Narratives of Sexual Danger in Late-Victorian London.* Chicago, 1992.

Walser, Karin. *Dienstmädchen. Frauenarbeit und Weiblichkeitsbilder um 1900.* Frankfurt/ Main, 1985.

Weber, Max. "The Formal Qualities of Modern Law." In *Max Weber on Law in Economy and Society,* trans. Edward Shils and Max Rheinstein, 301–321. Cambridge, MA, 1954.

———. "The Rational and Irrational Administration of Justice." In *Max Weber on Law in Economy and Society,* trans. Edward Shils and Max Rheinstein, 349–356. Cambridge, MA, 1954.

Weigel, Sigrid. *"Und selbst im Kerker frei . . . !"Schreiben im Gefängnis: Zur Theorie und Gattungsgeschichte der Gefängnisliteratur, 1750–1933.* Marburg, 1982.

Weikart, Richard. *Socialist Darwinism: Evolution in German Socialist Thought from Marx to Bernstein.* San Francisco, 1999.

Weiler, Inge. *Giftmordwissen und Giftmörderinnen. Eine diskursgeschichtliche Studie.* Tübingen, 1998.

Weingart, Peter, Jürgen Kroll, and Kurt Bayertz. *Rasse, Blut und Gene: Geschichte der Eugenik und Rassenhygiene in Deutschland.* Frankfurt/Main, 1988.

Weinkauff, Hermann. "Der Naturrechtsgedanke in der Rechtsprechung des Bundesgerichtshofes." *Neue Juristische Wochenschrift* 13 (1960): 1689–1696.

———. *Die Deutsche Justiz und der Nationalsozialismus. Ein Überblick.* Stuttgart, 1968.

———. *Die Deutsche Justiz und der Nationalsozialismus.* Stuttgart: Deutsche Verlags-Anstalt, 1968.

Weinke, Annette. *Die Verfolgung von NS-Tätern im geteilten Deutschland.* Paderborn, 2002.

Wendehorst, Alfred. *Geschichte der Friedrich-Alexander-Universität Erlangen-Nürnberg.* Munich, 1993.

Werle, Gerhard. *Justiz-Strafrecht und polizeiliche Verbrechensbekämpfung im Dritten Reich.* Berlin, 1989.

Wesel, Uwe. *Geschichte des Rechts. Von den Frühformen bis zum Vertrag von Maastricht.* Munich, 1997.

Wetzell, Richard F. "Criminal Law Reform in Imperial Germany." Ph.D. diss., Stanford University, 1991.

———. "The Medicalization of Criminal Law Reform in Imperial Germany." In *Institutions of Confinement: Hospitals, Asylums and Prisons in Western Europe and North America, 1500–1950*, ed. Norbert Finzsch and Robert Jütte, 275–284. New York, 1996.

———. *Inventing the Criminal: A History of German Criminology, 1880–1945.* Chapel Hill, 2000.

———. "From Retributive Justice to Social Defense: Penal Reform in Fin-de-Siècle Germany." In *Germany at the Fin de Siècle: Culture, Politics, and Ideas*, ed. Suzanne Marchand and David Lindenfeld, 59–77. Baton Rouge, 2004.

———. "Criminology in Weimar and Nazi Germany." In *Criminals and Their Scientists: The History of Criminology in International Perspective*, ed. Peter Becker and Richard F. Wetzell, 401–423. New York, 2006.

———. "Psychiatry and Criminal Justice in Modern Germany, 1880–1933." *Journal of European Studies* 39 (2009): 270–289.

Whitman, James Q. *Harsh Justice: Criminal Punishment and the Widening Gap Between America and Europe.* Oxford, 2003.

Wieacker, Franz. *Privatrechtsgeschichte der Neuzeit. Unter besonderer Berücksichtigung der deutschen Entwicklung*, 2nd ed. Göttingen, 1967.

Wiener, Martin J. *Reconstructing the Criminal: Culture, Law and Policy in England, 1830–1914.* Cambridge, 1990.

Wierling, Dorothee. *Mädchen für Alles: Arbeitsalltag und Lebensgeschichte städtischer Dienstmädchen um der Jahrhundertwende.* Berlin, 1987.

———. "Die Jugend als innerer Feind: Konflikte in der Erziehungsdiktatur der sechziger Jahre," in *Sozialgeschichte der DDR*, ed. Hartmut Kaelble, Jürgen Kocka, and Hartmut Zwahr, 404–425. Stuttgart, 1994.

———. "Der Staat, die Jugend und der Westen: Texte zu Konflikten der 1960er Jahre." In *Akten, Eingaben, Schaufenster: Die DDR und ihre Texte: Erkundungen zu Herrschaft und Alltag*, ed. Alf Lüdtke and Peter Becker, 223–240. Berlin, 1997.

———. "The Hitler Youth Generation in the GDR: Insecurities, Ambitions and Dilemmas." In *Dictatorship as Experience: Towards a Socio-Cultural History of the GDR*, ed. Konrad Jarausch, 307–324. New York, 1999.

Wilhelm, Uwe. *Das Deutsche Kaiserreich und seine Justiz: Justizkritik—politische Strafrechtssprechung—Justizpolitik.* Berlin: Duncker & Humblot, 2010.

Wilhelmus, Wolfgang, Dagmar Szöllösi, and Gabriele Langer, eds. *Universität Greifswald 525 Jahre.* Berlin/East, 1982.

Wilkinson, Molly. *Training Socialist Citizens: Sports and the State in East Germany.* Leiden, 2008.

Willing, Matthias. *Das Bewahrungsgesetz (1918–1967).* Göttingen, 2003.

Wilson, James Q., and Richard J. Hernstein. *Crime and Human Nature.* New York, 1985.

Winker, Gabriele, and Nina Degele. *Intersektionalität: Zur Analyse sozialer Ungleichheiten.* Bielefeld, 2009.

Winkler, Karl Tilman. "Reformers United: The American and German Juvenile Court, 1882–1923." In *Institutions of Confinement: Hospitals and Prisons in Western Europe and North America, 1500–1950*, ed. Norbert Finzsch and Robert Jütte, 235–274. New York, 1996.

Witter, Katharina. "Funktion und Organisation der Zuchthäuser im kapitalistischen Deutschland, dargelegt am Beispiel des Zuchthauses Untermassfeld." Master's Thesis (Diplomarbeit), Berlin/East, 1982.

Wittern, Renate, ed. *Die Professoren der Friedrich-Alexander-Universität Erlangen 1763–1960.* Vol. 1, *Theologische Fakultät, Juristische Fakultät.* Erlangen, 1993.

Wolff, Jörg. *Jugendliche vor Gericht: Nationalsozialistische Jugendstrafrechtspolitik und Justizalltag.* Munich, 1992.

Wolff, Jörg, and Christine Dörner. "Jugendstrafrecht zwischen Weimar und Nationalsozialismus." *Recht der Jugend und des Bildungswesens* 38 (1990): 54.

Wolff, Jörg, et al. *Das Jugendstrafrecht zwischen Nationalsozialismus und Demokratie: Die Rückkehr der Normalität.* Baden Baden, 1997.

Wolgast, Eike. *Die Universität Heidelberg 1386–1986.* Berlin, 1986.

Worm, Manfred. *SPD und Strafrechtsreform: Die Stellung der Sozialdemokratischen Partei Deutschlands zur Strafrechtsreform unter Berücksichtigung ihrer Wandlung von einer Klassenkampfpartei zur Volkspartei.* Munich, 1968.

Wrobel, Hans. *Verurteilt zur Demokratie: Justiz und Justizpolitik in Deutschland 1945–1949.* Heidelberg, 1989.

Zarusky, Jürgen. "Walter Wagners Volksgerichtshof-Studie von 1974 im Kontext der Forschungsentwicklung." In *Der Volksgerichtshof im nationalsozialistischen Staat,* ed. Walter Wagner, 993–1023. 2nd, expanded edition. Munich, 2011.

Zeller, Bernhard, ed. *Alfred Döblin 1878–1978: Eine Ausstellung des Deutschen Literaturarchivs im Schiller-Nationalmuseum Marbach am Neckar.* München, 1978.

Ziemann, Benjamin, Richard F. Wetzell, Dirk Schumann and Kerstin Brückweh, "The Scientization of the Social in Comparative Perspective." In *Engineering Society: The Role of the Human and Social Sciences in Modern Societies, 1880–1980,* ed. Kerstin Brückweh, et al., 1–40. Houndmills, 2012.

Zimmermann, Verena. *Den neuen Menschen schaffen: Die Umerziehung von schwererziehbaren und straffälligen Jugendlichen in der DDR (1945–1990).* Cologne, 2004.

Zull, Gertraud. *Das Bild vom Dienstmädchen um die Jahrhundertwende. Eine Untersuchung der stereotypen Vorstellungen über den Charakter und soziale Lage des städtischen weiblichen Hauspersonals.* Munich, 1984.

INDEX